W9-AWH-682

The
Random
House
Basic Dictionary

Italian-English
English-Italian

The Random House Basic Dictionary

Italian-English
English-Italian

by Robert A. Hall, Jr.

Professor of Linguistics, Cornell University

BALLANTINE BOOKS • NEW YORK

Copyright © 1981, 1967, 1957 by Random House, Inc.

All rights reserved under International and Pan-American Copyright Conventions. Published in the United States by Ballantine Books, a division of Random House, Inc., New York, and simultaneously in Canada by Random House of Canada Limited, Toronto.

Library of Congress Catalog Card Number: 67-20649

ISBN 0-345-34603-3

This edition published by arrangement with Random House, Inc. Previously published as *The Italian Vest Pocket Dictionary* and *The Random House Italian Dictionary*.

Manufactured in the United States of America

First Ballantine Books Edition: August 1981
Eleventh Printing: August 1993

Concise Pronunciation Guide

Italian Letter	Pronunciation
a	Like English *a* in *father*.
b	As in English.
c	Before *e* or *i*, and sometimes at the end of words, like English *ch*. Elsewhere, like English *k*.
ch	Before *e* or *i*, like English *k*.
ci	Before *a*, *o*, or *u*, like English *ch*.
d	As in English.
é	("close *e*") Like English *ay* in *day*, but with no final *y*-like glide.
è	("open *e*") Like English *e* in *bet*.
e	Like English *e* in *bet*.
f	As in English.
g	Before *e* or *i*, like English *g* in *gem*. Elsewhere, like English *g* in *go*.
gh	Before *e* or *i*, like English *g* in *go*.
gi	Before *a*, *o*, or *u*, like English *g* in *gem*.
gl	Before *i*, normally like English *lli* in *million*.
gli	Before *a*, *e*, *o*, or *u*, like English *lli* in *million*.
gn	Like English *ny* in *canyon*.
h	After *c* and *g*, indicates "hard" pronunciation of preceding consonant letter. Elsewhere, silent.
i	After *c*, *g*, and (normally) *sc*, before *a*, *o*, or *u*, indicates "soft" pronunciation of preceding consonant letter or letters.

Italian Letter	Pronunciation
	Elsewhere: When unstressed and before or after another vowel, like English *y*. Otherwise, like English *i* in *machine*, but with no final *y*-like glide.
j	At the end of words, when replacing *ii* in some noun plurals, like Italian *i*. Otherwise, like English *y*.
k	As in English.
l	Like English *l* in *like*, but with the tongue behind the upper front teeth.
m	As in English.
n	As in English.
ó	("close *o*") Like English *o* in *go*, but with no final *w*-like glide.
ò	("open *o*") Like English *o* in *bought*.
o	Like English *o* in *bought*.
p	As in English.
qu	Like English *qu* in *quick*.
r	Not at all like American English *r*; a quick flap of the tip of the tongue on the gumridge.
s	Between vowels, like English *s* in *lease* (in southern Italy); like *s* in *please* (in northern Italy); sometimes like *s* in *lease* and sometimes like *s* in *please* (in central Italy). Before *b*, *d*, *g*, *l*, *m*, *n*, *r*, *v*, like English *z*. Elsewhere, like English *s* in *same*, *stick*.

Italian Letter	Pronunciation
sc	Before *e* or *i*, and occasionally at the end of words, like English *sh*. Elsewhere, like English *sk*.
sch	Before *e* or *i*, like English *sk*.
sci	Before *a*, *o*, or *u*, like English *sh*.
t	As in English.
u	When unstressed and

Italian Letter	Pronunciation
	before or after another vowel, like English *w*. Otherwise, like English *oo* in *boot*, but without final *w*-like glide.
v	As in English.
w	Rare; like English *v*.
x	Rare; like English *x*.
z	Like English *ts* in *cats* or like English *dz* in *adze*.

Consonant Length

All Italian consonants occur both single (short) and double (long); in the latter instance, the time of their pronunciation lasts from one-and-a-half to two times that of the single consonants.

Italian Accentuation

In most conventional writing and printing, spoken stress is marked by a grave accent (`` ` ``), but only when it falls on the last syllable of a word: *città*, *vendè*, *lunedì*, *cantò*, *tribù*. An accent is placed over the vowel letter of some words to distinguish them from others having the same spelling and pronunciation but differing in meaning: *è* "is" versus *e* "and". In other instances, stress is usually left unmarked, although it may fall on any syllable up to the sixth from the end.

However, Italians are very sensitive to misplaced stress, even though accent marks are not customarily used in Italian spelling. In this dictionary, therefore, as in most Italian dictionaries, the occurrence of stress is indicated with an accent mark whenever it does not fall on the next-to-the-last syllable, and also in all words ending in *-ia*, *-io*. In addition, the presence of the open varieties of *e* and *o*, to which Italians are also sensitive, is marked by a grave accent (`` ` ``), in all its occurrences, even in the next-to-the-last syllable.

Noun and Adjective Plurals

Virtually all Italian nouns form their plurals by changing the final vowel. The following are the principal patterns of noun plural formation:

Final Vowel		Examples	
Singular	Plural	Singular	Plural
-a (f.)	-e	ròsa	ròse
-a (m.)	-i	dramma	drammi
-o (m.)	-i	libro	libri
-o (m.)	-a (f.)	bràccio	bràccia
-e (m., f.)	-i (m., f.)	flume	flumi
		parte	parti

Nouns ending in unstressed -i, in stressed vowels, or in consonants; family names; and abbreviations are normally unchanged in the plural: *crisi, città, tram; Scaglione; auto, ràdio.*

Adjectives ending in -o follow the pattern of *libro* for the masculine and that of *rosa* for the feminine; those ending in -e follow the pattern of *flume, parte* for both masculine and feminine.

Regular Verbs

Infinitive	Present	Future	Preterite	Past Part.
cantare	canto	canterò	cantai	cantato
dormire	dormo	dormirò	dormìi	dormito
finire	finisco	finirò	finìi	finito
temere	temo	temerò	temèi	temuto
véndere	vendo	venderò	vendèi	venduto

Irregular Verbs

Infinitive	Present	Future	Preterite	Past Part.
accéndere	accendo	accenderò	accesi	acceso
andare	vado	andrò	andai	andato
aprire	apro	aprirò	apèrsi	apèrto
avere	ò (ho)	avrò	èbbi	avuto
bere	bevo	berrò	bevvi	bevuto
cadere	cado	cadrò	caddi	caduto
cìngere	cingo	cingerò	cinsi	cinto
cógliere	colgo	coglierò	colsi	colto
concèdere	concedo	concederò	concèssi	concèsso
condurre	conduco	condurrò	condussi	condotto
dare	do	darò	diedi	dato
diféndere	difendo	difenderò	difesi	difeso
dire	dico	dirò	dissi	detto
dovere	devo	dovrò	dovèi	dovuto
èssere	sono	sarò	fui	stato
fare	fàccio	farò	feci	fatto
fóndere	fondo	fonderò	fusi	fuso
giacere	giàccio	giacerò	giacqui	giaciuto
morire	muòio	morirò	morìi	mòrto
nàscere	nasco	nascerò	nacqui	nato
parere	paio	parrò	parsi	parso
porre	pongo	porrò	posi	posto
potere	pòsso	potrò	potèi	potuto
rèndere	rèndo	renderò	resi	reso
salire	salgo	salirò	salìi	salito
sapere	sò	saprò	seppi	saputo
stare	sto	starò	stetti	stato
scégliere	scelgo	sceglierò	scelsi	scelto
tenere	tengo	terrò	tenni	tenuto
trarre	traggo	trarrò	trassi	tratto
uscire	esco	uscirò	uscìi	uscito
valere	valgo	varrò	valsi	valso
vedere	vedo	vedrò	vidi	visto or veduto
venire	vengo	verrò	venni	venuto
vìvere	vivo	vivrò	vissi	vissuto
volere	vòglio	vorrò	vòlli	voluto

Abbreviations

abbr.	abbreviation
adj.	adjective
adv.	adverb
Amer.	American
Brit.	British
comm.	commercial
conj.	conjunction
eccles.	ecclesiastical
econ.	economics
f.	feminine
fam.	familiar
fig.	figuratively
geom.	geometry
gram.	grammar; grammatical
interj.	interjection
intr.	intransitive
lit.	literally
m.	masculine
math.	mathematics
med.	medicine
mil.	military
n.	noun
naut.	nautical
num.	number
pl.	plural
pred.	predicate
prep.	preposition
pron.	pronoun; pronunciation
refl.	reflexive
sg.	singular
tr.	transitive (used only with verbs which also have reflexive use to indicate intransitive meaning)
typogr.	typography
vb.	verb

Useful Phrases

Good day. Buòn giorno.
Good evening. Buòna sera.
Good night. Buòna nòtte.
Good-bye. Arrivederci.
How are you? Come sta?
Fine, thank you. Bène, gràzie.
Glad to meet you. Piacere.
Thank you very much. Molte gràzie.
You're welcome. Prègo.
Please. Prègo.
Good luck. Buòna fortuna.
To your health. Salute.

Please help me. M'aiuti, per favore.
Do you understand? Capisce?
I don't understand. Non capisco.
Speak slowly, please. Parli adàgio, per favore.
Please repeat. Ripeta, per favore.
I don't speak Italian. Non parlo italiano.
Do you speak English? Parla inglese?
Does anyone here speak English? C'è qualcuno che parla inglese?
How do you say…in Italian? Come si dice…in italiano?

What is your name? Come si chiama?
My name is… Mi chiamo…
I am an American. Sono americano.

How is the weather? Che tèmpo fa?
What time is it? Che ora è?
What is it? Che còsa è?

How much does this cost? Quanto còsta questo?
It is too expensive. E troppo caro.
I want to buy… Vorrèi comprare…
I want to eat. Vorrèi mangiare.
Can you recommend a restaurant? Può raccomandare un ristorante?
I am hungry. Ò fame.
I am thirsty. Ò sete.
Check, please. Il conto, per favore.
Is there a hotel here? C'è un albèrgo qui?

Where is...? Dov'è...?
What is the way to...? Qual'è la strada per...?
Take me to... Mi conduca a...
I need... Ò bisogno di...
I am ill. Sono malato.
Please call a doctor. Chiami un mèdico, per favore.
I want to send a telegram. Vorrèi spedire un telegramma.
Where can I change money? Dove posso far cambiare del denaro?
Will you accept checks? Accètta assegni?
What is the postage? Quanto còsta l'affrancatura?

Right away. Sùbito.
Help! Aiuto!
Come in. Avanti.
Hello (on telephone). Pronto.
Stop. Si fermi.
Hurry. Fàccia prèsto.
Go on. Avanti.
Right. A dèstra.
Left. A sinistra.
Straight ahead. Sèmpre diritto.

Signs

Attenzione Caution
Perìcolo Danger
Uscita Exit
Entrata Entrance
Alt, Alto, Fermatevi Stop
Chiuso Closed
Apèrto Open
Rallentatevi Slow down
Sènso ùnico One way (street)
È vietato fumare No smoking
È vietato entrare No admittance
Signore Women
Signori, Uòmini Men
Gabinetto (di decènza), Cèsso
  Toilet

Weights and Measures

The Italians use the *Metric System* of weights and measures, which is a decimal system in which multiples are shown by the prefixes: *deci-* (one tenth); *centi-* (one hundredth); *milli-* (one thousandth); *deca-* (ten); *etto-* (hundred); *chilo-* abbreviated *k.*) (thousand).

1 centìmetro	.3937 inches
1 mètro	39.37 inches
1 chilòmetro (abbr. *km.*)	.621 mile
1 centigramma	.1543 grain
1 gramma	15.432 grains
1 ettogramma (abbr. *etto*)	3.527 ounces
1 chilogramma (abbr. *kg.*)	2.2046 pounds
1 tonnellata	2204 pounds
1 centilitro	.338 ounces
1 litro	1.0567 quart (liquid); .908 quart (dry)
1 chilolitro	264.18 gallons

Numerals

Cardinal

1	uno, una	18	diciòtto	101	centuno
2	due	19	diciannòve	102	centodue
3	tre	20	venti	200	duecènto
4	quattro	21	ventuno, ventuna	300	trecènto
5	cinque	22	ventidue	400	quattrocènto
6	sèi	28	ventòtto	500	cinquecènto
7	sètte	30	trenta	600	seicènto
8	òtto	31	trentuno, trentuna	700	settecènto
9	nòve	32	trentadue	800	ottocènto
10	dièci	38	trentòtto	900	novecènto
11	ùndici	40	quaranta	1,000	mille
12	dódici	50	cinquanta	2,000	duemila
13	trédici	60	sessanta	3,000	tremila
14	quattòrdici	70	settanta	100,000	centomila
15	quìndici	80	ottanta	1,000,000	un milione
16	sédici	90	novanta	2,000,000	due milioni
17	diciassètte	100	cènto		

Ordinal

1st	primo	15th	decimoquinto
2nd	secondo		or quindicésimo
3rd	tèrzo	16th	decimosèsto
4th	quarto		or sedicésimo
5th	quinto	17th	decimosèttimo
6th	sèsto		or diciassettésimo
7th	sèttimo	18th	decimottavo
8th	ottavo		or diciottésimo
9th	nòno	19th	decimonòno
10th	dècimo		or diciannovésimo
11th	decimoprimo	20th	ventésimo
	or undicésimo	21st	ventésimoprimo
12th	decimosecondo	30th	trentésimo
	or dodicésimo	40th	quarantésimo
13th	decimotèrzo	100th	centésimo
	or tredicésimo	1000th	millésimo
14th	decimoquarto		
	or quattordicésimo		

Days of the Week

Monday	lunedì
Tuesday	martedì
Wednesday	mercoledì
Thursday	giovedì
Friday	venerdì
Saturday	sàbato
Sunday	doménica

Months

January	gennaio	July	lùglio
February	febbraio	August	agosto
March	marzo	September	settèmbre
April	aprile	October	ottobre
May	màggio	November	novèmbre
June	giugno	December	dicèmbre

Centuries

In Italian, centuries may be referred to by the equivalent of ordinal numeral plus the word for century: *il sècolo decimottavo* "the eighteenth century," etc. For the centuries from 1200 A.D. to the present, it is also common to refer to them by the cardinal numbers for the "hundreds" present in each century-name, thus:

il Duecènto	=	the thirteenth century	=	the '200's
il Trecènto	=	the fourteenth century	=	the '300's
il Quattrocènto	=	the fifteenth century	=	the '400's
il Cinquecènto	=	the sixteenth century	=	the '500's
il Seicènto	=	the seventeenth century	=	the '600's
il Settecènto	=	the eighteenth century	=	the '700's
l'Ottocènto	=	the nineteenth century	=	the '800's
il Novecènto	=	the twentieth century	=	the '900's

Italy

Population 50,762,000
Approximate Length 760 miles
Approximate Width 100 to 150 miles
Square Miles 116,294
Capital Rome (Roma)

Regions and Provinces

Region	Population	Constituent-Provinces
Abruzzi	1,213,002	Chieti, L'Aquila, Pescara, Teramo
Basilicata	648,085	Matera, Potenza
Calabria	2,045,215	Catanzaro, Cosenza, Reggio, Calabria
Campania	4,756,094	Avellino, Benevento, Caserta, Napoli, Salerno
Emilia-Romagna	3,646,507	Bologna, Ferrara, Forlì, Modena, Parma, Piacenza, Ravenna, Reggio Emilia
Friuli-Venezia Giulia	1,205,222	Gorizia, Trieste, Udine
Lazio (Latium)	3,922,783	Frosinone, Latina, Rieti, Roma, Viterbo
Liguria	1,717,630	Genova, Imperia, La Spezia, Savona
Lombardia (Lombardy)	7,390,492	Bergamo, Brescia, Como, Cremona, Mantova, Milano, Pavia, Sondrio, Varese
Marche (Marches)	1,347,234	Ancona, Ascoli Piceno, Macerata, Pesaro Urbino
Molise	371,775	Campobasso
Piemonte (Piedmont)	3,889,962	Alessandria, Asti, Cuneo, Novara, Turino, Vercelli
Puglia (Apulia)	3,220,485	Bari, Brindisi, Foggia, Lecce, Taranto
Sardegna (Sardinia)	1,413,289	Cagliari, Nuoro, Sassari

Region	Population	Constituent-Provinces
Sicilia (Sicily)	4,711,783	Agrigento, Caltanissetta, Catania, Enna, Messina, Palermo, Ragusa, Siracusa, Trapani
Trentino-Alto Adige	785,491	Bolzano, Trento
Toscana (Tuscany)	3,267,374	Arezzo, Firenze, Grosseto, Livorno, Lucca, Massa, Pisa, Pistoia, Siena
Umbria	788,546	Perugia, Terni
Valle d'Aosta	99,754	Aosta
Veneto (Venetia)	3,833,837	Belluno, Padova, Rovigo, Treviso, Venezia, Verona, Vicenza

Major Cities

City	Population	Location
Roma (Rome)	2,328,930	W. Central
Milano (Milan)	1,643,402	N.W.
Napoli (Naples)	1,198,233	S.W.
Torino (Turin)	1,096,958	N.W.
Genova (Genoa)	814,232	N.W.
Palermo	604,475	S. (N.W. Sicily)
Bologna	469,170	N. Central
Firenze (Florence)	451,730	N. Central
Catania	376,239	S. (E. Sicily)
Venezia (Venice)	353,018	N.E.
Bari	320,049	S.E.
Messina	258,118	S. (N.E. Sicily)
Verona	230,907	N.E.
Padova (Padua)	205,057	N.E.
Taranto	197,716	S.E.
Cagliari	191,439	W. (S. Sardinia)
Brescia	182,232	N.
Livorno (Leghorn)	164,808	N.W.
Ferrara	156,038	N.E.
Parma	155,132	N. Central
Reggio di Calabria	155,039	S.
Modena	147,501	N. Central
La Spezia	125,661	N.W.
Reggio nell'Emilia	119,912	N. Central
Bergamo	117,773	N.
Perugia	115,852	Central
Ancona	102,604	E. Central
Pescara	100,363	E. Central
Bolzano (Bozen)	83,956	N.
Trento (Trient)	74,766	N.

Legal Holidays In Italy

All Sundays
January 1, New Year's Day
January 6, Epiphany
March 19, Saint Joseph's Day
April 25, Liberation of Italy
Monday after Easter Sunday

Ascension Day
Corpus Christi Day

May 1, Labor Day
June 2, Day of the Republic
June 29, Saints Peter's & Paul's Day
August 15, Assumption of Mary
November 1, All Saint's Day
December 8, Immaculate Conception of Mary
December 25, Christmas
December 26

Most businesses are closed on the afternoon of the following traditional holidays:
The last day before Lent (Mardi Gras)
Thursday of Holy Week
November 2, All Souls' Day
December 24, Christmas Eve
December 31, New Year's Eve

Italian Family Names

In its simplest form, an Italian proper name consists of given name (*prenome*) plus family name (*cognome*): *Giovanni Rossi*. It may, however, contain more than one of each type of name: *Luigi Maria Franceschini-Petrocchi*. If more than one family name is present, both are used or else only the first: *il signore Franceschini-Petrocchi*, or *il signor Franceschini*, but not *il signor Petrocchi*.

A woman, on marrying, adds her husband's family name preceding her own: *Giuseppina Bianchi*, on marrying Mr. Bracciolini, becomes *Giuseppina Bracciolini-Bianchi*. She will often, however, be referred to simply as *la signora Bracciolini* after her marriage. The American English order for a married woman's name, given name plus maiden name plus husband's family name, is found in Italian only in an archaic construction in which the woman's maiden name is followed by *in* plus her husband's family name: *Giuseppina Bianchi in Bracciolini*.

In traditional Italian usage, a person's given name precedes his or her family name, as in English: *Giuliano Bàrtoli Pierina Cardinali*. A modern habit, of placing the family name before the given name, is by now almost universal in lists, directories and official documents, and is being used increasingly even in everyday situations: *Bàrtoli Giuliano, Cardinali Pierina*.

Italian-English

A

a, *prep.* at; in; to; by.
àbaco, *n.m.* abacus.
abate, *n.m.* abbot.
abbàcchio, *n.m.* lamb.
abbagliare, *vb.* dazzle.
abbaiamento, *n.m.* bark; barking.
abbaiare, *vb.* bark, bay.
abbaino, *n.m.* dormer.
abbandonare, *vb.* abandon, forsake, relinquish, vacate.
abbandonato, *adj.* abandoned.
abbandono, *n.m.* abandon, abandonment.
abbassamento, *n.m.* lowering, abasement.
abbassare, *vb.* lower, abase; debase; (*refl.*) stoop; subside.
abbassato, *adj.* lowered; downcast.
abbastanza, *adv.* enough.
abbàttere, *vb.* knock down, fell; dishearten; (*refl.*) droop.
abbattimento, *n.m.* disheartenment, dismay, dejection.
abbattuto, *adj.* despondent.
abbazia, *n.f.* abbey.
abbellimento, *n.m.* embellishment.
abbellire, *vb.* beautify, embellish.
abbigliare, *vb.* dress up, accouter.
abbigliamento maschile, *n.m.* menswear.
abbigliatura, *n.f.* accouterments.
abbonacciare, *vb.* becalm.
abbonamento, *n.m.* subscription. biglietto d'a., season ticket.
abbonarsi, *vb.* subscribe.
abbondante, *adj.* abundant, plentiful.
abbondantemente, *adv.* abundantly.
abbondanza, *n.f.* abundance, plenty.
abbondare, *vb.* abound.
abbordare, *vb.* accost.
abborracciare, *vb.* bungle.
abbozzare, *vb.* sketch.
abbozzo, *n.m.* sketch, draft.
abbracciare, *vb.* embrace, clasp, hug.
abbraccio, *n.m.* embrace, clasp, hug.
abbreviamento, *n.m.* abridgement.
abbreviare, *vb.* abbreviate, abridge, shorten.
abbreviatura, *n.f.* abbreviation.
abbronzare, *vb.* tan.
abbronzato, *adj.* sunburnt.
abbronzatura, *n.f.* sunburn, tan.
abbrustolire, *vb.* toast.
abbrutire, *vb.* brutalize.
abdicare, *vb.* abdicate.
abdicazione, *n.f.* abdication.
aberrante, *adj.* aberrant.

aberrare, *vb.* be aberrant.
aberrazione, *n.f.* aberration.
abete, *n.m.* fir.
abiètto, *adj.* abject.
àbile, *adj.* skilful, clever, able, adroit, capable, cunning, deft.
abilità, *n.f.* ability, skill, cleverness, adeptness, cunning.
abilmente, *adv.* skilfully, ably, adeptly, capably.
Abissinia, *n.f.* Abyssinia.
abissino, *n.* and *adj.* Abyssinian.
abisso, *n.m.* abyss, chasm.
abitàbile, *adj.* habitable.
abitante, *n.m.* inhabitant, dweller, resident.
abitare, *vb.* live, dwell, reside, inhabit.
abitazione, *n.f.* dwelling, habitation, residence.
àbito, *n.m.* dress, suit, habit.
abituale, *adj.* habitual, usual, accustomed.
abituare, *vb.* accustom, habituate.
abituarsi a, *vb.* get accustomed to.
abitùdine, *n.f.* habit.
abiura, *n.f.* abjuration.
abiurare, *vb.* abjure.
ablativo, *n.m.* and *adj.* ablative.
abluzione, *n.f.* ablution.
abnegare, *vb.* abnegate.
abnegazione, *n.f.* abnegation.
abolimento, *n.m.* abolition.
abolire, *vb.* abolish.
abominare, *vb.* abominate, loathe.
abominazione, *n.f.* abomination.
abominévole, *adj.* abominable, loathsome.
aborrimento, *n.m.* abhorrence.
aborrire, *vb.* abhor.
abortire, *vb.* abort; be abortive.
abortivo, *adj.* abortive.
aborto, *n.m.* abortion.
abrasione, *n.f.* abrasion.
abrasivo, *n.m.* and *adj.* abrasive.
abrogare, *vb.* abrogate.
abrogazione, *n.f.* abrogation.
àbside, *n.f.* apse.
a buòn mercato, *adv.* cheap; cheaply.
abusare di, *vb.* abuse, misuse.
abusivamente, *adv.* abusively.
abusivo, *adj.* abusive.
abuso, *n.m.* abuse.
acanto, *n.m.* acanthus.
a cavalcioni, *adv.* astride.
accadèmia, *n.f.* academy.
accadèmico, *adj.* academic.
accadere, *vb.* happen, befall, occur, take place.
accamparsi, *vb.* camp, encamp.
accampamento, *n.m.* camp, encampment.
accanto, *adv.* beside, alongside.

accanto a, *prep.* beside, next to, alongside.
accantonamento, *n.m.* cantonment.
accaparrare, *vb.* corner.
accarezzare, *vb.* caress, fondle, stroke.
accecare, *vb.* blind.
accelerare, *vb.* accelerate, speed up.
accelerato, *n.m.* local.
acceleratore, *n.m.* accelerator.
accelerazione, *n.f.* acceleration.
accèndere, *vb.* light, switch on, ignite, kindle.
accendisigaro, *n.m.* cigar-lighter, cigarette-lighter.
accennare, *vb.* hint.
accensione, *n.f.* ignition.
accentare, *vb.* accent, stress.
accènto, *n.m.* accent, stress.
accentuare, *vb.* accent.
accerchiare, *vb.* encircle, ring around.
accertarsi, *vb.* ascertain.
accessìbile, *adj.* accessible.
accèsso, *n.m.* access, approach; fit.
accessòrio, 1. *adj.* accessory; attachment. 2. *n.m.* accessory; adjunct.
accetta, *n.f.* hatchet.
accettàbile, *adj.* acceptable.
accettabilità, *n.f.* acceptability.
accettabilmente, *adv.* acceptably.
accettare, *vb.* accept.
accettazione, *n.f.* acceptance.
accètto, *adj.* acceptable.
acciàio, *n.m.* steel.
accidentale, *adj.* accidental.
accidentalmente, *adv.* accidentally.
acciugato, *adj.* frowning, glum.
acciuga, *n.f.* anchovy.
acclamare, *vb.* acclaim.
acclamazione, *n.f.* acclamation.
acclimare, *vb.* acclimate.
acclimatare, *vb.* acclimate.
acclività, *n.f.* acclivity.
acchiùdere, *vb.* enclose.
accogliènza, *n.f.* reception.
accògliere, *vb.* receive, entertain.
accòlito, *n.m.* acolyte.
accolata, *n.f.* accolade.
accomodante, *adj.* accommodating.
accomodare, *vb.* accommodate; mend; (*refl.*) make oneself comfortable; compromise.
accomodazione, *n.f.* accommodation.
accompagnamento, *n.m.* accompaniment.
accompagnare, *vb.* accompany.
accompagnatore, *n.m.* accompanist.
acconciare, *vb.* fix.
acconciatura, *n.f.* hair-do.

accondiscendénza, n.f. condescension.

accondiscéndere, vb. condescend.

acconsentire, vb. consent.

accontentare, vb. content.

accoppiare, vb. couple; mate.

accorciare, vb. shorten, curtail.

accordare, vb. tune.

accòrdo, n.m. agreement, accord; compact; concord; chord. d'a., in agreement.

accosciarsi, vb. squat.

accreditare, vb. accredit.

accréscere, vb. accrue, increase, boost, enhance, heighten.

accrescimento, n.m. increase, accretion, accrual, boost.

accucciarsi, vb. crouch.

accumulare, vb. accumulate.

accumulativo, adj. accumulative.

accumulatore, n.m. battery, accumulator.

accumulazione, n.f. accumulation.

accuratamente, adv. accurately, carefully.

accuratezza, n.f. accuracy, carefulness.

accurato, adj. accurate, careful.

accusa, n.f. accusation, indictment.

accusare, vb. accuse, arraign, indict. a. ricevuta di, acknowledge receipt of.

accusativo, n.m. and adj. accusative.

accusato, n.m. accused.

accusatore, n.m. accuser.

acerbità, n.f. acerbity.

acèrbo, adj. sour, unripe.

àcero, n.m. maple.

acetato, n.m. acetate.

acètico, adj. acetic.

acetilène, n.m. acetylene.

aceto, n.m. vinegar.

acidificare, vb. acidify.

acidità, n.f. acidity.

àcido, n.m. and adj. acid, sour.

acidòsi, n.f. acidosis.

acidulo, adj. acidulous.

acme, n.f. acme.

acne, n.f. acne.

acqua, n.f. water.

acquaforte, n.f. etching.

acquáio, n.m. sink.

acquarèllo, n.m. watercolor.

acquàrio, n.m. aquarium.

acquàtico, adj. aquatic.

acquavite, n.f. brandy.

acquazzone, n.m. heavy shower, cloudburst.

acquedotto, n.m. aqueduct.

àcqueo, adj. aqueous.

acquetare, vb. appease, quiet.

acquiescenza, n.f. acquiescence.

acquietarsi, vb. calm down, acquiesce.

acquisitivo, adj. acquisitive.

acquistare, vb. acquire.

acquisto, n.m. acquisition.

acre, adj. acrid, acrimonious, tart.

acrèdine, n.f. acrimony.

acrimònia, n.f. acrimony.

acro, n.m. acre.

acròbata, n.m. acrobat.

acròstico, n.m. acrostic.

acume, n.m. acumen.

acupunctura, n.f. acupuncture.

acùstica, n.f. acoustics.

acutamente, adv. acutely, sharply.

acutezza, n.f. acuteness, sharpness.

acuto, adj. acute, sharp, keen, pointed, shrewd.

ad, prep. at; in; to; by.

adàgio, 1. n.m. adage. 2. adv. slowly; gently.

adamantino, adj. adamant.

adattàbile, adj. adaptable.

adattabilità, n.f. adaptability.

adattamento, n. adaptation; fitting.

adattare, vb. adapt.

adattévole, adj. adaptive.

adatto, adj. fit, suitable.

addetto, 1. n.m. attaché. 2. adj. assigned, employed.

addìo, interj. hello; good-bye, adieu, farewell.

additare, vb. point out.

addizionale, adj. additional.

addizionare, vb. add.

addizione, n.f. addition.

addolorare, vb. grieve, tr.; a. ricevuta di, (refl.) sorrow.

addolorato, adj. sorrowful.

addome, n.m. abdomen.

addomesticare, vb. tame.

addomesticato, adj. tame.

addominale, adj. abdominal.

addormentarsi, vb. fall asleep.

addottrinare, vb. indoctrinate.

addurre, vb. lead up, bring up, adduce.

adenòide, adj. adenoid.

adeguatamente, adv. adequately.

adeguato, adj. adequate.

aderènte, n.m. adherent, member (of association, etc.).

aderènza, n.f. adherence, support; relation.

aderire, vb. adhere, cling, stick, support, join.

adescare, vb. allure, entice, lure.

adescatore, adj. alluring.

adesione, n.f. adhesion; intention to join (association, etc.).

adesività, n.f. adhesive.

adesivo, n.m. and adj. adhesive.

adèsso, adv. now.

adiacènte, adj. adjacent, adjoining.

adirarsi, vb. get angry.

adirato, adj. angry, cross.

adolescènte, n. and adj. adolescent.

adolescènza, n.f. adolescence.

adoperare, vb. use.

adoràbile, adj. adorable.

adorare, vb. adore, worship.

adorazione, n.f. adoration, worship.

adornamento, n.m. adornment.

adorno, adj. adorned.

adottare, vb. adopt.

adozione, n.f. adoption.

adrenalina, n.f. adrenalin.

adulare, vb. adulate, flatter, fawn upon.

adulatore, n.m. flatterer.

adulazione, n.f. adulation, flattery.

adùltera, n.f. adulteress.

adulterante, n. and adj. adulterant.

adulterare, vb. adulterate.

adultèrio, n.m. adultery.

adùltero, n.m. adulterer.

adulto, n. (m.) and adj. adult, grown-up.

adunata, n.f. gathering, meeting.

aerare, vb. aerate, air.

aerazione, n.f. aeration.

aèreo, 1. n.m. aircraft, airplane. 2. adj. aerial.

aerodinàmico, adj. streamlined.

aeronàutica, n.f. aeronautics.

aeroplano, n.m. airplane.

aeroporto, n.m. airport.

aeroscalo, n.m. airport.

affàbile, adj. affable.

affabilità, n.f. affability.

affabilmente, adv. affably.

affaccendato, adj. busy.

affamato, adj. famished, ravenous.

affare, n.m. affair, concern; bargain, deal; (pl.) business.

affascinante, adj. fascinating, glamorous.

affascinare, vb. fascinate, allure, captivate, charm.

affaticare, vb. fatigue.

afferènte, adj. afferent.

affermare, vb. affirm, state.

affermativamente, adv. affirmatively.

affermativo, adj. affirmative.

affermazione, n.f. affirmation, statement.

afferrare, vb. grasp, grip, seize, catch, snatch.

affettare, vb. affect; slice.

affettato, adj. affected; finicky, prim.

affettazione, n.f. affectation; frill.

affettuosamente, adv. affectionately.

affettuoso, adj. affectionate.

affezione, n.f. affection, attachment.

affibbiare, vb. buckle.

affidare, vb. entrust.

affiggere, vb. post.

affigliare, vb. affiliate.

affigliazione, n.f. affiliation.

affine, adj. related, akin, allied.

affinità, n.f. affinity.

affissare, vb. affix.

affisso, n.m. affix.

affittare, vb. lease, let, rent.

affitto, *n.m.* lease, rent.

affliggere, *vb.* afflict, distress.

afflizione, *n.f.* affliction, distress.

affluente, *n.m.* tributary.

affluire, *vb.* rush.

afflusso, *n.m.* rush.

affollare, *vb.* crowd.

affollarsi, *vb.* come together in crowds, flock.

affondare, *vb.* sink.

affrancare, *vb.* enfranchise.

affrancatura, *n.f.* postage.

affresco, *n.m.* fresco.

affrettare, *vb.* hasten, haste, hurry, quicken, speed.

affrettatamente, *adv.* hastily.

affrettato, *adj.* hasty.

affrontare, *vb.* face.

aforismo, *n.m.* aphorism.

affrontare, *vb.* face, go to meet; affront, insult.

affronto, *n.m.* affront, insult.

Àfrica, *n.f.* Africa.

africano, *n.* and *adj.* African.

àgata, *n.f.* agate.

àgave, *n.f.* century plant.

agènda, *n.f.* note-book.

agènte, *n.m.* agent. **a. di càmbio**, stockbroker.

agenzìa, *n.f.* agency.

agganciare, *vb.* clasp.

aggettivo, *n.m.* adjective.

aggiornamento, *n.m.* adjournment.

aggiornare, *vb.* adjourn; bring up to date.

aggiùngere, *vb.* add.

aggiunto, 1. *n.* and *adj.* adjunct. 2. *adj.* added, extra.

aggiustamento, *n.m.* adjustment.

aggiustare, *vb.* adjust.

aggiustatore, *n.m.* adjuster.

aggiustatura, *n.f.* adjustment.

agglutinare, *vb.* agglutinate.

agglutinazione, *n.f.* agglutination.

aggravamento, *n.m.* aggravation.

aggravare, *vb.* aggravate.

aggregare, *vb.* aggregate.

aggregato, *n.m.* aggregate.

aggregazione, *n.f.* aggregation.

aggressione, *n.f.* aggression.

aggressivamente, *adv.* aggressively.

aggressività, *n.f.* aggressiveness.

aggressivo, *adj.* aggressive.

aggressore, *n.m.* aggressor.

aggrottare, *vb.* wrinkle. **a. le cìglia**, frown, scowl.

aggrovigliare, *vb.* snarl, tangle.

àgile, *adj.* agile, nimble.

agilità, *n.f.* agility.

àgio, *n.m.* ease, leisure.

agire, *vb.* act.

agitare, *vb.* agitate; wave, flourish; stir; *(refl.)* fidget, toss.

agitatore, *n.m.* agitator.

agitazione, *n.f.* agitation.

àglio, *n.m.* garlic.

agnèllo, *n.m.* lamb.

agnòstico, *n.* and *adj.* agnostic.

ago, *n.f.* needle. **a. da rammendo**, darning-needle.

agonìa, *n.f.* agony.

agonizzante, *adj.* agonized.

agonizzare, *vb.* be in agony.

agopuntura, *n.f.* acupuncture.

agosto, *n.m.* August.

agràrio, *adj.* agrarian.

agricoltore, *n.m.* farmer.

agricultura, *n.f.* agriculture, farming.

agrifòglio, *n.m.* holly.

agrimensore, *n.m.* surveyor.

aguzzare, *vb.* sharpen.

ahi, *interj.* ouch!

Aia, *n.f.* l'A., The Hague.

airone, *n.m.* heron.

aiutante, *n.m.* assistant, helper, adjutant, aide.

aiutare, *vb.* help, aid, assist, befriend.

aiuto, *n.m.* help, aid, assistance.

ala, *n.f.* wing.

alacrità, *n.f.* alacrity.

alambicco, *n.m.* still.

alba, *n.f.* dawn, daybreak.

albèrgo, *n.m.* hotel, hostelry.

àlbero, *n.m.* tree; mast, shaft, spar.

albicòcca, *n.f.* apricot.

albino, *n.m.* and *adj.* albino.

album, *n.m.* album.

albume, *n.m.* albumen.

àlcali, *n.m.* alkali.

alcalino, *adj.* alkaline.

alce, *n.m.* elk.

àlcole, *n.m.* alcohol.

àlcool, *n.m.* alcohol.

alc(o)òlico, *adj.* alcoholic.

alcòva, *n.f.* alcove.

alcuni, *adj.* some.

alfabètico, *adj.* alphabetical.

alfabèto, *n.m.* alphabet.

alfalfa, *n.f.* alfalfa.

alfière, *n.m.* ensign.

àlgebra, *n.f.* algebra.

àlias, *adv.* alias.

alibi, *n.m.* alibi.

alienare, *vb.* alienate, estrange.

alièno, *adj.* alien, foreign, strange.

alimentare, 1. *vb.* feed, nourish. 2. *adj.* pertaining to food, alimentary.

alimentàrio, *adj.* alimentary.

alimento, *n.m.* food, nourishment.

aliscafo, *n.m.* hovercraft.

allacciare, *vb.* enlace.

allargare, *vb.* broaden, widen.

allarmare, *vb.* alarm, startle.

allarme, *n.m.* alarm, alert.

allarme d'incèndio, *n.m.* fire alarm.

allarmista, *n.m.* alarmist.

alleanza, *n.f.* alliance.

alleare, *vb.* ally.

alleato, 1. *n.m.* ally. 2. *adj.* allied.

allegare, *vb.* allege.

allegazione, *n.f.* allegation.

alleggerire, *vb.* lighten.

allegorìa, *n.f.* allegory.

allegrìa, *n.f.* merriment, cheerfulness, mirth.

allegro, *adj.* lively, merry, cheerful, frisky, jolly.

allenare, *vb.* train, coach.

allenatore, *n.m.* trainer, coach.

allentamento, *n.m.* letdown.

allentare, *vb.* loosen, relax.

allergìa, *n.f.* allergy.

allevare, *vb.* train, breed, foster, nurture, raise, rear.

allevatore, *n.m.* trainer, breeder.

alleviare, *vb.* alleviate, allay, relieve.

allietare, *vb.* gladden.

alligatore, *n.m.* alligator.

allineare, *vb.* align, line up.

allòdola, *n.f.* lark.

alloggiare, *vb.* lodge, put up, accommodate, billet.

allòggio, *n.m.* lodging, accommodation, billet.

allontanarsi, *vb.* go away, stray.

allora, *adv.* then.

allòro, *n.m.* laurel.

allucinazione, *n.f.* hallucination.

allùdere, *vb.* allude.

allume, *n.m.* alum.

alluminio, *n.m.* aluminum.

allungare, *vb.* lengthen, elongate, reach out.

allusione, *n.f.* allusion, reference.

almanacco, *n.m.* almanac.

alpaca, *n.m.* alpaca.

Alpi, *n.f.* (*pl.*) Alps.

alpino, *adj.* Alpine.

alt, *interj.* halt!

alta fedeltà, *n.f.* high fidelity.

altalena, *n.f.* seesaw; swing.

altamente, *adv.* highly.

altare, *n.m.* altar.

alterare, *vb.* alter.

alterazione, *n.f.* alteration.

alternare, *vb.* alternate.

alternativa, *n.f.* alternative.

alternativo, *adj.* alternative, alternate.

altezza, *n.f.* height; Highness.

altitùdine, *n.f.* altitude.

alto, *adj.* high, lofty, tall; loud. **in a.**, *adv.* on high, aloft.

altoparlante, *n.m.* loudspeaker.

altopiano, *n.m.* plateau.

altrimenti, *adv.* otherwise, else.

altro, *adj.* other, else.

altrove, *adv.* elsewhere.

altruismo, *n.m.* altruism.

altura, *n.f.* height.

alunno, *n.m.* pupil.

alveare, *n.m.* beehive.

alzaia, *n.f.* hawser.

alzare, *vb.* raise.

alzarsi, *vb.* get up, rise.

amàbile, *adj.* amiable, likable, lovable.

amaca, *n.f.* hammock.

amàlgama, *n.m.* amalgam.

amalgamare, *vb.* amalgamate.

amante, 1. *n.m.* lover; *f.* mistress. 2. *adj.* fond.

amaramente, adv. bitterly.

amare, vb. love.

amareggiare, vb. embitter.

amarezza, n.f. bitterness.

amaro, adj. bitter.

ambasciata, n.f. embassy; message.

ambasciatore, n.m. ambassador.

ambedue, adj. and pron. both.

ambidestro, adj. ambidextrous.

ambiente, n.m. environment, habitat.

ambiguità, n.f. ambiguity.

ambiguo, adj. ambiguous.

ambizione, n.f. ambition.

ambizioso, adj. ambitious.

ambra, n.f. amber.

ambulanza, n.f. ambulance.

ambulatòrio, n. and adj. ambulatory.

Amburgo, n.m. Hamburg.

ameba, n.f. amoeba.

amenità, n.f. amenity.

América, n.f. America.

americano, n. and adj. American.

ametista, n.f. amethyst.

amica, n.f. friend.

amichévole, adj. friendly, amicable.

amichevolezza, n.f. friendliness.

amicizia, n.f. friendship, amity.

amico, 1. n.m. friend. 2. adj. friendly.

àmido, n.m. starch.

ammaccare, vb. bruise.

ammaccatura, n.f. bruise.

ammalato, adj. sick.

ammaliare, vb. bewitch.

ammassare, vb. amass, hoard; lump.

ammasso, n.m. hoard, pile.

ammenda, n.f. fine.

amméttere, vb. admit.

ammiccare, vb. wink.

amministrare, vb. administer, manage.

amministrativo, adj. administrative.

amministratore, n.m. administrator, executive, manager.

amministrazione, n.f. administration, management.

ammiràbile, adj. admirable.

ammirabilmente, adv. admirably.

ammiràglia, n.f. nave a., flagship.

ammiragliato, n.m. admiralty.

ammiràglio, n.m. admiral.

ammirare, vb. admire.

ammiratore, n.m. admirer.

ammirazione, n.f. admiration.

ammirévole, adj. admirable.

ammissìbile, adj. admissible.

ammissione, n.f. admission, admittance.

ammobiliare, vb. furnish.

ammollire, vb. soften, mollify.

ammoníaca, n.f. ammonia.

ammonimento, n.m. warning.

ammonire, vb. admonish, warn, caution.

ammonizione, n.f. admonition.

ammontare, vb. amount.

ammorbidire, vb. soften; baste.

ammortire, vb. deaden.

ammortizzare, vb. amortize.

ammucchiare, vb. heap, pile, stack.

ammuffito, adj. musty.

ammutinamento, n.m. mutiny.

amnesia, n.f. amnesia.

amniocentèsi, n.f. amniocentesis.

amnistia, n.f. amnesty.

amorale, adj. amoral.

amore, n.m. love.

amorfo, adj. amorphous.

amoroso, adj. amorous, of love.

amovìbile, adj. removable.

ampère, n.m. ampere.

ampiezza, n.f. breadth.

ampio, adj. ample; extensive; broad, wide.

amplesso, n.m. (sexual) embrace.

ampliare, vb. amplify.

amplificare, vb. amplify.

ampollina, n.f. cruet.

ampolloso, adj. stilted.

amputare, vb. amputate.

amputato, 1. n.m. amputee. 2. adj. amputated.

anacronismo, n.m. anachronism.

analfabèta, n. and adj. illiterate.

analfabetismo, n.m. illiteracy.

anàlisi, n.f. analysis.

analista, n.m. analyst.

analítico, adj. analytic.

analizzare, vb. analyze.

analogia, n.f. analogy.

análogo, adj. analogous.

ananás, n.m. pineapple.

anarchia, n.f. anarchy.

anatomia, n.f. anatomy.

anca, n.f. haunch, hip.

ancella, n.f. handmaid.

anche, adv. also, too; even.

anchilòstoma, n.m. hookworm.

ància, n.f. reed.

ancora, adv. still, yet.

àncora, n.f. anchor.

ancorare, vb. anchor.

ancoràggio, n.m. anchorage.

andare, vb. go; fare; (health). a. bene a, fit; become. a. a zonzo, loaf, loiter, lounge; saunter.

andàrsene, vb. go away.

andatura, n.f. gait.

anèddoto, n.m. anecdote.

anelare, vb. pant.

anèllo, n.m. ring, link.

anemia, n.f. anemia.

anestesia, n.f. anesthesia.

anestètico, n.m. and adj. anesthetic.

anestetista, n.m. anesthetist.

anéto, n.m. dill.

anfìbio, 1. n.m. amphibian. 2. adj. amphibious.

anfiteatro, n.m. amphitheater.

àngelo, n.m. angel.

angolare, adj. angular.

àngolo, n.m. angle, corner.

angòscia, n.f. anguish, heartache.

anguilla, n.f. eel.

ànice, n.m. anise.

anile, n.m. anil, bluing.

anilìna, n.f. aniline.

ànima, n.f. soul.

animale, n.m. and adj. animal.

animare, vb. animate.

animazione, n.f. animation.

ànimo, n.m. spirit, animus, mind.

animosità, n.f. animosity.

ànitra, n.f. duck.

annali, n.m. (pl.) annals.

annegare, vb. drown.

annerire, vb. blacken.

annessione, n.f. annexation.

annèsso, n.m. annex.

annèttere, vb. annex.

annichilire, vb. annihilate.

annidarsi, vb. nestle.

anniversàrio, n.m. anniversary.

anno, n.m. year.

annobilire, vb. ennoble.

annoiare, vb. annoy, bore, harass.

annotare, vb. annotate.

annotazione, n.f. annotation.

annuale, n.m. and adj. annual, yearly.

annualità, n.f. annuity.

annunciare, vb. announce.

annunciatore, n.m. announcer.

annunciatrice, n.f. announcer.

annullamento, n.m. annulment, cancellation, nullification.

annullare, vb. annul, cancel, nullify.

annunziare, vb. announce.

annunzio, n.m. announcement, advertisement.

ànnuo, adj. annual.

ànodo, n.m. anode.

anomalìa, n.f. anomaly.

anòmalo, adj. anomalous.

anònimo, adj. anonymous.

anormale, adj. abnormal.

anormalità, n.f. abnormality.

anormalmente, adv. abnormally.

ansando, adj. panting, breathless.

ansante, adj. panting, out of breath.

ansare, vb. pant, be out of breath.

ànsia, n.f. anxiety.

ansietà, n.f. anxiety, concern, worry.

ansioso, adj. anxious.

antico, adj. ancient, antique.

antiàcido, n.m. antacid.

antagonismo, n.m. antagonism.

antagonista, n.m. antagonist, opponent, villain.

antàrtico, n.m. and adj. antarctic.

antecedente, adj. antecedent.

antenato, n.m. ancestor, forebear, forefather.

antenna, n.f. antenna; (radio) aerial.

anteprima, *n.f.* preview.

anteriore, *adj.* anterior, previous, fore.

antiàcido, *adj.* antacid.

antiaèreo, *adj.* antiaircraft.

anticamente, *adv.* in ancient times, formerly.

anticàmera, *n.f.* anteroom.

anticipare, *vb.* anticipate; advance (payment).

anticipato, *adj.* anticipated, foregone.

anticipazione, *n.f.* anticipation.

anticipo, *n.m.* advance payment; down payment. in a., beforehand.

anticlericale, *adj.* anticlerical.

antico, *adj.* ancient, antique.

anticòrpo, *n.m.* antibody.

antidoto, *n.m.* antidote.

antifona, *n.f.* anthem.

antilope, *n.f.* antelope.

antimònio, *n.m.* antimony.

antinucleare, *adj.* antinuclear.

antipasto, *n.m.* hors d'oeuvres, appetizer.

antipatia, *n.f.* antipathy, dislike.

antipàtico, *adj.* disagreeable, nasty.

antiquato, *adj.* antiquated.

antiquità, *n.f.* antiquity.

antisèttico, *n.m. and adj.* antiseptic.

antisociale, *adj.* antisocial.

antitossina, *n.f.* antitoxin.

antologia, *n.f.* anthology.

antrace, *n.m.* anthrax.

antracite, *n.f.* anthracite.

antropologia, *n.f.* anthropology.

antropològico, *adj.* anthropological.

apatia, *n.f.* apathy.

apàtico, *adj.* apathetic.

ape, *n.f.* bee.

apèrto, *adj.* open, overt.

apertura, *n.f.* opening, aperture, gap.

apiàrio, *n.m.* apiary.

àpice, *n.m.* apex.

apogèo, *n.m.* apogee, high point, heyday.

apologia, *n.f.* apology.

apoplessia, *n.f.* apoplexy.

apoplèttico, *adj.* apoplectic.

apòstata, *n.m.* apostate.

apostòlico, *adj.* apostolic.

apòstolo, *n.m.* apostle.

appaciamento, *n.m.* appeasement.

appannare, *vb.* tarnish.

appannatura, *n.f.* tarnish.

apparato, *n.m.* apparatus.

apparècchio, *n.m.* apparatus.

apparènte, *adj.* apparent.

apparènza, *n.f.* appearance, guise.

apparire, *vb.* appear.

apparizione, *n.f.* apparition.

appartamento, *n.m.* apartment, flat.

appartenènza, *n.f.* belonging, appurtenance.

appartenere, *vb.* belong, pertain.

appassionato, *adj.* passionate.

appassire, *vb.* fade, wilt.

appellante, *n.m.* appellant.

appellare, *vb.* appeal.

appèllo, *n.m.* appeal, call, roll-call.

appena, *adv.* hardly, scarcely, just, barely.

appendectomia, *n.f.* appendectomy.

appendice, *n.f.* appendix, appendage.

appendicite, *n.f.* appendicitis.

appetito, *n.m.* appetite.

appezzamento, *n.m.* lot, plot.

appiattire, *vb.* flatten.

appiccicare, *vb.* stick.

applaudire, *vb.* applaud, cheer, clap.

applàuso, *n.m.* applause, cheer, plaudit.

applicàbile, *adj.* applicable.

applicare, *vb.* apply.

applicazione, *n.f.* application.

appoggiare, *vb.* support, back (up), lean.

appòggio, *n.m.* support, backing; foothold, footing; furtherance.

appollaiarsi, *vb.* roost, perch.

apportare, *vb.* bring, fetch.

apposizione, *n.f.* apposition.

appòsta, *adv.* on purpose, advisedly, deliberately.

apprendista, *n.m.* apprentice.

apprezzàbile, *adj.* appreciable.

apprezzamento, *n.m.* appreciation.

apprezzare, *vb.* appreciate, value, prize.

approfittare, *vb.* profit.

approfondire, *vb.* deepen.

appropriato, *adj.* appropriate.

appropriarsi, *vb.* appropriate.

approssimare, *vb.* approximate.

approssimativamente, *adv.* approximately.

approssimativo, *adj.* approximate.

approssimazione, *n.f.* approximation.

approvare, *vb.* approve.

approvazione, *n.f.* approval, approbation.

appuntamento, *n.m.* appointment, date, engagement, rendezvous, tryst.

aprile, *n.m.* April.

aprire, *vb.* open, unlock.

apriscàtole, *n.m.* can-opener.

àquila, *n.f.* eagle.

aquilino, *adj.* aquiline.

aquilone, *n.m.* kite.

aquilòtto, *n.m.* eaglet.

aràbile, *adj.* arable.

àrabo, 1. *n.* Arab. 2. *adj.* Arabic.

archidde, *n.f.* peanut.

aragosta, *n.f.* lobster.

araldica, *n.f.* heraldry.

araldico, *adj.* heraldic.

araldo, *n.m.* herald.

arància, *n.f.* orange.

aranciata, *n.f.* orangeade.

aràncio, *n.m.* orange tree.

arare, *vb.* plow.

aratro, *n.m.* plow.

arbitrare, *vb.* arbitrate.

arbitràrio, *adj.* arbitrary, high-handed.

arbitrato, *n.m.* arbitration.

àrbitro, *n.m.* arbiter, arbitrator, judge, referee, umpire.

arbòreo, *adj.* arboreal.

arbusto, *n.m.* shrub.

arca, *n.f.* ark.

arcàico, *adj.* archaic.

archeologia, *n.f.* archaeology.

archetto, *n.m.* little bow. gambe ad a., bow legs.

architetto, *n.m.* architect.

architettònico, *adj.* architectural.

architettura, *n.f.* architecture.

archiviare, *vb.* file.

archivio, *n.m.* archives, file.

arcidiòcesi, *n.f.* archdiocese.

arcidùca, *n.m.* archduke.

arcière, *n.m.* archer.

arcipèlago, *n.m.* archipelago.

arcivéscovo, *n.m.* archbishop.

arco, *n.m.* arc, arch; bow. tiro dell'a., archery.

arcobaleno, *n.m.* rainbow.

ardènte, *adj.* ardent, burning.

àrdere, *vb.* burn.

ardèsia, *n.f.* slate.

ardimento, *n.m.* boldness.

ardire, *vb.* be bold, dare.

arditamente, *adv.* boldly.

ardito, *adj.* bold.

ardore, *n.m.* ardor.

àrduo, *adj.* arduous, difficult.

àrea, *n.f.* area.

àrem, *n.m.* harem.

arena, *n.f.* sand, arena.

arenarsi, *vb.* get stranded.

argènteo, *adj.* silver.

Argentina, *n.f.* Argentine.

argentino, *adj.* silvery; Argentine.

argènto, *n.m.* silver.

argilla, *n.f.* clay.

argillòso, *adj.* clayey.

àrgine, *n.m.* embankment.

argomento, *n.m.* argument, topic.

arguire, *vb.* argue; deduce, conclude.

ària, *n.f.* air, (music) aria.

àrido, *adj.* arid.

aringa, *n.f.* herring.

arioso, *adj.* airy.

aristòcrate, *n.m.* aristocrat.

aristocràtico, *adj.* aristocratic.

aristocrazia, *n.f.* aristocracy.

aritmètica, *n.f.* arithmetic.

Arlecchino, *n.m.* Harlequin.

arma, *n.f.* arm (weapon). a. da fuòco, firearm.

armàdio, *n.m.* clothes-closet.

armamento, *n.m.* armament.

arma nucleare, *n.f.* nuclear weapon.

armare, *vb.* arm.

armatura, *n.f.* armor.

armeria, *n.f.* armory.

armistizio, n.m. armistice.
armonia, n.f. harmony.
armònica, n.f. harmonica.
armònico, adj. harmonic.
armonioso, adj. harmonious, dulcet.
armonizzare, vb. harmonize.
àrnica, n.f. arnica.
aròma, n.m. aroma.
aromàtico, adj. aromatic.
arpa, n.f. harp.
arrabbiarsi, vb. get angry.
arrabbiato, adj. angry.
arraffare, vb. grab.
arrampicarsi, vb. climb, creep, clamber up, scramble up.
arrampicatore, n.m. climber.
arrèndersi, vb. surrender.
arrestare, vb. arrest, apprehend; (refl.) stall.
arrèsto, n.m. arrest.
arretrato, adj. out-of-date.
arricchire, vb. enrich.
arricciare, vb. curl.
arringa, n.f. harangue.
arringare, vb. harangue.
arrischiare, vb. risk.
arrivare, vb. arrive.
arrivista, n.m. or f. social climber.
arrivo, n.m. arrival.
arrogante, adj. arrogant.
arroganza, n.f. arrogance.
arrogarsi, vb. arrogate, assume.
arrolamento, n.m. enlistment.
arrolare, vb. enlist.
arrossire, vb. blush.
arrostire, vb. roast.
arròsto, n.m. roast.
arrotolare, vb. roll up, coil.
arruffare, vb. ruffle, bristle.
arrugginire, vb. rust.
arrugginito, adj. rusty.
arruolare, vb. enroll; levy.
arsenale, n.m. arsenal; dockyard, navy yard.
arsènico, n.m. arsenic.
arte, n.f. art, trade, craft, craftsmanship, guild.
artèria, n.f. artery.
arteriale, adj. arterial.
arteriosclerosi, n.f. arteriosclerosis.
artesiano, adj. artesian.
àrtico, adj. Arctic.
articolare, vb. articulate.
articolato, adj. articulate.
articolazione, n.f. articulation; joint.
artìcolo, n.m. article, item. a. di fondo, editorial.
artificiale, adj. artificial.
artificialità, n.f. artificiality.
artifìcio, n.m. artifice.
artigiano, n.m. artisan, craftsman.
artiglière, n.m. gunner.
artiglieria, n.f. artillery.
artìglio, n.m. talon, claw.
artista, n.m. or f. artist.
artìstico, adj. artistic.
arto, n.m. limb.
artrite, n.f. arthritis.
arzillo, adj. spry.
asbèsto, n.m. asbestos.

ascèlla, n.f. armpit.
Ascensione, n.f. (eccles.) Ascension, Assumption.
ascensore, n.m. elevator, lift.
ascèsso, n.m. abscess.
ascètico, n.m. and adj. ascetic.
àscia, n.f. axe.
asciugamani, n.m. handtowel.
asciugapiatti, n.m. dishtowel.
asciugare, vb. dry, blot, wipe.
asciugatòio, n.m. towel.
asciutto, adj. dry.
ascoltare, vb. listen to, hearken to, hark.
ascrìvere, vb. ascribe.
asfalto, n.m. asphalt.
asfìssia, n.f. asphyxia.
asfissiare, vb. asphyxiate, smother.
Asia, n.f. Asia.
asiàtico, adj. Asian.
asimmetrìa, n.f. asymmetry.
àsino, n.m. ass, donkey.
asma, n.m. asthma. a. del fièno, hay fever.
asmàtico, adj. asthmatic.
aspàrago, n.m. asparagus.
asperità, n.f. asperity.
aspettare, vb. await, wait (for); (refl.) expect.
aspettativa, n.f. expectation, expectancy.
aspètto, n.m. aspect, appearance, look; meaning.
aspirante, n.m. aspirant.
aspirare, vb. aspire, aspirate.
aspirato, adj. aspirate (consonant).
aspiratore, n.m. aspirator.
aspirazione, n.f. aspiration, suction.
aspirina, n.f. aspirin.
asprezza, n.f. harshness.
aspro, adj. harsh.
assaggiare, vb. test, try, assay, sample.
assalire, vb. assail, attack, beset.
assalitore, n.m. assailant, attacker.
assaltare, vb. assault.
assalto, n.m. assault, bout, round.
assassinare, vb. assassinate.
assassinio, n.m. assassination, murder.
assassino, n.m. assassin, murderer.
asse, 1. n.m. axis, axle. 2. n.f. board, plank.
asse a rotelle, n.m. skateboard.
assediante, n.m. besieger.
assediare, vb. besiege, beset.
assèdio, n.m. siege.
assegnàbile, adj. assignable.
assegnamento, n.m. assignment.
assegnare, vb. assign, allot, allocate.
assegnazione, n.f. assignment, allotment.
assegno, n.m. check; allowance.
assegno (per) viaggiatori, n.m. travelers' check.

assemblèa, n.f. assembly, gathering, meeting.
assennato, adj. sensible.
assènso, n.m. assent.
assente, 1. n. absentee. 2. adj. absent.
assentire, vb. assent.
assenza, n.f. absence.
assènzio, n.m. absinthe.
asserire, vb. assert.
asservire, vb. enslave.
asserzione, n.f. assertion.
assessore, n.m. assessor.
asseverare, vb. asseverate.
asseverazione, n.f. asseveration.
assicurare, vb. assure, insure.
assicurazione, n.f. assurance, insurance.
assiduamente, adv. assiduously.
assìduo, adj. assiduous.
assimilare, vb. assimilate.
assimilativo, adj. assimilative.
assimilazione, n.f. assimilation.
assiòma, n.m. axiom.
assistènte, n. and adj. assistant.
assistente mèdico, n.m. paramedic.
assistènza, n.f. attendance, assistance, relief. a. sociale, social work.
assistere, vb. be present.
asso, n.m. ace.
associare, vb. associate, affiliate.
associazione, n.f. association, affiliation.
assoggettare, vb. subject.
assolo, n.m. solo.
assolutamente, adv. absolutely.
assolutezza, n.f. absoluteness.
assolutismo, n.m. absolutism.
assoluto, adj. absolute.
assoluzione, n.f. absolution, acquittal.
assòlvere, vb. absolve, acquit.
assomiglianza, n.f. likeness.
assonanza, n.f. assonance.
assopirsi, vb. drowse.
assorbènte, 1. n.m. absorbent. 2. adj. absorbent, absorbing.
assorbimento, n.m. absorption.
assorbire, vb. absorb.
assorbito, adj. absorbed.
assordare, vb. deafen.
assortimento, n.m. assortment.
assortire, vb. assort, sort.
assortito, adj. assorted.
assorto, adj. absorbed.
assùmere, vb. assume, take on.
assurdamente, adv. absurdly.
assurdità, n.f. absurdity, nonsense.
assurdo, 1. n.m. absurdity. 2. adj. absurd, preposterous.
astèmio, adj. abstemious.
astenersi, vb. abstain, refrain.
asterisco, n.m. asterisk.
asteròide, n.m. asteroid.
astigmatismo, n.m. astigmatism.
astinènza, n.f. abstinence.

àstio, *n.m.* grudge.

astrale, *adj.* astral, of the stars.

astrarre, *vb.* abstract.

astratto, *adj.* abstract, abstracted.

astrazione, *n.f.* abstraction.

astringènte, *adj.* astringent.

astro, *n.m.* star, aster.

astrologia, *n.f.* astrology.

astronauta, *n.m.* astronaut.

astronomia, *n.f.* astronomy.

astruso, *adj.* abstruse.

astuccio, *n.m.* case.

astuto, *adj.* astute, artful, clever, canny, cunning, designing.

astùzia, *n.f.* guile.

atassia, *n.f.* ataxia.

àteo, 1. *n.m.* atheist. 2. *adj.* atheistic, godless.

atlante, *n.m.* atlas.

atlàntico, *adj.* Atlantic.

atlèta, *n.m.* athlete.

atlètico, *adj.* athletic.

atletismo, *n.m.* athletics.

atmosfèra, *n.f.* atmosphere.

atmosfèrico, *adj.* atmospheric.

atòllo, *n.m.* atoll.

atòmico, *adj.* atomic.

àtomo, *n.m.* atom.

atonale, *adj.* atonal.

atroce, *adj.* atrocious, heinous.

atrocità, *n.f.* atrocity.

atrofia, *n.f.* atrophy.

atropina, *n.f.* atropine.

attaccàbile, *adj.* assailable.

attaccamento, *n.m.* attachment.

attaccapanni, *n.m.* coathanger.

attaccare, *vb.* attach, fasten, hitch, tack, stick; attack, assail.

attaccaticcio, *adj.* sticky.

attacco, *n.m.* attack, onslaught.

atteggiamento, *n.m.* attitude.

atteggiarsi, *vb.* take an attitude.

attentamente, *adv.* attentively, carefully.

attènto, *adj.* attentive, careful, thoughtful.

attenuare, *vb.* attenuate.

attenzione, *n.f.* attention, carefulness, notice.

atterràggio, *n.m.* landing. pista d'a., landing strip, runway.

atterrare, *vb.* land.

atterrire, *vb.* terrify.

attesa, *n.f.* wait. in a. di, while waiting for, pending.

attestare, *vb.* attest, vouch for.

àttimo, *n.m.* instant.

attinio, *n.m.* actinium.

attirare, *vb.* attract, entice, lure, decoy.

attitùdine, *n.f.* aptitude.

attivamente, *adv.* actively, busily.

attivare, *vb.* activate.

attivatore, *n.m.* activator.

attivazione, *n.f.* activation.

attivismo, *n.m.* activism.

attività, *n.f.* activity.

attivo, 1. *n.m.* asset. 2. *adj.* active, busy.

attizzare, *vb.* stir, poke.

atto, 1. *n.m.* act, deed. 2. *adj.* apt, fitted.

attore, *n.m.* actor; plaintiff.

attraènte, *adj.* attractive, engaging, fetching.

attrarre, *vb.* attract.

attraversare, *vb.* cross, go through, pass through.

attravèrso, *adv. and prep.* across, through.

attrazione, *n.f.* attraction.

attrezzare, *vb.* rig.

attrezzatura, *n.f.* rig.

attribuìbile, *adj.* attributable.

attribuire, *vb.* attribute.

attribuzione, *n.f.* attribution.

attrice, *n.f.* actress.

attrizione, *n.f.* attrition.

attualità, *n.f.* reality, current significance; (*pl.*) newsreel.

attuare, *vb.* actuate.

attuàrio, *n.m.* actuary.

attutire, *vb.* silence.

audace, *adj.* audacious, bold, daring.

audàcia, *n.f.* audacity, boldness, daring.

audiovisivo, *adj.* audiovisual.

auditòrio, *n.m.* auditorium.

audizione, *n.f.* audition.

augurare, *vb.* augur; wish.

àula, *n.f.* hall; classroom.

aumentare, *vb.* augment, increase, raise, enhance; escalate.

aumènto, *n.m.* increase, raise, rise.

àureo, *n.m.* golden.

auréola, *n.f.* halo.

auriga, *n.m.* charioteer.

ausiliare, *n.m. and adj.* auxiliary.

auspicio, *n.m.* auspice.

austerità, *n.f.* austerity.

austèro, *adj.* austere.

Austria, *n.f.* Austria.

austrìaco, *adj.* Austrian.

autenticare, *vb.* authenticate.

autenticità, *n.f.* authenticity.

autèntico, *adj.* authentic.

autista, *n.m.* chauffeur, (auto) driver.

àuto, *n.f.* auto.

autobiografia, *n.f.* autobiography.

àutobus, *n.m.* bus.

autocarro, *n.m.* truck, lorry.

autòcrate, *n.m.* autocrat.

autocrazia, *n.f.* autocracy.

autògrafo, *n.m.* autograph.

autolinea, *n.f.* bus line.

autòma, *n.m.* automaton, robot.

automaticamente, *adv.* automatically.

automàtico, *adj.* automatic.

automòbile, *n.f.* automobile.

automobilista, *n.m.* motorist.

automobilìstico, *adj.* pertaining to automobiles, automotive.

automotrice, *n.f.* railcar.

autonomia, *n.f.* autonomy.

autònomo, *adj.* autonomous.

autoparcheggio, *n.m.* parking area.

autopsia, *n.f.* autopsy.

autore, *n.m.* author.

autorévole, *adj.* authoritative.

autorevolmente, *adv.* authoritatively.

autorimessa, *n.f.* garage.

autorità, *n.f.* authority.

autoritàrio, *adj.* authoritarian.

autorizzare, *vb.* authorize, empower, entitle.

autorizzazione, *n.f.* authorization.

autotreno, *n.m.* trailer truck.

autunno, *n.m.* autumn, fall.

avambràccio, *n.m.* forearm.

avamposto, *n.m.* outpost.

avana, *adj.* brown, beige.

avanguàrdia, *n.f.* vanguard.

avanti, 1. *adv.* in front, ahead, onward, forward, before; (clock) fast. 2. *prep.* before, in front of. 3. *interj.* come in!

avanzamento, *n.m.* advancement.

avanzare, *vb.* advance; be left over.

avanzato, *adj.* advanced.

avanzo, *n.m.* relic, left-over, surplus.

avaria, *n.f.* damage.

avariare, *vb.* damage.

avarìzia, *n.f.* avarice.

avaro, 1. *n.m.* miser. 2. *adj.* avaricious, miserly, grasping, stingy.

avemmaria, *n.f.* Hail Mary.

avena, *n.f.* oats.

avere, *vb.* have.

aviàrio, *n.m.* aviary.

aviatore, *n.m.* aviator, flier.

aviatrice, *n.f.* aviatrix.

aviazione, *n.f.* aviation.

àvido, *adj.* avid, greedy.

aviogètto, *n.m.* jet plane.

aviolinea, *n.f.* air line.

aviorimessa, *n.f.* hangar.

aviotrasportato, *adj.* airborne.

avòrio, *n.m.* ivory.

avornièllo, *n.m.* laburnum.

avvelenare, *vb.* poison.

avvenimento, *n.m.* event, happening, occurrence.

avvenire, *n.m.* future, futurity.

avventato, *adj.* reckless.

avventìzio, *adj.* adventitious.

avvènto, *n.m.* advent.

avventore, *n.m.* regular customer.

avventura, *n.f.* adventure.

avventurare, *vb.* adventure; risk.

avventurière, *n.m.* adventurer.

avventurosamente, *adv.* adventurously.

avventuroso, *adj.* adventurous, enterprising, venturesome.

avverbiale, *adj.* adverbial.

avvèrbio, *n.m.* adverb.

avversamente, *adv.* adversely.

avversàrio, *n.* adversary.

avversione, *n.f.* aversion.

avversità, n.f. adversity, hardship.

avvèrso, adj. adverse; averse.

avvertire, vb. warn, alert, advert.

avvicinarsi a, vb. approach.

avvilimento, n.m. abasement.

avvilire, vb. abase, debase.

avviluppare, vb. envelop.

avvisare, vb. inform, advise.

avviso, n.m. advice; news, information, notice, notification; warning.

avvitare, vb. screw.

avvizzire, vb. wither.

avvocato, n.m. advocate, lawyer.

avvòlgere, vb. wrap up, enfold, wind.

ayatolla(h), n.m. ayatollah.

aziènda, n.f. firm, concern.

azione, n.f. action; share (of stock).

azionists, n.m. stockholder.

azzuffarsi, vb. get into a scrap.

azzurro, adj. blue, azure.

B

babbo, n.m. dad, daddy, pop, pa.

babbuino, n.m. baboon.

bacca, n.f. berry.

baccano, n.m. uproar, racket, row.

baccellière, n.m. bachelor.

baccèllo, n.m. pod, shell.

bacchetta, n.f. wand, (conductor's) baton.

baciare, vb. kiss.

bacillo, n.m. bacillus.

bacino, n.m. basin, dock. b. di carenaggio, dry dock.

bàcio, n.m. kiss.

bada, n. a b., at bay.

badare, vb. heed, look out, mind.

badessa, n.f. abbess.

badìa, n.f. abbey.

baffi, n.m.pl. mustache.

bagàglio, n.m. baggage, luggage.

bagliore, n.m. glare.

bagnante, n.m. or f. bather.

bagnare, vb. bathe, soak.

bagnino, n.m. bath attendant, life-guard.

bagno, n.m. bath.

bàia, n.f. bay.

baio, adj. bay (color).

baionetta, n.f. bayonet.

balaùstra, n.f. balustrade.

balaustrata, n.f. balustrade.

balbettare, vb. babble, stammer.

balbetto, n.m. babble.

balbuziènte, n.m. stammerer, stutterer, babbler.

balcone, n.m. balcony.

baldacchino, n.m. canopy.

baldòria, n.f. carousing, revelry, spree.

balena, n.f. whale.

balenare, vb. flash.

baleno, n.m. flash.

bàlia, n.f. nurse.

ballstica, n.f. ballistics.

balla, n.f. bale.

ballàbile, n.m. dance tune.

ballare, vb. dance.

ballata, n.f. ballad, ballade.

ballatòio, n. catwalk.

ballerina, n.f. dancer, ballerina.

ballerino, n.m. dancer.

ballo, n.m. dance, dancing; ballet; ball.

balneare, adj. pertaining to baths or bathing.

balsàmico, adj. balmy, balsamous.

bàlsamo, n.m. balsam, balm.

baluardo, n.m. bulwark.

balzare, vb. bound, leap, dart.

balzo, n.m. bound, leap, dart.

bambina, n.f. child, little girl.

bambinaia, n.f. nurse.

bambinesco, adj. childish, babyish.

bambino, n.m. child, little boy.

bàmbola, n.f. doll.

bambù, n.m. bamboo.

banale, adj. banal, commonplace, hackneyed.

banalità, n.f. banality, platitude.

banana, n.f. banana.

banca, n.f. bank.

bancàrio, adj. pertaining to banks.

bancarotta, n.f. bankruptcy.

banchetto, n.m. banquet, feast.

banchière, n.m. banker.

banchina, n.f. pier.

banco, n.m. bank; bench; counter, stall.

banconota, n.f. bank note.

banda, n.f. band, gang; fillet.

bandièra, n.f. banner, flag, ensign.

bandire, vb. banish, exile.

bandista, n.m. bandsman.

bandito, n.m. bandit, outlaw.

banditore, n.m. crier, auctioneer.

bando, n.m. banishment, exile.

bar, n.m. bar.

bara, n.f. bier, pall.

barattare, vb. barter, swap.

baratterìa, n.f. graft.

baratto, n.m. barter, swap.

barba, n.f. beard.

barbabiètola, n.f. beet.

barbàrie, n.f. barbarism.

barbarismo, n.m. barbarism.

bàrbaro, 1. n. barbarian. 2. adj. barbarous.

barbazzale, n.m. curb.

barbetta, n.f. little beard, goatee.

barbière, n.m. barber.

barbitùrico, n.m. barbiturate.

barbuto, adj. bearded.

barca, n.f. boat.

barcollare, vb. stagger, totter.

bardare, vb. caparison, harness.

bardatura, n.f. caparison; harness.

barèlla, n.f. litter, stretcher.

barile, n.m. barrel, cask.

barlletto, n.m. keg.

bàrio, n.m. barium.

barista, n.m. bartender.

baritono, n.m. and adj. baritone.

barlume, n.m. glimmer, gleam.

baròcco, adj. baroque.

baromètrico, adj. barometric.

baròmetro, n.m. barometer.

baronale, adj. baronial.

barone, n.m. baron.

baronessa, n.f. baroness.

barricata, n.f. barricade.

barrièra, n.f. barrier.

basare, vb. base, ground.

base, n.f. base, basis, footing, ground.

basetta, n.f. whisker.

Basilèa, n.f. Basel.

bassezza, n.f. baseness.

basso, 1. n.m. bass. 2. adj. low, vile, base; bass.

bassofondo, n.m. slum.

bastardo, n.m. and adj. bastard, mongrel.

bastare, vb. suffict, be enough.

bastione, n.m. rampart.

bastonare, vb. club.

bastone, n.m. baton, stick, club, staff, rod, bat, cane.

battàglia, n.f. battle.

battaglièro, adj. bellicose, warlike, combative.

battàglio, n.m. clapper.

battaglione, n.m. battalion.

battèllo, n.m. boat. b. a remi, rowboat.

bàttere, vb. beat, batter.

battería, n.f. battery.

battèrio, n.m. bacterium. battèri, pl. bacteria.

batteriologìa, n.f. bacteriology.

batteriòlogo, n.m. bacteriologist.

battesimale, adj. baptismal.

battésimo, n.m. baptism, christening.

battezzare, vb. baptize, christen.

battibecco, n.m. squabble.

battipalo, n.m. ram.

battista, n.m. Baptist.

battistèro, n.m. baptistery.

bàttito, n.m. beat.

battuto, adj. beaten.

batùffolo, n.m. wad.

baùle, n.m. trunk.

bauxite, n.f. bauxite.

bauva, n.f. drivel.

bavaglino, n.m. bib.

bavàglio, n.m. gag.

bazàr, n.m. bazaar.

bazzècola, n.f. trifle.

beatamente, adv. blissfully.

beatificare, vb. beatify.

beatitùdine, n.f. bliss, beatitude.

beato, adj. blissful, blessed.

beccare, vb. peck.

becco, n.m. beak, bill; burner; spout.

Befana, n.f. old woman who

brings presents on Twelfth Night.

beffa, *n.f.* gibe.

beffarsi di, *vb.* gibe at, jeer at, mock.

belga, *adj.* Belgian.

Belgio, *n.m.* Belgium.

belletto, *n.m.* make-up.

bellezza, *n.f.* beauty. **salone di b.**, beauty parlor.

bellicosamente, *adv.* belligerently.

bellicoso, *adj.* bellicose, belligerent.

belligerante, *adj.* belligerent.

belligeranza, *n.f.* belligerence.

bellimbusto, *n.m.* dandy.

bellino, *adj.* cunning, cute, pretty, good-looking.

bello, *adj.* beautiful, fine, fair, handsome, lovely.

bellumore, *n.m.* way, wit.

benché, *conj.* although.

benda, *n.f.* bandage; blindfold; headband.

bendare, *vb.* blindfold.

bene, **1.** *n.m.* good, asset. **b. mobile**, chattel. **2.** *adv.* well.

benedetto, *adj.* blessed.

benedire, *vb.* bless.

benedizione, *n.f.* benediction, blessing.

benefattore, *n.m.* benefactor.

benefattrice, *n.f.* benefactress.

beneficare, *vb.* benefit.

beneficiario, *n.m.* beneficiary.

benefico, *adj.* beneficent.

benessere, *n.m.* welfare.

benevolenza, *n.f.* benevolence.

benevolmente, *adv.* benevolently.

benèvolo, *adj.* benevolent, kindly.

beni, *n.m.pl.* goods, estate.

benignità, *n.f.* benignity.

benigno, *adj.* benign.

benvenuto, *adj.* welcome.

benzina, *n.f.* benzine, gasoline.

bere, *vb.* drink.

beri-beri, *n.m.* beriberi.

Berna, *n.f.* Bern.

berretto, *n.m.* cap.

bersaglio, *n.m.* target.

bestémmia, *n.f.* blasphemy, curse-word, expletive, oath.

bestemmiare, *vb.* blaspheme, curse, swear.

bestemmiatore, *n.m.* blasphemer.

bestia, *n.f.* beast.

bestiale, *adj.* bestial, beastly.

bestiame, *n.m.* cattle; animals, livestock.

bèttola, *n.f.* (low-class) wineshop.

bevanda, *n.f.* beverage, drink.

bevibile, *adj.* drinkable.

biancheria, *n.f.* linen, laundry.

bianco, *adj.* white, blank.

biancospino, *n.m.* hawthorn.

biasimare, *vb.* blame.

biasimo, *n.* blame.

Bibbia, *n.f.* Bible.

bibita, *n.f.* drink.

biblico, *adj.* Biblical.

bibliografia, *n.f.* bibliography.

biblioteca, *n.f.* library.

bibliotecario, *n.m.* librarian.

bicarbonato, *n.m.* bicarbonate.

bicchiere, *n.m.* glass.

bicentennale, *adj.* bicentennial.

bicicletta, *n.f.* bicycle.

bicipite, *n.m.* biceps.

bidello, *n.m.* janitor.

bidone, *n.m.* large can.

biennale, *adj.* biennial; biannual.

biennio, *n.m.* two-year period.

bietta, *n.f.* wedge, cleat.

bifocale, *adj.* bifocal.

biforcazione, *n.f.* crotch; junction.

bigamia, *n.f.* bigamy.

bigamo, **1.** *n.* bigamist. **2.** *adj.* bigamous.

bighellone, *n.m.* gadabout, loafer.

bigliettaio, *n.m.* ticket agent; (tram, bus) conductor.

biglietto, *n.m.* note; (money) bill; card; ticket. **b. di visita**, calling card.

bigotteria, *n.f.* bigotry.

bigottismo, *n.m.* bigotry.

bigotto, **1.** *n.* bigot. **2.** *adj.* bigoted.

bilancia, *n.f.* balance, scales.

bilanciare, *vb.* balance.

bilaterale, *adj.* bilateral.

bile, *n.f.* bile.

biliardo, *n.m.* billiards.

biliare, *adj.* bilious.

bilingue, *adj.* bilingual.

bilione, *n.m.* billion.

bilioso, *adj.* bilious.

bimbo, *n.m.* child, baby.

bimensile, *adj.* bimonthly (twice a month).

bimestrale, *adj.* bimonthly (every two months).

bimestre, *n.m.* two months' period.

bimetallico, *adj.* bimetallic.

binario, *n.m.* track.

binda, *n.f.* jack.

binòcolo, *n.m.* binoculars, spyglasses. **b. da teatro**, operaglasses.

binoculare, *adj.* binocular.

biochimica, *n.f.* biochemistry.

biografia, *n.f.* biography.

biografico, *adj.* biographical.

biografo, *n.m.* biographer.

biologia, *n.f.* biology.

biologicamente, *adv.* biologically.

biologico, *adj.* biological.

biondo, *adj.* blond(e), fair.

biossido, *n.m.* dioxide.

bipede, *n.m. and adj.* biped.

birichinata, *n.f.* prank.

birichino, *adj.* naughty.

birra, *n.f.* ale, beer.

birraio, *n.m.* brewer.

bisbigliare, *vb.* whisper.

bisbiglio, *n.m.* whisper.

biscòtto, *n.m.* cracker, biscuit, cookie.

bisecare, *vb.* bisect.

bisestile, *adj.* **anno b.**, leap year.

bisettimanale, *adj.* twice weekly, biweekly.

bismuto, *n.m.* bismuth.

bisognare, *vb.* be necessary.

bisogno, *n.m.* need, want.

bisognoso, *adj.* needy.

bisonte, *n.m.* bison.

bistecca, *n.f.* beefsteak, steak.

bisticciarsi, *vb.* quarrel, argue, bicker.

bisticcio, *n.m.* quarrel, argument; pun.

bistrattare, *vb.* mistreat.

bivacco, *n.m.* bivouac.

bivio, *n.m.* (road) fork, junction.

bizzeffe, *n.f.pl.* **a b.**, galore.

blandire, *vb.* blandish, coax.

blando, *adj.* bland; suave.

blatta, *n.f.* cockroach.

bleso, *adj.* lisping.

blindato, *adj.* armored. **carro b.**, tank.

bloccare, *vb.* block.

blocco, *n.m.* bloc; block; blockade.

blu, *adj.* blue.

blue jeans, *n.m.pl.* blue jeans.

bluff, *n.m.* bluff (at cards, etc.).

bluffare, *vb.* bluff (at cards, etc.).

bluffatore, *n.m.* bluffer.

blusa, *n.f.* blouse.

boa, *n.f.* buoy.

bobina, *n.f.* bobbin, reel, spool; coil.

bocca, *n.f.* mouth. **a b. aperta**, open-mouthed, agape.

boccaporto, *n.m.* hatch, hatchway.

boccheggiamento, *n.m.* gasp.

boccheggiare, *vb.* gasp.

boccia, *n.f.* bowl.

bocciare, *vb.* fail, flunk.

boccone, *n.m.* morsel, swallow.

boemo, *n.m. and adj.* Bohemian.

boia, *n.m.* executioner.

boicottaggio, *n.m.* boycott.

boicottare, *vb.* boycott.

boliviano, *adj.* Bolivian.

bolla, *n.f.* bubble.

bollare, *vb.* stamp.

bollettino, *n.m.* bulletin.

bollire, *vb.* boil.

bollo, *n.m.* stamp.

bolo, *n.m.* cud.

bomba, *n.f.* bomb; bombshell. **b. al neutron**, neutron bomb.

bombardamento, *n.m.* bombardment.

bombardare, *vb.* bombard, shell.

bombardiere, *n.m.* bomber, bombardier.

bomboletta nebulizzante, *n.f.* aerosol bomb.

bonifica, *n.f.* reclamation.

bonificare, *vb.* reclaim.

bontà, *n.f.* goodness.

borbottamento, *n.m.* mumbling, gibberish.

borbottare, *vb.* mutter.

bordata, *n.f.* broadside.

bordèllo, *n.m.* brothel.

bordo, *n.m.* board (side of ship); edge, brink, rim. **a b. di,** *prep.* aboard, on board (of).

borghese, *adj.* bourgeois, middle-class.

borghesìa, *n.f.* bourgeoisie, middle class.

borgo, *n.m.* village, burg, borough.

borgognone, *n.m.* iceberg.

bòrico, *adj.* boric.

borsa, *n.f.* bag, brief-case, pouch, purse; fellowship; stock exchange. **b. di studio,** scholarship.

borsaiòlo, *n.m.* pickpocket.

borsetta, *n.f.* little bag, purse, handbag.

boschetto, *n.m.* grove.

bosco, *n.m.* wood.

boscoso, *adj.* wooded.

botànica, *n.f.* botany.

botànico, *adj.* botanical.

bottaio, *n.m.* cooper.

bòtte, *n.f.* cask, hogshead.

bottega, *n.f.* shop.

botteghino, *n.m.* box-office.

bottiglia, *n.f.* bottle, jar.

bottino, *n.m.* booty, plunder, loot.

bottone, *n.m.* button.

bovaro, *n.m.* cattleman.

bovino, *adj.* bovine.

bòzze, *n.f.pl.* proof. **b. in colonna,** galley-proof. **b. impaginate,** page-proof.

bòzzolo, *n.m.* cocoon.

braccialetto, *n.m.* bracelet.

bracciata, *n.f.* armful.

braccio, *n.m.* arm; fathom.

brace, *n.f.* embers.

brache, *n.f.pl.* breeches, pants.

brama, *n.f.* ardent desire, craving, eagerness, longing.

bramare, *vb.* desire ardently, covet, crave, long for, yearn for.

bramosamente, *adv.* desirously, covetously, eagerly.

bramoso, *adj.* desirous, covetous, eager.

brànchia, *n.f.* gill.

brandire, *vb.* brandish.

brano, *n.m.* passage, excerpt.

Brasile, *n.m.* Brazil.

brasiliano, *adj.* Brazilian.

bravata, *n.f.* bravado.

bravo, 1. *n.* henchman. **2.** *adj.* fine.

brèccia, *n.f.* breach.

brefotròfio, *n.m.* foundling hospital.

Brètone, *n.m.* Briton.

brève, *adj.* brief, short.

brevemente, *adv.* briefly.

brevettare, *vb.* patent.

brevetto, *n.m.* patent.

brevità, *n.f.* brevity, briefness.

brezza, *n.f.* breeze.

briccone, *n.m.* rascal, rogue.

bricconesco, *adj.* roguish.

briciola, *n.f.* crumb.

brigantino, *n.m.* brig.

brigata, *n.f.* brigade.

briglia, *n.f.* bridle.

brillante, *adj.* brilliant.

brillare, *vb.* shine.

brina, *n.f.* frost.

brindare, *vb.* toast.

brindisi, *n.m.* toast, health.

brio, *n.m.* vim, verve.

brioso, *adj.* lively, sprightly.

britànnico, *adj.* British.

brivido, *n.m.* shudder, shiver, chill.

bròcca, *n.f.* jug, pitcher.

broccato, *n.m.* brocade.

bròdo, *n.m.* broth, bouillon. **b. ristretto,** consommé.

bronchiale, *adj.* bronchial.

bronchite, *n.f.* bronchitis.

brontolamento, *n.m.* grumble.

brontolare, *vb.* grumble, growl; rumble.

brontolìo, *n.m.* rumble.

bronzo, *n.m.* bronze.

brucare, *vb.* browse.

bruciare, *vb.* burn, scorch.

bruciatura, *n.f.* burn.

bruciore di stòmaco, *n.m.* heartburn.

bruco, *n.m.* caterpillar, cankerworm.

brughièra, *n.f.* heath, moor.

bruna, *n.f.* brunette.

brunire, *vb.* burnish.

bruno, *adj.* brown.

bruscamente, *adv.* brusquely.

brusco, *adj.* brusque.

bruscolo, *n.m.* cinder.

brutale, *adj.* brutal.

brutalità, *n.f.* brutality.

bruto, *n.m. and adj.* brute.

bruttezza, *n.f.* ugliness.

brutto, *adj.* ugly, homely.

buca, *n.f.* pit, pot-hole.

bucato, *n.m.* laundry.

bùccia, *n.f.* hull, husk, peel, rind, skin.

bùccina, *n.f.* bugle.

buco, *n.m.* hole.

budèllo, *n.m.* bowel, intestine, gut.

budino, *n.m.* pudding.

bue, *n.m.* ox; beef.

bùfalo, *n.m.* buffalo.

buffonata, *n.f.* antic.

buffone, *n.m.* buffoon, jester.

bugìa, *n.f.* lie, fabrication, falsehood.

bugiardo, 1. *n.m.* liar. **2.** *adj.* lying.

bùio, 1. *n.m.* darkness. **2.** *adj.* dark.

bulbo, *n.m.* bulb.

bulletta, *n.f.* tack.

bungalò, *n.m.* bungalow.

buongustaio, *n.m.* gourmet.

buòn mercato, *n.m.* cheapness.

buòno, 1. *n.m.* bond. **2.** *adj.* good.

burattino, *n.m.* puppet.

bùrbero, *adj.* gruff.

burla, *n.f.* trick, practical joke, prank.

burlone, *n.m.* joker.

burro, *n.m.* butter.

burrone, *n.m.* ravine, canyon, gulch, gully.

bussare, *vb.* knock.

bussata, *n.f.* knock.

bùssola, *n.f.* compass.

busta, *n.f.* envelope.

busto, *n.m.* bust; bodice, corset.

buttare, *vb.* throw, toss.

C

C (on water faucets) = **caldo,** *adj.* hot.

cabina, *n.f.* cabin, stateroom.

cablogramma, *n.m.* cablegram.

cacao, *n.m.* cocoa.

càccia, *n.m.* fighter plane.

càccia, *n.f.* hunt, hunting, chase.

cacciare, *vb.* hunt, chase; stick; shove.

cacciatore, *n.m.* hunter, chaser.

cacciatorpedinière, *n.m.* destroyer.

cacciatrice, *n.f.* huntress.

cacciavite, *n.m.* screw-driver.

cachì, *n.m.* khaki.

càcio, *n.m.* cheese.

cacofonìa, *n.f.* cacophony.

cacto, *n.m.* cactus.

cadauno, 1. *adj.* each; apiece. **2.** *pron.* each one.

cadàvere, *n.m.* cadaver, corpse.

cadavèrico, *adj.* cadaverous.

cadènza, *n.f.* cadence, cadenza.

cadere, *vb.* fall. **lasciar c.,** drop.

cadetto, *n.m.* cadet.

còdmio, *n.m.* cadmium.

caduta, *n.f.* fall.

caffè, *n.m.* coffee; café; buffet.

caffeina, *n.f.* caffeine.

cagionare, *vb.* occasion, cause.

cagna, *n.f.* bitch.

caimano, *n.m.* cayman.

calabrone, *n.m.* bumblebee, hornet.

calafatare, *vb.* calk.

calafato, *n.m.* calker.

calamità, *n.f.* calamity, woe.

calamitoso, *adj.* calamitous.

calapranzi, *n.m.* dumbwaiter.

calare, *vb.* lower.

calcagno, *n.m.* heel.

calcare, *adj.* calcareous. **pietra c.,** limestone.

calce, *n.f.* lime.

calcificare, *vb.* calcify.

calcina, *n.f.* mortar.

càlcio, *n.m.* calcium; kick; football; butt (of gun).

calcolàbile, *adj.* calculable.

calcolare, *vb.* calculate.

calcolatore, 1. *adj.* calculating. **2.** *n.m.* computer.

calcolatrice elettrònica, *n.f.* computer.

càlcolo, *n.m.* calculus; calculation. **c. biliare,** gallstone.

caldaia, *n.f.* boiler, caldron, furnace.

caldo, 1. *n.m.* heat. **2.** *adj.* hot, warm.

caleidoscòpio, n.m. kaleido-scope.

calendàrio, n.m. calendar.

caletta, n.f. joggle.

càlibro, n.m. caliber; calipers.

càlice, n.m. chalice; calyx.

calicò, n.m. calico.

callifugo, n.m. corn-plaster.

calligrafia, n.f. calligraphy, handwriting.

callista, n.m. chiropodist.

callo, n.m. callus, corn.

callosità, n.f. callousness.

calloso, adj. callous, horny.

calma, n.f. calm, composure; stillness.

calmare, vb. calm, soothe; still.

calmo, adj. calm, composed; still.

calore, n.m. heat, warmth.

caloria, n.f. calorie.

calòrico, adj. caloric.

calorìfero, n.m. heater.

calorìmetro, n.m. calorimeter.

caloroso, adj. warm.

calpestare, vb. tread on.

calunnia, n.f. calumny, slan-der, slur.

calunniare, vb. calumniate, slander, slur.

Calvàrio, n.m. Calvary.

calvìzie, n.f.sg. baldness.

calvo, adj. bald.

calza, n.f. stocking, (pl.) hose.

calzare, vb. shoe.

calzetteria, n.f. hosiery.

calzino, n.m. sock.

calzolaio, n.m. shoemaker, cobbler.

calzoni, n.m.pl. trousers.

camaleonte, n.m. chameleon.

cambiamento, n.m. change, shift.

cambiare, vb. change, shift.

cambiavalute, n.m. mon-eychanger.

cambio, n.m. change; relief. c. di velocità, n.f. gearshift.

cambrì, n.m. cambric.

camèlia, n.f. camelia.

càmera, n.f. room, chamber; (legislative) house.

camerata, n.m. comrade, buddy, pal.

cameratismo, n.m. camarade-rie, comradeship.

camerièra, n.f. chambermaid, waitress; stewardess, flight attendant.

camerière, n.m. manservant; waiter; bellboy; steward, flight attendant; valet.

càmice, n.m. smock.

camìcia, n.f. shirt.

camiciòla, n.f. undershirt.

camiciòtto, n.m. smock.

camino, n.m. chimney.

camioncino, n.m. light truck; utility.

camione, n.m. truck.

cammèllo, n.m. camel.

cammèo, n.m. cameo.

camminare, vb. walk, step.

cammino, n.m. road.

camòscio, n.m. chamois.

campagna, n.f. country, coun-tryside; campaign.

campana, n.f. bell.

campanèllo, n.m. (little) bell.

campanette, n.f.pl. glocken-spiel.

campanile, n.m. bell-tower, belfry, steeple.

campeggiare, vb. camp.

campeggiatore, n.m. camper.

campeggio, n.m. camping.

campionàrio, adj. pertaining to samples.

campionato, n.m. champion-ship.

campione, n.m. champion; sample.

campo, n.m. field.

camposanto, n.m. cemetery, churchyard, graveyard.

camuffamento, n.m. disguise, camouflage.

camuffare, vb. disguise, cam-ouflage.

Cànada, n.m. Canada.

canadese, adj. Canadian.

canale, n.m. canal, channel, duct, inlet.

canalizzare, vb. canalize.

cànapa, n.f. hemp.

Canàrie, n.f.pl. Canary Is-lands.

canarino, n.m. canary.

cancellare, vb. cancel, erase, delete, efface, obliterate.

cancellatura, n.f. erasure.

cancelleria, n.f. chancellery. oggetti di c., stationery.

cancellière, n.m. chancellor.

cancèllo, n.m. gate.

cancrena, n.f. gangrene.

cancrenoso, adj. gangrenous.

cancro, n.m. cancer, canker.

candela, n.f. candle. c. d'accen-sione, spark-plug.

candelabro, n.m. candelabrum.

candelière, n.m. candlestick.

candidamente, adv. candidly.

candidato, n.m. candidate, nominee.

candidatura, n.f. candidacy.

càndido, adj. candid.

candito, adj. candied.

candore, n.m. candor.

cane, n.m. dog, hound, cock (of gun). c. poliziotto, police dog, bloodhound.

canfora, n.f. camphor.

canguro, n.m. kangaroo.

canile, n.m. doghouse, kennel.

canino, adj. canine.

canna, n.f. reed, cane.

cannèlla, n.f. cinnamon.

cannibale, n.m. cannibal.

cannone, n.m. cannon.

cannoneggiamento, n.m. can-nonade.

cannonièra, n.f. gunboat.

cannonière, n.m. cannoneer.

cannuccia di paglia, n.f. straw (for drinking).

canòa, n.f. canoe.

cànone, n.m. canon; rent.

canònico, 1. n.m. canon. 2. adj. canonical.

canonizzare, vb. canonize.

canovaccio, n.m. canvas.

cantare, vb. sing, chant; (hen, goose) cackle; (rooster) crow.

cantatore, n.m. singer.

cantatrice, n.f. singer.

canticchiare, vb. hum, croon.

cantina, n.f. basement; can-teen.

canto, n.m. corner; song, sing-ing, chant.

cantuccio, n.m. nook.

canzone, n.f. song.

caos, n.m. chaos.

caòtico, adj. chaotic.

capace, adj. capable, able.

capacità, n.f. capacity, ability.

capanna, n.f. cabin, hut, shack.

capàrbio, adj. wilful.

capello, n.m. hair.

capestro, n.m. halter.

capezzale, n.m. al c. di, at the bedside of.

capézzolo, n.m. nipple.

capillare, adj. capillary.

capire, vb. understand.

capitale, 1. adj. capital (city). 2. n.m. capital (money). 3. adj. capital.

capitalismo, n.m. capitalism.

capitalista, n.m. capitalist.

capitalìstico, adj. capitalistic.

capitalizzare, vb. capitalize.

capitalizzazione, n.f. capital-ization.

capitano, n.m. captain.

capitare, vb. happen, befall.

capitolare, vb. capitulate.

capitolo, n.m. chapter.

capitombolare, vb. tumble.

capitómbolo, n.m. tumble.

capo, n.m. head, chief, chief-tain, head-man, leader, prin-cipal.

capobanda, n.m. bandmaster; gang leader.

capofitto, adv. a c., headlong.

capolavoro, n.m. masterpiece.

capolinea, n.m. terminus.

caporale, n.m. corporal.

capotreno, n.m. conductor (of train).

capovòlgere, vb. overturn, up-set, capsize.

cappa, n.f. cape.

cappèlla, n.f. chapel.

cappellano, n.m. chaplain.

cappellièra, n.f. hatbox, band-box.

cappèllo, n.m. hat, bonnet.

càppio, n.m. loop.

cappone, n.m. capon.

cappuccio, n.m. hood.

capra, n.f. goat.

capraio, n.m. goat-herd.

capretto, n.m. kid.

capriccio, n.m. caprice, whim.

capricciosamente, adv. capri-ciously.

capricciosità, n.f. capricious-ness.

capriccioso, adj. capricious, fanciful, flighty, tempera-mental.

caprifòglio, n.m. honeysuckle.

capriòla, n.f. caper; somersault.

càpsula, n.f. capsule.

capzioso, adj. captious.

carabìna, n.f. carbine.

caraffa, n.f. carafe, decanter.

caramèlla, n.f. caramel.

caramente, adv. dearly.

carato, n.m. carat.

caràttere, n.m. character.

caratterìstica, n.f. characteristic.

caratteristicamente, adv. characteristically.

caratterìstico, adj. characteristic.

caratterizzare, vb. characterize.

caratterizzazione, n.f. characterization.

carbónchio, n.m. carbuncle.

carbóne, n.m. charcoal; coal.

carbònio, n.m. carbon.

carbonizzare, vb. char.

carburante, n.m. fuel.

carburatore, n.m. carburetor.

carburo, n.m. carbide.

carcàssa, n.f. carcass; hulk.

càrcere, n.m. jail.

carcerière, n.m. jailer.

carcinogènico, adj. carcinogenic.

carciòfo, n.m. artichoke.

cardellìno, n.m. goldfinch.

cardìaco, adj. cardiac.

cardinale, n.m. and adj. cardinal.

càrdine, n.m. hinge.

carenare, vb. careen.

carestìa, n.f. famine.

carézza, n.f. caress; endearment.

cariarsi, vb. decay.

càrica, n.f. charge.

caricare, vb. load, charge; (watch) wind.

caricatura, n.f. caricature.

càrico, 1. n.m. load, cargo, charge, freight. 2. adj. loaded, fraught.

càrie, n.f. caries, decay.

cariglione, n.m. carillon.

carisma, n.m. charisma.

carità, n.f. charity, charitableness.

caritatévole, adj. charitable, benevolent.

caritatevolmente, adv. charitably, benevolently.

carlinga, n.f. cockpit.

carnale, adj. carnal.

carne, n.f. meat; flesh.

carnéfice, n.m. executioner.

carnevale, n.m. carnival.

carnìvoro, adj. carnivorous.

carnoso, adj. fleshy.

caro, adj. dear, expensive.

carosèllo, n.m. carousel, merry-go-round.

caròta, n.f. carrot.

carovana, n.f. caravan, trailer.

carpìre, vb. seize, grab.

carretta per bagagli, n.f. baggage cart.

carrettata, n.f. carload.

carrettière, n.m. carter, drayman.

carrièra, n.f. career.

carro, n.m. car; cart, wagon; chariot; dray, van. c. armato, tank. c. fùnebre, hearse. c. di scorta, tender.

carròzza, n.f. carriage, coach, (railroad) car. c. lètti, sleeper. c. ristorante, diner.

carrozzèlla, n.f. baby-carriage, perambulator.

carrozzìno, n.m. side-car.

carta, n.f. paper; card; chart; map; charter. c. a carbone, carbon paper. c. assorbente, blotter, blotting paper. c. di crèdito, credit card. c. da lèttere, notepaper. c. velina, tissue-paper; onionskin. c. da parati, wallpaper. c. intestata, letterhead.

cartèlla, n.f. portfolio; folder.

cartèllo, n.m. cartel; placard, poster, sign. c. pubblicitàrio, billboard.

cartilàgine, n.f. cartilage, gristle.

cartolaio, n.m. stationer.

cartolerìa, n.f. stationery store.

cartoncino, n.m. thin cardboard.

cartone, n.m. cardboard, pasteboard; cartoon (picture).

cartuccia, n.f. cartridge.

carvì, n.m. caraway.

casa, n.f. house, home. in c., indoors. c. colònica, farmhouse.

casàccio, n.m. a c., haphazard, helter-skelter, at random.

casalìngo, adj. home; homelike.

cascata, n.f. cascade, waterfall.

casèlla, n.f. pigeonhole; P.O. box.

casèrma, n.f. barracks.

casétta, n.f. cottage.

casimiro, n.m. cashmere.

casìno, n.m. casino.

caso, n.m. case; happening; chance. per c., by accident.

cassa, n.f. case; chest; box; cashier's office or desk. c. da mòrto, coffin. c. di risparmio, savings bank.

cassafòrte, n.f. strongbox; safe.

cassare, vb. overrule.

casseruòla, n.f. casserole.

cassetta, n.f. box; cassette.

cassettina, n.f. casket.

cassetto, n.m. drawer; till.

cassière, n.m. cashier; teller.

cassone, n.m. caisson.

casta, n.f. caste.

castagna, 1. n.m. chestnut. 2. adj. tan.

castello, n.m. castle, château. c. di prua, forecastle.

castigare, vb. castigate, chastise, chasten.

castigo, n.m. chastisement.

castità, n.f. chastity.

casto, adj. chaste.

castòro, n.m. beaver.

castrare, vb. castrate, emasculate; geld.

castrone, n.m. gelding, wether.

casuale, adj. casual; perfunctory.

casualmente, adv. casually.

casùpola, n.f. hut.

cataclisma, n.m. cataclysm.

catacomba, n.f. catacomb.

catàlogo, n.m. catalogue.

catapulta, n.f. catapult.

catarro, n.m. catarrh; cold.

catarsi, n.f. catharsis.

catàstrofe, n.f. catastrophe.

catechismo, n.m. catechism.

catechizzare, vb. catechize.

categorìa, n.f. category.

categòrico, adj. categorical.

catena, n.f. chain; range.

catenaccio, n.m. bolt.

cateratta, n.f. cataract; floodgate.

catino, n.m. basin.

càtodo, n.m. cathode.

catrame, n.m. tar.

cattedrale, n.f. cathedral.

cattivèria, n.f. badness, mischief.

cattìvo, adj. bad, evil; mischievous.

cattolicismo, n.m. Catholicism.

cattòlico, adj. Catholic.

cattura, n.f. capture.

catturare, vb. capture.

catturatore, n.m. capturer, captor.

càusa, n.f. cause; lawsuit; case. a c. di, because of.

causalità, n.f. causality, causation.

causare, vb. cause, bring about; encompass.

càustico, adj. caustic.

cautèla, n.f. caution.

cautèrio, n.m. cautery.

cauterizzare, vb. cauterize.

càuto, adj. cautious; gingerly.

cauzione, n.f. bail; security.

cava, n.f. quarry.

cavalcare, vb. ride (horseback).

cavalcata, n.f. cavalcade.

cavalcavìa, n.m. overpass.

cavalière, n.m. knight, cavalier, horseman, rider.

cavalla, n.f. mare.

cavalleresco, adj. chivalric.

cavallerìa, n.f. cavalry; chivalry.

cavalletta, n.f. grasshopper.

cavalletto, n.m. easel.

cavallo, n.m. horse; (chess) knight. c. a dòndolo, rocking-horse; hobby-horse. c. da guerra, warhorse, charger. c.-vapore, horsepower.

cavatappi, n.m.sg. corkscrew.

cavèrna, n.f. cavern, cave.

cavezza, n.f. halter.

caviale, n.m. caviar.

caviglia, n.f. ankle.

cavità, n.f. cavity; hole.

cavo, 1. *n.m.* hollow; cable. 2. *adj.* hollow.

cavolfiore, *n.m.* cauliflower.

càvolo, *n.m.* cabbage; kale.

cecità, *n.f.* blindness.

cèdere, *vb.* yield, cede, surrender, give in; back down; subside.

cèdola, *n.f.* coupon.

cèdro, *n.m.* cedar.

celamento, *n.m.* concealment.

celare, *vb.* conceal.

celebrante, *n.m.* celebrant.

celebrare, *vb.* celebrate.

celebrazione, *n.f.* celebration.

cèlebre, *adj.* celebrated, famous.

celebrità, *n.f.* celebrity.

celerità, *n.f.* speed, quickness, celerity.

celèste, *adj.* celestial.

cèlia, *n.f.* joke, banter, chaff.

celiare, *vb.* joke, banter, chaff.

celibato, *n.m.* celibacy.

cèlibe, *adj.* celibate; single, unmarried.

cèlla, *n.f.* cell.

cellòfane, *n.m.* cellophane.

cèllula, *n.f.* cell.

cellulare, *adj.* cellular.

celluloïde, *n.f.* celluloid.

cellulosa, *n.f.* cellulose.

cèltico, *adj.* Celtic.

cementare, *vb.* cement.

cemento, *n.m.* cement, concrete.

cena, *n.f.* supper.

cenàcolo, *n.m.* coterie; Last Supper.

cèncio, *n.m.* rag.

cencioso, *adj.* ragged.

cènere, *n.f.* ashes.

cenno, *n.m.* sign, hint.

censimento, *n.m.* census.

censore, *n.m.* censor.

censòrio, *adj.* censorious.

censura, *n.f.* censure; censorship.

censurare, *vb.* censor.

centenàrio, *n.m. and adj.* centenary.

centennale, *n.m. and adj.* centennial.

centésimo, 1. *n.m.* cent; 100th part. 2. *adj.* hundredth.

centìgrado, *adj.* centigrade.

centinaio, *n.m.* group of 100.

cènto, *num.* hundred.

centrale, *adj.* central.

centralino, *n.m.* switchboard.

centralizzare, *vb.* centralize.

cèntro, *n.m.* center. **c. da tàvola,** centerpiece.

ceppi, *n.m.pl.* fetters.

ceppo, *n.m.* log, stump.

cera, *n.f.* wax; beeswax; mien.

ceralacca, *n.f.* sealing-wax.

ceràmica, *n.f.* ceramics.

ceràmico, *adj.* ceramic.

cerbiàttolo, *n.m.* fawn.

cercare, *vb.* seek, look for, hunt for.

cérchio, *n.m.* circle; hoop; ring.

cereale, *n.m. and adj.* cereal.

cerebrale, *adj.* cerebral.

cerimònia, *n.f.* ceremony.

cerimoniale, *adj.* ceremonial.

cerimonioso, *adj.* ceremonious.

certamente, *adv.* certainly.

certezza, *n.f.* certainty, certitude.

certificare, *vb.* certify.

certificato, *n.m.* certificate.

certificazione, *n.f.* certification.

cèrto, *adj.* certain, sure.

cèrva, *n.f.* doe; hind; roe.

cervèllo, *n.m.* brain.

cervicale, *adj.* cervical.

cervice, *n.f.* cervix.

cèrvo, *n.m.* stag; deer.

cesellare, *vb.* chisel.

cesèllo, *n.m.* chisel.

cesòie, *n.f.pl.* shears.

cespùglio, *n.m.* bush.

cespuglioso, *adj.* bushy.

cessare, *vb.* cease, stop, quit.

cessazione, *n.f.* cessation.

cessione, *n.f.* cession.

cesta, *n.f.* basket; hamper.

cèto, *n.m.* class.

cetriòlo, *n.m.* cucumber.

che, 1. *pron.* who; which; what. 2. *prep.* than. 3. *conj.* that.

chè, *conj.* for.

cherubino, *n.m.* cherub.

chi, *pron.* who; whom.

chiàcchiera, *n.f.* chatter, chat.

chiacchierare, *vb.* chatter, chat, gab.

chiacchierone, *n.m.* chatterbox.

chiamare, *vb.* call, summon.

chiamata, *n.f.* call, summons.

chiaramente, *adv.* clearly.

chiarezza, *n.f.* clearness.

chiarificare, *vb.* clarify.

chiarificazione, *n.f.* clarification.

chiarimento, *n.m.* enlightenment.

chiarina, *n.f.* clarion.

chiarire, *vb.* clear, clear up.

chiarità, *n.f.* clarity.

chiaro, *adj.* clear, bright, lucid, plain. **c. di luna,** moonlight.

chiarore, *n.m.* brightness.

chiaroveggènte, *n. and adj.* clairvoyant; fortune-teller.

chiaroveggènza, *n.f.* clairvoyance.

chiasso, *n.m.* uproar, fuss, hullabaloo.

chiassoso, *adj.* uproarious; obstreperous.

chiatta, *n.f.* barge.

chiave, *n.f.* key; clef. **c. inglese,** wrench.

chicco, *n.m.* grain; seed.

chièdere, *vb.* ask for, request, beg.

chièsa, *n.f.* church.

chiglia, *n.f.* keel.

chilociclo, *n.m.* kilocycle.

chilogramma, *n.m.* kilogram.

chilometràggio, *n.m.* distance in kilometers.

chilòmetro, *n.m.* kilometer.

chilowatt, *n.m.* kilowatt.

chìmica, *n.f.* chemistry.

chimicamente, *adv.* chemically.

chìmico, 1. *n.* chemist. 2. *adj.* chemical.

chimioterapia, *f.* chemotherapy.

chimono, *n.m.* kimono.

chinino, *n.m.* quinine.

chiocciare, *vb.* cluck.

chiòdo, *n.m.* nail; spike; clove.

chiòsa, *n.f.* gloss.

chiosare, *vb.* gloss.

chiòsco, *n.m.* kiosk.

chiòstro, *n.m.* cloister.

chirurgìa, *n.f.* surgery.

chirurgo, *n.m.* surgeon.

chitarra, *n.f.* guitar.

chiùdere, *vb.* close, shut. **c. a chiave,** lock.

chiunque, *pron.* whoever; whomever.

chiusa, *n.f.* lock.

chiusura, *n.f.* closure; fastening. **c. lampo,** zipper.

ci, *pron.* us; to us.

ci, *pro-phrase* (replaces phrases introduced by prepositions of place) here, there; to it; at it.

ciabattino, *n.m.* cobbler.

ciambellano, *n.m.* chamberlain.

cianfrusàglia, *n.f.* gimcrack; trash.

ciao, *interj.* hi!; so long!

ciarlatanismo, *n.m.* charlatanism.

ciarlatano, *n.m.* charlatan, mountebank.

ciascuno, *pron.* each one.

cibo, *n.m.* food.

cicala, *n.f.* cicada.

cicatrice, *n.f.* scar.

cicatrizzare, *vb.* scar.

cicisbèo, *n.m.* gigolo.

ciclamato, *m.* cyclamate.

ciclista, *n.m. or f.* bicyclist.

ciclo, *n.m.* cycle.

ciclomotore, *n.m.* moped.

ciclone, *n.m.* cyclone.

ciclotrone, *n.m.* cyclotron.

cicòria, *n.f.* chicory.

cicuta, *n.f.* hemlock.

ciecamente, *adv.* blindly.

cièco, *adj.* blind.

cièlo, *n.m.* heaven; sky.

cifra, *n.f.* cipher; figure.

cifràrio, *n.m.* code.

ciglio, *n.m.* eyelash, cilia.

cigno, *n.m.* swan.

cigolare, *vb.* creak, squeak.

cigolio, *n.m.* squeak.

ciliare, *adj.* ciliary.

ciliègia, *n.f.* cherry.

ciliègio, *n.m.* cherry-tree.

cilindrico, *adj.* cylindrical.

cilindro, *n.m.* cylinder.

cima, *n.f.* peak.

cimare, *vb.* clip, trim.

cimice, *n.f.* bedbug.

ciminièra, *n.f.* smoke-stack; funnel.

cimitèro, *n.m.* cemetery; churchyard.

Cina, *n.f.* China.
cincigila, *n.f.* chinchilla.
cincona, *n.f.* cinchona.
cinèllo, *n.m.* cymbal.
cinema, *n.m.* cinema, movies; (movie) theater.
cinematogràfico, *adj.* cinematic, of the movies.
cinematògrafo, *n.m.* cinema, movies; (movie) theater.
cinese, *adj.* Chinese.
cinètico, *adj.* kinetic.
cingere, *vb.* gird.
cinghia, *n.f.* strap.
cinguettare, *vb.* chirp.
cinguettio, *n.m.* chirping.
cinico, 1. *n.m.* cynic. 2. *adj.* cynical.
ciniglia, *n.f.* chenille.
cinismo, *n.m.* cynicism.
cinnamòmo, *n.m.* cinnamon.
cinquanta, *num.* fifty.
cinque, *num.* five.
cintura, *n.f.* belt, girdle, sash; waist.
ciò, *pron.* this; that; it.
ciòcco, *n.m.* log.
cioccolato, *n.m.* chocolate.
cioè, *conj.* that is; namely.
ciòttolo, *n.m.* pebble, stone; cobblestone.
cipolla, *n.f.* onion; chive.
cipresso, *n.m.* cypress.
cipria, *n.f.* face-powder.
circo, *n.m.* circus.
circolare, 1. *n.m. and adj.* circular. 2. *vb.* circulate.
circolatòrio, *adj.* circulatory.
circolazione, *n.f.* circulation; currency.
circolo, *n.m.* circle, club.
circoncidere, *vb.* circumcise.
circoncisione, *n.f.* circumcision.
circondare, *vb.* surround, encompass.
circonferenza, *n.f.* circumference, girth.
circonlocuzione, *n.f.* circumlocution.
circoscrivere, *vb.* circumscribe.
circonvenire, *vb.* circumvent.
circonvenzione, *n.f.* circumvention.
circospetto, *adj.* circumspect.
circostanza, *n.f.* circumstance.
circostanziale, *adj.* circumstantial.
circostanziatamente, *adv.* circumstantially.
circuito, *n.m.* circuit.
cirripede, *n.m.* barnacle.
cirrosi, *n.f.* cirrhosis.
ciste, *n.f.* cyst.
cistèrna, *n.f.* cistern.
citare, *vb.* cite; quote; summon.
citazione, *n.f.* citation; quotation; summons.
citrico, *adj.* citric.
citrullo, *n.m.* fool.
città, *n.f.* city, town. **c. universitària,** campus.
cittadella, *n.f.* citadel.

cittadina, *n.f.* woman citizen; small city.
cittadinanza, *n.f.* citizenship; citizenry.
cittadino, *n.m.* citizen.
ciuffo, *n.m.* tuft.
ciuffolotto, *n.m.* bullfinch.
civetta, *n.f.* owl; coquette, flirt.
civettare, *vb.* coquet, flirt.
civetteria, *n.f.* coquetry.
civico, *adj.* civic.
civile, 1. *n. and adj.* civilian. 2. *adj.* civil; civilized.
civilizzare, *vb.* civilize.
civiltà, *n.f.* civilization; civility.
clacson, *n.m.* klaxon; horn.
clamore, *n.m.* clamor.
clamoroso, *adj.* noisy, blatant, clamorous, obstreperous.
clandestinamente, *adv.* clandestinely.
clandestino, *adj.* clandestine.
clangore, *n.m.* clangor.
claretto, *n.m.* claret.
clarinettista, *n.m.* clarinetist.
clarinetto, *n.m.* clarinet.
classe, *n.f.* class.
classicismo, *n.m.* classicism.
clàssico, *adj.* classic; classical.
classificàbile, *adj.* classifiable.
classificare, *vb.* classify, class; grade.
classificazione, *n.f.* classification.
clàusola, *n.f.* clause.
claustrofobia, *n.f.* claustrophobia.
clava, *n.f.* cudgel, nightstick.
clavicèmbalo, *n.m.* harpsichord.
clavicola, *n.f.* collarbone.
clemènte, *adj.* lenient.
clemènza, *n.f.* clemency.
cleptòmane, *n.m.* kleptomaniac.
cleptomania, *n.f.* kleptomania.
clericale, *adj.* clerical.
clericalismo, *n.m.* clericalism.
clèro, *n.m.* clergy.
cliènte, *n.m.* client, customer; guest.
clientèla, *n.f.* clientele.
clima, *n.m.* climate.
climàtico, *adj.* climatic.
clinica, *n.f.* clinic.
clinicamente, *adv.* clinically.
clinico, *adj.* clinical.
clistère, *n.m.* enema.
clòro, *n.m.* chlorine.
clorofilla, *n.f.* chlorophyll.
cloroformio, *n.m.* chloroform.
cloruro, *n.m.* chloride.
coagulare, *vb.* coagulate.
coagulazione, *n.f.* coagulation.
coalizione, *n.f.* coalition.
coalizzarsi, *vb.* coalesce.
cobalto, *n.m.* cobalt.
cobra, *n.m.* cobra.
cocaina, *n.f.* cocaine.
cocchière, *n.m.* coachman.
cocchio, *n.m.* coach.
coccinella, *n.f.* ladybug.
cocco, *n.m.* coconut tree.
coccodrillo, *n.m.* crocodile.
cocktail, *n.m.* cocktail.

coda, *n.f.* tail.
codardia, *n.f.* cowardice.
codardo, 1. *n.m.* coward. 2. *adj.* cowardly, craven.
codeina, *n.f.* codeine.
còdice, *n.m.* codex; code. **c. (di avviamento) postale,** zip code.
codificare, *vb.* codify.
coeguale, *adj.* coequal.
coercitivo, *adj.* coercive, compulsive.
coercizione, *n.f.* coercion, duress.
coerènte, *adj.* coherent; consistent.
coesione, *n.f.* cohesion.
coesistènza, *n.f.* coexistence.
coesistere, *vb.* coexist.
coesivo, *adj.* cohesive.
còfano, *n.m.* coffer; (auto) hood; (Brit.) bonnet.
còffa, *n.f.* crow's-nest.
cogitare, *vb.* cogitate.
cògliere, *vb.* pick, pluck, gather, cull.
cognata, *n.f.* sister-in-law.
cognato, *n.m.* brother-in-law.
cognome, *n.m.* family name, surname.
coincidènte, *adj.* coincident; coincidental.
coincidènza, *n.f.* coincidence; (transport) connection.
coincidere, *vb.* coincide; connect.
coinvòlgere, *vb.* involve.
colare, *vb.* strain.
colatòio, *n.m.* colander.
colazione, *n.f.* light meal; lunch. **prima c.,** breakfast.
colèra, *n.m.* cholera.
colino, *n.m.* strainer.
còlla, *n.f.* glue, paste.
collaborare, *vb.* collaborate.
collaboratore, *n.m.* collaborator.
collaborazione, *n.f.* collaboration.
collana, *n.f.* necklace.
collant, *n.m.* panty hose.
collare, 1. *n.m.* collar. 2. *vb.* glue.
collasso, *n.m.* collapse.
collaterale, *n.m. and adj.* collateral.
collaudare, *vb.* test.
collazionare, *vb.* collate.
collèga, *n.m.* colleague.
collegamento, *n.m.* connection, liaison.
collegare, *vb.* connect, link.
còllera, *n.f.* choler, anger, wrath.
collèrico, *adj.* choleric.
collettivamente, *adv.* collectively, jointly.
collettivo, *adj.* collective, joint.
colletto, *n.m.* collar.
collezione, *n.f.* collection.
collezionista, *n.m.* collector.
collina, *n.f.* hill.
còllo, *n.m.* neck; package.
collocare, *vb.* locate; place.
colloquiale, *adj.* colloquial.

colloquialismo, *n.m.* colloquialism.

colloquialmente, *adv.* colloquially.

collòquio, *n.m.* colloquy; interview.

collusione, *n.f.* collusion.

colombo, *n.m.* dove.

colònia, *n.f.* colony, settlement.

Colònia, *n.f.* Cologne.

coloniale, *adj.* colonial.

colonizzare, *vb.* colonize.

colonizzazione, *n.f.* colonization.

colonna, *n.f.* column; (*typogr.*) galley.

colonnèllo, *n.m.* colonel.

colòno, *n.m.* colonist, settler; farmer.

colorare, *vb.* stain.

colorazione, *n.f.* coloration.

colore, *n.m.* color, hue; paint; stain; suit. **di c.,** colored.

colorire, *vb.* color.

colorito, *n.m.* coloring, complexion.

coloritura, *n.f.* coloring.

colossale, *adj.* colossal.

colpa, *n.f.* fault, guilt.

colpetto, *n.m.* little blow, tap.

colpévole, **1.** *n.m.* culprit. **2.** *adj.* guilty, culpable.

colpevolmente, *adv.* guiltily.

colpire, *vb.* hit, strike, rap, smite.

colpito, *adj.* stricken.

colpo, *n.m.* blow; stroke; clout, hit, rap; shot.

coltèllo, *n.m.* knife. **c. a serramànico,** jack-knife.

coltivare, *vb.* cultivate, till; grow, raise.

coltivatore, *n.m.* cultivator.

coltivazione, *n.f.* cultivation.

colto, *adj.* cultured, cultivated, educated.

coltrone, *n.m.* quilt.

còma, *n.m.* coma.

comandamento, *n.m.* commandment.

comandante, *n.m.* commander.

comandare, *vb.* command, order, bid.

comando, *n.m.* command.

comare, *n.f.* godmother.

combattènte, *n.m.* combatant, fighter.

combàttere, *vb.* combat, fight, battle.

combattimento, *n.m.* combat, fight, fray.

combinare, *vb.* combine.

combinazione, *n.f.* combination; union suit.

combriccola, *n.f.* coterie.

combustibile, **1.** *n.m.* fuel. **2.** *adj.* combustible.

combustione, *n.f.* combustion.

come, **1.** *adv.* how. **2.** *prep. and conj.* like; as.

cometa, *n.f.* comet.

còmico, **1.** *n.* comedian. **2.** *adj.* comic, comical, funny.

cominciamento, *n.m.* beginning; commencement.

cominciare, *vb.* begin, commence, start.

comitato, *n.m.* committee, board, commission.

commèdia, *n.f.* comedy.

commemorare, *vb.* commemorate.

commemorativo, *adj.* commemorative, memorial.

commemorazione, *n.f.* commemoration.

commentare, *vb.* comment.

commento, *n.m.* comment; commentary.

commerciale, *adj.* commercial.

commercialismo, *n.m.* commercialism.

commercializzare, *vb.* commercialize.

commercialmente, *adv.* commercially.

commerciante, *n.m.* business man, merchant, trader.

commerciare, *vb.* trade.

commèrcio, *n.m.* commerce, trade.

commesso, *n.m.* salesman. **c. viaggiatore,** travelling salesman.

commèttere, *vb.* commit.

commiato, *n.m.* leave.

commiserare, *vb.* commiserate.

commisurato, *adj.* commensurate.

commissariato, *n.m.* commissary.

commissàrio, *n.m.* commissioner.

commissione, *n.f.* commission; committee; errand.

commovènte, *adj.* moving; affecting; touching.

commozione, *n.f.* commotion, stir.

commuòvere, *vb.* move; affect; touch (emotionally).

commutare, *vb.* commute.

commutazione, *n.f.* commutation.

comodamente, *adv.* comfortably.

còmodo, **1.** *n.m.* ease; leisure. **2.** *adj.* comfortable; leisurely; snug.

compaesano, *n.m.* compatriot.

compagna, *n.f.* companion.

compagnia, *n.f.* company, companionship.

compagno, *n.m.* companion; mate; partner.

comparàbile, *adj.* comparable.

comparare, *vb.* compare.

comparativamente, *adv.* comparatively.

comparativo, *adj.* comparative.

compare, *n.m.* godfather; crony.

compassione, *n.f.* compassion.

compassionévole, *adj.* compassionate.

compassionevolmente, *adv.* compassionately.

compasso, *n.m.* compass.

compatibile, *adj.* compatible.

compatriòta, *n.m.* compatriot, fellow-countryman.

compattezza, *n.f.* compactness.

compatto, *adj.* compact.

compensare, *vb.* compensate.

compensativo, *adj.* compensatory.

compensazione, *n.f.* compensation. **stanza di c.,** clearing-house.

compènso, *n.m.* compensation.

competènte, *adj.* competent, (law) cognizant.

competentemente, *adv.* competently.

competènza, *n.f.* competence, fitness, (legal) cognizance.

compètere, *vb.* compete; be within the province of.

compilare, *vb.* compile.

complimento, *n.m.* completion, achievement, accomplishment.

compire, *vb.* complete, finish, accomplish, achieve.

compito, *adj.* accomplished.

còmpito, *n.m.* task, assignment.

compleanno, *n.m.* birthday.

complemento, *n.m.* complement.

complessità, *n.f.* complexity.

complesso, *n.m. and adj.* complex.

completamente, *adv.* completely; altogether; outright; wholly; quite; throughout; utterly.

completamento, *n.m.* completion.

completare, *vb.* complete.

completezza, *n.f.* completeness.

complèto, *adj.* complete; thorough; utter.

complicare, *vb.* complicate.

complicato, *adj.* complicated, involved, intricate.

complicazione, *n.f.* complication; intricacy.

còmplice, *n.m. and f.* accomplice.

complicità, *n.f.* complicity.

complimentare, *vb.* compliment.

complimento, *n.m.* compliment.

complòtto, *n.m.* plot.

componènte, *n.m. and adj.* component.

comporre, *vb.* compose.

comportamento, *n.m.* behavior.

comportare, *vb.* entail, involve; (*refl.*) behave, act.

compositore, *n.m.* composer.

composizione, *n.f.* composition.

compostezza, *n.f.* composure.

composto, **1.** *n.m.* compound. **2.** *adj.* composed; compound; composite.

compra, *n.f.* purchase.

comprare, *vb.* buy; purchase.

compratore, n.m. buyer, purchaser.

compréndere, vb. comprehend; comprise.

comprensibile, adj. comprehensible.

comprensione, n.f. comprehension, understanding.

comprensivo, adj. comprehensive.

compreso, adj. comprised; including.

compressione, n.f. compression.

compresso, adj. compressed.

compressore, n.m. compressor.

comprimere, vb. compress.

compromesso, n.m. compromise.

comprométtere, vb. compromise, endanger.

comprovare, vb. prove.

compunzione, n.f. compunction.

computare, vb. compute.

computazione, n.f. computation.

comunale, adj. communal.

comune, adj. common.

comunella, n.f. master-key.

comunemente, adv. commonly.

comunicabile, adj. communicable.

comunicante, n.m. communicant.

comunicare, vb. communicate; (refl.) take communion.

comunicativo, adj. communicative.

comunicato, n.m. communiqué.

comunicazione, n.f. communication.

comunione, n.f. communion.

comunismo, n.m. communism.

comunista, n.m. or f. communist.

comunistico, adj. communist.

comunità, n.f. community.

comunque, adv. however; howsoever.

con, prep. with.

concavo, adj. concave.

concédere, vb. grant, concede, allow.

concentramento, n.m. concentration.

concentrare, vb. concentrate.

concentrazione, n.f. concentration.

concepibile, adj. conceivable.

concepibilmente, adv. conceivably.

concepire, vb. conceive.

concernere, vb. concern.

concertare, vb. concert.

concerto, n.m. concert; concerto.

concessione, n.f. concession; grant, bestowal.

concetto, n.m. concept.

conchiglia, n.f. conch-shell.

conciare, vb. tan.

conciliare, vb. conciliate.

conciliativo, adj. conciliatory.

conciliatore, n.m. conciliator.

conciliazione, n.f. conciliation.

concime, n.m. compost, manure.

concisamente, adv. concisely.

concisione, n.f. concision, conciseness.

conciso, adj. concise.

conclave, n.m. conclave.

concludere, vb. conclude.

conclusione, n.f. conclusion.

conclusivamente, adv. conclusively.

conclusivo, adj. conclusive.

concomitante, adj. concomitant.

concordare, vb. agree.

concordato, n.m. concordat.

concorde, adj. concordant, agreeing.

concorrente, n. competitor; (sports) entrant.

concorrenza, n.f. concurrence; competition.

concorrere, vb. compete; concur.

concorso, n.m. competition; tournament; contribution; concurrence; rush (of people).

concozione, n.f. concoction.

concretamente, adv. concretely.

concretezza, n.f. concreteness.

concreto, adj. concrete.

concubina, n.f. concubine.

concuocere, vb. concoct.

concupiscente, adj. lustful.

concupiscenza, n.f. lust.

concussione, n.f. concussion.

condanna, n.f. condemnation; doom; conviction; sentence.

condannabile, adj. condemnable.

condannare, vb. condemn, doom; sentence.

condannato, n.m. convict.

condensare, vb. condense; thicken.

condensatore, n.m. condenser.

condensazione, n.f. condensation.

condimento, n.m. condiment, seasoning; dressing, relish.

condire, vb. season, use condiments.

condividere, vb. share.

condizionale, adj. conditional.

condizionalmente, adv. conditionally.

condizionare, vb. condition.

condizione, n.f. condition; status.

condoglianza, n.f. condolence.

condolere, vb. condole.

condominio, n.m. condominium.

condonare, vb. condone.

condotta, n.f. conduct, behavior; bearing, deportment.

condotto, n.m. conduct.

conducente, n.m. driver.

condurre, vb. conduct, lead; conduce; (refl.) behave.

conduttività, n.f. conductivity.

conduttivo, adj. conductive.

conduttore, n.m. conductor.

conduttura, n.f. flue.

confederarsi, vb. confederate.

confederato, n.m. confederate.

confederazione, n.f. confederation, confederacy.

conferenza, n.f. conference; lecture.

conferenziere, n.m. lecturer.

conferire, vb. confer, bestow.

conferma, n.f. confirmation.

confermare, vb. confirm.

confessare, vb. confess, admit; avow.

confessionale, n.m. and adj. confessional.

confessione, n.f. confession, admission, avowal.

confessore, n.m. confessor.

confetteria, n.f. confectionery, confectioner's shop.

confettiere, n.m. confectioner.

confetto, n.m. candy; confection.

confettura, n.f. candy; confection.

confezione, n.f. ready-to-wear dress.

confidare, vb. confide, entrust; rely.

confidente, 1. n.m. or f. confidant. 2. adj. confident.

confidentemente, adv. confidently.

confidenza, n.f. confidence.

confidenziale, adj. confidential.

confinare, vb. abut; border; confine; verge.

confine, n.m. boundary, border.

confisca, n.f. confiscation.

confiscare, vb. confiscate.

conflagrazione, n.f. conflagration.

conflitto, n.m. conflict, strife.

confóndere, vb. confuse, confound, addle, bewilder, befuddle.

conformarsi, vb. conform.

conformazione, n.f. conformation.

conforme, adj. in accordance, in conformity.

conformemente, adv. accordingly, in conformity.

conformista, n.m. conformer, conformist.

conformità, n.f. conformity, accordance.

confortare, vb. comfort; encourage.

confortatore, n.m. comforter.

conforto, n.m. comfort; encouragement.

confrontare, vb. compare; confront.

confronto, n.m. comparison; collation.

confusione, n.f. confusion, blur, mix-up, turmoil.

confuso, adj. confused, addled, bewildered.

confutare, *vb.* disprove, refute.

confutazione, *n.f.* disproof, refutation; rebuttal.

congedare, *vb.* dismiss.

congedo, *n.m.* dismissal; leave.

congegno, *n.m.* contrivance, device, contraption, gadget; gearing.

congelamento, *n.m.* congealment; frostbite.

congelare, *vb.* congeal.

congelatore, *n.m.* freezer.

congenitamente, *adv.* congenitally.

congènito, *adj.* congenital.

congestione, *n.f.* congestion.

congettura, *n.f.* conjecture, surmise.

congetturare, *vb.* conjecture, surmise.

congiùngere, *vb.* join, splice.

congiuntamente, *adv.* conjointly.

congiuntivite, *n.f.* conjunctivitis.

congiuntivo, 1. *n.m.* (gram.) subjunctive. 2. *adj.* (verbs) subjunctive; (pronouns) conjunctive.

congiunto, *adj.* joint.

congiunzione, *n.f.* conjunction; join.

congiura, *n.f.* conspiracy.

congiurare, *vb.* conspire.

congiurato, *n.m.* conspirator.

conglomerare, *vb.* conglomerate.

conglomerato, *n.m. and adj.* conglomerate.

conglomerazione, *n.f.* conglomeration.

congratularsi con, *vb.* congratulate.

congratulatòrio, *adj.* congratulatory.

congregarsi, *vb.* congregate.

congregazione, *n.f.* congregation.

congrèsso, *n.m.* congress; convention.

coniare, *vb.* coin, mint.

cònico, *adj.* conic.

coniglièra, *n.f.* hutch.

coniglietto, *n.m.* little rabbit, bunny.

coniglio, *n.m.* rabbit.

cònio, *n.m.* coinage.

coniugale, *adj.* conjugal.

coniugare, *vb.* conjugate.

coniugazione, *n.f.* conjugation.

connessione, *n.f.* connection.

connèsso, *adj.* related.

connèttere, *vb.* connect.

connivènte, *adj.* conniving.

connivènza, *n.f.* connivance.

connotare, *vb.* connote.

connotazione, *n.f.* connotation.

connubiale, *adj.* connubial.

còno, *n.m.* cone.

conoscènza, *n.f.* acquaintance, knowledge, cognizance.

conóscere, *vb.* know, be acquainted with.

conoscitore, *n.m.* connoisseur.

conosciuto, *adj.* known, acquainted.

conquista, *n.f.* conquest.

conquistàbile, *adj.* conquerable.

conquistare, *vb.* conquer.

conquistatore, *n.m.* conqueror.

consacrare, *vb.* consecrate.

consacrazione, *n.f.* consecration.

consapévole, *adj.* conscious, aware.

consciamente, *adv.* consciously.

cònscio, *adj.* conscious, aware.

consecutivamente, *adv.* consecutively.

consecutivo, *adv.* consecutive.

consegna, *n.f.* consignment, delivery.

consegnare, *vb.* consign, deliver.

consènso, *n.m.* concurrence, agreement, assent, consent; consensus.

consentire, *vb.* consent, accede.

conseguènte, *adj.* consequent.

conseguentemente, *adv.* consequently.

conseguènza, *n.f.* consequence.

conseguenziale, *adj.* consequential.

consèrva, *n.f.* jam, preserves; compote.

conservare, *vb.* conserve, keep, preserve, retain, store.

conservativo, *adj.* preservative.

conservatore, *n.m. and adj.* conservative.

conservatòrio, *n.m.* conservatory.

conservazione, *n.f.* conservation, preservation.

consideràbile, *adj.* considerable.

considerabilmente, *adv.* considerably.

considerare, *vb.* consider.

considerazione, *n.f.* consideration.

considerévole, *adj.* considerable.

consigliare, *vb.* advise, counsel.

consigliatamente, *adv.* advisedly.

consigliatore, *n.m.* adviser.

consigliére, *n.m.* councilor, counselor.

consiglio, *n.m.* advice, counsel; council; board.

consistènza, *n.f.* consistency.

consistere, *vb.* consist.

consolare, *adj.* consular.

consolare, *vb.* console, comfort, solace.

consolato, *n.m.* consulate; consulship.

consolatore, *n.m.* consoler, comforter.

consolazione, *n.f.* consolation, solace.

cònsole, *n.m.* consul.

consolidare, *vb.* consolidate.

consòlida reale, *n.f.* larkspur.

consonante, *n.f. and adj.* consonant.

consòrte, *n.m. and f.* consort, mate.

consòrzio, *n.m.* syndicate; trust.

consorzio automobilístico, *n.m.* car pool.

consuèto, *n.m.* customary.

consuetùdine, *n.f.* custom.

consultare, *vb.* consult.

consultatore, *n.m.* consultant.

consultazione, *n.f.* consultation.

consulto, *n.m.* consultation.

consumare, *vb.* consume; expend, wear out.

consumato, *adj.* consummate.

consumatore, *n.m.* consumer.

consumazione, *n.f.* consummation.

consumo, *n.m.* consumption; wear.

contàbile, *n.m.* bookkeeper.

contabilità, *n.f.* accounting, bookkeeping.

contadino, 1. *n.* peasant; countryman; farmer. 2. *adj.* peasant; rustic.

contàgio, *n.m.* contagion.

contagioso, *adj.* contagious.

contagocce, *n.m.* dropper.

contaminare, *vb.* contaminate; pollute.

contanti, *n.m.pl.* cash.

contare, *vb.* count; c. su count on, rely on.

contatore, *n.m.* meter.

contatto, *n.m.* contact.

conte, *n.m.* count, earl.

contèa, *n.f.* county.

contemplare, *vb.* contemplate.

contemplativo, *adj.* contemplative.

contemplazione, *n.f.* contemplation.

contemporàneo, *adj.* contemporary.

contendènte, *n.m.* contender.

contèndere, *vb.* contend.

contenere, *vb.* contain.

contentezza, *n.f.* contentment, gladness.

contènto, *adj.* glad, happy, content.

contenzione, *n.f.* contention.

contesa, *n.f.* contest.

contessa, *n.f.* countess.

contestàbile, *adj.* contestable.

contestare, *vb.* contest.

contesto, *n.m.* context.

contiguo, *adj.* contiguous.

continentale, *adj.* continental.

continènte, 1. *n.m.* continent. 2. *adj.* continent, chaste.

continènza, *n.f.* continence.

contingènte, *adj.* contingent.

contingènza, *n.f.* contingency.

continuamente, *adv.* continually.

continuare, *vb.* continue.

continuazione, *n.f.* continuation.

continuità, *n.f.* continuity.

continuo, *adj.* continual, continuous. **corrènte contìnua**, direct current.

conto, *n.m.* account; bill; check; count. **rèndere c. di**, account for. **rèndersi c. di**, realize.

contòrcere, *vb.* contort; *(refl.)* writhe.

contórno, *n.m.* contour; sidedish.

contorsióne, *n.f.* contortion.

contorsionìsta, *n.m.* contortionist.

contrabbandière, *n.m.* smuggler.

contrabbàndo, *n.m.* contraband, smuggling.

contraddicìbile, *adj.* contradictable.

contraddìre, *vb.* contradict, gainsay.

contraddittòrio, *adj.* contradictory.

contraddizióne, *n.f.* contradiction.

contraffàre, *vb.* counterfeit; forge; imitate; impersonate.

contraffattóre, *n.m.* forger; impersonator.

contraffazióne, *n.f.* forgery; impersonation.

contraffòrte, *n.m.* buttress.

contràlto, *n.m.* contralto; alto.

contrappéso, *n.m.* counterbalance.

contrariàre, *vb.* spite.

contràrio, *adj.* contrary; reverse.

contràrre, *vb.* contract; *(refl.)* shrink.

contrastàre, *vb.* contrast.

contràsto, *n.m.* contrast.

contrattàcco, *n.m.* counterattack.

contrattatóre, *n.m.* contractor.

contràtto, *n.m.* contract.

contravventóre, *n.m.* violator.

contravvenzióne, *n.f.* misdemeanor, violation.

contrazióne, *n.f.* contraction.

contribuènte, *n.m.* taxpayer.

contribuìre, *vb.* contribute.

contributìvo, *adj.* contributive.

contribùto, *n.m.* contribution.

contributóre, *n.m.* contribution.

contributòrio, *adj.* contributory.

contribuzióne, *n.f.* contribution.

contrìto, *adj.* contrite.

contrizióne, *n.f.* contrition.

contro, *prep.* against, versus. **c. assegno**, C.O.D.

controazióne, *n.f.* counteraction.

controcurva, *n.f.* reverse curve.

controffensìva, *n.f.* counteroffensive.

controllàbile, *adj.* controllable.

controllàre, *vb.* check, inspect; audit.

contròllo, *n.m.* check; restraint; inspection; audit.

contròllo delle nàscite, *n.m.* birth control, contraception.

controllóre, *n.m.* controller; inspector; auditor; ticket-collector.

contromandàre, *vb.* countermand.

contromàrca, *n.f.* check.

contropartìta, *n.f.* counterpart.

Controrifórma, *n.f.* Counter-Reformation.

controvèrsia, *n.f.* controversy.

controvèrso, *adj.* controversial.

contumàce, *adj.* defaulting.

contumàcia, *n.f.* default.

contusióne, *n.f.* contusion.

convalescènte, *adj.* convalescent.

convalescènza, *n.f.* convalescence.

conveniènte, *adj.* convenient; advisable; suitable, fitting.

convenientemènte, *adv.* conveniently.

conveniènza, *n.f.* convenience; advisability; suitability; propriety.

convenìre, *vb.* come together, convene; be suitable; become; befit.

convènto, *n.m.* convent; monastery.

convenzionàle, *adj.* conventional.

convenzionalmènte, *adv.* conventionally.

convenzióne, *n.f.* convention; covenant.

convergènte, *adj.* convergent.

convergènza, *n.f.* convergence.

convèrgere, *vb.* converge.

conversàre, *vb.* converse.

conversatóre, *n.m.* conversationalist.

convèrso, *adj.* converse.

convertìbile, *adj.* convertible.

convertìre, *vb.* convey.

convertitríce, *n.f.* converter.

convèsso, *adj.* convex.

convincènte, *adj.* convincing, cogent.

convìncere, *vb.* convince.

convinzióne, *n.f.* conviction.

conviviàle, *adj.* convivial.

convocàre, *vb.* convoke.

convocazióne, *n.f.* convocation.

convogliàre, *vb.* convoy.

convòglio, *n.m.* convoy, train, procession.

convulsióne, *n.f.* convulsion.

convulsìvo, *adj.* convulsive.

cooperàre, *vb.* cooperate.

cooperatìva, *n.f.* cooperative.

cooperativamènte, *adv.* cooperatively.

cooperatìvo, *adj.* cooperative.

coordinàre, *vb.* coordinate.

coordinatóre, *n.m.* coordinator.

coordinazióne, *n.f.* coordination.

coòrte, *n.m.* cohort.

copèrchio, *n.m.* lid.

copèrta, *n.f.* cover, blanket.

copertìna, *n.f.* cover (of book).

copertùra, *n.f.* cover, covering.

còpia, *n.f.* copy; copiousness.

copiàre, *vb.* copy.

copiatóre, *n.m.* copier.

copiosamènte, *adv.* copiously.

copiosità, *n.f.* copiousness.

copióso, *adj.* copious.

copìsta, *n.m.* copyist.

còppa, *n.f.* cup, mug, flagon, goblet.

còppia, *n.f.* couple.

coprifuòco, *n.m.* curfew.

coprìre, *vb.* cover.

coràggio, *n.m.* courage, bravery; gameness; gallantry; mettle.

coraggiosamènte, *adv.* courageously, gamely, gallantly.

coraggióso, *adj.* brave, courageous; game; gallant.

coràle, *adj.* choral.

coràllo, *n.m.* coral.

còrda, *n.f.* string, rope, cord; chord.

cordiàle, *n.m. and adj.* cordial, hearty.

cordialità, *n.f.* cordiality.

cordialmènte, *adv.* cordially.

cordiglièra, *n.f.* ladder; run.

cordóne, *n.m.* cordon.

cordovàno, *n.m.* cordovan.

Corèa, *n.f.* Korea.

coreggiàto, *n.m.* flail.

coreografìa, *n.f.* choreography.

coreògrafo, *n.m.* choreographer.

coriàndoli, *n.m.pl.* confetti.

corìsta, *n.m.* chorister.

cornamùsa, *n.f.* bagpipe.

còrnea, *n.f.* cornea.

cornétta, *n.f.* cornet.

cornettìsta, *n.m.* cornetist.

cornìce, *n.f.* frame, mantel.

cornicióne, *n.m.* cornice.

còrno, *n.m.* horn.

cornucòpia, *n.m. or f.* cornucopia.

còro, *n.m.* chorus, choir; chancel.

corollàrio, *n.m.* corollary.

coróna, *n.f.* crown. **c. nobiliare**, coronet.

coronàrio, *adj.* coronary.

còrpo, *n.m.* body; corps.

corporàle, *adj.* corporal.

corporàto, *adj.* corporate.

corporazióne, *n.f.* corporation; guild.

corpòreo, *adj.* corporeal, bodily.

corpulènto, *adj.* corpulent, burly, portly.

corpùscolo, *n.m.* corpuscle.

corredàre, *vb.* equip, outfit, provide.

corrèdo, *n.m.* equipment, outfit.

corrèggere, *vb.* correct, amend, right.

correlazióne, *n.f.* correlation.

corrènte, 1. *n.f.* current; stream. **c. alternàta**, alternating current. **c. contìnua**, direct current. **c. d'ària**, draft.

2. *adj.* current: (in dates) instant.

correntemente, *adv.* currently.

correntista, *n.m.* depositor.

córrere, *vb.* run; race.

correttamente, *adv.* correctly.

correttezza, *n.f.* correctness.

correttivo, *adj.* corrective.

corrètto, *adj.* correct, right.

correzione, *n.f.* correction.

corridolo, *n.m.* corridor, hallway; lobby.

corridore, *n.m.* runner.

corrière, *n.m.* courier.

corrispondènte, **1.** *n.* correspondent. **2.** *adj.* corresponding; correspondent.

corrispondènza, *n.f.* correspondence.

corrispóndere, *vb.* correspond.

corroborare, *vb.* corroborate.

corroborativo, *adj.* corroborative.

corroborazione, *n.f.* corroboration.

corródere, *vb.* corrode.

corrómpere, *vb.* corrupt; bribe.

corrosione, *n.f.* corrosion.

corrugare, *vb.* corrugate, wrinkle.

corruttibile, *adj.* corruptible.

corruttivo, *adj.* corruptive.

corruttore, *n.m.* corrupter; briber.

corruzione, *n.f.* corruption; bribery.

corsa, *n.f.* race; ride; trip.

corso, *n.m.* course.

còrso, *adj.* Corsican.

corte, *n.f.* court.

cortéccia, *n.f.* bark.

corteggiamento, *n.m.* courting, courtship.

corteggiare, *vb.* court, woo.

corteggiatore, *n.m.* wooer, beau, suitor.

cortèo, *n.m.* cortege, procession; pageant.

cortese, *adj.* courteous, accommodating, polite.

cortesia, *n.f.* courtesy, politeness.

cortigiana, *n.f.* courtesan, prostitute.

cortigiano, *n.m.* courtier.

cortile, *n.m.* courtyard, patio.

cortina, *n.f.* curtain.

corto, *adj.* short; stupid; (of sea) choppy.

corvetta, *n.f.* corvette.

corvino, *adj.* raven.

còrvo, *n.m.* crow; raven.

còsa, *n.f.* thing.

còscia, *n.f.* thigh.

coscènza, *n.f.* consciousness; conscience.

coscienziosamente, *adv.* conscientiously.

coscienzioso, *adj.* conscientious, painstaking.

coscritto, *n.m. and adj.* conscript.

coscrizione, *n.f.* conscription.

così, *adv.* so, thus.

cosmètico, *n.m. and adj.* cosmetic.

còsmico, *adj.* cosmic.

còsmo, *n.m.* cosmos.

cosmopolita, *adj.* cosmopolitan.

cóso, *n.m.* thingumajig.

cospargere, *vb.* scatter, intersperse, sprinkle, strew.

cospicuamente, *adv.* conspicuously.

cospicuità, *n.f.* conspicuousness.

cospicuo, *adj.* conspicuous.

còsta, *n.f.* coast.

costante, *adj.* constant, fixed, firm.

costantemente, *adv.* constantly.

costanza, *n.f.* constancy.

costare, *vb.* cost.

costellazione, *n.f.* constellation.

costernare, *vb.* dismay.

costernazione, *n.f.* consternation, dismay.

costièro, *adj.* coastal.

costituènte, *adj.* constituent.

costituire, *vb.* constitute.

costituzionale, *adj.* constitutional.

costituzione, *n.f.* constitution.

còsto, *n.m.* cost, expense.

còstola, *n.f.* rib.

costoletta, *n.f.* cutlet; chop.

costosamente, *adv.* expensively.

costosità, *n.f.* costliness.

costoso, *adj.* costly, dear, expensive, valuable.

costringere, *vb.* force, coerce, compel, constrict, constrain.

costruire, *vb.* construct, build, erect.

costruttivamente, *adv.* constructively.

costruttivo, *adj.* constructive.

costruttore, *n.m.* builder, constructor.

costruzione, *n.f.* construction, erection.

costume, *n.m.* costume, garb; custom: (pl.) mores.

còte, *n.f.* hone.

cotiglione, *n.m.* cotillion.

cotone, *n.m.* cotton.

cotonina, *n.f.* cotton cloth, cretonne.

còtto, *adj.* cooked; done.

cottro, *n.m.* cutter.

covare, *vb.* brood, hatch; smolder.

covata, *n.f.* brood.

covo, *n.m.* den, lair.

covone, *n.m.* sheaf.

crampo, *n.m.* cramp.

crànio, *n.m.* cranium, skull.

cratère, *n.m.* crater.

cravatta, *n.f.* necktie.

creare, *vb.* create.

creativo, *adj.* creative.

creatore, *n.m.* creator.

creatura, *n.f.* creature.

creazione, *n.f.* creation.

credènte, *n.m.* believer.

credènza, *n.f.* belief, credence; cupboard; dresser.

credenziali, *n.f.pl.* credentials.

crédere, *vb.* believe, think.

credibile, *adj.* credible, believable.

credibilità, *n.f.* credibility.

crédito, *n.m.* credit.

creditore, *n.m.* creditor.

crédo, *n.m.* credo, creed.

credulità, *n.f.* credulity.

crèdulo, *adj.* credulous, gullible.

credulone, *n.m.* dupe.

crèma, *n.f.* cream.

crema caramella, *n.f.* custard.

cremagliera, *n.f.* rack.

cremare, *vb.* cremate.

crematòrio, *adj.* crematory.

cremazione, *n.f.* cremation.

cremeria, *n.f.* creamery.

cremisi, *adj.* crimson.

creosòto, *n.m.* creosote.

crèpa, *n.f.* crack, chink.

crepàccio, *n.m.* crevasse.

crepacuòre, *n.m.* heartbreak.

crepùscolo, *n.m.* twilight, dusk.

créscere, *vb.* grow.

créscita, *n.f.* growth.

crespo, **1.** *n.m.* crepe. **2.** *adj.* wavy; crisp.

cresta, *n.f.* crest, ridge; (rooster's) comb.

crèta, *n.f.* clay.

cricca, *n.f.* clique, clan.

cricco, *n.m.* jack.

criminale, *adj.* criminal.

criminologia, *n.f.* criminology.

criminòlogo, *n.m.* criminologist.

crine, *n.f.* hair.

crinièra, *n.f.* mane.

criochirurgia, *n.f.* cryosurgery.

cripta, *n.f.* crypt.

crisàlide, *n.f.* chrysalis.

crisantèmo, *n.m.* chrysanthemum.

crisi, *n.f.* crisis.

cristalleria, *n.f.pl.* glassware.

cristallino, *adj.* crystalline.

cristallizzare, *vb.* crystallize.

cristallo, *n.m.* crystal; cut glass.

cristianésimo, *n.m.* Christianity.

cristianità, *n.f.* Christendom.

cristiano, *n. and adj.* Christian.

critèrio, *n.m.* criterion.

critica, *n.f.* criticism, critique, fault finding.

criticare, *vb.* criticize.

critico, **1.** *n.* critic. **2.** *adj.* critical.

crittografia, *n.f.* cryptography.

crivellare, *vb.* sift; screen.

crivèllo, *n.m.* sieve; screen.

croccante, *adj.* crisp.

crocchetta, *n.f.* croquette.

croce, *n.f.* cross.

crocefissione, *n.f.* crucifixion.

crocefisso, *n.m.* crucifix.

crocevia, *n.f.* crossroads.

crociata, *n.f.* crusade.

crociato, *n.m.* crusader.

crocicchio, *n.m.* crossroads.

crocièra, n.f. crusade.

crocifiggere, vb. crucify.

crogiòlo, n.m. crucible.

crollare, vb. collapse, crash.

cròllo, n.m. collapse, crash.

cromàtico, adj. chromatic.

cròmo, n.m. chrome, chromium.

cromosòma, n.m. chromosome.

crònaca, n.f. chronicle.

cronicamente, adv. chronically.

crònico, adj. chronic.

cronista, n.m. chronicler; (newspaper) columnist; (radio) commentator.

cronologìa, n.f. chronology.

cronològico, adj. chronological.

crosta, n.f. crust; scab.

crostàceo, n.m. and adj. crustacean.

crostino, n.m. crouton; canapé.

crostoso, adj. crusty.

crùccio, n.m. chagrin.

cruciale, adj. crucial.

cruciverba, n.m. cross-word puzzle.

crudèle, adj. cruel.

crudeltà, n.f. cruelty.

crudezza, n.f. crudeness.

crudità, n.f. crudity.

crudo, adj. crude, raw.

crumiro, n.m. scab, strikebreaker.

crup, n.m. croup.

crusca, n.f. bran.

cruscòtto, n.m. dashboard.

cùbico, adj. cubic.

cubìcolo, n.m. cubicle.

cubismo, n.m. cubism.

cubo, n.m. cube.

cubo per flash, n.m. flashcube.

cuccetta, n.f. berth, bunk.

cucchiàia, n.f. spoon; scoop.

cucchiaiata, n.f. spoonful.

cucchiaìno, n.m. (small) spoon.

cucciòlo, n.m. puppy.

cucìna, n.f. kitchen; cuisine; cooking. c. econòmica, range. libro di c., cookbook.

cucinare, vb. cook.

cucìre, vb. sew.

cucitura, n.f. sewing; seam.

cùculo, n.m. cuckoo.

cuffia, n.f. cap; hood; earphone.

cugìna, n.f. cousin.

cugìno, n.m. cousin.

cùi, pron. which; to which; whom; to whom; of which; whose.

calice, n.m. gnat.

culinàrio, adj. culinary.

culla, n.f. cradle.

cullare, vb. cradle, lull.

culminante, adj. culminating, climactic.

culminare, vb. culminate.

culminazione, n.f. culmination.

cùlmine, n.m. top; summit; climax.

culo, n.m. posterior.

culto, n.m. cult; worship.

cultura, n.f. culture.

culturale, adj. cultural.

cumulativo, adj. cumulative.

cuneo, n.m. wedge.

cunetta, n.f. gutter.

cuòco, n.m. cook, chef.

cuòio, n.m. leather.

cuòre, n.m. heart.

cupè, n.m. coupé.

cupidìgia, n.f. greed, cupidity.

cupo, adj. sullen.

cùpola, n.f. cupola, dome.

cura, n.f. care; cure; worry.

curare, vb. care for, take care of, nurse, nurture, tend; (refl.) care.

curatore, n.m. curator.

curiosità, n.f. curiosity, curio.

curioso, adj. curious.

curricolo, n.m. curriculum.

curva, n.f. curve.

curvare, vb. curve, bend, warp; hunch; (refl.) stoop.

curvatura, n.f. curvature; crook.

curvo, adj. curved, bent; stooped.

cuscinetto, n.m. pad; stamp pad; (machinery) bearing. stato c., buffer state. c. a rotolamento, roller bearing. c. a sfere, ball bearing.

cuscino, n.m. cushion.

custòde, n.m. custodian, guardian, keeper.

custòdia, n.f. custody, charge.

custodire, vb. guard.

cutàneo, adj. cutaneous.

cutìcola, n.f. cuticle.

D

da, prep. from; by; for; fit for, suitable for; characteristic of; at . . .'s (house, shop, etc.).

dado, n.m. die (pl. dice).

daga, n.f. dagger.

dàina, n.f. hind.

dàino, n.m. buck.

dàlia, n.f. dahlia.

dama, n.f. lady; checkers.

damasco, n.m. damask.

damerìno, n.m. dandy, fop.

damigèlla, n.f. damsel. d. d'onore, maid of honor, bridesmaid.

danese, adj. Danish.

Danimarca, n.f. Denmark.

dannare, vb. damn.

dannazione, n.f. damnation.

danneggiare, vb. harm, damage, injure; mar.

danno, n.m. harm, damage, detriment, hurt, injury.

dannoso, adj. harmful, baneful, detrimental, hurtful, injurious.

danza, n.f. dance.

danzare, vb. dance.

dappertutto, adv. everywhere; throughout.

dardo, n.m. dart.

dare, vb. give.

data, n.f. date.

datare, vb. date.

dati, n.m.pl. data.

datore, n.m. giver. d. di lavoro, employer.

dàttero, n.m. date.

dattilògrafa, vb. typist.

dattilografare, vb. type.

davanti, 1. n.m. front. 2. adv. before. d. a, prep. before.

davanzale, n.m. sill.

davvero, adv. indeed, really.

dàzio, n.m. excise.

dèa, n.f. goddess.

debilitare, vb. debilitate.

debitamente, adv. duly.

dèbito, 1. n.m. debt, debit. 2. adj. due.

debitore, n.m. debtor.

dèbole, adj. weak, feeble, faint, frail, puny.

debolezza, n.f. weakness, feebleness, failing, frailty.

debolmente, adv. weakly, faintly.

debuttante, n. debutant(e).

debutto, n.m. debut.

decalcomanìa, n.f. decalcomania.

decadènte, adj. decadent.

decadènza, n.f. decay, decadence, decline.

decadere, vb. decay, decline, lapse.

decaffeinizzato, adj. decaffeinated.

decano, n.m. dean.

decapitare, vb. behead, decapitate.

deceduto, adj. deceased.

decènnio, n.m. decade.

decènte, adj. decent.

decentramento, n.m. decentralization.

decentrare, vb. decentralize.

decènza, n.f. decency.

dècibel, n.m. decibel.

decìdere, vb. decide; (refl.) decide, make up one's mind, resolve.

deciduo, adj. deciduous.

decifrare, vb. decipher, decode.

decimale, adj. decimal.

decimare, vb. decimate.

dècimo, adj. tenth.

decimonòno, adj. nineteenth.

decimosèsto, adj. sixteenth.

decimotèrzo, adj. thirteenth.

decimottavo, adj. eighteenth.

decisione, n.f. decision, resolve.

decisivo, adj. decisive.

declamare, vb. delaim.

declamazione, n.f. declamation.

declinare, vb. decline.

declinazione, n.f. declension.

decomporre, vb. decompose, decay.

decomposizione, n.f. decomposition, decay.

decongestionante, adj. decongestant.

decorare, vb. decorate.

decorativo, adj. decorative.

decoratore, n.m. decorator.

decorazione, n.f. decoration.

decòro, n.m. decorum.
decoroso, adj. decorous.
decrèpito, adj. decrepit.
decretare, vb. decree; enact.
decreto, n.m. decree; enactment.
dèdica, n.f. dedication.
dedicare, vb. dedicate, devote; (refl.) become addicted.
dedurre, vb. deduce, deduct.
deduttivo, adj. deductive.
deduzione, n.f. deduction.
deferènte, adj. deferent.
deferènza, n.f. deference.
defezione, n.f. defection.
deficiènte, adj. deficient.
deficiènza, n.f. deficiency.
déficit, n.m. deficit.
definire, vb. define.
definitivamente, adj. definitely.
definitivo, adj. definitive.
definito, adj. definite; finite.
definizione, n.f. definition.
deflazionare, vb. deflate.
deflazione, n.f. deflation.
deflèttere, vb. deflect.
deformare, vb. deform.
deforme, adj. deformed.
deformità, n.f. deformity.
defraudare, vb. defraud.
defunto, adj. defunct, deceased.
degenerare, vb. degenerate.
degenerato, n.m. and adj. degenerate.
degenerazione, n.f. degeneration.
degènte, adj. bedridden.
degnarsi, vb. deign.
degno, adj. worthy.
degradare, vb. degrade, demote.
degradazione, n.f. degradation.
deificare, vb. deify.
deità, n.f. deity.
delegare, vb. delegate.
delegato, n.m. delegate.
delegazione, n.f. delegation.
delfino, n.m. dolphin.
deliberare, vb. deliberate.
deliberatamente, adv. deliberately.
deliberativo, adj. deliberative.
deliberato, adj. deliberate.
deliberazione, n.f. advisement; deliberation.
delicatezza, n.f. delicacy.
delicato, adj. delicate, dainty.
delineare, vb. delineate.
delinquènte, n.m. delinquent.
delinquènza, n.f. delinquency.
delirante, adj. delirious.
delirare, vb. be delirious, rave.
delirio, n.m. delirium.
delitto, n.m. crime.
delizioso, adj. delicious.
delùdere, vb. delude; disappoint.
delusione, n.f. delusion; disappointment.
demagògo, n.m. demagogue.
demarcazione, n.f. demarcation.
demènte, adj. demented.
demeritare, vb. forfeit.

demèrito, n.m. demerit.
democràtico, 1. n.m. democrat. 2. adj. democratic.
democrazìa, n.f. democracy.
demolire, vb. demolish.
demolizione, n.f. demolition.
demonìaco, adj. demoniacal, fiendish.
demònio, n.m. demon, fiend.
demoralizzare, vb. demoralize.
denaro, n.m. money.
denaturare, vb. denature.
denigrare, vb. denigrate, blacken, slander, cast aspersions on, belittle.
denigrazione, n.f. slander, aspersion.
denominatore, n.m. denominator.
denominazione, n.f. denomination.
densità, n.f. density.
dènso, adj. dense, thick.
dentale, adj. dental.
dènte, n.m. tooth; cog.
dentellare, vb. indent.
dentellatura, n.f. indentation.
dentièra, n.f. denture; gearing. ferrovìa a d., cog railway.
dentifricio, n.m. dentifrice.
dentista, n.m. dentist.
dèntro, adv. and prep. inside, within.
denudare, vb. denude.
denùncia, n.f. denunciation.
denunciare, vb. denounce; report.
deodorante, n.m. deodorant.
deodorare, vb. deodorize.
deperìbile, adj. perishable.
deplorare, vb. deplore.
deplorévole, adj. deplorable.
deporre, vb. depose; put down, set down; lay.
deportare, vb. deport.
deportazione, n.f. deportation.
depositante, n.m. depositor.
depositare, vb. deposit.
depòsito, n.m. deposit; depot. d. bagagli, checkroom.
deposizione, n.f. deposition, statement.
depravare, vb. deprave.
depravazione, n.f. depravity.
deprecare, vb. deprecate, decry.
depredamento, n.m. depredation.
depressione, n.f. depression.
deprezzamento, n.m. depreciation.
deprezzare, vb. depreciate, cheapen.
deprìmere, vb. depress.
deputato, n.m. deputy, representative.
deragliare, vb. derail.
derelitto, adj. derelict.
deridere, vb. deride, mock, laugh at, ridicule.
derisione, n.f. derision, mockery.
derisivo, adj. derisive.
deriva, n.f. drift. alla d., adrift.
derivare, vb. derive.

derivativo, adj. derivative.
derivazione, n.f. derivation.
dermatologìa, n.f. dermatology.
derogatòrio, adj. derogatory.
derubare, vb. rob.
descrittivo, adj. descriptive.
descrizione, n.f. description.
desecrare, vb. desecrate.
desensibilizzare, vb. desensitize.
desèrto, n.m. desert; wilderness.
desideràbile, adj. desirable.
desiderabilità, n.f. desirability.
desiderare, vb. desire, want, wish.
desidèrio, n.m. desire, wish.
desideroso, adj. desirous.
designare, vb. designate, nominate.
designato, n.m. nominee.
designazione, n.f. designation.
desinènza, n.f. ending.
desìstere, vb. desist.
desolare, vb. desolate.
desolato, adj. desolate.
desolazione, n.f. desolation.
dèspota, n.m. despot.
destinare, vb. destine.
destinatàrio, n.m. addressee.
destinazione, n.f. destination.
destino, n.m. destiny, doom.
destituito, adj. destitute.
destituzione, n.f. destitution.
dèstra, n.f. right.
destramente, adv. skillfully, dexterously.
destrezza, n.f. adroitness, adeptness, dexterity, skill.
dèstro, adj. adroit, adept, deft, skilful, dexterous, handy; right.
destròrso, adj. and adv. clockwise.
desùmere, vb. gather; infer.
detenere, vb. detain.
detenzione, n.f. detention.
detergènte, n.m. and adj. detergent.
deteriorare, vb. deteriorate.
deteriorazione, n.f. deterioration.
determinare, vb. determine.
determinazione, n.f. determination.
determinìsmo, n.m. determinism.
detestare, vb. detest, abhor.
detestazione, n.f. detestation, abhorrence.
detonare, vb. detonate.
detonazione, n.f. detonation, report.
detrarre, vb. detract.
detrimento, n.m. detriment.
detrìti, n.m.pl. debris.
detronizzare, vb. dethrone.
dettagliare, vb. detail.
dettàglio, n.m. detail. al d., at retail.
dettare, vb. dictate.
dettatura, n.f. dictation.
devastare, vb. devastate, ravage.

devastazione, *n.f.* devastation, havoc, ravage.

deviare, *vb.* deviate.

deviazione, *n.f.* deviation, detour.

devio, *adj.* devious.

devitalizzare, *vb.* devitalize.

dev.mo (for devotissimo, *adj.*): Vostro d., yours truly.

devòto, *adj.* devout, devoted, godly.

devozione, *n.f.* devotion.

di, *prep.* of; than.

diabète, *n.m.* diabetes.

diabòlico, *adj.* diabolic, devilish.

diàccio, *adj.* icy.

diàcono, *n.m.* deacon.

diadèma, *n.m.* diadem, coronet.

diaframma, *n.m.* diaphragm; midriff.

diagnosi, *n.f.* diagnosis.

diagnosticare, *vb.* diagnose.

diagnòstico, *adj.* diagnostic.

diagonale, *adj.* diagonal.

diagonalmente, *adv.* diagonally.

diagramma, *n.m.* diagram.

dialètto, *n.m.* dialect.

dialogo, *n.m.* dialogue.

diamante, *n.m.* diamond.

diametrale, *adj.* diametrical.

diametro, *n.m.* diameter.

diamine!, *interj.* the dickens!

diàrio, *n.m.* diary.

diarrèa, *n.f.* diarrhea.

diatermia, *n.f.* diathermy.

diatriba, *n.f.* diatribe.

diàvolo, *n.m.* devil.

dibàttere, *vb.* debate; (*refl.*) flounder.

dibattimento, *n.m.* debate.

di buon' ora, *adv.* early.

dicèmbre, *n.m.* December.

diceria, *n.f.* gossip, rumor.

dichiarare, *vb.* declare, explain. d. ricevuta di, acknowledge receipt of.

dichiarativo, *adj.* declarative.

dichiarazione, *n.f.* declaration; explanation.

diciannòve, *num.* nineteen.

diciannovèsimo, *adj.* nineteenth.

diciassètte, *num.* seventeen.

diciassettèsimo, *adj.* seventeenth.

diciottèsimo, *adj.* eighteenth.

diciòtto, *num.* eighteen.

didàttico, *adj.* didactic.

dièci, *num.* ten.

dièsis, *n.m.* sharp (music).

dièta, *n.f.* diet.

dietètica, *n.f.* dietetics.

dietètico, *adj.* dietetic, dietary.

dietista, *n.m.* dietitian.

diètro a, *prep.* behind.

difèndere, *vb.* defend, advocate.

difensìbile, *adj.* defensible.

difensivo, *adj.* defensive.

difensore, *n.m.* defender, advocate.

difesa, *n.f.* defense, advocacy.

difètto, *n.m.* defect, fault, flaw.

difettoso, *adj.* defective, faulty.

diffamare, *vb.* defame, libel, malign.

diffamatòrio, *adj.* defamatory, libelous.

diffamazione, *n.f.* defamation.

differènte, *adj.* different.

differènza, *n.f.* difference.

differenziale, *adj.* differential.

differenziare, *vb.* differentiate.

differire, *vb.* defer, put off; differ.

difficile, *adj.* difficult.

difficoltà, *n.f.* difficulty.

difficoltoso, *adj.* fussy.

diffidare di, *vb.* mistrust.

diffóndere, *vb.* diffuse, spread; (*refl.*) expatiate, dwell upon.

diffusione, *n.f.* diffusion.

diffuso, *adj.* diffuse, widespread.

difterite, *n.f.* diphtheria.

diga, *n.f.* dike, dam, levee.

digeribile, *adj.* digestible.

digerire, *vb.* digest.

digestione, *n.f.* digestion.

digestivo, *adj.* digestive.

digitale, 1. *n.f.* digitalis, foxglove. 2. *adj.* digital.

digiunare, *vb.* fast.

digiuno, *n.m.* fast.

dignificare, *vb.* dignify.

dignità, *n.f.* dignity.

dignitàrio, *n.m.* dignitary.

dignitoso, *adj.* dignified.

digredire, *vb.* digress.

digressione, *n.f.* digression.

digressivo, *adj.* discursive.

digrignare, *vb.* gnash.

dilapidato, *adj.* dilapidated.

dilapidazione, *n.f.* dilapidation, disrepair.

dilatare, *vb.* dilate.

dilatòrio, *adj.* dilatory.

dilemma, *n.m.* dilemma.

dilettante, *n.m.* amateur.

dilettévole, *adj.* delightful, delectable.

dilètto, 1. *n.m.* delight. 2. *adj.* beloved, darling.

diligènte, *adj.* diligent.

diligènza, *n.f.* diligence.

diluire, *vb.* dilute.

diluviare, *vb.* rain cats and dogs.

diluvio, *n.m.* deluge.

diluzione, *n.f.* dilution.

dimenare, *vb.* wag; (*refl.*) toss about; flounce.

dimensione, *n.f.* dimension.

dimenticare, *vb.* forget.

diméntico, *adj.* forgetful.

diméttere, *vb.* dismiss; (*refl.*) resign, quit.

dimezzare, *vb.* halve, cut in half.

diminuire, *vb.* diminish, lessen, abate, decrease, dwindle, let up, subside.

diminutivo, *n.m. and adj.* diminutive.

diminuzione, *n.f.* diminution, lessening, abatement, decrease.

dimissione, *n.f.* resignation.

dimora, *n.f.* abode, dwelling.

dimostràbile, *adj.* demonstrable.

dimostrare, *vb.* demonstrate.

dimostrativo, *adj.* demonstrative.

dimostratore, *n.m.* demonstrator.

dimostrazione, *n.f.* demonstration.

dinàmica, *n.f.* dynamics.

dinàmico, *adj.* dynamic.

dinamite, *n.f.* dynamite.

dinamo, *n.f.* dynamo.

dinastia, *n.f.* dynasty.

diniègo, *n.m.* denial.

dinosauro, *n.m.* dinosaur.

dintorni, *n.m.pl.* environs, surroundings.

dio, *n.m.* god.

diòcesi, *n.f.* diocese, bishopric.

dipanare, *vb.* reel off, unwind.

dipartimentale, *adj.* departmental.

dipartimento, *n.m.* department.

dipendènte, *n.m. and adj.* dependent.

dipendènza, *n.f.* dependence.

dipèndere, *vb.* depend.

dipingere, *vb.* paint, depict.

dipinto, *n.m.* painting.

diplòma, *n.m.* diploma.

diplomàtico, 1. *n.m.* diplomat. 2. *adj.* diplomatic.

diplomazia, *n.f.* diplomacy.

dipòrto, *n.m.* sport.

diramazione, *n.f.* junction.

dire, *vb.* say.

direttamente, *adv.* directly.

direttissimo, *n.m.* express train.

direttivo, *adj.* directive, directional.

dirètto, *adj.* direct; directed; bound; lineal; right; through.

direttorato, *n.m.* directorate.

direttore, *n.m.* director; conductor; editor; manager; principal.

direzione, *n.f.* direction, management.

dirigere, *vb.* direct; manage; aim; conduct; steer; edit.

dirigìbile, *n.m. and adj.* dirigible.

dirimpètto, *adv.* d. a, *prep.* opposite; facing.

diritti, *n.m.pl.* tax; dues. d. d'autore, copyright.

diritto, 1. *n.m.* right; law. 2. *adj., adv.* straight; upright.

dirottatore, *n.m.* hijacker.

disaccòrdo, *n.m.* discord, variance.

disadatto, *n.m.* unfit.

disagio, *n.m.* discomfort.

disapprovare, *vb.* disapprove.

disapprovazione, *n.f.* disapproval.

disarmare, *vb.* disarm.

disarmo, *n.m.* disarmament.

disastro, *n.m.* disaster, debacle.

disastroso, *adj.* disastrous.
discendènte, *n.f.* descendant.
discépolo, *n.m.* disciple.
discèrnere, *vb.* discern.
discesa, *n.f.* descent.
disciplina, *n.f.* discipline.
disciplinare, 1. *adj.* disciplinary. 2. *vb.* discipline.
disco, 1. *n.m.* disc, record. 2. *adj.* disco (music).
disconóscere, *vb.* disavow, disclaim, disown.
disconoscimento, *n.m.* disavowal, disclaimer.
discordante, *adj.* discordant.
discordare, *vb.* disagree, be discordant.
discòrdia, *n.f.* discord.
discórrere, *vb.* discourse.
discorso, *n.m.* speech, discourse, talk, address.
discotèca, *n.f.* record library; discotheque.
discrédito, *n.m.* discredit.
discrepante, *adj.* discrepant.
discrepanza, *n.f.* discrepancy.
discreto, *adj.* discreet; moderate; fair.
discrezione, *n.f.* discretion.
discriminare, *vb.* discriminate.
discriminazione, *n.f.* discrimination.
discussione, *n.f.* discussion.
discusso, *adj.* moot.
discùtere, *vb.* discuss.
discutibile, *adj.* debatable.
disdegnare, *vb.* disdain, spurn.
disdegno, *n.m.* disdain, scorn.
disdegnoso, *adj.* disdainful, scornful.
disegnare, *vb.* design; draw.
disegnatore, *n.m.* designer; draftsman.
disegno, *n.m.* picture; cartoon; design; drawing.
diseredare, *vb.* disinherit.
disertare, *vb.* desert.
disertore, *n.m.* deserter.
diserzione, *n.f.* desertion.
disfare, *vb.* undo.
disfatta, *n.f.* defeat.
disfattismo, *n.m.* defeatism.
disfigurare, *vb.* disfigure.
disgrazia, *n.f.* misfortune, mishap, accident; disgrace.
disgraziato, *adj.* unfortunate, unlucky.
disgustare, *vb.* disgust.
disgusto, *n.m.* disgust, distaste.
disgustoso, *adj.* disgusting, distasteful, nasty.
disidratare, *vb.* dehydrate.
disillùdere, *vb.* disillusion.
disillusione, *n.f.* disillusion.
disimballare, *vb.* unpack.
disimpegnare, *vb.* disengage.
disincanto, *n.m.* disenchantment.
disinfettante, *n.m.* disinfectant.
disinfettare, *vb.* disinfect.
disingannare, *vb.* undeceive, disabuse.
disintegrare, *vb.* disintegrate.
disinteressato, *adj.* disinterested.

dislessia, *n.f.* dyslexia.
dislocamento, *n.m.* displacement.
disobbediènte, *adj.* disobedient.
disoccupato, *adj.* unemployed.
disonestà, *n.f.* dishonesty.
disonèsto, *adj.* dishonest; foul.
disonorante, *adj.* disgraceful.
disonorare, *vb.* dishonor, disgrace.
disonore, *n.m.* dishonor, disgrace.
disonorévole, *adj.* dishonorable, discreditable, disreputable.
disórdine, *n.m.* disorder.
disordinato, *adj.* disorderly.
disórdine, *n.m.* disorder, litter.
disorganizzare, *vb.* disorganize.
disparato, *adj.* disparate.
dispari, *adj.* odd.
disparità, *n.f.* disparity.
disparte: in d., *adv.* apart, aloof.
dispensa, *n.f.* pantry.
dispensàbile, *adj.* dispensable.
dispensare, *vb.* dispense.
dispensario, *n.m.* dispensary.
dispensazione, *n.f.* dispensation.
dispepsia, *n.f.* dyspepsia.
dispèptico, *adj.* dyspeptic.
disperare, *vb.* despair.
disperato, 1. *n.* desperado. 2. *adj.* desperate; forlorn, hopeless.
disperazione, *n.f.* desperation, despair, hopelessness.
disperdere, *vb.* disperse.
dispersione, *n.f.* dispersal.
dispetto, *n.m.* spite.
dispiacente, *adj.* sorry; displeasing.
dispiacere, 1. *n.m.* displeasure. 2. *vb.* displease.
disponibile, *adj.* available; disposable.
disporre, *vb.* dispose, arrange; range.
disposizione, *n.f.* disposition; disposal.
dispòtico, *adj.* despotic.
dispotismo, *n.m.* despotism.
disprezzare, *vb.* despise, disparage, scorn, slight.
disprezzo, *n.m.* contempt, scorn, slight.
disputa, *n.f.* dispute.
disputàbile, *adj.* disputable.
disputare, *vb.* dispute.
dissecare, *vb.* dissect.
disseminare, *vb.* disseminate.
dissenso, *n.m.* dissent, disagreement, dissension.
dissenteria, *n.f.* dysentery.
dissentire, *vb.* dissent, disagree.
disserrare, *vb.* unlock.
dissertazione, *n.f.* dissertation.
disservizio, *n.m.* disservice, bad service.
dissetare, *vb.* quench (one's) thirst.
dissezione, *n.f.* dissection.

dissìmile, *adj.* dissimilar, unlike.
dissimulare, *vb.* dissimulate, dissemble.
dissipare, *vb.* dissipate, dispel.
dissipazione, *n.f.* dissipation.
dissociare, *vb.* dissociate.
dissolutezza, *n.f.* dissoluteness, dissipation.
dissoluto, *adj.* dissolute, dissipated.
dissoluzione, *n.f.* dissolution.
dissòlvere, *vb.* dissolve.
dissonante, *adj.* dissonant.
dissonanza, *n.f.* dissonance.
dissotterrare, *vb.* unearth.
dissuadere, *vb.* dissuade.
distaccamento, *n.m.* detachment *(mil.).* **distaccare**, *vb.* detach.
distacco, *n.m.* detachment.
distante, *adj.* distant.
distare, *vb.* be distant.
distèndere, *vb.* distend.
distensione, *n.f.* détente.
distesa, *n.f.* expanse; extent; spread.
disteso, *adj.* spread.
distillare, *vb.* distill.
distillatore, *n.m.* distiller.
distilleria, *n.f.* distillery.
distillazione, *n.f.* distillation.
distinguere, *vb.* distinguish.
distintamente, *adv.* distinctly.
distintivo, 1. *n.m.* badge. 2. *adj.* distinctive.
distinto, *adj.* distinct.
distinzione, *n.f.* distinction.
distògliere, *vb.* deter.
distòrcere, *vb.* distort.
distrarre, *vb.* distract.
distratto, *adj.* absentminded.
distrazione, *n.f.* distraction.
distretto, *n.m.* district.
distribuire, *vb.* distribute, apportion, deal out, dole out.
distributore, *n.m.* distributor.
distribuzione, *n.f.* distribution; deal.
districare, *vb.* disentangle, extricate, unravel.
distrùggere, *vb.* destroy.
distruttibile, *adj.* destructible.
distruttivo, *adj.* destructive.
distruzione, *n.f.* destruction.
disturbare, *vb.* disturb, trouble.
disturbo, *n.m.* disturbance, trouble.
disubbidienza, *n.f.* disobedience.
disubbidire, *vb.* disobey.
disuguale, *adj.* uneven.
disunire, *vb.* disunite.
disuso, *n.m.* disuse.
ditale, *n.m.* thimble.
dito, *n.m.* finger. **d. del piede**, toe.
ditta, *n.f.* firm.
dittafono, *n.m.* dictaphone.
dittatore, *n.m.* dictator.
dittatoriale, *adj.* dictatorial.
dittatura, *n.f.* dictatorship.
diva, *n.f.* famous singer, diva.
divagare, *vb.* ramble, get off the subject.

divampare, vb. burst into flames.

divano, n.m. divan, davenport, lounge.

divenire, vb. become; get.

diventare, vb. become; get.

divergènte, adj. divergent.

divergènza, n.f. divergence.

divèrgere, vb. diverge.

diversione, n.f. diversion.

diversità, n.f. diversity.

diversivo, n.m. relief.

divèrso, adj. diverse, different.

divertimento, n.m. amusement, hobby, recreation, entertainment, fun.

divertire, vb. amuse, divert, entertain; (refl.) have a good time.

dividèndo, n.m. dividend.

divìdere, vb. divide, split.

divièto, n.m. prohibition.

divinare, vb. divine.

divinità, n.f. divinity.

divino, adj. divine, godlike.

divisa, n.f. uniform.

divisìbile, adj. divisible.

divisione, n.f. division.

divisòrio, adj. dividing.

divorare, vb. devour.

divorziare, vb. divorce.

divòrzio, n.m. divorce.

divulgare, vb. divulge.

dizionàrio, n.m. dictionary.

dizione, n.f. diction.

dòccia, n.f. shower.

dòcile, adj. docile, tame, submissive, amenable.

documentare, vb. document.

documentàrio, adj. documentary.

documentazione, n.f. documentation.

documento, n.m. document.

dodicèsimo, adj. twelfth.

dòdici, num. twelve.

dogana, n.f. customs, customshouse.

doganière, n.m. customs officer.

dògma, n.m. dogma.

dogmaticità, n.f. assertiveness.

dogmàtico, adj. dogmatic, assertive.

dogmatismo, n.m. dogmatism.

dolce, 1. n.m. candy, bonbon. 2. adj. sweet.

dolcemente, adv. sweetly, soothingly.

dolcezza, n.f. sweetness.

dolènte, adj. sore.

dolere, vb. hurt, pain; (refl.) complain.

dòllaro, n.m. dollar.

dolore, n.m. sorrow, pain, ache, grief.

doloróso, adj. dolorous, sorrowful, mournful, painful, grievous.

domanda, n.f. question; request; application; demand; query.

domandare, vb. ask; demand; request; query; (refl.) wonder.

domani, n.m. and adv. tomorrow.

domare, vb. tame.

domènica, n.f. Sunday.

domèstica, n.f. housemaid.

domesticare, vb. domesticate.

domèstico, 1. n. servant. 2. adj. domestic.

domicìlio, n.m. domicile.

dominante, adj. dominant.

dominare, vb. dominate, sway.

dominazione, n.f. domination.

dominio, n.m. domain, dominion.

dòmino, n.m. domino.

donare, vb. donate.

donatore, n.m. giver.

donazione, n.f. donation.

donchisciottesco, adj. quixotic.

donde, adv. whence.

dondolare, vb. rock, swing.

dònna, n.f. woman.

dònnola, n.f. weasel.

dono, n.m. gift, grant, present.

dopo, 1. adv. afterwards. 2. prep. after. d. che, conj. after.

doppiamente, adv. doubly.

doppiare, vb. double.

dóppio, adj. double; duplex.

dorare, vb. gild.

dorato, adj. gilt.

doratura, n.f. gilt.

dormire, vb. sleep.

dormitòrio, n.m. dormitory.

dorsale, adj. dorsal, pertaining to the back.

dòrso, n.m. back.

dosare, vb. dose.

dosatura, n.f. dosage.

dòse, n.f. dose.

dòsso, n.m. back.

dotare, vb. endow.

dotato, adj. gifted.

dotazione, n.f. endowment.

dòte, n.f. dowry.

dòtto, 1. n. scholar. 2. adj. learned.

dottorato, n.m. doctorate.

dottore, n.m. doctor.

dottrina, n.f. doctrine; learning.

dottrinàrio, adj. doctrinaire.

dove, adv. where.

dovere, 1. n.m. duty. 2. vb. owe; be supposed to; have to: ought; must.

dovunque, adv. wherever.

dovuto, adj. due, owing.

dozzina, n.f. dozen.

draga, n.f. dredge.

dragare, vb. dredge.

dragone, n.m. dragon.

dramma, n.m. dram; drama, play.

drammàtica, n.f. dramatics.

drammàtico, adj. dramatic.

drammatizzare, vb. dramatize.

drammaturgìa, n.f. dramaturgy, play-writing.

drammaturgo, n.m. dramatist, playwright.

drappeggiare, vb. drape.

drappéggio, n.m. drapery, drapes.

drappèllo, n.m. platoon.

dràstico, adj. drastic.

drenàggio, n.m. drainage.

drizza, n.f. halyard.

drizzare, vb. straighten.

dròga, n.f. drug.

dromedàrio, n.m. dromedary.

duale, n.m. and adj. dual.

dualismo, n.m. dualism.

dùbbio, 1. n.m. doubt. 2. adj. doubtful, dubious.

dubbióso, adj. doubtful.

dubitare, vb. doubt.

duca, n.m. duke.

ducato, n.m. duchy, dukedom.

duce, n.m. (Fascist) leader.

duchessa, n.f. duchess.

due, num. two.

duellante, n.m. duellist.

duellare, vb. duel.

duèllo, n.m. duel.

duétto, n.m. duet.

duna, n.f. dune.

dunque, adv. therefore; so; then.

duplicare, vb. duplicate.

duplicazione, n.f. duplication.

duplicità, n.f. duplicity, double-dealing.

duràbile, adj. durable, enduring.

durabilità, n.f. durability.

duramente, adv. hard.

durante, prep. during.

durare, vb. endure, last.

durata, n.f. duration.

durévole, adj. lasting.

durezza, n.f. hardness.

duro, adj. hard.

dùttile, adj. ductile.

E

e, conj. and.

èbano, n.m. ebony.

ebràico, n. and adj. Hebrew, Hebraic; Jewish.

ebrèo, n. and adj. Hebrew; Jew(ish).

eccèdere, vb. exceed.

eccellènte, adj. excellent.

eccellènza, n.f. excellence.

Eccellènza, n.f. Excellency.

eccèllere, vb. excel.

eccentricità, n.f. eccentricity.

eccèntrico, adj. eccentric.

eccessivo, adj. excessive.

eccèsso, n.m. excess.

eccètto, prep. except; but.

eccettuare, vb. except.

eccezionale, adj. exceptional.

eccezione, n.f. exception.

eccitàbile, adj. excitable, highstrung, hot-headed.

eccitamento, n.m. excitement.

eccitare, vb. excite.

eccitazione, n.f. excitement.

ecclesiàstico, 1. n. ecclesiastic, cleric, clergyman. 2. adj. ecclesiastical.

ècco, vb. here is; there is; lo; behold.

echeggiare, vb. echo.

eclissare, vb. eclipse.

eclissi, n.f. eclipse.

eco, *n.m.* echo.

ecologìa, *n.f.* ecology.

ecològico, *adj.* ecological.

economìa, *n.f.* economy, thrift. e. polìtica, economics.

economicamente, *adv.* economically, cheaply.

econòmico, *adj.* economic, economical, cheap.

economista, *n.m.* economist.

economizzare, *vb.* economize, save.

ecumènico, *adj.* ecumenical.

eczèma, *n.m.* eczema.

ed, *conj.* and.

èdera, *n.f.* ivy.

edificare, *vb.* edify, build.

edifìcio, *n.m.* edifice, building.

editore, *n.m.* publisher.

editoriale, *adj.* editorial.

editto, *n.m.* edict.

edizione, *n.f.* edition, publication.

edonismo, *n.m.* hedonism.

educare, *vb.* educate, train.

educativo, *adj.* educational.

educatore, *n.m.* educator.

educazione, *n.f.* education, breeding, manners.

effeminato, *adj.* effeminate.

effervescènza, *n.f.* effervescence.

effettivamente, *adv.* effectively; in effect.

effettività, *n.f.* effectiveness.

effettivo, *adj.* effective.

effetto, *n.m.* effect.

effettuare, *vb.* effect, bring about, contrive.

efficace, *adj.* efficacious, effectual.

efficàcia, *n.f.* efficacy.

efficiènte, *adj.* efficient.

efficientemente, *adv.* efficiently.

efficiènza, *n.f.* efficiency.

effìgie, *n.f.* effigy.

effìmero, *adj.* ephemeral.

egemonìa, *n.f.* hegemony.

ègida, *n.f.* aegis, auspices, protection.

Egitto, *n.m.* Egypt.

egiziano, *adj.* Egyptian.

egli, *pron.* he.

egoismo, *n.m.* egoism, selfishness.

egoìstico, *adj.* selfish.

egotismo, *n.m.* egotism.

egotista, *n.m.* egotist.

eiaculare, *vb.* ejaculate.

elaborare, *vb.* elaborate.

elaborato, *adj.* elaborate.

elaborazione, *n.f.* data processing.

elasticità, *n.f.* elasticity.

elàstico, *n.m. and adj.* elastic.

elefante, *n.m.* elephant.

elefantesco, *adj.* elephantine.

elegante, *adj.* elegant, smart.

eleganza, *n.f.* elegance.

elèggere, *vb.* elect.

eleggìbile, *adj.* eligible.

eleggibilità, *n.f.* eligibility.

elegìa, *n.f.* elegy.

elegìaco, *adj.* elegiac.

elementare, *adj.* elemental, elementary.

elemento, *n.m.* element.

elemòsina, *n.f.* charity, alms, dole.

elencare, *vb.* list, itemize.

elènco, *n.m.* list. e. telefònico, telephone directory.

elettivo, *adj.* elective.

elettricista, *n.m.* electrician.

elettricità, *n.f.* electricity.

elèttrico, *adj.* electric, electrical.

elettrocardiogramma, *n.m.* electrocardiogram.

elettrocuzione, *n.f.* electrocution.

elèttrodo, *n.m.* electrode.

elettrodomèstici, *n.m.pl.* electric household appliances.

elettròlisi, *n.f.* electrolysis.

elettromotrice, *n.f.* electric railcar.

elettrone, *n.m.* electron.

elettrònica, *n.f.* electronics.

elettrònico, *adj.* electronic.

elettrotreno, *n.m.* express train of electric railcars.

elevare, *vb.* elevate.

elevazione, *n.f.* elevation.

elezione, *n.f.* election.

èlica, *n.f.* propeller.

elicòttero, *n.m.* helicopter.

eliminare, *vb.* eliminate.

eliminazione, *n.f.* elimination.

èlio, *n.m.* helium.

eliocèntrico, *adj.* heliocentric.

elìògrafo, *n.m.* heliograph.

eliotipìa, *n.f.* blueprint.

eliotròpio, *n.m.* heliotrope.

elisir, *n.m.* elixir.

ella, *pron.f.* she; (very formal) you.

ellènico, *adj.* Hellenic.

ellenismo, *n.m.* Hellenism.

èlmo, *n.m.* helmet.

elocuzione, *n.f.* elocution.

elogiare, *vb.* eulogize.

elògio, *n.m.* eulogy.

eloquènte, *adj.* eloquent.

eloquentemente, *adv.* eloquently.

eloquènza, *n.f.* eloquence.

èlsa, *n.f.* hilt.

elucidare, *vb.* elucidate.

elùdere, *vb.* elude, dodge, evade.

elusivo, *adj.* elusive.

emaciato, *adj.* emaciated.

emanare, *vb.* emanate.

emancipare, *vb.* emancipate.

emancipatore, *n.m.* emancipator.

emancipazione, *n.f.* emancipation.

ematite, *n.f.* hematite.

embargo, *n.m.* embargo.

emblèma, *n.m.* emblem, badge.

emblemàtico, *adj.* emblematic.

embriologìa, *n.f.* embryology.

embrionale, *adj.* embryonic.

embrione, *n.m.* embryo.

emendamento, *n.m.* amendment.

emendare, *vb.* amend, emend.

emergènte, *adj.* emergent.

emergènza, *n.f.* emergency.

emèrgere, *vb.* emerge.

emètico, *adj.* emetic.

emèttere, *vb.* emit; send forth; issue; utter.

emicrània, *n.f.* migraine.

emigrante, *n.m. and adj.* emigrant.

emigrare, *vb.* emigrate.

emigrazione, *n.f.* emigration.

eminènte, *adj.* eminent.

eminènza, *n.f.* eminence.

emisfèrio, *n.m.* hemisphere.

emissàrio, *n.m.* emissary.

emissione, *n.f.* issue.

emofìlia, *n.f.* hemophilia.

emoglobina, *n.f.* hemoglobin.

emolliènte, *n.m. and adj.* emollient.

emolumento, *n.m.* emolument.

emorragìa, *n.f.* hemorrhage.

emorròide, *n.f.* hemorrhoid, pile.

emotivo, *adj.* emotional.

emozionàbile, *adj.* emotional.

emozione, *n.f.* emotion.

emplastro, *adj.* plaster.

èmpio, *adj.* impious, blasphemous, godless.

empìrico, *adj.* empirical. rimèdio e., nostrum.

emulare, *vb.* emulate.

emulsione, *n.f.* emulsion.

encefalite, *n.f.* encephalitis.

encèfalo, *n.m.* encephalon.

enciclica, *n.f.* encyclical.

enciclopedìa, *n.f.* encyclopaedia.

endèmico, *adj.* endemic.

endòcrino, *adj.* endocrine.

endovenoso, *adj.* intravenous.

energìa, *n.f.* energy.

enèrgico, *adj.* energetic.

ènfasi, *n.f.* emphasis.

enfàtico, *adj.* emphatic.

enimma, *n.m.* enigma, riddle.

enimmàtico, *adj.* enigmatic.

ennè, *n.m.* henna.

enòrme, *adj.* enormous.

enormità, *n.f.* enormity.

enteroclisma, *n.m.* enema, colonic irrigation.

entità, *n.f.* entity.

entrare, *vb.* enter.

entrata, *n.f.* entrance, entry; admission; revenue; input.

entro, *prep.* in; within.

entusiasmo, *n.m.* enthusiasm.

entusiasta, *n.m. or f.* enthusiast, devotee.

entusiàstico, *adj.* enthusiastic.

enumerare, *vb.* enumerate.

enumerazione, *n.f.* enumeration.

enunciare, *vb.* enunciate.

enunciazione, *n.f.* enunciation.

epàtica, *n.f.* hepatica.

epàtico, *adj.* hepatic.

eperlano, *n.m.* smelt.

èpico, *adj.* epic.

epicurèo, *n.m.* epicure.

epidemìa, *n.f.* epidemic.

epidèmico, *adj.* epidemic.

epidèrmide, n.f. epidermis.
epigramma, n.m. epigram.
epilessia, n.f. epilepsy.
epilogo, n.m. epilogue.
episòdio, n.m. episode.
epistola, n.f. epistle.
epitàffio, n.m. epitaph.
epiteto, n.m. epithet.
epitomare, vb. epitomize.
epitome, n.f. epitome.
època, n.f. epoch.
epopéa, n.f. epic.
equanimità, n.f. equanimity.
equatore, n.m. equator.
equatoriale, adj. equatorial.
equazione, n.f. equation.
equèstre, adj. equestrian.
equidistante, adj. equidistant.
equilaterale, adj. equilateral.
equilibrare, vb. balance, equilibrate.
equilibrato, adj. balanced; level.
equilibrio, n.m. balance, equilibrium; poise.
equinòzio, n.m. equinox.
equipaggiare, vb. rig.
equipàggio, n.m. crew; equipment; rig.
equità, n.f. equity.
equitazione, n.f. equitation, horsemanship.
equivalènte, adj. equivalent.
equivalere, vb. be equivalent.
equìvoco, 1. n.m. mistake. 2. adj. equivocal.
èquo, adj. equable, equitable, fair, just.
èra, n.f. era.
èrba, n.f. grass; herb.
erbàccia, n.f. weed.
erbàceo, adj. herbaceous.
erbàrio, n.m. herbarium.
erboso, adj. grassy.
ercùleo, adj. Herculean.
erède, n.m. heir.
ereditá, n.f. heredity; heritage; inheritance.
ereditare, vb. inherit.
ereditàrio, adj. hereditary.
ereditièra, n.f. heiress.
eremita, n.m. hermit.
eremitàggio, n.m. hermitage.
eresia, n.f. heresy.
erètico, 1. n. heretic. 2. adj. heretical.
erètto, adj. erect, upright.
erezione, n.f. erection.
èrgere, vb. raise.
èrica, n.f. heather.
erìgere, vb. erect, raise.
ermellino, n.m. ermine.
ermètico, adj. hermetic.
èrnia, n.f. hernia.
eròdere, vb. erode.
eròe, n.m. hero.
eroicamente, adv. heroically.
eròico, adj. heroic.
eroìna, n.f. heroine; heroin.
eroismo, n.m. heroism.
erosione, n.f. erosion.
erosivo, adj. erosive.
eròtico, adj. erotic.
èrpete, n.f. herpes, shingles.
erpicare, vb. harrow.

èrpice, n.m. harrow.
errante, adj. errant.
errare, vb. err, make a mistake, be wrong; wander; rove.
erràtico, adj. erratic.
errato, adj. wrong, mistaken.
erròneo, adj. erroneous, mistaken.
errore, n.m. error, mistake, blunder, slip.
èrto, adj. steep.
erudito, 1. n. scholar. 2. adj. erudite.
erudizione, n.f. erudition, scholarship.
eruttare, vb. erupt.
eruzione, n.f. eruption; rash.
esagerare, vb. exaggerate.
esagerazione, n.f. exaggeration.
esàgono, n.m. hexagon.
esalare, vb. exhale.
esalazione, n.f. fume.
esaltare, vb. exalt, elate.
esaltato, adj. exalted, elated.
esaltazione, n.f. exaltation, elation.
esame, n.m. examination; canvass; survey.
esaminare, vb. examine; canvass; survey.
esangue, adj. bloodless.
esasperare, vb. exasperate.
esasperazione, n.f. exasperation.
esattamente, adv. exactly.
esatto, adj. exact.
esauriènte, adj. exhaustive; indepth.
esaurimento, n.m. exhaustion.
esaurire, vb. exhaust, deplete.
esca, n.f. bait; tinder.
eschimese, n.m. Eskimo pie.
esclamare, vb. exclaim.
esclamazione, n.f. exclamation.
escludere, vb. exclude.
esclusione, n.f. exclusion.
esclusivo, adj. exclusive.
escogitare, vb. excogitate, devise.
escoriare, vb. excoriate.
escremento, n.m. excrement.
esculènto, adj. esculent.
escursione, n.f. excursion, jaunt, junket, outing.
esecràbile, adj. execrable.
esecutivo, adj. executive.
esecutore, n.m. executor.
esecuzione, n.f. execution, enforcement; performance, rendition.
eseguire, vb. execute, enforce; perform.
esèmpio, n.m. example.
esemplare, 1. n.m. copy. 2. adj. exemplary.
esemplificare, vb. exemplify.
esentare, vb. exempt; dispense.
esènte, adj. exempt; immune. e. da dogana, duty-free.
esercitare, vb. exercise; exert; drill, practice.
esercitazione, n.f. practice, drill.

esèrcito, n.m. army.
esercìzio, n.m. exercise.
esibire, vb. exhibit, display.
esibizione, n.f. exhibition, display.
esibizionismo, n.m. exhibitionism.
esigènza, n.f. exigency; requirement.
esigere, vb. exact, require, demand.
esilarare, vb. exhilarate.
esilare, vb. exile, banish.
esìlio, n.m. exile, banishment.
esistènte, adj. existent, extant.
esistènza, n.f. existence, being.
esistere, vb. exist.
esitante, adj. hesitant.
esitare, vb. hesitate, falter, waver.
esitazione, n.f. hesitation.
èsodo, n.m. exodus.
esòfago, n.m. esophagus.
esonerare, vb. exonerate.
esorbitante, adj. exorbitant.
esorcizzare, vb. exorcise.
esortare, vb. exhort; plead with.
esortativo, adj. exhortatory.
esortazione, n.f. exhortation.
esotèrico, adj. esoteric.
esòtico, adj. exotic.
espàndere, vb. expand.
espansione, n.f. expansion.
espansivo, adj. expansive, effusive.
espatriato, adj. expatriate.
espediènte, n.m. and adj. expedient; makeshift.
espèllere, vb. expel, drive out, eject, evict, oust.
esperiènza, n.f. experience.
esperimentare, n.m. experiment; experience.
espèrto, n.m. and adj. expert; experienced, practiced, proficient.
espettorare, vb. expectorate.
espiare, vb. expiate, atone for.
espiazione, n.f. expiation, atonement.
espirare, vb. expire.
espirazione, n.f. expiration.
espletivo, adj. expletive.
esplicativo, adj. explanatory.
esplìcito, adj. explicit.
esplòdere, vb. explode.
esplorare, vb. explore.
esplorativo, adj. exploratory.
esploratore, n.m. explorer; scout.
esplorazione, n.f. exploration.
esplosione, n.f. explosion, blast.
esplosivo, n.m. and adj. explosive.
esponènte, n.m. exponent.
esporre, vb. expose.
esportare, vb. export.
esportazione, n.f. export, exportation.
espositivo, adj. expository.
esposizione, n.f. exposition; exposé; exposure; show.
esposto, n.m. exposé.

espressamente, adv. expressly.

espressione, n.f. expression.

espressivo, adj. expressive.

esprèsso, n.m. and adj. express; special delivery; coffee 'espresso.'

esprimere, vb. express.

espropriare, vb. expropriate.

espulsione, n.f. expulsion, ejection, eviction, ouster.

espingere, vb. expunge.

espurgare, vb. expurgate.

essa, pron.f.sg. she; it.

esse, pron.f.pl. they.

essènza, n.f. essence.

essenziale, adj. essential.

essenzialmente, adv. essentially.

èssere, 1. n. being. 2. vb. be.

essi, pron.m.pl. they.

essiccatòlo, n.m. drier.

esso, pron.m.sg. he; it.

essudato, n.m. exudation.

èst, n.m. east.

èstasi, n.f. ecstasy, rapture.

estasiare, vb. send into ecstasies, enrapture.

estate, n.f. summer.

estemporàneo, adj. extemporaneous.

estensione, n.f. extent; extension; range.

estenuare, vb. extenuate.

esteriore, adj. exterior, outer, outward.

esteriormente, adv. outwardly.

estèrno, adj. external, outside.

èstero, 1. n.m. foreign parts 2. adj. foreign; external.

estesamente, adv. extensively.

esteso, adj. extensive; far-flung.

estètica, n.f. aesthetics.

estètico, adj. aesthetic.

estinguere, vb. extinguish, quench.

estinto, adj. extinct.

estinzione, n.f. extinction.

estirpare, vb. extirpate.

estivo, adj. of summer.

estòllere, vb. extol.

estòrcere, vb. extort.

estorsione, n.f. extortion.

estra-, prefix. extra-.

estradare, vb. extradite.

estradizione, n.f. extradition.

estràneo, adj. extraneous.

estrarre, vb. extract.

estratto, n.m. extract.

estrazione, n.f. extraction.

estremamente, adv. extremely, exceedingly.

estremità, n.f. extremity; end; butt.

estrèmo, 1. n. fullback. 2. adj. extreme, utmost.

estrovertito, adj. extrovert.

estuàrio, n.m. estuary.

esuberante, adj. exuberant; ebullient.

esultante, adj. exultant.

esultare, vb. exult.

esumare, vb. exhume; resurrect.

età, n.f. age.

ètere, n.m. ether.

etèreo, adj. ethereal.

eternamente, adv. eternally, forevermore.

eternità, n.f. eternity; eon.

etèrno, adj. eternal.

eterodossia, n.f. heterodoxy.

eterodòsso, adj. heterodox.

eterogèneo, adj. heterogeneous, motley.

eterosessuale, adj. heterosexual.

ètica, n.f. ethics.

etichetta, n.f. label; docket; sticker; tag.

ètico, adj. ethical; hectic.

etílico, adj. ethyl.

etimologia, n.f. etymology.

ètnico, adj. ethnic.

èttaro, n.m. hectare.

ètto, n.m. hectogram.

ettogramma, n.m. hectogram.

eucalitto, n.m. eucalyptus.

eufònico, adj. euphonious.

eugenètica, n.f. eugenics.

eugènico, adj. eugenic.

eunuco, n.m. eunuch.

Europa, n.f. Europe.

europèo, adj. and n. European.

eutanasia, n.f. euthanasia.

evacuare, vb. evacuate.

evanescènte, adj. evanescent.

evangelista, n.m. evangelist.

evaporare, vb. evaporate.

evaporazione, n.f. evaporation.

evasione, n.f. evasion; escape.

evasivo, adj. evasive.

evènto, n.m. outcome.

evidènte, adj. evident.

evidentemente, adv. evidently.

evidènza, n.f. evidence.

evitàbile, adj. avoidable.

evitare, vb. avoid, evade, eschew, obviate.

evocare, vb. evoke.

evoluzione, n.f. evolution.

evoluzionista, n.m. evolutionist.

evòlvere, vb. evolve.

evviva, interj. hurrah (for).

extra, adj. extra.

F

F (on water faucets) = freddo, adj. cold.

fa, adv. ago.

fàbbrica, n.f. factory; mill; (architecture) fabric.

fabbricante, n.m. manufacturer.

fabbricare, vb. build; manufacture, fabricate.

fabbricazione, n.f. manufacture; fabrication.

fabbro, n.m. smith. f. ferraio, blacksmith.

faccendière, n.m. busybody.

faccetta, n.f. facet.

facchino, n.m. porter.

faccia, n.f. face.

facciata, n.f. facade.

faceto, adj. facetious, witty, humorous.

faciale, adj. facial.

facile, adj. easy, facile.

facilità, n.f. facility, ease, easiness.

facilitare, vb. facilitate.

facilmente, adv. easily.

facoltà, n.f. faculty, knack, power.

facoltativo, adj. optional.

facsimile, n.m. facsimile.

factotum, n.m. handy-man; jack-of-all-trades.

fagiano, n.m. pheasant.

fagiòlo, n.m. string bean.

faglia, n.f. faille.

fagòtto, n.m. bassoon.

falce, n.f. scythe.

falciare, vb. mow.

falco, n.f. hawk.

falcone, n.m. falcon.

falconeria, n.f. falconry.

falegname, n.m. carpenter.

falla, n.f. leak.

fallace, adj. fallacious.

fallàcia, n.f. fallacy.

fallibile, adj. fallible.

fallimento, n.m. bankruptcy; failure.

fallire, vb. fail; go bankrupt.

fallito, adj. bankrupt.

fallòcrate, n.m. macho.

falò, n.m. bonfire.

falsetto, n.m. falsetto.

falsificare, vb. falsify, fake, counterfeit.

falsificatore, n.f. faker.

falsificazione, n.f. falsification.

falsità, n.f. falsity.

falso, 1. n.m. counterfeit, fake. 2. adj. false, counterfeit.

fama, n.f. fame.

fame, n.f. hunger; starvation. aver f., be hungry.

famigerato, adj. notorious.

famiglia, n.f. family; household.

familiare, adj. familiar, well-known; acquainted.

familiarità, n.f. familiarity.

familiarizzare, vb. familiarize.

famoso, adj. famous, famed.

fanale, n.m. lamp; light. f. anteriore, headlight.

fanàtico, n.m. and adj. fanatic, fanatical.

fanatismo, n.m. fanaticism.

fanciulla, n.f. maiden; girl.

fanciullescamente, adv. childishly; boyishly.

fanciullesco, adj. childish; boyish.

fanciullezza, n.f. childhood; boyhood; girlhood.

fanciullo, n.m. child; boy.

fandònia, n.f. fib; story, tale; (pl.) nonsense.

fanfara, n.f. fanfare.

fanghiglia, n.f. slush.

fango, n.m. mud, mire.

fangoso, adj. muddy.

fantascienza, n.f. science fiction.

fantasia, n.f. fantasy, imagination. di f., fancy.

fantasma, n.m. phantom.

fantasticheria, *n.f.* reverie, daydream.

fantastico, *adj.* fantastic.

fante, *n.m.* infantryman.

fanteria, *n.f.* infantry.

fantino, *n.m.* jockey.

fantoccio, *n.m.* puppet, dummy.

faraona, *n.f.* guinea fowl.

fardello, *n.m.* burden.

fare, *vb.* do; make. **f. a meno di,** go without. **f. finta di,** pretend to.

faretra, *n.f.* quiver (arrowcase).

farfalla, *n.f.* butterfly.

farina, *n.f.* flour; farina; meal.

farmacia, *n.f.* drug store, pharmacy.

farmacista, *n.m.* druggist, pharmacist.

faro, *n.m.* beacon, lighthouse.

farsa, *n.f.* farce.

farsesco, *adj.* farcical.

fascino, *n.m.* fascination; charm; glamor.

fascio, *n.m.* bundle; sheaf; Fascist group.

fascismo, *n.m.* fascism.

fascista, *n. and adj.* fascist.

fase, *n.f.* phase, stage.

fastidio, *n.m.* annoyance, bother, trouble, unpleasantness, nuisance.

fastidioso, *adj.* fastidious; bothersome, troublesome.

fasto, *n.m.* pomp.

fastoso, *adj.* pompous.

fata, *n.f.* fairy.

fatale, *adj.* fatal; fateful.

fatalità, *n.f.* fatality.

fatalmente, *vb.* fatally.

fatica, *n.f.* fatigue; toil, hard work.

faticare, *vb.* toil.

fato, *n.m.* fate.

fattibile, *adj.* feasible.

fatto, *n.m.* fact; deed, feat.

fattore, *n.m.* maker; factor; steward; granger.

fattoria, *n.f.* farm; grange; homestead; ranch; station.

fattura, *n.f.* invoice.

fatturare, *vb.* invoice.

fatuo, *adj.* fatuous.

fava, *n.f.* bean.

favo, *n.m.* honeycomb.

favola, *n.f.* fable.

favoloso, *adj.* fabulous.

favore, *n.m.* favor; behalf. **a f. di,** in behalf of. **per f.,** please.

favorévole, *adj.* favorable, auspicious.

favorire, *vb.* favor.

favoritismo, *n.m.* favoritism.

favorito, *n.m. and adj.* favorite.

fazione, *n.f.* faction.

fazzoletti detergenti, *n.m.pl.* facial tissues.

fazzoletto, *n.m.* handkerchief.

febbraio, *n.m.* February.

febbre, *n.f.* fever.

febbrile, *adj.* feverish.

febbrilmente, *adv.* feverishly.

feccia, *n.f.* dregs; lees; *(pl.)* faeces.

fecondo, *adj.* fecund.

fede, *n.f.* faith, creed.

fededegno, *adj.* trustworthy, reliable.

fedele, *adj.* faithful, true.

fedeltà, *n.f.* faithfulness, allegiance, fidelity.

federa, *n.f.* pillowcase.

federale, *adj.* federal.

federazione, *n.f.* federation.

fegato, *n.m.* liver; pluck, guts.

felce, *n.f.* fern.

felice, *adj.* happy, felicitous.

felicemente, *adv.* happily.

felicità, *n.f.* felicity, happiness.

felicitare, *vb.* congratulate; felicitate; compliment.

felicitazione, *n.f.* congratulation; felicitation.

felino, *adj.* feline.

fellone, *n.m.* felon.

fellonia, *n.f.* felony.

feltro, *n.m.* felt.

femmina, *n.f.* female.

femminile, *adj.* female, feminine.

femminilità, *n.f.* femininity.

fendere, *vb.* split, cleave, crack.

fenditura, *n.f.* split, cleft, crack.

fenomenale, *adj.* phenomenal.

fenomeno, *n.m.* phenomenon.

feriale, *adj.* of a weekday.

ferire, *vb.* wound, injure.

ferita, *n.f.* wound, injury.

ferito, *n.m.* wounded person, casualty.

feritòia, *n.f.* loophole.

ferma biancheria, *n.m.* clothespin.

fermamente, *adv.* firmly, fast.

fermare, *vb.* stop, halt, stay.

fermata, *n.f.* stop, halt. **f. intermèdia,** stop-over.

fermatura, *n.f.* fastening.

fermentare, *vb.* ferment.

fermentazione, *n.f.* fermentation.

fermento, *n.m.* ferment.

fermezza, *n.f.* firmness.

fermo, *adj.* firm, fixed, fast, steady. **f. pòsta,** general delivery. **mettere il f. su,** garnishee.

feroce, *adj.* ferocious, fierce.

ferocemente, *adv.* ferociously.

feròcia, *n.f.* ferocity.

ferramenta, *n.f.pl.* hardware.

ferrare, *vb.* shoe.

ferreo, *adj.* iron.

ferrièra, *n.f.* ironworks.

ferro, *n.m.* iron. **f. da stirare,** flat-iron. **f. di cavallo,** horseshoe.

ferrovia, *n.f.* railroad.

ferroviàrio, *adj.* railroad.

fertile, *adj.* fertile.

fertilità, *n.f.* fertility.

fertilizzante, *n.m.* fertilizer.

fertilizzare, *vb.* fertilize.

fertilizzazione, *n.f.* fertilization.

fervente, *adj.* fervent.

ferventemente, *adv.* fervently.

fervido, *adj.* fervid.

fervore, *n.m.* fervor, fervency.

fesso, *adj.* cracked; crazy.

fessura, *n.f.* split, cleavage, cranny, fissure; slit; slot.

festa, *n.f.* feast, festival, fête, holiday, vacation.

festività, *n.f.* festivity.

festivo, *adj.* festive. **giorno f.,** holiday.

festone, *n.m.* festoon.

fetale, *adj.* fetal.

feticcio, *n.m.* fetish.

fetido, *adj.* fetid.

feto, *n.m.* fetus.

fetta, *n.f.* slice, fillet.

feudale, *adj.* feudal.

feudalismo, *n.m.* feudalism.

feudo, *n.m.* fief, feud.

fiacco, *adj.* limp.

fiaccola, *n.f.* torch.

fiamma, *n.f.* flame, blaze.

fiammante, *adj.* flaming.

fiammeggiare, *vb.* flame, blaze; flare.

fiammifero, *n.m.* match.

fiammingo, 1. *n.* Fleming; flamingo. **2.** *adj.* Flemish.

fiancheggiare, *vb.* flank.

fianco, *n.m.* flank; hip; side. **di f. a,** beside, abreast of.

fiasco, *n.m.* flask; fiasco; flop.

fiato, *n.m.* breath.

fibbia, *n.f.* buckle.

fibra, *n.f.* fiber.

fibroso, *adj.* fibrous.

ficcare, *vb.* put; thrust, stick, shove.

fico, *n.m.* fig.

fidanzamento, *n.m.* betrothal, engagement.

fidanzare, *vb.* betroth, affiance; *(refl.)* get engaged.

fidanzata, *n.f.* fiancée.

fidanzato, *n.m.* fiancé.

fidatezza, *n.f.* dependability.

fidènte, *adj.* reliant.

fido, *adj.* dependable.

fiducia, *n.f.* trust.

fiele, *n.m.* gall. **vescica del f.,** gall-bladder.

fienile, *n.m.* hayloft.

fieno, *n.m.* hay.

fiera, *n.f.* fair. **f. campionària,** sample fair.

figlia, *n.f.* daughter.

figliare, *vb.* have a litter.

figliata, *n.f.* litter.

figlio, *n.m.* son.

figliòccio, *n.m.* godchild.

figura, *n.f.* figure.

figurare, *vb.* figure.

figurarsi, *vb.* imagine, fancy, envisage.

figuratamente, *adv.* figuratively.

figurato, *adj.* figurative.

figurina, *n.f.* figurine.

fila, *n.f.* file; line; row; rank; tier.

filàccia inglese, *n.f.* lint.

filamento, *n.m.* filament.

filantropia, *n.f.* philanthropy.

filare, *vb.* spin.

filatèlica, *n.f.* philately.

filato, *n.m.* yarn.

filetto, *n.m.* fillet.
filiale, *adj.* filial.
filigrana, *n.f.sg.* filigree.
filo, *n.m.* thread; string; clew; wire.
filobus, *n.m.* trolley-bus.
filone, *n.m.* vein, lode.
filosofia, *n.f.* philosophy.
filosòfico, *adj.* philosophical.
filòsofo, *n.m.* philosopher.
filovìa, *n.f.* trolley-bus line.
filtrare, *vb.* filter.
filtro, *n.m.* filter.
filza, *n.f.* string; collection; file.
finale, 1. *n.m.* finale. 2. *adj.* final, eventual.
finalista, *n.m.* finalist.
finalità, *n.f.* finality; purpose.
finalmente, *adv.* finally.
finanza, *n.f.* finance.
finanziàrio, *adj.* financial.
finanzière, *n.m.* financier.
finchè, *conj.* till, until.
fine, *n.m.* purpose; *f.* end, finish.
finèstra, *n.f.* window.
finezza, *n.f.* finesse.
fingere, *vb.* pretend, feign, assume, make believe.
finire, *vb.* end, finish.
fino, *adj.* fine; pure.
fino a. *prep.* as far as; until, till. f. dove? how far? f. a quando? how long?
finòcchio, *n.m.* fennel; (slang) pederast.
finora, *adv.* up to now, so far, hereto, hitherto.
finta, *n.f.* pretense, make-believe.
finto, *adj.* pretended, fictional, mock, make-believe.
finzione, *n.f.* fiction; figment.
fiòcco, *n.m.* flake; (boat) jib. f. da cipria, powder-puff.
fiòcina, *n.f.* harpoon.
fiocinare, *vb.* harpoon.
fiòco, *adj.* hoarse.
fionda, *n.f.* sling.
fioraio, *n.m.* florist.
fiore, *n.m.* flower, bloom, blossom.
fiorentino, *adj.* Florentine.
fioretto, *n.m.* foil.
fiori, *n.m.pl.* clubs (cards).
fiorire, *vb.* flower, bloom, blossom; flourish.
fiorito, *adj.* flowery.
fiòtto, *n.m.* stream.
Firènze, *n.f.* Florence.
firma, *n.f.* signature.
firmare, *vb.* sign; endorse.
fisarmònica, *n.f.* accordion.
fiscale, *adj.* fiscal.
fischiare, *vb.* whistle.
fischio, *n.m.* whistle.
fisica, *n.f.* physics.
fisico, 1. *n.m.* physicist; physique. 2. *adj.* physical.
fisiologia, *n.f.* physiology.
fisioterapìa, *n.f.* physiotherapy.
fissare, *vb.* fix; set; appoint; assess (a fine); fasten.

fissazione, *n.f.* fixation.
fissione, *n.f.* fission.
fisso, *adj.* fixed; set.
fittiziamente, *adv.* fictitiously.
fittizio, *adj.* fictitious.
fitto, *adj.* thick.
fiume, *n.m.* river.
fiumicino, *n.m.* stream, creek.
fiutare, *vb.* smell.
fiuto, *n.m.* scent; smell; flair.
flàccido, *adj.* flaccid.
flagellante, *n.m.* flagellant.
flagellare, *vb.* flagellate.
flagrante, *adj.* flagrant.
flagrantemente, *adv.* flagrantly.
flan, *n.m.* custard.
flanèlla, *n.f.* flannel.
flàuto, *n.m.* flute.
flèmma, *n.m.* phlegm.
flemmàtico, *adj.* phlegmatic.
flessìbile, *adj.* flexible; limp.
flessibilità, *n.f.* flexibility.
flessione, *n.f.* inflection.
flessuoso, *adj.* lithe.
flèttere, *vb.* flex.
flirt, *n.m.* flirtation.
flirtare, *vb.* flirt.
floreale, *adj.* floral.
flòscio, *adj.* soft; flabby.
flòtta, *n.f.* fleet.
fluente, *adj.* glib.
fluidità, *n.f.* fluidity.
flùido, *n.m. and adj.* fluid.
fluorescènte, *adj.* fluorescent.
fluoroscòpio, *n.m.* fluoroscope.
flusso, *n.m.* flux.
fluttuare, *vb.* fluctuate.
fluttuazione, *n.f.* fluctuation.
fobìa, *n.f.* phobia.
fòca, *n.f.* seal.
focàccia, *n.f.* cake.
focale, *adj.* focal.
focolare, *n.m.* fireplace, hearth.
focoso, *adj.* fiery.
fòdera, *n.f.* lining.
fòdero, *n.m.* sheath.
foggia, *n.f.* shape, guise.
foggiare, *vb.* make; forge; shape.
fòglia, *n.f.* leaf; blade (of grass); foil.
fogliame, *n.m.* foliage.
fòglio, *n.m.* sheet.
fogliolina, *n.f.* leaflet.
fogliuto, *adj.* leafy.
fogna, *n.f.* drain; sewer.
folclore, *n.m.* folklore.
fòlio, *n.m.* folio.
fòlla, *n.f.* crowd; crush; mob.
folle, *adj.* crazy; mad.
folletto, *n.m.* elf, hobgoblin.
follìa, *n.f.* folly.
follicolo, *n.m.* follicle.
folto, *adj.* thick; bushy.
fomentare, *vb.* foment.
fondamentale, *adj.* fundamental, basic.
fondamento, *n.m.* foundation.
fondare, *vb.* found.
fondatore, *n.m.* founder.
fondazione, *n.m.* foundation.
fondènte, *n.m.* fondant.

fóndere, *vb.* melt; (metal) cast; fuse; (ore) smelt.
fonderìa, *n.f.* foundry.
fondina, *n.f.* holster.
fonditore, *n.m.* melter; smelter; caster.
fondo, *n.m.* bottom; fund.
fonètico, *adj.* phonetic.
fontana, *n.f.* fountain.
fonte, *n.f.* spring; source.
foràggio, *n.m.* forage; fodder.
forare, *vb.* bore, pierce, puncture.
foratura, *n.f.* puncture.
fòrbici, *n.f.pl.* scissors.
forca, *n.f.* pitchfork; gallows.
forchetta, *n.f.* fork.
forcina, *n.f.* hairpin, bobby pin.
fòrcipe, *n.m.* forceps.
forènse, *adj.* forensic.
foresta, *n.f.* forest, wood.
forestièro, 1. *n.* foreigner. 2. *adj.* foreign.
fórfora, *n.f.* dandruff.
forma, *n.f.* form, mold, shape; (shoe) last.
formàggio, *n.m.* cheese.
formaldèide, *n.f.* formaldehyde.
formale, *adj.* formal.
formalità, *n.f.* formality.
formalmente, *adv.* formally.
formare, *vb.* form, mold, shape; (telephone) dial (a number).
formativo, *adj.* formative.
formato, *n.m.* format.
formazione, *n.f.* formation.
formica, *n.f.* ant.
formicolare, *vb.* swarm.
formidàbile, *adj.* formidable.
fòrmula, *n.f.* formula.
formulare, *vb.* formulate.
formulazione, *n.f.* formulation.
fornace, *n.m.* furnace; kiln.
fornaio, *n.m.* baker.
fornèllo, *n.m.* stove.
fornire, *vb.* furnish, equip, supply.
fornitura, *n.f.* supply.
forno, *n.m.* oven; bakery.
foro, *n.m.* hole, bore, vent.
fòro, *n.m.* forum.
forse, *adv.* perhaps, maybe, possibly.
forsizia, *n.f.* forsythia.
forte, 1. *n.m.* forte. 2. *adj.* strong; loud. 3. *adv.* loud.
fortemente, *adv.* strongly; hard.
fortezza, *n.f.* fort, fortress; fortitude.
fortificare, *vb.* fortify.
fortificazione, *n.f.* fortification.
fortùito, *adj.* fortuitous, chance.
fortuna, *n.f.* fortune, luck.
fortunato, *adj.* fortunate, lucky.
forùncolo, *n.m.* boil; pimple.
fòrza, *n.f.* force, strength.
forzare, *vb.* force.
forzato, *adj.* forced; forcible.
foschìa, *n.f.* fog.

fosco, *adj.* dark, dreary, dusky, grim, somber.

fosforo, *n.m.* phosphorus.

fossa, *n.f.* moat.

fossato, *n.m.* ditch.

fossetta, *n.f.* dimple.

fossile, *n.m. and adj.* fossil.

fossilizzare, *vb.* fossilize.

fosso, *n.m.* ditch.

fotocopia, *n.f.* photocopy.

fotocopiatore, *n.m.* photocopier.

fotoelèttrico, *adj.* photoelectric.

fotogènico, *adj.* photogenic.

fotografare, *vb.* photograph.

fotografia, *n.f.* photograph; photography.

fotògrafo, *n.m.* photographer.

fra, *prep.* between, among, amid. f. pòco, soon, by-and-by, presently.

fracassare, *vb.* smash.

fracasso, *n.m.* uproar, fuss, ado, fracas.

fràgile, *adj.* fragile, brittle, frail.

fràgola, *n.f.* strawberry.

fragore, *n.m.* clang, crash.

fragrante, *adj.* fragrant.

fragranza, *n.f.* fragrance.

fraintèndere, *vb.* misunderstand, misconstrue.

frammentàrio, *adj.* fragmentary.

frammento, *n.m.* fragment.

frana, *n.f.* landslide.

francamente, *adv.* frankly, candidly.

francese, 1. *n.m.* Frenchman; *f.* Frenchwoman. **2.** *adj.* French.

franchezza, *n.m.* frankness, candidness, directness.

Francia, *n.f.* France.

franco, *adj.* frank, candid, straightforward.

francobollo, *n.m.* postage stamp.

frangènte, *n.m.* breaker; *(pl.)* surf.

frangia, *n.f.* fringe; (hair-do) bang.

frangionde, *n.m.* breakwater.

frantumare, *vb.* shatter, smash.

frase, *n.f.* phrase; sentence.

frassino, *n.m.* ash-tree.

frastagliare, *vb.* indent.

frastuono, *n.m.* uproar, racket.

frate, *n.m.* friar.

fratellanza, *n.f.* brotherhood.

fratellastro, *n.m.* half-brother; step-brother.

fratèllo, *n.m.* brother.

fraternamente, *adv.* fraternally.

fraternità, *n.f.* fraternity.

fraternizzare, *vb.* fraternize.

fratèrno, *adj.* brotherly, fraternal.

fratricida, *n.m.* fratricide (person).

fratricìdio, *n.m.* fratricide (act).

frattèmpo, *n.m.* meantime, meanwhile, interim.

frattura, *n.f.* fracture.

fratturare, *vb.* fracture.

fraudolentemente, *adv.* fraudulently.

fraudolento, *adj.* fraudulent.

frazione, *n.f.* fraction.

fréccia, *n.f.* arrow; directional signal.

freddamente, *adv.* coldly.

freddezza, *n.f.* coldness.

freddo, 1. *n.m.* cold; chill. **2.** *adj.* cold, chilly. aver f., feel cold. far f., be cold.

freddura, *n.f.* pun.

fregare, *vb.* rub.

fregata, *n.f.* rub; frigate.

frèmito, *n.m.* thrill.

frenare, *vb.* brake; check.

frenesia, *n.f.* frenzy.

frenètico, *adj.* frantic, frenzied.

freno, *n.m.* brake; check.

frequentare, *vb.* frequent, attend, haunt.

frequentatore, *n.m.* habitué.

frequente, *adj.* frequent.

frequentemente, *adv.* frequently.

frequenza, *n.* frequency.

freschezza, *n.f.* freshness.

fresco, 1. *n.m.* coolness. **2.** *adj.* cool; fresh.

fretta, *n.f.* haste, hurry, hustle, rush.

frettolosamente, *adv.* hastily.

frettoloso, *adj.* hasty, cursory.

fricassèa, *n.f.* fricassee.

friggere, *vb.* fry.

frìgido, *adj.* frigid.

frigorìfero, *n.m.* refrigerator; freezer.

frittata, *n.f.* omelet.

frittèlla, *n.f.* fritter, pancake.

frivolezza, *n.f.* frivolousness.

frivolità, *n.f.* frivolity.

frìvolo, *adj.* frivolous.

frizione, *n.f.* friction; rubbing; (auto) clutch.

fròde, *n.f.* fraud.

frontale, *adj.* frontal; head on.

fronte, *n.m.* forehead, brow; front.

fronteggiare, *vb.* face.

frontièra, *n.f.* frontier, border.

fròttola, *n.f.* fib, canard; *(pl.)* nonsense.

frugale, *adj.* frugal.

frugalità, *n.f.* frugality.

fruizione, *n.f.* fruition.

frumento, *n.m.* wheat.

frusciare, *vb.* rustle.

fruscio, *n.m.* rustle.

frusta, *n.f.* lash, whip.

frustare, *vb.* lash, whip.

frustino, *n.m.* horsewhip.

frustrare, *vb.* frustrate, foil, thwart.

frustrazione, *n.f.* frustration.

frutteto, *n.m.* orchard.

fruttificare, *vb.* fructify.

frutto, *n.m.* fruit.

fruttuoso, *adj.* fruitful.

fucilare, *vb.* shoot.

fucile, *n.m.* gun, rifle.

fucilerìa, *n.f.* fusillade.

fucina, *n.f.* forge, smithy.

fuco, *n.m.* drone.

fùcsia, *n.f.* fuchsia.

fuga, *n.f.* flight, escape, getaway; fugue.

fugace, *adj.* fleeting.

fuggire, *vb.* flee; elope; run away.

fuggitivo, *n.m. and adj.* fugitive.

fùlcro, *n.m.* fulcrum.

fulgore, *n.m.* radiance.

fuliggine, *n.f.* soot.

fulminare, *vb.* fulminate.

fulminazione, *n.f.* fulmination.

fùlmine, *n.m.* (bolt of) lightning; thunderbolt.

fumaiòlo, *n.m.* smokestack.

fumare, *vb.* smoke.

fumetto, *n.m.* comic strip. giornalino a fumetti, comic book.

fumigare, *vb.* fumigate.

fumigatore, *n.m.* fumigator.

fumo, *n.m.* smoke.

fune, *n.f.* rope.

fùnebre, *adj.* funeral.

funerale, *n.m.* funeral.

funèreo, *adj.* funereal.

fungicida, *n.f.* fungicide.

fungo, *n.m.* fungus; mushroom.

funivia, *n.f.* cableway.

funzionale, *adj.* functional.

funzionare, *vb.* function; work; run.

funzionàrio, *n.m.* functionary, official.

funzione, *n.f.* function.

fuòchi d'artifìcio, *m.pl.* fireworks.

fuochista, *n.m.* fireman.

fuòco, *n.m.* fire, blaze; focus.

fuòri, *adv.* out; outside; forth. f. di, outside.

fuoruscito, *n.m.* exile.

furbo, *adj.* crafty, tricky, sly, shrewd.

furfante, *n.m.* blackguard, scoundrel, villain.

furgone, *n.m.* van.

furia, *n.f.* fury.

furioso, *adj.* furious; wild.

furore, *n.m.* furor, fury.

furtivamente, *adv.* stealthily.

furtivo, *adj.* stealthy.

furto, *n.m.* theft, burglary, larceny, robbery.

fusibile, 1. *n.m.* fuse. **2.** *adj.* easily melted.

fusione, *n.f.* fusion, merger; (nuclear) meltdown.

fuso, *adj.* molten.

fusollèra, *n.f.* fuselage.

fustigare, *vb.* flog.

fùtile, *adj.* futile.

futilità, *n.f.* futility.

futuro, *n.m. and adj.* future.

futurologìa, *n.f.* futurology.

G

gabardina, *n.f.* gabardine.

gabbia, *n.f.* cage.

gabbiano, *n.m.* gull.

gabinetto, n.m. cabinet; toilet; closet; office.
gagliardo, adj. sturdy.
galamente, adv. gaily.
galezza, n.f. gaiety.
gaio, adj. gay, cheerful, jolly, blithe, debonair.
gala, n.f. frill; gala.
galante, adj. gallant.
galàssia, n.f. galaxy.
galatèo, n.m. etiquette, good manners.
galèa, n.f. galley.
galeone, n.m. galleon.
galla, n.f. a g., afloat.
galleggiare, vb. float.
galleria, n.f. gallery; tunnel; arcade.
gàllico, adj. Gallic.
gallina, n.f. hen.
gallismo, n.m. machismo.
gallo, n.m. rooster, cock.
gallone, n.m. stripe; chevron; gallon.
galoppare, vb. gallop.
galòppo, n.m. gallop.
galòscia, n.f. galosh.
galvanizzare, vb. galvanize.
galvanoplàstica, n.f. electroplating.
gamba, n.f. leg.
gamberetto, n.m. shrimp.
gambo, n.m. stalk.
gamma, n.f. scale; gamut.
gancio, n.m. clip; clasp; hook.
gànghero, n.m. hinge.
gara, n.f. competition.
garantire, vb. guarantee.
garanzia, n.f. guarantee; guaranty; bail.
garbuglio, n.m. tangle.
gardènia, n.f. gardenia.
gareggiare, vb. vie, compete.
gargarismo, n.m. gargle.
gargarizzare, vb. gargle.
garofano, n.m. carnation.
garrotta, n.f. garrote.
gàrrulo, adj. garrulous.
garza, n.f. gauze; cheesecloth.
gas, n.m. gas.
gassoso, adj. gassy, gaseous.
gàstrico, adj. gastric.
gastrite, n.f. gastritis.
gastronomia, n.f. gastronomy.
gastronòmico, adj. gastronomic.
gatta, n.f. cat.
gattino, n.m. kitten.
gatto, n.m. cat, tomcat.
gavòtta, n.f. gavotte.
gazzèlla, n.f. gazelle.
gazzetta, n.f. gazette.
gelare, vb. freeze.
gelatina, n.f. gelatine; jelly.
gelatinoso, adj. gelatinous.
gelato, n.m. ice cream.
gèlido, adj. chilly, frosty.
gelone, n.m. chilblain.
gelosia, n.f. jealousy.
geloso, adj. jealous.
gelsomino, n.m. jasmine.
gemèllo, n.m. twin.
gèmere, vb. groan, moan.
gèmito, n.m. moan, groan.
gèmma, n.f. gem; bud.

gemmare, vb. bud.
gène, n.m. gene.
genealogia, n.f. genealogy, pedigree.
genealògico, adj. genealogical.
generale, n.m. and adj. general.
generalità, n.f. generality.
generalizzare, vb. generalize.
generalizzazione, n.f. generalization.
generalmente, adv. generally.
generare, vb. generate, beget, breed, engender.
generatore, n.m. generator.
generazione, n.f. generation.
gènere, n.m. kind, gender, genre, genus. g. alimentari, foodstuffs.
genèrico, adj. generic.
gènero, n.m. son-in-law.
generosamente, adv. generously.
generosità, n.f. generosity.
generoso, adj. generous.
genètica, n.f. genetics.
genètico, adj. genetic.
genicidio, n.m. genocide.
gènio, n.m. genius; engineering.
genitale, adj. genital.
genitali, n.m.pl. genitals.
genitivo, n.m. and adj. genitive.
genitore, n.m. parent.
gennaio, n.m. January.
Gènova, n.f. Genoa.
genovese, adj. Genoese.
gènte, n.f. people, folks.
gentile, adj. gentile; nice, kind.
gentilezza, n.f. kindness.
gentiluòmo, n.m. gentleman.
genuflèttersi, vb. genuflect.
genuinamente, adv. genuinely.
genuinità, n.f. genuineness.
genuino, adj. genuine.
genziana, n.f. gentian.
geografia, n.f. geography.
geogràfico, adj. geographical.
geògrafo, n.m. geographer.
geometria, n.f. geometry.
geomètrico, adj. geometric.
geopolitica, n.f. geopolitics.
gerànio, n.m. geranium.
gerarchia, n.f. hierarchy.
geràrchico, adj. hierarchical.
gèrgo, n.m. jargon, slang.
Germània, n.f. Germany.
germànico, adj. Germanic.
gèrme, n.m. germ.
germicida, n.m. germicide.
germinale, adj. germinal.
germinare, vb. germinate.
germogliare, vb. sprout.
germòglio, n.m. sprout; shoot.
geroglifico, adj. hieroglyphic.
Gerusalèmme, n.f. Jerusalem.
gesso, n.m. chalk; gypsum.
gessoso, adj. chalky.
gestazione, n.f. gestation.
gesticolare, vb. gesticulate.
gesticolazione, n.f. gesticulation.
gèsto, n.m. gesture.
Gesù, n.m. Jesus.
gesuita, n.m. Jesuit.

gettare, vb. throw, hurl; cast; dash; flip.
gètto, n.m. throw; cast; jet.
gettone, n.m. token.
gheriglio, n.m. kernel.
ghermire, vb. snatch.
gherone, n.m. gusset.
ghette, f.pl. panty hose.
ghiacciaia, n.f. ice-box.
ghiacciaio, n.m. glacier.
ghiàccio, n.m. ice.
ghiaia, n.f. gravel.
ghianda, n.f. acorn.
ghiandaia, n.f. jay.
ghiàndola, n.f. gland.
ghigliottina, n.f. guillotine.
ghingano, n.m. gingham.
ghiotto, adj. gluttonous.
ghiottone, 1. n.m. gutton, gourmand. 2. adj. greedy.
ghiottoneria, n.f. greediness.
ghirlanda, n.f. garland, wreath.
ghisa, n.f. cast iron.
già, 1. adj. former; sometime. 2. adv. already, formerly.
giacca, n.f. coat, jacket.
giacchè, conj. since.
giacchetta, n.f. jacket.
giacchio, n.m. dragnet.
giacere, vb. lie.
giacinto, n.m. hyacinth.
giada, n.f. jade.
giaguaro, n.m. jaguar.
giallo, adj. yellow.
giàmbico, adj. iambic.
Giappone, n.m. Japan.
giapponese, adj. Japanese.
giara, n.f. jar.
giardinetta, n.f. station wagon.
giardinière, n.m. gardener.
giardino, n.m. garden. g. d'infanzia, kindergarten.
giarrettièra, n.f. garter.
giavazzo, n.m. jet.
giavellòtto, n.m. javelin.
gibbone, n.m. gibbon.
giga, n.f. jig.
gigante, n.m. giant.
giganteseo, adj. gigantic; giant.
giglio, n.m. lily.
gilè, n.m. vest; waistcoat.
ginnòto, n.m. electric eel.
ginecologia, n.f. gynaecology.
ginepro, n.m. juniper.
Ginevra, n.f. Geneva.
ginevrino, adj. Genevan.
ginnàsio, n.m. high school.
ginnasta, n.m. gymnast.
ginnàstica, n.f. gymnastics.
ginnàstico, adj. gymnastic.
ginòcchio, n.m. knee.
giocare, vb. play. g. d'azzardo, gamble.
giocatore, n.m. player. g. d'azzardo, gambler.
giocàttolo, n.m. toy.
giòco, n.m. game. g. d'azzardo, game of chance; gambling.
giocondo, adj. jocund.
giogo, n.m. yoke.
giòia, n.f. joy, glee.
gioielleria, n.f. jewelry.
gioiellière, n.m. jeweler.
gioièllo, n.m. jewel.

giòire, vb. rejoice; gloat.

giolóso, adj. joyful, happy, blithe, gleeful.

giornaìe, n.m. news-vendor.

giornàle, n.m. newspaper; journal; daily.

giornaliéro, adj. daily.

giornalismo, n.m. journalism.

giornalista, n.m. journalist.

giornata, n.f. day.

giórno, n.m. day. g. feriàle, weekday; workday. g. festivo, holiday.

gióvane, adj. young.

giovanile, adj. youthful; juvenile.

giovedì, n.m. Thursday.

giovénca, n.f. heifer.

gioviàle, adj. jovial.

giovinézza, n.f. youth.

giradischi, n.m. record player.

giraffa, n.f. giraffe.

giràre, vb. turn, revolve, spin, whirl; crank; endorse.

giràta, n.f. endorsement.

giretto, n.m. spin.

giro, n.m. turn; revolution; round. prèndere in g., make fun of; kid.

giroscòpio, n.m. gyroscope.

girovago, adj. itinerant.

gita, n.f. outing; picnic.

giù, adv. down.

giubilànte, adj. jubilant.

giubilèo, n.m. jubilee.

giudaismo, n.m. Judaism.

giudèo, n.m. Jew.

giudicàre, vb. judge; deem.

giùdice, n.m. judge.

giudiziàrio, adj. judiciary; judicial.

giudizio, n.m. judgment, discernment.

giudizióso, adj. judicious.

giùgno, n.m. June.

giugulàre, adj. jugular.

giuncàta, n.f. junket.

giunchiglia, n.f. jonquil.

giùnco, n.m. rush.

giùngere, vb. join; arrive.

giungla, n.f. jungle.

giuntùra, n.f. juncture, joint.

giuramento, n.m. oath.

giuràre, vb. swear.

giuràto, n.m. juror.

giuria, n.f. jury.

giurisdizióne, n.f. jurisdiction.

giurisprudènza, n.f. jurisprudence.

giurista, n.m. jurist.

giustacuòre, n.m. jerkin.

giustamente, adv. justly, fairly.

giustézza, n.f. fairness.

giustificàbile, adj. justifiable.

giustificàre, vb. justify.

giustificazióne, n.f. justification.

giustìzia, n.f. justice; righteousness.

giustiziàre, vb. execute.

giùsto, adj. just, fair; even, right; righteous; sound.

gl', def. art. m.pl. the.

glaciàle, adj. glacial. zòna g., frigid zone.

gladiòlo, n.m. gladiolus.

glàndola, n.f. gland.

glandolàre, adj. glandular.

glaucòma, n.m. glaucoma.

gli, 1. def. art. m.pl. the. 2. pron. 3. sg.m. dative. to him.

glicerina, n.f. glycerine.

globàle, adj. global.

glòbo, n.m. globe. g. dell'òcchio, eyeball.

globulàre, adj. globular.

glòbulo, n.m. globule.

glòria, n.f. glory.

gloriàrsi, vb. glory.

glorificàre, vb. glorify.

glorificazióne, n.f. glorification.

glorióso, adj. glorious.

glossàrio, n.m. glossary.

glucòsio, n.m. glucose.

glutinóso, adj. glutinous.

gnòcco, n.m. dumpling.

gòbba, n.f. hunchback (woman); hump; hunch.

gòbbo, n.m. humpback, hunchback.

gòccia, n.f. drop.

gocciamento, n.m. dripping.

gocciolàre, vb. drip.

godére, vb. enjoy; (refl.) bask in.

godìbile, adj. enjoyable.

godimento, n.m. enjoyment.

goffàggine, n.f. clumsiness.

gòffo, adj. awkward, clumsy, gawky, uncouth.

gòla, n.f. throat; gorge; gullet.

gòlf, n.m. golf; sweater.

gòlfo, n.m. gulf.

gòmena, n.f. hawser.

gòmito, n.m. elbow.

gòmma, n.f. gum; rubber. g. lacca, shellac.

gommóso, adj. gummy.

góndola, n.f. gondola.

gondolière, n.m. gondolier.

gonfiamento, n.m. inflation; swelling up.

gonfiàre, vb. inflate; swell; bloat; (refl.) bulge.

gònfio, adj. inflated; swollen; baggy.

gong, n.m. gong.

gònna, n.f. skirt.

gonnèlla, n.f. gown; petticoat.

gonorrèa, n.f. gonorrhea.

gorgogliàre, vb. gurgle.

gorgòglio, n.m. gurgle.

gorilla, n.m. gorilla.

gòtico, adj. Gothic.

governante, n.f. governess.

governàre, vb. govern.

governativo, adj. governmental.

governatoràto, n.m. governorship.

governatóre, n.m. governor.

governatoriàle, adj. gubernatorial.

govèrno, n.m. government.

gozzo, n.m. goiter.

gozzoviglia, n.f. revel.

gozzovigliàre, vb. revel.

gracchiàre, vb. caw.

gràcchio, n.m. grackle.

gracidàre, vb. croak.

gradàle, n.m. grail.

gradatamente, adv. by degrees.

gradévole, adj. pleasing; acceptable; agreeable.

gradevolmente, adv. pleasingly; agreeably; acceptably.

gradino, n.m. step.

grado, n.m. degree; grade; rank.

graduàle, adj. gradual.

gradualmente, adv. gradually.

graduàre, vb. graduate.

graduazióne, n.f. foreclosure.

graffiàre, vb. scratch.

graffiatura, n.f. scratch.

gràfico, 1. n.m. graph. 2. adj. graphic.

grafite, n.f. graphite.

grafologìa, n.f. graphology.

grammàtica, n.f. grammar.

grammaticàle, adj. grammatical.

grammàtico, n.m. grammarian.

grammo, n.m. gram.

grammòfono, n.m. gramophone, phonograph.

granàio, n.m. granary; barn.

granàta, n.f. grenade.

granatina, n.f. grenadine.

granàto, n.m. garnet.

Gran Bretagna, n.f. Great Britain.

grànchio, n.m. crab.

grande, adj. big; large; great; grand.

grandézza, n.f. greatness, grandeur; size; magnitude.

grandinàre, vb. hail.

grandinàta, n.f. hailstorm.

gràndine, n.f. hail.

grandiosamente, adv. grandiosely, grandly.

grandióso, adj. grandiose.

granìto, n.m. granite.

gràno, n.m. grain; bead. g. saraceno, buckwheat.

granturco, n.m. corn; maize.

granulàre, 1. adj. granular. 2. vb. granulate.

granulazióne, n.f. granulation.

granèllo, n.m. granule.

grappa, n.f. clamp.

gràppolo, n.m. bunch, cluster.

grassatóre, n.m. highway robber.

grassazióne, n.f. hold-up.

grassétto, adj. chubby; boldface.

grasso, 1. n.m. fat; grease. 2. adj. fat; stout; fatty; greasy.

grassòccio, adj. plump, buxom.

gràta, n.f. lattice.

graticola, n.f. grate; grill; grid; gridiron; griddle; broiler.

gratificàre, vb. gratify.

gratificazióne, n.f. gratification; bonus.

gratitùdine, n.f. gratitude.

gràto, adj. grateful, thankful; pleasing.

grattacièlo, n.m. skyscraper.

grattùgia, n.f. grater.

grattugiàre, vb. grate.

gratuitamente, *adv.* gratis.

gratùito, *adj.* free, gratis, complimentary, gratuitous.

grave, *adj.* grave; grievous.

gravemente, *adj.* gravely.

gràvida, *adj.f.* pregnant, big with child.

gravidanza, *n.f.* pregnancy.

gravità, *n.f.* gravity.

gravitare, *vb.* gravitate.

gravitazione, *n.f.* gravitation.

gràzia, *n.f.* grace.

gràzie, *interj.* thanks!

graziosamente, *adv.* graciously.

grazioso, *adj.* gracious; pretty; becoming; comely.

Grècia, *n.f.* Greece.

grèco, *adj.* Greek.

gregàrio, *adj.* gregarious.

gregge, *n.m.* flock, herd.

grembiule, *n.m.* apron.

grèmbo, *n.m.* lap.

gretto, *adj.* mean; shabby.

grezzo, *adj.* raw.

gridare, *vb.* cry; shout, yell.

grido, *n.m.* cry; shout, yell.

grigiastro, *adj.* grayish.

grìgio, *adj.* gray; drab.

grilletto, *n.m.* trigger.

grillo, *n.m.* cricket.

grisou, *n.m.* firedamp.

gròg, *n.m.* grog.

gronda, *n.f.* eaves.

grondaia, *n.f.* gutter.

grossagrana, *n.f.* grosgrain.

grosso, *adj.* big; large; fat.

grossolanamente, *adv.* grossly.

grossolanità, *n.f.* coarseness; grossness.

grossolano, *adj.* coarse; gross.

grotta, *n.f.* grotto.

grottesco, *adj.* grotesque.

groviglio, *n.m.* ravel, tangle, snarl.

gru, *n.f.* crane; derrick.

grùccia, *n.f.* crutch.

grugnire, *vb.* grunt.

grugnito, *n.m.* grunt.

grumo, *n.m.* clot.

gruppo, *n.m.* group, clump, cluster; gang.

guadagnare, *vb.* earn; gain.

guadagno, *n.m.* gain, profit; *(pl.)* earnings.

guado, *n.m.* ford.

guaina, *n.f.* sheath.

guaio, *n.m.* trouble, woe.

guància, *n.f.* cheek; jowl.

guanciale, *n.m.* pillow.

guanto, *n.m.* glove; gauntlet.

guardacòste, *adj.* coast guard.

guardare, *vb.* look at; guard; gaze; regard; watch; *(refl.)* beware.

guardaròba, *n.f.* cloakroom; wardrobe.

guàrdia, *n.f.* guard; watch.

guardiano, *n.m.* guardian; caretaker; watchman.

guardina, *n.f.* guard-house.

guardingo, *adj.* guarded.

guaribile, *adj.* curable.

guarigione, *n.f.* cure, recovery.

guarire, *vb.* cure, heal.

guarnigione, *n.f.* garrison.

guarnire, *vb.* garnish.

guarnizione, *n.f.* garnishment; gasket.

guastare, *vb.* spoil, mar.

guazzabùglio, *n.m.* mess; hash.

guèrra, *n.f.* war.

guerresco, *adj.* warlike.

guerrièro, *n.m.* warrior.

guerriglia, *n.f.* guerrilla.

guerriglièer, *n.m.* guerrilla fighter.

gufo, *n.m.* owl.

gùglia, *n.f.* spire.

guida, *n.f.* guide; guidance; leadership; guidebook; directory.

guidare, *vb.* guide; drive (auto).

guinzàglio, *n.m.* leash.

guru, *n.m.* guru.

gùscio, *n.m.* shell.

gustare, *vb.* taste.

gustativo, *adj.* gustatory, involving taste.

gusto, *n.m.* taste; gusto; relish.

gustoso, *adj.* tasty, appetizing, palatable.

gutturale, *adj.* guttural.

H, I

hascisc, *n.m.* hashish.

hertz, *n.m.* hertz.

i, *def. art. m.pl.* the.

iato, *n.m.* hiatus.

ibernazione, *n.f.* hibernation.

ibisco, *n.m.* hibiscus.

ibridazione, *n.f.* cross-fertilization.

ìbrido, *adj.* hybrid.

icòne, *n.f.* icon.

iddìo, *n.m.* god.

idèa, *n.f.* idea.

ideale, *adj.* ideal.

idealismo, *n.m.* idealism.

idealista, *n.m.* idealist.

idealìstico, *adj.* idealistic.

idealizzare, *vb.* idealize.

idealmente, *adv.* ideally.

idèntico, *adj.* identical.

identificàbile, *adj.* identifiable.

identificare, *vb.* identify.

identificazione, *n.f.* identification.

identità, *n.f.* identity.

ideologia, *n.f.* ideology.

idìllico, *adj.* idyllic.

idìllo, *n.m.* idyll.

idìoma, *n.m.* idiom.

idiòta, **1.** *n.m.* idiot. **2.** *adj.* idiotic.

idiozìa, *n.f.* idiocy.

idòlatra, *n.m. or f.* idolater.

idolatrare, *vb.* idolize.

idolatrìa, *n.* idolatry.

idolo, *n.m.* idol.

idoneltà, *n.f.* fitness.

idòneo, *adj.* fit; qualified.

idrante, *n.m.* hydrant.

idrato di carbone, *n.m.* carbohydrate.

idràulico, **1.** *n.m.* plumber. **2.** *adj.* hydraulic.

idroclòrico, *adj.* hydrochloric.

idroelèttrico, *adj.* hydroelectric.

idrofobìa, *n.f.* hydrophobia.

idrògeno, *n.m.* hydrogen.

idropisìa, *n.f.* dropsy.

idroscalo, *n.m.* seaplane airport.

idroterapèutica, *n.f.* hydrotherapy.

idrovolante, *n.m.* seaplane; hydroplane.

ièna, *n.f.* hyena.

ièri, *n.m. and adv.* yesterday.

igiène, *n.f.* hygiene; sanitation.

igiènico, *adj.* hygienic; sanitary.

ignaro, *adj.* ignorant.

ignòbile, *adj.* ignoble.

ignominioso, *adj.* ignominious.

ignorante, *adj.* ignorant.

ignorantone, *n.m.* ignoramus.

ignoranza, *n.f.* ignorance.

ignòto, *adj.* unknown.

il, *def. art. m.sg.* the.

ilare, *adj.* hilarious.

ilarità, *n.f.* hilarity.

illècito, *adj.* illicit.

illegale, *adj.* illegal.

illeggìbile, *adj.* illegible.

illeggìbilmente, *adv.* illegibly.

illegittimità, *n.f.* illegitimacy.

illegìttimo, *adj.* illegitimate.

illimitatamente, *adv.* boundlessly.

illimitato, *adj.* unlimited; boundless; limitless.

illògico, *adj.* illogical.

illuminare, *vb.* illuminate; light up; brighten; enlighten.

illuminazione, *n.f.* illumination.

illusione, *n.f.* illusion.

illusòrio, *adj.* illusory; illusive.

illustrare, *vb.* illustrate.

illustrativo, *adj.* illustrative.

illustrazione, *n.f.* illustration.

illustre, *adj.* illustrious.

imam, *n.m.* imam.

imbecuccare, *vb.* wrap up.

imballàggio, *n.m.* packing.

imballare, *vb.* pack.

imbalsamare, *vb.* embalm.

imbarazzare, *vb.* embarrass.

imbarazzo, *n.m.* embarrassment.

imbarcare, *vb.* embark.

imbastire, *vb.* baste.

imbavagliare, *vb.* gag.

imbecille, *n.m. and adj.* imbecile; half-wit; moron.

imbèrbe, *adj.* beardless.

imbiancare, *vb.* whiten; bleach.

imboccatura, *n.f.* mouthpiece; nozzle.

imboscata, *n.f.* ambush. tendere un' i., to ambush.

imbottire, *vb.* pad; stuff.

imbottita, *n.f.* quilt.

imbottitura, *n.f.* wadding; padding; batting.

imbrattare, *vb.* soil; stain; daub.

imbrattatura, *n.f.* daub.

imbrogliare, *vb.* embroil; entangle.

imbuto, *n.m.* funnel.

imitare, *vb.* imitate; mimic.

imitativo, *adj.* imitative.

imitatore, *n.m.* mimic; imitator.

imitazione, *n.f.* imitation.

immacolato, *adj.* immaculate.

immagazzinare, *vb.* store.

immaginabile, *adj.* imaginable.

immaginare, *vb.* imagine; fancy.

immaginario, *adj.* imaginary.

immaginativo, *adj.* imaginative.

immaginazione, *n.f.* fancy, imagination.

immagine, *n.f.* image.

immaginoso, *adj.* fanciful.

immane, *adj.* huge.

immanente, *adj.* immanent.

immateriale, *adj.* immaterial.

immaturo, *adj.* immature.

immediatamente, *adv.* immediately, instantly; directly; forthwith; presently.

immediato, *adj.* immediate, instant.

immenso, *adj.* immense.

immergere, *vb.* immerse, dip.

immigrante, *n. and adj.* immigrant.

immigrare, *vb.* immigrate.

imminente, *adj.* imminent.

immischiarsi, *vb.* interfere, meddle, tamper.

immobile, *adj.* immobile, motionless, immovable.

immobilizzare, *vb.* immobilize.

immoderato, *adj.* immoderate.

immodestia, *n.f.* immodesty.

immodesto, *adj.* immodest.

immorale, *adj.* immoral.

immoralità, *n.f.* immorality.

immoralmente, *adv.* immorally.

immortalare, *vb.* immortalize.

immortale, *adj.* immortal, deathless.

immortalità, *n.f.* immortality.

immune, *adj.* immune.

immunità, *n.f.* immunity.

immunizzare, *vb.* immunize.

immutabile, *adj.* immutable.

impaginare, *vb.* arrange in pages.

impalare, *vb.* impale.

impalcatura, *n.f.* scaffolding.

impallidire, *vb.* pale; blanch; fade.

impantanarsi, *vb.* bog down.

imparare, *vb.* learn.

imparentato, *adj.* related, kindred.

impartire, *vb.* impart.

imparziale, *adj.* impartial.

impastare, *vb.* knead.

impaziente, *adj.* impatient, eager.

impazientemente, *adv.* impatiently, eagerly.

impazienza, *n.f.* impatience, eagerness.

impazzito, *adj.* gone crazy, deranged.

impedimento, *n.m.* impediment, hindrance.

impedire, *vb.* impede, hinder, hamper, avert, balk, forestall, prevent.

impegnare, *vb.* pledge; pawn.

impegno, *n.m.* undertaking, commitment.

impellere, *vb.* impel.

impenetrabile, *adj.* impenetrable.

impenitente, *adj.* impenitent.

impennarsi, *vb.* rear.

imperativo, *n.m. and adj.* imperative.

imperatore, *n.m.* emperor.

imperatrice, *n.f.* empress.

impercettibile, *adj.* imperceptible.

imperfetto, *adj.* imperfect.

imperfezione, *n.f.* imperfection.

imperiale, *adj.* imperial.

imperialismo, *n.m.* imperialism.

imperioso, *adj.* imperious.

imperituro, *adj.* imperishable; immortal.

impermeabile, 1. *n.m.* raincoat. 2. *adj.* water-proof.

impero, *n.m.* empire.

impersonale, *adj.* impersonal.

impersonare, *vb.* impersonate.

impersonatore, *n.m.* impersonator.

impertinente, *adj.* impertinent.

impertinenza, *n.f.* impertinence.

impervio, *adj.* impervious.

impeto, *n.m.* impetus.

impetuosamente, *adv.* impetuously; boisterously.

impetuoso, *adj.* impetuous; boisterous; dashing; heady.

impiallacciare, *vb.* veneer.

impiantare, *vb.* implant.

impianto, *n.m.* installation; plant.

impiccagione, *n.f.* hanging.

impiccare, *vb.* hang.

impiccatore, *n.m.* hangman.

impiccio, *n.m.* jam, fix, pickle, predicament, scrape.

impiegare, *vb.* employ; use.

impiegato, *n.f.* employee.

impiegato, *n.m.* employee, clerk.

impiego, *n.m.* employment, job.

implacabile, *adj.* implacable.

implicare, *vb.* implicate; imply; involve.

implicazione, *n.f.* implication.

implicito, *adj.* implicit, implied.

implorare, *vb.* implore, beg, plead with.

imponderabile, *adj.* imponderable.

imporre, *vb.* impose; levy.

importante, *adj.* important, momentous.

importanza, *n.f.* importance.

importare, *vb.* import; be important, matter.

importazione, *n.f.* import, importation.

importunare, *vb.* importune.

importuno, *adj.* importunate.

imposizione, *n.f.* imposition.

impossibile, *adj.* impossible.

impossibilità, *n.f.* impossibility.

imposta, *n.f.* tax, duty, levy. i. sul valore aggiunto, value-added tax.

impostare, *vb.* mail, post.

impostura, *n.f.* imposture, humbug.

impotente, *adj.* impotent, powerless, helpless.

impotenza, *n.f.* impotence.

impoverire, *vb.* impoverish.

impregnare, *vb.* impregnate.

imprenditore, *n.m.* contractor; entrepreneur. i. di pompe funebri, undertaker.

impresa, *n.f.* enterprise, undertaking; feat.

impresario, *n.m.* impresario, theatrical manager.

impressionante, *adj.* impressive.

impressionare, *vb.* impress.

impressione, *n.f.* impression.

imprigionare, *vb.* imprison.

imprimere, *vb.* impress.

improbabile, *adj.* improbable, unlikely.

impronta, *n.f.* mark; print. i. digitale, fingerprint.

improprio, *adj.* improper.

improvvisare, *vb.* improvise.

improvviso, 1. *n.m.* impromptu. 2. *adj.* unforeseen; sudden, abrupt.

impudente, *adj.* impudent, cocky.

impudicizia, *n.f.* immodesty, shamelessness.

impudico, *adj.* immodest, shameless; lewd.

impugnare, *vb.* impugn.

impulsivo, *adj.* impulsive.

impulso, *n.m.* impulse.

impunità, *n.f.* impunity.

impurità, *n.f.* impurity.

impuro, *adj.* impure.

imputare, *vb.* impute; accuse; impeach.

imputato, *n.m.* defendant.

imputridire, *vb.* rot; *(refl.)* go rotten; (egg) addle.

in, *prep.* in; into.

inabile, *adj.* ineligible; unfitted.

inalare, *vb.* inhale.

inalienabile, *adj.* inalienable.

inamidare, *vb.* starch.

inane, *adj.* inane.

inaridire, *vb.* parch.

inaspettatamente, *adv.* unexpectedly.

inaspettato, *adj.* unexpected.

inattivo, *adj.* inactive, dormant.

inaugurale, *adj.* inaugural.

inaugurare, *vb.* inaugurate.

inaugurazione, n.f. inauguration.

inavveduto, adj. inadvertent.

incandescènte, adj. incandescent, glowing.

incandescènza, n.f. incandescence, glow.

incantamento, n.m. incantation.

incantare, vb. enchant, charm.

incantatore, n.m. enchanter, charmer.

incantatrice, n.f. enchantress, charmer.

incantésimo, n.m. spell.

incantévole, adj. enchanting.

incanto, n.m. enchantment, charm.

incapace, adj. unable.

incapacità, n.f. incapacity; disability.

incarcerare, vb. incarcerate.

incaricare, vb. charge, entrust, commission.

incàrico, n.m. charge; commission, task, assignment.

incarnato, adj. incarnate.

incarnazione, n.f. incarnation.

incartamento, n.m. dossier.

incatenare, vb. chain.

incatramare, vb. tar.

incavo, n.m. dent.

incendiàrio, n.m. and adj. incendiary.

incèndio, n.m. fire. **i. doloso,** arson.

incènso, n.m. incense, frankincense.

incentivo, n.m. incentive.

incerare, vb. wax.

incertezza, n.f. uncertainty, suspense.

incèrto, adj. uncertain.

incespicare, vb. stumble, falter.

incessante, adj. incessant, ceaseless.

incèsto, n.m. incest.

inchièsta, n.f. inquiry; inquest.

inchinarsi, vb. bow.

inchino, n.m. bow.

inchiodare, vb. nail.

inchiòstro, n.m. ink.

inciampare, vb. stumble.

incidentale, adv. incidental.

incidentalmente, adv. incidentally.

incidènte, n.m. accident; incident.

incidènza, n.f. incidence.

incidere, vb. incise, engrave; record.

incinta, adj.f. pregnant.

incipiènte, adj. incipient.

incipriare, vb. powder.

incisione, n.f. incision; engraving; gravure; recording.

incisivo, adj. incisive. **dènte i.,** incisor.

incisore, n.m. engraver.

incitare, vb. incite.

inclinare, vb. incline; list; slant; tilt; tip.

inclinazione, n.f. inclination; tilt; list; penchant.

inclùdere, vb. include.

inclusivo, adj. inclusive.

incògnito, adj. incognito.

incollare, vb. glue, paste.

incollatura, n.f. sizing.

incolpare, vb. blame, accuse.

incolpato, n.m. accused, blamed.

incolpatore, n.m. blamer, accuser.

incombènte, adj. incumbent.

incombustibile, adj. fireproof, incombustible.

incominciare, vb. begin.

incomodare, vb. inconvenience.

incòmodo, adj. inconvenient.

incomparàbile, adj. incomparable.

incompetènte, adj. unqualified.

incondizionato, adj. unqualified.

incònscio, adj. unconscious.

inconsiderato, adj. rash.

incontrare, vb. meet, encounter.

incontro, 1. n.m. meeting, encounter; match. 2. adv. towards; to meet.

incoraggiamento, n.m. encouragement, urging, abetment.

incoraggiare, vb. encourage, urge, abet.

incoraggiatore, n.m. encourager, urger, abettor.

incorniciare, vb. frame.

incoronare, vb. crown.

incoronazione, n.f. coronation.

incorporare, vb. incorporate; embody.

incorpòreo, adj. incorporeal; disembodied.

incorreggibile, adj. incorrigible.

incórrere, vb. incur.

incostante, adj. inconstant, fickle.

incostanza, n.f. inconstancy, fickleness.

incredibile, adj. incredible.

incredulità, n.f. incredulity.

incrèdulo, adj. incredulous.

incremento, n.m. increment.

increspare, vb. ruffle.

increspatura, n.f. ruffle; ripple.

incriminare, vb. incriminate.

incriminazione, n.f. incrimination.

incrociare, vb. cross; intersect; cruise.

incrociato, adj. crossed; crisscross.

incrociatore, n.m. cruiser.

incrocio, n.m. crossing; cross; intersection.

incrostare, vb. incrust.

incubatrice, n.f. incubator.

incubo, n.m. nightmare.

incudine, n.f. anvil.

inculcare, vb. inculcate.

incuneare, vb. wedge.

incurabile, adj. incurable.

incurante, adj. not caring, nonchalant.

incursione, n.f. inroad, raid.

indebitato, adj. indebted.

indebolire, vb. weaken; sap.

indefinitamente, adv. indefinitely.

indefinito, adj. indefinite.

indegnità, n.f. indignity; unworthiness.

indegno, adj. unworthy.

indelèbile, adj. indelible.

indennità, n.f. indemnity.

indennizzare, vb. indemnify.

India, n.f. India.

indiana, n.f. chintz.

indiano, adj. Indian.

indicare, vb. indicate, point to.

indicativo, n.m. and adj. indicative.

indicatore, n.m. indicator.

indicazione, n.f. indication.

indice, n.m. index; forefinger.

indietrato, n.m. arrears.

indietreggiare, vb. back (up); go backwards; recoil.

indiètro, adv. backwards; aft; behind; slow.

indifferente, adj. indifferent, casual, nonchalant.

indifferentemente, adv. indifferently, casually.

indifferènza, n.f. indifference, casualness, disregard.

indigeno, 1. n.m. aborigine, native. 2. adj. indigenous, aboriginal, native.

indigente, adj. indigent.

indigestione, n.f. indigestion.

indignato, adj. indignant.

indignazione, n.f. indignation.

indimenticàbile, adj. unforgettable.

indipendènte, adj. independent.

indipendènza, n.f. independence.

indiretto, adj. indirect.

indirizzare, vb. address.

indirizzo, n.m. address; direction.

indiscreto, adj. indiscreet.

indiscrezione, n.f. indiscretion.

indispensàbile, adj. indispensable.

indisposizione, n.f. indisposition; distemper.

indisposto, adj. indisposed, unwell.

indistinto, adj. indistinct, blurred.

individuale, adj. individual.

individualità, n.f. individuality.

individualmente, adv. individually.

individuo, n.m. individual; fellow.

indivisibile, adj. indivisible.

indolènte, adj. indolent.

Indonèsia, n.f. Indonesia.

indorare, vb. gild.

indossare, vb. put on, don.

indovinare, vb. guess.

indovinèllo, n.m. riddle, conundrum, puzzle.

indugiare, vb. delay, loiter, dally, dawdle, lag, linger.

indùgio, n.m. delay.

indulgènte, adj. indulgent.

indulgènza, n.f. indulgence.

indùlgere, vb. indulge.

indurìre, vb. harden, steel.

indùrre, vb. induce.

indùstria, n.f. industry.

industriàle, 1. n. industrialist. 2. adj. industrial, manufacturing.

industrióso, adj. industrious.

induttìvo, adj. inductive.

induzióne, n.f. induction.

inebbriànte, adj. inebriating, heady.

inebbriàre, vb. inebriate, intoxicate.

inegùale, adj. unequal.

ineleggìbile, adj. ineligible.

inerènte, adj. inherent.

inèrte, adj. inert.

inèrzia, n.f. inertia.

inespèrto, adj. inexperienced, callow.

inesplicàbile, adj. inexplicable.

inespugnàbile, adj. impregnable.

inestimàbile, adj. priceless.

inètto, adj. inept.

inevitàbile, adj. inevitable.

infallìbile, adj. infallible.

infàme, adj. infamous.

infàmia, n.f. infamy.

infànte, n.m. infant.

infantìle, adj. infantile, childish, childlike, babyish.

infantilità, n.f. childishness.

infànzia, n.f. infancy, childhood.

infarcìre, vb. stuff, cram.

infastidìre, vb. annoy, bother, irk, be troublesome.

infaticàbile, adj. indefatigable.

infatuàre, vb. infatuate.

infàusto, adj. ill-omened, ominous.

infedéle, n. and adj. unfaithful, infidel.

infedeltà, n.f. infidelity.

infelìce, adj. unhappy; unlucky.

inferènza, n.f. inference.

inferióre, adj. inferior, lower; under.

inferiorità, n.f. inferiority.

inferìre, vb. infer.

infermerìa, n.f. infirmary.

infermièra, n.f. nurse.

infermità, n.f. infirmity.

infèrmo, adj. infirm.

infernàle, adj. infernal, hellish.

infèrno, n.m. hell.

inferriàta, n.f. grating.

infestàre, vb. infest.

infettàre, vb. infect.

infettìvo, adj. infectious.

infètto, adj. infected.

infezióne, n.f. infection.

infiammàbile, adj. inflammable.

infiammàre, vb. inflame.

infiammatòrio, adj. inflammatory.

infiammazióne, n.f. inflammation.

infilàre, vb. string, thread.

infiltràre, vb. infiltrate.

infiltrazióne, n.f. infiltration; leakage.

infinità, n.f. infinity.

infinitesimàle, adj. infinitesimal.

infinìto, 1. n.m. infinite; infinitive. 2. adj. infinite.

infìsso, n.m. fixture.

inflazióne, n.f. inflation.

inflessióne, n.f. inflection.

inflìggere, vb. inflict.

inflizióne, n.f. infliction.

influènte, adj. influential.

influènza, n.f. influence; influenza; grippe.

influsso, n.m. influence.

infoltìre, vb. thicken.

inforcatura, n.f. crotch.

informàre, vb. inform; acquaint, appraise; (refl.) inquire.

informàtica, n.f. computer science.

informatizzàre, vb. computerize.

informazióne, n.f. piece of information; (pl.) information.

infórme, adj. formless.

infornàta, n.f. batch.

infossàto, adj. sunken.

inframettènte, adj. meddlesome, officious.

inframméttere, vb. interject; (refl.) meddle.

infràngere, vb. infringe.

infruttuóso, adj. fruitless, unsuccessful.

infuòri, adv. all'i. di, except for, outside of.

infuriàre, vb. become infuriated, rage.

ingabbiàre, vb. cage.

ingannàre, vb. deceive, trick, fool, beguile, cheat, bluff, double-cross, hoax, hoodwink, mislead.

ingannatóre, 1. n.m. deceiver, cheater. 2. adj. deceitful.

ingannévole, adj. deceptive, treacherous.

ingànno, n.m. deceit, deception, trickery, bluff, hocus-pocus.

ingarbugliàre, vb. tangle; garble.

ingegnère, n.m. engineer.

ingegnerìa, n.f. engineering.

ingegnosaménte, adv. cleverly, ingeniously.

ingegnosità, n.f. cleverness, ingeniousness.

ingegnóso, adj. clever, ingenious.

ingènuo, adj. naïve; artless.

ingerènza, n.f. interference.

Inghilterra, n.f. England.

inghiottìre, vb. swallow; gulp.

inginocchiàrsi, vb. kneel.

ingiùngere, vb. enjoin.

ingiunzióne, n.f. injunction.

ingiùria, n.f. insult, abuse.

ingiuriàre, vb. insult, abuse.

ingiuriosaménte, adv. insultingly.

ingiurióso, adj. insulting, abusive.

ingiustificàto, adj. unwarranted.

ingiustìzia, n.f. injustice.

ingiùsto, adj. unjust, unfair.

inglése, 1. n.m. or f. Englishman; Englishwoman. 2. adj. English.

ingollàre, vb. gobble, gulp down.

ingombrànte, adj. cumbersome.

ingombràre, vb. encumber, clog, clutter.

ingozzàre, vb. guzzle.

ingranàggio, n.m. gear, gearing.

ingranàre, vb. mesh.

ingrandiménto, n.m. enlargement, aggrandizement.

ingrandìre, vb. enlarge, aggrandize, magnify.

ingranditóre, n.m. enlarger.

ingrassàre, vb. fatten.

ingravidàre, vb. render pregnant, impregnate.

ingrediènte, n.m. ingredient.

ingrèsso, n.m. entrance, entry.

ingròsso, n.m. all'i., wholesale.

inguìne, n.m. groin.

inibìre, vb. inhibit.

inibizióne, n.f. inhibition.

iniettàre, vb. inject.

iniezióne, n.f. injection.

inimicìzia, n.f. enmity; feud.

inimitàbile, adj. inimitable.

iniquità, n.f. iniquity.

inìquo, adj. unrighteous.

iniziàle, n.f. and adj. initial.

iniziàre, vb. initiate, begin, start.

iniziatìva, n.f. initiative.

iniziazióne, n.f. initiation.

inìzio, n.m. beginning, inception, start.

innaffiàre, vb. water.

innalzàre, vb. raise, hoist.

innamoràre, vb. enamor.

innamoràrsi, vb. fall in love.

innamoràta, n.f. sweetheart.

innamoràto, n.m. sweetheart.

innàrio, n.m. hymnal.

innestàre, vb. graft.

innèsto, n.m. graft.

inno, n.m. hymn. i. nazionale, national anthem.

innocènte, adj. innocent; harmless; blameless.

innocènza, n.f. innocence.

innòcuo, adj. innocuous, harmless.

innovazióne, n.f. innovation.

innumerévole, adj. innumerable, countless, myriad.

inoculàre, vb. inoculate.

inoculazióne, n.f. inoculation.

inoltre, adv. besides, furthermore.

inondàre, vb. inundate, flood, swamp.

inondazióne, n.f. inundation, flood.

inorridìre, vb. be horrified.

inossidàbile, adj. rust-proof.

inquietare, vb. worry; (refl.) be concerned.

inquièto, adj. uneasy.

inquilino, n.m. occupant, tenant.

inquinamento, n.m., pollution.

inquisizione, n.f. inquisition.

insaccare, vb. put in a bag.

insalata, n.f. salad.

insanguinato, adj. gory.

insània, n.f insanity.

insano, adj. insane.

insaporire, vb. flavor.

insaputa, n.f. all'i. di, without the knowledge of.

insediamento, n.m. installation.

insediare, vb. install.

insegna, n.f. standard; signboard; coat of arms; ensign; (pl.) insignia.

insegnante, n.m. or f. teacher.

insegnare, vb. teach.

inseguimento, n.m. pursuit.

inseguire, vb. follow, pursue.

insensibile, adj. insensible, insensitive, unfeeling.

insensibilità, n.f. insensitivity, callousness.

inseparàbile, adj. inseparable.

inserire, vb. insert, put in.

inservibile, adj. unusable.

inserzione, n.f. insertion; advertisement.

inserzionista, n.m. advertiser.

insetticida, adj. pólvere i., insecticide.

insètto, n.m. insect, bug.

insidioso, adj. insidious.

insième, 1. n.m. ensemble. 2. adv. together.

insignificante, adj. insignificant.

insignificanza, n.f. insignificance.

insinuare, vb. insinuate.

insinuazione, n.f. insinuation, innuendo.

insipido, adj. insipid, tasteless.

insistènte, adj. insistent.

insistènza, n.f. insistence.

insistere, vb. insist.

insoddisfazione, n.f. dissatisfaction.

insoffribile, adj. insufferable.

insolente, adj. insolent, insulting, abusive.

insolentemente, adv. insolently.

insolènza, n.f. insolence.

insòlito, adj. unusual.

insònnia, n.f. insomnia.

instàbile, adj. unsteady.

installare, vb. install.

installazione, n.f. installation.

insù, adv. all'i., uphill; upwards.

insufficiènte, adj. insufficient.

insulare, adj. insular.

insulina, n.f. insulin.

insulso, adj. dull, insipid.

insultare, vb. insult, abuse.

insulto, n.m. insult, abuse.

insuperàbile, adj. insuperable.

insurrezione, n.f. insurrection.

intaccare, vb. notch, nick.

intangibile, adj. intangible.

intascare, vb. pocket.

intatto, adj. intact.

integrale, adj. integral.

integrare, vb. integrate.

integrità, n.f. integrity.

intellètto, n.m. intellect; understanding.

intellettuale, adj. intellectual.

intelligènte, adj. intelligent, smart.

intelligènza, n.f. intelligence; wit.

intelligènzia, n.f. intelligentsia.

intelligibile, adj. intelligible.

intensificare, vb. intensify.

intensivo, adj. intensive.

intènso, adj. intense.

intènto, n.m. and adj. intent.

intenzionale, adj. intentional.

intenzionalmente, adv. intentionally, designedly.

intenzione, n.f. intention.

interamente, adv. entirely, wholly.

intercèdere, vb. intercede.

intercettare, vb. intercept.

interdetto, 1. n.m. interdict. 2. adj. speechless.

interdire, vb. interdict.

interessante, adj. interesting.

interessare, vb. interest, concern; affect; (refl.) concern oneself.

interèsse, n.m. interest, concern.

interfàcie, n.f. interface.

interferènza, n.f. interference.

interiezione, n.f. interjection.

interiora, f.pl. entrails.

interiore, adj. interior, inner, inside.

interlùdio, n.m. interlude.

intermediàrio, 1. n.m. intermediary, mediator, go-between. 2. adj. intermediary.

intermèdio, adj. intermediate.

intermissione, n.f. intermission.

intermittènte, adj. intermittent.

internare, vb. intern.

internazionale, adj. international.

internazionalismo, n.m. internationalism.

intèrno, 1. n.m. inside. 2. adj. internal; inner, inside; inland.

intero, adj. entire, whole.

interporre, vb. interpose.

interpretare, vb. interpret, construe.

interpretazione, n.f. interpretation.

intèrprete, n.m. interpreter.

interrogare, vb. interrogate, question.

interrogativo, adj. interrogative.

interrogazione, n.f. interrogation.

interrómpere, vb. interrupt; discontinue.

interruttore, n.m. switch.

interruzione, n.f. interruption, break.

intersecare, vb. intersect.

intersezione, n.f. intersection.

intervallo, n.m. interval; headway.

intervenire, vb. intervene.

intervento, n.m. intervention.

intervista, n.f. interview.

intervistare, vb. interview.

intestino, 1. n.m. intestine, bowel, gut. 2. adj. intestine.

intimamente, adv. intimately; inwardly.

intimidazione, n.f. intimidation.

intimidire, vb. intimidate, daunt.

intimità, n.f. intimacy; privacy.

intimo, adj. intimate; inward. più i., innermost.

intitolare, vb. entitle.

intollerante, adj. intolerant.

intonacare, vb. plaster.

intònaco, n.m. plaster.

intonare, vb. intone.

intonazione, n.f. intonation.

intontito, adj. groggy.

intorno, adv. around; about; round. i. a, prep. around; about; round.

intossicare, vb. intoxicate.

intossicazione, n.f. intoxication.

intràlcio, n.m. hindrance.

intrappolare, vb. entrap.

intraprèndere, vb. undertake.

intravedere, vb. glimpse.

intrecciare, vb. braid.

intréccio, n.m. plot.

intrepidamente, adv. dauntlessly, fearlessly.

intrepidezza, n.f. intrepidity, fearlessness.

intrèpido, adj. intrepid, dauntless, fearless.

intricato, adj. intricate.

intrigare, vb. intrigue.

intrigo, n.m. intrigue.

intrìnseco, adj. intrinsic.

introdurre, vb. introduce.

introduttivo, adj. introductory.

introduzione, n.f. introduction.

introspezione, n.f. introspection.

introvertito, adj. introvert.

intrudere, vb. intrude, obtrude.

intruso, n.m. intruder.

intuire, vb. sense.

intuitivo, adj. intuitive.

intuizione, n.f. intuition.

inumano, adj. inhuman.

inumidire, vb. dampen, humidify, moisten, wet.

inùtile, adj. useless, needless.

invàdere, vb. invade, overrun.

invàlido, 1. n. invalid. 2. adj. disabled; invalid.

invano, adv. in vain.

invariàbile, adj. invariable.

invasione, n.f. invasion.

invasore, n.m. invader.

invecchiare, *vb.* grow old, age.

invece, *adv.* instead.

inventare, *vb.* invent.

inventàrio, *n.m.* inventory.

inventìvo, *adj.* inventive.

inventore, *n.m.* inventor.

invenzione, *n.f.* invention.

invernale, *adj.* of winter, wintry.

invèrno, *n.m.* winter.

invèrso, *adj.* inverse.

invertebrato, *n.m. and adj.* invertebrate.

investigare, *vb.* investigate.

investigazione, *n.f.* investigation; inquiry.

investimento, *n.m.* investment.

investire, *vb.* invest; run into.

inveterato, *adj.* inveterate.

invettiva, *n.f.* invective.

inviare, *vb.* send.

inviato, *n.m.* envoy.

invidia, *n.f.* envy.

invidiàbile, *adj.* enviable.

invidiare, *vb.* envy, begrudge.

invidioso, *adj.* envious.

invigorire, *vb.* invigorate.

iniluppare, *vb.* enmesh.

invincìbile, *adj.* invincible.

invisìbile, *adj.* invisible.

invitare, *vb.* invite, ask.

invito, *n.m.* invitation; bid.

invocare, *vb.* invoke.

invocazione, *n.f.* invocation.

involontàrio, *adj.* involuntary.

involucro, *n.m.* wrapping.

invulneràbile, *adj.* invulnerable.

inzuppare, *vb.* drench; soak, dunk.

io, 1. *pron.* I. 2. *n.* ego.

iòdio, *n.m.* iodine.

iperacidità, *n.f.* hyperacidity.

ipèrbole, *n.f.* hyperbole.

ipercrìtico, *adj.* hypercritical.

ipersensìtivo, *adj.* hypersensitive.

ipertensione, *n.f.* hypertension.

ipnòsi, *n.f.* hypnosis.

ipnòtico, *adj.* hypnotic.

ipnotismo, *n.m.* hypnotism.

ipnotizzare, *vb.* hypnotize.

ipocondria, *n.f.* hypochondria.

ipocondrìaco, *n.m. and adj.* hypochondriac.

ipocrisìa, *n.f.* hypocrisy, cant.

ipòcrita, *n.m.* hypocrite.

ipòcrito, *adj.* hypocritical.

ipodèrmico, *adj.* hypodermic.

ipotèca, *n.f.* mortgage.

ipotecare, *vb.* mortgage.

ipotenusa, *n.f.* hypotenuse.

ipòtesi, *n.f.* hypothesis.

ipotètico, *adj.* hypothetical.

ippodromo, *n.m.* hippodrome; race-track.

ippopòtamo, *n.m.* hippopotamus.

ira, *n.f.* anger, ire, wrath.

Iràk, *n.m.* Iraq.

irato, *adj.* irate, wrathful.

iride, *n.f.* iris.

irìdio, *n.m.* iridium.

iris, *n.f.* iris.

Irlanda, *n.f.* Ireland.

irlandese, *adj.* Irish.

ironìa, *n.f.* irony.

irònico, *adj.* ironical.

irradiare, *vb.* beam, shine, radiate.

irradiazione, *n.f.* radiation.

irrazionale, *adj.* irrational.

irrefutàbile, *adj.* irrefutable.

irregolare, *adj.* irregular; fitful.

irregolarità, *n.f.* irregularity.

irreprensìbile, *adj.* irreprehensible, faultless.

irreprensibilmente, *adv.* irreprehensibly, faultlessly.

irrequièto, *adj.* restless.

irresistìbile, *adj.* irresistible.

irresponsàbile, *adj.* irresponsible.

irrevocàbile, *adj.* irrevocable.

irriconoscìbile, *adj.* unrecognizable.

irrigare, *vb.* irrigate.

irrigazione, *n.f.* irrigation.

irrigidire, *vb.* stiffen.

irrispettoso, *adj.* disrespectful.

irritàbile, *adj.* irritable, on edge, edgy, fretful.

irritabilità, *n.f.* irritability, fretfulness.

irritabilmente, *adv.* irritably, fretfully.

irritante, *adj.* irritant.

irritare, *vb. tr.* irritate, fret, gall, vex.

irritato, *adj.* irritated, cross.

irritazione, *n.f.* irritation.

irriverènte, *adj.* irreverent.

irsuto, *adj.* hirsute.

iscrìvere, *vb.* inscribe; enroll, register.

iscrizione, *n.f.* inscription; enrollment, registration.

isola, *n.f.* island.

isolamento, *n.m.* isolation; insulation.

isolare, *vb.* isolate; insulate.

isolatore, *n.m.* insulator.

isolazione, *n.f.* isolation.

isolazionista, *n.m.* isolationist.

isolotto salvagènte, *n.m.* safety island.

isòscele, *adj.* isosceles.

ispànico, *adj.* Hispanic.

ispettore, *n.m.* inspector.

ispezionare, *vb.* inspect.

ispezione, *n.f.* inspection.

ìspido, *adj.* shaggy.

ispirare, *vb.* inspire.

ispirazione, *n.f.* inspiration.

Israèle, *n.m.* Israel.

israeliano, *adj.* Israeli.

israelita, *n.m.* Israelite.

israelìtico, *adj.* Israelite.

istantànea, *n.f.* snapshot.

istantàneo, *adj.* instantaneous.

istante, *n.m.* instant.

istanza, *n.f.* instance.

isterectomìa, *n.f.* hysterectomy.

istèrico, *adj.* hysterical.

isterismo, *n.m.* hysteria, hysterics.

istigare, *vb.* instigate.

istillare, *vb.* instill.

istintivo, *adj.* instinctive.

istinto, *n.m.* instinct.

istituto, *n.m.* institute.

istituzione, *n.f.* institution.

istmo, *n.m.* isthmus.

istriònica, *n.f.* histrionics.

istriònico, *adj.* histrionic.

istruire, *vb.* instruct.

istruttivo, *adj.* instruction.

istruttore, *n.m.* instructor.

istruttrice, *n.f.* instructress.

istruzione, *n.f.* instruction.

Itàlia, *n.f.* Italy.

italiano, *n.m. and adj.* Italian.

itàlico, *adj.* Italic.

itineràrio, *n.m.* itinerary.

itterizia, *n.f.* jaundice.

ittiologìa, *n.f.* ichthyology.

iuniore, *adj.* junior.

iuta, *n.f.* jute.

J, K

jarda, *n.f.* yard.

jeans, *m.pl.* jeans.

Jugoslàvia, *n.f.* Yugoslavia.

jugoslavo, *adj.* Yugoslav.

karakiri, *n.m.* harakiri.

karate, *n.m.* karate.

kg., *abbr.* kilogram.

kilohertz, *n.m.* kilohertz.

km., *abbr.* kilometer.

kohl, *n.m.* mascara.

kw., *abbr.* kilowatt.

L

l', 1. *def. art.* the. 2. *pron.* 3. *sg.* him; her.

la, 1. *pron.* her; it; you. 2. *def. art. f.* the.

là, *adv.* there.

labbro, *n.m.* lip. l. **leporino,** hairlip.

labirinto, *n.m.* labyrinth, maze.

laboratòrio, *n.m.* laboratory.

laborioso, *adj.* laborious.

lacca, *n.f.* lacquer.

laccare, *vb.* lacquer.

lacchè, *n.m.* lackey, flunkey.

làccio, *n.m.* string; trap; noose; lariat, lasso; loop.

lacerare, *vb.* lacerate.

lacerazione, *n.f.* laceration.

lacònico, *adj.* laconic.

lacuale, *adj.* lake.

ladro, *n.m.* thief, burglar.

ladrone, *n.m.* robber.

lagnanza, *n.f.* complaint, grievance.

lagnarsi, *vb.* complain.

lago, *n.m.* lake.

làgrima, *n.f.* tear.

laguna, *n.f.* lagoon.

laicato, *n.m.* laity.

làico, 1. *n.* layman. 2. *adj.* lay.

lama, *n.f.* blade.

lambire, *vb.* lap.

lamentare, *vb.* lament, bewail.

lamentazione, *n.f.* lamentation.

lamentévole, *adj.* lamentable.

lamento, *n.m.* lament.

laminare, *vb.* laminate.

làmpada, n.f. lamp.
lampadàrio, n.m. chandelier.
lampadina, n.f. light bulb. l. tascàbile, flashlight.
lampeggiare, vb. lighten.
lampeggiatore, n.m. blinker.
lampo, n.m. (flash of) lightning.
lampone, n.m. raspberry.
lana, n.f. wool. l. di acciaio n.f. steel wool.
lancetta, n.f. lancet.
lància, n.f. lance, spear; launch.
lanciafiamme, n.m. flamethrower.
lanciare, vb. hurl, cast, chuck, fling, launch, pitch, sling, throw.
lanciatore, n.m. pitcher.
lànguido, adj. languid; lackadaisical.
languire, vb. languish, pine.
languore, n.m. languor.
lanolina, n.f. lanolin.
lantèrna, n.f. lantern.
lanugine, n.f. down, fuzz.
lanuginoso, adj. fluffy, downy; fuzzy.
lapidare, vb. stone.
làpis, n.m. pencil.
largamente, adv. broadly, widely.
larghezza, n.f. breadth; width.
largo, adj. broad, wide; (music) largo.
laringe, n.f. larynx.
laringite, n.f. laryngitis.
larva, n.f. larva; grub; ghost.
lasciare, vb. let; leave; quit. l. stare, let alone.
làscito, n.m. legacy.
lascivo, adj. lascivious, lecherous.
làser, n.m. laser.
lassativo, n.m. and adj. laxative.
lassitùdine, n.f. lassitude.
lastra, n.f. plate; sheet; slab.
latènte, adj. latent.
laterale, adj. lateral.
latino, n.m. and adj. Latin.
latitanza, n.f. hiding (used of criminals).
latitùdine, n.f. latitude.
lato, n.m. side.
latrare, vb. howl, bay.
latrato, n.m. howl, bay.
latrina, n.f. latrine, lavatory, toilet, privy.
latta, n.f. tin.
lattaia, n.f. milkmaid, dairymaid.
lattaio, n.m. milkman, dairyman.
latte, n.m. milk.
làtteo, adj. milky.
latteria, n.f. dairy; milk-bar.
làttico, adj. lactic.
lattòsio, n.m. lactose.
lattuga, n.f. lettuce.
làudano, n.m. laudanum.
laudativo, adj. laudatory.
làurea, n.f. degree.
laurearsi, vb. graduate.

laureato, adj. laureate.
làuro, n.m. laurel; bay.
lava, n.f. lava.
lavabiancheria, n.m. washing machine.
lavabo, n.m. wash-basin.
lavagna, n.f. blackboard; slate.
lavanda, n.f. lavender.
lavandaia, n.f. laundress.
lavandaio, n.m. laundryman.
lavanderia, n.f. laundry.
lavandino, n.m. sink.
lavare, vb. wash, launder.
lavatòio, n.m. washroom.
lavorare, vb. work.
lavoratore, n.m. worker.
lavoro, n.m. work.
laziale, adj. of Latium.
Làzio, n.m. Latium.
le, 1. def. art. f.pl. the. 2. pron. 3. sg. dative to her; 3. pl.f. them.
leale, adj. loyal.
lealista, n.m. loyalist.
lealtà, n.f. loyalty.
lebbra, n.f. leprosy.
lebbroso, 1. n. leper. 2. adj. leprous.
leccare, vb. lick.
lega, n.f. league; alloy.
legale, adj. legal, lawful.
legalizzare, vb. legalize.
legame, n.m. tie, bond, link.
legamento, n.m. ligament.
legare, vb. bequeath, leave (in will); bind, tie.
legato, n.m. bequest, legacy.
legatore, n.m. bookbinder.
legatoria, n.f. bindery, bookbindery.
legatura, n.f. ligature; (music) slur.
legazione, n.f. legation.
legge, n.f. law.
leggenda, n.f. legend.
leggendàrio, adj. legendary.
lèggere, vb. read.
leggerezza, n.f. lightness; levity.
leggiadro, adj. lovely.
leggibile, adj. legible.
leggeramente, adv. lightly; flippantly.
leggèro, adj. light; flippant.
legione, n.f. legion.
legislatore, n.m. legislator.
legislazione, n.f. legislation.
legittimo, adj. legitimate, lawful.
legna, n.f. firewood.
legname, n.m. lumber, timber.
legume, n.m. vegetable, legume.
lei, pron. she; her; you.
lembo, n.m. hem; flap.
lentamente, adv. slowly.
lente, n.f. lens; eyeglass.
lentezza, n.f. slowness.
lenticchia, n.f. lentil.
lentiggine, n.f. freckle.
lentigginoso, adj. freckled.
lento, adj. slow, slack, sluggish.
lenzuola, n.f.pl. sheets, bedclothes.

lenzuòlo, n.m. sheet.
leone, n.m. lion.
leopardo, n.m. leopard.
lèpre, n.f. hare.
lèsbica, n.f. lesbian.
lèsbico, adj. lesbian.
lesione, n.f. lesion.
lèssico, n.m. lexicon.
letale, adj. lethal.
letame, n.m. dung, manure, muck.
letargia, n.f. lethargy.
letàrgico, n.m. lethargic.
lèttera, n.f. letter.
letterale, adj. literal.
letteràrio, adj. literary.
letteratezza, n.f. literacy.
letterato, adj. literate.
letteratura, n.f. literature.
letterecci, n.m.pl. bedding.
lettièra, n.f. bedstead; litter; (animal's) bed.
lettino, n.m. cot.
lètto, n.m. bed; couch. l. ad acqua, waterbed. l. del mare, seabed.
lettore, n.m. reader.
lettura, n.f. reading.
leucèmia, n.f. leukemia.
lèva, n.f. lever; levy.
levare, vb. raise; (refl.) get up, arise.
levatrice, n.f. midwife.
levigare, vb. smooth.
levigato, adj. smooth.
levrière, n.m. greyhound.
lezione, n.f. lesson.
li, pron. 3. pl.m. them.
lì, adv. there.
libagione, n.f. libation.
libbra, n.f. pound.
liberale, adj. liberal, generous, bounteous.
liberalismo, n.m. liberalism.
liberalità, n.f. liberality, generosity, bounty.
liberare, vb. liberate, deliver, free, relieve, release, rescue.
liberazione, n.f. liberation, deliverance, relief, release, rescue.
libero, adj. free.
libertà, n.f. liberty, freedom.
libertino, n.m. and adj. libertine.
libidinoso, adj. libidinous.
libraio, n.m. bookseller.
libreria, n.f. bookstore.
libretto, n.m. booklet; (opera) libretto.
libro, n.m. book. l. in brossura, paperback.
licenza, n.f. license; furlough; leave.
licenziamento, n.m. discharge.
licenziare, vb. discharge, fire, sack.
licenzioso, adj. licentious.
licèo, n.m. high school.
lido, n.m. beach, shore, seashore.
lietamente, adv. gladly.
lièto, adj. glad, happy.
lièvito, n.m. leaven.

lignàggio, *n.m.* lineage, ancestry.

lignite, *n.f.* lignite.

ligure, *adj.* Ligurian.

ligustro, *n.m.* privet.

lillà, *n.m.* lilac.

lima, *n.f.* file.

limare, *vb.* file.

limatura, *n.f.* filings.

limbo, *n.m.* limbo.

limitare, *vb.* limit.

limitazione, *n.f.* limitation.

limite, *n.m.* limit, bound.

limonata, *n.f.* lemonade.

limone, *n.m.* lemon.

limpido, *adj.* limpid.

lince, *n.f.* lynx. **l. persiana**, caracul.

linciare, *vb.* lynch.

lindezza, *n.f.* neatness.

lindo, *adj.* neat.

linea, *n.f.* line; figure.

lineare, *adj.* linear.

linfa, *n.f.* lymph; sap.

lingeria, *n.f.* lingerie.

lingua, *n.f.* tongue, language.

linguaggio, *n.m.* language.

linguista, *n.m.* linguist.

linguistica, *n.f.* linguistics.

linguistico, *adj.* linguistic.

linimento, *n.m.* liniment.

lino, *n.m.* linen.

liquefare, *vb.* liquefy.

liquidare, *vb.* liquidate.

liquidazione, *n.f.* liquidation.

liquido, *n.m. and adj.* liquid.

liquirizia, *n.f.* licorice.

liquore, *n.m.* liquor; liqueur.

lira, *n.f.* lira; lyre.

liricismo, *n.m.* lyricism.

lirico, *adj.* lyric; operatic.

lisciare, *vb.* smooth.

liscio, *adj.* smooth, sleek.

lista, *n.f.* list; menu, bill of fare; stripe.

listello, *n.m.* lath.

litania, *n.f.* litany.

lite, *n.f.* fight, quarrel, struggle, affray, brawl, row.

litigante, *n.m.* litigant.

litigare, *vb.* quarrel, bicker, row.

litigioso, *adj.* quarrelsome, argumentative, rowdy.

litografare, *vb.* lithograph.

litografia, *n.f.* lithography, lithograph.

litro, *n.m.* liter.

liturgia, *n.f.* liturgy.

liturgico, *adj.* liturgical.

liuto, *n.m.* lute.

livellare, *vb.* level.

livellatrice, *n.f.* bulldozer.

livello, *n.m.* level.

livido, *adj.* livid.

Livorno, *n.m.* Leghorn.

livrea, *n.f.* livery.

lo, **1.** *pron.* him; it; you. **2.** *def. art. m.* the.

lobo, *n.m.* lobe.

locale, *adj.* local.

località, *n.f.* locality, locale.

localizzare, *vb.* localize.

locanda, *n.f.* inn.

locomotiva, *n.f.* locomotive, engine.

locomotore, *n.m.* locomotive.

locomozione, *n.f.* locomotion.

locusta, *n.f.* locust.

locuzione, *n.f.* expression.

lodare, *vb.* praise, commend, laud.

lode, *n.f.* praise, commendation.

lodévole, *adj.* praiseworthy, commendable, laudable.

lodevolmente, *adv.* praiseworthily, commendably.

lòggia, *n.f.* loge.

loggione, *n.m.* top gallery.

lògica, *n.f.* logic.

lògico, *adj.* logical.

logorare, *vb.* wear out.

lògoro, *adj.* worn-out, shabby.

lombàggine, *n.f.* lumbago.

Lombardia, *n.f.* Lombardy.

lombardo, *adj.* Lombard.

lombata, *n.f.* loin.

lombo, *n.m.* loin; sirloin.

lombrico, *n.m.* earthworm.

londinese, *adj.* of London.

Londra, *n.f.* London.

longevità, *n.f.* longevity.

longèvo, *adj.* long-lived.

longitudinale, *adj.* longitudinal.

longitùdine, *n.f.* longitude.

lontano, **1.** *adj.* distant, far. **2.** *adv.* far away, far off, afar.

lòppa, *n.f.* chaff.

loquace, *adj.* loquacious, talkative.

lordo, *adj.* soiled; (weight) gross.

loro, *pron.* they; their; theirs; them; to them; you; your; yours; to you.

losanga, *n.f.* lozenge.

lòto, *n.m.* lotus; mud, mire.

lotta, *n.f.* struggle, fight.

lottare, *vb.* struggle, wrestle.

lotteria, *n.f.* lottery, raffle.

lotto, *n.m.* lot.

lozione, *n.f.* lotion.

lubrificante, *n.m. and adj.* lubricant.

lubrificare, *vb.* lubricate, grease, oil.

lucchetto, *n.m.* padlock.

luccicare, *vb.* twinkle.

lucciola, *n.f.* firefly; glowworm.

luce, *n.f.* light.

lucernàrio, *n.m.* skylight.

lucèrtola, *n.f.* lizard.

lucidare, *vb.* polish, shine.

lucidatura, *n.f.* polish.

lucidezza, *n.f.* shininess, gloss.

luci di città, *n.f.pl.* parking lights.

lùcido, **1.** *n.m.* polish. **2.** *adj.* shiny, glossy.

lucrativo, *adj.* lucrative.

lucrosamente, *adv.* gainfully.

lucroso, *adj.* gainful.

lùglio, *n.m.* July.

lùi, *pron.* he; him.

lumaca, *n.f.* snail.

luminoso, *adj.* luminous, bright, light, shining.

lunare, *adj.* lunar.

lunàtico, *n.m. and adj.* lunatic.

lunedì, *n.m.* Monday.

lunga, *n.f.* **di gran l.** by far.

lungamente, *adv.* long.

lunghezza, *n.f.* length.

lungo, **1.** *adj.* long. **2.** *prep.* along.

luogo, *n.m.* place. **l. comune**, cliché. **aver l.**, take place.

lupa, *n.f.* she-wolf.

lupo, *n.m.* wolf.

lùppolo, *n.m.* hop.

lusingare, *vb.* flatter, cajole.

lusingatore, *n.m.* flatterer.

lusinghe, *n.f.pl.* flattery.

lusinghièro, *adj.* flattering.

lusso, *n.m.* luxury. **di l.**, de luxe.

lussuoso, *adj.* luxurious.

lussureggiante, *adj.* luxuriant, lush.

lustrascarpe, *n.m.* bootblack.

lustro, *n.m.* luster.

luterano, *adj.* Lutheran.

lutto, *n.m.* mourning.

M

ma, *conj.* but.

macabro, *adj.* macabre.

maccheroni, *n.m.pl.* macaroni.

màcchia, *n.f.* spot, blemish, stain, blot; underbrush, brushwood.

macchiare, *vb.* spot, blot.

macchietta, *n.f.* flock.

macchiettato, *adj.* spotted, dappled.

màcchina, *n.f.* machine; engine. **m. a copiare**, photocopier. **m. da scrivere**, typewriter.

macchinista, *n.m.* engineer; machinist.

macellaio, *n.m.* butcher.

macellare, *vb.* butcher, slaughter.

macèllo, *n.m.* butchery, slaughter.

màcina, *n.f.* grindstone.

macinare, *vb.* grind, mill.

madornale, *adv.* gross.

madre, *n.f.* mother; (cheque) stub.

madrigale, *n.m.* madrigal.

madrina, *n.f.* godmother.

maestà, *n.f.* majesty.

maestoso, *adj.* majestic.

maestra, *n.f.* teacher.

maestro, *n.m.* master, teacher.

mafia, *f.* mafia.

magari, *adv.* perhaps even.

magazzinàggio, *n.m.* storage.

magazzino, *n.m.* storehouse; (arms) depot, armory.

maggese, *n.f.* fallow field. **a m.**, fallow.

màggio, *n.m.* May.

maggioranza, *n.f.* majority.

maggiordòmo, *n.m.* butler.

maggiore, **1.** *n.m.* major; elder;

senior. 2. adj. greater; elder; greatest; eldest.

maggiormente, adv. mostly.

magia, n.f. magic.

magico, adj. magic.

magistrato, n.m. magistrate.

magistratura, n.f. judiciary.

maglia, n.f. mesh; jersey.

maglietta, n.f. T-shirt.

magnanimo, adj. magnanimous, high-minded.

magnate, n.m. magnate.

magnesio, n.m. magnesium.

magnete, n.m. magnet.

magnetico, adj. magnetic.

magnetofono, n.m. tape recorder.

magnificenza, n.f. magnificence.

magnifico, adj. magnificent.

magniloquente, adj. grandiloquent.

mago, n.m. magician.

magro, adj. lean, gaunt, meager, spare, thin.

mai, adv. ever; never.

maiale, n.m. hog, pig; pork.

maionese, n.f. mayonnaise.

malamente, adv. badly.

malaria, n.f. malaria.

malato, adj. sick, ill, ailing.

malattia, n.f. sickness, malady, illness, ailment, disease.

malaugurio, n.m. ill omen, jinx.

malavita, n.f. underworld.

maldicenza, n.f. scandal.

male, 1. n.m. evil; pain, ache, hurt. m. di mare, seasickness. 2. adv. badly.

maledetto, adj. accursed.

maledire, vb. curse.

maledizione, n.f. curse.

malevolenza, n.f. malice.

malevolo, adj. malevolent.

malfattore, n.m. ruffian.

malgrado, prep. despite.

maligno, adj. malignant.

malinconia, n.f. melancholy.

malinconico, adj. melancholy.

malizia, n.f. mischief.

malizioso, adj. mischievous.

malleabile, adj. malleable.

mallevadore, n.m. guarantor; sponsor.

malore, n.m. illness.

malto, n.m. malt.

maltrattare, vb. maltreat, mistreat.

malvagio, adj. wicked, fell.

malvagità, n.f. wickedness.

malvarosa, n.f. hollyhock.

mamma, n.f. mother.

mammella, n.f. breast; udder.

mammifero, n.m. mammal.

manata, n.f. handful.

mancanza, n.f. lack; failure; shortage. in m. di, failing; lacking.

mancare, vb. be missing, be lacking; fail.

mancia, n.f. tip, gratuity.

mancorrente, n.m. hand-rail.

mandare, vb. send.

mandato, n.m. mandate; warrant.

mandolino, n.m. mandolin.

mandorla, n.f. almond.

mandorlo, n.m. almond-tree.

mandra, n.f. herd, drove.

maneggiare, vb. handle.

manette, n.f.pl. handcuffs.

manganese, n.m. manganese.

mangiabile, adj. edible, eatable.

mangiare, vb. eat.

mangiatoia, n.f. manger.

mania, n.f. mania, craze, fad.

maniaco, n.m. and adj. maniac.

manica, n.f. sleeve.

manico, n.m. handle, haft.

manicomio, n.m. madhouse, (insane) asylum.

manicotto, n.m. muff.

manicure, n.f. manicure.

maniera, n.f. manner, way, fashion.

manierismo, n.m. mannerism.

manifestare, vb. manifest, evince.

manifesto, 1. n.m. manifesto. 2. adj. manifest.

maniglia, n.f. handle.

manipolare, vb. manipulate.

mannaia, n.f. axe, chopper, cleaver.

mano, n.f. hand.

manodopera, n.f. labor.

manoscritto, n.m. and adj. manuscript.

manovella, n.f. handle, crank.

manovra, n.f. maneuver.

manovrare, vb. maneuver.

mansueto, adj. tame.

mantello, n.m. cloak, mantle, wrap.

mantenere, vb. maintain, keep.

mantenimento, n.m. maintenance.

mantice, n.m. bellows.

Mantova, n.f. Mantua.

mantovano, adj. Mantuan.

manuale, 1. n.m. manual, handbook. 2. adj. manual.

manubrio, n.m. handle-bar.

marca, n.f. brand.

marcare, vb. mark.

marchese, n.m. marquis.

marchigiano, adj. of the Marche.

marchio, n.m. stamp, hallmark.

marcia, n.f. march.

marciapiede, n.m. sidewalk.

marciare, vb. march.

marcio, adj. rotten, decayed; (egg) addled.

marcire, vb. rot, decay.

mare, n.m. sea.

marea, n.f. tide.

maresciallo, n.m. marshal.

margarina, n.f. margarine.

margherita, n.f. daisy.

marginale, adj. marginal, borderline.

margine, n.m. margin, edge.

marijuana, n.f. marijuana.

marina, n.f. navy; marine.

marinaio, n.m. mariner, sailor.

marinare, vb. marinate.

marino, adj. marine.

marionetta, n.f. marionette.

maritale, adj. marital.

maritare, vb. marry.

marito, n.m. husband.

marittimo, adj. maritime; marine.

marmellata, n.f. marmalade; jam.

marmo, n.m. marble.

marmocchio, n.m. brat.

marmotta, n.f. ground hog.

maroso, n.m. billow.

marrone, n.m. maroon; chestnut.

marrubio, n.f. horehound.

Marsiglia, n.f. Marseilles.

martedì, n.m. Tuesday.

martellare, vb. hammer.

martello, n.m. hammer.

martinello, n.m. jack.

martire, n.m. martyr.

martirio, n.m. martyrdom.

marziale, adj. martial.

marzo, n.m. March.

mascalzone, n.m. scoundrel, blackguard; crook.

mascella, n.f. jaw.

maschera, n.f. mask; usher. m. antigas, gas mask.

mascherare, vb. mask.

mascherata, n.f. masquerade.

maschile, adj. masculine.

maschio, 1. n. male; cock; buck. 2. adj. masculine; male.

massa, n.f. mass; bulk; lump.

massacrare, vb. massacre, slaughter.

massacro, n.m. massacre, slaughter.

massaggiare, vb. massage.

massaggiatore, n.m. masseur.

massaggio, n.m. massage.

massaia, n.f. housekeeper; housewife.

massiccio, adj. massive.

massima, n.f. maxim.

massimo, n.m. and adj. maximum.

masticare, vb. chew, masticate.

masticatore, n.m. chewer.

mastro, n.m. master. libro m., ledger.

matassa, n.f. skein, hank.

matematica, n.f. mathematics.

matematico, adj. mathematical.

materasso, n.m. mattress.

materia, n.f. matter; subject.

materiale, n.m. and adj. material.

materialismo, n.m. materialism.

materializzare, vb. materialize.

maternità, n.f. maternity.

materno, adj. maternal.

matita, n.f. pencil; crayon.

matriarcato, n.m. matriarchy.

matricola, n.f. freshman.

matrigna, n.f. stepmother.

matrimonio, n.m. matrimony, marriage; match.

matrona, n.f. matron.

mattatoio, n.m. stockyards.

mattina, n.f. morning.

mattinata, *n.f.* morning; matinée.

mattino, *n.m.* morning.

mattone, *n.m.* brick.

maturare, *vb.* ripen; mature.

maturato, *adj.* ripened; mellow.

maturità, *n.f.* maturity.

maturo, *adj.* mature; ripe; grown.

mausolèo, *n.m.* mausoleum.

mazza, *n.f.* bludgeon, cudgel.

mazzo, *n.m.* bunch; (cards) pack.

me, *pron.* me.

meccànico, 1. *n.m.* mechanic. **2.** *adj.* mechanical.

meccanismo, *n.m.* mechanism, machinery.

meccanizzare, *vb.* mechanize.

medàglia, *n.f.* medal.

medaglione, *n.m.* medallion; locket.

mèdia, *n.f.* average; mean.

mediano, *adj.* median.

mediatore, *n.m.* ombudsman.

medicare, *vb.* medicate.

medicina, *n.f.* medicine.

mèdico, 1. *n.* doctor, physician. **2.** *adj.* medical.

mèdio, *adj.* middle; average; medium; mean; mid-.

mediocre, *adj.* mediocre.

mediocrità, *n.f.* mediocrity.

medioevale, *adj.* mediaeval.

medioèvo, *n.m.* Middle Ages.

Medio Oriente, *n.m.* Middle East.

meditare, *vb.* meditate, muse.

meditazione *n.f.* meditation.

mediterràneo, *n.m. and adj.* Mediterranean.

medusa, *n.f.* jellyfish.

megàfono, *n.m.* megaphone.

megahertz, *n.m.* megahertz.

mèglio, *adv.* better. **il m.,** (the) best.

mela, *n.f.* apple.

melancònico, *adj.* melancholy, dismal.

melanzana, *n.f.* eggplant.

melassa, *n.f.* molasses.

mellone, *n.m.* melon; cantaloupe.

melma, *n.f.* muck, mire, ooze, slime.

melo, *n.m.* apple-tree.

melodia, *n.f.* melody, tune.

melodioso, *adj.* melodious, tuneful.

melodramma, *n.m.* melodrama.

membrana, *n.f.* membrane.

mèmbro, *n.m.* member; limb.

memoràbile, *adj.* memorable.

mèmore, *adj.* mindful.

memòria, *n.f.* memory; memoir; record.

memoriale, *n.m.* memorial.

menare, *vb.* lead.

mènda, *n.f.* fault, defect, imperfection.

mendace, *adj.* mendacious, lying.

mendicante, *n.m. and adj.* beggar, mendicant.

mendicare, *vb.* beg.

mèndico, *n.m.* mendicant.

menestrèllo, *n.m.* minstrel.

meno, *adv. and prep.* minus; less. **a m. di,** without. **a m. che . . . non,** unless.

menomare, *vb.* diminish, reduce; impair.

menopàusa, *n.f.* menopause.

mensile, *adj.* monthly.

mènsola, *n.f.* bracket.

menta, *n.f.* mint.

mentale, *adj.* mental.

mentalità, *n.f.* mentality.

mente, *n.f.* mind.

mentire, *vb.* lie.

mento, *n.m.* chin.

mentòlo, *n.m.* menthol.

mentre, *conj.* while.

menzionare, *vb.* mention.

menzione, *n.f.* mention.

menzogna, *n.f.* lie, untruth.

menzognèro, *adj.* lying, untruthful.

meramente, *adv.* merely.

meraviglia, *n.f.* marvel, wonder; amazement, astonishment.

meravigliare, *bv.* amaze, astonish; (refl.) be amazed, marvel, wonder.

meraviglioso, *adj.* marvelous, wonderful, amazing.

mercante, *n.m.* merchant.

mercanteggiare, *vb.* bargain, haggle.

mercantile, *adj.* mercantile.

mercanzia, *n.f.* merchandise.

mercato, *n.m.* market.

mèrce, *n.f.* commodity; ware. (*pl.*) goods; freight.

mercenàrio, 1. *n.* hireling; mercenary. **2.** *adj.* mercenary.

merceria, *n.f.* haberdashery.

merciàio, *n.m.* haberdasher.

mercoledì, *n.m.* Wednesday.

mercùrio, *n.m.* mercury.

merènda, *n.f.* light meal, collation.

meretrice, *n.f.* harlot.

meridionale, *adj.* southern.

meringa, *n.f.* meringue.

meritare, *vb.* deserve, merit, earn.

meritévole, *adj.* deserving.

mèrito, *n.m.* merit.

meritòrio, *adj.* meritorious.

merletto, *n.m.* lace.

mèrlo, *n.m.* blackbird.

merluzzo, *n.m.* cod, codfish.

mèro, *adj.* mere.

meschino, *adj.* mean, petty; paltry, shabby, beggarly, picayune, trivial.

mescolanza, *n.f.* mixture, admixture, blend.

mescolare, *vb.* mix, blend, mingle; alloy.

mese, *n.m.* month.

messa, *n.f.* mass.

messaggèro, *n.m.* messenger.

messàggio, *n.m.* message.

messicano, *adj.* Mexican.

Mèssico, *n.m.* Mexico.

mesticcio, *n.m.* half-breed.

mèstola, *n.f.* ladle.

mèstolo, *n.m.* ladle, dipper.

mestruazione, *n.f.* menstruation.

mèta, *n.f.* goal.

metà, *n.f.* half.

metabolismo, *n.m.* metabolism.

metafisica, *n.f.* metaphysics.

metàllico, *adj.* metallic.

metallo, *n.m.* metal.

metamòrfosi, *n.f.* metamorphosis.

mètano, *n.m.* methane, firedamp.

metèora, *n.f.* meteor.

meteorologia, *n.f.* meteorology.

meticoloso, *adj.* meticulous.

mètodo, *n.m.* method.

metràggio, *n.m.* length in meters; footage.

mètrico, *adj.* metric.

mètro, *n.m.* meter.

metròpoli, *n.f.* metropolis.

metropolitana, *n.f.* subway.

metropolitano, *adj.* metropolitan.

méttere, *vb.* place, put, set, lay.

mezzaluna, *n.f.* half-moon.

mezzanino, *n.m.* mezzanine.

mezzanòtte, *n.f.* midnight.

mezzaria, *n.f.* center line.

mèzzo, 1. *n.m.* middle; medium; means. **in m. a,** amid. **2.** *adj.* half; mid-.

mezzogiorno, *n.m.* noon; south.

mi, *pron.* me; to me.

microfilm, *n.m.* microfilm.

microforma, *n.f.* microform.

microscheda, *n.f.* microfiche.

microscòpico, *adj.* microscopic.

microscòpio, *n.m.* microscope.

midollo, *n.m.* marrow.

miele, *n.m.* honey.

mietere, *vb.* reap.

miglio, *n.m.* mile.

miglioramento, *n.m.* improvement.

migliorare, *vb.* improve, better, ameliorate, amend.

migliore, *adj.* better. **il m.,** (the) best.

migrare, *vb.* migrate.

migratòrio, *adj.* migratory.

migrazione, *n.f.* migration.

milanese, *adj.* Milanese.

Milano, *n.f.* Milan.

miliare, *adj.* **pietra m.,** milestone.

milionàrio, *n.m.* millionaire.

milione, *n.m.* million.

militante, *adj.* militant.

militare, *adj.* military.

militarismo, *n.m.* militarism.

milite, *n.m.* soldier.

milizia, *n.f.* militia.

millantare, *vb.* bluster, brag.

millantatore, *n.m.* braggart.

millanteria, *n.f.* bluster, brag.

mille, *num.* thousand.

millimetro, *n.m.* millimeter.

mimetismo, *n.m.* mimicry; camouflage.

mimetizzare, *vb.* camouflage.

mina, *n.f.* mine.

minàccia, *n.f.* menace, threat.

minacciare, *vb.* menace, threaten.

minare, *vb.* mine.

minatore, *n.m.* miner.

minerale, *n.m. and adj.* mineral, ore.

minerário, *adj.* mining.

minèstra, *n.f.* soup.

miniatura, *n.f.* miniature.

miniaturizzare, *vb.* miniaturize.

minièra, *n.f.* mine.

minimamente, *adv.* least.

minimo, 1. *n.m.* minimum. 2. *adj.* least, minimum.

ministèro, *n.m.* ministry.

ministrare, *vb.* minister.

ministro, *n.m.* minister.

minoranza, *n.f.* minority.

minore, *adj.* minor, lesser; younger, junior.

minorenne, *n.m. and adj.* minor.

minorità, *n.f.* minority.

minùgia, *n.f.pl.* catgut.

minùscolo, *adj.* tiny.

minuto, *n.m. and adj.* minute. al m., at retail.

mio, *adj.* my; mine.

miope, *adj.* short-sighted.

miopia, *n.f.* myopia.

miosòtide, *n.f.* forget-me-not.

mira, *n.f.* aim.

miràcolo, *n.m.* miracle.

miracoloso, *adj.* miraculous.

miràggio, *n.m.* mirage.

mirare, *vb.* aim.

miriade, *n.f.* myriad.

mirto, *n.m.* myrtle.

miscellàneo, *adj.* miscellaneous.

miscredènte, *n. and adj.* miscreant; infidel.

miscùglio, *n.m.* mixture; medley; hodge-podge.

misèria, *n.f.* poverty, want; misery.

misericòrdia, *n.f.* mercy.

misero, *adj.* miserable, wretched.

missile, *n.m.* missile.

missionàrio, *n.m. and adj.* missionary.

missione, *n.f.* mission.

misterioso, *adj.* mysterious.

mistèro, *n.m.* mystery.

mistico, *adj.* mystic.

mistificare, *vb.* mystify.

misto, *adj.* mixed; coeducational.

mistura, *n.f.* mixture.

misura, *n.f.* measure; size.

misuramento, *n.m.* measurement.

misurare, *vb.* measure, gauge.

misuratore, *adj.* measuring.

mite, *adj.* gentle; meek; mild.

mitemente, *adv.* mildly, gently.

mitezza, *n.f.* mildness, meekness.

mitico, *adj.* mythical.

mitigare, *vb.* mitigate, soften, lessen, assuage.

mito, *n.m.* myth.

mitologia, *n.f.* mythology.

mitràglia, *n.f.* grapeshot.

mitragliatrice, *n.f.* machine gun.

mòbile, 1. *n.m.* piece of furniture. 2. *adj.* movable, mobile.

mobilia, *n.f.* furnishings.

mobilitare, *vb.* mobilize.

mobilitazione, *n.f.* mobilization.

mòda, *n.f.* mode, fashion. alla m., fashionable, modish.

modellare, *vb.* model, mold.

modèllo, *n.m.* model, pattern.

moderare, *vb.* moderate.

moderato, *adj.* moderate.

moderazione, *n.f.* moderation.

modèrno, *adj.* modern.

modèstia, *n.f.* modesty.

modèsto, *adj.* modest, demure; plain.

modificare, *vb.* modify.

modista, *n.m. or f.* milliner.

modisteria, *n.f.* millinery.

mòdo, *n.m.* manner; mode; way. m. di vivere, life style.

modulare, *vb.* modulate.

mòdulo, *n.m.* blank form.

moffetta, *n.f.* skunk.

mògano, *n.m.* mahogany.

mòggio, *n.m.* bushel.

mòglie, *n.f.* wife.

molare, *adj.* molar.

molècola, *n.f.* molecule.

molestare, *vb.* molest.

molle, *adj.* soft.

mòlo, *n.m.* jetty, mole, pier.

molòsso, *n.m.* bulldog.

moltéplice, *adj.* multiple, manifold.

molteplicità, *n.f.* multiplicity.

moltiplicare, *vb.* multiply.

moltiplicazione, *n.f.* multiplication.

moltitùdine, *n.f.* multitude, host.

molto, 1. *adj.* much; *(pl.)* many, plenty of. 2. *adv.* very; much.

momentàneo, *adj.* momentary.

momènto, *n.m.* moment.

mònaca, *n.f.* nun.

mònaco, *n.m.* monk.

Mònaco di Bavièra, *n.m.* Munich.

monarca, *n.m.* monarch.

monarchia, *n.f.* monarchy.

monastèro, *n.m.* monastery.

moncone, *n.m.* stump.

mondano, *adj.* worldly.

mondiale, *adj.* world-wide.

mondo, *n.m.* world.

monèllo, *n.m.* gamin, urchin.

monèta, *n.f.* coin.

monetàrio, *adj.* monetary.

monitore, *n.m.* monitor.

monòcolo, *n.m.* monocle.

monòlogo, *n.m.* monologue.

monoplano, *n.m.* monoplane.

monopolizzare, *vb.* monopolize.

monopòlio, *n.m.* monopoly.

monosìllabo, *n.m.* monosyllable.

monòssido, *n.m.* monoxide.

monotonìa, *n.f.* monotony, dullness.

monòtono, *adj.* monotonous, dull, dreary, humdrum.

monsone, *n.m.* monsoon.

montàggio, *n.m.* assembly.

montagna, *n.f.* mountain.

montagnoso, *adj.* mountainous.

montanaro, *n.m.* mountaineer.

montare, *vb.* mount; set.

monte, *n.m.* mount, mountain.

montone, *n.m.* ram.

montuoso, *adj.* mountainous.

monumentale, *adj.* monumental.

monumento, *n.m.* monument, memorial.

mòra, *n.f.* blackberry.

morale, 1. *n.m.* morale. 2. *n.f. and adj.* moral.

moralista, *n.m.* moralist.

moralità, *n.f.* morality.

moralmente, *adj.* morally.

mòrbido, *adj.* soft.

morbillo, *n.m.* measles.

morboso, *adj.* morbid.

mordace, *adj.* scathing.

mòrdere, *vb.* bite.

morfina, *n.f.* morphine.

mormorare, *vb.* murmur.

mormorìo, *n.m.* murmur.

mòrso, *n.m.* bite; (harness) bit.

mortale, *adj.* mortal, deadly, deathly, fatal.

mortalità, *n.f.* mortality.

mòrte, *n.f.* death, demise.

mortificare, *vb.* mortify.

mòrto, *adj.* dead.

mortuàrio, *adj.* mortuary.

mosàico, *n.m.* mosaic.

mosca, *n.f.* fly. m. cavallina, horsefly.

mostarda, *n.f.* mustard.

mostra, *n.f.* show, exhibit, exhibition.

mostrare, *vb.* show, exhibit.

mostro, *n.m.* monster.

mostruosità, *n.f.* monstrosity, freak.

mostruoso, *adj.* monstrous, freak.

motivare, *vb.* motivate.

motivo, *n.m.* motive; motif; sake.

mòto, *n.m.* motion.

motocicletta, *n.f.* motorcycle.

motocultura, *n.f.* motorized farming.

motore, 1. *n.m.* motor. 2. *adj.* motive.

motorizzare, *vb.* motorize.

motoscafo, *n.m.* motor-boat.

motto, *n.m.* motto, quip, slogan.

movimento, *n.m.* movement.

mozione, *n.f.* motion.

mozzare, *vb.* lop off.

mozzicone, *n.m.* stub.

mozzo, *n.m.* deck-hand.

mòzzo, *n.m.* hub.

mùcchio, n.m. heap, pile, stack.

muco, n.m. mucus.

mucoso, adj. mucous.

muffa, n.f. mold. m. bianca, mildew.

muffito, adj. moldy.

mugghiare, vb. bellow, low.

mùgghio, n.m. bellow.

muggire, vb. bellow.

muggito, n.m. bellow.

mughetto, n.m. lily of the valley.

mugnaio, n.m. miller.

mulatto, n.m. mulatto.

mulino, n.m. mill.

mulla(h), n.f. mullah.

mulo, n.m. mule.

multa, n.f. fine.

multare, vb. fine.

multicolore, adj. multicolored, motley.

multinazionale, adj. multinational.

mùltiplo, adj. multiple.

mùmmia, n.f. mummy.

mùngere, vb. milk.

municipale, adj. municipal.

munificènte, adj. munificent.

munizione, n.f. munition, ammunition.

muòvere, vb. move, stir; (refl.) budge.

murale, adj. mural.

muratore, n.m. bricklayer, mason.

muratura, n.f. masonry, bricklaying.

muro, n.m. wall.

musa, n.f. muse.

muschio, n.m. moss.

muscolare, adj. muscular.

mùscolo, n.m. muscle.

musèo, n.m. museum.

museruòla, n.f. muzzle.

mùsica, n.f. music. m. da càmera, chamber music.

musicale, adj. musical.

musicista, n.m. musician.

muso, n.m. muzzle.

mussolina, n.f. muslin.

muta, n.f. pack (of dogs).

mutabilità, n.f. changeability.

mutamento, n.m. change.

mutare, vb. change.

mutazione, n.f. mutation.

mutévole, adj. changeable.

mutilare, vb. mutilate.

mutilato, n.m. amputee.

muto, adj. mute, dumb.

mùtuo, adj. mutual.

N

nàcchere, n.f.pl. castanets.

nafta, n.f. naphtha.

nàilon, n.m. nylon.

nano, n.m. dwarf, midget.

napoletano, adj. Neapolitan.

Nàpoli, n.f. Naples.

narcìso, n.m. narcissus, daffodil.

narcòtico, n.m. and adj. narcotic.

narice, n.f. nostril.

narrare, vb. narrate, relate.

narrativo, adj. narrative.

narrazione, n.f. narration, relation.

nasale, adj. nasal.

nàscere, vb. come into being; be born; arise.

nàscita, n.f. birth.

nascóndere, vb. hide; (refl.) lurk.

nascondiglio, n.m. hide-out, cache.

naso, n.m. nose.

naspo, n.m. reel.

nastro, n.m. ribbon; tape. n. televisio, videotape.

natale, adj. natal.

Natale, n.m. Christmas.

natalità, n.f. birth rate.

nàtica, n.f. buttock.

natività, n.f. nativity.

nativo, adj. native.

nato, adj. born.

natura, n.f. nature. n. mòrta, still life.

naturale, adj. natural.

naturalezza, n.f. naturalness.

naturalista, n.m. naturalist.

naturalizzare, vb. naturalize.

naufragare, vb. wreck.

naufràgio, n.m. shipwreck.

nàufrago, n.m. castaway.

nàusea, n.f. nausea.

nauseante, adj. nauseating.

nàutico, adj. nautical.

navale, adj. naval.

navata, n.f. aisle; nave.

nave, n.f. ship, vessel.

navigàbile, adj. navigable.

navigare, vb. navigate; sail.

navigatore, n.m. navigator.

navigazione, n.f. navigation.

nazionale, adj. national.

nazionalismo, n.m. nationalism.

nazionalità, n.f. nationality.

nazionalizzare, vb. nationalize.

nazionalizzazione, n.f. nationalization.

nazione, n.f. nation.

ne, pro-phrase (replaces phrases introduced by di and by da when meaning "from") some; any; thereof; of it (him, her); about it (him, her); from there.

nè, conj. neither; nor.

nébbia, n.f. fog, haze, mist.

nebbioso, adj. foggy, hazy, misty.

nebulizzare, vb. atomize (liquids); spray.

nebulosa, n.f. nebula.

nebulóso, adj. nebulous.

necessàrio, adj. necessary, needful, requisite.

necessità, n.f. necessity.

necrològio, n.m. obituary.

nefàrio, adj. nefarious.

negare, vb. deny.

negativa, n.f. negative.

negativo, adj. negative.

negligènte, adj. remiss.

negligènza, n.f. oversight.

negoziante, n.m. dealer.

negoziare, vb. negotiate.

negoziazione, n.f. negotiation.

negòzio, n.m. store, shop.

negra, n.f. Black (woman).

negro, n.m. Black (man or person).

nemico, n.m. and adj. enemy, foe.

neòfita, n.m. neophyte.

nèon, n.m. neon.

nepotismo, n.m. nepotism.

nèrbo, n.m. sinew.

nero, adj. black.

nèrvo, n.m. nerve.

nervoso, adj. nervous, jittery.

nessuno, 1. adj. no; (after negative) any. 2. pron. nobody, no one; none.

nèttare, n.m. nectar.

netto, adj. clean; clear-cut; net.

neurologìa, n.f. neurology.

neutralità, n.f. neutrality.

neutralizzare, vb. neutralize, counteract.

neutro, n.m. and adj. neutral.

neutrone, n.m. neutron.

neve, n.f. snow.

nevicare, vb. snow.

nevischio, n.m. sleet.

nevralgìa, n.f. neuralgia.

nevròtico, adj. neurotic.

nìbbio, n.m. kite.

nichel, n.m. nickel.

nicotìna, n.f. nicotine.

nìdo, n.m. nest, aerie.

niènte, pron. nothing. n. affatto, adv. not at all.

ninfa, n.f. nymph.

ninna-nanna, n.f. lullaby.

ninnolo, n.m. trinket.

nipote, n.m. and f. nephew; niece; grandson; granddaughter.

nitrato, n.m. nitrate.

nitrògeno, n.m. nitrogen.

nò, interj. no.

nòbile, n. and adj. noble.

nobilmente, adv. nobly.

nobiltà, n.f. nobility.

nobiluòmo, n.m. nobleman.

nòcca, n.f. knuckle; fetlock.

nocciòla, n.f. nut; hazelnut.

nocciòlo, n.m. hazel; (fig.) kernel.

noce, n. 1. m. nut-tree; walnut. n. americano, hickory. 2. f. nut; walnut.

nocivo, adj. harmful, injurious.

nòdo, n.m. knot, gnarl, kink, node. n. scorsòio, slipknot; noose.

nodoso, adj. knotty.

noi, pron. we; us.

nòia, n.f. boredom, ennui.

noleggiare, vb. hire.

noléggio, n.m. rental.

nòlo, n.m. hire.

nòmade, n.m. nomad.

nome, n.m. name; given name.

nomìgnolo, n.m. nickname.

nòmina, n.f. nomination, appointment.

nominale, adj. nominal.

nominare, vb. nominate, name, appoint.

non, adv. not.

non allineato, adj. non-aligned.

noncurante, adj. easy-going.

nondimeno, adv. nonetheless, nevertheless, all the same.

nonna, n.f. grandmother.

nonno, n.m. grandfather.

nono, adj. ninth.

nonostante, prep. notwithstanding.

non ti scordar di me, n.m. forget-me-not.

nord, n.m. north.

nord-est, n.m. northeast.

nord-ovest, n.m. northwest.

norma, n.f. norm; standard.

normale, adj. normal; standard.

normalmente, adv. normally.

norvegese, adj. Norwegian.

Norvègia, n.f. Norway.

nostalgia, n.f. nostalgia; homesickness.

nòstro, adj. our; ours.

nostròmo, n.m. boatswain.

nòta, n.f. note; footnote.

notaio, n.m. notary.

notare, vb. note.

notazione, n.f. notation.

notévole, adj. notable, noticeable, remarkable.

notificare, vb. notify.

notificazione, n.f. notification.

notizia, n.f. piece of news.

noto, adj. noted, well-known.

notorietà, n.f. notoriety.

notòrio, adj. notorious.

notturno, 1. n.m. nocturne. 2. adj. nocturnal.

novanta, num. ninety.

novantésimo, adj. ninetieth.

nòve, num. nine.

novellìstica, n.f. novel-writting, fiction.

novèmbre, n.m. November.

novèna, n.f. novena.

novità, n.f. novelty.

novìzio, n.m. novice.

novocaìna, n.f. novocaine.

nozione, n.f. notion.

nòzze, n.f. pl. wedding.

nube, n.f. cloud.

nucleare, adj. nuclear.

nùcleo, n.m. nucleus.

nudità, n.f. nudity, bareness.

nudo, adj. naked, nude, bare.

nulla, pron. nothing.

nullità, n.f. nonentity.

nullo, adj. void.

numerare, vb. number.

numèrico, adj. numerical.

nùmero, n.m. number.

numeroso, adj. numerous.

nùnzio, n.m. nuncio.

nuòcere, vb. harm, injure.

nuòra, n.f. daughter-in-law.

nuotare, vb. swim.

nuòvo, adj. new. di n., anew; again.

nutrice, n.f. nurse.

nutriènte, adj. nutritious.

nutrimento, n.m. nourishment; feed.

nutrire, vb. nourish; feed.

nutrizione, n.f. nutrition.

nùvola, n.f. cloud.

nuvolosità, n.f. cloudiness.

nuvoloso, adj. cloudy.

nuziale, adj. nuptial, bridal.

O

o, conj. or. o . . . o, either . . . or.

oasi, n.f. oasis.

obbediènte, adj. obedient, compliant.

obbediènza, n.f. obedience, compliance.

obbedire, vb. obey, comply.

obbligare, vb. oblige.

obbligatòrio, adj. obligatory, binding, compulsory, mandatory.

obbligazione, n.f. obligation; bond, debenture.

obelisco, n.m. obelisk.

obèso, adj. obese.

òbice, n.m. howitzer.

obiettare, vb. object, demur.

obiettivo, 1. n.m. objective. 2. adj. objective; factual.

obiezione, n.f. objection.

oblazione, n.f. fine paid voluntarily.

oblìo, n.m. oblivion.

obliquo, adj. oblique, slant.

oblò, n.m. porthole.

oblungo, adj. oblong.

òbolo, n.m. obol; mite.

òca, n.f. goose.

occasionale, adj. occasional.

occasione, n.f. occasion, opportunity, chance; bargain.

occhiali, n.m.pl. eyeglasses, spectacles.

occhiata, n.f. glance, look.

occhièllo, n.m. button-hole; eyelet.

òcchio, n.m. eye. o. della màstica, armhole. o. pesto, black eye.

occidentale, adj. occidental, western.

occidènte, n.m. Occident, west.

occulto, adj. occult.

occupante, n.m. occupant.

occupare, vb. occupy.

occupato, adj. busy.

occupazione, n.f. occupation, job.

ocèano, n.m. ocean.

oculare, adj. ocular. testimone o., eye-witness.

oculìsta, n.m. oculist.

od, conj. or.

odiare, vb. hate.

òdio, n.m. hate, hatred.

odioso, adj. hateful, invidious, odious, obnoxious.

odontoiatrìa, f. dentistry.

odore, n.m. odor, scent, smell.

offèndere, vb. offend.

offensiva, n.f. offensive.

offensivo, adj. offensive, objectionable.

offensore, n.m. offender.

offerènte, n.m. bidder.

offèrta, n.f. offer; bid.

offesa, n.f. offense.

officiare, adv. officiate.

offrire, vb. offer, tender; bid.

oftàlmico, adj. ophthalmic.

oggètto, n.m. object.

òggi, n.m.and adv. today.

ogni, adj. each, every.

ogniqualvòlta, adv. whenever.

ognuno, pron. everybody, everyone.

Olanda, n.f. Holland.

olandese, 1. n.m. Dutchman. 2. adj. Dutch.

oleoso, adj. oily.

olfattòrio, adj. olfactory.

oligarchìa, n.f. oligarchy.

òlio, n.m. oil.

olìva, n.f. olive.

olìvo, n.m. olive-tree.

olmo, n.m. elm.

olocàusto, n.m. holocaust.

olografìa, n.f. holography.

ologramma, n.m. hologram.

oltràggio, n.m. outrage.

oltraggioso, adj. outrageous.

oltre, adv. and prep. beyond; besides, further.

oltrepassare, vb. pass beyond; outrun.

omàggio, n.m. homage; gift, present.

ombelìco, n.m. navel.

ombra, n.f. shade; shadow.

ombreggiare, vb. shade.

ombrèllo, n.m. umbrella.

ombroso, adj. shady.

omelìa, n.f. homily.

ométtere, vb. omit, leave out; overlook.

omicìda, n.m. homicide (person).

omicìdio, n.m. homicide, manslaughter.

omissione, n.f. omission.

òmnibus, n.m. local (train).

omogèneo, adj. homogeneous.

omogenizzare, vb. homogenize.

omologare, vb. probate.

omologazione, n.f. probate.

omònimo, 1. n.m. homonym; namesake. 2. adj. homonymous, of the same name.

omosessuale, adj. homosexual.

òncia, n.f. ounce.

onda, n.f. wave.

ondare, vb. surge.

ondeggiare, vb. undulate.

ònere, n.m. burden, onus.

oneroso, adj. burdensome.

onestà, n.f. honesty.

onestamente, adv. honestly, decently.

onèsto, adj. honest, decent, above board.

onnipotènte, adj. almighty, omnipotent.

onorare, vb. honor.

onoràrio, 1. n.m. honorarium, fee. 2. adj. honorary.

onore, n.m. honor.

onorévole, adj. honorable, decent.

onorevolezza, *n.f.* honorableness, decency.

opacità, *n.f.* opacity.

opaco, *adj.* opaque.

opale, *n.m.* opal.

òpera, *n.f.* work; opera.

operàio, *n.m.* worker.

operare, *vb.* operate.

operativo, *adj.* operative.

operatore, *n.m.* operator.

operazione, *n.f.* operation; transaction.

operetta, *n.f.* operetta; musical comedy.

operoso, *adj.* industrious.

opinione, *n.f.* opinion.

opporre, *vb.* oppose; *(refl.)* object.

opportunamente, *adv.* advisably.

opportunismo, *n.m.* opportunism.

opportunità, *n.f.* desirability; suitability; advisability; expediency.

opportuno, *adj.* fitting; desirable; advisable; expedient.

opposizione, *n.f.* opposition.

oppressione, *n.f.* oppression.

opposto, *n.m. and adj.* opposite.

oppressivo, *adj.* oppressive.

oppresso, *adj.* oppressed, downtrodden.

oppressore, *n.m.* oppressor.

opprimènte, *adj.* oppressive, burdensome.

opprimere, *vb.* oppress.

optometrìa, *n.f.* optometry.

opulento, *adj.* opulent, affluent.

opulènza, *n.f.* opulence, affluence.

opùscolo, *n.m.* pamphlet.

opzione, *n.f.* option.

ora, **1.** *n.f.* hour; o'clock; time. che o. è? what time is it? **2.** *adv.* now.

oràcolo, *n.m.* oracle.

orale, *adj.* oral.

oràrio, *n.m.* timetable, schedule.

oratore, *n.m.* orator, speaker.

oratòria, *n.f.* oratory.

orazione, *n.f.* oration.

orbare, *vb.* bereave.

òrbita, *n.f.* orbit; socket.

orchèstra, *n.f.* orchestra.

orchidèa, *n.f.* orchid.

òrda, *n.f.* horde.

ordàlia, *n.f.* ordeal.

ordinamento, *n.m.* arrangement.

ordinanza, *n.f.* ordinance.

ordinare, *vb.* order, arrange, array; ordain; tidy, trim.

ordinàrio, *n.m.* ordinary.

ordinato, *adj.* orderly, tidy, trim.

ordinazione, *n.f.* ordination.

òrdine, *n.m.* order, array; fiat.

orecchino, *n.m.* ear-ring.

orècchio, *n.m.* ear.

orecchioni, *n.m.pl.* mumps.

oréfice, *n.m.* goldsmith.

òrfano, *n.m.* orphan.

orfanotròfio, *n.m.* orphanage.

orgànico, *adj.* organic.

organismo, *n.m.* organism.

organista, *n.m.* organist.

organizzare, *vb.* organize.

organizzazione, *n.f.* organization.

òrgano, *n.m.* organ.

organza, *n.f.* organdy.

òrgia, *n.f.* orgy, debauch.

orgòglio, *n.m.* pride.

orgoglioso, *adj.* proud.

orientale, *adj.* Oriental; eastern.

orientamento, *n.m.* orientation; bearings.

orientare, *vb.* orient.

orientazione, *n.f.* orientation.

oriènte, *n.m.* Orient; east.

originale, *adj.* original, novel.

originalità, *n.f.* originality.

origine, *n.f.* origin.

origliare, *vb.* eavesdrop.

orina, *n.f.* urine.

orinare, *vb.* urinate.

orinatòio, *n.m.* urinal.

orizzontale, *adj.* horizontal; level.

orizzonte, *n.m.* horizon.

orlare, *vb.* hem; edge.

orlatura, *n.f.* edging.

orlo, *n.m.* brink, brim, edge, rim, verge; hem. **o. a giorno,** hemstitch.

orma, *n.f.* footstep; footprint.

ormeggiare, *vb.* moor.

ormeggio, *n.m.* mooring.

ormone, *n.m.* hormone.

ornamentale, *adj.* ornamental.

ornamento, *n.m.* ornament.

ornare, *vb.* ornament, adorn.

ornato, *adj.* ornate.

ornitologìa, *n.f.* ornithology.

òro, *n.m.* gold.

orologiaio, *n.m.* watchmaker.

orològio, *n.m.* clock; watch. **o. a pòlvere,** hourglass.

or' ora, *adv.* just now.

oròscopo, *n.m.* horoscope.

orrèndo, *adj.* ghastly, gruesome.

orribile, *adj.* horrible, grisly.

òrrido, *adj.* horrid.

orrore, *n.m.* horror.

orso, *n.m.* bear.

ortènsia, *n.f.* hydrangea.

orticultura, *n.f.* horticulture.

òrto, *n.m.* orchard; garden.

ortodòsso, *adj.* orthodox.

ortografìa, *n.f.* orthography, spelling.

ortopèdico, *adj.* orthopedic.

orzaiòlo, *n.m.* sty.

orzo, *n.m.* barley.

osare, *vb.* dare; venture.

oscèno, *adj.* obscene.

oscillare, *vb.* oscillate, sway.

oscuramento, *n.m.* darkening; blackout.

oscurare, *vb.* darken, obscure, dim, shade.

oscurità, *n.f.* darkness, obscurity, dimness, gloom.

oscuro, *adj.* dark, obscure, dim, gloomy.

osmòsi, *n.f.* osmosis.

ospedale, *n.m.* hospital.

ospedalizzare, *vb.* hospitalize.

ospedalizzazione, *n.f.* hospitalization.

ospitale, *adj.* hospitable.

ospitalità, *n.f.* hospitality.

òspite, *n.* **1.** *m.* host; guest; visitor; lodger. **2.** *f.* hostess; guest; visitor.

ossatura, *n.f.* framework.

ossequioso, *adj.* obsequious.

osservanza, *n.f.* observance.

osservare, *vb.* observe, notice, remark.

osservatore, *n.m.* observer.

osservatòrio, *n.m.* observatory.

osservazione, *n.f.* observation, remark.

ossessione, *n.f.* obsession.

òssia, *conj.* or.

ossìgeno, *n.m.* oxygen.

òsso, *n.m.* bone.

ossuto, *adj.* bony.

ostacolare, *vb.* hinder, bar, block, interfere with, obstruct.

ostàcolo, *n.m.* obstacle, bar, hindrance, block, snag.

ostàggio, *n.m.* hostage.

òste, *n.m.* innkeeper.

ostensibile, *adj.* ostensible.

ostentare, *vb.* show off, display, flaunt.

ostentato, *adj.* ostentatious.

ostentazione, *n.f.* ostentation, display.

osterìa, *n.f.* tavern.

ostètrico, **1.** *n.m.* obstetrician. **2.** *adj.* obstetrical.

òstia, *n.f.* Host.

ostile, *adj.* hostile, antagonistic.

ostilità, *n.f.* hostility.

ostinato, *adj.* obstinate, dogged, headstrong; obdurate.

ostracizzare, *vb.* ostracize.

òstrica, *n.f.* oyster.

ostruire, *vb.* obstruct.

ostruzione, *n.f.* obstruction.

ottàgono, *n.m.* octagon.

ottanta, *num.* eighty, fourscore.

ottantèsimo, *adj.* eightieth.

ottava, *n.f.* eight; octave.

ottavino, *n.m.* piccolo.

ottavo, *adj.* eight.

ottenere, *vb.* obtain, get.

òttica, *n.f.* optics.

òttico, **1.** *n.m.* optician. **2.** *adj.* optic.

ottimismo, *n.m.* optimism.

ottimistico, *adj.* optimistic.

òtto, *num.* eight.

ottobre, *n.m.* October.

ottone, *n.m.* brass.

ottopode, *n.m.* octopus.

ottùndere, *vb.* dull.

otturare, *vb.* stop up; fill.

otturatore, *n.m.* shutter.

otturazione, *n.f.* filling.

ottusamente, *adv.* bluntly, obtusely.

ottusità, n.f. obtuseness, dullness, bluntness.
ottuso, adj. obtuse, dull, blunt.
ovaia, n.f. ovary.
ovale, n.m. and adj. oval.
ovazione, n.f. ovation.
ovatta, n.f. wadding.
òvest, n. west.
òvvio, adj. obvious.
oziare, vb. loaf.
òzio, n.m. idleness.
ozioso, adj. idle.

P

pacca, n.f. smack.
pacco, n.m. package, pack, parcel.
pace, n.f. peace.
pacificare, vb. pacify.
pacificatore, n.m. pacifier.
pacifico, adj. pacific, peaceful.
pacifismo, n.m. pacifism.
pacifista, n.m. pacifist.
padèlla, n.f. pan, frying pan.
padiglione, n.m. pavilion; stand.
Pàdova, n.f. Padua.
padovano, adj. Paduan.
padre, n.m. father.
padrino, n.m. godfather.
padrona, n.f. mistress; landlady.
padronanza, n.f. mastery.
padrone, n.m. boss, employer; landlord; master.
paesàggio, n.m. landscape, scenery.
paese, n.m. country.
paga, n.f. pay.
pagamento, n.m. payment.
pagano, n. and adj. pagan, heathen.
pagare, vb. pay, defray.
pàggio, n.m. page.
pàgina, n.f. page.
pàgine centrali, n.f.pl. centerfold.
pàglia, n.f. straw. p. di acciaio, n.f. steel wool.
pagliaccesco, adj. clownish.
pagliàccio, n.m. clown.
pagnòtta, n.f. loaf.
pagòda, n.f. pagoda.
paio, n.m. pair, couple.
pala, n.f. shovel.
palafitta, n.f. pile.
palafrenière, n.m. groom.
pàlato, n.m. palate.
palazzo, n.m. palace; large building; mansion. p. di giustizia, courthouse.
palco, n.m. antler; box (in theater).
palcoscènico, n.m. stage.
palèstra, n.f. gymnasium.
palla, n.f. ball.
pallacanestro, n.f. basketball.
pallamaglio, n.m. croquet.
pallidezza, n.f. paleness.
pàllido, adj. pale, pallid, wan, pasty.
pallinacci, n.m.pl. buckshot.
pallini, n.m.pl. shot.

pallone, n.m. balloon.
pallòttola, n.f. bullet; ball.
palma, n.f. palm.
palo, n.m. pole, post, stake.
pàlpebra, n.f. eyelid.
palpitare, vb. palpitate.
palude, n.f. swamp, bog, marsh.
panacèa, n.f. panacea.
pancetta, n.f. bacon.
pància, n.f. paunch, belly.
panciòtto, n.m. vest.
pane, n.m. bread, loaf. p. abbrustolito, toast.
pànfilo, n.m. yacht.
pànico, n.m. panic.
panino, n.m. roll, biscuit.
panna, n.f. cream.
pannaiòlo, n.m. clothier; draper.
pannèllo, n.m. panel.
pannolino, n.m. diaper; sanitary napkin.
pannolino, n.m. diaper.
panorama, n.m. panorama.
pantaloni, n.m.(pl.) trousers, pants, breeches.
pantano, n.m. bog.
pantèra, n.f. panther.
pantòfola, n.f. slipper.
pantomima, n.f. pantomime.
papa, n.m. pope.
papà, n.m. papa.
papale, adj. papal.
pàpera, n.f. goose.
paperetto, n.m. gosling.
pàpero, n.m. gander.
pappa, n.f. gruel.
pappagallo, n.m. parrot; parakeet.
paràbola, n.f. parabola.
parabrezza, n.m. windshield, windscreen.
paracadute, n.m. parachute.
paradiso, n.m. paradise.
paradòsso, n.m. paradox.
parafango, n.m. mudguard; fender.
paraffina, n.f. paraffin.
parafrasare, vb. paraphrase.
parafrasi, n.f. paraphrase.
parafulmine, n.m. lightning-rod.
parafuòco, n.m. firescreen.
paragonàbile, adj. comparable.
paragonare, vb. compare.
paragone, n.m. comparison.
paràgrafo, n.m. paragraph.
paràlisi, n.f. paralysis.
paralizzare, vb. paralyze.
parallelo, n.m. and adj. parallel.
paralume, n.m. shade.
paramèdico, n.m. paramedic.
parametro, n.m. parameter.
parapiglia, n.m. scramble.
parassita, n.m. parasite.
parata, n.f. parade.
paratia, n.f. bulkhead.
paravènto, n.m. screen; windshield.
parcheggiamento, n.m. parking.
parcare, vb. park.
parcheggio, n.m. parking.
parco, n.m. park.

parécchio, adj. some; considerable; (pl.) several.
parènte, n.m. relative.
parentela, n.f. kin, kindred; relationship.
parèntesi, n.f. parenthesis. p. quadra, bracket.
parere, 1. n.m. opinion. 2. vb. appear, seem.
pari, 1. n.m. peer. 2. n.f. par. 3. adj. even, equal.
pària, n.m. pariah, outcast.
Parigi, n.f. Paris.
parigino, adj. Parisian.
parità, n.f. parity. p. àurea, gold standard.
parlamentare, 1. adj. parliamentary. 2. vb. parley.
parlamento, n.m. parliament, legislature; parley.
parlare, vb. speak, talk.
parmigiano, adj. Parmesan.
parodia, n.f. parody.
parodiare, vb. parody.
paròla, n.f. word.
parossismo, n.m. paroxysm.
parròcchia, n.f. parish.
parrocchiale, adj. parochial.
pàrroco, n.m. parish priest; parson.
parrucca, n.f. wig.
parrucchière, n.m. hairdresser; barber.
parsimònia, n.f. parsimony.
parte, n.f. part; share. a p., apart. p. del discorso, part of speech.
partecipante, n.m. participant.
partecipare, vb. participate, partake.
partecipazione, n.f. participation.
partènza, n.f. departure.
particèlla, n.f. particle.
participio, n.m. participle.
particolare, adj. particular.
particolareggiato, adj. detailed; circumstantial.
partigiano, n.m. and adj. partisan.
partire, vb. depart, leave.
partita, n.f. game.
partito, n.m. party.
partitura, n.f. score.
partizione, n.f. partition.
parto, n.m. childbirth.
partorire, vb. bear, give birth to.
parziale, adj. partial.
parzialità, n.f. partiality, bias.
pàscere, vb. graze.
pàscolo, n.m. pasture; grazing.
Pasqua, n.f. Easter.
pasquinata, n.f. lampoon.
passàbile, adj. passable.
passàggio, n.m. passage; aisle; crossing. p. a livèllo, grade crossing.
passante, n.m. passer-by.
passapòrto, n.m. passport.
passare, vb. pass; spend.
passatèmpo, n.m. pastime.
passato, 1. n.m. past; purée. 2. adj. past, over, bygone.
passeggiare, vb. walk, stroll.

passeggiata, *n.f.* walk, stroll; ride.

passeggèro, *n.m.* passenger.

passeggiatore, *n.m.* stroller.

passerélla, *n.f.* gangway.

pàssero, *n.m.* sparrow.

passione, *n.f.* passion; fondness.

passivo, *n.m. and adj.* passive.

passo, *n.m.* pass; pace; step; tread.

pasta, *n.f.* paste; dough, batter. **p. asciutta,** macaroni. **p. frolla,** frosting.

pasteurizzare, *vb.* pasteurize.

pasticca, *n.f.* pastille, lozenge, tablet.

pasticceria, *n.f.* pastry; pastryshop.

pasticcio, *n.f.* mess; pasty.

pastiglia, *n.f.* pastille.

pasto, *n.m.* meal.

pastore, *n.m.* shepherd; pastor.

patata, *n.f.* potato.

patènte, *n.m.* license.

paternità, *n.f.* paternity, fatherhood.

patèrno, *adj.* paternal, fatherly.

patètico, *adj.* pathetic.

patibolo, *n.m.* scaffold.

patinoso, *adj.* furry.

patologia, *n.f.* pathology.

pàtos, *n.f.* pathos.

pàtria, *n.f.* country; fatherland, homeland.

patriarca, *n.m.* patriarch.

patrigno, *n.m.* stepfather.

patrimònio, *n.m.* patrimony, inheritance; estate.

patriòta, *n.m.* patriot.

patriòttico, *adj.* patriotic.

patriottismo, *n.m.* patriotism.

patronato, *n.m.* patronage.

patròno, *n.m.* patron.

pattinare, *vb.* skate.

pàttino, *n.m.* skate.

patto, *n.m.* pact; compact.

pattuglia, *n.f.* patrol.

paúra, *n.f.* fear. **aver p.,** be afraid.

pauroso, *adj.* fearful.

pàusa, *n.f.* pause.

pavimentare, *vb.* pave.

pavimentazione, *n.f.* flooring.

pavimento, *n.m.* floor.

pavone, *n.m.* peacock.

pavoneggiarsi, *vb.* strut.

paziènte, *adj.* patient.

paziènza, *n.f.* patience.

pazzia, *n.f.* insanity, madness, lunacy.

pazzo, *adj.* crazy, insane, mad.

peccaminoso, *adj.* sinful.

peccare, *vb.* sin.

peccato, *n.m.* sin; pity; shame. **che p.!** what a pity!

peccatore, *n.m.* sinner.

pece, *n.f.* pitch.

pechblenda, *n.f.* pitchblende.

pècora, *n.f.* sheep, ewe.

peculiare, *adj.* peculiar.

peculiarità, *n.f.* peculiarity.

pecuniàrio, *adj.* pecuniary.

pedagogia, *n.f.* pedagogy.

pedagògo, *n.m.* pedagogue.

pedale, *n.m.* pedal.

pedante, *n.m.* pedant.

pedèstre, *adj.* pedestrian.

pediàtra, *n.m.* pediatrician.

pedina, *n.f.* pawn.

pedonale, *adj.* pedestrian.

pedone, *n.m.* pedestrian.

pèggio, *adv.* worse. **il p.,** worst.

peggiore, *adj.* worse. **il p.,** the worst.

pegno, *n.m.* pledge; pawn.

pelare, *vb.* skin, peel.

pèlle, *n.f.* skin, hide. **p. verniciata,** patent leather.

pellegrinàggio, *n.m.* pilgrimage.

pellegrino, *n.m.* pilgrim.

pelliccia, *n.f.* fur.

pellicciaio, *n.m.* furrier.

pellicola, *n.f.* film, movie.

pellirossa, *n.m.* (American) Indian.

pelo, *n.m.* hair.

peloso, *adj.* hairy.

peluria, *n.f.* down.

pèlvi, *n.f.* pelvis.

pena, *n.f.* pain; penalty.

pendènte, **1.** *n.m.* pendant. **2.** *adj.* pending.

pendènza, *n.f.* slope.

pèndere, *vb.* hang.

pendìo, *n.m.* slope, slant, incline.

penetrante, *adj.* penetrating, discerning.

penetrare, *vb.* penetrate.

penetrazione, *n.f.* penetration, insight.

penicillina, *n.f.* penicillin.

penisola, *n.f.* peninsula.

penitènte, *n.m. and adj.* penitent.

penitènza, *n.f.* penitence, penance.

penna, *n.f.* feather, plume; pen. **p. stilogràfica,** fountain pen.

pennèllo, *n.m.* brush.

pennuto, *adj.* feathered.

pensare, *vb.* think.

pensatore, *n.m.* thinker.

pensièro, *n.m.* thought.

pensilina, *n.f.* marquee.

pensionante, *n.m.* boarder.

pensione, *n.f.* pension, boarding house.

pensoso, *adj.* pensive, thoughtful.

pentimento, *n.m.* repentance.

pentirsi, *vb.* repent, rue.

pèntola, *n.f.* kettle, pot. **p. a pressione,** pressure cooker.

penùria, *n.f.* penury.

penzolare, *vb.* dangle.

pepe, *n.m.* pepper.

pepita, *n.f.* nugget.

per, *prep.* for; through; by; per.

pera, *n.f.* pear.

per cènto, *adv.* per cent.

percentuale, *n.m.* percentage.

percettibile, *adj.* perceptible.

percezione, *n.f.* perception.

perché, **1.** *adv.* why. **2.** *conj.* because; for.

perciò, *adv.* therefore.

percorrènza, *n.f.* distance travelled.

percorso, *n.m.* passage (of time); lapse; route.

percòssa, *n.f.* blow; (*pl.*) beating.

percuòtere, *vb.* hit, strike, maul; tap.

pèrdere, *vb.* lose; miss; forfeit; leak.

pèrdita, *n.f.* loss; bereavement; forfeiture; leakage.

perdizione, *n.f.* perdition.

perdonare, *vb.* pardon, forgive.

perdono, *n.m.* pardon, forgiveness.

perènne, *adj.* perennial.

perentòrio, *adj.* peremptory.

perfettamente, *adv.* perfectly.

perfètto, *adj.* perfect, flawless.

perfezionare, *vb.* perfect.

perfezione, *n.f.* perfection.

perfino, *adv.* even.

perforare, *vb.* punch.

perforazione, *n.f.* perforation.

pergamena, *n.f.* parchment.

pergolato, *n.m.* arbor, bower.

pericolo, *n.m.* danger, peril, jeopardy.

pericoloso, *adj.* dangerous, perilous.

periferia, *n.f.* periphery, outskirts.

perimetro, *n.m.* perimeter.

periòdico, **1.** *n.m.* periodical, magazine. **2.** *adj.* periodical; periodic; serial.

periodo, *n.m.* period, term.

perire, *vb.* perish.

pèrla, *n.f.* pearl.

permanènte, *adj.* permanent.

permanènza, *n.f.* stay.

permeare, *vb.* permeate.

permesso, *n.m.* permission, leave, license.

permèttere, *vb.* permit, let, allow.

permissibile, *adj.* permissible.

pernàcchia, *n.f.* Bronx cheer.

pernice, *n.f.* partridge.

pernicioso, *adj.* pernicious.

pèrno, *n.m.* pivot.

pero, *n.m.* pear-tree.

però, *adv.* however; though.

perpendicolare, *n.m. and adj.* perpendicular.

perpetrare, *vb.* perpetrate.

perpètuo, *adj.* perpetual.

perplessità, *n.f.* perplexity, bafflement, bewilderment, quandary.

perplèsso, *adj.* perplexed, baffled, bewildered.

persecuzione, *n.f.* persecution.

perseguire, *vb.* pursue.

perseguitare, *vb.* persecute.

perseveranza, *n.f.* perseverance.

perseverare, *vb.* persevere.

pèrsico, *adj.* pesce p., bass (fish); perch.

persistènte, *adj.* persistent.

persistere, vb. persist.
persona, n.f. person. p. anziana, senior citizen.
personaggio, n.m. personage.
personale, 1. n.m. personnel, staff. 2. adj. personal.
personalità, n.f. personality.
personalmente, adv. personally.
persuadere, vb. persuade.
persuasivo, adj. persuasive.
pèrtica, n.f. perch; pole.
pertinènte, adj. pertinent, relevant.
perturbare, vb. perturb.
pervàdere, vb. pervade.
perversione, n.f. perversion.
pervèrso, adj. perverse.
pervertire, vb. pervert, debauch.
pesante, adj. heavy.
pesare, vb. weigh; balance.
pesca, n.f. fishing.
pèsca, n.f. peach.
pescàggio, n.m. draft.
pescare, vb. fish; angle.
pescatore, n.m. fisherman.
pesce, n.m. fish. p. rosso, goldfish. p. spada, swordfish.
pescecane, n.m. shark; profiteer.
peschièra, n.f. fishery.
pesciolino, n.f. minnow.
pescivéndola, n.f. fishwife.
pescivéndolo, n.m. fishmonger.
pèsco, n.m. peach-tree.
peso, n.m. weight. p. màssimo, heavyweight. p. lòrdo, gross weight.
pessimismo, n.m. pessimism.
pestare, vb. pound.
pèste, n.f. plague.
pestilènza, n.f. pestilence.
pesto, adj. pounded, crushed. òcchio p., black eye.
pètalo, n.m. petal.
petardo, n.m. firecracker.
petizione, n.f. petition.
petròlio, n.m. petroleum. p. raffinato, kerosene.
pettégola, n.f. gossip.
pettegolare, vb. gossip.
pettegolezzo, n.m. gossip.
pettègolo, 1. n.m. gossip. 2. adj. gossipy.
pettinare, vb. comb.
pettinatura, n.f. coiffure, hairdo.
pèttine, n.m. comb.
pettirosso, n.m. robin.
pètto, n.m. chest; bosom; (meat) brisket.
petulante, adj. petulant.
petulanza, n.f. petulance, buff.
pèzza, n.f. patch.
pezzettino, n.m. little bit, mite.
pezzetto, n.m. scrap.
pèzzo, n.m. piece, bit, chunk. p. di ricàmbio, spare part. p. gròsso, big shot.
piacere, 1. n.m. pleasure. 2. vb. please.
piacévole, adj. pleasing, pleasant, agreeable, genial.

piacevolezza, n.f. pleasing quality, geniality.
piacevolmente, adv. pleasingly, agreeably, genially.
piaga, n.f. sore; wound.
piagnucolare, vb. whimper, snivel, blubber.
piagnucolone, n.m. whiner, whimperer, sniveler, complainer.
piagnucoloso, adj. maudlin.
pialla, n.f. plane.
piallàccio, n.m. veneer.
piallare, vb. plane.
pianeta, n.m. planet.
piàngere, vb. weep, cry, bewail, mourn.
pianista, n.m. pianist.
piano, 1. n.m. plan; story; floor; plane. 2. adj. level, flat.
pianofòrte, n.m. piano.
pianta, n.f. plant; plan, plot; map.
piantagione, n.f. plantation.
piantare, vb. plant.
piantatore, n.m. planter.
pianto, n.m. crying, weeping.
pianura, n.f. plain.
pianuzza, n.f. halibut.
piattaforma, n.f. platform, dais.
piattino, n.m. saucer.
piatto, 1. n.m. dish, plate; cymbal. 2. adj. flat.
piazza, n.f. square.
piazzale, n.m. large square.
piccante, adj. piquant.
picchetto, n.m. picket.
picchiare, vb. hit, smack, sock, clout, cuff, rap.
picchiata, n.f. nose dive.
picchiatore, n.m. divebomber.
picchio, n.m. blow, rap.
piccione, n.m. pigeon. p. viaggiatore, homing pigeon, carrier pigeon.
picco, n.m. peak, crag.
piccolo, adv. little, small, petty.
piccone, n.m. pick.
pidòcchio, n.m. louse.
piède, n.m. foot. p. stòrto, clubfoot.
piedestallo, n.m. pedestal.
piega, n.f. fold, crease, pleat, tuck.
piegare, vb. fold, bend, crease.
pieghévole, adj. pliable, pliant.
Piemonte, n.m. Piedmont.
piemontese, adj. Piedmontese.
pienamente, adv. fully.
pienezza, n.f. fullness.
pieno, adj. full.
pietà, n.f. mercy, pity, piety.
pietoso, adj. merciful, pitiful.
piètra, n.f. stone. p. angolare, cornerstone. p. focaia, flint.
pietrificare, vb. petrify.
piffero, n.m. fife, fifer, piper.
pigiama, n.m.pl. pyjamas.
pigione, n.f. rent.
pigmento, n.m. pigment.
pigro, adj. lazy.
pila, n.f. battery. p. a secco, dry cell.
pilastro, n.m. pillar.

pillola, n.f. pill.
pilone, n.m. pier; pillar.
pilòta, n.m. pilot.
pinna, n.f. fin.
pinnàcolo, n.m. pinnacle.
pino, n.m. pine.
pinta, n.f. pint.
pinze, n.f.pl. pincers, pliers.
pinzette, n.f.pl. pliers.
pìo, adj. pious.
pioggerèlla, n.f. drizzle.
piòggia, n.f. rain.
piombo, n.m. lead.
pionière, n.m. pioneer.
piòta, n.f. turf, sod.
piòvere, vb. rain.
piovigginare, vb. drizzle.
piovoso, adj. rainy.
pipa, n.f. pipe.
pipistrèllo, n.m. bat.
pipita, n.f. hangnail.
piràmide, n.f. pyramid.
pirata, n.m. pirate.
piròscafo, n.m. steamship.
pisèllo, n.m. pea.
pisolino, n.m. doze, snooze, nap.
pista, n.f. (race) track; (race) course; (cinder) path. p. d'atterràggio, landing strip, runway.
pistola, n.f. pistol.
pistone, n.m. piston.
pittore, n.m. painter.
pittoresco, adj. picturesque.
pittura, n.f. painting.
più, 1. adv. more; per di p., moreover; per lo p., mostly. 2. prep. plus.
piuma, n.f. plume, feather.
piumàggio, n.m. plumage.
piumato, adj. plumed, feathered.
piumino, n.m. feathers.
piumoso, adj. feathery.
piuòlo, n.m. peg, rung.
piuttosto, adv. rather.
pizza, n.f. pizza.
pizzicòtto, n.m. nip, pinch.
pizzo, n.m. lace.
placare, vb. appease, placate.
placatore, n.m. appeaser.
plàcido, adj. placid.
plàgio, n.m. plagiarism.
planetàrio, 1. n.m. planetarium. 2. adj. planetary.
plasma, n.m. plasma.
plàstica, n.f. plastic.
plàstico, adj. plastic.
plàtino, n.m. platinum.
plausibile, adj. plausible.
plebàglia, n.f. mob, rabble.
plebiscito, n.m. plebiscite.
pleurìte, n.f. pleurisy.
plotone, n.m. platoon.
plùmbeo, adj. leaden.
plurale, n.m. and adj. plural.
plutocrate, n.m. plutocrat.
pneumàtico, 1. n. tire. 2. adj. pneumatic.
po', n.m. un p., a little, somewhat.
pòchi, adj. and pron. pl. few.
pòco, n. and adv. little. fra p.,

in a short time, presently, soon.

poèma, *n.m.* poem.

poesìa, *n.f.* poem; poetry.

poèta, *n.f.* poet.

poetéssa, *n.f.* woman poet.

poètico, *adj.* poetic.

pòi, *adv.* then.

poìana, *n.f.* buzzard.

poichè, *conj.* since.

polacca, *n.f.* polonaise.

polacco, *adj.* Polish.

polare, *adj.* polar.

poligamia, *n.f.* polygamy.

poliglòtto, *adj.* polyglot.

poligono, *n.m.* polygon.

politica, *n.f.* politics; policy.

politico, 1. *n.m.* politician. **2.** *adj.* politic, political.

polizìa, *n.f.* police.

poliziòtto, *n.m.* policeman, cop.

polizza, *n.f.* policy.

pollame, *n.m.* poultry.

pòllice, *n.m.* thumb; big toe; inch.

pòlline, *n.m.* pollen.

pollo, *n.m.* chicken, fowl.

polmonàre, *adj.* pulmonary.

polmóne, *n.m.* lung.

polmonìte, *n.f.* pneumonia.

pòlo, *n.m.* pole.

Polònia, *n.f.* Poland.

polpa, *n.f.* pulp.

polpétta, *n.f.* meat-ball; croquette.

polsino, *n.m.* cuff.

polso, *n.m.* wrist; pulse.

poltróna, *n.f.* armchair, easychair.

pólvere, *n.m.* dust; powder.

polverizzare, *vb.* pulverize; powder.

polveroso, *adj.* dusty.

pomerìggio, *n.m.* afternoon.

pomo, *n.m.* apple.

pomodòro, *n.m.* tomato.

pompa, *n.f.* pump; pomp. **p. da incèndio,** fire engine.

pompare, *vb.* pump.

pompèlmo, *n.m.* grapefruit.

pompière, *n.m.* fireman.

pompóso, *adj.* pompous.

pónce, *n.m.* punch.

ponderàre, *vb.* ponder.

ponderóso, *adj.* ponderous.

ponte, *n.m.* bridge; deck; span. **p. levatòio,** drawbridge. **p. sospeso,** suspension bridge.

pontéfice, *n.m.* pontiff.

pontile, *n.m.* gangplank.

pontóne, *n.m.* pontoon.

popelìna, *n.f.* broadcloth.

popolàre, *adj.* popular.

popolarità, *n.f.* popularity.

popolazióne, *n.f.* population.

pòpolo, *n.m.* people, folk.

poppa, *n.f.* stern; breast.

pòrca, *n.f.* sow; ridge.

porcellàna, *n.f.* porcelain, china.

porcellìno, *n.m.* piglet. **p. d'India,** guinea pig.

porcile, *n.m.* sty.

pòrco, *n.m.* hog, pig, swine.

pornografìa, *n.f.* pornography.

pòro, *n.m.* pore.

poróso, *adj.* porous.

pórpora, *n.f.* purple.

porre, *vb.* put, place, set, lay.

pòrro, *n.m.* leek.

pòrta, *n.f.* door; gate; gateway; goal.

portabagagli, *n.m.* porter.

portacénere, *n.m.* ash-tray.

portaèrei, *n.m.* aircraft carrier, flat-top.

portafògli, *n.m.* billfold, wallet; pocketbook.

portafòglio, *n.m.* portfolio.

portafortuna, *n.m.* good-luck charm; mascot.

portale, *n.m.* portal.

portare, *vb.* carry, bear, bring; wear.

portasigarette, *n.m.* cigaretteholder.

portàta, *n.f.* reach; range; scope.

portàtile, *adj.* portable.

portatóre, *n.m.* carrier, bearer.

portavóce, *n.m.* spokesman, mouthpiece.

pòrtico, *n.m.* portico, porch.

portièra, *n.f.* door.

portière, *n.m.* goal-keeper; porter.

portinàio, *n.m.* doorman, concierge.

portinerìa, *n.f.* concierge's office.

pòrto, *n.m.* port, harbor, haven, inlet.

Portogallo, *n.m.* Portugal.

portoghése, *adj.* Portuguese.

portóne, *n.m.* gate.

porzióne, *n.f.* portion, helping, share.

pòsa, *n.f.* pose; exposure.

posàre, *vb.* pose.

posàrsi, *vb.* perch.

posaterìa, *n.f.* cutlery.

posatóio, *n.m.* perch.

poscrìtto, *n.m.* postscript.

positìvo, *adj.* positive.

posizióne, *n.f.* position.

posporre, *vb.* postpone.

possedére, *vb.* possess, own.

possènte, *adj.* powerful.

possessìvo, *adj.* possessive.

possèsso, *n.m.* possession, belonging.

possessóre, *n.m.* possessor, owner.

possìbile, *adj.* possible.

possibilità, *n.f.* possibility.

possibilménte, *adv.* possibly.

pòsta, *n.f.* mail, post.

postàle, *adj.* postal.

postéggio, *n.m.* parking.

pòsteri, *n.m.pl.* posterity.

posterióre, *adj.* posterior, rear, back, hind.

posterità, *n.f.* posterity.

postìno, *n.m.* mailman, postman.

pòsto, *n.m.* place; post; room; spout.

potàssio, *n.m.* potassium.

potènte, *adj.* powerful, potent, forcible, mighty.

potènza, *n.f.* power, might.

potenziàle, *n.m. and adj.* potential.

potére, 1. *n.m.* power. **2.** *vb.* be able, can, may.

pòvero, 1. *n.m.* poor man, pauper. **2.** *adj.* poor.

povertà, *n.f.* poverty.

pozióne, *n.f.* potion.

pozzànghera, *n.f.* puddle.

pozzo, *n.m.* well; shaft. **p. nero,** cesspool.

prammàtico, *adj.* pragmatic.

pranzare, *vb.* dine.

pranzo, *n.m.* dinner.

praterìa, *n.f.* prairie.

pràtica, *n.f.* practice.

praticàbile, *adj.* passable; practicable.

praticaménte, *adv.* practically.

praticàre, *vb.* practice.

pràtico, *adj.* practical, businesslike. **p. di,** skilled in; acquainted with, familiar with.

prato, *n.m.* meadow, field; lawn.

preàmbolo, *n.m.* preamble.

preavvertìre, *vb.* forewarn.

precàrio, *adj.* precarious.

precauzióne, *n.f.* precaution.

precedènte, 1. *n.m.* precedent. **2.** *adj.* preceding, former, previous.

precedènza, *n.f.* precedence, right of way.

precèdere, *vb.* precede, go before, (in time) antedate.

precètto, *n.m.* precept.

precìnto, *n.m.* precinct.

precipitàre, *vb.* precipitate; *(refl.)* rush.

precipìzio, *n.m.* precipice.

precisióne, *n.f.* precision.

precìso, *adj.* precise.

preclùdere, *vb.* preclude.

precòce, *adj.* precocious.

precursóre, *n.m.* precursor, forerunner, harbinger.

prèda, *n.f.* prey.

predàre, *vb.* plunder, forage.

predatòrio, *adj.* predatory.

predecessóre, *n.m.* predecessor.

predestinazióne, *n.f.* predestination.

predicàre, *vb.* preach.

predicato, *n.m.* predicate.

predicatóre, *n.m.* preacher.

predilètto, *n. and adj.* favorite, darling.

predilezióne, *n.f.* predilection.

predire, *vb.* predict, foretell.

predisporre, *vb.* predispose, bias.

predominànte, *adj.* predominant.

predominìo, *n.m.* dominance.

prefabbricato, *adj.* prefabricated.

prefazióne, *n.f.* preface, foreword.

preferènza, *n.f.* preference.

preferìbile, *adj.* preferable.

preferire, vb. prefer.

prefetto, n.m. prefect.

prefisso, n.m. prefix. p. telese-lettivo, area code.

pregare, vb. pray, beg.

preghiera, n.f. prayer, request, plea.

pregiudicare, vb. prejudice.

pregiudizio, n.m. prejudice, bias.

pregna, adj.f. pregnant.

pregustare, vb. foretaste.

pregustazione, n.f. foretaste.

preistorico, adj. prehistoric.

preliminare, adj. preliminary.

preludio, n.m. prelude.

prematuro, adj. premature.

premeditare, vb. premeditate.

premere, vb. press.

premessa, n.f. premise.

premiare, vb. award (a prize to); reward.

premio, n.m. prize, award, premium.

premonizione, n.f. premonition.

premurosamente, adv. considerately.

premuroso, adj. considerate.

prenatale, adj. prenatal.

prendere, vb. take; get; catch.

prenotare, vb. reserve.

prenotazione, n.f. reservation.

preoccupare, vb. worry.

preoccupazione, n.f. worry.

preparare, vb. prepare.

preparatòrio, adj. preparatory.

preparazione, n.f. preparation.

preponderante, adj. preponderant.

preposizione, n.f. preposition.

prepotènte, 1. adj. overbearing, tyrannical. 2. n. bully.

prerogativa, n.f. prerogative.

presa, n.f. grasp, grip, hold; (electrical) outlet; socket. p. di tèrra, (electrical) ground.

presàgio, n.m. omen, portent.

presagire, vb. presage, predict, forebode, foreshadow, portend.

prescrivere, vb. prescribe.

prescrizione, n.f. prescription.

presentàbile, adj. presentable.

presentare, vb. present, introduce.

presentazione, n.f. presentation, introduction.

presènte, adj. present.

presentimento, n.m. presentiment, foreboding.

presentire, vb. forebode.

presènza, n.f. presence.

preservare, vb. preserve.

presidènte, n.m. president, chairman.

presidentessa, n.f. chair-woman.

presidènza, n.f. presidency, chairmanship.

presièdere, vb. preside.

prèssa, n.f. press.

pressappòco, adv. about, approximately.

pressione, n.f. pressure.

prèsso a, prep. near; by.

prestare, vb. lend, loan.

prestigio, n.m. prestige.

prèstito, n.m. loan.

prèsto, adv. soon, quickly; early.

presùmere, vb. presume.

presuntuosità, n.f. presumptuousness, forwardness.

presuntuoso, adj. presumptuous.

presunzione, n.f. presumption.

presupporre, vb. presuppose.

prète, n.m. priest.

pretèndere, vb. pretend; claim.

pretenzioso, adj. pretentious.

pretesa, n.f. pretense.

pretèsto, n.m. pretext.

prevalènte, adj. prevalent.

prevalere, vb. prevail.

prevedere, vb. foresee, forecast.

prevedìbile, adj. foreseeable.

preventivo, 1. n.m. estimate; budget; deterrent. 2. adj. preventive.

prevenzione, n.f. prevention.

previdènza, n.f. foresight.

previsione, n.f. forecast.

prezioso, adj. precious, valuable.

prezzémolo, n.m. parsley.

prèzzo, n.m. price, charge; fare; rate.

prigione, n.f. prison, jail.

prigionìa, n.f. imprisonment, captivity.

prigionièro, n.m. and adj. prisoner, captive.

prima, 1. n. première. 2. adv. first; before; beforehand. p. che, conj. before. p. di, prep. before.

primàrio, adj. primary.

primato, n.m. record.

primavera, n.f. spring.

primitivo, adj. primitive; original.

primo, adj. first; foremost; prime.

principale, adj. principal, chief, main, prime.

principalmente, adv. principally, chiefly, mainly.

principe, n.m. prince.

principessa, n.f. princess.

principiante, n.m. beginner.

principiare, vb. begin.

principio, n.m. beginning; principle.

priorità, n.f. priority.

prisma, n.m. prism.

privare, vb. deprive, bereave.

privato, adj. private.

privazione, n.f. deprivation.

privilègio, n.m. privilege.

privo, adj. devoid, void, lacking (in); destitute.

probàbile, adj. probable.

probabilità, n.f. probability, likelihood.

probità, n.f. probity.

problèma, n.m. problem.

procèdere, vb. proceed.

procedimento, n.m. proceeding; procedure.

procedura, n.f. procedure.

processione, n.f. procession.

procèsso, n.m. process; trial.

proclamare, vb. proclaim.

proclamazione, n.f. proclamation.

procrastinare, vb. procrastinate.

procura, n.f. proxy.

procurare, vb. procure.

procuratore, n.m. attorney; proxy.

prodezza, n.f. prowess.

prodigalità, n.f. prodigality, extravagance.

prodigare, vb. lavish.

prodigio, n.m. prodigy.

prodigo, adj. prodigal, extravagant, lavish.

proditòrio, adj. treacherous.

prodotto, n.m. product.

produrre, vb. produce.

produttivo, adj. productive.

produzione, n.f. production, output, yield.

profanare, vb. profane, defile.

profano, adj. profane.

proferire, vb. utter.

professare, vb. profess.

professionale, adj. professional.

professione, n.f. profession, calling, occupation.

professionista, n.m. professional; practitioner.

professore, n.m. professor.

profèta, n.m. prophet.

profètico, adj. prophetic.

profetizzare, vb. prophesy.

profezìa, n.f. prophecy.

profilo, n.m. profile.

profitto, n.m. profit.

profondamente, adv. deeply, profoundly.

profondità, n.f. profundity, depth.

profondo, adj. deep, profound; in-depth.

profumare, vb. perfume.

profumo, n.m. perfume, scent.

profuso, adj. profuse.

progettare, vb. project, plan.

progètto, n.m. project, plan, scheme. p. di legge, (legislative) bill.

prognosi, n.f. prognosis.

programma, n.m. program.

progredire, vb. progress, advance.

progredito, adj. progressed; advanced.

progressivo, adj. progressive.

progrèsso, n.m. progress, headway.

proibire, vb. prohibit, forbid, ban.

proibitivo, adj. prohibitive.

proibizione, n.f. prohibition, band.

proiettare, vb. project.

proièttile, n.m. projectile.

proiettore, n.m. projector.

proiezione, n.f. projection.

pròle, n.f. offspring, issue.
proliferazione, n.f. proliferation.
prolifico, adj. prolific.
pròlogo, n.m. prologue.
prolungamento, n.m. prolongation, extension.
prolungare, vb. prolong, extend.
promessa, n.f. promise.
prométtere, vb. promise.
prominènte, adj. prominent.
promiscuo, adj. promiscuous.
promozione, n.f. promotion.
promulgare, vb. promulgate.
promuòvere, vb. promote.
pronome, n.m. pronoun.
pronosticare, vb. forecast.
pronosticatore, n.m. forecaster.
prontamente, adv. readily.
pronto, 1. adj. ready; prompt; quick; willing. 2. interj. (telephone) hello.
promùncia, n.f. pronunciation.
promunciare, vb. pronounce.
propaganda, n.f. propaganda.
propagare, vb. propagate.
propèndere, vb. incline.
propensione, n.f. propensity.
propènso, adj. inclined.
propizio, adj. propitious, favorable.
proponènte, n.m. proponent.
proporre, vb. propose.
proporzionato, adj. proportionate.
proporzione, n.f. proportion.
propòsito, n.m. purpose. a p., apropos. di p., on purpose.
proposizione, n.f. sentence.
propòsta, n.f. proposal; proposition.
proprietà, n.f. property, belongings.
proprietàrio, n.m. proprietor.
pròprio, 1. adj. proper; own. 2. adv. just; right; quite.
propugnare, vb. advocate.
propugnatore, n.m. advocate.
propugnazione, n.f. advocacy.
pròra, n.f. prow, bow.
pròroga, n.f. delay; extension.
prorogare, vb. delay; extend.
prorómpere, vb. burst forth.
pròsa, n.f. prose.
prosàico, adj. prosaic.
prosciutto, n.m. ham.
proscrìvere, vb. proscribe.
prosperare, vb. prosper, thrive.
prosperità, n.f. prosperity, boom.
pròspero, adj. prosperous.
prospettiva, n.f. perspective.
prospettivo, adj. prospective.
prospètto, n.m. prospect.
prossimità, n.f. proximity, nearness, closeness.
pròssimo, 1. n. neighbor. 2. adj. next; nearest; forthcoming.
prostituta, n.f. prostitute.
prostrare, vb. prostrate.
prostrato, adj. prostrate.
protèggere, vb. protect, shield.
proteìna, n.f. protein.

protèsta, n.f. protest.
protestante, n.m. and adj. Protestant.
protestantésimo, n.m. Protestantism.
protestare, vb. protest.
protettivo, adj. protective.
protettore, n.m. protector.
protezione, n.f. protection.
protocòllo, n.m. protocol.
protone, n.m. proton.
protrarre, vb. protract.
protuberanza, n.f. protuberance, swelling, bulge, lump.
pròva, n.f. proof; test; ordeal; rehearsal; probation; trial. p. conclusiva, acid test. p. generale, dress rehearsal.
provare, vb. try; essay; rehearse; test.
proverbiale, adj. proverbial.
provèrbio, n.m. proverb, adage.
provincia, n.f. province.
provinciale, adj. provincial.
provocante, adj. defiant.
provocare, vb. provoke.
provocazione, n.f. provocation.
provvedere, vb. provide, supply.
provvidènza, n.f. providence.
provvisòrio, adj. temporary, acting, interim.
provvista, n.f. provision; supply, store, stock.
prudènte, adj. prudent.
prudènza, n.f. prudence.
prùdere, vb. itch.
prudore, n.m. itch.
prugna, n.f. plum.
prurire, vb. itch.
prurito, n.m. itch.
pseudònimo, n.m. pseudonym.
psichedèlico, adj. psychedelic.
psichiatra, n.m. psychiatrist.
psichiatria, n.f. psychiatry.
psicoanàlisi, n.f. psychoanalysis.
psicologia, n.f. psychology.
psicològico, adj. psychological.
psicòsi, n.f. psychosis.
ptomaìna, n.f. ptomaine.
pubblicare, vb. publish.
pubblicazione, n.f. publication.
pubblicità, n.f. publicity; advertising.
pùbblico, n. and adj. public.
pugilato, n.m. boxing.
pugilatore, n.m. boxer.
pugilìstico, adj. pugilistic, fistic.
Pùglie, n.f.pl. Apulia.
pugliese, adj. Apulian.
pugnace, adj. pugnacious.
pugnalare, vb. stab.
pugnalata, n.f. stab.
pugnale, n.m. dagger.
pugno, n.m. fist; punch.
pula, n.f. chaff.
pulce, n.f. flea.
pulcino, n.m. chick.
puledro, n.m. colt.
puléggia, n.f. pulley.
pulire, vb. clean; polish. p. a secco, dry-clean.

pulito, adj. clean; polished.
pulitore, n.m. cleaner.
pulitura, n.f. cleaning. p. a secco, dry-cleaning.
pulizia, n.f. cleanliness.
pullman, n.m. de luxe bus.
pùlpito, n.m. pulpit.
pàlsar, n.m. pulsar.
pulsare, vb. pulsate.
pungènte, adj. pungent, sharp, biting.
pùngere, vb. prick, sting.
pungiglione, n.m. sting.
pùngolo, n.m. goad.
punire, vb. punish, chastise.
punitivo, adj. punitive.
punizione, n.f. punishment, chastisement.
punta, n.f. tip.
puntare, vb. point; aim; wager, stake.
puntata, n.f. installment.
punteggiare, vb. punctuate.
punteggiatura, n.f. punctuation.
puntellare, vb. prop.
puntèllo, n.m. prop.
puntina, n.f. needle.
punto, n.m. point; period; dot; stitch. p. di vista, viewpoint; standpoint. due punti, colon. p. mòrto, stalemate, deadlock. p. esclamativo, exclamation point. p. e virgola, semicolon.
puntuale, adj. punctual.
puntura, n.f. puncture; sting.
pupàttola, n.f. doll.
pupillo, n.m. ward.
purchè, conj. provided that.
purezza, n.f. purity.
purga, n.f. purge.
purgante, n.m. and adj. purgative, laxative.
purgare, vb. purge.
purgativo, adj. cathartic.
purificare, vb. purify.
purità, n.f. purity.
puro, adj. pure.
putrefatto, adj. rotten, decayed.
putrefazione, n.f. rot.
pùtrido, adj. decayed, putrid, rotten; (egg) addled.
puttana, n.f. whore, tart.
puzzare, vb. stink, smell.
puzzo, n.m. stench, smell.
puzzolènte, adj. stinking, noisome.
puzzone, n.m. skunk.

Q

qua, adv. hither.
quadràngolo, n.m. quadrangle.
quadrante, n.m. quadrant; dial.
quadrare, vb. square.
quadrato, 1. n.m. square; ring. 2. adj. square.
quadrifònico, adj. quadraphonic.
quadro, n.m. picture; table; cadre.

quadro generale, n.m. overview.
quadrùpede, n.m. quadruped.
quàglia, n.f. quail.
quagliare, vb. curdle.
quagliata, n.f. curd, clabber.
qualche, adj. some.
qualcosa, pron. something; anything.
qualcuno, pron. somebody; anybody.
quale, adj. which. **il q.,** which; who.
qualifica, n.f. qualification.
qualificare, vb. qualify.
qualificazione, n.f. qualification.
qualità, n.f. quality.
qualunque, adj. whatever; whichever.
quando, adv. when. **di q. in q.,** from time to time, occasionally.
quantità, n.f. quantity, amount.
quanto, adj. and adv. how much; how many. **in q. che,** in so far as.
quantunque, conj. although.
quaranta, num. forty.
quarantèsimo, adj. fortieth.
quarantena, n.f. quarantine.
quarésima, n.f. Lent.
quartetto, n.m. quartet.
quartière, n.m. quarter. **q. generale,** headquarters.
quarto, 1. n. quarter. 2. adj. fourth.
quarzo, n.m. quartz.
quasar, n.m. quasar.
quasi, 1. adv. almost, nearly. 2. conj. as if.
quattòrdici, num. fourteen.
quattro, num. four.
quegli, adj.m.pl. those.
quel, adj.m.pl. those.
quel, adj.m.sg. that.
quella, adj. and pron. f.sg. that.
quelle, adj. and pron. f.pl. those.
quelli, pron.m.pl. those.
quello, 1. adj. that. 2. pron. that one; the former.
quèrcia, n.f. oak.
questa, adj. and pron. f.sg. this.
queste, adj. and pron. f.pl. these.
questi, pron. m.sg. this man.
questionàrio, n.m. questionnaire.
questione, n.f. question.
questo, 1. adj. this. 2. pron. this one; the latter.
quèstua, n.f. (church) collection.
qui, adv. here.
quietanza, n.f. receipt.
quiète, n.f. quiet, stillness.
quièto, adj. quiet.
quindi, adv. hence, therefore.
quindicèsimo, adj. fifteenth.
quindici, num. fifteen.
quindicinale, adj. fortnightly, bimonthly.
quintetto, n.m. quintet.

quinto, adj. fifth.
quota, n.f. quota; dues; fee.
quotidianamente, adv. daily.
quotidiano, n.m. and adj. daily, everyday.

R

rabàrbaro, n.m. rhubarb.
rabberciare, vb. botch.
ràbbia, n.f. anger, rage; rabies.
rabbino, n.m. rabbi.
rabbioso, adj. rabid.
rabbrividire, vb. shudder; shiver.
racchetta, n.f. racket.
raccògliere, vb. collect, gather; harvest, reap.
raccòlta, n.f. collection, gathering; harvest, crop.
raccòlto, n.m. crop, harvest.
raccomandare, vb. recommend; commend.
raccomandazione, n.f. recommendation.
raccontare, vb. tell, narrate.
racconto, n.m. story, tale, account, narrative.
raccorciamento, n.m. abbreviation; shortening.
raccorciare, vb. abbreviate; shorten.
raddrizzare, vb. straighten.
ràdere, vb. shave.
radiatore, n.m. radiator.
radicale, n.m. and adj. radical.
radicchiella, n.f. dandelion.
radice, n.f. root.
ràdio, n. 1. n.m. radium. 2. f. radio, wireless.
radioattivo, adj. radio-active.
radiocorrière, n.m. radio news.
radiofònico, adj. radio.
radiotelemetria, n.f. radar.
radiotelèmetro, n.m. radar.
rado, adj. sparse.
radunare, vb. gather; muster.
raduno, n.m. rally.
radura, n.f. glade, clearing.
ràfano, n.m. horse-radish.
raffazzonamento, n.m. reworking; patchwork.
raffermo, adj. stale.
ràffica, n.f. gust; squall; blast.
raffinare, vb. refine.
raffinatezza, n.f. refinement.
ràffio, n.m. claw.
rafforzare, vb. strengthen.
raffreddare, vb. chill.
raffreddore, n.m. cold.
raffrenare, vb. restrain, curb.
ragazza, n.f. girl, lass.
ragazzo, n.m. boy, lad.
raggiante, adj. radiant, beaming.
ràggio, n.m. spoke; ray, beam; shaft; radius.
raggiùngere, vb. arrive at, achieve, attain; reach; overtake.
raggiungibile, adj. attainable.
raggiungimento, n.m. achievement, attainment.
raggrumarsi, vb. clot.

raggruppare, vb. group.
ragionare, vb. reason; talk.
ragione, n.f. reason. **aver r.,** be right.
ragioneria, n.f. accounting.
ragionévole, adj. reasonable.
ragionière, n.m. accountant.
ragliare, vb. bray.
raglio, n.m. bray.
ragnatelo, n.m. cobweb.
ragno, n.m. spider.
ràion, n.m. rayon.
rallegrare, vb. cheer up, rejoice.
rallentare, vb. slow down, slacken.
ramaiuolo, n.m. ladle, scoop.
ramanzina, n.f. scolding.
rame, n.m. copper.
rammendare, vb. mend, darn.
rammendatura, n.f. mend, darn.
rammentare, vb. remind; (refl.) recollect.
ramo, n.m. branch, bough, limb.
ramolàccio, n.m. radish.
ramoscèllo, n.m. twig; sprig.
rana, n.f. frog.
ràncido, adj. rancid.
ràncio, n.m. mess.
rancore, n.m. rancor.
rango, n.m. rank.
rannicchiarsi, vb. huddle.
rannuvolarsi, vb. cloud over.
ranòcchio, n.m. frog.
ràntolo, n.m. rattle.
rannùncolo, n.m. buttercup.
rapa, n.f. turnip.
rapidamente, vb. rapidly, quickly, fast.
ràpido, 1. n.m. limited (train). 2. adj. rapid, fast, quick, speedy.
rapimento, n.m. abduction, kidnapping.
rapina, n.f. rapine, plunder. **uccèllo di r.,** n.m. bird of prey.
rapire, vb. abduct, kidnap.
rapitore, n.m. abductor, kidnapper.
rappezzare, vb. patch.
rapporto, n.m. relation; report; rapport; ratio; intercourse.
rappresàglia, n.f. reprisal, retaliation.
rappresentare, vb. represent; perform.
rappresentativo, adj. representative.
rappresentazione, n.f. representation; performance.
raramente, adv. rarely, seldom.
raro, adj. rare.
raschiare, vb. scrape; scratch out; erase.
raschino, n.m. eraser.
rasentare, vb. skirt, skim.
raso, n.m. satin.
rassegnarsi, vb. resign oneself.
rassegnazione, n.f. resignation.
rassicurare, vb. reassure.
rassomigliare, vb. resemble.
rastrellare, vb. rake.

rastrellièra, n.f. rack.
rastrèllo, n.m. rake.
rata, n.f. installment.
ratificare, vb. ratify.
ratto, n.m. rat; abduction.
rattoppare, vb. patch.
rattristare, vb. sadden.
rhuco, adj. hoarse, raucous.
ravanèllo, n.m. radish.
ravvivamento, n.m. revival.
ravvivare, vb. enliven; revive.
razionale, adj. rational.
razionare, vb. ration.
razione, n.f. ration.
razza, n.f. race, breed, kind.
razzo, n.m. rocket.
re, n.m. king.
reagire, vb. react.
reale, adj. real; royal.
realista, n.m. realist.
realizzare, vb. realize; fulfill.
realizzazione, n.f. realization; fulfillment.
realmente, adv. really.
realtà, n.f. reality.
reame, n.m. realm.
reattore, n.m. reactor; jet.
reazionàrio, adj. reactionary.
reazione, n.f. reaction.
recare, vb. reach; hand (over); (refl.) go, betake oneself.
recèdere, vb. recede.
recensione, n.f. review.
recensire, vb. review.
recènte, adj. recent; latter.
recentemente, adv. recently, lately.
recinto, n.m. enclosure, fence.
recipiènte, n.m. vessel; beaker; bin; container; holder.
recitare, vb. act; play; recite.
recitazione, n.f. recitation; acting.
reclamante, n.m. claimant.
reclamare, vb. claim.
réclame, n.f. advertising.
reclamizzare, vb. advertise.
reclamo, n.m. claim.
reclinare, vb. recline.
rèchuta, n.f. recruit.
reclutare, vb. recruit.
rèddito, n.m. income.
redentore, n.m. redeemer.
redenzione, n.f. redemption.
redigere, vb. draw up, draft; edit.
redimere, vb. redeem, reclaim.
rèdina, n.f. rein.
regalare, vb. present.
regale, adj. regal.
regalità, n.f. royalty.
regalo, n.m. present.
reggènte, n.m. regent.
règgere, vb. hold up; wield.
reggimento, n.m. regiment.
reggipètto, n.m. brassière.
reggiseno, n.m. brassière.
regime, n.m. regime, rule; diet.
regina, n.f. queen.
règio, adj. royal.
regione, n.f. region.
registrare, vb. register; record; (luggage) check.
registratore a filo, n.m. wire recorder.

registratore magnètico, n.m. tape recorder.
registrazione, n.f. registration.
registro, n.m. register; record.
regnare, vb. reign, rule.
regno, n.m. kingdom, realm, reign.
règola, n.f. rule; (pl.) menstruation.
regolamento, n.m. regulation.
regolare, 1. adj. regular. 2. vb. regulate, rule; set.
regolarità, n.f. regularity.
regolatore, n.m. regulator.
règolo, n.m. ruler. **r. calcolatore,** slide-rule.
reiterare, vb. reiterate.
relatività, n.f. relativity.
relativo, adj. relative.
relazione, n.f. relation; liaison.
religione, n.f. religion.
religioso, adj. religious.
reliquia, n.f. relic.
remare, vb. row.
remata, n.f. row.
reminiscènza, n.f. reminiscence.
remo, n.m. oar, paddle.
remòto, adj. remote.
rena, n.f. sand.
rèndere, vb. render; give back. **r. conto di,** account for.
rendiconto, n.m. statement.
rendimento, n.m. output.
rène, n.f. kidney.
reniforme, adj. kidney-shaped.
rènna, n.f. reindeer.
renoso, adj. sandy.
repellènte, adj. repulsive.
repertòrio, n.m. repertoire.
rèplica, n.f. reply, rejoinder; repeat performance.
replicare, vb. reply, rejoin; repeat.
repressione, n.f. repression.
reprimere, vb. repress.
repùbblica, n.f. republic; commonwealth.
repubblicano, adj. republican.
repulsivo, adj. repulsive; forbidding.
requisire, vb. requisition, commandeer.
requisito, n.m. requirement, qualification.
requisizione, n.f. requisition.
rescindere, vb. rescind.
residènte, adj. resident.
residènza, n.f. residence.
residuo, n.m. residue.
rèsina, n.f. rosin.
resistènza, n.f. resistance.
resistere, vb. resist.
respingènte, n.m. bumper, buffer.
respingere, vb. reject, repel, repulse.
respirare, vb. breathe.
respirazione, n.f. respiration.
respiro, n.m. breath, breathing.
responsàbile, adj. responsible, accountable, answerable, liable; amenable.
responsabilità, n.f. responsibility, liability.

responsivo, adj. responsive.
restare, vb. remain, stay.
restaurare, vb. restore.
restaurazione, n.f. restoration.
restituire, vb. restore; refund.
restituzione, n.f. restitution.
rèsto, n.m. remainder, remnant; change.
restringere, vb. restrict.
restrizione, n.f. restriction.
retàggio, n.m. inheritance.
rete, n.f. net; netting; network.
reticella, n.f. luggage rack.
reticènte, adj. reticent.
reticènza, n.f. reticence.
rètina, n.f. retina.
retribuzione, n.f. retribution.
retroattivo, adj. retroactive.
retroguàrdia, n.f. rear-guard.
retroscèna, n.f. backstage.
retrospettivo, adj. retrospective.
retrotèrra, n.f. hinterland.
retrovisore, adj. specchio **r.,** rear-view mirror.
rettàngolo, n.m. rectangle.
rettificare, vb. rectify.
rettificatrice, n.f. rectifier.
rèttile, n.m. reptile.
rettilineo, n.m. straightaway.
rètto, adj. straight.
rettòrica, n.f. rhetoric.
rettòrico, adj. rhetorical.
reumàtico, adj. rheumatic.
reumatismo, n.m. rheumatism.
reverèndo, adj. reverend.
revisione, n.f. revision.
revisore, n.m. (accounts) auditor; (proof) proof-reader.
rèvoca, n.f. revocation.
revocare, vb. revoke.
riabilitare, vb. rehabilitate.
riassùmere, vb. make a résumé of, summarize.
riassunto, n.m. abstract, résumé.
ribadire, vb. rivet.
ribalta, n.f. footlights.
ribàttere, vb. retort.
ribellarsi, vb. rebel, revolt.
ribèlle, 1. n.m. rebel, insurgent. 2. adj. rebellious, insurgent; refractory.
ribellione, n.f. rebellion.
ribes, n.m. gooseberry; currant.
ricadere, vb. relapse.
ricaduta, n.f. relapse.
ricalcitrante, adj. recalcitrant.
ricamare, vb. embroider.
ricambiare, vb. reciprocate, retaliate.
ricàmbio, n.m. exchange. **di r.,** spare.
ricamo, n.m. embroidery.
ricapitolare, vb. recapitulate, sum up.
ricattare, vb. blackmail.
ricattatore, n.m. blackmailer, extortioner.
ricatto, n.m. blackmail.
ricchezza, n.f. riches, wealth.
riccio, n.m. hedgehog.
ricciolo, n.m. curl.
ricciuto, adj. curly.

ricco, adj. rich, wealthy.

ricerca, n.f. search, quest; research.

ricercare, vb. search.

ricercato, adj. recherché; far-fetched.

ricetta, n.f. recipe.

ricettacolo, n.m. receptacle.

ricettivo, adj. receptive.

ricevente, n.m. recipient.

ricevere, vb. receive, get.

ricevimento, n.m. reception, party.

ricevitore, n.m. receiver.

ricevuta, n.f. receipt.

richiamare, vb. recall.

richiedente, n.m. applicant.

richiedere, vb. request, ask for; demand; entail; require.

richiesta, n.f. request; demand.

riciclare, vb. recycle.

ricompensa, n.f. recompense, reward.

ricompensare, vb. recompense, reward.

riconciliare, vb. reconcile.

ricongiungersi, vb. rejoin.

riconoscere, vb. recognize; acknowledge.

riconoscimento, n.m. recognition.

ricordare, vb. remember, recollect.

ricordo, n.m. remembrance, souvenir, keepsake, memento; record.

ricorrere, vb. recur; resort; have recourse.

ricorso, n.m. recourse; resort.

ricostruire, vb. reconstruct, rebuild.

ricoverare, vb. shelter.

ricovero, n.m. shelter.

ricuperare, vb. recover, recuperate; retrieve.

ricupero, n.m. recovery.

ridacchiare, vb. giggle, chortle.

ridere, vb. laugh.

ridicolo, 1. n. ridicule. 2. adj. ridiculous, laughable, ludicrous.

ridire, vb. say again.

ridotto, n.m. redoubt; foyer.

ridurre, vb. reduce, curtail; (music) arrange.

riduttore, n.m. adapter.

riduzione, n.f. reduction; (music) arrangement.

riempire, vb. fill.

rientranza, n.f. recess.

riesame, n.m. review.

riesaminare, vb. re-examine, review.

riferimento, n.m. reference.

riferire, vb. refer; (refl.) relate.

rifiutare, vb. refuse, decline.

rifiuto, n.m. refusal.

rifiuti, n.m.pl. refuse, garbage. r. nucleari, nuclear waste.

riflessione, n.f. reflection.

riflesso, n.m. reflection, glint; reflex.

riflettere, vb. reflect.

rifluire, vb. ebb.

riflusso, n.m. ebb.

riforma, n.f. reform, reformation.

riformare, vb. reform.

rifuggire, vb. shrink.

rifugiarsi, vb. take refuge.

rifugiato, n.m. refugee.

rifugio, n.m. refuge, shelter, asylum, haven.

riga, n.f. line, file, row.

rigaglie, n.f.pl. giblets.

rigettare, vb. reject.

rigidezza, n.f. rigidity, stiffness.

rigido, adj. rigid, stiff.

rigo, n.m. line; staff.

rigoglioso, adj. luxuriant.

rigore, n.m. rigor.

rigoroso, adj. rigorous, stringent.

riguardare, vb. regard, concern.

riguardo, n.m. regard. r. a, regarding.

rilassamento, n.m. relaxation, laxity.

rilassato, adj. relaxed, lax.

rilegare, vb. bind.

rilegatura, n.f. binding.

rilevamento, n.m. survey.

rilevante, adj. relevant, germane.

rilucente, adj. shiny, lustrous.

riluttante, adj. reluctant, loath.

riluttanza, n.f. reluctance.

rima, n.f. rhyme.

rimandare, vb. postpone, put off.

rimando, n.m. reference.

rimanente, n.m. remainder, rest.

rimanere, vb. remain, stay, abide.

rimarchévole, adj. noteworthy, remarkable.

rimare, vb. rhyme.

rimbalzare, vb. bounce, rebound.

rimbalzo, n.m. bounce, rebound.

rimbambimento, n.m. dotage.

rimbambirsi, vb. grow childish (in old age).

rimboccare, vb. tuck.

rimborsare, vb. reimburse, repay.

rimediare, vb. remedy.

rimedio, n.m. remedy.

rimettere, vb. put back; remit; reinstate; (refl.) get back.

rimodernare, vb. modernize, renovate.

rimorchiare, vb. tow.

rimorchiatore, n.m. tugboat.

rimorchio, n.m. trailer.

rimorso, n.m. remorse.

rimozione, n.f. removal.

rimpatriare, vb. repatriate.

rimpiàngere, vb. regret.

rimpianto, n.m. regret.

rimpiazzare, vb. replace.

rimpinzare, vb. cram, stuff.

rimproverare, vb. reprove, chide, rebuke, reproach, reprimand, upbraid.

rimprovero, n.m. rebuke, reproof, reproach, reprimand.

rimuovere, vb. remove.

rinascere, vb. be reborn.

rinascimento, n.m. renaissance.

rinascita, n.f. rebirth.

rinato, adj. born-again.

rinchiudere, vb. enclose.

rincréscere, vb. cause regret.

rincrescimento, n.m. regret.

rinforzare, vb. reinforce.

rinforzo, n.m. reinforcement.

rinfrescare, vb. cool; refresh; freshen.

ringhiare, vb. snarl.

ringhiera, n.f. railing, banister.

ringhio, n.m. snarl.

ringiovanire, vb. rejuvenate.

ringraziare, vb. thank.

rinnovamento, n.m. renewal.

rinnovare, vb. renew.

rinoceronte, n.m. rhinoceros.

rinomanza, n.f. renown.

rinomato, adj. renowned.

rintocco, n.m. knell.

rintracciare, vb. trace.

rinúncia, n.f. waiver.

rinunciare, vb. renounce, forego; waive.

rione, n.m. ward.

ripagare, vb. repay.

riparare, vb. repair, recondition.

riparazione, n.f. repair, reparation, redress.

ripercussione, n.f. repercussion.

ripètere, vb. repeat.

ripetizione, n.f. repetition.

ripetutamente, adv. repeatedly, again and again.

ripiano, n.m. ledge.

ripido, adj. steep; abrupt.

ripieno, 1. n.f. stuffing. 2. adj. stuffed.

riposante, adj. restful.

riposare, vb. rest, repose.

riposo, n.m. repose, rest, leisure.

riprendere, vb. retake; resume; reprehend.

riprensíbile, adj. reprehensible.

ripresa, n.f. revival; (music) repeat.

riprodurre, vb. reproduce.

riproduzione, n.f. reproduction.

riproduzione esatta, n.f. clone.

ripudiare, vb. repudiate.

ripudio, n.m. repudiation.

ripugnante, adj. repugnant, abhorrent.

ripugnanza, n.f. repugnance, abhorrence, loathing.

ripulsa, n.f. rebuff, repulse.

riputare, vb. repute.

riputazione, n.f. reputation, standing.

risanare, vb. heal.

risata, n.f. burst of laughter.

risatina, n.f. snicker.

riscaldare, vb. warm up, heat; (refl.) warm oneself; bask.

riscattare, vb. ransom.

riscatto, *n.m.* ransom.

rischiare, *vb.* risk, hazard; stake; venture.

rischio, *n.m.* risk, hazard, venture.

rischioso, *adj.* risky, hazardous.

risciacquare, *vb.* rinse.

riscuòtere, *vb.* shake; collect; cash.

risèrva, *n.f.* reserve.

riservare, *vb.* reserve.

riservato, *adj.* reserved, aloof.

risièdere, *vb.* reside.

riso, *n.m.* laughter; rice.

risoluto, *adj.* resolute, determined.

risoluzione, *n.f.* resolution.

risòlvere, *vb.* resolve, solve.

risonante, *adj.* resonant.

risonanza, *n.f.* resonance.

risonare, *vb.* resound, ring out.

risorgènte, *adj.* resurgent.

risorsa, *n.f.* resource.

risparmiare, *vb.* save.

risparmio, *n.m.* saving(s).

rispettàbile, *adj.* respectable.

rispettare, *vb.* respect.

rispettivo, *adj.* respective.

rispetto, *n.m.* respect, regard.

rispettoso, *adj.* respectful.

risplendènte, *adj.* resplendent, beaming, effulgent.

risplèndere, *vb.* be resplendent, shine, beam, glitter.

rispóndere, *vb.* answer, respond, reply.

risposta, *n.f.* answer, response, reply.

rissa, *n.f.* brawl, fight, affray.

ristorante, *n.m.* restaurant.

ristorare, *vb.* restore, refresh.

ristoratore, *n.m.* restaurant.

ristòro, *n.m.* refreshment.

risultare, *vb.* result; appear; be evident.

risultato, *n.m.* result, outgrowth.

risurrezione, *n.f.* resurrection.

risvegliare, *vb.* rouse.

risvòlta, *n.f.* lapel.

ritaglio, *n.m.* clipping, cutting.

ritardare, *vb.* delay, retard.

ritardo, *n.m.* delay, lag. in r., delayed, late.

ritenere, *vb.* retain.

ritenzione, *n.f.* retention.

ritirare, *vb.* retire, withdraw; (*refl.*) retreat, pull back, back out; flinch.

ritirata, *n.f.* retreat; toilet.

ritmico, *adj.* rhythmical.

ritmo, *n.m.* rhythm.

rito, *n.m.* rite.

ritornare, *vb.* return; revert.

ritorno, *n.m.* return.

ritrarre, *vb.* retract, pull back.

ritrasméttere, *vb.* relay.

ritrattare, *vb.* portray; retract.

ritratto, *n.m.* portrait.

ritroso, *adj.* unwilling, balky.

ritrovato, *n.m.* finding.

ritròvo, *n.m.* meeting-place, hang-out. r. notturno, cabaret.

rituale, *n.m. and adj.* ritual.

riunione, *n.f.* reunion; meeting, assembly.

riunire, *vb.* reunite; join; assemble; (*refl.*) meet, foregather.

riuscire, *vb.* succeed; turn out.

riuscita, *n.f.* success.

riuscito, *adj.* successful.

riva, *n.f.* bank; strand.

rivale, *n. and adj.* rival.

rivaleggiare, *vb.* rival.

rivalità, *n.f.* rivalry.

rivedere, *vb.* see again; review.

rivelare, *vb.* reveal, disclose.

rivelazione, *n.f.* revelation, disclosure, exposure.

rivendicare, *vb.* vindicate.

riverberare, *vb.* reverberate.

riverènte, *adj.* reverent.

riverènza, *n.f.* reverence; bow, curtsy, obeisance.

riverire, *vb.* revere.

rivestitura, *n.f.* facing.

rivista, *n.f.* magazine; review; revue; musical comedy; muster.

rivòlta, *n.f.* revolt.

rivoltare, *vb.* revolt.

rivoltèlla, *n.f.* revolver.

rivoluzionàrio, *adj.* revolutionary.

rivoluzione, *n.f.* revolution.

ròba, *n.f.* stuff. r. da chiodi, junk; nonsense.

robustezza, *n.f.* hardiness.

robusto, *adj.* robust, strong, hardy, hale, stalwart, sturdy.

ròcca, *n.f.* fortress; rock.

roccaforte, *n.f.* stronghold.

rocchetto, *n.m.* reel; spool.

ròccia, *n.f.* rock.

roccioso, *adj.* rocky.

rock, *n.m. and adj.* rock (music).

ródere, *vb.* gnaw, champ.

roditore, *n.m.* rodent.

rognone, *n.m.* kidney.

Roma, *n.f.* Rome.

romano, *adj.* Roman.

romàntico, *adj.* romantic.

romanzière, *n.m.* novelist.

romanzo, *n.m.* novel; romance.

romitàggio, *n.m.* hermitage.

rómpere, *vb.* break.

rompìbile, *adj.* breakable.

rompicollo, *adv.* a r., breakneck.

róndine, *n.f.* swallow.

ronzare, *vb.* buzz, drone; hum.

ronzino, *n.m.* nag.

ronzio, *n.m.* buzz, drone, hum.

ròsa, 1. *n.* rose. 2. *adj.* pink.

rosàrio, *n.m.* rosary.

ròseo, *adj.* rosy.

rosicchiare, *vb.* nibble.

rosolìa, *n.f.* German measles.

rossetto, *n.m.* lipstick; rouge.

rosso, *adj.* red.

rossore, *n.m.* blush.

rosticcerìa, *n.f.* grillroom.

rotàia, *n.f.* rail.

rotare, *vb.* rotate.

rotatòrio, *adj.* rotatory.

rotazione, *n.f.* rotation.

rotèlla, *n.f.* roller. r. del ginòcchio, knee-cap.

rotolare, *vb.* roll.

ròtolo, *n.m.* roll; scroll.

rotondo, *adj.* round.

rotta, *n.f.* rout.

rotto, *adj.* broken.

rottura, *n.f.* break, breakage; rupture.

rovesciare, *vb.* reverse; spill.

rovèscio, *n.m.* reverse; downpour. a r., backhand.

rovina, *n.f.* ruin, downfall, wreck.

rovinare, *vb.* ruin, wreck.

rovinoso, *adj.* ruinous.

rovo, *n.m.* briar.

rozzo, *adj.* rough.

rubacchiare, *vb.* pilfer.

rubare, *vb.* rob, steal, burglarize, filch.

rubicondo, *adj.* rubicund, ruddy, florid.

rubinetto, *n.m.* faucet, tap; cock.

rubino, *n.m.* ruby.

rude, *adj.* rude, rough, curt, abrupt, blunt.

rùdere, *n.m.* ruin.

rudezza, *n.f.* roughness, curtness, abruptness.

rudimento, *n.m.* rudiment.

ruga, *n.f.* wrinkle.

rùggine, *n.f.* rust.

rugginoso, *adj.* rusty.

ruggire, *vb.* roar.

ruggito, *n.m.* roar.

rugiada, *n.f.* dew.

rugiadoso, *adj.* dewy.

rullare, *vb.* roll.

rullìo, *n.m.* roll.

rullo, *n.m.* roller.

ruminare, *vb.* chew the cud.

rumore, *n.m.* noise, clatter, din.

rumoroso, *adj.* noisy, blatant.

ruòlo, *n.m.* list, roll; ròle.

ruòta, *n.f.* wheel.

rupe, *n.f.* cliff, rock.

rurale, *adj.* rural.

ruscèllo, *n.m.* brook.

russare, *vb.* snore.

Rùssia, *n.f.* Russia.

russo, *adj.* Russian.

rùstico, *n.m. and adj.* rustic.

ruttare, *vb.* belch.

rutto, *n.m.* belch.

rùvido, *adj.* rough.

S

sàbato, *n.m.* Saturday.

sàbbia, *n.f.* sand; grit.

sabbioso, *adj.* sandy.

sabotàggio, *n.m.* sabotage.

sabotare, *vb.* sabotage.

sabotatore, *n.m.* saboteur.

saccarina, *n.f.* saccharine.

saccarino, *adj.* saccharine.

saccheggiare, *vb.* sack, pillage, plunder.

sacchèggio, *n.m.* sack, pillage.

sacco, *n.m.* sack, bag. s. a

aria, (automobile) airbag. s.
da montagna, backpack.
sacramento, n.m. sacrament.
sacrificare, vb. sacrifice.
sacrificio, n.m. sacrifice.
sacrilègio, n.m. sacrilege.
sacrilego, adj. sacrilegious.
sacro, adj. sacred.
sadismo, n.m. sadism.
saggezza, n.f. wisdom.
saggiare, vb. sample, try, assay, test.
sàggio, 1. n.m. essay; sample, specimen; assay, test. 2. adj. wise, sage.
saggista, n.m. essayist.
sàgoma, n.f. loading gauge.
sagrestano, n.m. sacristan, sexton.
sagrestia, n.f. sacristy, vestry.
saia, n.f. denim.
sala, n.f. hall; room.
salame, n.m. salami; bologna.
salamòia, n.f. pickle.
salare, vb. salt.
salàrio, n.m. wages.
salato, adj. salty; briny.
saldare, vb. solder; (comm.) settle; balance.
saldatura, n.f. solder.
saldo, 1. n.f. (comm.) balance. 2. adj. steady, steadfast.
sale, n.m. salt.
sàlice, n.m. willow.
salire, vb. go up, ascend, mount.
saliscendi, n.m. latch.
salita, n.f. ascent.
saliva, n.f. saliva.
salmo, n.m. psalm.
salmone, n.m. salmon.
salone, n.m. salon; lounge.
salottino, n.m. boudoir.
salòtto, n.m. parlor.
salpare, vb. set sail.
salsa, n.f. sauce.
salsiccia, n.f. sausage.
salso, adj. salt, salty.
saltare, vb. jump, leap, bound, hop, gambol, skip, spring, vault.
salto, n.m. jump, leap, bound, hop, gambol, spring, vault. s. mortale, somersault.
saltuàrio, adj. desultory.
salubre, adj. salubrious, healthful.
salutare, 1. adj. salutary, beneficial. 2. vb. greet, salute, hail.
salutazione, n.f. salutation.
salute, n.f. health.
saluto, n.m. greeting, salute, salutation.
salvagente, n.m. life-buoy; life-preserver. isolòtto s., safety island.
salvare, vb. save, salvage.
salvaguardare, vb. safeguard.
salvaguàrdia, n.f. safeguard.
salvatàggio, n.m. salvage.
salvatore, n.m. savior.
salvezza, n.f. salvation.
salvo, 1. adj. safe. 2. prep. except, but, save.
sambuco, n.m. elder tree.

sanatòrio, n.m. sanatorium.
sàndalo, n.m. sandal.
sangue, n.m. blood; gore.
sanguinare, vb. bleed.
sanguinàrio, adj. bloodthirsty, sanguinary.
sanguinoso, adj. bloody.
sanguisuga, n.f. leech.
sanità, n.f. sanity.
sanitàrio, adj. sanitary.
sano, adj. healthy, sound, sane, wholesome.
santificare, vb. sanctify, hallow.
santità, n.f. holiness, sanctity.
santo, 1. n. saint. 2. adj. holy, sainted.
santuàrio, vb. sanctuary, shrine.
sanzionare, vb. sanction.
sanzione, n.f. sanction.
sapere, vb. know; know how to; savor, taste.
sapone, n.m. soap.
sapore, n.m. taste, flavor, savor.
saporito, adj. savory, tasty.
saporoso, adj. tasty, luscious.
sarcasmo, n.m. sarcasm.
sarcàstico, adj. sarcastic.
Sardegna, n.f. Sardinia.
sardèlla, n.f. sardine.
sardo, adj. Sardinian.
sarta, n.f. dressmaker.
sarto, n.m. tailor.
sasso, n.m. rock, boulder, stone.
satèllite, n.m. satellite.
sàtira, n.f. satire.
satireggiare, vb. satirize.
saturare, vb. saturate.
saturazione, n.f. saturation, glut.
saziare, vb. satiate, sate, cloy.
sbadato, adj. careless, heedless.
sbadigliare, vb. yawn.
sbadiglio, n.m. yawn.
sbagliare, vb. err, blunder, make a mistake, slip.
sbàglio, n.m. mistake.
sbalordire, vb. astound, dumbfound.
sbalzellone, n.m. jerk.
sbandare, vb. disband.
sbarazzare, vb. rid.
sbarcare, vb. disembark, land.
sbarco, n.m. disembarkation, landing.
sbarra, n.f. bar, rail.
sbarramento, n.m. fuòco di s., barrage.
sbarrare, vb. bar.
sbàttere, vb. slam, bang.
sbavare, vb. drivel.
sbirciare, vb. peek, look sideways.
sbocco, n.m. outlet.
sborsare, vb. disburse, pay out.
sbraitare, vb. squall.
sbriciolare, vb. crumble.
sbrigare, vb. expedite.
sbrinamento, n.m. defrosting (refrigerator.)
sbrinare, vb. defrost (refrigerator.)

sbucciare, vb. peel, pare.
sbuffare, vb. puff, chug.
sbuffo, n.m. puff, chug.
scabroso, adj. rugged.
scacchi, n.m.pl. chess.
scacchièra, n.f. chessboard, checkerboard.
scacco, n.m. chessman. s. matto, checkmate.
scadènza, n.f. maturity.
scadere, vb. fall due.
scaffale, n.m. shelf; bookcase.
scafo, n.m. hull.
scagliare, vb. hurl, sling.
scaglione, n.m. echelon.
scala, n.f. staircase; scale. s. a piuòli, ladder.
scalare, vb. scale, climb.
scalèo, n.m. stepladder.
scalo, n.m. station. s. mèrci, freight station. s. di smistamento, marshalling yards, freight yard.
scalzo, adj. barefoot.
scambiàbile, adj. exchangeable.
scambiare, vb. exchange.
scàmbio, n.m. exchange; (railroad) switch; points.
scampanare, vb. chime, peal.
scampanellata, n.f. ring.
scampanio, n.m. chime, peal.
scampo, n.m. escape.
scandagliare, vb. take soundings, sound out, fathom.
scàndalo, n.m. scandal.
scandaloso, adj. scandalous.
scandire, vb. scan (poetry).
scanso, n.m. avoidance. a s. di, so as to avoid.
scapaccione, n.m. cuff.
scappare, vb. escape.
scappata, n.f. escapade.
scappatòia, n.f. means of escape, loophole.
scarafàggio, n.m. beetle.
scaramuccia, n.f. skirmish.
scaramucciare, vb. skirmish.
scàrica, n.f. discharge.
scaricare, vb. unload, discharge, dump.
scàrico, n.m. discharge; spillway.
scarlattina, n.f. scarlet fever.
scarlatto, n.m. and adj. scarlet.
scarpa, n.f. shoe.
scarseggiare, vb. be scarce.
scarsezza, n.f. scarcity, dearth.
scarsità, n.f. scarcity, dearth.
scarso, adj. scarce, meager, scant.
scartamento, n.m. gauge.
scartare, vb. discard, scrap.
scarti, n.m.pl. rubbish.
scàtola, n.f. box; can.
scattare, vb. spring up; burst forth; spurt; dash.
scatto, n.m. spring; spurt; dash.
scavare, vb. excavate, dig out; burrow, delve.
scavo, n.m. excavation.
scégliere, vb. choose, pick, select.

scelta, n.f. choice, selection; triage.

scelto, adj. select, choice.

scèna, n.f. scene.

scenàrio, n.m. scenario.

scéndere, vb. descend, go down, get down, alight.

scervellato, adj. harebrained, madcap.

scèttico, 1. n. skeptic. 2. adj. skeptical.

scheda, n.f. card; form; ballot.

schedàrio, n.m. card-file.

schedina, n.f. (filing) card.

scheggia, n.f. chip, splinter.

scheggiare, vb. chip, splinter.

schèletro, n.m. skeleton.

scherma, n.f. fencing.

schermidore, n.m. fencer.

schermire, vb. fence.

schermo, n.m. screen.

schernire, vb. mock, scoff at, taunt.

scherno, n.m. mockery.

scherzare, vb. joke, jest, banter.

scherzo, n.m. joke, jest, banter; play; (music) scherzo.

scherzoso, adj. joking, playful.

schiaccianoci, n.m. nutcracker.

schiacciare, vb. crush, mash.

schiaffeggiare, vb. slap, buffet, smack.

schiaffo, n.m. slap, buffet.

schiarire, vb. clear up.

schiavitù, n.f. slavery.

schiavo, n.m. slave.

schièna, n.f. back.

schifoso, adj. loathsome.

schioccare, vb. snap.

schiuma, n.f. foam, froth, lather, suds. **s. per capelli**, hairspray.

schivare, vb. avoid, dodge, shun.

schizzare, vb. sketch; squirt.

schizzinoso, adj. squeamish.

schizzo, n.m. splash, splotch, dab; sketch, outline.

sci, n.m. ski.

scia, n.f. wake.

sciàbola, n.f. saber.

sciacallo, n.m. jackal.

scialacquare, vb. squander.

sciallo, n.m. shawl.

sciamare, vb. swarm.

sciame, n.m. swarm.

sciampagna, n.f. champagne.

sciampò, n.m. shampoo.

sciancato, 1. n. cripple. 2. adj. crippled.

sciare, vb. ski.

sciarpa, n.f. scarf, muffler.

sciàtica, n.f. sciatica.

sciatto, adj. sloppy; dowdy.

scientifico, adj. scientific.

scienza, n.f. science.

scienziato, n.m. scientist.

scimmia, n.f. ape; monkey.

scimpanzè, n.m. chimpanzee.

scindere, vb. split.

scintilla, n.f. spark.

scintillare, vb. sparkle, glitter, glisten.

scintillio, n.m. sparkle, glitter.

sciòcco, adj. stupid, foolish, dumb, silly.

sciògliere, vb. untie; loosen; resolve; dissolve; melt.

scioglimento, n.m. dénouement.

sciòlto, adj. loose.

scioperare, vb. strike.

sciòpero, n.m. strike.

sciroppo, n.m. syrup.

scissione, n.f. division; cleavage; split.

sciupare, vb. spoil; waste; fritter away.

sciupone, n.m. spendthrift.

scivolare, vb. slip; slide; glide.

scivolone, n.m. slip.

scodella, n.f. bowl.

scòglio, n.m. reef.

scolàttolo, n.m. squirrel.

scolare, vb. drain.

scolaro, n.m. pupil.

scollato, adj. décolleté.

scolorimento, n.m. discoloration.

scolorire, vb. discolor.

scolpare, vb. exculpate.

scolpire, vb. carve.

scommessa, n.f. bet, wager.

scomméttere, vb. bet, wager.

scomodità, n.f. inconvenience.

scomparire, vb. disappear.

scomparsa, n.f. disappearance.

scompartimento, n.m. compartment.

scompigliare, vb. disarrange.

scompiglio, n.m. disarray.

scomposto, adj. unseemly. **stare s.**, slouch.

scomunica, n.f. excommunication.

scomunicare, vb. excommunicate.

sconcertante, adj. disconcerting, upsetting, bewildering.

sconcertare, vb. disconcert, upset, faze, abash.

sconfiggere, vb. defeat.

sconfinato, adj. unbounded.

sconfitta, n.f. defeat, discomfiture.

scongiurare, vb. conjure.

sconnesso, adj. disconnected, disjointed.

sconnèttere, vb. disconnect.

sconosciuto, adj. unknown.

sconsolato, adj. disconsolate, comfortless.

scontare, vb. discount.

scontentare, vb. discontent.

scontènto, 1. n.m. discontent. 2. adj. discontented, disgruntled.

sconto, n.m. discount, rebate.

scontrarsi, vb. collide.

scontrino, n.m. check.

scontro, n.m. collision.

sconveniènte, adj. unbecoming, improper, unseemly.

sconvolgere, vb. upset, overturn; overthrow; derange; unsettle.

sconvolgimento, n.m. upset, overturn; overthrow; derangement.

scopa, n.f. broom.

scoperta, n.f. discovery.

scopèrto, adj. uncovered, bare.

scopetta, n.f. whisk-broom.

scòpo, n.m. purpose, aim.

scoppiare, vb. burst, explode.

scoppiettare, vb. pop.

scòppio, n.m. outbreak; explosion.

scoprimento, n.m. detection.

scoprire, vb. discover, uncover, bare, detect.

scopritore, n.m. discoverer.

scoraggiamento, n.m. discouragement, dejection.

scoraggiare, vb. discourage, dishearten.

scoraggiato, adj. discouraged, dejected, downhearted.

scorato, adj. broken-hearted.

scòrgere, vb. perceive, discern.

scórrere, vb. flow; peruse.

scorreria, n.f. foray.

scorrévole, adj. fluent.

scorrevolezza, n.f. fluency.

scorsòio, adj. running.

scòrta, n.f. escort.

scortare, vb. escort.

scortese, adj. discourteous, impolite.

scortesia, n.f. discourtesy.

scorticare, vb. flay.

scorza, n.f. bark.

scosceso, adj. steep.

scòssa, n.f. jolt; shake; shock.

scottare, vb. scald.

scottatura, n.f. scald.

Scòzia, n.f. Scotland.

scozzese, adj. Scotch.

screditare, vb. discredit, debunk.

scremare, vb. skim.

screpolare, vb. chap.

screpolatura, n.f. chapping; crevice.

scriba, n.m. scribe.

scribacchiare, vb. scribble.

scricchiolare, vb. creak.

scrigno, n.m. strong-box, safe, coffer.

scritto, n.m. writing.

scrittore, n.m. writer.

scrittura, n.f. writing; scripture.

scrivania, n.f. desk.

scrivere, vb. write.

scrofa, n.f. sow.

scròscio, n.m. gust.

scrostare, vb. scale.

scrùpolo, n.m. scruple.

scrupoloso, adj. scrupulous.

scrutare, vb. scrutinize, scan.

scudo, n.m. shield, escutcheon.

sculacciare, vb. spank.

sculacciata, n.f. spanking.

scultore, n.m. sculptor, carver.

scultura, n.f. sculpture, carving.

scuòla, n.f. school.

scuòtere, vb. shake, jog, jar; wag; (refl.) bestir oneself.

scuretto, n.m. shutter.

scusa, n.f. excuse, apology.

scusàbile, adj. excusable.

scusare, *vb.* excuse; *(refl.)* apologize.

sdraiarsi, *vb.* stretch out, sprawl.

sdrucciolare, *vb.* slide, slip.

sdrucciolévole, *adj.* slippery.

se, *conj.* if; whether.

sè, *pron.* himself; herself; itself; themselves.

sebbène, *conj.* although.

seccare, *vb.* dry; bore; hassle.

seccatura, *n.f.* bore, nuisance; hassle.

secchezza, *n.f.* dryness.

sécchia, *n.f.* bucket, pail, hod.

secco, *adj.* dry.

secolare, *adj.* secular; century-long.

sècolo, *n.m.* century.

secondàrio, *adj.* secondary.

secondo, **1.** *n.* second; half-back; mate. **2.** *adj.* second. **3.** *prep.* according to.

sèdano, *n.m.* celery.

sedativo, *n.m. and adj.* sedative.

sede, *n.f.* seat. **Santa S.,** Holy See.

sedere, *vb.* sit.

sèdia, *n.f.* chair, seat. **s. a dóndolo,** rocker.

sedicésimo, *adj.* sixteenth.

sédici, *num.* sixteen.

seducènte, *adj.* seductive, alluring.

sedurre, *vb.* seduce.

seduta, *n.f.* sitting.

sega, *n.f.* saw.

ségale, *n.f.* rye.

segare, *vb.* saw.

seggiovia, *n.f.* ski-lift.

seghettato, *adj.* jagged.

segmento, *n.m.* segment.

segnalare, *vb.* signal.

segnale, *n.m.* signal.

segnare, *vb.* mark; score.

segno, *n.m.* sign, cue, mark, token.

sego, *n.m.* tallow.

segregare, *vb.* segregate.

segretària, *n.f.* secretary.

segretàrio, *n.m.* secretary.

segreto, *n.m. and adj.* secret.

seguace, *n.m.* follower, hanger-on.

seguènte, *adj.* next.

seguire, *vb.* follow.

séguito, *n.m.* retinue, suite.

sèi, *num.* six.

selce, *n.f.* flint.

selciato, *n.m.* pavement.

selettivo, *adj.* selective.

selezione, *n.f.* selection.

sèlla, *n.f.* saddle.

sellare, *vb.* saddle.

selvaggina, *n.f.* game.

selvàggio, *n.m. and adj.* savage, wild.

selvàtico, *adj.* wild.

selvaticume, *n.m.* wildlife.

semàforo, *n.m.* traffic light.

semàntica, *n.f.* semantics.

semàntico, *adj.* semantic.

sembrare, *vb.* seem.

seme, *n.m.* seed.

semèstre, *n.m.* semester.

semicérchio, *n.m.* semicircle.

semidìo, *n.m.* demigod.

seminare, *vb.* sow.

seminàrio, *n.m.* seminary.

semplice, *adj.* simple, plain; no-frills.

semplicemente, *adv.* simply.

semplicità, *n.f.* simplicity.

semplificare, *vb.* simplify.

sèmpre, *adv.* always, ever; still, yet.

sempreverde, *adj.* evergreen.

sènape, *n.f.* mustard.

senato, *n.m.* senate.

senatore, *n.m.* senator.

senile, *adj.* senile.

senno, *n.m.* sense.

seno, *n.m.* breast, bosom. **s. frontale,** sinus.

sensale, *n.m.* broker.

sensazionale, *adj.* sensational, lurid.

sensazione, *n.f.* sensation.

senseria, *n.f.* brokerage.

sensìbile, *adj.* sensitive, sympathetic.

sensitivo, *adj.* sensitive.

sènso, *n.m.* sense; direction. **s. unico,** one-way (street).

sensuale, *adj.* sensual.

sentièro, *n.m.* path, trail.

sentimentale, *adj.* sentimental.

sentimento, *n.m.* feeling, sentiment.

sentire, *vb.* feel; hear.

sènza, *prep.* without. **s. piombo,** unleaded (gasoline).

separare, *vb.* separate, part.

separato, *adj.* separate.

separazione, *n.f.* separation, parting.

sepoltura, *n.f.* burial, interment.

seppellire, *vb.* bury, entomb, inter.

sequèstro, *n.m.* lien.

sera, *n.f.* evening.

serbare, *vb.* keep, preserve.

serbatòio, *n.m.* reservoir; cistern; tank.

serenata, *n.f.* serenade.

sereno, **1.** *n.f.* clear sky. **2.** *adj.* serene; clear; cloudless.

sergènte, *n.m.* sergeant.

seriamente, *adv.* seriously.

sèrie, *n.f.* series; row; array; set; suite; succession.

serietà, *n.f.* seriousness, earnestness.

sèrio, *adj.* serious, earnest. **sul s.,** earnestly.

sermone, *n.m.* sermon.

sèrpe, *n.m.* snake.

serpènte, *n.m.* serpent.

sèrra, *n.f.* greenhouse, hothouse.

serràglio, *n.m.* menagerie.

serratura, *n.f.* lock.

servile, *adj.* servile, menial, subservient.

servitù, *n.f.* servitude, bondage; servants.

servizièvole, *adj.* helpful, obliging.

servìzio, *n.m.* service; employ.

sèrvo, *n.m.* servant.

sessanta, *num.* sixty.

sessantésimo, *adj.* sixtieth.

sessione, *n.f.* session.

sessismo, *n.m.* sexism.

sessista, *adj.* sexist.

sèsso, *n.m.* sex.

sessuale, *adj.* sexual.

sèsto, *num.* sixth.

seta, *n.f.* silk.

setàceo, *adj.* silken.

sete, *n.f.* thirsty.

sétola, *n.f.* bristle.

setoloso, *adj.* bristly.

sètta, *n.f.* sect, denomination.

settanta, *num.* seventy.

settantésimo, *adj.* seventieth.

sètte, *num.* seven.

settèmbre, *n.m.* September.

settentrionale, *adj.* northern.

settimana, *n.f.* week.

settimanale, *n.m. and adj.* weekly.

sèttimo, *adj.* seventh.

severità, *n.f.* severity.

severo, *adj.* severe, dour, stern, strict.

sezionale, *adj.* sectional.

sezione, *n.f.* section.

sfacèlo, *n.m.* breakdown, ruin, debacle.

sfavore, *n.m.* disfavor, disgrace.

sfavorévole, *adj.* unfavorable.

sfèra, *n.f.* sphere.

sfèrza, *n.f.* whip, scourge, lash.

sferzare, *vb.* lash, whip, scourge.

sfìda, *n.f.* challenge, dare, defiance.

sfidare, *vb.* defy, challenge, dare.

sfidatore, *n.m.* defier, challenger.

sfidùcia, *n.f.* distrust.

sfilare, *vb.* defile; file off.

sfinito, *adj.* tired out; jaded.

sfiorare, *vb.* touch lightly, brush against, dab at, skim.

sfogare, *vb.* vent.

sfogo, *n.m.* expression; outlet; scope; vent.

sfondo, *n.m.* background.

sfortuna, *n.f.* misfortune, bad luck.

sfortunato, *adj.* unfortunate.

sforzare, *vb.* strain.

sforzarsi, *vb.* make an effort, endeavor, strive.

sforzo, *n.m.* effort, endeavor, exertion; stress.

sfregiare, *vb.* deface.

sfrontatezza, *n.f.* effrontery.

sfruttamento, *n.m.* exploitation.

sfruttare, *vb.* exploit.

sfuggire, *vb.* escape.

sfumatura, *n.f.* nuance.

sgabèllo, *n.m.* stool; footstool.

sgarberia, *n.f.* indignity.

sgargiante, *adj.* flamboyant, garish.

sghignazzare, vb. guffaw.

sghignazzata, n.f. guffaw.

sgomberare, vb. clear.

sgombro, n.m. mackerel.

sgonfiare, vb. deflate.

sgòrbia, n.f. gouge.

sgòrbio, n.m. blotch; daub; scrawl.

sgorgare, vb. empty, disgorge; gush, well forth.

sgradévole, adj. disagreeable.

sgranocchiare, vb. munch.

sgraziato, adj. graceless.

sgridare, vb. scold, bawl out, berate, chide.

sguardo, n.m. look, glance.

sì, pron. himself; herself; itself; themselves; yourself; yourselves.

sì, interj. yes.

sia, conj. either; or.

sibilare, vb. hiss.

sibilo, n.m. hiss.

siccità, n.f. dryness, drought.

Sicilia, n.f. Sicily.

siciliano, adj. Sicilian.

sicuramente, adv. surely; securely; assuredly.

sicurezza, n.f. safety, security, surety.

sicuro, adj. sure; secure; assured; safe.

sidro, n.m. cider.

siepe, n.f. hedge.

siero, n.m. buttermilk; whey; serum.

sifilide, n.f. syphilis.

sifilitico, adj. syphilitic.

sifone, n.m. syphon.

Sig., n.m. (abbr. for Signore) Mr.

sigaretta, n.f. cigarette.

sigaro, n.m. cigar.

sigillare, vb. seal.

sigillo, n.m. seal; cachet.

significare, vb. signify, mean, betoken, purport.

significativo, adj. significant.

significato, n.m. significance, meaning, import, purport.

signora, n.f. lady; Mrs.; madam.

signore, n.f.pl. (on toilets) ladies.

signore, n.m. gentleman; lord; Mr.; sir.

signoria, n.f. lordship.

silenziatore, n.m. silencer, muffler.

silenzio, n.m. silence.

silenzioso, adj. silent, quiet, noiseless.

sillaba, n.f. syllable.

silo, n.m. silo.

silòfono, n.m. xylophone.

silvicultore, n.m. forester.

silvicultura, n.f. forestry.

simbòlico, adj. symbolic.

simbolo, n.m. symbol.

similcuoio, n.m. artificial leather.

simile, adj. similar, alike, like.

similmente, adv. similarly, alike, likewise.

simpatia, n.f. sympathy.

simpàtico, adj. likeable, aggreable, pleasant, congenial.

simpatizzare, vb. sympathize.

simulare, vb. simulate.

simultàneo, adj. simultaneous.

sinceramente, adv. sincerely.

sincerità, n.f. sincerity.

sincero, adj. sincere, heartfelt.

sincronizzare, vb. synchronize.

sincrono, adj. synchronous.

sindacato, n.m. union.

sindaco, n.m. mayor.

sindrome, n.f. syndrome.

sinfonia, n.f. symphony; overture.

sinfònico, adj. symphonic.

singhiozzare, vb. sob.

singhiozzo, n.m. sob.

singolare, adj. singular.

singulto, n.m. hiccup.

sinistra, n.f. left.

sinistro, 1. n.m. accident. 2. adj. left; sinister.

sinistròrso, adj. and adv. counter-clockwise.

sino, prep. as far as, up to, till. s. da, since.

sinònimo, 1. n.m. synonym. 2. adj. synonymous.

sintesi, n.f. synthesis.

sintètico, adj. synthetic.

sintomo, n.m. symptom.

sintonizzare, vb. tune in.

sinuoso, adj. sinuous.

sipàrio, n.m. curtain.

sirèna, n.f. siren; mermaid.

siringa, n.f. syringe.

sistèma, n.m. system.

sistemare, vb. put in order, arrange, settle, fix up.

sistemàtico, adj. systematic.

sito, n.m. site.

situare, vb. situate.

situazione, n.f. situation, location.

slanciarsi, vb. rush, dash.

slancio, n.m. rush, dash; impetus; élan.

slavo, adj. Slavic.

sleale, adj. disloyal.

slealtà, n.f. disloyalty.

slitta, n.f. sleigh, sled.

slittamento, n.m. skid.

slittare, vb. slide, skid.

slogare, vb. dislocate.

sloggiare, vb. dislodge.

smaltare, vb. enamel, glaze.

smalto, n.m. enamel, glaze.

smantellare, vb. dismantle.

smarrire, vb. mislay, misplace, lose.

smarrito, adj. stray.

smascherare, vb. unmask.

smembrare, vb. dismember.

smentire, vb. give the lie to, belie.

smeraldo, n.m. emerald.

smeriglio, n.m. emery.

smèttere, vb. stop, quit.

smilitarizzare, vb. demilitarize.

smilzo, adj. gangling.

smobilitare, vb. demobilize.

smobilitazione, n.f. demobilization.

smontare, vb. dismount, alight, disassemble.

smorfia, n.f. grimace.

snaturare, vb. denaturalize.

snervamento, n.m. enervation.

snervare, vb. enervate.

sobbalzare, vb. jounce, jolt; throb.

sobbalzo, n.m. jounce, jolt.

sobborgo, n.m. suburb, (pl.) outskirts.

sobrio, adj. sober, somber.

socchiuso, adj. half-closed, ajar.

soccómbere, vb. succumb.

soccórrere, vb. succor, relieve.

soccorso, n.m. succor, relief.

sociale, adj. social.

socialismo, n.m. socialism.

socialista, n. and adj. socialist.

società, n.f. society; company.

S. delle Nazioni, League of Nations.

sociévole, adj. sociable, companionable.

socio, n.m. member; fellow; partner.

sociologia, n.f. sociology.

soda, n.f. soda.

soddisfacènte, adj. satisfactory.

soddisfare, vb. satisfy.

soddisfazione, n.f. satisfaction.

sòdio, n.m. sodium.

sòdo, adj. hard-boiled.

sofà, n.m. sofa.

sofà, n.m. davenport.

soffiare, vb. blow.

soffietto, n.m. bellows.

soffitta, n.f. attic, garret.

soffitto, n.m. ceiling.

soffocare, vb. suffocate, choke, smother, stifle.

soffrire, vb. suffer, tolerate, put up with.

sofisma, n.m. chicanery.

sofisticato, adj. sophisticated.

soggètto, 1. n.m. subject. 2. adj. subject, liable.

soggezione, n.f. awe; uneasiness.

sogghignare, vb. sneer.

sogghigno, n.m. sneer.

soggiogare, vb. subjugate, subdue.

soggiornare, vb. sojourn, stay.

soggiorno, n.m. sojourn, stay.

sògliola, n.f. sole.

sognare, vb. dream.

sognatore, n.m. dreamer.

sogno, n.m. dream.

solaio, n.m. loft.

solamente, vb. only, alone.

solare, adj. solar.

solatìo, adj. sunny.

solco, n.m. furrow; groove; rut.

soldato, n.m. soldier. s. sémplice, private.

soldo, n.m. penny.

sole, n.m. sun; sunshine.

solenne, adj. solemn.

solennità, n.f. solemnity.

solere, vb. be in the habit of, be accustomed to.

solidificare, vb. solidify.

solidità, n.f. solidity.

sòlido, n.m. and adj. solid.

solista, n.m. or f. soloist.

solitàrio, adj. solitary, lone, lonely, lonesome.

sòlito, adj. usual, habitual, accustomed.

solitúdine, n.f. solitude, privacy.

sollecitare, vb. solicit; urge.

sollécito, adj. solicitous.

solleticare, vb. ticklish.

sollevare, vb. raise, lift, heave; relieve, ease.

sollevazione, n.f. uprising.

sollièvo, n.m. relief.

solo, adj. alone, sole, only, single.

soltanto, adv. only.

solùbile, adj. soluble.

soluzione, n.f. solution.

solvènte, n.m. and adj. solvent.

somaro, n.m. donkey.

somiglianza, n.f. likeness, similarity.

somma, n.f. sum, amount, quantity.

sommare, vb. sum up, add.

sommàrio, n.m. and adj. summary.

sommèrgere, vb. submerge.

sommergìbile, n.m. submarine.

sommersione, n.f. submersion.

sommità, n.f. summit, top.

sondare, vb. probe; sound.

sonnecchiare, vb. doze, nap, drowse.

sonnellino, n.m. nap, doze.

sonno, n.m. sleep, slumber.

sonnolènto, adj. somnolent, drowsy, sleepy.

sonnolènza, n.f. somnolence, drowsiness.

sontuoso, adj. sumptuous.

soppiantare, vb. supplant, supersede.

soppiatto, adj. di s., stealthily.

sopportàbile, adj. bearable.

sopportare, vb. support, bear; abide, endure.

sopportazione, n.f. endurance.

soppressione, n.f. suppression.

sopprimere, vb. suppress, put down, quell.

sopra, adv. and prep. over, above; upon.

sopràbito, n.m. overcoat, top-coat.

sopracciglio, n.m. eyebrow.

sopraddetto, adj. aforesaid.

sopraffare, vb. overcome, overwhelm.

sopraindicato, adj. aforementioned.

soprannaturale, adj. supernatural.

soprano, n.m. soprano.

sopratutto, adv. above all.

sopravvivènza, n.f. survival.

sopravvivère, vb. survive, outlive.

sorbetto, n.m. sherry.

sórcio, n.m. mouse.

sòrdido, adj. sordid.

sordità, n.f. deafness.

sordo, adj. deaf.

sordomuto, n.m. deaf-mute.

sorèlla, n.f. sister.

sorgènte, n.f. source; spring; headwater(s).

sórgere, vb. rise, spring.

sormontare, vb. surmount.

sorpassare, vb. pass; surpass; cross over.

sorpasso, n.m. passing.

sorprèndere, vb. surprise.

sorpresa, n.f. surprise, astonishment.

sorrìdere, vb. smile.

sorriso, n.m. smile.

sorseggiare, vb. sip.

sorso, n.m. swallow; sip.

sòrta, n.f. sort.

sòrte, n.f. luck; lot.

sorteggio, n.m. drawing.

sorveglianza, n.f. surveillance, supervision.

sorvegliare, vb. oversee, supervise.

sospèndere, vb. suspend, discontinue.

sospensione, n.f. suspension; abeyance; stay.

sospettare, vb. suspect.

sospètto, 1. n.m. suspicion, hunch. 2. adj. suspicious, suspect.

sospettosamente, adv. suspiciously, askance.

sospettoso, adj. suspicious, distrustful.

sospirare, vb. sigh.

sospiro, n.m. sigh.

sòsta, n.f. stopping.

sostantivo, n.m. noun.

sostanza, n.f. substance.

sostanziale, adj. substantial.

sostare, vb. stop.

sostegno, n.m. backing, support; foothold.

sostenere, vb. uphold, sustain; maintain; support, back (up).

sostenitore, n.m. upholder, backer, sponsor.

sostituire, vb. substitute, replace.

sostituto, n.m. substitute, alternate.

sostituzione, n.f. substitution.

sottana, n.f. petticoat; skirt.

sotterfugio, n.m. subterfuge.

sotterràneo, adj. underground.

sottile, adj. subtle; thin, slim.

sotto, adv. and prep. under, underneath, below, beneath.

sottolineare, vb. underline.

sottomarino, adj. submarine.

sottomèttere, vb. submit.

sottomissione, n.f. submission.

sottopassàggio, n.m. underpass.

sottoporre, vb. subject.

sottoscritto, adj. undersigned.

sottoscrivere, vb. subscribe; sign.

sottosopra, adv. upside down, topsy-turvy.

sottotenènte, n.m. second lieutenant.

sottovalutare, vb. underestimate.

sottovènto, 1. n.m. lee. 2. adv. leeward.

sottovèste, n.f. slip; (pl.) underwear.

sottrarre, vb. subtract, deduct; (refl.) get out of, shirk.

sottufficiale, n.m. non-commissioned officer.

soviètico, adj. soviet.

sovranità, n.f. sovereignty.

sovrano, n.m. and adj. sovereign, ruler.

sovrintendènte, n.m. superintendent.

sovrumano, adj. superhuman.

sovvenzione, n.f. subvention.

sovversivo, adj. subversive.

sovvertire, vb. subvert; overthrow.

spaccare, vb. split.

spàccio, n.m. sale; shop.

spada, n.f. sword.

spadroneggiare, vb. act as if one owned the place; be bossy, domineer.

spaghetti, n.m.pl. spaghetti.

Spagna, n.f. Spain.

spagnuòlo, 1. n.m. Spaniard. 2. adj. Spanish.

spago, n.m. twine.

spalancare, vb. open wide.

spalla, n.f. shoulder.

spalleggiare, vb. back (up).

spalmare, vb. smear.

spanna, n.f. span.

spàragi, n.m. (pl.) asparagus.

sparare, vb. fire, shoot.

spàrgere, vb. scatter.

sparire, vb. disappear.

sparlare, vb. speak ill.

sparo, n.m. shot.

sparuto, adj. haggard.

spàsimo, n.m. spasm, pang.

spasmòdico, adj. spasmodic.

spassionato, adj. dispassionate.

spauràcchio, n.m. scarecrow.

spaventare, vb. frighten, alarm, appal, scare.

spavènto, n.m. fright, scare.

spaventoso, adj. fearful, frightful.

spàzio, n.m. space.

spazioso, adj. spacious, capacious; roomy, commodious.

spazzacamino, n.m. chimney-sweep.

spazzamine, n.m. nave s., mine-sweeper.

spazzare, vb. sweep.

spazzatura, n.f. sweepings, dust.

spazzino, n.m. street-cleaner; scavenger.

spàzzola, n.f. brush.

spazzolare, vb. brush.

specchio, n.m. mirror, looking-glass.

speciale, adj. special, especial.

specialista, n.m. specialist.

specialità, n.f. specialty.

specialmente, adv. specially, especially.

spècie, n.f. species.

specificare, *vb.* specify.

specifico, *adj.* specific.

speculare, *vb.* speculate.

speculazione, *n.f.* speculation.

spedire, *vb.* send, despatch, ship; remit.

speditore, *n.m.* sender, shipper, dispatcher.

spedizione, *n.f.* expedition; despatch; shipment; remittance.

spedizioniere, *n.m.* shipping agent.

spegnere, *vb.* put out; douse; switch off.

spendere, *vb.* spend; expend.

spensieratamente, *adv.* thoughtlessly, heedlessly, carelessly.

spensieratezza, *n.f.* thoughtlessness, heedlessness, carelessness.

spensierato, *adj.* thoughtless, heedless, careless, happy-go-lucky.

speranza, *n.f.* hope.

sperare, *vb.* hope.

spergiurare, *vb.* perjure oneself.

spergiuro, *n.m.* perjury.

sperimentale, *adj.* experimental; tentative.

sperimentare, *vb.* experiment.

sperone, *n.m.* spur.

spesa, *n.f.* expense, expenditure.

spesso, 1. *adj.* thick. 2. *adv.* often.

spessore, *n.m.* thickness.

spettacolare, *adj.* spectacular.

spettacolo, *n.m.* spectacle, show.

spettatore, *n.m.* spectator, onlooker, bystander.

spettro, *n.m.* specter, ghost; spectrum.

spezie, *n.f.pl.* spice.

spiacciare, *vb.* squash.

spiacévole, *adj.* unpleasant.

spiàggia, *n.f.* beach, shore.

spiare, *vb.* spy.

spiccagnolo, *adj.* freestone.

spidocchiare, *vb.* delouse.

spiegare, *vb.* explain; spread; unfold; unfurl.

spiegazione, *n.f.* explanation.

spiegazzare, *vb.* crinkle, crease, crumple.

spietato, *adj.* pitiless, merciless, ruthless.

spiga, *n.f.* ear (of grain).

spilla, *n.f.* brooch.

spillo, *n.m.* pin. s. **di sicurezza**, safety-pin.

spina, *n.f.* thorn; spine; (electric) plug. s. **dorsale**, backbone.

spinaci, *n.m.pl.* spinach.

spinetta, *n.f.* spinet.

spingere, *vb.* push, jostle, shove; thrust; urge.

spinta, *n.f.* push, shove; thrust.

spionàggio, *n.m.* espionage.

spione, *n.m.* spy.

spira, *n.f.* spire, coil.

spirale, *n.m. and adj.* spiral.

spiritismo, *n.m.* spiritualism.

spirito, *n.m.* spirit; wit.

spiritoso, *adj.* witty.

spirituale, *adj.* spiritual.

splèndere, *vb.* shine.

splèndido, *adj.* splendid, gorgeous.

splendore, *n.m.* splendor, brilliance.

spodestare, *vb.* dispossess.

spogliare, *vb.* unclothe; divest, despoil, strip; harry.

spola spaziale, *n.f.* space shuttle.

spoletta, *n.f.* fuse.

sponda, *n.f.* shore.

spontaneità, *n.f.* spontaneity.

spontàneo, *adj.* spontaneous.

spopolare, *vb.* depopulate.

spòra, *n.f.* spore.

sporàdico, *adj.* sporadic.

sporcare, *vb.* foul, soil.

spòrco, *adj.* dirty, foul, soiled.

spòrgere, *vb.* put out; project.

sportivo, 1. *n.* sportsman. 2. *adj.* sport.

sposa, *n.f.* bride, spouse.

sposalizio, *n.m.* wedding, espousal.

sposare, *vb.* marry, espouse.

sposi, *n.m.pl.* bride and groom; newlyweds.

sposo, *n.m.* bridegroom, spouse.

spostamento, *n.m.* displacement.

spostare, *vb.* displace.

sprecare, *vb.* waste.

sprèco, *n.m.* waste.

spregévole, *adj.* contemptible, despicable, mean.

spregiare, *vb.* despise.

spregiudicato, *adj.* broadminded.

sprèmere, *vb.* squeeze.

spremuta, *n.f.* squash.

sprezzante, *adj.* contemptuous, despising, scornful.

sprezzantemente, *adv.* contemptuously.

sprigionare, *vb.* release.

spruzzare, *vb.* spray.

sprofondarsi, *vb.* subside; sink.

spronare, *vb.* spur.

sprone, *n.m.* spur.

sproporzionato, *adj.* disproportionate.

sproporzione, *n.f.* disproportion.

spruzzare, *vb.* spout; spurt; splash; spatter.

spruzzo, *n.m.* splash, spatter.

spugna, *n.f.* sponge.

spuma, *n.f.* foam, froth.

spuntare, *vb.* appear; dawn.

spuntino, *n.m.* snack.

spùrio, *adj.* spurious.

sputacchiera, *n.f.* spittoon, cuspidor.

sputare, *vb.* spit.

squadra, *n.f.* squad, gang; team.

squadrone, *n.m.* squadron.

squalifica, *n.f.* disqualification.

squalificare, *vb.* disqualify.

squàllido, *adj.* squalid, bleak.

squallore, *n.m.* squalor, bleakness.

squama, *n.f.* scale.

squarciare, *vb.* gash, slash.

squàrcio, *n.m.* gash, slash.

squillare, *vb.* blare.

squillo, *n.m.* blare.

squisitezza, *n.f.* exquisiteness, daintiness, delicacy.

squisito, *adj.* exquisite, dainty, delicate.

Sra., *n.f.* (abbr. for Signora) Mrs.

sradicare, *vb.* eradicate; uproot.

sradicatore, *n.m.* eradicator.

sregolatezza, *n.f.* dissipation, debauchery.

stàbile, *adj.* stable.

stabilimento, *n.m.* establishment.

stabilire, *vb.* establish; set; appoint; settle.

stabilità, *n.f.* stability.

stabilizzare, *vb.* stabilize.

staccare, *vb.* detach, sever.

stacciare, *vb.* sift.

stàccio, *n.m.* sieve.

stàdio, *n.m.* stadium; stage.

staffière, *n.m.* footman; groom.

stagione, *n.f.* season.

stagnante, *adj.* stagnant.

stagnare, *vb.* stagnate.

stagnino, *n.m.* tinsmith; plumber.

stagno, *n.m.* pond; pool; tin.

stalla, *n.f.* stable.

stallo, *n.m.* stall.

stallone, *n.m.* stallion.

stame, *n.m.* stamen.

stamigna, *n.m.* bunting.

stampa, *n.f.* press; printing.

stampare, *vb.* print.

stampèlla, *n.f.* crutch.

stampino, *n.m.* stencil.

stampo, *n.m.* stamp; mold; die.

stancare, *vb.* tire.

stanco, *adj.* tired, fagged, weary.

standardizzare, *vb.* standardize.

stanga, *n.f.* shaft.

stanghetta, *n.f.* hang-over.

stantuffo, *n.m.* piston.

stanza, *n.f.* room. s. **da bagno**, bathroom. s. **da lètto**, bedroom.

stanziamento, *n.m.* appropriation.

stanziare, *vb.* appropriate.

stare, *vb.* stand; be.

starnutire, *vb.* sneeze.

starnuto, *n.m.* sneeze.

stasera, *adv.* tonight.

stàtico, *adj.* static.

statistica, *n.f.* statistics.

stato, *n.m.* state; estate.

stàtua, *n.f.* statue.

statura, *n.f.* stature.

statuto, *n.f.* statute.

stazionàrio, *adj.* stationary.

stazione, *n.f.* station; resort. s. balneare, bathing resort.

stecca, *n.f.* stick; cue; slat; splint.

stella, *n.f.* star.

stellare, *adj.* stellar.

stelo, *n.m.* stem.

stèmma, *n.m.* coat of arms.

stèndere, *vb.* extend; spread; draw up; *(refl.)* span.

stenografa, *n.f.* stenographer.

stenografia, *n.f.* stenography, shorthand.

stentatamente, *adv.* with difficulty.

stèrco, *n.m.* dung.

stereofònico, *adj.* stereophonic.

stereotipia, *n.f.* stereotype.

stèrile, *adj.* sterile, barren.

sterilità, *n.f.* sterility, barrenness.

sterilizzare, *vb.* sterilize.

sterlina, *n.f.* pound sterling.

sterminare, *vb.* exterminate.

sterminio, *n.m.* extermination.

stesso, *adj.* same; self.

stetoscòpio, *n.m.* stethoscope.

stia, *n.f.* hen-coop.

stigma, *n.m.* stigma.

stile, *n.m.* style.

stima, *n.f.* esteem, estimate, appraisal.

stimàbile, *adj.* estimable.

stimare, *vb.* esteem, estimate, appraise, deem, value.

stimmate, *n.f.pl.* stigmata.

stimolante, *n.m. and adj.* stimulant.

stimolare, *vb.* stimulate, goad.

stimolo, *n.m.* stimulus, goad.

stinco, *n.m.* shin.

stipèndio, *n.m.* salary.

stipettaio, *n.m.* cabinetmaker.

stipite, *n.m.* jamb.

stipo, *n.m.* cabinet.

stipulare, *vb.* stipulate.

stirare, *vb.* iron.

stirpe, *f.* lineage; stock.

stitichezza, *n.f.* constipation.

stitico, *adj.* constipated.

stiva, *n.f.* hold (of boat).

stivale, *n.m.* boot.

stivatore, *n.m.* stevedore.

stizzoso, *adj.* peevish.

Stoccarda, *n.f.* Stuttgart.

Stoccolma, *n.f.* Stockholm.

stoffa, *n.f.* cloth, stuff, material, fabric.

stòico, 1. *n.* stoic, 2. *adj.* stoical.

stòla, *n.f.* stole.

stòlido, *adj.* stolid.

stolto, 1. *n.m.* fool, dunce. 2. *adj.* foolish.

stòmaco, *n.m.* stomach.

stòrcere, *vb.* sprain.

stordimento, *n.m.* dizziness.

stordire, *vb.* stun.

stordito, *adj.* stunned, dizzy.

stòria, *n.f.* history; story, yarn.

stòrico, 1. *n.* historian. 2. *adj.* historic, historical.

stornare, *vb.* turn away; divert.

storpiare, *vb.* maim.

stòrta, *n.f.* sprain.

stòrto, *adj.* crooked.

stoviglie, *n.f.pl.* earthenware, pottery.

stra-, *prefix*, extra-.

stràbico, *adj.* cross-eyed.

straccio, *n.m.* rag; clout.

straccione, *n.m.* ragamuffin.

strada, *n.f.* road, street. s. maestra, highway.

stradale, *adj.* pertaining to roads.

strafottènte, *adj.* inconsiderate.

strale, *n.m.* arrow; shaft.

stranezza, *n.f.* strangeness, oddity.

strangolare, *vb.* strangle, choke.

stranièro, 1. *n.* stranger; foreigner. 2. *adj.* strange; foreign.

strano, *adj.* strange, odd, peculiar, queer, quaint, weird.

straordinàrio, *adj.* extraordinary; extra.

strappare, *vb.* tear, rip rend; snatch, wrench.

strapazzate, *adj.* uòva s., scrambled eggs.

straripare, *vb.* overflow.

stratagèmma, *n.m.* stratagem.

strategia, *n.f.* strategy.

stratègico, *adj.* strategic.

strato, *n.m.* stratum, layer; coating.

stratosfèra, *n.f.* stratosphere.

strattone, *n.m.* jerk.

stravagante, *adj.* extravagant.

stravaganza, *n.f.* extravagance.

straziante, *adj.* heart-rending.

straziato, *adj.* heartbroken.

strega, *n.f.* witch, hag.

stregare, *vb.* bewitch.

stregone, *n.m.* wizard.

stregoneria, *n.f.* sorcery.

strènuo, *adj.* strenuous.

streptocòcco, *n.m.* streptococcus.

stretta, *n.f.* clasp; squeeze. s. di mano, hand-shake.

stretto, 1. *n.m.* strait. 2. *adj.* narrow, tight.

stria, *n.f.* streak.

stridulo, *adj.* shrill, strident.

strigliare, *vb.* curry.

strillare, *vb.* scream, shriek.

strillo, *n.m.* scream, shriek.

strinare, *vb.* singe.

stringere, *vb.* hold tight; clasp; clench; squeeze; press; tighten. s. la mano a, shake hands with.

striscia, *n.f.* strip; stripe; band; slip.

strisciare, *vb.* creep.

strofinàccio, *n.m.* wiper; dustcloth; dishcloth.

strofinare, *vb.* rub; wipe.

strumentale, *adj.* instrumental.

strumento, *n.m.* instrument; implement.

strutto, *n.m.* lard.

struttura, *n.f.* structure.

struzzo, *n.m.* ostrich.

stucco, *n.m.* stucco.

studènte, *n.m.* student.

studentessa, *n.f.* student.

studiare, *vb.* study.

stùdio, *n.m.* study; studio.

studioso, *adj.* studious.

stufa, *n.f.* stove.

stufare, *vb.* stew.

stufato, *n.m.* stew.

stuòia, *n.f.* mat.

stuoino, *n.m.* door-mat.

stupèndo, *adj.* stupendous.

stupidità, *n.f.* stupidity, dumbness, backwardness.

stùpido, *adj.* stupid, dumb, backward.

stupire, *vb.* amaze, astonish, astound, surprise, daze.

stupirsi, *vb.* be amazed, be astonished, be surprised.

stupore, *n.m.* daze, stupor; astonishment, amazement, wonder.

sturare, *vb.* uncork.

su, *prep. and adv.* on; upon; up.

subcosciènte, *adj.* subconscious.

subire, *vb.* undergo.

sùbito, *adv.* immediately.

sublimare, *vb.* sublimate.

sublimato, *n.m. and adj.* sublimate.

sublime, *adj.* sublime.

subnormale, *adj.* subnormal.

subordinato, *n.m. and adj.* subordinate.

succèdere, *vb.* succeed; happen, occur.

successione, *n.f.* succession.

successivo, *adj.* successive; subsequent.

successo, *n.m.* success.

successore, *n.m.* successor.

succhiare, *vb.* suck.

succhièllo, *n.m.* auger, gimlet.

succo, *n.m.* juice.

succoso, *adj.* juicy.

succursale, *n.f.* branch.

sud, *n.m.* south. polo s., South Pole.

sudare, *vb.* sweat, perspire, swelter.

sudàrio, *n.m.* shroud.

suddetto, *adj.* aforesaid.

sùddito, *n.m.* subject.

sud-èst, *n.m.* southeast.

sùdicio, *adj.* dirty, dingy, filthy, grimy.

sudiciume, *n.m.* dirt, filth, grime.

sudore, *n.m.* sweat, perspiration.

sud-òvest, *n.m.* southwest.

sufficiènte, *adj.* sufficient, adequate, enough.

sufficientemente, *adv.* sufficiently, adequately.

sufficiènza, *n.f.* sufficiency, adequacy.

suggellare, *vb.* seal.

suggèllo, *n.m.* seal.

suggerimento, *n.m.* suggestion.
suggerire, *vb.* suggest.
suggeritore, *n.m.* prompter.
sùghero, *n.m.* cork.
sugo, *n.m.* sauce. **s. di carne,** gravy.
suicidarsi, *vb.* commit suicide.
suicìdio, *n.m.* suicide.
suindicato, *adj.* aforementioned.
sultanina, *adj.* **uva s.,** sultana raisin.
sunto, *n.m.* abstract, résumé.
suo, *adj.* his; her; hers; its; your; yours.
suòcera, *n.f.* mother-in-law.
suòcero, *n.m.* father-in-law.
suòla, *n.f.* sole.
suòlo, *n.m.* soil.
suonare, *vb.* sound; ring; play.
suonatore, *n.m.* player.
suòno, *n.m.* sound; ring.
superare, *vb.* overcome; surpass, exceed; excel; top; pass (exam.).
supèrbia, *n.f.* haughtiness, pride.
supèrbo, *adj.* haughty, proud; superb.
superficiale, *adj.* superficial.
superficie, *n.f.* surface.
supèrfluo, *adj.* superfluous.
superiore, *adj.* superior; upper.
superiorità, *n.f.* superiority.
superlativo, *n.m. and adj.* superlative.
superstar, *n.f.* superstar.
superstizione, *n.f.* superstition.
superstizioso, *adj.* superstitious.
superuòmo, *n.m.* superman.
supplemento, *n.m.* supplement.
sùpplica, *n.f.* supplication, entreaty.
supplicare, *vb.* supplicate, beseech, entreat.
supplichévole, *adj.* beseeching.
supplichevolmente, *adv.* beseechingly.
supplire, *vb.* replace; make up for; eke out.
supporre, *vb.* suppose.
supposizione, *n.f.* supposition, assumption.
suppurare, *vb.* suppurate, fester.
supremazia, *n.f.* supremacy, ascendancy.
suprèmo, *adj.* supreme, paramount.
surgelamento, *n.m.* deep freeze.
surrenale, *adj.* adrenal.
susina, *n.f.* plum.
susino, *n.m.* plum-tree.
sussidiare, *vb.* subsidize.
sussìdio, *n.m.* subsidy.
sussultare, *vb.* start.
sussulto, *n.m.* start.
svaligiare, *vb.* rob completely.
svalutare, *vb.* devalue.
svanire, *vb.* vanish.
svantàggio, *n.m.* disadvantage, drawback, handicap.
svariato, *adj.* varied.

svedese, **1.** *n.* Swede. **2.** *adj.* Swedish.
svegliare, *vb.* awaken, wake up, arouse; *(refl.)* awake.
svèglio, *adj.* awake.
svelto, *adj.* quick; slender.
svenimento, *n.m.* faint, swoon.
svenire, *vb.* faint, swoon.
sventolare, *vb.* wave; fan.
svernare, *vb.* winter; hibernate.
svestire, *vb.* undress; *(refl.)* disrobe.
Svèzia, *n.f.* Sweden.
sviarsi, *vb.* lose one's way, go astray.
sviato, *adj.* lost; stray.
svignàrsela, *vb. (fam.)* abscond.
sviluppare, *vb.* develop.
sviluppatore, *n.m.* developer.
sviluppo, *n.m.* development, growth.
sviscerare, *vb.* eviscerate.
svista, *n.f.* blunder.
Svizzera, *n.f.* Switzerland.
svìzzero, *n. and adj.* Swiss.
svogliato, *adj.* listless.
svolazzare, *vb.* flutter.
svòlta, *n.f.* turn.

T

tabacco, *n.m.* tobacco.
tabernàcolo, *n.m.* tabernacle.
tacca, *n.f.* nick, notch.
taccagno, *adj.* niggardly.
tacchino, *n.m.* turkey, gobbler.
tacco, *n.m.* heel.
taccuino, *n.m.* note-book.
tacere, *vb.* be quiet, keep quiet.
tachìmetro, *n.m.* speedometer.
tàfano, *n.m.* gadfly.
tafferùglio, *n.m.* scuffle, scrap.
tagliando, *n.m.* coupon.
tagliare, *vb.* cut; carve; chop; clip; hack; hew.
tagliatèlle, *n.f.pl.* noodles.
tagliatore, *n.m.* cutter.
tàglio, *n.m.* cut.
tale, *adj.* such.
talènto, *n.m.* talent.
tallone, *n.m.* heel.
talpa, *n.f.* mole.
tamburo, *n.m.* drum; drummer. **t. maggiore,** drum major.
tana, *n.f.* burrow, den, lair.
tànghero, *n.m.* boor, cold.
tangìbile, *adj.* tangible.
tappare, *vb.* plug, stop up.
tappeto, *n.m.* carpet, rug.
tappezzare, *vb.* upholster.
tappezzerìa, *n.f.* tapestry, hanging; wallcovering.
tappezzière, *n.m.* upholsterer.
tappo, *n.m.* cork, stopper, plug.
tarchiato, *adj.* squat, stocky.
tardi, *adv.* late.
tardivo, *adj.* tardy, late.
tardo, *adj.* late.
targa, *n.f.* plate.
tariffa, *n.f.* tariff; fare.
tarma, *n.f.* moth.
tartagliare, *vb.* stutter.
tartaruga, *n.f.* turtle.

tasca, *n.f.* pocket.
tascàbile, *adj.* pocket size.
tassa, *n.f.* tax; fee. **t. di scambio,** sales tax.
tassàllo, *n.m.* dowel.
tassì, *n.m.* taxicab.
tasso, *n.m.* badger.
tastièra, *n.f.* keyboard.
tasto, *n.m.* key.
tastoni, *adv.* **andare a t.,** grope.
tatto, *n.m.* tact; feel.
tàvola, *n.f.* table; board; plank.
tavoletta, *n.f.* tablet.
tavolòzza, *n.f.* palette.
tazza, *n.f.* cup.
te, *pron.* **2.** *sg.* thee; you.
tè, *n.m.* tea.
teatro, *n.m.* theater.
tècnica, *n.f.* technique.
tècnico, *adj.* technical.
tedesco, *n. and adj.* German.
tèdio, *n.m.* tedium.
tedioso, *adj.* tedious.
tégola, *n.f.* tile.
teièra, *n.f.* tea-pot.
tela, *n.f.* cloth; web. **t. cerata,** oil-cloth. **t. da fusto,** buckram.
telaio, *n.m.* loom; frame; chassis.
telefonare, *vb.* telephone.
telefonata, *n.f.* telephone call.
telèfono, *n.m.* telephone.
telegrafare, *vb.* telegraph.
telègrafo, *n.m.* telegraph.
telegramma, *n.m.* telegram.
teleschermo, *n.m.* television screen.
telescòpio, *n.m.* telescope.
telescrivente, *n.f.* teletype.
televisione, *n.f.* television.
televisore, *n.m.* television set.
tèma, *n.m.* theme.
temerarietà, *n.f.* rashness, foolhardiness.
temeràrio, **1.** *n.m.* daredevil. **2.** *adj.* rash, foolhardy.
temere, *vb.* fear, dread.
temperamento, *n.m.* temperament.
temperanza, *n.f.* temperance.
temperare, *vb.* temper.
temperato, *adj.* temperate.
temperatura, *n.f.* temperature.
temperino, *n.m.* pen-knife.
tempèsta, *n.f.* tempest, storm, gale.
tempestoso, *adj.* tempestuous, stormy, gusty.
tèmpia, *n.f.* temple.
tèmpio, *n.m.* temple.
tèmpo, *n.m.* time; weather.
tenace, *adj.* tenacious, dogged.
tènda, *n.f.* tent; awning; booth.
tendènte, *adj.* tending, conducive.
tendènza, *n.f.* tendency, trend.
tèndere, *vb.* tend, conduce; stretch.
tèndine, *n.m.* tendon.
tènebre, *n.f.pl.* darkness.
tenebroso, *adj.* dark.
tenènte, *n.m.* lieutenant.

teneramente, *adv.* tenderly, fondly.

tenere, *vb.* hold; keep.

tenerezza, *n.f.* tenderness, fondness.

tènero, *adj.* tender, fond.

tenore, *n.m.* tenor.

tensione, *n.f.* tension, strain, stress.

tentare, *vb.* attempt, try; tempt.

tentativo, 1. *n.m.* attempt. 2. *adj.* tentative.

tentazione, *n.f.* temptation.

tènue, *adj.* tenuous, flimsy.

teologìa, *n.f.* theology.

teòlogo, *n.m.* theologian.

teorìa, *n.f.* theory.

teòrico, *adj.* theoretical.

teppista, *n.m.* hoodlum.

terapìa, *n.f.* therapy.

tergicristallo, *n.m.* windshield-wiper.

terminale, *adj.* terminal.

terminare, *vb.* terminate, end, finish.

tèrmine, *n.m.* end; terminus; term; deadline; abutment.

termòmetro, *n.m.* thermometer.

termosifone, *n.m.* heating system.

tèrra, *n.f.* earth, ground, land.

terrazza, *n.f.* terrace.

terremòto, *n.m.* earthquake.

terreno, 1. *n.m.* soil, terrain; lot. 2. *adj.* earthy, earthly.

terribile, *adj.* terrible, awful, frightful, dire, dreadful.

terribilmente, *adv.* terribly, awfully, dreadfully.

terrìccio, *n.m.* loam.

territòrio, *n.m.* territory.

terrore, *n.m.* terror, fear, awe.

tèrzo, *adj.* third.

Terzo Mondo, *n.m.* Third World.

tesa, *n.f.* (hat) brim.

teso, *adj.* tight, taut, tense, up-tight.

tesorière, *n.m.* treasurer.

tesòro, *n.m.* treasure; treasury.

tèssera, *n.f.* card; ticket.

tèssere, *vb.* weave.

tèssile, *adj.* textile.

tessitore, *n.m.* weaver.

tessitura, *n.f.* texture; weaving.

tessuto, *n.m.* tissue; textile.

tèsta, *n.f.* head. t. di sbarco, bridgehead. tener t. a, cope with.

testamento, *n.m.* testament, will.

testardo, *adj.* stubborn, head-strong, self-willed.

testata carica, *n.f.* warhead.

testàtico, *n.m.* poll-tax.

testimòne, *n.m.* witness. t. oculare, eyewitness.

testimonianza, *n.f.* testimony.

testimoniare, *vb.* testify.

tèsto, *n.m.* text.

tètano, *n.m.* tetanus, lockjaw.

tetraone, *n.m.* grouse.

tètto, *n.m.* roof.

tettòia, *n.f.* shed.

thè, *n.m.* tea.

ti, *pron.* 2. *sg.* thee; you.

tièpido, *adj.* tepid, lukewarm.

tifo, *n.m.* typhus.

tifoìdeo, *adj.* typhoid.

tifoso, *n.m.* fan, enthusiast.

tiglio, *n.m.* lime-tree; linden.

tiglioso, *adj.* tough, leathery.

tigre, *n.m.* tiger.

timbrare, *vb.* stamp.

timbro, *n.m.* stamp.

timidamente, *adv.* timidly, shyly, bashfully.

timidezza, *n.f.* timidity, shyness, bashfulness.

timido, *adj.* timid, shy, bashful, coy; chicken-hearted; diffident.

timone, *n.m.* helm; rudder; (wagon) pole.

timonière, *n.m.* steersman, helmsman; coxswain.

timore, *n.m.* fear, apprehension, dread.

timoroso, *adj.* timorous, fearful, apprehensive.

tìmpano, *n.m.* ear-drum; kettle-drum.

tìngere, *vb.* dye.

tino, *n.m.* vat.

tinta, *n.f.* tint, shade.

tintinnare, *vb.* tinkle, jingle.

tintore, *n.m.* dyer; dry-cleaner.

tintura, *n.f.* dye.

tìpico, *adj.* typical.

tipo, *n.m.* type.

tirannìa, *n.f.* tyranny.

tiranno, *n.m.* tyrant.

tirare, *vb.* draw, pull, tag.

tirata, *n.f.* pull.

tiratura, *n.f.* printing.

tìrchio, *adj.* stingy.

tiro, *n.m.* trick.

tisi, *n.f.* consumption, tuberculosis.

tìsico, *adj.* consumptive.

titolare, 1. *n.* incumbent. 2. *adj.* titular.

tìtolo, *n.m.* title, headline, heading, caption.

tizio, *n.m.* chap, fellow, guy.

toccare, *vb.* touch.

tocco, *n.m.* touch.

tògliere, *vb.* take away, remove.

tollerante, *adj.* tolerant.

tolleranza, *n.f.* tolerance.

tollerare, *vb.* tolerate, stand.

tomba, *n.f.* tomb, grave.

tombale, *adj.* pertaining to a tomb or grave.

tondo, *adj.* round.

tonfo, *n.m.* splash; thud.

tònica, *n.f.* (music) tonic.

tònico, *adj.* and *adj.* tonic.

tonnellata, *n.f.* ton.

tonno, *n.m.* tuna.

tòno, *n.m.* tone, pitch.

tonsilla, *n.f.* tonsil.

topo, *n.m.* mouse.

tòrcere, *vb.* twist, wring.

torinese, *adj.* Turinese.

Torino, *n.f.* Turin.

torlo, *n.m.* yolk.

tormentare, *vb.* torment; fret; nag; tease.

tormento, *n.m.* torment.

tormentoso, *adj.* excruciating.

tornare, *vb.* return.

tornasole, *n.m.* litmus.

tórnio, *n.m.* lathe.

tòro, *n.m.* bull.

torre, *n.f.* tower.

torrefazione, *n.f.* roasting (of coffee).

torrènte, *n.m.* torrent; mountain stream.

torretta, *n.f.* turret.

tórsolo, *n.m.* core.

tòrta, *n.f.* cake, tart, pie.

tòrto, *n.m.* wrong. aver t., be wrong.

tortura, *n.f.* torture.

torturare, *vb.* torture.

tosare, *vb.* clip, shear.

tosatore, *n.m.* clipper.

tosatura, *n.f.* clipping.

Toscana, *n.f.* Tuscany.

toscano, *adj.* Tuscan.

tosse, *n.f.* cough.

tossicòmane, *n.m.* drug addict.

tossire, *vb.* cough.

totale, *n.m.* and *adj.* total.

totalità, *n.f.* totality, entirety.

totalitàrio, *adj.* totalitarian.

tovàglia, *n.f.* tablecloth.

tovagliolino, *n.m.* little napkin; doily.

tovagliòlo, *n.m.* napkin.

tòzzo, *adj.* stocky, chunky.

tra, *prep.* between, among, amid.

traballare, *vb.* reel, stagger, lurch.

traboccare, *vb.* overflow.

tràccia, *n.f.* trace.

tradimento, *n.m.* betrayal, treason.

tradire, *vb.* betray.

traditore, *n.m.* traitor.

tradizionale, *adj.* traditional.

tradizione, *n.f.* tradition.

tradurre, *vb.* translate.

traduzione, *n.f.* translation.

tràffico, *n.m.* traffic.

trafìggere, *vb.* transfix, spear.

traforare, *vb.* pierce; tunnel.

traforo, *n.m.* tunnel.

tragèdia, *n.f.* tragedy.

traghetto, *n.m.* ferry.

tràgico, *adj.* tragic.

traguardo di puntamento, *n.m.* bombsight.

tram, *n.m.* street-car, trolley-car.

trambusto, *n.m.* flurry.

tramestìo, *n.m.* bustle.

tramezzino, *n.m.* sandwich.

trampolino, *n.m.* springboard.

tranne, *prep.* except.

tranquillità, *n.f.* tranquillity.

tranquillo, *adj.* tranquil, quiet, peaceful.

transatlàntico, 1. *n.m.* liner. 2. *adj.* transatlantic.

transizione, *n.f.* transition.

transvestito, *adj.* transvestite.

tranvìa, *n.f.* tramway, streetcar line.

tranvìàrio, *adj.* tramway.
trapànare, *n.f.* drill.
tràpano, *n.m.* drill.
trapasso, *n.m.* death, passage; (property) conveyance.
tràppola, *n.f.* pitfall, snare, trap.
trapunta, *n.f.* quilt.
trasalìre, *vb.* give a start.
trasandato, *adj.* sloppy.
trascinare, *vb.* drag, haul, lug.
trascinarsi, *vb.* crawl.
trascórrere, *vb.* elapse, pass.
trascuràbile, *adj.* negligible.
trascurare, *vb.* neglect, disregard, ignore, overlook.
trascuratamente, *adv.* negligently, carelessly.
trascuratezza, *n.f.* negligence, carelessness.
trascurato, *adj.* negligent, careless, frowzy, sloppy, slovenly.
trasferimento, *n.m.* transfer.
trasferire, *vb.* transfer.
trasformare, *vb.* transform.
trasfusione, *n.f.* transfusion.
traslòco, *n.m.* move; (household goods) moving.
trasméttere, *vb.* transmit, broadcast, convey.
trasmettitore, *n.m.* transmitter, broadcaster.
trasmissione, *n.f.* transmission. t. radiofònica, broadcast.
trasparènte, *adj.* transparent.
trasportare, *vb.* transport, carry, haul, convey.
trasportatore, *n.m.* conveyor.
traspòrto, *n.m.* transport; transportation; carriage; cartage; haulage.
trastullare, *vb.* amuse; (*refl.*) toy.
trastullo, *n.m.* toy.
trasudare, *vb.* ooze, seep.
tratta, *n.f.* draft.
trattamento, *n.m.* treatment.
trattare, *vb.* treat; deal.
trattato, *n.m.* treaty; treatise.
trattenere, *vb.* entertain; refrain; restrain; withhold; (*refl.*) forbear.
trattenimento, *n.m.* entertainment.
tratto, *n.m.* trait; feature; dash; stretch; tract. t. d'unione, hyphen.
trattore, *n.m.* restaurant-keeper.
trattorìa, *n.f.* restaurant.
trattrìce, *n.f.* tractor.
travasare, *vb.* scoop; pour off.
trave, *n.f.* beam, girder.
travèrso, *adv.* dì travèrso, awry.
travestimento, *n.m.* disguise; travesty.
travestire, *vb.* disguise; travesty.
travicèllo, *n.m.* joist, rafter.
tre, *num.* three.
tréccia, *n.f.* braid.
tredicèsimo, *adj.* thirteenth.
trédici, *num.* thirteen.
trégua, *n.f.* truce; respite.

tremare, *vb.* tremble, quake, shake.
tremèndo, *adj.* tremendous; awesome.
trèmito, *n.m.* trembling, quake.
tremolare, *vb.* tremble, flicker, quaver.
tremolìo, *n.m.* trembling, flicker.
treno, *n.m.* train.
trenta, *num.* thirty.
trentèsimo, *adj.* thirtieth.
tresca, *n.f.* intrigue; (illicit) love affair.
trescone, *n.m.* reel (dance).
triàngolo, *n.m.* triangle.
tribade, *n.f.* Lesbian.
tribolazione, *n.f.* tribulation.
tribórdo, *n.m.* starboard.
tribù, *n.f.* tribe, clan.
tribuna, *n.f.* stand, grandstand.
tributàrio, *n.m. and adj.* tributary.
tributo, *n.m.* tribute.
trichèco, *n.m.* walrus.
trifòglio, *n.m.* clover.
trimestrale, *adj.* every three months, quarterly.
trimèstre, *n.m.* three-month period, quarter; (school) term.
trincèa, *n.f.* trench; cutting.
trincerare, *vb.* entrench.
trinciante, *n.m.* carving-knife.
trinciare, *vb.* carve, cut up.
trionfale, *adj.* triumphal.
trionfante, *adj.* triumphal.
trionfare, *vb.* triumph.
trionfo, *n.m.* triumph.
triplicare, *vb.* triple.
triplice, *adj.* triple.
triste, *adj.* sad, gloomy, depressed, doleful, glum.
tristezza, *n.f.* sadness, gloom, glumness.
tritare, *vb.* pound, mangle.
trito, *adj.* trite.
triturare, *vb.* mince.
trivèllo, *n.m.* auger, borer.
trofèo, *n.m.* trophy.
trògolo, *n.m.* trough.
tròia, *n.f.* sow.
tromba, *n.f.* trumpet.
trombaio, *n.m.* plumber.
trombettière, *n.m.* trumpeter.
tronco, *n.m.* trunk; log.
tròno, *n.m.* throne.
tròpico, 1. *n.m.* tropic. 2. *adj.* tropical.
troppo, 1. *adj.* too many; too much. 2. *adv.* too.
tròta, *n.f.* trout.
trottare, *vb.* trot.
tròtto, *n.m.* trot.
trovare, *vb.* find, locate; (*refl.*) be; be located; happen to be.
trovatèllo, *n.m.* foundling.
trucco, *n.m.* trick.
trucidare, *vb.* slay.
truffare, *vb.* cheat, swindle.
truffatore, *n.m.* cheater; swindler.
truppa, *n.f.* troop.
tu, *pron.* 2. *sg.* thou; you.

tubercolòsi, *n.f.* tuberculosis.
tubo, *n.m.* tube, pipe.
tuffare, *vb.* plunge; dip; dunk; (*refl.*) dive.
tuffatore, *n.m.* diver; dive-bomber.
tuffo, *n.m.* dive, plunge.
tugùrio, *n.m.* hovel.
tulipano, *n.m.* tulip.
tumore, *n.m.* tumor.
tùmulo, *n.m.* mound.
tumulto, *n.m.* tumult, uproar, hubbub, riot.
tumultuare, *vb.* riot.
tuo, *adj.* thy; your.
tuonare, *vb.* thunder.
tuòno, *n.m.* thunder.
turbante, *n.m.* turban.
turbina, *n.f.* turbine.
turbinare, *vb.* whirl, gyrate, swirl.
tùrbine, *n.m.* whirlwind.
turbo-èlica, *n.f.* turbo-prop.
turbolènto, *adj.* turbulent; boisterous.
turboreattore, *n.m.* turbojet.
Turchìa, *n.f.* Turkey.
turco, 1. *n.m.* Turk. 2. *adj.* Turkish.
turismo, *n.m.* sightseeing, tourism.
turista, *n.m.* tourist.
turìstico, *adj.* tourist.
turno, *n.m.* turn, shift.
tuta, *n.f.* overalls; dungarees.
tutèla, *n.f.* guardianship.
tutore, *n.m.* guardian.
tuttavìa, *adv.* however; yet.
tutto, 1. *adj.* all; whole. t. a un tratto, all of a sudden. 2. *pron.* everything.

U

ubbidìre, *vb.* obey.
ubbriachezza, *n.f.* drunkenness, intoxication.
ubbrìaco, *adj.* drunk, drunken.
ubbriacone, *n.m.* drunkard, inebriate.
uccellièra, *n.f.* bird-house, aviary.
uccellino, *n.m.* fledgling.
uccèllo, *n.m.* bird. u. dì rapìna, bird of prey.
uccìdere, *vb.* kill.
uccisore, *n.m.* killer.
udìbile, *adj.* audible.
udiènza, *n.f.* audience, interview, hearing.
udìre, *vb.* hearing.
udìtivo, *adj.* auditory.
udìto, *n.m.* hearing.
uditore, *n.m.* hearer, auditor.
uditòrio, *n.m.* audience.
uditrice, *n.f.* hearer, auditor.
ufficiale, 1. *n.m.* officer, official. 2. *adj.* official.
ufficio, *n.m.* office, bureau.
ùgola, *n.f.* uvula.
uguaglianza, *n.f.* equality.
uguagliare, *vb.* equal, equalize, equate, match.
uguale, *adj.* equal.

ùlcera, n.f. ulcer.

ulterióre, adj. ulterior, further.

ùltimo, adj. last, end, hindmost, ultimate.

umanaménte, adv. humanly.

umanésimo, n.m. humanism.

umanista, n.m. humanist.

umanità, n.f. humanity, mankind.

umanitàrio, adj. humanitarian, humane.

umano, adj. human.

umbro, adj. Umbrian.

umidità, n.f. dampness, humidity, moisture.

ùmido, adj. damp, humid, moist, wet.

umìle, adj. humble, lowly.

umiliare, vb. humiliate, humble; (refl.) grovel.

umiliazióne, n.f. humiliation.

umiltà, n.f. humility.

umóre, n.m. humor.

umorismo, n.m. humor.

umorista, n.m. humorist.

umorìstico, adj. humorous, jocular.

unànime, adj. unanimous.

uncinare, vb. hook.

uncìno, n.m. hook, grapple.

undicèsimo, adj. eleventh.

ùndici, num. eleven.

ùngere, vb. grease; smear; anoint; oil.

unghérese, adj. Hungarian.

Unghería, n.f. Hungary.

ùnghia, n.f. fingernail.

unguènto, n.m. unguent, salve, ointment.

ùnico, adj. only; unique; single; sole.

unificare, vb. unify.

unifórme, 1. n.m. uniform. 2. adj. uniform, even.

uniformità, n.f. uniformity, evenness.

unilaterale, adj. unilateral, one-sided.

unióne, n.f. union.

unire, vb. unite.

unisessuale, adj. unisex.

unità, n.f. unity; unit.

universale, adj. universal.

università, n.f. university, college.

universitàrio, adj. pertaining to a university, collegiate.

univèrso, n.m. universe.

uno m., una f. 1. art. a, an. 2. num. one.

untuóso, adj. greasy.

uòmo, n.m. man.

uòpo, n.m. purpose.

uòvo, n.m. egg. u. affogato, poached egg.

uragàno, n.m. hurricane.

uranìnite, n.f. pitchblende.

urbàno, adj. urban.

urgènte, adj. urgent, pressing.

urgènza, n.f. urgency.

urlare, vb. yell, holler, bawl, shout, cry, howl.

urlo, n.m. yell, shout, howl.

urna, n.f. urn.

urtare, vb. bump; shock; clash.

urto, n.m. bump; shock; impact; clash.

usànza, n.f. usage.

usare, vb. use.

usclère, n.m. usher; bailiff.

uscìta, n.f. exit.

usignuòlo, n.m. nightingale.

uso, n.m. use; custom.

usuàle, adj. usual.

usùra, n.f. usury.

usurpare, vb. usurp, encroach upon.

utensìle, n.m. utensil, tool.

utènte, n.m. user.

ùtero, n.m. uterus, womb.

utile, adj. useful, helpful.

utilità, n.f. utility, usefulness, helpfulness.

utilizzare, vb. utilize.

uva, n.f. grape.

V

va bene, interj. O.K.

vacante, adj. vacant.

vacanza, n.f. holiday, (pl.) vacation.

vacca, n.f. cow.

vaccaro, n.m. cowboy, cowhand.

vacchetta, n.f. cowhide.

vaccinare, vb. vaccinate.

vaccinazióne, n.f. vaccination.

vaccìnio, n.m. huckleberry.

vaccìno, n.m. vaccine.

vacillare, vb. vacillate, waver.

vàcuo, adj. vacuous.

vagabóndo, n.m. vagabond, hobo, bum, tramp.

vagare, vb. wander around, gallivant, ramble, roam.

vàglia, n.m. money-order.

vàglio, n.m. sieve.

vago, adj. vague, dreamy, hazy; (poetical) charming.

vagóne, n.m. car; coach. v. ristorante, dining car. v. lètti, sleeper.

vaiòlo, n.m. smallpox.

valanga, n.f. avalanche.

valere, vb. be worth.

vàlido, adj. valid.

valigetta, n.f. little suitcase; handbag.

valìgia, n.f. suitcase, valise.

valle, n.f. valley.

valletta, n.f. vale, dale, glen.

valóre, n.m. valor; value, worth.

valoróso, adj. valiant.

valùta, n.f. currency.

valutare, vb. evaluate, estimate, value.

valutazióne, n.f. evaluation, estimate.

vàlvola, n.f. valve; (radio) tube.

vàlzer, n.m. waltz.

vampiro, n.m. vampire.

vanaglorióso, adj. vainglorious, boastful.

vàndalo, n.m. vandal.

vanga, n.f. spade.

vangèlo, n.m. gospel.

vanìglia, n.f. vanilla.

vanità, n.f. vanity, conceit.

vanitóso, adj. vain, conceited.

vano, 1. n.m. room. 2. adj. vain.

vantàggio, n.m. advantage, benefit, profit. trarre v. da, benefit by.

vantaggiosaménte, adv. advantageously.

vantaggióso, adj. advantageous, beneficial, profitable.

vantare, vb. boast.

vantatóre, n.m. boaster.

vantería, n.f. boast, boasting, boastfulness.

vanto, n.m. boast.

vapóre, n.m. vapor, steam.

varare, vb. launch.

variare, vb. vary.

variazióne, n.f. variation.

varicèlla, n.f. chicken-pox.

varietà, n.f. variety.

vàrio, adj. various.

varo, n.m. launching.

vasca, n.f. tub.

vasellame, n.m. crockery, earthenware.

vasectomìa, n.f. vasectomy.

vaso, n.m. vase. v. da nòtte, chamber-pot.

vassallo, n.m. vassal.

vassóio, n.m. tray.

vasto, adj. vast.

vècchia, n.f. old woman, crone.

vècchio, adj. old, aged, elderly.

vedere, vb. see, behold.

vèdova, n.f. widow.

vèdovo, n.m. widower.

veduta, n.f. view.

veemènte, adj. vehement.

veemènza, n.f. vehemence.

vegetale, adj. vegetable.

vèglia, n.f. vigil; wake.

vegliare, vb. be awake.

veìcolo, n.m. vehicle.

vela, n.f. sail.

velato, adj. veiled, filmy.

veleno, n.m. poison, venom.

velenóso, adj. poisonous, venomous.

vèllo, n.m. fleece.

vellóso, adj. fleecy.

velluto, n.m. velvet.

velo, n.m. veil.

velóce, adj. swift, fleet, speedy.

velocista, n.m. sprinter.

velocità, n.f. velocity, speed.

vena, n.f. vein.

vendèmmia, n.f. vintage.

vèndere, vb. sell.

vendetta, n.f. revenge, vengeance.

vendicare, vb. avenge, revenge.

vendicatóre, n.m. avenger.

vèndita, n.f. sale. v. all'asta, auction.

venerdì, n.m. Friday. v. santo, Good Friday.

venèreo, adj. venereal.

Venèzia, n.f. Venice.

venezìano, adj. Venetian.

venìre, vb. come.

ventàglio, n.m. fan.

ventèsimo, adj. twentieth.

venti, num. twenty.

ventilare, *vb.* ventilate.

ventilazione, *n.f.* ventilation.

ventina, *n.f.* score.

vènto, *n.m.* wind.

ventoso, *adj.* windy, breezy.

vèntre, *n.m.* belly.

ventriglio, *n.m.* gizzard.

ventura, *n.f.* venture.

venuta, *n.f.* coming.

veramente, *adv.* truly, really, actually.

veranda, *n.f.* porch.

verbale, 1. *n.m.* minutes. 2. *adj.* verbal.

vèrbo, *n.m.* verb.

verboso, *adj.* verbose, wordy.

verde, *adj.* green. **al v.,** broke, penniless.

verdetto, *n.m.* verdict.

verdura, *n.f.* vegetables.

verga, *n.f.* rod, switch.

vérgine, *n.f.* virgin.

vergogna, *n.f.* shame.

vergognarsi di, *vb.* be ashamed of.

vergognoso, *adj.* ashamed; shameful.

verìdico, *adj.* truthful.

verifica, *n.f.* verification, check, audit.

verificare, *vb.* verify, check, audit.

verità, *n.f.* truth, reality, actuality.

vèrme, *n.m.* worm.

vermiglio, *adj.* vermilion.

vernàcolo, *n.m. and adj.* vernacular.

vernice, *n.f.* varnish, glaze.

verniciare, *vb.* varnish, glaze.

vero, *adj.* true, real, actual; very.

vèrro, *n.m.* boar.

versamento, *n.m.* payment.

versare, *vb.* pour; pay in; shed.

versàtile, *adj.* versatile.

versato, *adj.* versed, conversant.

versificare, *vb.* versify.

versione, *n.f.* version.

vèrso, 1. *n.m.* verse; song; (hen, goose) cackle. 2. *prep.* toward.

versucci, *n.m.pl.* doggerel.

vertebrato, *n.m. and adj.* vertebrate.

verticale, *adj.* vergical.

vertigine, *n.f.* vertigo, dizziness.

vertiginoso, *adj.* vertiginous, dizzy.

verzura, *n.f.* greenery.

vescica, *n.f.* bladder; blister.

vescovato, *n.m.* bishopric.

véscovo, *n.m.* bishop.

vèspa, *n.f.* wasp.

vespasiano, *n.m.* public urinal.

vèspri, *n.m.pl.* vespers.

vestàglia, *n.f.* dressing-gown, bathrobe, negligée.

vèste, *n.f.* dress, garb, apparel, robe.

vestiarista, *n.m.* costumer.

vestibolo, *n.m.* vestibule, hallway.

vestiglo, *n.m.* vestige.

vestimento, *n.m.* clothing, garb, apparel.

vestire, *vb.* dress, clothe, garb, apparel.

vestito, 1. *n.m.* dress, suit, garment; (pl.) clothes, clothing. 2. *adj.* clad, clothed.

Vesùvio, *n.m.* Vesuvius.

veterano, *n.m.* veteran.

veterinàrio, *n.m. and adj.* veterinary.

vèto, *n.m.* veto.

vetraio, *n.m.* glazier.

vetro, *n.m.* glass, pane.

vetroso, *adj.* glassy.

vetta, *n.f.* summit.

vettovàglie, *n.f.pl.* victuals.

vettura, *n.f.* carriage; car.

vezzeggiare, *vb.* fondle, coddle, pet.

vi, *pron.* 2. *pl.* you.

vi, *pro-phrase* (replaces phrases introduced by prepositions of place) there; to it; at it.

via, 1. *n.f.* way, road, street. 2. *adv.* away; off. 3. *prep.* via.

viadotto, *n.m.* viaduct.

viaggiare, *vb.* journey, travel, tour, voyage.

viaggiatore, *n.m.* traveller.

viàggio, *n.m.* journey, trip, travel, tour, voyage.

viale, *n.m.* avenue, boulevard; drive(way); (in garden) alley.

vibrare, *vb.* vibrate.

vibrazione, *n.f.* vibration.

vicàrio, *n.m.* vicar.

vicinanza, *n.f.* neighborhood, vicinity.

vicino, 1. *n.m.* neighbor. 2. *adj.* nearby, neighboring, close. **vicino a,** *prep.* near, about. 3. *adv.* near, close.

vico, *n.m.* hamlet.

vicolo, *n.m.* alley. **v. cièco,** blind alley, dead end.

videodisco, *n.m.* videodisc.

vietare, *vb.* forbid, veto.

vietato, *adj.* forbidden.

vigilante, *adj.* vigilant, alert, watchful.

vigilare, *vb.* watch, look out.

vigile, *n.m.* policeman.

vigilia, *n.f.* vigil; eve.

vigliacco, *n.m.* cad.

vigna, *n.f.* vineyard.

vigore, *n.m.* vigor, force.

vigorìa, *n.f.* forcefulness.

vigoroso, *adj.* vigorous, forceful, lusty.

vile, *adj.* vile.

villàggio, *n.m.* village.

villano, *adj.* inconsiderate.

villetta, *n.f.* cottage.

vincere, *vb.* conquer, overcome, overpower, beat, vanquish, win.

vincibile, *adj.* conquerable.

vincitore, *n.m.* victor, conqueror, winner.

vincolare, *vb.* bind.

vincolo, *n.m.* bind, link.

vino, *n.m.* wine. **v. di Xeres,** sherry.

viòla, *n.f.* viola; viol; violet.

violare, *vb.* violate; rape.

violatore, *n.m.* violator.

violazione, *n.f.* violation, breach.

violènto, *adj.* violent.

violènza, *n.f.* violence.

violino, *n.m.* violin, fiddle.

violoncellista, *n.m.* cellist.

violoncèllo, *n.m.* cello.

viòttolo, *n.m.* byway, lane.

vipera, *n.f.* adder, viper.

virare, *vb.* tack, veer.

virgola, *n.f.* comma.

virile, *adj.* virile, manly.

virilità, *n.f.* virility, manhood.

virtù, *n.f.* virtue.

virtuale, *adj.* virtual.

virtuoso, *adj.* virtuous.

vischi, *n.m.* whisky.

vischio, *n.m.* bird-lime; mistletoe.

viscoso, *adj.* viscous, sticky.

visibile, *adj.* visible.

visione, *n.f.* vision.

visita, *n.f.* visit.

visitare, *vb.* visit.

visivo, *adj.* of vision.

viso, *n.m.* face, countenance.

visone, *n.m.* mink.

vista, *n.f.* sight; eyesight; view.

vistare, *vb.* visa.

visto, *n.m.* visa.

vistosamente, *adv.* gaudily.

vistosità, *n.f.* flashiness, gaudiness.

vistoso, *adj.* flashy, gaudy.

visuale, *adj.* visual.

vita, *n.f.* life; livelihood; living; waist.

vitale, *adj.* vital.

vitalità, *n.f.* vitality.

vitalizio, *adj.* for life.

vitamina, *n.f.* vitamin.

vite, *n.f.* vine; grapevine; screw.

vitèllo, *n.m.* calf; veal.

vitreo, *adj.* glassy, of glass.

vittima, *n.f.* victim.

vitto, *n.m.* food, victuals, board.

vittòria, *n.f.* victory.

vittorioso, *adj.* victorious.

viva, *interj.* hurrah (for).

vivace, *adj.* vivacious, lively, brisk.

vivacemente, *adv.* vivaciously, briskly.

vivacità, *n.f.* vivacity, liveliness, briskness.

vivaio, *n.m.* hatchery, nursery.

vivènte, *adj.* living, alive.

vivere, *vb.* live, be alive.

vivido, *adj.* vivid.

vivo, *adj.* live.

viziare, *vb.* vitiate.

vizio, *n.m.* vice.

vizioso, *adj.* vicious.

vocabolàrio, *n.m.* vocabulary.

vocale, 1. *n.f.* vowel. 2. *adj.* vocal.

vocazione, *n.f.* vocation, calling.

voce, *n.f.* voice; word, rumor, report.

vociare, *vb.* vociferate.

voga, *n.f.* vogue.

vòglia, *n.f.* wish, desire; birthmark.

voi, *pron.* 2. *pl.* you.

volante, *n.m.* steering-wheel; flounce.

volare, *vb.* fly.

volerci, *vb.* be necessary.

volgare, *adj.* vulgar; common; vernacular.

volgarità, *n.f.* vulgarity, commonness.

volgo, *n.m.* rabble.

volo, *n.m.* flight. **v. noleggiato,** charter flight.

volontà, *n.f.* will.

volontàrio, 1. *n.m.* volunteer. 2. *adj.* voluntary.

volpe, *n.f.* fox.

volpino, *adj.* foxy.

vòlta, *n.f.* time; vault.

voltafaccia, *n.m.* about-face.

voltàggio, *n.m.* voltage.

volteggiare, *vb.* hover; turn; vault.

volume, *n.m.* volume, bulk.

voluminoso, *adj.* voluminous, bulky.

vòmere, *n.m.* coulter; plowshare.

vomitare, *vb.* vomit, disgorge.

vòmite, *n.m.* vomit.

vòrtice, *n.m.* vortex, whirlpool, eddy.

vòstro, *adj.* your; yours.

votante, *n.m.* voter.

votare, *vb.* vote.

votazione, *n.f.* voting, ballot.

voto, *n.m.* vow; wish; mark; grade.

vulcano, *n.m.* volcano.

vulneràbile, *adj.* vulnerable.

vuotare, *vb.* empty.

vuòto, 1. *n.m.* emptiness; vacuum. 2. *adj* empty, blank, vacant.

W, Z

W., abbr. for **evviva** hurrah for.

W.C., abbr. for water-closet (toilet).

zaffiro, *n.m.* sapphire.

zàino, *n.m.* knapsack.

zampa, *n.f.* paw.

zampillare, *vb.* gush; squirt.

zampogna, *n.f.* bagpipe.

zàngola, *n.f.* churn.

zanna, *n.f.* fang.

zanzara, *n.f.* mosquito.

zanzarièra, *n.f.* mosquito-net.

zappa, *n.f.* hoe.

zappare, *vb.* hoe.

zàttera, *n.f.* raft.

zavorra, *n.f.* ballast.

zèbra, *n.f.* zebra.

zecca, *n.f.* mint.

zèffiro, *n.m.* zephyr.

zelante, *n.m.* zealous.

zèlo, *n.m.* zeal.

zènzero, *n.m.* ginger.

zeppo, *adj.* chock full.

zèro, *n.m.* zero; cipher.

zia, *n.f.* aunt.

zibellino, *n.m.* sable.

zinco, *n.m.* zinc.

zingara, *n.f.* gypsy woman.

zingaro, *n.m.* gypsy.

zio, *n.m.* uncle.

zitèlla, *n.f.* old maid, spinster.

zitto, *adj.* silent.

zòccolo, *n.m.* hoof; wooden shoe; baseboard.

zòlla, *n.f.* clod, sod.

zòna, *n.f.* zone.

zoològico, *adj.* zoological.

zoologia, *n.f.* zoology.

zoppicamento, *n.m.* limp.

zoppicare, *vb.* limp, hobble.

zòppo, *adj.* lame.

zòtico, 1. *n.* boor. 2. *adj.* boorish.

zoticone, *n.m.* lout.

zucca, *n.f.* gourd, pumpkin, squash.

zùcchero, *n.m.* sugar.

zuppa, *n.f.* soup.

Zurigo, *n.m.* Zurich.

English-Italian

A

a, *art.* un *m.*, una *f.*

abacus, *n.* àbaco *m.*

abandon, 1. *n.* abbandono *m.* 2. *vb.* abbandonare.

abandoned, *adj.* abbandonato.

abandonment, *n.* abbandono *m.*

abase, *vb.* abbassare, avvilire.

abasement, *n.* abbassamento *m.*, avvilimento *m.*

abash, *vb.* sconcertare.

abate, *vb.* diminuire.

abatement, *n.* diminuzione *f.*

abbess, *n.* badessa *f.*

abbey, *n.* badìa *f.*, abbazìa *f.*

abbot, *n.* abate *m.*

abbreviate, *vb.* abbreviare, raccorciare.

abbreviation, *n.* abbreviatura *f.*, raccorciamento *m.*

abdicate, *vb.* abdicare.

abdication, *n.* abdicazione *f.*

abdomen, *n.* addòme *m.*

abdominal, *adj.* addominale.

abduct, *vb.* rapire.

abduction, *n.* rapimento *m.*, ratto *m.*

abductor, *n.* rapitore *m.*

aberrant, *adj.* aberrante.

aberration, *n.* aberrazione *f.*

abet, *vb.* incoraggiare.

abetment, *n.* incoraggiamento *m.*

abettor, *n.* incoraggiatore *m.*

abeyance, *n.* sospensione *f.*

abhor, *vb.* aborrire, detestare.

abhorrence, *n.* aborrimento *m.*, detestazione *f.*, ripugnanza *f.*

abhorrent, *adj.* ripugnante.

abide, *vb.* (dwell) abitare; (remain) rimanere; (tolerate) sopportare.

abiding, *adj.* permanènte, costante.

ability, *n.* abilità *f.*, capacità *f.*

abject, *adj.* abiètto.

abjuration, *n.* abiura *f.*

abjure, *vb.* abiurare.

abjurer, *n.* chi abiura.

ablative, *adj. and n.* ablativo (*m.*).

ablaze, *adj.* in fiamme.

able, *adj.* àbile, capace (di); (be a.) potere.

able-bodied, *adj.* forte, robusto.

ablution, *n.* abluzione *f.*

ably, *adv.* abilmente.

abnegate, *vb.* abnegare.

abnegation, *n.* abnegazione *f.*

abnormal, *adj.* anormale.

abnormality, *n.* anormalità *f.*

abnormally, *adv.* anormalmente.

aboard, 1. *adv.* (naut.) a bordo; (all a.) in carrozza. 2. *prep.* a bordo di.

abode, *n.* dimora *f.*

abolish, *vb.* abolire.

abolishment, *n.* abolimento *m.*

abolition, *n.* abolizione *f.*

abominable, *adj.* abominévole.

abominate, *vb.* abominare.

abomination, *n.* abominazione *f.*

aboriginal, *adj.* indigeno.

aborigine, *n.* indigeno *m.*

abort, *vb.* abortire.

abortion, *n.* aborto *m.*

abortive, *adj.* abortivo.

abound, *vb.* abbondare.

about, 1. *adv.* (approximately) pressappòco, all'incirca; (around) intorno; (be a. to) stare per. 2. *prep.* (concerning; around) intorno a; (near) vicino a.

about-face, *n.* voltafàccia *m.*

above, *adv. and prep.* sopra.

aboveboard, 1. *adj.* sincèro, onèsto. 2. *adv.* apertamente, onestamente.

abrasion, *n.* abrasione *f.*

abrasive, *n. and adj.* abrasivo (*m.*).

abreast, *adv. and prep.* di fianco (a).

abridge, *vb.* abbreviare.

abridgment, *n.* abbreviamento *m.*

abroad, *adv.* all'èstero.

abrogate, *vb.* abrogare.

abrogation, *n.* abrogazione *f.*

abrupt, *adj.* (sudden) improvviso; (steep) ripido; (curt) rude.

abruptly, *adv.* (suddenly) all'improvviso, improvvisamente; (curtly) rudemente.

abruptness, *n.* rudezza *f.*

abscess, *n.* ascèsso *m.*

abscond, *vb.* sparire; (fam.) svignàrsela.

absence, *n.* assènza *f.*

absent, *adj.* assènte.

absentee, *n.* assènte *m.*

absent-minded, *adj.* distratto.

absinthe, *n.* assènzio *m.*

absolute, *adj.* assoluto.

absolutely, *adv.* assolutamente.

absoluteness, *n.* assolutezza *f.*

absolution, *n.* assoluzione *f.*

absolutism, *n.* assolutismo *m.*

absolve, *vb.* assòlvere.

absorb, *vb.* assorbire.

absorbed, *adj.* (lit.) assorbito; (fig.) assorto.

absorbent, *n. and adj.* assorbènte *m.*

absorbing, *adj.* assorbènte.

absorption, *n.* assorbimento *m.*

abstain, *vb.* astenersi.

abstemious, *adj.* astèmio.

abstinence, *n.* astinènza *f.*

abstract, 1. *n.* (book, article) riassunto *m.*, sunto *m.* 2. *adj.* astratto. 3. *vb.* astrarre, riassùmere.

abstracted, *adj.* astratto.

abstraction, *n.* astrazione *f.*

abstruse, *adj.* astruso.

absurd, *adj.* assurdo.

absurdity, *n.* assurdità *f.*, assurdo *m.*

absurdly, *adv.* assurdamente.

abundance, *n.* abbondanza *f.*

abundant, *adj.* abbondante.

abundantly, *adv.* abbondantemente.

abuse, 1. *n.* (misuse) abuso *m.*; (insult) insulto *m.*, ingiùria *f.* 2. *vb.* abusare (di), insultare, ingiuriare.

abusive, *adj.* (misusing) abusivo; (insulting) insolente, ingiurioso.

abusively, *adv.* abusivamente, insolentemente, ingiuriosamente.

abut, *vb.* confinare con.

abutment, *n.* tèrmine *m.*

abyss, *n.* abisso *m.*

Abyssinia, *n.* Abissinia *f.*

Abyssinian, *n. and adj.* abissino.

academic, *adj.* accadèmico.

academic freedom, *n.* libertà d'insegnamento *f.*

academy, *n.* accadèmia *f.*

acanthus, *n.* acanto *m.*

accede, *vb.* consentire.

accelerate, *vb.* accelerare.

acceleration, *n.* accelerazione *f.*

accelerator, *n.* acceleratore *m.*

accent, *n.* accènto *m.*

accentuate, *vb.* (lit.) accentare; (fig.) accentuare.

accept, *vb.* accettare.

acceptability, *n.* accettabilità.

acceptable, *adj.* accètto, accettàbile, gradévole.

acceptably, *adv.* accettabilmente.

acceptance, *n.* accettazione *f.*

access, *n.* accèsso *m.*

accessible, *adj.* accessìbile.

accessory, *n. and adj.* accessòrio (*m.*).

accident, *n.* incidènte *m.*, sinistro *m.*; (by a.) per caso.

accidental, *adj.* accidentale.

accidentally, *adv.* accidentalmente.

acclaim, *vb.* acclamare.

acclamation, *n.* acclamazione *f.*

acclimate, *vb.* acclimare, acclimatare.

acclivity, *n.* acclività *f.*

accolade, *n.* accollata *f.*

accommodate, *vb.* accomodare; (lodge) alloggiare.

accommodating, *adj.* accomodante, cortese.

accommodation, *n.* accomodazione *f.*; (lodging) allòggio *m.*

accompaniment, *n.* accompagnamento *m.*

accompanist, *n.* accompagnatore *m.*

accompany, *vb.* accompagnare.

accomplice, *n.* còmplice *m.* and *f.*

accomplish, *vb.* compire.

accomplished, *adj.* compìto.

accomplishment, *n.* compimento *m.*

accord, n. accòrdo m.

accordance, n. conformità f.; **(in a. with)** conforme a.

accordingly, adv. (correspondingly) conformemente; (therefore) dunque.

according to, prep. secondo.

accordion, n. fisarmònica f.

accost, vb. abbordare.

account, n. (comm.) conto m.; (narrative) racconto m.

accountable for, adj. responsàbile di.

accountant, n. ragioniere.

account for, vb. rèndere conto di.

accounting, n. (occupation) ragionerìa f.; (procedure) contabilità f.

accouter, vb. abbigliare.

accouterments, n. abbigliatura f.sg.

accredit, vb. accreditare.

accretion, n. accrescimento m.

accrual, n. accrescimento m.

accrue, vb. accréscere.

accumulate, vb. accumulare.

accumulation, n. accumulazione f.

accumulative, adj. accumulativo.

accumulator, n. accumulatore m.

accuracy, n. accuratezza f.

accurate, adj. accurato.

accursed, adj. maledetto.

accusation, n. accusa f.

accusative, n. and adj. accusativo (m.).

accuse, vb. accusare, incolpare, imputare.

accused, n. accusato m., incolpato m.

accuser, n. accusatore m., incolpatore m.

accustom, vb. abituare.

accustomed, adj. sòlito, abituale; (be accustomed to) solere; (become accustomed to) abituarsi a.

ace, n. asso m.

acerbity, n. acerbità f.

acetate, n. acetato m.

acetic, adj. acètico.

acetylene, n. acetilène m.

ache, n. dolore m., male m.

achieve, vb. compire, raggiùngere.

achievement, n. compimento m., raggiungimento m.

acid, n. and adj. àcido (m.).

acidify, vb. acidificare.

acidity, n. acidità f.

acidosis, n. acidòsi f.

acid test, n. pròva conclusiva f.

acidulous, adj. acidulo.

acknowledge, vb. (recognize) riconóscere; (a. receipt of) accusare, dichiarare ricevuta di.

acme, n. acme f., punto culminante m.

acne, n. acne f.

acolyte, n. accòlito m.

acorn, n. ghianda f.

acoustics, n. acùstica f.sg.

acquaint, vb. informare, far sapere; (be acquainted with) conóscere.

acquaintance, n. conoscènza f.

acquainted, adj. conosciuto, familiare.

acquiesce, vb. acquietarsi, consentire tacitamente.

acquiescence, n. acquiescenza f.

acquire, vb. acquistare.

acquisition, n. acquisto m.

acquisitive, adj. acquisitivo.

acquit, v. assòlvere.

acquittal, n. assoluzione f.

acre, n. acro m.

acreage, n. estensione di terra f.

acrid, adj. acre.

acrimonious, adj. acre.

acrimony, n. acrèdine f., acrimònia f.

acrobat, n. acròbata m.

across, adv. and prep. attraverso.

acrostic, n. acròstico m.

act, 1. n. atto m. 2. vb. agire; (stage) recitare; (behave) comportarsi.

acting, 1. n. recitazione f. 2. adj. provvisòrio.

actinium, n. attìnio m.

action, n. azione f.

activate, vb. attivare.

activation, n. attivazione f.

activator, n. attivatore m.

active, adj. attivo.

activism, n. attivismo m.

activity, n. attività f.

actor, n. attore m.

actress, n. attrice f.

actual, adj. vero.

actuality, n. verità f.

actually, adv. veramente.

actuary, n. attuàrio m.

actuate, vb. attuare.

acumen, n. acume m.

acupuncture, n. agopuntura f.; acupuntura f.

acute, adj. acuto.

acutely, adv. acutamente.

acuteness, n. acutezza f.

adage, n. adàgio m., màssima f., provèrbio m.

adamant, adj. adamantino.

Adam's apple, n. pomo d'Adamo m.

adapt, vb. addattare.

adaptability, n. adattabilità f.

adaptable, adj. adattàbile.

adaptation, n. adattamento m.

adapter, n. riduttore m.

adaptive, adj. adattévole.

add, vb. (join) aggiùngere; (arith.) sommare, addizionare.

adder, n. vipera f.

addict, n. (drug a.) tossicòmane m.

addict oneself to, vb. dedicarsi a.

addition, n. addizione f.

additional, adj. addizionale.

addle, vb. confondere; (egg) imputridirsi.

addled, adj. confuso; (egg) màrcio, pùtrido.

address, 1. n. (on letters, etc.) indirizzo m.; (speech) discorso m. 2. vb. (a letter) indirizzare; (a person) indirizzarsi a.

addressee, n. destinatàrio m.

adduce, vb. addurre.

adenoid, 1. n. vegetazione adenòide f. 2. n. adenòide f.

adept, adj. dèstro, àbile.

adeptly, adv. destramente, abilmente.

adeptness, n. destrezza f., abilità f.

adequacy, n. sufficienza f.

adequate, adj. adeguato, sufficiènte.

adequately, adv. adeguatamente, sufficientemente.

adhere, vb. aderire.

adherence, n. aderènza f.

adherent, n. aderènte m.

adhesion, n. adesione f.

adhesive, n. and adj. adesivo (m.).

adhesiveness, n. adesività f.

adieu, interj. addìo.

adjacent, adj. adiacènte.

adjective, n. aggettivo m.

adjoin, vb. essere adiacènte a.

adjoining, adj. adiacènte.

adjourn, vb. aggiornare.

adjournment, n. aggiornamento m.

adjunct, n. and adj. aggiunto, accessòrio.

adjust, vb. aggiustare.

adjuster, n. aggiustatore m.

adjustment, n. (action) aggiustamento m.; (money) aggiustatura f.

adjutant, n. aiutante m., assistènte m.

administer, vb. amministrare.

administration, n. amministrazione f.

administrative, adj. amministrativo.

administrator, n. amministratore m.

admirable, adj. ammirévole, ammiràbile.

admirably, adv. ammirabilmente.

admiral, n. ammiràglio m.

admiralty, n. ammiragliato m., ministero della marina m.

admiration, n. ammirazione f.

admire, vb. ammirare.

admirer, n. ammiratore m.

admiringly, adv. con ammirazione.

admissible, adj. ammissibile.

admission, n. (entrance) ammissione f.; (entry) entrata f.; (confession) confessione f.

admit, vb. ammèttere.

admittance, n. ammissione f.; (entry) entrata f.

admittedly, adv. lo confèsso.

admixture, n. mescolanza f.

admonish, *vb.* ammonire.

admonition, *n.* ammonizione *f.*

ado, *n.* fracasso *m.*

adolescence, *n.* adolescènza *f.*

adolescent, *n. and adj.* adolescènte *(m.).*

adopt, *vb.* adottare.

adoption, *n.* adozione *f.*

adorable, *adj.* adoràbile.

adoration, *n.* adorazione *f.*

adore, *vb.* adorare.

adorn, *vb.* adornare, ornare.

adorned, *adj.* adorno.

adornment, *n.* adornamento *m.*

adrenal glands, *n.* ghiàndole surrenali *f.pl.*

adrenalin, *n.* adrenalina *f.*

adrift, *adv.* alla deriva.

adroit, *adj.* destro, àbile.

adulate, *vb.* adulare.

adulation, *n.* adulazione *f.*

adult, *n. and adj.* adulto.

adulterant, *n. and adj.* adulterante.

adulterate, *vb.* adulterare.

adulterer, *n.* adùltero *m.*

adulteress, *n.* adùltera *f.*

adultery, *n.* adultèrio *m.*

advance, 1. *n.* progresso *m.;* (pay) anticipo *m.;* (in a.) in anticipo. 2. *vb.* avanzare, progredire; (pay) anticipare.

advanced, *adj.* avanzato, progredito.

advancement, *n.* avanzamento *m.*

advantage, *n.* vantàggio *m.*

advantageous, *adj.* vantaggioso.

advantageously, *adv.* vantaggiosamente.

advent, *n.* avvènto *m.*

adventitious, *adj.* avventizio.

adventure, 1. *n.* avventura *f.* 2. *vb.* avventurare, rischiare.

adventurer, *n.* avventurière *m.*

adventurous, *adj.* avventuroso.

adventurously, *adv.* avventurosamente.

adverb, *n.* avvèrbio *m.*

adverbial, *adj.* avverbiale.

adversary, *n.* avversàrio *m.*

adverse, *adj.* avvèrso.

adversely, *adv.* avversamente.

adversity, *n.* avversità *f.*

advert, *vb.* avvertire.

advertise, *vb.* far réclame per, reclamizzare.

advertisement, *n.* réclame *f.,* pubblicità *f.;* (newspaper) annunzio *m.,* inserzione *f.*

advertiser, *n.* inserzionista *m.*

advertising, *n.* réclame *f.,* pubblicità *f.*

advice, *n.* consiglio *m.;* (news) avviso *m.*

advisability, *n.* convenienza *f.,* opportunità *f.*

advisable, *adj.* conveniente, opportuno.

advisably, *adv.* opportunamente.

advise, *adv.* consigliare; (inform) avvisare.

advisedly, *adv.* consigliatamente, apposta.

advisement, *n.* deliberazione *f.*

adviser, *n.* consigliatore *m.*

advocacy, *n.* difesa *f.,* propugnazione *f.*

advocate, 1. *n.* (law) avvocato *m.;* (defender) difensore *m.,* propugnatore *m.* 2. *vb.* propugnare, difèndere.

aegis, *n.* ègida *f.*

aerate, *vb.* aerare.

aeration, *n.* aerazione *f.*

aerial, *adj.* aèreo.

aerially, *adv.* perària.

aerie, *n.* nido *m.*

aeronautics, *n.* aeronàutica *f.*

aerosol bomb, *n.* bomboletta nebulizzante *f.*

aesthetic, *adj.* estètico.

aesthetics, *n.* estètica *f.*

afar, *adv.* lontano.

affability, *n.* affabilità *f.*

affable, *adj.* affàbile.

affably, *adv.* affabilmente.

affair, *n.* affare *m.*

affect, *vb.* (move) commuovere; (concern) interessare; (pretend) affettare.

affectation, *n.* affettazione *f.*

affected, *adj.* affettato.

affecting, *adj.* commovènte.

affection, *n.* affezione *f.*

affectionate, *adj.* affetuoso.

affectionately, *adv.* affettosamente.

afferent, *adj.* afferènte.

affiance, *vb.* fidanzare.

affidavit, *n.* dichiarazione giurata *f.*

affiliate, *vb.* affigliare, associare.

affiliation, *n.* affigliazione *f.,* associazione *f.*

affinity, *n.* affinità *f.*

affirm, *vb.* affermare.

affirmation, *n.* affermazione *f.*

affirmative, *adj.* affermativo.

affirmatively, *adv.* affermativamente.

affix, 1. *n.* affisso *m.* 2. *vb.* affissare.

afflict, *vb.* affliggere.

affliction, *n.* afflizione *f.*

affluence, *n.* opulènza *f.*

affluent, *adj.* opulènto.

afford, *vb.* (have the means to) avere i mezzi di.

affray, *n.* lite *f.,* rissa *f.*

affront, 1. *n.* affronto *m.* 2. *vb.* affrontare.

afield, *adv.* (far a.) lontano.

afire, *adv.* in fiamme.

afloat, *adv.* a galla.

aforementioned, *adj.* soprain-dicato, suindicato.

aforesaid, *adj.* sopraddetto, suddetto.

afraid, *pred.adj.* (be a.) aver paùra.

Africa, *n.* Àfrica *f.*

African, *n. and adj.* africano *(m.).*

aft, *adv.* indiètro.

after, 1. *prep.* dopo. 2. *conj.* dopo che.

aftereffect, *n.* effètto *m.*

aftermath, *n.* conseguènze *f.(pl.)*

afternoon, *n.* pomeriggio *m.*

afterthought, *n.* (as an a.) ripensàndoci.

afterward, *adv.* dopo.

afterwards, *adv.* dopo.

again, *adv.* di nuòvo; (again and again) ripetutamente.

against, *prep.* contro.

agape, *adv.* a bocca aperta.

agate, *n.* àgata *f.*

age, 1. *n.* età *f.* 2. *vb.* invecchiare.

aged, *adj.* vècchio.

ageism, *n.* discriminazione basata sull'età *f.*

ageless, *adj.* che non invècchia.

agency, *n.* agenzia *f.*

agenda, *n.* òrdine del giorno *m.*

agent, *n.* agènte *m.*

agglutinate, *vb.* agglutinare.

agglutination, *n.* agglutinazione *f.*

aggrandize, *vb.* ingrandire.

aggrandizement, *n.* ingrandimento *m.*

aggravate, *vb.* aggravare.

aggravation, *n.* aggravamento *m.*

aggregate, 1. *n.* aggregato *m.* 2. *vb.* aggregare.

aggregation, *n.* aggregazione *f.*

aggression, *n.* aggressione *f.*

aggressive, *adj.* aggressivo.

aggressively, *adv.* aggressivamente.

aggressiveness, *n.* aggressività *f.*

aggressor, *n.* aggressore *m.*

aghast, *adj.* sbalordito.

agile, *adj.* àgile.

agility, *n.* agilità *f.*

agitate, *vb.* agitare.

agitation, *n.* agitazione *f.*

agitator, *n.* agitatore *m.*

agnostic, *n. and adj.* agnòstico *(m.).*

ago, *adv.* fa *(always follows).*

agonized, *adj.* agonizzante.

agony, *n.* agonìa *f.;* (be in a.) agonizzare.

agrarian, *adj.* agràrio.

agree, *vb.* concordare, èssere d'accordo.

agreeable, *adj.* piacévole, gradévole; (of persons) simpàtico.

agreeably, *adv.* piacevolmente, gradevolment.

agreeing, *adj.* concòrde.

agreement, *n.* accòrdo *m.*

agriculture, *n.* agricultura *f.*

ahead, *adv.* avanti; (straight a.) sèmpre diritto.

aid, 1. *n.* aiuto *m.* 2. *vb.* aiutare.

aide, *n.* aiutante *m.*

ail, *vb.* èssere malato.

ailing, *adj.* malato.

ailment, *n.* malattìa *f.*

aim, 1. *n.* mira; (purpose) scòpo. 2. *vb.* (point) puntare; (direct) dirìgere; (look toward) mirare.

aimless, *adj.* senza scòpo.

aimlessly, *adv.* senza scòpo.

air, 1. *n.* ària *f.* 2. *vb.* aerare.

airbag, *n.* (in automobiles) sacco ad aria *m.*

air base, *n.* base aèrea *f.*

airborne, *adj.* aviotrasportato.

air-condition, *vb.* istallare un impianto di condizionamento d'ària in.

air-conditioned, *adj.* ad ària condizionata.

air-conditioning, *n.* condizionamento dell'ària *m.*

aircraft, *n.* aèreo *m.*

aircraft-carrier, *n.* portaèrei *m.*

air fleet, *n.* flotta aèrea *f.*

air gun, *n.* fucile ad ària compressa *m.*

airing, *n.* (walk) passeggiata *f.*

air line, *n.* aviolínea *f.*

air liner, *n.* aeroplano *m.*

air mail, *n.* posta aèrea *f.*

airplane, *n.* aeroplano *m.*

air pollution, *n.* inquinamento dell'aria *m.*

airport, *n.* aeropòrto *m.*, aeroscalo *m.*; (for seaplanes) idroscalo *m.*

air pressure, *n.* pressione dell'ària *f.*

air raid, *n.* attacco aèreo *m.*

air-sick, *adj.* (be a.) sentir nàusea (in un aeroplano).

airtight, *adj.* impermeàbile all'ària.

airy, *adj.* arioso.

aisle, *n.* passaggio *m.*; (church) navata *f.*

ajar, *adj.* socchiuso.

akin, *adj.* affine.

alacrity, *n.* alacrità *f.*

alarm, 1. *n.* allarme *m.* 2. *vb.* allarmare, spaventare.

alarmist, *n.* allarmista *m.*

albino, *n. and adj.* albino (*m.*).

album, *n.* album *m.*

albumen, *n.* albume *m.*

alcohol, *n.* àlcool, àlcole *m.*

alcoholic, *adj.* alc(o)òlico.

alcove, *n.* alcòva *f.*

ale, *n.* birra *f.*

alert, 1. *n.* allarme *m.* 2. *adj.* vigilante; (keen) acuto. 3. *vb.* avvertire.

alfalfa, *n.* alfalfa *f.*

algebra, *n.* àlgebra *f.*

alias, *adv.* àlias.

alibi, *n.* àlibi *m.*

alien, *n. and adj.* alièno (*m.*); (foreign) straniero (*m.*), forestiero (*m.*).

alienate, *vb.* alienare.

alight, *vb.* (dismount) smontare; (get down) scéndere.

align, *vb.* allineare.

alike, 1. *adj.* sìmile. 2. *adv.* similmente.

alimentary, *adj.* alimentare.

alimentary canal, *n.* canale alimentàrio *m.*

alive, *adj.* vivente; (be a.) vivere.

alkali, *n.* àlcali *m.*

alkaline, *adj.* alcalino.

all, *adj.* tutto; (above a.) sopratutto; (a. at once) tutt'a un tratto; (a. the same) nondimeno; (a. of you) voi tutti; (not at a.) niente affatto.

allay, *vb.* alleviare; (lessen) diminuire.

allegation, *n.* allegazione *f.*

allege, *vb.* allegare.

allegiance, *n.* fedeltà *f.*

allegory, *n.* allegorìa *f.*

allergy, *n.* allergìa *f.*

alleviate, *vb.* alleviare.

alley, *n.* vìcolo *m.*; (in garden) viale *m.*

alliance, *n.* alleanza *f.*

allied, *adj.* alleato; (related) affine.

alligator, *n.* alligatore *m.*

allocate, *vb.* assegnare.

allot, *vb.* assegnare, divìdere.

allotment, *n.* assegnazione *f.*

allow, *vb.* (permit) perméttere; (admit) amméttere; (grant) concèdere; (a. for) far dèbito conto di.

allowance, *n.* (money) assegno *m.*; (permission) permesso *m.*; (reduction) riduzione *f.*

alloy, 1. *n.* lega *f.* 2. *vb.* mescolare.

all right, *interj.* va bène.

allude, *vb.* allùdere.

allure, *vb.* affascinare, adescare.

alluring, *adj.* adescatore, seducènte.

allusion, *n.* allusione *f.*

ally, 1. *n.* alleato *m.* 2. *vb.* alleare.

almanac, *n.* almanacco *m.*

almighty, *adj.* onnipotente.

almond, *n.* màndorla *f.*

almond-tree, *n.* màndorlo *m.*

almost, *adv.* quasi.

alms, *n.* elemòsina *f.(sg.)*

aloft, *adv.* in alto.

alone, 1. *adj.* solo; (let a.) lasciare in pace. 2. *adv.* solamente.

along, *prep.* lungo; (come a.!) venite dunque!

alongside, 1. *adv.* accanto. 2. *prep.* accanto a.

aloof, 1. *adj.* riservato. 2. *adv.* in disparte.

aloud, *adv.* ad alta voce.

alpaca, *n.* alpaca *m.*

alphabet, *n.* alfabèto *m.*

alphabetical, *adj.* alfabètico.

alphabetize, *vb.* méttere in òrdine alfabètico.

Alps, *n.* Alpi *f.pl.*

already, *adv.* già, di già.

also, *adv.* anche.

altar, *n.* altare *m.*

alter, *vb.* alterare.

alteration, *n.* alterazione *f.*

alternate, 1. *n.* sostituto *m.* 2. *adj.* alternativo. 3. *vb.* alternare.

alternating current, *n.* corrente alternata *f.*

alternative, 1. *n.* alternativa *f.* 2. *adj.* alternativo.

although, *conj.* benchè, quantunque, sebbene.

altitude, *n.* altitùdine *f.*

alto, *n.* contralto *m.*

altogether, *adv.* completamente.

altruism, *n.* altruismo *m.*

alum, *n.* allume *m.*

aluminum, *n.* allumìnio *m.*

always, *adv.* sèmpre.

amalgam, *n.* amàlgama *m.*

amalgamate, *vb.* amalgamare.

amass, *vb.* ammassare.

amateur, *n.* dilettante *m. and f.*

amaze, *vb.* meravigliare, stupire; (be a.d.) meravigliarsi, stupirsi.

amazement, *n.* meraviglia *f.*, stupore *m.*

amazing, *adj.* meraviglioso.

ambassador, *n.* ambasciatore *m.*

amber, *n.* ambra *f.*

ambidextrous, *adj.* ambidèstro.

ambiguity, *n.* ambiguità *f.*

ambiguous, *adj.* ambìguo.

ambition, *n.* ambizione *f.*

ambitious, *adj.* ambizioso.

ambulance, *n.* ambulanza *f.*

ambulatory, *n. and adj.* ambulatòrio (*m.*).

ambush, 1. *n.* imboscata *f.* 2. *vb.* tendere un'imboscata a.

ameliorate, *vb.* migliorare.

amenable, *adj.* responsàbile, governàbile, dòcile.

amend, *vb.* emendare, corrèggere, migliorare.

amendment, *n.* emendamento *m.*

amenity, *n.* amenità *f.*

America, *n.* Amèrica *f.*

American, *n. and adj.* americano (*m.*).

amethyst, *n.* ametista *f.*

amiable, *adj.* amàbile.

amicable, *adj.* amichévole.

amid, *prep.* fra, tra, in mèzzo a.

amidships, *adv.* nel mezzo della nave.

amiss, *adv.* che non va bene; (be a.) non andar bene.

amity, *n.* amicizia *f.*

ammonia, *n.* ammoniaca *f.*

ammunition, *n.* munizione *f.*

amnesia, *n.* amnesìa *f.*

amnesty, *n.* amnistia *f.*

amniocentesis, *n.* amniocentèsi *f.*

amoeba, *n.* amèba *f.*

among, *prep.* fra, tra.

amoral, *adj.* amorale.

amorous, *adj.* amoroso.

amorphous, *adj.* amorfo.

amortize, *vb.* ammortizzare.

amount, 1. *n.* somma *f.*, quantità *f.* 2. *vb.* ammontare.

ampere, *n.* ampère *m.*

amphibian, *n.* anfìbio *m.*

amphibious, *adj.* anfìbio.

amphitheater, *n.* anfiteatro *m.*

ample, *adj.* àmpio.

amplify, *vb.* ampliare, amplificare.

amputate, *vb.* amputare.

amputee, *n.* amputato *m.*, mutilato *m.*

amuse, *vb.* divertire.

amusement, *n.* divertimento *m.*

an, *art.* un *m.*, una *f.*

anachronism, *n.* anacronismo *m.*

analogous, *adj.* anàlogo.

analogy, *n.* analogìa *f.*

analysis, *n.* anàlisi *f.*

analyst, *n.* analista *m.*

analytic, *adj.* analìtico.

analyze, *vb.* analizzare.

anarchy, *n.* anarchìa *f.*

anatomy, *n.* anatomìa *f.*

ancestor, *n.* antenato *m.*

ancestral, *adj.* degli antenati.

ancestry, *n.* lignàggio *m.*

anchor, 1. *n.* àncora *f.* 2. *vb.* ancorare.

anchorage, *n.* ancoràggio *m.*

anchovy, *n.* acciuga *f.*

ancient, *adj.* antico.

and, *conj.* e; (before vowels) ed.

anecdote, *n.* anèddoto *m.*

anemia, *n.* anemìa *f.*

anesthesia, *n.* anestesìa *f.*

anesthetic, *n. and adj.* anestètico *(m.)*.

anesthetist, *n.* anestetista *m. f.*

anew, *adv.* di nuòvo.

angel, *n.* àngelo *m.*

anger, *n.* ira *f.*, ràbbia *f.*

angle, 1. *n.* àngolo *m.* 2. *vb.* (fish) pescare.

angry, *adj.* adirato, arrabiato; (get a.) adirarsi, arrabbiarsi.

anguish, *n.* angóscia *f.*

angular, *adj.* angolare.

aniline, *n.* anilina *f.*

animal, *n. and adj.* animale *(m.)*.

animate, *vb.* animare.

animated, *adj.* animato.

animated cartoon, *n.* disegno animato *m.*

animation, *n.* animazione *f.*

animosity, *n.* animosità *f.*

animus, *n.* ànimo *m.*

anise, *n.* ànice *m.*

ankle, *n.* caviglia *f.*

annals, *n.* annali *m.(pl.)*

annex, 1. *n.* annèsso *m.* 2. *vb.* annèttere.

annexation, *n.* annessione *f.*

annihilate, *vb.* annichilire.

anniversary, *n.* anniversàrio *m.*

annotate, *vb.* annotare.

annotation, *n.* annotazione *f.*

announce, *vb.* annunziare, annunciare.

announcement, *n.* annunzio *m.*

announcer, *n.* annunciatore *m.*, annunciatrice *f.*

annoy, *vb.* infastidire.

annoyance, *n.* fastidio *m.*

annual, *n. and adj.* ànnuo *(m.)*, annuale *(m.)*.

annuity, *n.* annualità *f.*

annul, *vb.* annullare.

anode, *n.* ànodo *m.*

anoint, *vb.* ùngere.

anomalous, *adj.* anòmalo.

anomaly, *n.* anomalìa *f.*

anonymous, *adj.* anònimo.

another, *adj.* un altro *m.*, un'altra *f.*; (one a.) l'un l'altro.

answer, 1. *n.* risposta *f.* 2. *vb.* rispóndere.

answerable, *adj.* responsàbile.

ant, *n.* formica *f.*

antacid, 1. *n.* antàcido *m.* 2. *adj.* antiàcido.

antagonism, *n.* antagonismo *m.*

antagonist, *n.* antagonista *m.*

antagonistic, *adj.* ostile.

antagonize, *vb.* rèndere ostile.

antarctic, *n. and adj.* antàrtico *(m.)*.

antecedent, *adj.* antecedènte.

antedate, *vb.* precédere.

antelope, *n.* antìlope *f.*

antenna, *n.* antenna *f.*

anterior, *adj.* anteriore.

anteroom, *n.* anticàmera *f.*

anthem, *n.* (church music) antifona *f.*; (national a.) inno nazionale *m.*

anthology, *n.* antologìa *f.*

anthracite, *n.* antracite *f.*

anthropological, *adj.* antropològico.

anthropology, *n.* antropologìa *f.*

antiaircraft, *adj.* antiaèreo.

antibody, *n.* anticòrpo *m.*

antic, *n.* buffonata *f.*

anticipate, *vb.* anticipare.

anticipation, *n.* anticipazione *f.*

anticlerical, *adj.* anticlericale.

anticlimax, *n.* delusione *f.*

antidote, *n.* antìdoto *m.*

antimony, *n.* antimònio *m.*

antinuclear, *adj.* antinucleare.

antipathy, *n.* antipatìa *f.*

antiquated, *adj.* antiquato.

antique, 1. *n.* oggetto antico *m.* 2. *adj.* antico.

antiquity, *n.* antiquità *f.*

antiseptic, *n. and adj.* antisèttico *(m.)*.

antisocial, *adj.* antisociale.

antitoxin, *n.* antitossina *f.*

antler, *n.* palco *m.*

anvil, *n.* incùdine *f.*

anxiety, *n.* ànsia *f.*, ansietà *f.*

anxious, *adj.* ansioso.

any, 1. *adj.* (in questions, for "some") del, dello, dell' *m.sg.*, della, dell' *f.sg.*, dei, degli *m.pl.*, delle *f.pl.*; (not . . . any) non . . . nessun; (no matter which) non importa quale; (every) ogni. 2. *pron.* (any of it, any of them, with verb) ne.

anybody, *pron.* qualcuno; (after negative) nessuno; (no matter who) non importa chi.

anyhow, *adv.* in qualche manièra, a ogni modo.

anyone, *pron. see* anybody.

anything, *pron.* qualcosa, qualche còsa; (after negation) niènte; (no matter) non impòrta che còsa.

anyway, *adv. see* anyhow.

anywhere, *adv.* non impòrta dove.

apart, *adv.* a parte.

apartheid, *n.* segregazione razziale *f.*

apartment, *n.* appartamento *m.*

apathetic, *adj.* apàtico.

apathy, *n.* apatìa *f.*

ape, *n.* scimmia *f.*

aperture, *n.* apertura *f.*

apex, *n.* àpice *m.*

aphorism, *n.* aforismo *m.*

apiary, *n.* apiàrio *m.*

apiece, *adj.* l'uno, cadaùno.

apogee, *n.* apogèo *m.*

apologetic, *adj.* (be a.) scusarsi.

apologize for, *vb.* scusarsi di.

apology, *n.* (defense) apologìa *f.*; (excuse) scusa *f.*

apoplectic, *adj.* apoplèttico.

apoplexy, *n.* apoplessìa *f.*

apostate, *n.* apòsta ta *m.*

apostle, *n.* apòstolo *m.*

apostolic, *adj.* apostòlico.

appall, *vb.* spaventare.

apparatus, *n.* apparato *m.*, apparècchio *m.*

apparel, 1. *n.* vèste *f.*, vestimento *m.* 2. *vb.* vestire.

apparent, *adj.* apparènte.

apparition, *n.* apparizione *f.*

appeal, 1. *n.* appèllo *m.* 2. *vb.* appellare.

appear, *vb.* parere; (become visible) apparire; (seem) sembrare; (be evident) risultare.

appearance, *n.* apparènza *f.*; (looks) aspètto *m.*

appease, *vb.* placare, acquetare.

appeasement, *n.* appaciamento *m.*

appeaser, *n.* placatore *m.*

appellant, *n.* appellante *m.*

appellate, *adj.* d'appèllo.

appendage, *n.* appendice *f.*

appendectomy, *n.* appendectomìa *f.*

appendicitis, *n.* appendicite *f.*

appendix, *n.* appendice *f.*

appetite, *n.* appetito *m.*

appetizer, *n.* antipasto *m.*

appetizing, *adj.* gustoso.

applause, *n.* applàuso *m.*

apple, *n.* pomo *m.*, mela *f.*

applesauce, *n.* (lit.) consèrva di mele *f.*; (nonsense) fròttola *f.*

apple-tree, *n.* melo *m.*

appliance, *n.* apparècchio *m.*

appliances, *n.* (electric) eletrodomèstici *m.pl.*

applicable, *adj.* applicàbile.

applicant, *n.* richiedènte *m.*

application, *n.* (putting on) applicazione *f.*; (request) domanda *f.*

applied, *adj.* applicato; (a. work) ricamo applicato *m.*

apply, *vb.* (put on) applicare; (request) richièdere, fare una domanda.

appoint, *vb.* (a person) nominare; (time, place) fissare, stabilire.

appointment, *n.* (nomination) nòmina *f.;* (date) appuntamento *m.*

apportion, *vb.* distribuire.

apposition, *n.* apposizione *f.*

appraisal, *n.* stima *f.*

appraise, *vb.* stimare.

appreciable, *adj.* apprezzàbile.

appreciate, *vb.* apprezzare, tenere in giusto conto.

appreciation, *n.* apprezzamento *m.*

apprehend, *vb.* (fear) temere; (catch) arrestare.

apprehension, *n.* timore *m.*

apprehensive, *adj.* timoroso.

apprentice, *n.* apprendista *m.*

apprise, *vb.* informare.

approach, 1. *n.* accèsso *m.* 2. *vb.* avvicinarsi a.

approachable, *adj.* avvicinàbile.

approbation, *n.* approvazione *f.*

appropriate, 1. *adj.* appropriato. 2. *vb.* (take for oneself) appropriarsi; (set aside funds) stanziare.

appropriation, *n.* stanziamento *m.*

approval, *n.* approvazione *f.*

approve, *vb.* approvare.

approximate, 1. *vb.* approssimare. 2. *adj.* approssimativo.

approximately, *adv.* approssimativamente.

approximation, *n.* approssimazione *f.*

appurtenance, *n.* appartenènza *f.*

apricot, *n.* albicòcca *f.*

April, *n.* aprile *m.*

apron, *n.* grembiule *m.*

apropos, *adv.* a propòsito.

apse, *n.* àbside *f.*

apt, *adj.* atto; (quick at) pronto a.

aptitude, *n.* attitùdine *f.*

Apulia, *n.* le Pùglie *f.pl.*

Apulian, *adj.* pugliese.

aquarium, *n.* acquàrio *m.*

aquatic, *adj.* acquàtico.

aqueduct, *n.* acquedotto *m.*

aqueous, *adj.* àcqueo.

aquiline, *adj.* aquilino.

Arab, *n.* àrabo *m.*

Arabic, *adj.* àrabo.

arable, *adj.* aràbile.

arbiter, *n.* àrbitro *m.*

arbitrary, *adj.* arbitràrio.

arbitrate, *vb.* arbitrare.

arbitration, *n.* arbitrato *m.*

arbitrator, *n.* àrbitro *m.*

arbor, *n.* pergolato *m.*

arboreal, *adj.* arbòreo.

arc, *n.* arco *m.*

arcade, *n.* gallerìa *f.*

arch, *n.* arco *m.*

archaeology, *n.* archeologìa *f.*

archaic, *adj.* arcàico.

archbishop, *n.* arcivéscovo *m.*

archdiocese, *n.* arcidiòcesi *f.*

archduke, *n.* arciduca *m.*

archer, *n.* arcière *m.*

archery, *n.* tiro dell'arco *m.*

archipelago, *n.* arcipèlago *m.*

architect, *n.* architetto *m.*

architectural, *adj.* architettònico.

architecture, *n.* architettura *f.*

archives, *n.* archìvio *m.(sg.)*

archway, *n.* pòrtico *m.*

arctic, *adj.* àrtico.

ardent, *adj.* ardènte.

ardor, *n.* ardore *m.*

arduous, *adj.* àrduo.

area, *n.* àrea *f.*

area code, *n.* prefisso teleselettivo *m.*

arena, *n.* arena *f.*

Argentine, 1. *n.* Argentina *f.* 2. *adj.* argentino.

argue, *vb.* (draw a conclusion) arguire; (quarrel) bisticciarsi.

argument, *n.* (in debate) argomento *m.;* (quarrel) bisticcio *m.*

argumentative, *adj.* litigioso.

aria, *n.*ària *f.*

arid, *adj.* àrido.

arise, *vb.* (get up) levarsi; (come into being) nàscere.

aristocracy, *n.* aristocrazìa *f.*

aristocrat, *n.* aristocràtico *m.*

aristocratic, *adj.* aristocràtico.

arithmetic, *n.* aritmètica *f.*

ark, *n.* arca *f.*

arm, 1. *n.* (body part) bràccio *m.;* (weapon) arma *f.* 2. *vb.* armare.

armament, *n.* armamento *m.*

armchair, *n.* poltrona *f.*

armful, *n.* bracciata *f.*

armhole, *n.* òcchio della mànica *m.*

armistice, *n.* armistizio *m.*

armor, *n.* armatura *f.*

armored, *adj.* blindato.

armory, *n.* armerìa *f.;* magazzino *m.*

armpit, *n.* ascèlla *f.*

arms, *n.* (weapons) armi *f.pl.*

army, *n.* esèrcito *m.*

arnica, *n.* àrnica *f.*

aroma, *n.* aròma *m.*

aromatic, *adj.* aromàtico.

around, 1. *adv.* intorno. 2. *prep.* intorno a.

arouse, *vb.* svegliare.

arraign, *vb.* accusare.

arrange, *vb.* ordinare, disporre, sistemare; (music) ridurre.

arrangement, *n.* ordinamento *m.;* (music) riduzione *f.*

array, 1. *n.* òrdine *m.,* sèrie *f.* 2. *vb.* ordinare.

arrears, *n.* indietrato *m.(sg.)*

arrest, 1. *n.* arrèsto *m.* 2. *vb.* arrestare.

arrival, *n.* arrivo *m.*

arrive, *vb.* arrivare, giùngere.

arrogance, *n.* arroganza *f.*

arrogant, *adj.* arrogante.

arrogate, *vb.* arrogarsi.

arrow, *n.* frèccia *f.,* strale *m.*

arrowhead, *n.* punta di frèccia *f.*

arsenal, *n.* arsenale *m.*

arsenic, *n.* arsènico *m.*

arson, *n.* incèndio doloso *m.*

art, *n.* arte *f.;* (fine arts) bèlle arti *f.pl.*

arterial, *adj.* arteriale.

arteriosclerosis, *n.* arterioscleròsi *f.*

artery, *n.* artèria *f.*

artesian well, *n.* pozzo artesiano *m.*

artful, *adj.* astuto.

arthritis, *n.* artrite *f.*

artichoke, *n.* carciòfo *m.*

article, *n.* artìcolo *m.*

articulate, 1. *adj.* articolato. 2. *vb.* articolare.

articulation, *n.* articolazione *f.*

artifice, *n.* artifìcio *f.*

artificial, *adj.* artificiale.

artificiality, *n.* artificialità *f.*

artillery, *n.* artiglierìa *f.*

artisan, *n.* artigiano *m.*

artist, *n.* artista *m., f.*

artistic, *adj.* artìstico.

artistry, *n.* arte *f.*

artless, *adj.* ingènuo, senz'arte.

as, *prep. and conj.* come; (as if) quasi.

asbestos, *n.* asbèsto *m.*

ascend, *vb.* salire.

ascendancy, *n.* supremazìa *f.*

ascendant, *adj.* suprèmo.

ascent, *n.* salita *f.*

ascertain, *vb.* accertarsi.

ascetic, *n. and adj.* ascètico *(m.).*

ascribe, *vb.* ascrìvere.

ash, *n.* (tree) fràssino *m.*

ashamed, *adj.* vergognoso; (be a. of) vergognarsi di.

ashen, *adj.* di cènere.

ashes, *n.* cènere *f. (sg.).*

ashore, *adv.* a tèrra.

ash-tray, *n.* portacéneri *m.*

Asia, *n.* Àsia *f.*

Asian, *adj.* asiàtico.

aside, *adv.* a parte.

ask, *vb.* (question) domandare; (request) chièdere; (invite) invitare.

askance, *adv.* sospettosamente.

asleep, *adj.* addormentato; (fall a.) addormentarsi.

asparagus, *n.* aspàrago *m.,* spàragi *m.pl.*

aspect, *n.* aspètto *m.*

asperity, *n.* asperità *f.*

aspersion, *n.* denigrazione *f.*

asphalt, *n.* asfalto *m.*

asphyxia, *n.* asfissìa *f.*

asphyxiate, *vb.* asfissiare.

aspirant, *n.* aspirante *m.*

aspirate, 1. *n.* aspirata *f.* 2. *adj.* aspirato. 3. *vb.* aspirare.

aspiration, *n.* aspirazione *f.*

aspirator, *n.* aspiratore *m.*

aspire, *vb.* aspirare.

aspirin, *n.* aspirina *f.*

ass, *n.* àsino *m.*

assail, *vb.* assalire, attaccare.

assailable, *adj.* attaccàbile.

assailant, n. assalitore m.

assassin, n. assassino m.

assassinate, vb. assassinare.

assassination, n. assassinio m.

assault, 1. n. assalto m. 2. vb. assaltare.

assay, 1. n. sàggio m. 2. vb. saggiare, assaggiare.

assemblage, n. riunione f.

assemble, vb. (bring together) riunire; (come together) riunirsi.

assembly, n. riunione f., assemblèa f.; (autos, etc.) montàggio m.

assent, 1. n. assènso m. 2. vb. assentire.

assert, vb. asserire.

assertion, n. asserzione f.

assertive, adj. dogmàtico.

assertiveness, n. dogmaticità f.

assess, vb. (a fine) fissare (una multa); (property) stimare.

assessor, n. assessore m.

asset, n. (possession) bène m.; (in accounting) attivo m.

asseverate, vb. asseverare.

asseveration, n. asseverazione f.

assiduous, adj. assiduo.

assiduously, adv. assiduamente.

assign, vb. assegnare.

assignable, adj. assegnàbile.

assignation, n. assegnazione f.; (date) appuntamento m.

assigned, adj. addetto.

assignment, n. assegnamento m., assegnazione f., incàrico m.; (school) cómpito m.

assimilate, vb. assimilare.

assimilation, n. assimilazione f.

assimilative, adj. assimilativo.

assist, vb. aiutare.

assistance, n. aiuto m.

assistant, n. and adj. assistènte (m.).

associate, vb. associare, tr.; associarsi, intr.

association, n. associazione f.

assonance, n. assonanza f.

assort, vb. assortire.

assorted, adj. assortito.

assortment, n. assortimento m.

assuage, vb. (pain) mitigare; (desire) soddisfare.

assume, vb. assùmere; (appropriate) arrogarsi; (feign) fingere; (suppose) supporre.

assuming, adj. arrogante, presuntuoso.

assumption, n. supposizione f.; (eccles.) Ascensione f.

assurance, n. assicurazione f.

assure, vb. assicurare.

assured, adj. assicurato, sicuro.

assuredly, adv. sicuramente.

aster, n. astro m.

asterisk, n. asterisco m.

astern, adv. a poppa.

asteroid, n. asteròide m.

asthma, n. asma m.

astigmatism, n. astigmatismo m.

astir, adv. in mòto.

astonish, vb. sorprèndere, meravigliare.

astonishment, n. sorpresa f., meraviglia f.

astound, vb. stupire; (be a.ed) stupirsi.

astral, adj. astrale.

astray, 1. adj. sviato. 2. vb. (go a.) sviarsi.

astride, adv. a cavalcioni; prep. a cavalcioni di.

astringent, adj. astringènte.

astrology, n. astrologia f.

astronaut, n. astronauta m.

astronomy, n. astronomia f.

astute, adj. astuto.

asunder, adv. (in twain) in due; (in pieces) a pèzzi.

asylum, n. (refuge) rifùgio m.; (madhouse) manicòmio m.

asymmetry, n. asimmetria f.

at, prep. (time, place, price) ad (before vowels), a (before vowels or consonants); (at someone's house, shop, etc.) da.

ataxia, n. atassia f.

atheist, n. àteo m.

athlete, n. atlèta m.

athletic, adj. atlètico.

athletics, n. atletismo m.

athwart, adv. attravèrso.

Atlantic, adj. atlàntico.

Atlantic Ocean, n. Ocèano atlàntico m.

atlas, n. atlante m.

atmosphere, n. atmosfèra f.

atmospheric, adj. atmosfèrico.

atoll, n. atòllo m.

atom, n. àtomo m.

atomic, adj. atòmico.

atomize, vb. (liquids) nebulizzare.

atonal, adj. atonale.

atone for, vb. espiare.

atonement, n. espiazione f.

atrocious, adj. atroce.

atrocity, n. atrocità f.

atrophy, n. atrofia f.

atropine, n. atropina f.

attach, vb. attaccare.

attaché, n. addetto m.

attachment, n. (lit.) attaccamento m.; (liking) affezione f.; (equipment) accessòrio m.

attack, 1. n. attacco m. 2. vb. attaccare.

attacker, n. assalitore m.

attain, vb. raggiùngere.

attainable, adj. raggiungìbile.

attainment, n. raggiungimento m.

attempt, 1. n. tentativo m. 2. vb. tentare.

attend, vb. (give heed to) prestare attenzione a; (medical) curarsi di; (serve) servire; (meeting) assistere a; (lectures) frequentare; (see to) occuparsi di.

attendance, n. assistènza f.

attendant, n. and adj. assistènte (m.).

attention, n. attenzione f.; (pay a.) fare attenzione.

attentive, adj. attènto.

attentively, adv. attentamente.

attenuate, vb. attenuare.

attest, vb. attestare.

attic, n. soffitta f.

attire, 1. n. abbigliamento m. 2. vb. abbigliare.

attitude, n. atteggiamento m.; (take an a.) atteggiarsi.

attorney, n. procuratore m.

attract, vb. attrarre.

attraction, n. attrazione f.

attractive, adj. attraènte.

attributable, adj. attribuìbile.

attribute, vb. attribuire.

attribution, n. attribuzione f.

attrition, n. attrizione f.

attune, vb. armonizzare; (an instrument) accordare.

auction, n. vèndita all'asta f.

auctioneer, n. banditore m.

audacious, adj. audace.

audacity, n. audàcia f.

audible, adj. udìbile.

audience, n. (listeners) uditòrio m.; (interview) udiènza f.

audiovisual, adj. audiovisio.

audit, 1. n. verifica f., contròllo m. 2. vb. verificare, controllare.

audition, n. audizione f.

auditor, n. uditore m., uditrice f.; (accounts) revisore m., controllore m.

auditorium, n. auditòrio m.

auditory, adj. uditivo.

auger, n. succhièllo m., trivèllo m.

augment, vb. aumentare.

augur, vb. augurare.

August, n. agosto m.

aunt, n. zia f.

auspice, n. auspicio m.

auspicious, adj. favorévole.

austere, adj. austèro.

austerity, n. austerità f.

Austria, n. Àustria f.

Austrian, adj. austrìaco.

authentic, adj. autèntico.

authenticate, vb. autenticare.

authenticity, n. autenticità f.

author, n. autore m.

authoritarian, adj. autoritàrio.

authoritative, adj. autorévole.

authoritatively, adv. autorevolmente.

authority, n. autorità f.

authorization, n. autorizzazione f.

authorize, vb. autorizzare.

auto, n. àuto f.

autobiography, n. autobiografia f.

autocracy, n. autocrazia f.

autocrat, n. autòcrate m.

autograph, n. autògrafo m.

automatic, adj. automàtico.

automatically, adv. automaticamente.

automaton, n. autòma m.

automobile, n. automòbile f.

automotive, adj. automobilistico.

autonomous, adj. autònomo.

autonomy, n. autonomia f.

autopsy, n. autopsia f.

autumn, n. autunno m.

auxiliary, n. and adj. ausiliare (m.).

avail, vb. servire; (be of no a.) non servire a nulla.

available, adj. disponibile.

avalanche, n. valanga f.

avarice, n. avarizia f.

avaricious, adj. avaro.

avenge, vb. vendicare.

avenger, n. vendicatore m.

avenue, n. viale m.

average, 1. n. mèdia f. 2. adj. mèdio. 3. vb. fare la mèdia di.

averse, adj. avvèrso.

aversion, n. avversione f.

avert, vb. impedire.

aviary, n. aviàrio m., uccellièra f.

aviation, n. aviazione f.

aviator, n. aviatore m.

aviatrix, n. aviatrice f.

avid, adj. àvido.

avocation, n. divertimento m.

avoid, vb. evitare, scansare; (so as to a.) a scanso di.

avoidable, adj. evitàbile.

avoidance, n. scanso m.

avow, vb. confessare.

avowal, n. confessione f.

avowedly, adv. lo confesso.

await, vb. aspettare.

awake, 1. adj. sveglio. 2. vb. svegliare, tr.; svegliarsi, intr.

awaken, vb. see awake.

award, 1. n. prèmio m. 2. vb. conferire; (a. a prize to) premiare.

aware, adj. consapévole, cònscio.

awash, adv. al livèllo dell'acqua.

away, adv. via, lontano; (go a.) andàrsene.

awe, 1. n. terrore m., soggezione f. 2. vb. ispirare terrore a.

awesome, adj. tremèndo.

awful, adj. terrìbile.

awhile, adv. per un momento.

awkward, adj. gòffo; (difficult) difficile.

awning, n. tènda f.

awry, adv. di travèrso.

axe, n. àscia f.

axiom, n. assiòma m.

axis, n. asse m.

axle, n. asse m.

ayatollah, n. ayatollah m.

azure, adj. azzurro.

B

babble, 1. n. balbettìo m. 2. vb. balbettare.

babbler, n. balbuziènte m.

babe, n. bimbo m.; (girl) ragazza f.

baboon, n. babbuino m.

baby, n. bimbo m.; (b.-carriage) carrozzèlla f.

babyish, adj. bambinesco, infantile.

bachelor, n. scàpolo m.; (degree) baccellière m.

bacillus, n. bacillo m.

back, 1. n. dòsso m., dòrso m., schièna f. 2. adj. posteriore, 3. vb. (go backwards) indietreggiare; (support) appoggiare, sostenere, spalleggiare; (b. down) cèdere. 4. adv. indiètro.

backbone, n. spina dorsale, f.

backer, n. sostenitore m.

backfire, vb. scoppiare.

background, n. sfondo m.

backhand, n. rovèscio m.

backing, n. appòggio m., sostegno m.

backlash, n. reazione conservatrice f.

backlog, n. risèrve f.pl.

back out, vb. ritirarsi.

backpack, n. sacco da montagna m.

backstage, n. retroscèna f.

backward, 1. adj. stùpido. 2. adv. indiètro.

backwardness, n. stupidità f.

backwards, adv. indiètro.

backwater, n. acqua stagnante f.

backwoods, n. retrotèrra f.

bacon, n. pancetta f.

bacteria, n. battèri m.pl.

bacteriologist, n. batteriòlogo m.

bacteriology, n. batteriologìa f.

bacterium, n. battèrio m.

bad, adj. cattivo.

badge, n. emblèma f., distintivo m.

badger, n. tasso m.

badly, adv. male, malamente.

badness, n. cattivèria f.

bad-tempered, adj. di cattivo umore.

baffle, vb. (hinder) impedire; (perplex) rèndere perplèsso.

bafflement, n. perplessità f.

bag, 1. n. sacco m., borsa f.; (woman's purse) borsetta f. 2. vb. (get) ottenere; (put in a b.) insaccare.

baggage, n. bagàglio m.

baggage cart, n. (airport) carretta per bagagli f.

baggy, adj. gònfio.

bagpipe, n. cornamusa f., zampogna f.

bail, n. cauzione f., garanzia f.

bailiff, n. uscière m.

bail out, vb. (set free) fornire garanzia per; (empty out water) vuotare.

bait, n. esca f.

bake, vb. cuòcere al forno.

baker, n. fornaio m.

bakery, n. forno m.

baking, n. cottura al forno m.

balance, 1. n. (equilibrium) equilìbrio m.; (comm.) saldo m.; (scales) bilància f. 2. vb. bilanciare; (weigh) pesare; (make of equal weight) equilìbrare; (comm.) saldare.

balcony, n. balcone m.

bald, adj. calvo.

baldness, n. calvizie f.sg.

bale, n. balla f.

balk, vb. (hinder) impedire; (refuse to move) essere ritroso.

balky, adj. ritroso.

ball, n. palla f.; (bullet) pallòtola f.; (dance) ballo m.

ballad, n. ballata f.

ballade, n. ballata f.

ballast, n. zavorra f.

ball bearing, n. cuscinetto a sfere m.

ballerina, n. ballerina f.

ballet, n. ballo m.

ballistics, n. balìstica f.

balloon, n. pallone m.

ballot, n. (voting) votazione f.; (paper) scheda f.

ballroom, n. sala da ballo f.

balm, n. bàlsamo m.

balmy, adj. balsàmico.

balsam, n. bàlsamo m.

balustrade, n. balaùstra f., balaustrata f.

bamboo, n. bambù m.

ban, 1. n. proibizione f. 2. vb. proibire.

banal, adj. banale.

banana, n. banana f.

band, n. (group, including musical band) banda f.; (headband) benda f.; (ribbon) strìscia f.

bandage, n. benda f.

bandanna, n. fazzoletto multicolore m.

bandbox, n. cappellièra f.

bandit, n. bandito m.

bandmaster, n. capobanda m., maestro di banda m.

bandsman, n. bandista m.

bandstand, n. palco della banda musicale f.

baneful, adj. dannoso.

bang, 1. n. (hair-do) fràngia f.; (blow) colpo m. 2. vb. sbàttere. 3. interj. pum!

banish, vb. bandire, esiliare.

banishment, n. bando m., esilio m.

banister, n. ringhièra , f.

bank, 1. n. (institution) banca f., banco m.; (edge of water) riva f. 2. vb. (rely on) contare su; (airplane) inclinare.

bankbook, n. libretto di depòsito m.

banker, n. banchière m.

banking, n. operazioni bancàrie f.pl. 2. adj. bancàrio.

bank note, n. banconota f.

bankrupt, 1. adj. fallito. 2. vb. far fallire; (go b.) fallire.

bankruptcy, n. fallimento m., bancarotta f.

banner, n. bandièra f.

banquet, n. banchetto m.

banter, 1. n. scherzo m., cèlia f. 2. vb. scherzare, celiare.

baptism, n. battésimo m.

baptismal, adj. battesimale.

Baptist, n. battista m.

baptistery, n. battistèro m.

baptize, vb. battezzare.

bar, 1. n. sbarra f.; (obstacle) ostàcolo m.; (for drinks) bar m. 2. vb. sbarrare; ostacolare.

barb, n. punta ricurva f.

barbarian, n. bàrbaro m.

barbarism, n. barbàrie f.; (gram.) barbarismo m.

barbarous, adj. bàrbaro m.

barbecue, 1. n. animale arrostito intèro m. 2. vb. arrostire intèro.

barber, n. barbière m., parrucchière m.

barbiturate, n. barbitùrico m.

bare, 1. adj. nudo, scopèrto. 2. vb. scoprire.

bareback, adv. sènza sèlla.

barefoot, adj. scalzo.

barely, adv. appena.

bareness, n. nudità f.

bargain, 1. n. affare m.; (cheap purchase) occasione f. 2. vb. mercanteggiare.

barge, n. chiatta f.

baritone, n. and adj. baritono (m.).

barium, n. bàrio m.

bark, 1. n. (of tree) scorza f., cortèccia f.; (of dog) abbaiamento m. 2. vb. abbaiare.

barley, n. orzo m.

barn, n. granaio m.

barnacle, n. cirrípede m.

barnyard, n. cortile m.

barometer, n. baròmetro m.

barometric, adj. baromètrico.

baron, n. barone m.

baroness, n. baronessa f.

baronial, adj. baronale.

baroque, adj. baròcco.

barracks, n. casèrma f.sg.

barrage, n. fuoco di sbarramento m.

barred, adj. sbarrato; (excluded) escluso; (forbidden) vietato.

barrel, n. barile m.

barren, adj. stèrile.

barrenness, n. sterilità f.

barricade, n. barricata f.

barrier, n. barrièra f.

barroom, n. bèttola f., bar m.

bartender, n. barista m.

barter, 1. n. baratto m. 2. vb. barattare.

base, 1. n. base f. 2. adj. basso. 3. vb. basare.

baseball, n. baseball m.

baseboard, n. zòccolo m.

Basel, n. Basilèa f.

basement, n. cantina f.

baseness, n. bassezza f.

bashful, adj. tìmido.

bashfully, adv. timidamente.

bashfulness, n. timidezza f.

basic, adj. fondamentale.

basin, n. (wash) catino m.; (river) bacino m.

basis, n. base f.

bask, vb. riscaldarsi, godersi.

basket, n. cesta f.

basketball, n. pallacanestro m.

bass, n. (voice) basso m.; (fish) pesce pèrsico m.

bassinet, n. culla f.

bassoon, n. fagòtto m.

bastard, n. and adj. bastardo (m.).

baste, vb. (sewing) imbastire; (cooking) ammorbidire.

bat, n. (animal) pipistrèllo m.; (baseball) bastone m.

batch, n. infornata f.

bate, vb. diminuire.

bath, n. bagno m.

bathe, vb. (tr.) bagnare; (intr.) fare il bagno.

bather, n. bagnante m. or f.

bathing resort, n. stazione balneare f.

bathrobe, n. vestàglia f.

bathroom, n. stanza da bagno f.

bathtub, n. vasca da bagno f.

baton, n. (military) bastone m.; (conductor's) bacchetta f.

battalion, n. battaglione m.

batter, 1. n. (cooking) pasta f. 2. vb. bàttere.

battery, n. batterìa f., pila f.

batting, n. (cotton b.) imbottitura di cotone f.

battle, 1. n. battàglia f. 2. vb. combàttere.

battlefield, n. campo di battàglia m.

battleship, n. nave da guèrra f.

bauxite, n. bauxite m.

bawl, vb. urlare; (b. out) sgridare.

bay, 1. n. (geography) bàia f.; (plant) làuro m.; (howl) latrato m.; (at b.) a bada. 2. adj. (color) baio. 3. vb. latrare; abbaiare.

bayonet, n. baionetta f.

bazaar, n. bazàr m.

be, vb. èssere; (health) stare.

beach, n. spiàggia f., lido m.

beachhead, n. tèsta di sbarco f.

beacon, n. faro m.

bead, 1. n. grano m. 2. vb. ornare di grani.

beading, n. ornamento di grani m.

beady, adj. a forma di grano.

beak, n. becco m.

beaker, n. recipiènte m.

beam, 1. n. (construction) trave f.; (light) ràggio m. 2. vb. irradiare, risplèndere.

beaming, adj. raggiante, risplendènte.

bean, n. fagiòlo m., fava f.

bear, 1. n. (animal) orso m. 2. vb. (carry) portare; (endure) sopportare; (give birth to) partorire.

bearable, adj. sopportàbile.

beard, n. barba f.

bearded, adj. barbuto.

beardless, adj. imbèrbe.

bearer, n. portatore m.

bearing, n. (behavior) condotta f.; (position) orientamento m.; (machinery) cuscinetto m.

bearskin, n. pèlle d'orso f.

beast, n. bèstia f.

beat, 1. n. bàttito m. 2. vb. bàttere; (conquer) vincere.

beaten, adj. battuto.

beatify, vb. beatificare.

beating, n. percosse f.pl.; (defeat) disfatta f.

beatitude, n. beatitùdine f.

beau, n. (fop) damerino m.; (wooer) corteggiatore m.

beautiful, adj. bèllo; (excellent) eccellènte.

beautifully, adv. in bel modo, bène, eccellentemente.

beautify, vb. abbellire.

beauty, n. bellezza f.; (b. parlor) salone di bellezza m.

beaver, n. castòro m.

becalm, vb. abbonacciare.

because, conj. perché; (b. of) a causa di.

beckon, vb. far cenno, accennare.

become, vb. divenire, diventare; (be suitable for) convenire a; (be attractive on) stare bène a.

becoming, adj. grazioso.

bed, n. lètto m.; (for animals) lettièra f.

bedbug, n. cìmice f.

bedclothes, n. lenzuòla f.pl.

bedding, n. letterecci m.pl.

bedfellow, n. compagno di lètto m.

bedizen, vb. ornare.

bedridden, adj. degènte.

bedroom, n. stanza da lètto f.

bedside, n. (at the b. of) al capezzale di.

bedspread, n. copèrta da lètto f.

bedstead, n. lettièra f.

bedtime, n. ora d'andare a lètto m.

bee, n. ape f.

beef, n. bue m.

beefsteak, n. bistecca f.

beehive, n. alveare m.

beer, n. birra f.

beeswax, n. cera f.

beet, n. barbabiètola f.

beetle, n. scarafàggio m.

befall, vb. accadere, capitare.

befit, vb. convenire a.

befitting, adj. conveniènte.

before, 1. adv. (in front) avanti, davanti; (earlier) prima. 2. prep. avanti, davanti a, prima di. 3. conj. prima che.

beforehand, adv. prima, in anticipo.

befriend, vb. aiutare.

befuddle, vb. confóndere.

beg, vb. (ask alms) mendicare; (request) chièdere; (implore) pregare; implorare.

beget, vb. generare.

beggar, n. mendicante m.

beggarly, adj. meschino.

begin, vb. cominciare, incominciare, iniziare, principiare.

beginner, n. principiante m.

beginning, n. principio m., cominciamento m., inizio m.

begrudge, *vb.* invidiare.

beguile, *vb.* ingannare.

behalf, *n.* favore *m.;* **(on b. of)** da parte di; **(in b. of)** a favore di.

behave, *vb.* comportarsi, condursi.

behavior, *n.* comportamento *m.,* condotta *f.*

behead, *vb.* decapitare.

behind, 1. *adv.* indiètro. **2.** *prep.* diètro a.

behold, *vb.* vedere.

beige, *adj.* avana.

being, *n.* èssere *m.;* (existence) esistènza *f.*

bejewel, *vb.* ornare di gioièlli.

belated, *adj.* tardivo.

belch, 1. *n.* rutto *m.* **2.** *vb.* ruttare.

belfry, *n.* campanile *m.*

Belgian, *n.* and *adj.* bèlga.

Belgium, *n.* il Bèlgio *m.*

belie, *vb.* smentire.

belief, *n.* credènza *f.,* opinione *f.,* fede *f.*

believable, *adj.* credíbile.

believe, *vb.* crèdere; (make believe) fíngere.

believer, *n.* credènte *m.*

belittle, *vb.* denigrare.

bell, *n.* (house) campanèllo *m.;* (church) campana *f.*

bellboy, *n.* camerière *m.*

bell buoy, *n.* bòa a campana *f.*

bellicose, *adj.* bellicoso, battagliéro.

belligerence, *n.* belligeranza *f.*

belligerent, *adj.* belligerante, bellicoso.

belligerently, *adv.* bellicosamente.

bellow, 1. *n.* mùgghio *m.,* muggito *m.* **2.** *vb.* muggire, mugghiare.

bellows, *n.* (large) màntice *m.;* (small) soffietto *m.*

bell-tower, *n.* campanile *m.*

belly, *n.* vèntre *m.,* pància *f.*

belong, *vb.* appartenere.

belongings, *n.* possessi *m.pl.* proprietà *f.sg.*

beloved, *adj.* amato, dilètto.

below, *adv.* and *prep.* sotto.

belt, *n.* cintura *f.*

bench, *n.* banco *m.*

bend, *vb.* piegare; (curve) curvare.

beneath, *adv.* and *prep.* sotto.

benediction, *n.* benedizione *f.*

benefactor, *n.* benefattore *m.*

benefactress, *n.* benefattrice *f.*

beneficent, *adj.* benèfico.

beneficial, *adj.* vantaggioso, salutare.

beneficiary, *n.* beneficiàrio *m.*

benefit, 1. *n.* beneficio *m.,* vantaggio *m.* **2.** *vb.* beneficare, trarre vantaggio da *(intr.).*

benevolence, *n.* benevolènza *f.*

benevolent, *adj.* benevolo, caritatèvole.

benevolently, *adv.* benevolmente, caritatevolmente.

benign, *adj.* benigno.

benignity, *n.* benignità *f.*

bent, *adj.* piegato, curvo.

benzine, *n.* benzina *f.*

bequeath, *vb.* legare.

bequest, *n.* legato *m.*

berate, *vb.* sgridare.

bereave, *vb.* orbare, privare.

bereavement, *n.* pèrdita *f.*

beriberi, *n.* beri-bèri *m.*

Bern, *n.* Berna *f.*

berry, *n.* bacca *f.*

berth, *n.* cuccetta *f.*

beseech, *vb.* supplicare.

beseeching, *adj.* supplichévole.

beseechingly, *adv.* supplichevolmente.

beset, *vb.* assalire, assediare.

beside, *prep.* accanto a.

besides, 1. *adv.* inoltre. **2.** *prep.* oltre.

besiege, *vb.* assediare.

besieger, *n.* assediante *m.*

besmirch, *vb.* insudiciare; (dishonor) disonorare.

best, 1. *adj.* il migliore. **2.** *adv.* il mèglio. **3.** *vb.* víncere.

bestial, *adj.* bestiale.

bestir oneself, *vb.* scuòtersi.

best man, *n.* testimone dello sposo *m.*

bestow, *vb.* conferire.

bestowal, *n.* concessione *f.*

bet, 1. *n.* scommessa *f.* **2.** *vb.* scomméttere.

betake (oneself), *vb.* recarsi, andare.

betoken, *vb.* significare.

betray, *vb.* tradire.

betrayal, *n.* tradimento *m.*

betroth, *vb.* fidanzare.

betrothal, *n.* fidanzamento *m.*

better, 1. *adj.* migliore. **2.** *adv.* mèglio. **3.** *vb.* migliorare.

between, *prep.* fra, tra.

bevel, *n.* inclinazione *f.*

beverage, *n.* bevanda *f.*

bewail, *vb.* lamentare, piàngere.

beware, *vb.* guardarsi.

bewilder, *vb.* confóndere, rèndere perplèsso.

bewildered, *adj.* confuso, perplèsso.

bewildering, *adj.* sconcertante.

bewilderment, *n.* confusione *f.,* perplessità *f.*

bewitch, *vb.* ammaliare, stregare.

beyond, 1. *adv.* al di là oltre. **2.** *prep.* al di là di, oltre.

biannual, *adj.* biennale.

bias, 1. *n.* parzialità *f.,* pregiudizio *m.;* (on the b.) in sbieco. **2.** *vb.* predispore.

bib, *n.* bavaglino *m.*

Bible, *n.* Bíbbia *f.*

Biblical, *adj.* bíblico.

bibliography, *n.* bibliografia *f.*

bicarbonate, *n.* bicarbonato *m.*

bicentennial, *adj.* bicentennale.

biceps, *n.* bicípite *m.*

bicker, *vb.* litigare, bisticciarsi.

bicycle, *n.* bicicletta *f.*

bicyclist, *n.* ciclista *m.* or *f.*

bid, 1. *n.* (offer) offèrta *f.;* (in-vitation) invito *m.* **2.** *vb.* (offer) offrire; (command) comandare.

bidder, *n.* offerènte *m.*

bide, *vb.* aspettare.

biennial, *adj.* biennale.

bier, *n.* bara *f.*

bifocal, *adj.* bifocale.

big, *adj.* grande, gròsso; (pregnant) gràvida *f.;* **(b. shot)** pèzzo gròsso *m.*

bigamist, *n.* bígamo *m.*

bigamous, *adj.* bígamo.

bigamy, *n.* bigamía *f.*

bigot, *n.* bigòtto *m.*

bigoted, *adj.* bigòtto.

bigotry, *n.* bigotteria *f.,* bigottismo *m.*

bilateral, *adj.* bilaterale.

bile, *n.* bile *f.*

bilingual, *adj.* bilingue.

bilious, *adj.* (pertaining to bile) biliare; (temperament) bilioso.

bill, *n.* (bird) becco *m.;* (money) biglietto *m.;* (sum owed) conto *m.;* (legislative) progètto di legge *m.;* **(b. of fare)** lista *f.*

billboard, *n.* cartèllo pubblicitàrio *m.*

billet, 1. *n.* allòggio *m.* **2.** *vb.* alloggiare.

billfold, *n.* portafògli *m.*

billiard ball, *n.* palla da biliardo *f.*

billiards, *n.* biliardo *m.sg.*

billion, *n.* bilione *m.*

bill of health, *n.* certificato mèdico *m.*

bill of lading, *n.* polizza di càrico *f.*

bill of sale, *n.* manifèsto di vèndita *m.*

billow, *n.* maroso *m.*

bimetallic, *adj.* bimetàllico.

bimonthly, *adj.* (twice a month) bimensile, quindicinale; (every two months) bimestrale.

bin, *n.* recipiènte *m.*

bind, *vb.* legare; (oblige) obbligare; (a book) rilegare.

bindery, *n.* legatoría *f.*

binding, 1. *n.* (book) rilegatura *f.* **2.** *adj.* obbligatòrio.

binocular, 1. *n.* binòcolo *m.* **2.** *adj.* binoculare.

biochemistry, *n.* biochímica *f.*

biodegradable, *adj.* soggetto alla putrafazione.

biofeedback, *n.* informazione ricevuta da un organismo durante un processo biológico *f.*

biographer, *n.* biògrafo *m.*

biographical, *adj.* biogràfico.

biography, *n.* biografía *f.*

biological, *adj.* biológico.

biologically, *adv.* biologicamente.

biologist, *n.* biologia *f.*

bipartisan, *adj.* di tutti e due i partiti.

biped, *n.* and *adj.* bípede *(m.).*

bird, *n.* uccèllo *m.*

birdlike, *adj.* come un uccèllo.

bird of prey, *n.* uccèllo di rapina *m.*

birth, *n.* nàscita *f.*

birth control, *n.* controllo delle nàscite *m.*

birthday, *n.* compleanno *m.*

birthmark, *n.* vòglia *f.*

birthplace, *n.* luògo di nàscita *m.*

birth rate, *n.* natalità *f.*

birthright, *n.* diritto di primogenitura *m.*

biscuit, *n.* (roll) pannino *m.;* (cracker) biscòtto *m.*

bisect, *vb.* bisecare.

bishop, *n.* véscovo *m.*

bishopric, *n.* vescovato *m.*, diòcesi *f.*

bismuth, *n.* bismuto *m.*

bison, *n.* bisonte *m.*

bit, *n.* (piece) pèzzo *m.;* (a b. of) un po' di; (harness) mòrso *m.;* (computer) singola unità d'informazione *f.*

bitch, *n.* cagna *f.*

bite, 1. *n.* mòrso *m.* 2. *vb.* mòrdere.

biting, *adj.* pungènte.

bitter, *adj.* amaro.

bitterly, *adv.* amaramente.

bitterness, *n.* amarezza *f.*

bivouac, *n.* bivacco *m.*

biweekly, *adj.* (twice a week) bisettimanale; (every two weeks) quindicinale.

black, *adj.* nero.

Black, (*n.* and *adj.*) (person) negro *m.;* negra *f.*

blackberry, *n.* mòra *f.*

blackbird, *n.* mèrlo *m.*

blackboard, *n.* lavagna *f.*

blacken, *vb.* annerire.

black eye, *n.* òcchio pesto *m.*

blackguard, *n.* mascalzone *m.;* furfante *m.*

blackmail, 1. *n.* ricatto *m.* 2. *vb.* ricattare.

blackmailer, *n.* ricattatore *m.*

black market, *n.* mercato nero *m.*

blackout, *n.* oscuramento *m.*

blacksmith, *n.* fabbro ferraio *m.*

bladder, *n.* vescica *f.*

blade, *n.* (of cutting tool) lama *f.;* (grass) fòglia *f.*

blame, 1. *n.* biàsimo *m.* 2. *vb.* biasimare.

blameless, *adj.* innocènte.

blanch, *vb.* impallidire.

bland, *adj.* blando.

blank, 1. *n.* (empty space) spàzio bianco *m.;* (form) mòdulo *m.* 2. *adj.* (page) bianco; (empty) vuòto.

blanket, *n.* copèrta *f.*

blare, 1. *n.* squillo *m.* 2. *vb.* squillare.

blaspheme, *vb.* bestemmiare.

blasphemer, *n.* bestemmiatore *m.*

blasphemous, *adj.* èmpio.

blasphemy, *n.* bestèmmia *f.*

blast, 1. *n.* (of wind) ràffica *f.;*

(explosion) esplosione *f.* 2. *vb.* far saltare.

blatant, *adj.* clamoroso, rumoroso.

blaze, 1. *n.* fiamma *f.;* (fire) fuòco *m.* 2. *vb.* fiammeggiare.

bleach, *vb.* imbiancare.

bleachers, *n.* tribune *f.pl.*

bleak, *adj.* squàllido.

bleakness, *n.* squallore *m.*

bleed, *vb.* sanguinare.

blemish, *n.* màcchia *f.*

blend, 1. *n.* mescolanza *f.* 2. *vb.* mescolare.

bless, *vb.* benedire.

blessed, *adj.* benedetto, beato.

blessing, *n.* benedizione *f.*

blight, 1. *n.* malattìa *f.* 2. *vb.* (be b.ed) ammalare.

blind, 1. *adj.* cièco. 2. *vb.* accecare.

blindfold, 1. *n.* benda *f.* 2. *adj.* bendato. 3. *vb.* bendare.

blindly, *adv.* ciecamente.

blindness, *n.* cecità *f.*

blink, *vb.* sbàttere le pàlpebre.

blinker, *n.* (signal) lampeggiatore *m.*

bliss, *n.* beatitùdine *f.*

blissful, *adj.* beato.

blissfully, *adv.* beatamente.

blister, *n.* vescica *f.*

blithe, *adj.* gaio, gioioso.

blizzard, *n.* tempèsta di neve *f.*

bloat, *vb.* gonfiare.

bloc, *n.* blòcco *m.*

block, 1. *n.* blòcco *m.*, ostàcolo *m.* 2. *vb.* bloccare, ostacolare.

blockade, *n.* blòcco *m.*

blond, *adj.* biondo.

blood, *n.* sangue *m.*

bloodhound, *n.* cane poliziòtto *m.*

bloodless, *adj.* esangue, senza sangue.

blood plasma, *n.* plasma del sangue *m.*

blood poisoning, *n.* avvelenamento del sangue *m.*

blood pressure, *n.* pressione del sangue *f.*

bloodshed, *n.* spargimento di sangue *m.*

bloodshot, *adj.* infiammato.

bloodthirsty, *adj.* sanguinàrio.

bloody, *adj.* sanguinoso.

bloom, 1. *n.* fiore *m.* 2. *vb.* fiorire.

blossom, 1. *n.* fiore *m.* 2. *vb.* fiorire.

blot, 1. *n.* màcchia *f.* 2. *vb.* macchiare; (dry ink) asciugare.

blotch, *n.* (spot) màcchia *f.*, sgòrbio *m.*

blotchy, *adj.* macchiato.

blotter, *n.* carta assorbente *f.*

blouse, *n.* blusa *f.*

blow, 1. *n.* colpo *m.* 2. *vb.* soffiare.

blowout, *n.* scòppio d'un pneumàtico *m.*

blubber, 1. *n.* (whale fat) grasso di balena *f.* 2. *vb.* (snivel) piagnucolare.

bludgeon, *n.* mazza *f.*

blue, *adj.* azzurro, blu; (gloomy) triste.

bluebird, *n.* uccèllo azzurro *m.*

blue jeans, *n.* blue jeans *m.pl.*

blueprint, *n.* eliotipìa *f.;* (plan) piano *m.*

bluff, 1. *n.* (cliff) rupe scoscesa *f.;* (cards) bluff *m.;* (trickery) inganno *m.* 2. *adj.* franco. 3. *vb.* bluffare, ingannare.

bluffer, *n.* bluffatore *m.*

bluing, *n.* anile *m.*

blunder, 1. *n.* errore *m.;* svista *f.* 2. *vb.* sbagliare.

blunderer, *n.* stordito *m.*

blunt, *adj.* (dull) ottuso; (curt) rude.

bluntly, *adv.* ottusamente, rudemente.

bluntness, *n.* ottusità *f.*

blur, 1. *n.* confusione *f.* 2. *vb.* rèndere indistinto.

blush, 1. *n.* rossore *m.* 2. *vb.* arrossire.

bluster, 1. *n.* millanterìa *f.* 2. *vb.* millantare.

boar, *n.* vèrro *m.*

board, 1. *n.* (plank) asse *f.*, tàvola *f.;* (food) vitto *m.;* (committee) comitato *m.;* (council) consiglio *m.;* (of ship) bordo *m.* 2. *vb.* (go on b.) andare a bordo.

boarder, *n.* pensionante *m.*

boarding house, *n.* pensione *f.*

boast, 1. *n.* vanto *m.*, vanterìa *f.* 2. *vb.* vantare, *tr.*

boaster, *n.* vantatore *m.*

boastful, *adj.* vanaglorioso.

boastfulness, *n.* vanterìa *f.*

boat, *n.* barca *f.*, battèllo *m.*

boathouse, *n.* tettòia per barche.

boatswain, *n.* nostròmo *m.*

bob, *vb.* tagliare corto.

bobbin, *n.* bobina *f.*

bobby pin, *n.* forcina *f.*

bode, *vb.* presagire.

bodice, *n.* busto *m.*

bodily, *adj.* corpòreo.

body, *n.* còrpo *m.*

bodyguard, *n.* guàrdia del còrpo *f.*

bog, 1. *n.* pantano *m.*, palude *f.* 2. *vb.* (b. down) impantanarsi.

Bohemian, *n.* and *adj.* boemo (*m.*).

boil, 1. *n.* (med.) forùncolo *m.* 2. *vb.* bollire.

boiler, *n.* caldaia *f.*

boisterous, *adj.* impetuoso, turbolento.

boisterously, *adv.* impetuosamente.

bold, *adj.* ardito; (be b.) ardire.

boldface, *n.* (type) caràtteri grassi *m.pl.*

boldly, *adv.* arditamente.

boldness, *n.* ardimento *m.*

Bolivian, *adj.* boliviano.

bologna, *n.* salsiccia *f.*, salame *m.*

bolster, *vb.* appoggiare.

bolster up, *vb.* tenere su.

bolt, 1. *n.* catenàccio *m.* **2.** *vb.* (shut) chiùdere a catenàccio; (run away) fuggire.

bomb, *n.* bomba *f.*

bombard, *vb.* bombardare.

bombardier, *n.* bombardière *f.*

bombardment, *n.* bombardamento *m.*

bomber, *n.* bombardière *m.*

bombproof, *adj.* a pròva di bomba.

bombshell, *n.* bomba *f.*

bombsight, *n.* traguardo di puntamento *m.*

bonbon, *n.* dolce *m.*

bond, *n.* legame *m.*, obbligazione *f.*, vincolo *m.*, buòno *m.*

bondage, *n.* servitù *f.*

bonded, *adj.* vincolato.

bone, *n.* òsso *m.*

boneless, *adj.* sènza òssa.

bonfire, *n.* falò *m.*

bonnet, *n.* (headdress) cappèllo *m.*; (motor-car) còfano *m.*

bonus, *n.* gratificazione *f.*

bony, *adj.* ossuto.

book, *n.* libro *m.*

bookbinder, *n.* legatore *m.*

bookbindery, *n.* legatoria *f.*

bookcase, *n.* scaffale *m.*

bookkeeper, *n.* contàbile *m.*

bookkeeping, *n.* contabilità *f.*

booklet, *n.* libretto *m.*

bookseller, *n.* libraio *m.*

bookstore, *n.* librerìa *f.*

boom, *n.* prosperità *f.*

boon, *n.* dono *m.*

boor, *n.* zòtico *m.*

boorish, *adj.* zòtico.

boost, 1. *n.* (increase) accrescimento *m.*; (push) spinta *f.* **2.** *vb.* (increase) accréscere; (push) spingere; (praise) lodare.

booster, *n.* (telephone) amplificatore *m.*; (person) entusiasta *m.*

boot, *n.* stivale *m.*

bootblack, *n.* lustrascarpe *m.*

booth, *n.* tènda *f.*

booty, *n.* bottino *m.*

border, 1. *n.* confine *m.*, frontièra *f.* **2.** *vb.* confinare.

borderline, 1. *n.* linea di confine *f.* **2.** *adj.* marginale.

bore, 1. *n.* (hole) foro *m.*; (annoyance) seccatura *f.* **2.** *vb.* (make a hole) forare; (annoy) seccare.

boredom, *n.* nòia *f.*

boric, *adj.* bòrico.

boring, 1. *n.* (hole) foro *m.* **2.** *adj.* seccante.

born, *adj.* nato; (be b.) nàscere.

born-again, *adj.* rinato.

borough, *n.* borgo *m.*

borrow, *vb.* prendere in prèstito.

borrower, *n.* chi prende a prèstito.

bosom, *n.* pètto *m.*, seno *m.*

boss, *n.* padrone *m.*

bossy, *adj.* spadroneggiante.

botanical, *adj.* botànico.

botany, *n.* botànica *f.*

botch, *vb.* rabberciare.

both, *adj. and pron.* ambedue.

bother, 1. *n.* fastidio *m.* **2.** *vb.* infastidire.

bothersome, *adj.* fastidioso.

bottle, *n.* bottiglia *f.*

bottom, *n.* fondo *m.*

bottomless, *adj.* sènza fondo.

boudoir, *n.* salottino *m.*

bough, *n.* ramo *m.*

bouillon, *n.* bròdo *m.*

boulder, *n.* sasso *m.*

boulevard, *n.* viale *m.*

bounce, 1. *n.* rimbalzo *m.* **2.** *vb.* rimbalzare.

bound, 1. *n.* limite *m.*; (jump) balzo *m.*, salto *m.* **2.** *vb.* balzare, saltare.

boundary, *n.* confine *m.*

bound for, *adj.* diretto a.

boundless, *adj.* illimitato.

boundlessly, *adv.* illimitatamente.

bounteous, *adj.* liberale.

bounty, *n.* liberalità *f.*

bouquet, *n.* mazzo di fiori *m.*

bourgeois, *adj.* borghese.

bout, *n.* (boxing) assalto *m.*

bovine, *adj.* bovino.

bow, 1. *n.* (for arrows, violin) arco *m.*; (greeting) inchino *m.*; (of boat) pròra *f.* **2.** *vb.* inchinarsi.

bowels, *n.* budella *f.pl.*, intestini *m.pl.*

bowl, 1. *n.* (vessel) scodèlla *f.* **2.** *vb.* giocare alle bocce.

bowlegged, *adj.* colle gambe ad archetto.

bowler, *n.* giocatore di bocce *m.*

bowling, *n.* giòco delle bocce *f.*

box, 1. *n.* scàtola *f.*, cassetta *f.*; (theater) palco *m.*; (P.O.) casèlla postale *f.* **2.** *vb.* fare del pugilato.

boxcar, *n.* vagone mèrci *m.*

boxer, *n.* pugilatore *m.*

boxing, *n.* pugilato *m.*

box office, *n.* botteghino *m.*

boy, *n.* ragazzo *m.*, fanciullo *m.*

boycott, 1. *n.* boicottàggio *m.* **2.** *vb.* boicottare.

boyhood, *n.* fanciullezza *f.*

boyish, *adj.* fanciullesco.

boyishly, *adv.* fanciullescamente.

brace, 1. *n.* sostegno *m.* **2.** *vb.* sostenere.

bracelet, *n.* braccialetto *m.*

bracket, *n.* mènsola *f.*; (group) gruppo *m.*; (typography) parèntesi quadra *f.*

brag, *vb.* millantare.

braggart, *n.* millantatore *m.*

braid, 1. *n.* tréccia *f.* **2.** *vb.* intrecciare.

brain, *n.* cervèllo *m.*

brainy, *adj.* intelligènte.

brake, 1. *n.* freno *m.* **2.** *vb.* frenare.

bran, *n.* crusca *f.*

branch, *n.* ramo *m.*; (comm.) succursale *f.*

brand, *n.* marca *f.*

brandish, *vb.* brandire.

brand-new, *adj.* nuovissimo.

brandy, *n.* acquavite *f.*

brash, *adj.* impertinènte.

brass, *n.* ottone *m.*

brassiere, *n.* reggipètto *m.*, reggiseno *m.*

brat, *n.* marmòcchio *m.*

bravado, *n.* bravata *f.*

brave, *adj.* coraggioso.

bravery, *n.* coràggio *m.*

brawl, *n.* lite *f.*, rissa *f.*

brawn, *n.* fòrza muscolare *f.*

bray, 1. *n.* ràglio *m.* **2.** *vb.* ragliare.

brazen, *adj.* di ottone; (insolent) insolènte.

Brazil, *n.* il Brasile *m.*

Brazilian, *adj.* brasiliano.

breach, *n.* bréccia *f.*; (of law) violazione *f.*

bread, *n.* pane *m.*

breadth, *n.* larghezza *f.*, ampiezza *f.*

break, 1. *n.* rottura *f.*; interruzione *f.* **2.** *vb.* ròmpere.

breakable, *adj.* rompibile.

breakage, *n.* rottura *f.*

breaker, *n.* frangènte *m.*

breakfast, *n.* prima colazione *f.*

breakneck, *adv.* a rompicollo.

breakwater, *n.* frangi-onde *m.*

breast, *n.* seno *m.*, mammèlla *f.*, poppa *f.*; (chest) pètto *m.*

breath, *n.* fiato *m.*, respiro *m.*

breathe, *vb.* respirare.

breathing, *n.* respiro *m.*

breathless, *adj.* sènza fiato; ansante.

breathlessly, *adv.* ansando.

breeches, *n.* brache *f.pl.*, pantaloni *m.pl.*

breed, 1. *n.* razza *f.* **2.** *vb.* (beget) generare; (train) educare; (raise) allevare.

breeder, *n.* generatore *m.*, allevatore *m.*

breeding, *n.* educazione *f.*

breeze, *n.* brezza *f.*

breezy, *adj.* (windy) ventoso; (cool) fresco.

brevity, *n.* brevità *f.*

brew, *vb.* fabbricare la birra.

brewer, *n.* birraio *m.*, fabbricante di birra *m.*

brewery, *n.* fàbbrica di birra *f.*

briar, *n.* rovo *m.*

bribe, *vb.* corrómpere.

briber, *n.* corruttore *m.*

bribery, *n.* corruzione *f.*

brick, *n.* mattone *m.*

bricklayer, *n.* muratore *m.*

bricklaying, *n.* muratura *f.*

bricklike, *adj.* come un mattone.

bridal, *adj.* nuziale.

bride, *n.* sposa *f.*

bridegroom, *n.* sposo *m.*

bridesmaid, *n.* damigèlla d'onore *f.*

bridge, *n.* ponte *m.*

bridged, *adj.* connèsso.

bridgehead, n. tèsta di ponte f.

bridle, n. briglia f.

brief, adj. bréve.

brief case, n. borsa f.

briefly, adv. brevemente.

briefness, n. brevità f.

brier, n. rovo m.

brig, n. brigantino m.

brigade, n. brigata f.

bright, adj. chiaro; luminoso.

brighten, vb. illuminare.

brightness, n. chiarore m.

brilliance, n. splendore m.

brilliant, adj. brillante.

brim, n. (cup) orlo m.; (hat) tesa f.

brine, n. acqua salata f.

bring, vb. portare; apportare; (b. about) causare.

brink, n. orlo m.; bordo m.

briny, adj. salato.

brisk, adj. vivace.

brisket, n. (meat) pètto m.

briskly, adv. vivacemente.

briskness, n. vivacità f.

bristle, 1. n. sétola f. 2. vb. arruffare.

bristly, adj. setoloso.

Britain, n. (Great B.) la Gran Bretagna f.

British, adj. britànnico.

Briton, n. Brètone m.

brittle, adj. fràgile.

broad, adj. largo, àmpio.

broadcast, 1. n. trasmissione radiofònica f. 2. vb. trasméttere.

broadcaster, n. trasmettitore m.

broadcloth, n. popelina f.

broaden, vb. allargare.

broadly, adv. largamente.

broadminded, adv. spregiudicato.

broadside, n. bordata f.

brocade, n. broccato f.

brocaded, adj. di broccato.

broil, adv. mettere alla graticola.

broiler, n. graticola f.

broke, adj. al verde.

broken, adj. rotto.

broken-hearted, adj. scorato.

broker, n. sensale m.

brokerage, n. senseria f.

bronchial, adj. bronchiale.

bronchitis, n. bronchite f.

bronze, n. bronzo m.

brooch, n. spilla f.

brood, 1. n. covata f., famiglia f. 2. vb. covare.

brook, n. ruscèllo m.

broom, n. scopa f.

broomstick, n. mànico della scopa f.

broth, n. bròdo m.

brothel, n. bordèllo m.

brother, n. fratèllo m.

brotherhood, n. fratellanza f.

brother-in-law, n. cognato m.

brotherly, adj. fratèrno.

brow, n. fronte f.

brown, adj. bruno.

browse, vb. brucare.

bruise, 1. n. ammaccatura f. 2. vb. ammaccare.

brunette, n. bruna f.

brunt, n. urto m.

brush, 1. n. spàzzola f.; (artist's) pennèllo m. 2. vb. spazzolare; (b. against) sfiorare.

brushwood, n. màcchia f.

brusque, adj. brusco.

brusquely, adv. bruscamente.

brutal, adj. brutale.

brutality, n. brutalità f.

brutalize, vb. abbrutire.

brute, n. and adj. bruto (m.).

bubble, n. bolla f.

buck, n. dàino m.; (male) màschio m.

bucket, n. sécchia f.

buckle, 1. n. fibbia f. 2. vb. affibbiare.

buckram, n. tela da fusto f.

bucksaw, n. sega intelaiata f.

buckshot, n. pallinacci m.pl.

buckwheat, n. grano saraceno m.

bud, 1. n. gèmma f. 2. vb. gemmare.

budge, vb. muòversi.

budget, n. preventivo m.

buffalo, n. bùfalo m.

buffer, n. respingènte m.; (b. state) stato cuscinetto m.

buffet, 1. n. (slap) schiaffo m.; (eating place) caffè m. 2. vb. schiaffeggiare.

buffoon, n. buffone m.

bug, n. insètto m.

bugle, n. bùccina f.

build, vb. costruire, fabbricare.

builder, n. costruttore m.

building, n. edificio m.

bulb, n. (of plant) bulbo m.; (electric light) lampadina f.

bulge, 1. n. protuberanza f. 2. vb. gonfiarsi.

bulk, n. volume m., massa f.

bulkhead, n. paratìa f.

bulky, adj. voluminoso.

bull, n. tòro m.

bulldog, n. molòsso m.

bulldozer, n. livellatrice f.

bullet, n. pallòttola f.

bulletin, n. bollettino m.

bulletproof, adj. a pròva di fucile.

bullfinch, n. ciuffolòtto m.

bullion, n. (gold) oro in lingotti m.

bully, n. prepotènte m.

bulwark, n. baluardo m.

bum, n. vagabondo m.

bumblebee, n. calabrone m.

bump, 1. n. urto m. 2. vb. urtare.

bumper, n. respingènte m.

bun, n. panino m.

bunch, n. mazzo m., gràppolo m.

bundle, n. fàscio m.

bungalow, n. bungalò m.

bungle, vb. abborracciare.

bunion, n. infiammazione del pòllice del piède f.

bunk, n. (bed) cuccetta f.; (nonsense) fròttole f.pl.

bunny, n. coniglietto m.

bunting, n. stamigna f.

buoy, n. bòa f.

buoyant, adj. che può galleggiare; (cheerful) allegro.

burden, n. fardèllo m.; (b. of proof) ònere della pròva m.

burdensome, adj. opprimènte, oneroso.

bureau, n. ufficio m.

burglar, n. ladro m.

burglarize, vb. rubare.

burglary, n. furto m.

burial, n. sepoltura f.

burlap, n. canovàccio rozzo m.

burly, adj. corpulènto.

burn, 1. n. bruciatura f. 2. vb. bruciare, àrdere.

burner, n. bècco m.

burning, adj. bruciante, ardènte.

burnish, vb. brunire.

burrow, 1. n. tana f. 2. vb. scavare.

burst, 1. n. scatto m. 2. vb. scoppiare; (dash) scattare; (b. forth) prorómpere.

bury, vb. seppellire.

bus, n. àutobus m.; (trolley b.) filobus m.; (de luxe b.) pullman m.; (b. line) autolinea f.

bush, n. cespuglio m.

bushel, n. mòggio m.

bushy, adj. cespuglioso; (thick) folto.

busily, adv. attivamente.

business, n. affare m.; affari m.pl.

businesslike, adj. pràtico.

businessman, n. uòmo d'affari m.

businesswoman, n. dònna d'affari f.

bust, n. busto m.

bustle, n. tramestìo m.

busy, adj. occupato, affaccendato, attivo.

busybody, n. faccendière m.

but, 1. prep. eccètto, salvo. 2. conj. ma.

butcher, 1. n. macellaio m. 2. vb. macellare.

butchery, n. macèllo m.

butler, n. maggiordòmo m.

butt, n. estremità f.; (of gun) càlcio m.

butter, n. burro m.

buttercup, n. ranùncolo m.

butterfat, n. grasso del latte m.

butterfly, n. farfalla f.

buttermilk, n. sièro m.

buttock, n. nàtica f.

button, n. bottone m.

buttonhole, n. occhièllo m.

buttress, n. contrafforte m.

buxom, adj. grassòccio.

buy, vb. comprare.

buyer, n. compratore m.

buzz, 1. n. ronzìo m. 2. vb. ronzare.

buzzard, n. poiana f.

buzzer, n. campanèllo m.

buzz saw, n. sega circolare f.

by, prep. (through) per; (near)

prèsso a; (at) a; (indicating agent) da.

by-and-by, adv. fra pòco.

bygone, adj. passato.

by-law, n. legge particolare f.

by-pass, vb. evitare.

by-product, n. prodotto secondàrio m.

bystander, n. spettatore m.

byte, n. unità bàsica di dati f.

byway, n. viòttolo m.

C

cab, n. tassi m.

cabaret, n. ritròvo notturno m.

cabbage, n. càvolo m.

cabin, n. capanna f.; (on boat) cabina f.

cabinet, n. (furniture) stipo m.; (politics) gabinetto m.

cabinetmaker, n. stipettaio m.

cable, n. cavo m.

cablegram, n. cablogramma m.

cableway, n. funivia f.

cache, n. nascondiglio m.

cachet, n. sigillo m.

cackle, 1. n. vèrso m. 2. vb. cantare.

cacophony, n. cacofonia f.

cactus, n. cacto m.

cad, n. vigliacco m.

cadaver, n. cadàvero m.

cadaverous, adj. cadavèrico.

cadet, n. cadetto m.

cadence, n. cadènza f.

cadmium, n. càdmio m.

cadre, n. quadro m.

café, n. caffè m.

caffeine, n. caffeina f.

cage, 1. n. gàbbia f. 2. vb. ingabbiare.

caisson, n. cassone m.

cajole, vb. lusingare.

cake, n. tòrta f., focàccia f.

calamitous, adj. calamitoso.

calamity, n. calamità f.

calcify, vb. calcificare.

calcium, n. càlcio m.

calculable, adj. calcolàbile.

calculate, vb. calcolare.

calculating, adj. calcolatore; (c. machine) màcchina calcolatrice f.

calculation, n. càlcolo m.

calculus, n. càlcolo m.

caldron, n. caldaia f.

calendar, n. calendàrio m.

calf, n. vitèllo m.

calfskin, n. pèlle di vitèllo f.

caliber, n. càlibro m.

calico, n. calicò m.

caliper, n. càlibro m.

calisthenic, adj. ginnàstico.

calisthenics, n. ginnàstica f.

calk, vb. calafatare.

calker, n. calafato m.

call, 1. n. chiamata f., appèllo m. 2. vb. chiamare.

calligraphy, n. calligrafia f.

calling, n. vocazione f., professione f.

calling card, n. biglietto di vìsita m.

callous, adj. calloso; (unfeeling) insensibile.

callousness, n. callosità f., insensibilità f.

callow, adj. inespèrto.

callus, n. callo m.

calm, 1. n. calma f. 2. adj. calmo. 3. vb. calmare.

calmly, adv. con calmo.

calmness, n. calma f.

caloric, adj. calòrico.

calorie, n. caloria f.

calorimeter, n. calorìmetro m.

calumniate, vb. calunniare.

calumny, n. calùnnia f.

Calvary, n. Calvàrio m.

calve, vb. partorire.

calyx, n. càlice m.

camaraderie, n. cameratismo m.

cambric, n. cambrì m.

camel, n. cammèllo m.

camelia, n. camèlia f.

camel's hair, n. peli di cammèllo m.pl.

cameo, n. cammèo m.

camera, n. màcchina fotogràfica f.

camouflage, 1. n. camuffamento m., mimetismo m. 2. vb. camuffare, mimetizzare.

camp, 1. n. accampamento m. 2. vb. accamparsi; (sport) campeggiare.

campaign, n. campagna f.

camper, n. campeggiatore m.

camphor, n. cànfora f.

camping, n. campèggio m.

campus, n. città universitària f.

can, 1. n. (tin) scàtola f.; (large) bidone m. 2. vb. (be able) potere.

Canada, n. il Canadà m.

Canadian, adj. canadese.

canal, n. canale m.

canalize, vb. canalizzare.

canapé, n. crostino m.

canard, n. fròttola f.

canary, n. canarino m.

Canary Islands, n. Canàrie f.pl.

cancel, vb. annullare, cancellare, disdire.

cancellation, n. annullamento m.

cancer, n. cancro m.

candelabrum, n. candelabro m.

candid, adj. càndido, franco.

candidacy, n. candidatura f.

candidate, n. candidato m.

candidly, adv. candidamente, francamente.

candidness, n. franchezza f., candore m.

candied, adj. candito.

candle, n. candela f.

candlestick, n. candelière m.

candor, n. candore m.

cane, n. bastone m.; (plants) canna f.

canine, adj. canino.

canister, n. scàtola f.

canker, n. cancro m.

cankerworm, n. bruco m.

canned, adj. in scàtola.

canner, n. fabbricante di consèrve alimentari m.

cannery, n. stabilimento di consèrve alimentari m.

cannibal, n. cannibale m.

canning, n. preparazione di consèrve alimentari f.

cannon, n. cannone m.

cannonade, n. cannoneggiamento m.

cannoneer, n. cannonière m.

cannot, vb. non potere.

canny, adj. astuto.

canoe, n. canòa f.

canon, n. (rule, law) cànone m.; (person) canònico m.

canonical, adj. canònico.

canonize, vb. canonizzare.

can-opener, n. apriscàtole m.

canopy, n. baldacchino m.

cant, n. ipocrisia f.

can't, vb. non potere.

cantaloupe, n. mellone m.

canteen, n. cantina f.

canter, vb. andare al piccolo galòppo.

cantonment, n. accantonamento m.

canvas, n. canovàccio m.

canvass, 1. n. esame m. 2. vb. esaminare.

canyon, n. burrone m.

cap, n. berretto m.

capability, n. capacità f.

capable, adj. capace, àbile.

capably, adv. abilmente.

capacious, adj. spazioso.

capacity, n. capacità f.

caparison, 1. n. bardatura f. 2. vb. bardare.

cape, n. cappa f.

caper, 1. n. capriòla f. 2. vb. far capriòle.

capillary, adj. capillare.

capital, 1. n. (money) capitale m.; (city) capitale f. 2. adj. capitale.

capitalism, n. capitalismo m.

capitalist, n. capitalista m.

capitalistic, adj. capitalistico.

capitalization, n. capitalizzazione f.

capitalize, vb. capitalizzare.

capitulate, vb. capitolare.

capon, n. cappone m.

caprice, n. capriccio m.

capricious, adj. capriccioso.

capriciously, adv. capricciosamente.

capriciousness, n. capricciosità f.

capsize, vb. capovòlgere.

capsule, n. càpsula f.

captain, n. capitano m.

caption, n. titolo m.

captious, adj. capzioso.

captivate, vb. affascinare.

captive, n. and adj. prigionièro (m.).

captivity, n. prigionia f.

captor, n. catturatore m.

capture, 1. n. cattura f. 2. vb. catturare.

car, n. carro m., vettura f.;

(auto) automòbile *f.;* (railroad) vagone *m.*

caracul, *n.* lince persiana *f.*

carafe, *n.* caraffa *f.*

caramel, *n.* caramèlla *f.*

carat, *n.* carato *m.*

caravan, *n.* carovana *f.*

caraway, *n.* carvi *m.*

carbide, *n.* carburo *m.*

carbine, *n.* carabina *f.*

carbohydrate, *n.* idrato di carbònio *m.*

carbon, *n.* carbònio *m.*

carbon dioxide, *n.* biòssido di carbònio *m.*

carbon monoxide, *n.* monòssido di carbònio *m.*

carbon paper, *n.* carta a carbone *f.*

carbuncle, *n.* carbónchio *m.*

carburetor, *n.* carburatore *m.*

carcass, *n.* carcassa *f.*

carcinogenic, *adj.* carcinogènico.

card, *n.* carta *f.*, biglietto *m.;* (filing) schedina *f.*

cardboard, *n.* cartone *m.;* (thin) cartoncino *m.*

cardiac, *adj.* cardíaco.

cardigan, *n.* golf *m.*

cardinal, *adj. and n.* cardinale *(m).*

care, 1. *n.* cura *f.* 2. *vb.* curarsi; (take c. of) curare.

careen, *vb.* carenare.

career, *n.* carrièra *f.*

carefree, *adj.* sènza preoccupazioni.

careful, *adj.* accurato, attento.

carefully, *adv.* accuratamente, attentamente.

carefulness, *n.* accuratezza *f.,* attenzione *f.*

careless, *adj.* spensierato, trascurato.

carelessly, *adv.* spensieratamente, trascuratamente.

carelessness, *n.* spensieratezza *f.,* trascuratezza *f.*

caress, 1. *n.* carezza *f.* 2. *vb.* accarezzare.

caretaker, *n.* guardiano *m.*

cargo, *n.* càrico *m.*

caricature, *n.* caricatura *f.*

caries, *n.* càrie *f.*

carillon, *n.* cariglione *m.*

carload, *n.* carrettata *f.*

carnal, *adj.* carnale.

carnation, *n.* garòfano *m.*

carnival, *n.* carnevale *m.*

carnivorous, *adj.* carnivoro.

carol, 1. *n.* canto di Natale *m.* 2. *vb.* cantare.

carouse, *vb.* far baldòria.

carousel, *n.* carosèllo *m.*

carpenter, *n.* falegname *m.*

carpet, *n.* tappeto *m.*

carpeting, *n.* stoffa per tappeti *f.*

car pool, *n.* consòrzio automobilístico *m.*

carriage, *n.* (vehicle) vettura *f.;* (transportation) traspòrto *m.*

carrier, *n.* portatore *m.*

carrier pigeon, *n.* piccione viaggiatore *m.*

carrot, *n.* caròta *f.*

carry, *vb.* portare; (c. on) tinuare; (c. out) eseguire; (c. through) condurre a buon fine.

cart, *n.* carro *m.*

cartage, *n.* traspòrto *m.*

cartel, *n.* cartèllo *m.*

carter, *n.* carrettière *m.*

cartilage, *n.* cartilàgine *f.*

carton, *n.* scàtola di cartone *f.*

cartoon, *n.* (sketch) cartone *m.;* (picture) disegno *m.*

cartridge, *n.* cartùccia *f.*

carve, *vb.* (art) scolpire; (meat) tagliare, trinciare.

carver, *n.* scultore *m.*

carving, *n.* scultura *f.*

carving-knife, *n.* trinciante *m.*

cascade, *n.* cascata *f.*

case, *n.* (instance; state of things) caso *m.;* (law) càusa *f.;* (packing) cassa *f.;* (holder) astùccio *m.;* (in any c.) in ogni caso.

cash, 1. *n.* contanti *m.pl.* 2. *vb.* (cheque) riscuòtere.

cashier, *n.* cassière *m.;* (cashier's desk) cassa *f.*

cashmere, *n.* casimiro *f.*

casing, *n.* copertura *f.*

casino, *n.* casino *m.*

cask, *n.* barile *m.*

casket, *n.* cassettina *f.*

casserole, *n.* casseruòla *f.*

cassette, *n.* cassetta *f.*

cast, 1. *n.* (throw) gètto *m.* 2. *vb.* gettare; (metal) fóndere.

castanets, *n.* nàcchere *f.pl.*

castaway, *n.* nàufrago *m.*

caste, *n.* casta *f.*

caster, *n.* fonditore *m.*

castigate, *vb.* castigare.

cast iron, *n.* ghisa *f.*

castle, *n.* castèllo *m.*

castoff, *adj.* abbandonato.

casual, *adj.* (accidental) casuale; (nonchalant) indifferente.

casually, *adv.* casualmente, indifferentemente.

casualness, *n.* indifferenza *f.*

casualty, *n.* (accident) disgràzia *f.;* (injured person) ferito *m.*

cat, *n.* gatto *m.*, gatta *f.*

cataclysm, *n.* cataclisma *m.*

catacomb, *n.* catacomba *f.*

catalogue, *n.* catàlogo *m.*

catapult, *n.* catapulta *f.*

cataract, *n.* cateratta *f.*

catarrh, *n.* catarro *m.*

catastrophe, *n.* catàstrofe *f.*

catch, *vb.* afferrare; (sickness) prèndere.

catcher, *n.* chi affèrra, chi prende.

catchword, *n.* parola di richiamo *f.*

catchy, *adj.* melodioso.

catechism, *n.* catechismo *m.*

catechize, *vb.* catechizzare.

categorical, *adj.* categòrico.

category, *n.* categorìa *f.*

cater, *vb.* provvedere a.

caterpillar, *n.* bruco *m.*

catgut, *n.* minùgia *f.pl.*

catharsis, *n.* catarsi *f.*

cathartic, *adj.* purgativo.

cathedral, *n.* cattedrale *f.*

cathode, *n.* càtodo *m.*

Catholic, *adj.* cattòlico.

Catholicism, *n.* cattolicismo *m.*

cat nap, *n.* pisolino *m.*

catsup, *n.* salsa di pomodoro *f.*

cattle, *n.* bestiame *m.*

cattleman, *n.* bovaro *m.*

catwalk, *n.* ballatòio *m.*

cauliflower, *n.* cavolfiore *m.*

causation, *n.* causalità *f.*

cause, 1. *n.* càusa *f.* 2. *vb.* causare, cagionare.

causeway, *n.* strada selciata *f.*

caustic, *adj.* càustico, sarcàstico.

cauterize, *vb.* cauterizzare.

cautery, *n.* cautèrio *m.*

caution, 1. *n.* cautèla *f.* 2. *vb.* ammonire.

cautious, *adj.* càuto.

cavalcade, *n.* cavalcata *f.*

cavalier, *n.* cavalière *m.*

cavalry, *n.* cavallerìa *f.*

cave, *n.* cavèrna *f.*

cave-in, *n.* crollo *m.*

cavern, *n.* cavèrna *f.*

caviar, *n.* caviale *m.*

cavity, *n.* cavità *f.*

caw, *vb.* gracchiare.

cayman, *n.* caimano *m.*

cease, *vb.* cessare.

ceaseless, *adj.* incessante.

cedar, *n.* cedro *m.*

cede, *vb.* cèdere.

ceiling, *n.* soffitto *m.*

celebrant, *n.* celebrante *m.*

celebrate, *vb.* celebrare.

celebrated, *adj.* (famous) cèlebre.

celebration, *n.* celebrazione *f.*

celebrity, *n.* celebrità *f.*

celerity, *n.* celerità *f.*

celery, *n.* sèdano *m.*

celestial, *adj.* celèste.

celibacy, *n.* celibato *m.*

celibate, *adj.* cèlibe.

cell, *n.* (room) cèlla *f.;* (biology) cèllula *f.*

cellar, *n.* cantina *f.*

cellist, *n.* violoncellista *m.*

cello, *n.* violoncèllo *m.*

cellophane, *n.* cellòfane *f.*

cellular, *adj.* cellulare.

celluloid, *n.* cellulòide *f.*

cellulose, *n.* cellulosa *f.*

Celtic, *adj.* cèltico.

cement, 1. *n.* cemento *m.* 2. *vb.* cementare.

cemetery, *n.* cimitèro *m.*, camposanto *m.*

censor, 1. *n.* censore *m.* 2. *vb.* censurare.

censorious, *adj.* censòrio.

censorship, *n.* censura *f.*

censure, *n.* censura *f.*

census, *n.* censimento *m.*

cent, *n.* centèsimo *m.*

centenary, *adj. and n.* centenàrio *(m.)*

centennial, *adj. and n.* centennale *(m.)*

center, *n.* cèntro *m.*

centerfold, *n.* pàgine centrali *f.pl.*

centerpiece, *n.* centro da tàvola *m.*

centigrade, *adj.* centìgrado.

central, *adj.* centrale.

centralize, *vb.* centralizzare.

century, *n.* sècolo *m.*

century plant, *n.* àgave *f.*

ceramic, *adj.* ceràmico.

ceramics, *n.* ceràmica *f.*

cereal, *n. and adj.* cereale *(m.)*

cerebral, *adj.* cerebrale.

ceremonial, *adj.* cerimoniale.

ceremonious, *adj.* cerimonioso.

ceremony, *n.* cerimònia *f.*

certain, *adj.* cèrto.

certainly, *adv.* certamente.

certainty, *n.* certezza *f.*

certificate, *n.* certificato *m.*

certification, *n.* certificazione *f.*

certify, *vb.* certificare.

certitude, *n.* certezza *f.*

cervical, *adj.* cervicale.

cervix, *n.* cervice *f.*

cessation, *n.* cessazione *f.*

cession, *n.* cessione *f.*

cesspool, *n.* pozzo nero *m.*

chafe, *vb.* (warm) riscaldare; (irritate) irritare.

chaff, 1. *n.* pula *f.*, lòppa *f.*; (banter) cèlia *f.* 2. *vb.* celiare.

chagrin, *n.* crùccio *m.*

chain, 1. *n.* catena *f.* 2. *vb.* incatenare.

chain reaction, *n.* reazione a catena *f.*

chair, *n.* sèdia *f.*

chairman, *n.* presidènte *m.*

chairmanship, *n.* presidènza *f.*

chairperson, *n.* presidente *m.;* presidèntessa *f.*

chairwoman, *n.* presidèntessa *f.*

chalice, *n.* càlice *f.*

chalk, *n.* gesso *m.*

chalky, *adj.* gessoso.

challenge, 1. *n.* sfida *f.* 2. *vb.* sfidare.

challenger, *n.* sfidatore *m.*

chamber, *n.* càmera *f.;* (c.-pot) vaso da nòtte *m.*

chamberlain, *n.* ciambellano *m.*

chambermaid, *n.* camerièra *f.*

chamber music, *n.* mùsica da càmera *f.*

chameleon, *n.* camaleonte *m.*

chamois, *n.* camòscio *m.*

champ, *vb.* ròdere.

champagne, *n.* sciampagna *f.*

champion, *n.* campione *m.*

championship, *n.* campionato *m.*

chance, 1. *n.* caso *m.;* (opportunity) occasione *f.;* (by c.) per caso 2. *adj.* fortùito.

chancel, *n.* còro *m.*

chancellery, *n.* cancelleria *f.*

chancellor, *n.* cancellière *m.*

chandelier, *n.* lampadàrio *m.*

change, 1. *n.* cambio *m.,* cambiamento *m.,* mutamento *m.;* (small coins) moneta spicciola *f.;* (money due) rèsto *m.* 2. *vb.* cambiare, mutare.

changeability, *n.* mutabilità *f.*

changeable, *adj.* mutévole.

changer, *n.* (money-changer) cambiavalute *m.*

channel, *n.* canale *m.*

chant, 1. *n.* canto *m.* 2. *vb.* cantare.

chaos, *n.* càos *m.*

chaotic, *adj.* caòtico.

chap, 1. *n.* (on skin) screpolatura *f.;* (fellow) tizio *m.* 2. *vb.* screpolare.

chapel, *n.* cappèlla *f.*

chaplain, *n.* cappellano *m.*

chapter, *n.* capìtolo *m.*

char, *vb.* carbonizzare.

character, *n.* caràttere *m.*

characteristic, 1. *n.* caratterìstica *f.* 2. *adj.* caratterìstico.

characteristically, *adv.* caratterìsticamente.

characterization, *n.* caratterizzazione *f.*

characterize, *vb.* caratterizzare.

charcoal, *n.* carbone di legna *m.*

charge, 1. *n.* (load) càrico *m.;* (attack; gun) càrica *f.;* (price) prèzzo *m.;* (custody) custòdia *f.* 2. *vb.* (load) caricare; (set a price) far pagare.

charger, *n.* cavallo da guerra *m.*

chariot, *n.* carro *m.*

charioteer, *n.* auriga *m.*

charisma, *n.* carisma *m.*

charitable, *adj.* caritatévole.

charitableness, *n.* carità *f.*

charitably, *adv.* caritatevolmente.

charity, *n.* carità *f.*

charlatan, *n.* ciarlatano *m.*

charlatanism, *n.* ciarlatanismo *m.*

charm, 1. *n.* incanto *m.;* (good-luck c.) portafortuna *m.* 2. *vb.* incantare, affascinare.

charmer, *n.* incantatore *m.,* incantatrice *f.*

charming, *adj.* affascinante

chart, *n.* (map) carta *f.;* (graph) gràfico *m.*

charter, *n.* carta *f.*

charter flight, *n.* volo noleggiato *m.*

charwoman, *n.* domèstica *f.*

chase, 1. *n.* càccia *f.* 2. *vb.* cacciare.

chaser, *n.* cacciatore *m.*

chasm, *n.* abisso *m.*

chassis, *n.* telaio *m.*

chaste, *adj.* casto.

chasten, *vb.* castigare.

chasteness, *n.* castità *f.*

chastise, *vb.* castigare, punire.

chastisement, *n.* castigo *m.,* punizione *f.*

chastity, *n.* castità *f.*

chat, 1. *n.* chiàcchiera *f.* 2. *vb.* chiacchierare.

château, *n.* castèllo *m.*

chattel, *n.* bène mòbile *m.*

chatter, 1. *n.* chiàcchiera *f.* 2. *vb.* chiacchierare.

chatterbox, *n.* chiacchierone *m.*

chauffeur, *n.* autista *m.*

cheap, *adj.* a buòn mercato, econòmico.

cheapen, *vb.* (prices) calare; (depreciate) deprezzare.

cheaply, *adv.* a buòn mercato, economicamente.

cheapness, *n.* buòn mercato *m.*

cheat, *vb.* ingannare, truffare.

cheater, *n.* ingannatore *m.,* truffatore *m.*

check, 1. *n.* (restraint) freno *m.;* (verification) contròllo *m.;* (theater) contromarca *f.;* (clothes; luggage) scontrino *m.;* (bill) conto *m.;* (bank) assegno *m.* 2. *vb.* (restrain) frenare; (verify) controllare; (luggage) registrare.

checker, *n.* scacco *m.*

checkerboard, *n.* scacchièra *f.*

checkers, *n.* dama *f.*

checkmate, *n.* scacco matto *m.*

cheek, *n.* guància *f.*

cheer, 1. *n.* applàuso *m.* 2. *vb.* applaudire; (c. up) rallegrare, *tr.*

cheerful, *adj.* allegro.

cheerfulness, *n.* allegrìa *f.*

cheerless, *adj.* triste.

cheery, *adj.* allegro.

cheese, *n.* càcio *m.,* formàggio *m.*

cheesecloth, *n.* garza *f.*

cheesy, *adj.* di qualità inferiore.

chef, *n.* cuòco *m.*

chemical, *adj.* chìmico.

chemically, *adv.* chimicamente.

chemist, *n.* chìmico *m.*

chemistry, *n.* chìmica *f.*

chemotherapy, *n.* chimioterapìa *f.*

chenille, *n.* ciniglia *f.*

cheque, *n.* assegno *m.*

cherish, *vb.* tener caro.

cherry, *n.* ciliègia *f.*

cherry-tree, *n.* ciliègio *m.*

cherub, *n.* cherubino *m.*

chess, *n.* scacchi *m.pl.*

chessboard, *n.* scacchièra *f.*

chessman, *n.* scacco *m.*

chest, *n.* (box) cassa *f.;* (body) pètto *m.*

chestnut, *n.* (nut) castagna *f.;* (tree) castagno *m.*

chevron, *n.* gallone *m.*

chew, *vb.* masticare.

chewer, *n.* masticatore *m.*

chic, *adj.* alla mòda.

chicanery, *n.* sofisma *m.*

chick, *n.* pulcino *m.*

chicken, *n.* pollo *m.*

chicken-hearted, *adj.* tìmido.

chicken-pox, *n.* varicèlla *f.*

chicory, *n.* cicòria *f.*

chide, vb. rimproverare, sgridare.

chief, 1. n. capo m. 2. adj. principale.

chiefly, adv. principalmente.

chieftain, n. capo m.

chiffon, n. mussolina leggerissima f.

chilblain, n. gelone m.

child, n. bambino m., bambina f.

childbirth, n. parto m.

childhood, n. infànzia f.

childish, adj. infantile.

childishness, n. infantilità f.

childless, adj. sènza figli.

childlessness, n. stato di èssere sènza figli m.

childlike, adj. infantile.

chill, 1. n. freddo m.; (shiver) brivido m. 2. vb. raffreddare.

chilliness, n. freddo m.

chilly, adj. freddo, gèlido.

chime, 1. n. scampanìo m. 2. vb. scampanare.

chimney, n. camino m.

chimney-sweep, n. spazzacamino m.

chimpanzee, n. scimpanzè m.

chin, n. mento m.

China, n. (la) Cina f.

china, n. porcellana f.

chinchilla, n. cincìglia f.

Chinese, adj. cinese.

chink, n. crèpa f.

chintz, n. indiana f.

chip, 1. n. schèggia f. 2. vb. scheggiare.

chiropodist, n. callista m.

chiropractor, n. callista m.

chirp, 1. n. cinguettìo m. 2. vb. cinguettare.

chisel, 1. n. cesèllo m. 2. vb. cesellare.

chivalrous, adj. cavalleresco.

chivalry, n. cavalleria f.

chive, n. cipolla f.

chloride, n. cloruro m.

chlorine, n. clòro m.

chloroform, n. clorofòrmio m.

chlorophyll, n. clorofilla f.

chock full, adj. pieno zeppo.

chocolate, n. cioccolato m.

choice, 1. n. scelta f. 2. adj. scelto.

choir, n. còro m.

choke, vb. soffocare, strangolare.

choker, n. cravatta f.

choler, n. còllera f.

cholera, n. colèra f.

choleric, adj. collèrico.

choose, vb. scègliere.

chop, 1. n. (meat) costoietta f. 2. vb. tagliare.

chopper, n. (knife) mannaia f.

choppy, adj. (of sea) corto.

chopstick, n. bacchetta f.

choral, adj. corale.

chord, n. (string) còrda f.; (harmony) accòrdo m.

chore, n. faccènda di casa f.

choreographer, n. coreògrafo m.

choreography, n. coreografìa f.

chorister, n. corista m.

chortle, vb. ridacchiare.

chorus, n. còro m.

chowder, n. minestra di pesce f.

Christ, n. Cristo m.

christen, vb. battezzare.

Christendom, n. cristianità f.

christening, n. battésimo m.

Christian, n. and adj. cristiano.

Christianity, n. cristianésimo m.

Christmas, n. Natale m.

chromatic, adj. cromàtico.

chrome, chromium, n. cròmo m.

chromosome, n. cromosòma m.

chronic, adj. crònico.

chronically, adv. cronicamente.

chronicle, n. crònaca f.

chronological, adj. cronològico.

chronology, n. cronologìa f.

chrysalis, n. crisàlide f.

chrysanthemum, n. crisantèmo m.

chubby, adj. grassetto.

chuck, vb. (cluck) chiocciare; (throw) lanciare.

chuckle, vb. ridere sotto voce.

chug, 1. n. sbuffo m. 2. vb. sbuffare.

chum, n. compagno m.

chummy, adj. ìntimo.

chunk, n. pèzzo m.

chunky, adj. tozzo.

church, n. chièsa f.

churchman, n. prète m.

churchyard, n. cimitèro m., camposanto m.

churn, n. zàngola f.

chute, n. canale di scolo m.

cicada, n. cicala f.

cider, n. sidro m.

cigar, n. sìgaro m.

cigarette, n. sigaretta f.

cilia, n. ciglio m.

ciliary, adj. ciliare.

cinch, n. còsa cèrta f.

cinchona, n. cincona f.

cinder, n. brùscolo m.

cinema, n. cìnema m., cinematògrafo m.

cinematic, adj. cinematogràfico.

cinnamon, n. (tree) cinnamòmo m.; (spice) cannèlla f.

cipher, n. (zero) zèro m.; (figure, secret writing) cifra f.

circle, n. (figure) cèrchio m.; (group) circolo m.

circuit, n. circùito m.; (short c.) corto circùito m.

circuitous, adj. indiretto.

circuitously, adv. indirettamente.

circular, n. and adj. circolare (m.).

circularize, vb. mandare dei circolari a.

circulate, vb. circolare.

circulation, n. circolazione f.

circulatory, adj. circolatòrio.

circumcise, vb. circoncìdere.

circumcision, n. circoncisione f.

circumference, n. circonferènza f.

circumlocution, n. circonlocuzione f.

circumscribe, vb. circonscrìvere.

circumspect, adj. circospètto.

circumstance, n. circostanza f.

circumstantial, adj. circostanziale; (detailed) particolareggiato.

circumstantially, adv. circostanziatamente.

circumvent, vb. circonvenire, impedire.

circumvention, n. circonvenzione f.

circus, n. circo m.

cirrhosis, n. cirròsi f.

cistern, n. cistèrna f., serbatòio m.

citadel, n. cittadèlla f.

citation, n. citazione f.

cite, vb. citare.

citizen, n. cittadino m., cittadina f.

citizenry, n. cittadinanza f.

citizenship, n. cittadinanza f.

citric, adj. cìtrico.

city, n. città f.; (small c.) cittadina f.

civic, adj. cìvico.

civil, adj. civile.

civilian, n. and adj. civile.

civility, n. civiltà f.

civilization, n. civiltà f.

civilize, vb. civilizzare.

civilized, adj. civile.

clabber, n. quagliata f.

clad, adj. vestito.

claim, 1. n. reclamo m. 2. vb. reclamare.

claimant, n. reclamante m.

clairvoyance, n. chiaroveggènza f.

clairvoyant, n. and adj. chiaroveggènte m. and f.

clamber, vb. arrampicarsi.

clammy, adj. freddo e ùmido.

clamor, n. clamore m.

clamorous, adj. clamoroso.

clamp, n. grappa f.

clan, n. clan m., tribù f.; (clique) cricca f.

clandestine, adj. clandestino.

clandestinely, adv. clandestinamente.

clang, n. fragore m.

clangor, n. clangore m.

clap, vb. (applaud) applaudire; (hands) bàttere le mani.

clapboard, n. tègola di legno f.

clapper, n. battàglio m.

claret, n. claretto m.

clarification, n. chiarificazione f.

clarify, vb. chiarificare.

clarinet, n. clarinetto m.

clarinetist, n. clarinettista m.

clarion, n. chiarina f.

clarity, n. chiarità f.

clash, 1. *n.* urto *m.* 2. *vb.* urtarsi.

clasp, 1. *n.* gàncio *m.;* (hand) stretta di mano *f.;* (embrace) abbràccio *m.* 2. *vb.* agganciare, stringere, abbracciare.

class, 1. *n.* classe *f.;* (social) cèto *m.* 2. *vb.* classificare.

classic, classical, *adj.* clàssico.

classicism, *n.* classicismo *m.*

classifiable, *adj.* classificàbile.

classification, *n.* classificazione *f.*

classify, *vb.* classificare.

classmate, *n.* compagno di classe *m.*

classroom, *n.* àula *f.*

clatter, *n.* rumore *m.*

clause, *n.* clàusola *f.*

claustrophobia, *n.* claustrofobia *f.*

claw, *n.* artiglio *m.*, ràffio *m.*

claw-hammer, *n.* martèllo a ràffio *m.*

clay, *n.* argilla *f.*, creta *f.*

clayey, *adj.* argilloso.

clean, 1. *adj.* pulito, netto. 2. *vb.* pulire.

clean-cut, *adj.* netto.

cleaner, *n.* pulitore *m.*

cleanliness, cleanness, *n.* pulizia *f.*

cleanse, *vb.* pulire.

clear, 1. *adj.* chiaro. 2. *vb.* (clear up) chiarire; (profit) guadagnare; (pass beyond) sorpassare; (weather, *refl.*) schiarirsi; (leave free) sgomberare.

clearance, *n.* permesso di partire *m.*

clear-cut, *adj.* netto.

clearing, *n.* radura *f.*

clearing house, *n.* stanza di compensazione *f.*

clearly, *adv.* chiaramente.

clearness, *n.* chiarezza *f.*

cleat, *n.* bietta *f.*

cleavage, *n.* fessura *f.*, scissione *f.*

cleave, *vb.* fèndere.

cleaver, *n.* mannaia *f.*

clef, *n.* chiave *f.*

cleft, *n.* fenditura *f.*

clemency, *n.* clemènza *f.*

clench, *vb.* stringere.

clergy, *n.* clèro *m.*

clergyman, *n.* ecclesiàstico *m.*

clerical, *adj.* clericale.

clericalism, *n.* clericalismo *m.*

clerk, *n.* (clergyman) ecclesiàstico *m.;* (employee) impiegato *m.*

clerkship, *n.* posto d'impiegato *m.*

clever, *adj.* àbile, ingegnoso.

cleverly, *adv.* abilmente, ingegnosamente.

cleverness, *n.* abilità *f.*, ingegnosità *f.*

clew, *n.* filo *m.*

cliché, *n.* luògo comune *m.*

click, *n.* rumore secco *m.*

client, *n.* cliènte *m.*

clientele, *n.* clientèla *f.*

cliff, *n.* rupe *f.*

climactic, *adj.* culminante.

climate, *n.* clima *f.*

climatic, *adj.* climàtico.

climax, *n.* cùlmine *m.*

climb, *vb.* scalare, arrampicarsi su.

climber, *n.* arrampicatore *m.;* (social) arrivista *m.* or *f.*

clinch, *vb.* (grasp) afferrare; (confirm) confermare; (conclude) conclùdere.

cling, *vb.* aderire.

clinic, *n.* clìnica *f.*

clinical, *adj.* clìnico.

clinically, *adv.* clinicamente.

clip, 1. *n.* gàncio *m.* 2. *vb.* (hair) tagliare; (wool) tosare; (plants) cimare.

clipper, *n.* tosatore *m.*

clipping, *n.* tosatura *f.*

clique, *n.* cricca *f.*

cloak, *n.* mantèllo *m.;* (cloakroom) guardaròba *f.*

clock, *n.* orològio *m.;* (two o'c.) le due.

clockwise, *adj.* and /adv. destròrso.

clockwork, *n.* meccanismo d'orologerìa *m.*

clod, *n.* zòlla *f.;* (person) tànghero *m.*

clog, 1. *n.* (wooden shoe) zòccolo *m.* 2. *vb.* ingombrare.

cloister, *n.* chiòstro *m.*

clone, *n.* riproduzione esatta *f.*

close, 1. *adj.* (closed) chiuso; (narrow) stretto; (near) vicino; (secret) riservato; (compact) servato *m.* 3. *vb.* chiùdere. 3. *adv.* vicino. 4. *prep.* (c. to) vicino a.

closely, *adv.* da vicino.

closeness, *n.* prossimità *f;* (weather) pesantezza *f.;* (secrecy) riservatezza *f.*

closet, *n.* (toilet) gabinetto *m.;* (clothes) armàdio *m.*

closure, *n.* chiusura *f.*

clot, 1. *n.* grumo *m.* 2. *vb.* raggrumarsi.

cloth, *n.* stòffa *f.*, tela *f.*

clothe, *vb.* vestire.

clothes, *n.* vestiti *m.pl.*

clothespin, *n.* ferabiancherìa *m.*

clothier, *n.* pannaiòlo *m.*

clothing, *n.* vestiti *m.pl.*

cloud, 1. *n.* nùvola *f.*, nube *f.* 2. *vb.* (c. over) rannuvolarsi.

cloudburst, *n.* acquazzone *m.*

cloudiness, *n.* nuvolosità *f.*

cloudless, *adj.* senza nùvole, sereno.

cloudy, *adj.* nuvoloso.

clout, 1. *n.* (blow) colpo *m.;* (rag) stràccio *m.* 2. *vb.* picchiare.

clove, *n.* chiodo di garòfano *m.*

clover, *n.* trifòglio *m.*

clown, *n.* pagliàccio *m.*

clownish, *adj.* pagliaccesco.

cloy, *vb.* saziare.

club, 1. *n.* (group) circolo *m.;*

(stick) bastone *m.* 2. *vb.* bastonare.

clubfoot, *n.* piede stòrto *m.*

clubs, *n.* (cards) fiori *m.pl.*

clue, *n.* filo *m.*

clump, *n.* gruppo *m.*

clumsiness, *n.* goffàggine *f.*

clumsy, *adj.* goffo.

cluster, 1. *n.* gràppolo *m.;* (people) gruppo *m.* 2. *vb.* raggruppare.

clutch, 1. *n.* (claw) artiglio *m.;* (automobile) frizione *f.* 2. *vb.* afferrare.

clutter, *vb.* ingombrare.

coach, 1. *n.* (carriage) carrozza *f.;* (horse-drawn) còcchio *m.;* (train) vagone *m.;* (sports) allenatore *m.* 2. *vb.* (sports) allenare; (school) dare lezioni private a.

coachman, *n.* cocchière *m.*

coagulate, *vb.* coagulare.

coagulation, *n.* coagulazione *f.*

coal, *n.* carbone fòssile *m.*

coalesce, *vb.* coalizzarsi.

coalition, *n.* coalizione *f.*

coal oil, *n.* petròlio *m.*

coal tar, *n.* catrame *m.*

coarse, *adj.* grossolano.

coarsen, *vb.* rèndere grossolano.

coarseness, *n.* grossolanità *f.*

coast, *n.* còsta *f.*

coastal, *adj.* costièro.

coaster, *n.* (ship) nave costièra *f.*

coast guard, *n.* milizia guardacòste *f.*

coat, *n.* (of suit) giacca *f.;* (overcoat) sopràbito *m.*

coating, *n.* strato *m.*

coat of arms, *n.* insegna *f.*, stèmma *m.*

coax, *vb.* blandire.

cobalt, *n.* cobalto *m.*

cobbler, *n.* ciabattino *m.*, calzolaio *m.*

cobblestone, *n.* ciòttolo *m.*

cobra, *n.* còbra *m.*

cobweb, *n.* ragnatelo *m.*

cocaine, *n.* cocaìna *f.*

cock, 1. *n.* (rooster) gallo *m.;* (male) maschio *m.;* (of gun) cane *m.;* (tap) rubinetto *m.*

cocker spaniel, *n.* cocker *m.*

cockeyed, *adj.* (lit.) stràbico; (crazy) matto, pazzo.

cockhorse, *n.* cavallo a dóndolo *m.*

cockpit, *n.* carlinga *f.*

cockroach, *n.* blatta *f.*

cocksure, *adj.* presuntuoso.

cocktail, *n.* coctèl *m.*

cocky, *adj.* impudènte.

cocoa, *n.* cacao *m.*

coconut, *n.* (tree) còcco *m.;* (nut) noce di còcco *f.*

cocoon, *n.* bòzzolo *m.*

cod, *n.* merluzzo *m.*

C.O.D., *adv.* contro assegno.

coddle, *vb.* vezzeggiare.

code, *n.* (law) còdice *m.;* (secret) cifràrio *m.*

codeine, *n.* codeìna *f.*

codfish, n. merluzzo m.

codify, vb. codificare.

cod-liver oil, n. òlio di fègato di merluzzo m.

coeducation, n. insegnamento misto m.

coeducational, adj. misto.

coequal, adj. coeguale.

coerce, vb. costringere.

coercion, n. coercizione f.

coercive, adj. coercitivo.

coexist, vb. coesistere.

coffee, n. caffè m.

coffer, n. còfano m., scrigno m.

coffin, n. cassa da mòrto f.

cog, n. dente m.; (c. railway) ferrovia a dentiera f.

cogent, adj. convincente.

cogitate, vb. cogitare.

cognizance, n. conoscènza f.; (legal) competènza f.

cognizant, adj. competènte.

cogwheel, n. ruòta dentata f.

cohere, vb. èssere coerènte.

coherent, adj. coerènte.

cohesion, n. coesione f.

cohesive, adj. coesivo.

cohort, n. coòrte m.

coiffure, n. pettinatura f.

coil, 1. n. spira f.; (electr.) bobina f.; (induction c.) bobina d'induzione f. 2. vb. arrotolare.

coin, 1. n. moneta f. 2. vb. coniare.

coinage, n. cònio m.

coincide, vb. coincidere.

coincidence, n. coincidènza f.

coincident, adj. coincidènte.

coincidental, adj. coincidènte.

coincidentally, adv. per coincidènza.

colander, n. colatòio m.

cold, 1. n. (temperature) freddo m.; (med.) raffreddore m. 2. adj. freddo; (it is c.) fa freddo; (feel c.) aver freddo.

cold-blooded, adj. a sangue freddo.

coldly, adv. freddamente.

coldness, n. freddezza f.

collaborate, vb. collaborare.

collaboration, n. collaborazione f.

collaborator, n. collaboratore m.

collapse, 1. n. cròllo m.; (med.) collasso m. 2. vb. crollare.

collar, n. colletto m.; (dog's, priest's) collare m.

collarbone, n. clavicola f.

collate, vb. collazionare.

collateral, n. and adj. collaterale m.

collation, n. (comparison) confronto m.; (meal) merènda f.

colleague, n. collèga m.

collect, vb. raccògliere; (money) riscuòtere.

collection, n. raccòlta f., collezione f., (church) quèstua f.

collective, adj. collettivo.

collectively, adv. collettivamente.

collector, n. (art) collezionista m.; (tickets) controllore m.

college, n. università f.

collegiate, adj. universitàrio.

collide, vb. scontrarsi.

colliery, n. minièra di carbone f.

collision, n. scontro m.

colloquial, adj. colloquiale.

colloquialism, n. colloquialismo m.

colloquially, adv. colloquialmente.

colloquy, n. collòquio m.

collusion, n. collusione f.

Cologne, n. Colònia f.

colon, n. (writing) due punti m.pl.

colonel, n. colonnèllo m.

colonial, adj. coloniale.

colonist, n. colòno m.

colonization, n. colonizzazione f.

colonize, vb. colonizzare.

colony, n. colònia f.

color, 1. n. colore m. 2. vb. colorire.

coloration, n. colorazione f.

colored, adj. di colore.

colorful, adj. pittoresco.

coloring, n. coloritura f.

colorless, adj. sènza colore.

colossal, adj. colossale.

colt, n. puledro m.

column, n. colonna f.

columnist, n. cronista m.

coma, n. còma m.

comb, 1. n. pèttine m.; (rooster) cresta f. 2. vb. pettinare.

combat, 1. n. combattimento m. 2. vb. combàttere.

combatant, n. combattènte m.

combative, adj. battaglièro.

combination, n. combinazione f.

combination lock, n. serratura a combinazioni f.

combine, vb. combinare.

combustible, adj. combustibile.

combustion, n. combustione f.

come, vb. venire; (c. about) accadere; (c. across) incontrare, trovare; (c. away) andàrsene; (c. back) tornare; (c. down) scéndere; (c. in) entrare; (c. out) uscire; (c. up) salire.

comedian, n. còmico m.

comedienne, n. attrice còmica f.

comedy, n. commèdia f.

come in!, interj. avanti!

comely, adj. grazioso.

comet, n. cometa f.

comfort, 1. n. confòrto m. 2. vb. confortare, consolare.

comfortable, adj. còmodo.

comfortably, adv. comodamente.

comforter, n. confortatore m., consolatore m.

comfortingly, adv. in modo consolatore.

comfortless, adj. sconsolato.

comic, comical, adj. còmico.

comic book, n. giornalino a fumetti m.

comic strip, n. fumetto m.

coming, n. venuta f.

comma, n. virgola f.

command, 1. n. comando m. 2. vb. comandare.

commandeer, vb. requisire.

commander, n. comandante m.

commander in chief, n. comandante in capo m.

commandment, n. comandamento m.

commemorate, vb. commemorare.

commemoration, n. commemorazione f.

commemorative, adj. commemorativo.

commence, vb. cominciare.

commencement, n. cominciamento m.

commend, vb. raccomandare, lodare.

commendable, adj. lodévole.

commendably, adv. lodevolmente.

commendation, n. lòde f.

commensurate, adj. commisurato.

comment, 1. n. commento m. 2. vb. commentare.

commentary, n. commento m.

commentator, n. (radio) cronista m.

commerce, n. commèrcio m.

commercial, adj. commerciale.

commercialism, n. commercialismo m.

commercialize, vb. commercializzare.

commercially, adv. commercialmente.

commiserate, vb. commiserare.

commissary, n. commissariato m.

commission, 1. n. (committee, percentage) commissione f.; (assignment) incàrico m.; mandato m. 2. vb. incaricare.

commissioner, n. commissàrio m.

commit, vb. commèttere.

commitment, n. impegno m.

committee, n. comitato m., commissione f.

commodious, adj. spazioso.

commodity, n. mèrce f.

common, adj. comune; (vulgar) volgare.

commonly, adv. comunemente.

commonness, n. volgarità f.

commonplace, 1. n. luògo comune m. 2. adj. banale.

commonwealth, n. repùbblica f.

commotion, n. commozione f.

communal, adj. comunale.

commune, vb. comunicare.

communicable, adj. comunicàbile.

communicant, n. comunicante m.

communicate, vb. comunicare.

communication, *n.* comunicazione *f.*

communicative, *adj.* comunicativo.

communion, *n.* comunione *f.*; (take c.) comunicarsi.

communiqué, *n.* comunicato *m.*

communism, *n.* comunismo *m.*

communist, *n.* comunista *m. or f.*

communistic, *adj.* comunistico.

community, *n.* comunità *f.*

commutation, *n.* commutazione *f.*; (c. ticket) biglietto d'abbonamento *m.*

commute, *vb.* commutare; (travel) viaggiare regolarmente.

commuter, *n.* viaggiatore regolare *m.*

compact, **1.** *n.* accòrdo *m.*, patto *m.* **2.** *adj.* compatto.

compactness, *n.* compattezza *f.*

companion, *n.* compagno *m.*, compagna *f.*

companionable, *adj.* sociévole.

companionship, *n.* compagnia *f.*

company, *n.* compagnia *f.*, società *f.*

comparable, *adj.* paragonàbile, comparàbile.

comparative, *adj.* comparativo.

comparatively, *adv.* comparativamente.

compare, *vb.* paragonare, confrontare, comparare.

comparison, *n.* paragone *m.*, confronto *m.*

compartment, *n.* scompartimento *m.*

compass, *n.* (naut.) bùssola *f.*; (geom.) compasso *m.*

compassion, *n.* compassione *f.*

compassionate, *adj.* compassiónévole.

compassionately, *adv.* compassionevolmente.

compatible, *adj.* compatibile.

compatriot, *n.* compatriòta *m.*, compaesano *m.*

compel, *vb.* costringere.

compensate, *vb.* compensare.

compensation, *n.* compènso *m.*

compensatory, *adj.* compensativo.

compete, *vb.* compètere, concórrere, gareggiare.

competence, *n.* competènza *f.*

competent, *adj.* competènte.

competently, *adv.* competentemente.

competition, *n.* concorso *m.*, gara *f.*; (comm.) concorrènza *f.*

competitive, *adj.* di concorso, di concorrènza.

competitor, *n.* concorrènte *m.*

compile, *vb.* compilare.

complacency, *n.* contentezza di sè stesso *f.*

complacent, *adj.* contento di sè stesso.

complain, *vb.* lagnarsi, dolersi.

complainer, *n.* piagnucolone *m.*

complainingly, *adv.* lagnàndosi.

complaint, *n.* lagnanza *f.*; (sickness) malattìa *f.*

complement, *n.* complemento *m.*

complete, **1.** *adj.* complèto. **2.** *vb.* completare.

completely, *adv.* completamente.

completeness, *n.* completezza *f.*

completion, *n.* completamento *m.*

complex, *n. and adj.* complèsso (m.).

complexion, *n.* colorito *m.*

complexity, *n.* complessità *f.*

compliance, *n.* obbediènza *f.*

compliant, *adj.* obbediènte.

complicate, *vb.* complicare.

complicated, *adj.* complicato.

complication, *n.* complicazione *f.*

complicity, *n.* complicità *f.*

compliment, **1.** *n.* complimento *m.* **2.** *vb.* complimentare, felicitare.

complimentary, *adj.* gratùito.

comply, *vb.* obbedire.

component, *n. and adj.* componènte (m.).

comport oneself, *vb.* comportarsi.

compose, *vb.* comporre.

composed, *adj.* (made of) composto di; (calm) calmo.

composer, *n.* compositore *m.*

composite, *adj.* composto.

composition, *n.* composizione *f.*

compost, *n.* concime *m.*

composure, *n.* compostezza *f.*; calma *f.*

compote, *n.* consèrva *f.*

compound, *n. and adj.* composto (m.).

comprehend, *vb.* comprèndere.

comprehensible, *adj.* comprensìbile.

comprehension, *n.* comprensione *f.*

comprehensive, *adj.* comprensivo.

compress, *vb.* comprìmere.

compressed, *adj.* comprèsso.

compression, *n.* compressione *f.*

compressor, *n.* compressore *m.*

comprise, *vb.* comprèndere.

compromise, **1.** *n.* compromesso *m.* **2.** *vb.* accomodarsi; (endanger) comprométtere.

compromiser, *n.* chi fa un compromesso *m.*

compulsion, *n.* costrizione *f.*

compulsive, *adj.* coercitivo; (involuntary) involontàrio.

compulsory, *adj.* obbligatòrio.

compunction, *n.* compunzione *f.*

computation, *n.* computazione *f.*

compute, *vb.* computare.

computer, *n.* calcolatrice elettrònica *f.*; calcolatore *m.*

computer science, *n.* informàtica *f.*

computerize, *v.* informatizzare.

comrade, *n.* camerata *m.*

comradeship, *n.* cameratismo *m.*

concave, *adj.* concavo.

conceal, *vb.* celare.

concealment, *n.* celamento *m.*

concede, *vb.* concèdere.

conceit, *n.* vanità *f.*

conceited, *adj.* vanitoso.

conceivable, *adj.* concepìbile.

conceivably, *adv.* concepibilmente.

conceive, *vb.* concepire.

concentrate, *vb.* concentrare.

concentration, *n.* concentrazione *f.*, concentramento *m.*

concentration camp, *n.* campo di concentramento *m.*

concept, *n.* concètto *m.*

concern, **1.** *n.* (affair) affare *m.*; (interest) interèsse *m.*; (firm) aziènda *f.*; (worry) ansietà *f.* **2.** *vb.* concèrnere, interessare, riguardare; (c. oneself with) interessarsi di; (be c.ed over) inquietarsi di.

concerning, *prep.* riguardo a, concernènte.

concert, **1.** *n.* concèrto *m.* **2.** *vb.* concertare.

concession, *n.* concessione *f.*

conch-shell, *n.* conchiglia *f.*

concierge, *n.* portinaio *m.*; (c.'s office) portineria *f.*

conciliate, *vb.* conciliare.

conciliation, *n.* conciliazione *f.*

conciliator, *n.* conciliatore *m.*

conciliatory, *adj.* conciliativo.

concise, *adj.* conciso.

concisely, *adv.* concisamente.

conciseness, concision, *n.* concisione *f.*

conclave, *n.* conclave *m.*

conclude, *vb.* conclùdere.

conclusion, *n.* conclusione *f.*

conclusive, *adj.* conclusivo.

conclusively, *adv.* conclusivamente.

concoct, *vb.* concuòcere.

concoction, *n.* concozione *f.*

concomitant, *adj.* concomitante.

concord, *n.* accòrdo *m.*

concordant, *adj.* concòrde.

concordat, *n.* concordato *m.*

concourse, *n.* concorso *m.*

concrete, **1.** *n.* cemento *m.* **2.** *adj.* concrèto.

concretely, *adv.* concretamente.

concreteness, *n.* concretezza *f.*

concubine, *n.* concubina *f.*

concur, *vb.* (events) concórrere; (persons) essere d'accòrdo.

concurrence, *n.* concorrènza *f.*; (agreement) consènso *m.*

concurrent, *adj.* concorrènte.

concussion, *n.* concussione *f.*

condemn, vb. condannare.

condemnable, adj. condannàbile.

condemnation, n. condanna f.

condensation, n. condensazione f.

condense, vb. condensare.

condenser, n. condensatore m.

condescend, vb. accondiscéndere.

condescendingly, adv. con accondiscendènza.

condescension, n. accondiscendènza f.

condiment, 1. n. condimento m. 2. vb. condire.

condition, 1. n. condizione f. 2. vb. condizionare.

conditional, adj. condizionale.

conditionally, adv. condizionalmente.

condole, vb. condolersi.

condolence, n. condoglianza f.

condominium, n. condominio m.

condone, vb. condonare.

conduce, vb. condurre, tèndere.

conducive, adj. tendènte.

conduct, 1. n. condotta f. 2. vb. condurre.

conductive, adj. conduttivo.

conductivity, n. conduttività f.

conductor, n. conduttore m.; (orchestra) direttore m.; (train) capotreno m.; (tram, bus) bigliettàrio m.

conduit, n. condotto m.

cone, n. còno m.

confection, n. (dress) confezione f.; (candy) confetto m.; confettura f.

confectioner, n. confettière m.; (c. shop) confetteria f.

confectionery, n. (store) confetteria f.

confederacy, n. confederazione f.

confederate, 1. n. confederato m. 2. vb. confederarsi.

confederation, n. confederazione f.

confer, vb. conferire.

conference, n. conferènza f.

confess, vb. confessare.

confession, n. confessione f.

confessional, n. and adj. confessionale (m.).

confessor, n. confessore m.

confetti, n. coriàndoli m.pl.

confidant, n. confidènte m.

confidante, n. confidènte f.

confide, vb. confidare.

confidence, n. confidènza f.

confident, adj. confidènte.

confidential, adj. confidenziale.

confidentially, adv. in confidènza.

confidently, adv. confidentemente.

confine, vb. confinare.

confirm, vb. confermare.

confirmation, n. conferma f.

confiscate, vb. confiscare.

confiscation, n. confisca f.

conflagration, n. conflagrazione f.

conflict, 1. n. conflitto m. 2. vb. venire a conflitto.

conform, vb. conformarsi.

conformation, n. conformazione f.

conformer, conformist, n. conformista m.

conformity, n. conformità f.

confound, vb. confóndere.

confront, vb. confrontare.

confuse, vb. confóndere.

confusion, n. confusione f.

congeal, vb. congelare.

congealment, n. congelamento m.

congenial, adj. simpàtico.

congenital, adj. congènito.

congenitally, adv. congenitamente.

congestion, n. congestione f.

conglomerate, 1. n. and adj. conglomerato (m.). 2. vb. conglomerare.

conglomeration, n. conglomerazione f.

congratulate, vb. felicitare, congratularsi con.

congratulation, n. felicitazione f., congratulazione f.

congratulatory, adj. congratulatòrio.

congregate, vb. congregarsi.

congregation, n. congregazione f.

congress, n. congrèsso m., parlamento m.

congressional, adj. parlamentare.

conic, adj. cònico.

conjecture, 1. n. congettura f. 2. vb. congetturare.

conjugal, adj. coniugale.

conjugate, vb. coniugare.

conjugation, n. coniugazione f.

conjunction, n. congiunzione f.

conjunctive, adj. congiuntivo.

conjunctivitis, n. congiuntivite f.

conjure, vb. scongiurare.

connect, vb. collegare, connèttere; (transport) coincìdere.

connection, n. collegamento m., connessione f.; (transport) coincidènza f.

connivance, n. connivènza f.

connive, vb. essere connivènte.

connoisseur, n. conoscitore m.

connotation, n. connotazione f.

connote, vb. connotare.

connubial, adj. connubiale.

conquer, vb. vincere, conquistare.

conquerable, adj. vincibile, conquistàbile.

conqueror, n. vincitore m., conquistatore m.

conquest, n. conquista f.

conscience, n. cosciènza f.

conscientious, adj. coscienzioso.

conscientiously, adv. coscienziosamente.

conscious, adj. cònscio, consapévole.

consciously, adv. consciamente.

consciousness, n. cosciènza f.

conscript, n. coscritto m.

conscription, n. coscrizione f.

consecrate, vb. consacrare.

consecration, n. consacrazione f.

consecutive, adj. consecutivo.

consecutively, adv. consecutivamente.

consensus, n. consènso m.

consent, 1. n. consènso m. 2. vb. consentire, acconsentire.

consequence, n. conseguènza f.

consequent, adj. conseguènte.

consequential, adj. conseguenziale.

consequently, adv. conseguentemente, per conseguènza.

conservation, n. conservazione f.

conservative, n. and adj. conservatore (m.).

conservatism, n. conservatorismo m.

conservatory, n. conservatòrio m.

conserve, vb. conservare.

consider, vb. considerare.

considerable, adj. considerèvole, consideràbile; (a fair amount) parécchio.

considerably, adv. considerabilmente.

considerate, vb. premuroso.

considerately, adv. premurosamente.

consideration, n. considerazione f.

considering, adv. considerando.

consign, vb. consegnare.

consignment, n. consegna f.

consist, vb. consistere.

consistency, n. consistènza f.

consistent, adj. coerènte.

consolation, n. consolazione f.

console, vb. consolare.

consolidate, vb. consolidare.

consommé, n. bròdo ristretto m.

consonant, n. and adj. consonante (f.).

consort, n. consòrte m. and f.

conspicuous, adj. cospicuo.

conspicuously, adv. cospicuamente.

conspicuousness, n. cospicuità f.

conspiracy, n. congiura f.

conspirator, n. congiurato m.

conspire, vb. congiurare.

constancy, n. costanza f.

constant, adj. costante.

constantly, adv. costantemente.

constellation, n. costellazione f.

consternation, n. costernazione f.

constipated, adj. stìtico.

constipation, n. stitichezza f.

constituency, n. votanti m.pl.

constituent, adj. costituènte.

constitute, vb. costituire.

constitution, n. costituzione f.

constitutional, adj. costituzionale.

constrain, vb. costringere.

constraint, n. costrizione f.

constrict, vb. costringere.

construct, vb. costruire.

construction, n. costruzione f.; (interpretation) interpretazione f.

constructive, adj. costruttivo.

constructively, adv. costruttivamente.

constructor, n. costruttore m.

construe, vb. interpretare.

consul, n. cònsole m.

consular, adj. consolare.

consulate, n. consolato m.

consulship, n. consolato m.

consult, vb. consultare.

consultant, n. consultatore m.

consultation, n. consultazione f., consulto m.

consume, vb. consumare.

consumer, n. consumatore m.

consummate, adj. consumato.

consummation, n. consumazione f.

consumption, n. consumo m.; (tuberculosis) tisi f.; tuberculosi f.

consumptive, adj. tisico.

contact, 1. n. contatto m. 2. vb. venire a contatto con.

contagion, n. contàgio m.

contagious, adj. contagioso.

contain, vb. contenere.

container, n. recipiènte m.

contaminate, vb. contaminare.

contemplate, vb. contemplare.

contemplation, n. contemplazione f.

contemplative, adj. contemplativo.

contemporary, adj. contemporàneo.

contempt, n. disprèzzo m.

contemptible, adj. spregévole.

contemptuous, adj. sprezzante.

contemptuously, adv. sprezzantemente.

contend, vb. contèndere; (affirm) sostenere.

contender, n. contendènte m.

content, 1. adj. contento. 2. vb. accontentare.

contented, adj. contento.

contention, n. contenzione f.

contentment, n. contentamento m.

contest, 1. n. contesa f., gara f. 2. vb. contestare.

contestable, adj. contestàbile.

contestant, n. gareggiante m.

context, n. contèsto m.

contiguous, adj. contiguo.

continence, n. continènza f.

continent, n. and adj. continènte (m.).

continental, adj. continentale.

contingency, n. contingènza f.

contingent, adj. contingènte.

continual, adj. continuo.

continuation, n. continuazione f.

continue, vb. continuare.

continuity, n. continuità f.

continuous, adj. continuo.

continuously, adv. continuamente.

contort, vb. contòrcere.

contortion, n. contorsione f.

contortionist, n. contorsionista m.

contour, n. contorno m.

contraband, n. contrabbando m.

contraception, n. controllo delle nàscite m.

contract, 1. n. contratto m. 2. vb. contrarre; (agree, undertake) contrattare.

contraction, n. contrazione f.

contractor, n. contrattatore m., imprenditore, m.

contradict, vb. contraddire.

contradictable, adj. contraddicibile.

contradiction, n. contraddizione f.

contradictory, adj. contraddittòrio.

contralto, n. contralto m.

contraption, n. congegno m.

contrary, adj. contràrio.

contrast, 1. n. contrasto m. 2. vb. contrastare, intr.

contribute, vb. contribuire; (newspaper) collaborare.

contribution, n. contributo m., contribuzione f.

contributive, adj. contributivo.

contributor, n. contributore m.; (newspaper) collaboratore m.

contributory, adj. contributòrio.

contrite, adj. contrito.

contrition, n. contrizione f.

contrivance, n. congegno m.

contrive, vb. (invent) inventare; (bring about) effettuare.

control, 1. n. controllo m. 2. vb. controllare.

controllable, adj. controllàbile.

controller, n. controllore m.

controversial, adj. controvèrso.

controversy, n. controvèrsia f.

contusion, n. contusione f.

conundrum, n. indovinèllo m.

convalesce, vb. rimèttersi in salute.

convalescence, n. convalescènza f.

convalescent, adj. convalescènte.

convene, vb. convenire.

convenience, n. conveniènza f.

convenient, adj. conveniènte.

conveniently, adv. convenientemente.

convent, n. convènto m.

convention, n. convenzione f.; (meeting) congrèsso m.

conventional, adj. convenzionale.

conventionally, adv. convenzionalmente.

converge, vb. convèrgere.

convergence, n. convergènza f.

convergent, adj. convergènte.

conversant with, adj. versato in, pràtico di.

conversational, adj. di conversazione.

conversationalist, n. conversatore m.

converse, 1. adj. convèrso. 2. vb. conversare.

conversely, adv. per convèrso.

convert, vb. convertire.

converter, n. convertitrice f.

convertible, adj. convertìbile.

convex, adj. convèsso.

convey, vb. trasméttere, trasportare.

conveyance, n. traspòrto m.; (property) trapasso di proprietà m.

conveyor, n. trasportatore m.

convict, 1. n. condannato m. 2. vb. dichiarare colpévole.

conviction, n. (belief) convinzione f.; (law) condanna f.

convince, vb. convincere.

convincing, adj. convincènte.

convincingly, adv. in modo convincènte.

convivial, adj. conviviale.

convocation, n. convocazione f.

convoke, vb. convocare.

convoy, 1. n. convòglio m. 2. vb. convogliare.

convulse, vb. méttere in convulsioni.

convulsion, n. convulsione f.

convulsive, adj. convulsivo.

cook, 1. n. cuòco m. 2. vb. cucinare.

cookbook, n. libro di cucina m.

cookie, n. biscòtto m.

cool, 1. adj. fresco. 2. vb. rinfrescare.

cooler, n. frigorìfero m.

coolness, n. fresco m.; (fig.) indifferènza f.

coop, n. stìa f.

cooper, n. bottaio m.

cooperate, vb. cooperare.

cooperation, n. cooperazione f.

cooperative, 1. n. cooperativa f. 2. adj. cooperativo.

cooperatively, adv. cooperativamente.

coordinate, vb. coordinare.

coordination, n. coordinazione f.

coordinator, n. coordinatore m.

cop, n. poliziòtto m.

cope, vb. lottare; (c. with) tener tèsta a.

copier, n. macchina a copiare f.; copiatore m.

copious, adj. copioso.

copiously, adv. copiosamente.

copiousness, n. copiosità f., còpia f.

copper, n. rame m.

copperplate, n. calligrafìa f.

copy, 1. *n.* còpia *f.*; (of book) esemplare *m.* 2. *vb.* copiare.

copyist, *n.* copista *m.*

copyright, *n.* diritti d'autore *m.pl.*

coquetry, *n.* civetterìa *f.*

coquette, 1. *n.* civetta *f.* 2. *vb.* civettare.

coral, *n.* corallo *m.*

cord, *n.* còrda *f.*

cordial, *n. and adj.* cordiale *(m.).*

cordiality, *n.* cordialità *f.*

cordially, *adv.* cordialmente.

cordon, *n.* cordone *m.*

cordovan, *n.* cordovano *m.*

core, *n.* (fruit) tórsolo *m.*; (heart) cuòre *m.*

cork, *n.* sùghero *m.*; (of bottle) tappo *m.*

corkscrew, *n.* cavatappi *m.* (sg.)

corn, *n.* (grain) granturco *m.*; (on foot) callo *m.*

cornea, *n.* còrnea *f.*

corner, 1. *n.* àngolo *m.*, canto *m.* 2. *vb.* (comm.) accaparrare.

cornerstone, *n.* piètra angolare *f.*

cornet, *n.* cornetta *f.*

cornetist, *n.* cornettista *m.*

cornice, *n.* cornicione *m.*

corn-plaster, *n.* callifugo *m.*

cornstarch, *n.* farina di granturco *f.*

cornucopia, *n.* cornucòpia *m. or f.*

corollary, *n.* corollàrio *m.*

coronary, *adj.* coronàrio.

coronation, *n.* incoronazione *f.*

coronet, *n.* (noble's) corna nobiliare *f.*; (headdress) diadèma *m.*

corporal, 1. *n.* caporale *m.* 2. *adj.* corporale.

corporate, *adj.* corporato.

corporation, *n.* corporazione *f.*

corps, *n.* còrpo *m.*

corpse, *n.* cadàvere *m.*

corpulent, *adj.* corpulènto.

corpuscle, *n.* corpùscolo *m.*

correct, 1. *adj.* corrètto. 2. *vb.* corrèggere.

correction, *n.* correzione *f.*

corrective, *adj.* correttivo.

correctly, *adv.* correttamente.

correctness, *n.* correttezza *f.*

correlate, *vb.* mèttere in correlazione.

correlation, *n.* correlazione *f.*

correspond, *vb.* corrispóndere.

correspondence, *n.* corrispondènza *f.*

correspondent, *n. and adj.* corrispondènte *(m.).*

corridor, *n.* corridòio *m.*

corroborate, *vb.* corroborare.

corroboration, *n.* corroborazione *f.*

corroborative, *adj.* corroborativo.

corrode, *vb.* corródere.

corrosion, *n.* corrosione *f.*

corrugate, *vb.* corrugare.

corrupt, *vb.* corrómpere.

corrupter, *n.* corrutore *m.*

corruptible, *adj.* corruttibile.

corruption, *n.* corruzione *f.*

corruptive, *adj.* corruttivo.

corsage, *n.* fiori *m.pl.*

corset, *n.* busto *m.*

Corsican, *adj.* còrso.

cortège, *n.* cortèo *m.*

corvette, *n.* corvetta *f.*

cosmetic, *n. and adj.* cosmètico *(m.).*

cosmic, *adj.* còsmico.

cosmopolitan, *adj.* cosmopolita.

cosmos, *n.* còsmo *m.*

cost, 1. *n.* costo *m.* 2. *vb.* costare.

costliness, *n.* costosità *f.*

costly, *adj.* costoso.

costume, *n.* costume *m.*

costumer, *n.* vestiarista *m.*

cot, *n.* lettino *m.*

coterie, *n.* combriccola *f.*, cenàcolo *m.*

cotillion, *n.* cotiglione *m.*

cottage, *n.* villetta *f.*, casetta *f.*

cotton, *n.* cotone *m.*

cottonseed, *n.* seme di cotone *m.*

couch, *n.* lètto *m.*

cough, 1. *n.* tosse *f.* 2. *vb.* tossire.

could, *vb.* use past or conditional of potere.

coulter, *n.* vòmere *m.*

council, *n.* consiglio *m.*

councilman, *n.* consiglière *m.*

counsel, 1. *n.* consiglio *m.* 2. *vb.* consigliare.

counselor, *n.* consiglière *m.*

count, 1. *n.* conto *m.*; (noble) conte *m.* 2. *vb.* contare.

countenance, 1. *n.* viso *m.* 2. *vb.* approvare.

counter, *n.* banco *m.*

counteract, *vb.* neutralizzare.

counteraction, *n.* controazione *f.*

counterattack, *n.* contrattacco *m.*

counterbalance, *n.* contrappeso *m.*

counter-clockwise, *adj. and adv.* sinistròrso.

counterfeit, 1. *n. and adj.* falso *(m.).* 2. *vb.* contraffare, falsificare.

countermand, *vb.* contromandare.

counteroffensive, *n.* controffensiva *f.*

counterpart, *n.* contropartita *f.*

Counter-Reformation, *n.* Controriforma *f.*

countess, *n.* contessa *f.*

countless, *adj.* innumerévole.

country, *n.* (nation) paese *m.*; (opposed to city) campagna *f.*; (native land) pàtria *f.*

countryman, *n.* (of same country) compatriòta *m.*; (rustic) contadino *m.*

countryside, *n.* campagna *f.*

county, *n.* contèa *f.*

coupé, *n.* cupè *m.*

couple, 1. *n.* còppia *f.*, paio *m.* 2. *vb.* accoppiare.

coupon, *n.* tagliando *m.*, cèdola *f.*

courage, *n.* coràggio *m.*

courageous, *adj.* coraggioso.

courier, *n.* corrière *m.*

course, *n.* corso *m.*; (for races) pista *f.*

court, 1. *n.* corte *f.* 2. *vb.* corteggiare, far la corte a.

courteous, *adj.* cortese.

courtesan, *n.* cortigiana *f.*

courtesy, *n.* cortesìa *f.*

courthouse, *n.* palazzo di giustlzia *m.*

courtier, *n.* cortigiano *m.*

courtly, *adj.* cerimonioso.

courtmartial, *n.* corte marziale *f.*

courtroom, *n.* aula di udiènza *f.*

courtship, *n.* corteggiamento *m.*

courtyard, *n.* cortile *m.*

cousin, *n.* cugino *m.*, cugina *f.*

covenant, *n.* convenzione *f.*

cover, 1. *n.* copertura *f.*, (book) copertina. 2. *vb.* coprire.

covering, *n.* copertura *f.*

covet, *vb.* bramare.

covetous, *adj.* bramoso.

cow, 1. *n.* vacca *f.* 2. *vb.* intimidire.

coward, *n.* codardo *m.*

cowardice, *n.* codardìa *f.*

cowardly, *adj.* codardo.

cowboy, *n.* vaccaro *m.*

cower, *vb.* rannicchiarsi.

cow hand, *n.* vaccaro *m.*

cowhide, *n.* vacchetta *f.*

coxswain, *n.* timonière *m.*

coy, *adj.* tìmido.

crab, *n.* grànchio *m.*

crack, 1. *n.* fenditura *f.* 2. *vb.* fèndere.

cracked, *adj.* fesso.

cracker, *n.* biscòtto *m.*

crackup, *n.* incidènte *m.*

cradle, 1. *n.* culla *f.* 2. *vb.* cullare.

craft, *n.* arte *f.*

craftsman, *n.* artigiano *m.*

craftsmanship, *n.* arte *f.*

crafty, *adj.* furbo.

crag, *n.* picco *m.*

cram, *vb.* rimpinzare, infarcire.

cramp, *n.* crampo *m.*

crane, *n.* gru *f.*

cranium, *n.* crànio *m.*

crank, 1. *n.* (handle) manovella *f.*; (crackpot) pazzo *m.* 2. *vb.* girare.

cranky, *adj.* capriccioso.

cranny, *n.* fessura *f.*

crapshooter, *n.* giocatore di dadi *m.*

craps, *n.* giòco dei dadi *m.*

crash, 1. *n.* cròllo *m.* 2. *vb.* crollare.

crate, *n.* gabbietta da imballàggio *f.*

crater, *n.* cratère *m.*

crave, *vb.* bramare.

craven, *adj.* codardo.

craving, n. brama f.
crawl, vb. trascinarsi.
crayon, n. matita f.
crazed, adj. pazzo.
crazy, adj. pazzo, fòlle.
creak, vb. cigolare, scricchiolare.
creaky, adj. cigolante, scricchiolante.
cream, n. crèma f., panna f.
creamery, n. cremería f.
creamy, adj. ricco di panna.
crease, 1. n. pièga f. 2. vb. (fold) piegare; (crinkle) spiegazzare.
create, vb. creare.
creation, n. creazione f.
creative, adj. creativo.
creator, n. creatore m.
creature, n. creatura f.
credence, n. credènza f.
credentials, n. credenziali f.pl.
credibility, n. credibilità f.
credible, adj. credìbile.
credit, n. crèdito m.
creditable, adj. soddisfacènte.
creditably, adv. in modo soddisfacènte.
credit card, n. carta di crèdito f.
creditor, n. creditore m.
credo, n. crèdo m.
credulity, n. credulità f.
credulous, adj. crèdulo.
creed, n. crèdo m.; fède f.
creek, n. fiumicino m.; (mountain c.) torrènte m.
creep, vb. strisciare, arrampicarsi.
cremate, vb. cremare.
cremation, n. cremazione f.
crematory, 1. adj. crematòrio. 2. n. forno crematòrio m.
creosote, n. creosòto f.
crepe, n. crespo m.
crescent, n. mezzaluna f.
crest, n. cresta f.
crestfallen, adj. a cresta bassa, scoraggiaro.
cretonne, n. cotonina f.
crevasse, n. crepàccio m.
crevice, n. screpolatura f.
crew, n. equipàggio m.
crib, n. lettino da bimbo m.
cricket, n. grillo m.
crier, n. banditore m.
crime, n. delitto m.
criminal, n. and adj. criminale (m.).
criminologist, n. criminòlogo m.
criminology, n. criminologia f.
crimson, adj. cremisi.
cringe, vb. piegarsi.
crinkle, vb. spiegazzare.
cripple, 1. n. sciancato. 2. vb. rendere sciancato.
crippled, adj. sciancato.
crisis, n. crisi f.
crisp, adj. crespo; (bread, etc.) croccante.
crisscross, adj. incrociato.
criterion, n. critèrio m.
critic, n. crìtico m.
critical, adj. crìtico.

criticism, n. crìtica f.
criticize, vb. criticare.
critique, n. crìtica f.
croak, vb. gracidare.
crochet, vb. lavorare all'uncinetto.
crock, n. vaso di terracotta m.
crockery, n. vasellame m.
crocodile, n. coccodrillo m.
crocodile tears, n. làgrime di coccodrillo f.pl.
crone, n. vècchia f.
crony, n. compare m.
crook, n. (bend) curvatura f.; (scoundrel) mascalzone m.
crooked, adj. stòrto.
croon, vb. canticchiare.
crop, n. raccòlta f., raccòlto m.
croquet, n. pallamàglio m.
croquette, n. crocchetta f., polpetta f.
cross, 1. n. croce f.; (mixture) incròcio m. 2. adj. irritato, adirato. 3. vb. attraversare; (mix) incrociare.
crossbreed, 1. n. incròcio di razze m. 2. adj. di razza incrociata.
cross-examine, vb. esaminare in contraddittòrio.
cross-eyed, adj. stràbico.
cross-fertilization, n. ibridazione f.
crossing, n. incròcio m.; (grade c.) passàggio a livèllo m.
cross-purposes, be at, vb. fraintèndersi.
crossroads, n. crocicchio m., crocevìa f.
cross section, n. sezione f.
crossword puzzle, n. cruciverba m.
crotch, n. (tree) biforcazione f.; (human body) inforcatura f.
crouch, vb. accucciarsi.
croup, n. crup m.
crouton, n. crostino m.
crow, 1. n. còrvo m. 2. vb. cantare.
crowd, 1. n. fòlla f. 2. vb. affollare; (push) spingere.
crown, 1. n. corona f. 2. vb. incoronare.
crown prince, n. prìncipe ereditàrio m.
crow's-foot, n. zampa di gallina f.
crow's-nest, n. còffa f.
crucial, adj. cruciale.
crucible, n. crogiòlo m.
crucifix, n. crocefisso m.
crucifixion, n. crocefissione f.
crucify, vb. crocifìggere.
crude, adj. crudo.
crudeness, n. crudezza f.
crudity, n. crudità f.
cruel, adj. crudèle.
cruelty, n. crudeltà f.
cruet, n. ampollina f.
cruise, 1. n. crocièra f. 2. vb. incrociare.
cruiser, n. incrociatore m.
crumb, n. brìciola f.
crumble, vb. sbriciolare.

crumple, vb. spiegazzare.
crunch, vb. schiacciare rumorosamente.
crusade, n. crociata f.
crusader, n. crociato m.
crush, 1. n. fòlla f. 2. vb. schiacciare.
crust, n. crosta f.
crustacean, n. and adj. crostàceo (m.).
crusty, adj. crostoso; (manners) irritàbile.
crutch, n. grùccia f., stampèlla f.
cry, 1. n. grido m. 2. vb. (shout) gridare, urlare; (weep) piàngere.
crying, n. pianto m.
cryosurgery, n. criochirurgìa f.
crypt, n. cripta f.
cryptic, adj. breve ed oscuro.
cryptography, n. crittografìa f.
crystal, n. cristallo m.
crystalline, adj. cristallino.
crystallize, vb. cristallizzare.
cub, n. piccolo m.
cubbyhole, n. nascondiglio m.
cube, n. cubo m.
cubic, adj. cùbico.
cubicle, n. cubicolo m.
cubism, n. cubismo m.
cuckoo, 1. n. cuculo m. 2. adj. pazzo.
cucumber, n. cetriòlo m.
cud, n. bòlo m.; (chew the c.) ruminare.
cuddle, vb. accarezzare.
cudgel, n. clava f., mazza f.
cue, n. segno m.; (billiards) stecca f.
cuff, 1. n. (shirt) polsino m.; (blow) scapaccione m. 2. vb. picchiare.
cuisine, n. cucina f.
culinary, adj. culinàrio.
cull, vb. cògliere.
culminate, vb. culminare.
culmination, n. culminazione f.
culpable, adj. colpévole.
culprit, n. colpévole m.
cult, n. culto m.
cultivate, vb. coltivare.
cultivated, adj. colto.
cultivation, n. coltivazione f.
cultivator, n. coltivatore m.
cultural, adj. culturale.
culture, n. cultura f.
cultured, adj. colto.
cumbersome, adj. ingombrante.
cumulative, adj. cumulativo.
cunning, 1. n. abilità f. 2. adj. astuto, àbile; (attractive) attraènte, bellino.
cup, n. tazza f.
cupboard, n. credènza f.
cupidity, n. cupidìgia f.
cupola, n. cùpola f.
curable, adj. guarìbile.
curator, n. curatore m.
curb, 1. n. (sidewalk) cordone m.; (harness) barbazzale m. 2. vb. raffrenare.
curbstone, n. bordo di piètre m.

curd, n. quagliata f.

curdle, vb. quagliare.

cure, 1. n. cura f., guarigione f. 2. vb. guarire.

curfew, n. coprifuòco m.

curio, n. curiosità f.

curiosity, n. curiosità f.

curious, adj. curioso; (queer) strano.

curl, 1. n. ricciolo m. 2. vb. arricciare.

curly, adj. ricciuto.

currant, n. ribes m.

currency, n. circolazione f.; (money) valuta f.

current, n. and adj. corrènte (f.).

currently, adv. correntemente.

curriculum, n. curricolo m.

curry, vb. (horse) strigliare.

curse, 1. n. maledizione f. 2. vb. maledire.

cursed, adj. maledetto.

curse-word, n. bestémmia f.

cursory, adj. frettoloso.

curt, adj. asciutto, breve.

curtail, vb. accorciare, ridurre.

curtain, n. cortina f.; (theater) sipàrio m.

curtsy, n. riverènza f.

curvature, n. curvatura f.

curve, 1. n. curva f. 2. vb. curvare.

cushion, n. cuscino m.

cuspidor, n. sputacchièra f.

custard, n. crema caramella f.

custodian, n. custòde m.

custody, n. custòdia f.

custom, n. costume m., consuetùdine f., uso m.

customary, adj. consuèto.

customer, n. cliènte m.; (regular c.) avventore m.

customs-house, customs, n. dogana f.

customs-officer, n. doganière m.

cut, 1. n. tàglio m. 2. vb. tagliare.

cutaneous, adj. cutàneo.

cute, adj. attraènte, bellino.

cut glass, n. cristallo m.

cuticle, n. cuticola f.

cutlet, n. costoletta f.

cutlery, n. posatería f.

cutout, n. interruttore m.

cutter, n. tagliatore m.; (boat) cottro m.

cutthroat, n. assassino m.

cutting, n. (railway) trincèa f.; (newspaper) ritàglio m.

cyclamate, n. ciclamato m.

cycle, 1. n. ciclo m.; (bicycle) bicicletta f. 2. vb. andare in bicicletta.

cyclist, n. ciclista m.

cyclone, n. ciclone m.

cyclotron, n. ciclotrone m.

cylinder, n. cilindro m.

cylindrical, adj. cilìndrico.

cymbal, n. piatto m., cinèllo m.

cynic, n. cìnico m.

cynical, adj. cìnico.

cynicism, n. cinismo m.

cypress, n. ciprèsso m.

cyst, n. ciste f.

D

dab, 1. n. schizzo m. 2. vb. sfiorare.

dabble, vb. essere un dilettante.

dad, n. babbo m.

daffodil, n. narciso m.

daffy, adj. pazzo.

dagger, n. daga f., pugnale m.

dahlia, n. dàlia f.

daily, 1. n. (newspaper) giornale m. 2. adj. giornalièro, quotidiano. 3. adv. quotidianamente.

daintiness, n. squisitezza f.

dainty, adj. squisito, delicato.

dairy, n. latteria f.

dairymaid, n. lattaia f.

dairyman, n. lattaio m.

dais, n. piattaforma f.

daisy, n. margherita f.

dale, n. valletta f.

dally, vb. indugiare.

dam, n. diga f.

damage, 1. n. danno m., avaria f. 2. vb. danneggiare, avariare.

damask, n. damasco m.

dame, vb. dannare; (curse) maledire.

damnation, n. dannazione f.

damp, 1. n. umidità f. 2. adj. ùmido.

dampen, vb. inumidire.

dampness, n. umidità f.

damsel, n. damigèlla f.

dance, 1. n. ballo m., danza f.; (d. tune) ballàbile m. 2. vb. ballare, danzare.

dancer, n. ballerino m., ballerina f.

dancing, n. ballo m.

dandelion, n. radicchièlla f.

dandruff, n. fòrfora f.

dandy, 1. n. damerino m., bel-limbusto m. 2. adj. òttimo.

danger, n. pericolo m.

dangerous, adj. pericoloso.

dangle, vb. penzolare.

Danish, adj. danese.

dapper, adj. piccolo e vivace.

dappled, adj. macchiettato.

dare, 1. n. sfida f. 2. vb. osare; (challenge) sfidare.

daredevil, n. temeràrio m.

daring, 1. n. audàcia f. 2. adj. audace.

dark, 1. n. oscurità f. 2. adj. oscuro, bùio, tenebroso.

darken, vb. oscurare.

dark horse, n. candidato sconosciuto m.

darkness, n. oscurità f., bùio m., tènebre f.pl.

darkroom, n. càmera oscura f.

darling, n. and adj. prediletto.

darn, 1. n. rammendatura f. 2. vb. rammendare.

darning needle, n. ago da rammendo m.

dart, 1. n. dardo m.; (movement) balzo m. 2. balzare.

dash, 1. n. (energy) slàncio m., scatto m.; (pen) tratto m. 2. vb. (throw) gettare; (destroy) distrùggere; (rush) slanciarsi; (spurt) scattare.

dashboard, n. cruscòtto m.

dashing, adj. impetuoso.

data, n. dati m.pl.

data processing, n. elaborazione f.

date, 1. n. data f.; (appointment) appuntamento m.; (fruit) dàttero m. 2. vb. datare.

date line, n. linea del cambiamento di data f.

daub, 1. n. imbrattatura f. 2. vb. imbrattare.

daughter, n. figlia f.

daughter-in-law, n. nuòra f.

daunt, vb. intimidire.

dauntless, adj. intrèpido.

dauntlessly, adv. intrepidamente.

davenport, n. divano m., sofaletto m.

dawdle, vb. indugiare.

dawn, 1. n. alba f. 2. vb. spuntare.

day, n. giorno m.; (span of day) giornata f.

daybreak, n. alba f.

daydream, n. fantasticheria f.

daylight, n. luce del giorno f.

daylight-saving time, n. ora d'estate f.

daze, 1. n. stupore m. 2. vb. stupire.

dazzle, vb. abbagliare.

deacon, n. diàcono m.

dead, n. and adj. mòrto (m.).

deaden, vb. ammortire.

dead end, n. vicolo cièco m.

dead letter, n. léttera mòrta f.

deadline, n. lìmite m.

deadlock, n. punto mòrto m.

deadly, adj. mortale.

deadwood, n. legno mòrto m.

deaf, adj. sordo.

deafen, vb. assordare.

deaf-mute, n. and adj. sordomuto (m.).

deafness, n. sordità f.

deal, 1. n. (amount) quantità f.; (business) affare m.; (cards) distribuzione f. 2. vb. (d. with) trattare con; (d. out) distribuire.

dealer, n. negoziante m.

dean, n. decano m.

dear, adj. caro.

dearly, adv. caramente.

dearth, n. scarsezza f., scarsità f.

death, n. mòrte f.

deathless, adj. immortale, imperituro.

deathly, adj. mortale.

débâcle, n. sfacèlo m., disastro m.

debase, vb. abbassare, avvilire.

debatable, adj. discutibile.

debate, 1. *n.* dibattimento *m.*
2. *vb.* dibàttere.

debater, *n.* dibattènte *m.*

debauch, 1. *n.* òrgia *f.*, sregolatezza *f.* 2. *vb.* pervertire.

debenture, *n.* obbligazione *f.*

debilitate, *vb.* debilitare.

debit, *n.* dèbito *m.*

debonair, *adj.* gaio.

debris, *n.* detriti *m.pl.*

debt, *n.* dèbito *m.*

debtor, *n.* debitore *m.*

debunk, *vb.* screditare.

debut, *n.* debutto *m.*

debutante, *n.* debuttante *f.*

decade, *n.* decènnio *m.*

decadence, *n.* decadènza *f.*

decadent, *adj.* decadènte.

decaffeinated, *adj.* decaffeinizzato.

decalcomania, *n.* decalcomania *f.*

decanter, *n.* caraffa *f.*

decapitate, *vb.* decapitare.

decay, 1. *n.* decadènza *f.*, decomposizione *f.*; (teeth) càrie *f.* 2. *vb.* decadere, decomporre, marcire; (teeth) cariarsi.

deceased, *n. and adj.* deceduto (*m.*), defunto (*m.*)

deceit, *n.* inganno *m.*

deceitful, *adj.* ingannatore.

deceive, *vb.* ingannare.

deceiver, *n.* ingannatore *m.*

December, *n.* dicèmbre *m.*

decency, *n.* (modesty) decènza *f.*; (honorable behavior) onorevolezza *f.*

decent, *adj.* (modest) decènte; (honorable) onorévole.

decentralization, *n.* decentramento *m.*

decentralize, *vb.* decentrare.

deception, *n.* inganno *m.*

deceptive, *adj.* ingannévole.

decibel, *n.* dècibel *m.*

decide, *vb.* decidere.

deciduous, *adj.* deciduo.

decimal, *adj.* decimale.

decimate, *vb.* decimare.

decipher, *vb.* decifrare.

decision, *n.* decisione *f.*

decisive, *adj.* decisivo.

deck, *n.* ponte *m.*

deck-hand, *n.* mozzo *m.*

declaim, *vb.* declamare.

declamation, *n.* declamazione *f.*

declaration, *n.* dichiarazione *f.*

declarative, *adj.* dichiarativo.

declare, *vb.* dichiarare.

declension, *n.* declinazione *f.*

decline, 1. *n.* decadènza *f.* 2. *vb.* declinare; (refuse) rifiutare; (decay) decadere.

decode, *vb.* decifrare.

décolleté, *adj.* scollato.

decompose, *vb.* decomporre.

decomposition, *n.* decomposizione *f.*

decongestant, *adj.* decongestionante.

décor, *n.* messa in scena *f.*

decorate, *vb.* decorare.

---

decoration, *n.* decorazione *f.*

decorative, *adj.* decorativo.

decorator, *n.* decoratore *m.*

decorous, *adj.* decoroso.

decorum, *n.* decòro *m.*

decoy, *vb.* attirare.

decrease, 1. *n.* diminuzione *f.* 2. *vb.* diminuire.

decree, 1. *n.* decreto *m.* 2. *vb.* decretare.

decrepit, *adj.* decrèpito.

decry, *vb.* deprecare.

dedicate, *vb.* dedicare.

dedication, *n.* dèdica *f.*

deduce, *vb.* dedurre.

deduct, *vb.* dedurre, sottrarre.

deduction, *n.* deduzione *f.*

deductive, *adj.* deduttivo.

deed, *n.* atto *m.*, fatto *m.*

deem, *vb.* giudicare, stimare.

deep, *adj.* profondo.

deepen, *vb.* approfondire.

deep freeze, *n.* surgelamento *m.*

deeply, *adv.* profondamente.

deep-rooted, *adj.* profondamente radicato.

deer, *n.* cèrvo *m.*

deerskin, *n.* pèlle di dàino *f.*

deface, *vb.* sfregiare.

defamation, *n.* diffamazione *f.*

defame, *vb.* diffamare.

default, 1. *n.* contumàcia *f.* 2. *n.* rèndersi contumace; (comm.) mancar di pagare.

defaulting, *adj.* contumace.

defeat, 1. *n.* sconfitta *f.*, disfatta *f.* 2. *vb.* sconfiggere.

defeatism, *n.* disfattismo *m.*

defect, *n.* difètto *m.*, mènda *f.*

defection, *n.* defezione *f.*

defective, *adj.* difettoso.

defend, *vb.* difèndere.

defendant, *n.* imputato *m.*

defender, *n.* difensore *m.*

defense, *n.* difesa *f.*

defenseless, *adj.* sènza difesa.

defensible, *adj.* difensibile.

defensive, *adj.* difensivo.

defer, *vb.* (put off) differire; (conform) conformarsi.

deference, *n.* deferènza *f.*

deferential, *adj.* deferènte.

defiance, *n.* sfida *f.*

defiant, *adj.* provocante.

deficiency, *n.* deficiènza *f.*

deficient, *adj.* deficiènte.

deficit, *n.* déficit *m.*

defile, *vb.* (march) sfilare; (foul) profanare.

define, *vb.* definire.

definite, *adj.* definito.

definitely, *adj.* definitivamente.

definition, *n.* definizione *f.*

definitive, *adj.* definitivo.

deflate, *vb.* sgonfiare; (econ.) deflazionare.

deflation, *n.* deflazione *f.*

deflect, *vb.* deflèttere.

deform, *vb.* deformare.

deformed, *adj.* deforme.

deformity, *n.* diffomità *f.*

defraud, *vb.* defraudare.

defray, *vb.* pagare.

---

defrost, *vb.* tògliere il ghiàccio a, (d. refrigerator) sbrinare.

defrosting, *n.* (refrigerator) sbrinamento *m.*

deft, *adj.* dèstro, àbile.

defy, *vb.* sfidare.

degenerate, 1. *n. and adj.* degenerato (*m.*). 2. *vb.* degenerare.

degeneration, *n.* degenerazione *f.*

degradation, *n.* degradazione *f.*

degrade, *vb.* degradare.

degree, *n.* grado *m.;* (university) làurea *f.*

dehydrate, *vb.* disidratare.

deify, *vb.* deificare.

deign, *vb.* degnarsi.

deity, *n.* deità *f.*

dejected, *adj.* scoraggiato.

dejection, *n.* scoraggiamento *m.*, abbattimento *m.*

delay, 1. *n.* indùgio *m.*, ritardo *m.* 2. *vb.* indugiare, ritardare.

delectable, *adj.* dilettévole.

delegate, 1. *n.* delegato *m.* 2. *vb.* delegare.

delegation, *n.* delegazione *f.*

delete, *vb.* cancellare.

deliberate, 1. *adj.* deliberato. 2. *vb.* deliberare.

deliberately, *adv.* deliberatamente, appòsta.

deliberation, *n.* deliberazione *f.*

deliberative, *adj.* deliberativo.

delicacy, *n.* delicatezza *f.*

delicate, *adj.* delicato.

delicious, *adj.* delizioso.

delight, *n.* dilètto *m.*

delightful, *adj.* dilettévole.

delineate, *vb.* delineare.

delinquency, *n.* delinquènza *f.*

delinquent, *n. and adj.* delinquènte (*m.*).

delirious, 1. *adj.* delirante. 2. *vb.* (be d.) delirare.

delirium, *n.* delirio *m.*

deliver, *vb.* (set free) liberare; (hand over) consegnare.

deliverance, *n.* liberazione *f.*

delivery, *n.* consegna *f.*

delouse, *vb.* spidocchiare.

delude, *vb.* delùdere.

deluge, *n.* dilùvio *m.*

delusion, *n.* delusione *f.*

de luxe, *adj.* di lusso.

delve, *vb.* scavare.

demagogue, *n.* demagògo *m.*

demand, 1. *n.* domanda *f.*, richièsta *f.* 2. *vb.* domandare, richièdere, esìgere.

demarcation, *n.* demarcazione *f.*

demean (oneself), *vb.* abbassarsi.

demeanor, *n.* condotta *f.*

demented, *adj.* demènte.

demerit, *n.* demèrito *m.*

demigod, *n.* semidio *m.*

demilitarize, *vb.* smilitarizzare.

demise, *n.* mòrte *f.*

demobilization, *n.* smobilitazione *f.*

demobilize, *vb.* smobilitare.

democracy, *n.* democrazia *f.*

democrat, *n.* democràtico *m.*

democratic, *adj.* democràtico.

demolish, *vb.* demolire.

demolition, *n.* demolizione *f.*

demon, *n.* demònio *m.*

demonstrable, *adj.* dimostràbile.

demonstrate, *vb.* dimostrare.

demonstration, *n.* dimostrazione *f.*

demonstrative, *adj.* dimostrativo.

demonstrator, *n.* dimostratore *m.*

demoralize, *vb.* demoralizzare.

demote, *vb.* degradare.

demur, *vb.* obiettare.

demure, *adj.* modesto.

den, *n.* tana *f.*, covo *m.*

denaturalize, *vb.* snaturare.

denature, *vb.* denaturare.

denial, *n.* diniègo *m.*

denim, *n.* saia *f.*

Denmark, *n.* Danimarca *f.*

denomination, *n.* denominazione *f.*; (church) sètta *f.*

denominator, *n.* denominatore *m.*

denote, *vb.* denotare.

dénouement, *n.* scioglimento *m.*

denounce, *vb.* denunciare.

dense, *adj.* dènso.

density, *n.* densità *f.*

dent, *n.* incavo *m.*

dental, *adj.* dentale.

dentifrice, *n.* dentifricio *m.*

dentist, *n.* dentista *m.*

dentistry, *n.* odontoiatria *f.*

denture, *n.* dentièra *f.*

denude, *vb.* denudare.

denunciation, *n.* denùncia *f.*

deny, *vb.* negare.

deodorant, *n. and adj.* deodorante (*m.*).

deodorize, *vb.* deodorare.

depart, *vb.* partire.

department, *n.* dipartimento *m.*

departmental, *adj.* dipartimentale.

departure, *n.* partènza *f.*

depend, *vb.* dipèndere.

dependability, *n.* fidatezza *f.*

dependable, *adj.* fido.

dependence, *n.* dipendènza *f.*

dependent, *n. and adj.* dipendènte (*m.*).

depict, *vb.* dipìngere.

depiction, *n.* rappresentazione *f.*

deplete, *vb.* esaurire.

deplorable, *adj.* deplorévole.

deplore, *vb.* deplorare.

depopulate, *vb.* spopolare.

deport, *vb.* deportare.

deportation, *n.* deportazione *f.*

deportment, *n.* condotta *f.*

depose, *vb.* deporre.

deposit, 1. *n.* depòsito. 2. *vb.* depositare.

deposition, *n.* deposizione *f.*

depositor, *n.* depositante *m.*, correntista *m.*

depository, *n.* depòsito *m.*

depot, *n.* (military) depòsito *m.*; (railroad) stazione *f.*

deprave, *vb.* depravare.

depravity, *n.* depravazione *f.*

deprecate, *vb.* deprecare.

depreciate, *vb.* deprezzare.

depreciation, *n.* deprezzamento *m.*

depredation, *n.* depredamento *m.*

depress, *vb.* deprimere.

depression, *n.* depressione *f.*

deprivation, *n.* privazione *f.*

deprive, *vb.* privare.

depth, *n.* profondità *f.*

depth charge, *n.* bomba di profondità *f.*

deputy, *n.* deputato *m.*

derail, *vb.* deragliare.

derange, *vb.* far impazzire.

deranged, *adj.* impazzito.

derelict, *adj.* derelitto.

dereliction, *n.* negligènza del dovere *f.*

deride, *vb.* deridere.

derision, *n.* derisione *f.*

derisive, *adj.* derisivo.

derivation, *n.* derivazione *f.*

derivative, *adj.* derivativo.

derive, *vb.* derivare.

dermatology, *n.* dermatologia *f.*

derogatory, *adj.* derogatòrio.

derrick, *n.* gru *f.*

descend, *vb.* scéndere.

descendant, *n.* discendènte *m.*

descent, *n.* discesa *f.*

describe, *vb.* descrivere.

description, *n.* descrizione *f.*

descriptive, *adj.* descrittivo.

desecrate, *vb.* desecrare.

desensitize, *vb.* desensibilizzare.

desert, 1. *n.* desèrto *m.*; (merit) mèrito *m.* 2. *vb.* disertare.

deserter, *n.* disertore *m.*

desertion, *n.* diserzione *f.*

deserve, *vb.* meritare.

deserving, *adj.* meritévole.

design, 1. *n.* disegno *m.* 2. *vb.* disegnare.

designate, *vb.* designare.

designation, *n.* designazione *f.*

designedly, *adv.* intenzionalmente.

designer, *n.* disegnatore *m.*

designing, *adj.* astuto.

desirability, *n.* desiderabilità *f.*

desirable, *adj.* desideràbile.

desire, 1. *n.* desidèrio *m.* 2. *vb.* desiderare.

desirous, *adj.* desideroso.

desist, *vb.* desistere.

desk, *n.* scrivania *f.*

desolate, 1. *adj.* desolato. 2. *vb.* desolare.

desolation, *n.* desolazione *f.*

despair, 1. *n.* disperazione *f.* 2. *vb.* disperare.

despatch, dispatch, 1. *n.* spedizione *f.*; (speed) prontezza *f.* 2. *vb.* spedire.

desperado, *n.* disperato *m.*

desperate, *adj.* disperato.

desperation, *n.* disperazione *f.*

despicable, *adj.* spregévole.

despise, *vb.* disprezzare, spregiare.

despite, *prep.* malgrado.

despondent, *adj.* abbattuto.

despot, *n.* dèspota *m.*

despotic, *adj.* dispòtico.

despotism, *n.* dispotismo *m.*

dessert, *n.* dessert *m.* (French pronunciation).

destination, *n.* destinazione *f.*

destine, *vb.* destinare.

destiny, *n.* destino *m.*

destitute, *adj.* destituito.

destitution, *n.* destituzione *f.*

destroy, *vb.* distrùggere.

destroyer, *n.* cacciatorpedinière *m.*

destructible, *adj.* distruttibile.

destruction, *n.* distruzione *f.*

destructive, *adj.* distruttivo.

desultory, *adj.* saltuàrio.

detach, *vb.* staccare, distaccare.

detachment, *n.* distacco *m.*; (mil.) distaccamento *m.*

detail, 1. *n.* dettaglio *m.* 2. *vb.* dettagliare.

detain, *vb.* detenere.

detect, *vb.* scoprire.

detection, *n.* scoprimento *m.*

detective, *n.* detective *m.* (English pron.).

detente, *n.* distensione *f.*

detention, *n.* detenzione *f.*

deter, *vb.* distògliere.

detergent, *n. and adj.* detergènte (*m.*)

deteriorate, *vb.* deteriorare.

deterioration, *n.* deteriorazione *f.*

determination, *n.* determinazione *f.*

determine, *vb.* determinare.

determined, *adj.* risoluto.

determinism, *n.* determinismo *m.*

deterrence, *n.* preventivo *m.*

detest, *vb.* detestare.

detestation, *n.* detestazione *f.*

dethrone, *vb.* detronizzare.

detonate, *vb.* detonare.

detonation, *n.* detonazione *f.*

detour, *n.* deviazione *f.*

detract, *vb.* detrarre.

detriment, *n.* detrimento *m.*, danno *m.*

detrimental, *adj.* dannoso.

devaluate, *vb.* svalutare.

devastate, *vb.* devastare.

devastation, *n.* devastazione *f.*

develop, *vb.* sviluppare.

developer, *n.* sviluppatore *m.*

developing nation, *n.* nazione in corso di sviluppo *f.*

development, *n.* sviluppo *m.*

deviate, *vb.* deviare.

deviation, *n.* deviazione *f.*

device, *n.* congegno *m.*

devil, *n.* diàvolo *m.*

devilish, *adj.* diabòlico.

devious, *adj.* dèvio.

devise, *vb.* escogitare.

devitalize, *vb.* devitalizzare.

devoid, *adj.* privo.

devote, *vb.* dedicare.

devoted, *adj.* devòto.

devotee, *n.* entusiasta *m. or f.*

devotion, *n.* devozione *f.*

devour, *vb.* divorare.

devout, *adj.* devòto.

dew, *n.* rugiada *f.*

dewy, *adj.* rugiadoso.

dexterity, *n.* destrezza *f.*

dexterous, *adj.* dèstro.

diabetes, *n.* diabète *f.*

diabolic, *adj.* diabòlico.

diadem, *n.* diadèma *m.*

diagnose, *vb.* diagnosticare.

diagnosis, *n.* diàgnosi *f.*

diagnostic, *adj.* diagnòstico.

diagonal, *adj.* diagonale.

diagonally, *adv.* diagonalmente.

diagram, *n.* diagramma *m.*

dial, 1. *n.* quadrante *m.;* (telephone) disco combinatore *m.* 2. *vb.* (telephone) formare (un numero).

dialect, *n.* dialètto *m.*

dialogue, *n.* diàlogo *m.*

diameter, *n.* diàmetro *m.*

diametrical, *adj.* diametrale.

diamond, *n.* diamante *m.*

diaper, *n.* pannilino *m.,* pannolino *m.*

diaphragm, *n.* diaframma *m.*

diarrhea, *n.* diarrèa *f.*

diary, *n.* diàrio *m.*

diathermy, *n.* diatermìa *f.*

diatribe, *n.* diatrìba *f.*

dice, *n.* dadi *m.pl.*

dickens (the), *interj.* diàmine!

dicker, *vb.* mercanteggiare.

dictaphone, *n.* dittàfono *m.*

dictate, *vb.* dettare.

dictation, *n.* dettatura *f.*

dictator, *n.* dittatore *m.*

dictatorial, *adj.* dittatoriale.

dictatorship, *n.* dittatura *f.*

diction, *n.* dizione *f.*

dictionary, *n.* dizionàrio *m.*

didactic, *adj.* didàttico.

die, 1. *n.* (gaming cube) dado *m.;* (stamper) stampo *m.* 2. *vb.* morire.

die-hard, *adj.* oltremodo conservatore.

diet, *n.* dièta *f.,* regime *m.*

dietary, *adj.* dietètico.

dietetic, *adj.* dietètico.

dietetics, *n.* dietètica *f.*

dietitian, *n.* dietista *m.*

differ, *vb.* differire.

difference, *n.* differènza *f.*

different, *adj.* differènte, divèrso.

differential, *adj.* differenziale.

differentiate, *vb.* differenziare.

difficult, *adj.* difficile.

difficulty, *n.* difficoltà *f.*

diffident, *adj.* tìmido.

diffuse, 1. *adj.* diffuso. 2. *vb.* diffóndere.

diffusion, *n.* diffusione *f.*

dig, *vb.* scavare.

digest, *vb.* digerire.

digestible, *adj.* digeribile.

digestion, *n.* digestione *f.*

digestive, *adj.* digestivo.

digital, *adj.* digitale.

digitalis, *n.* digitale *f.*

dignified, *adj.* dignitoso.

dignify, *vb.* dignificare.

dignitary, *n.* dignitàrio *m.*

dignity, *n.* dignità *f.*

digress, *vb.* digredire.

digression, *n.* digressione *f.*

dike, *n.* diga *f.*

dilapidated, *adj.* dilapidato.

dilapidation, *n.* dilapidazione *f.*

dilate, *vb.* dilatare.

dilatory, *adj.* dilatòrio.

dilemma, *n.* dilemma *m.*

dilettante, *n.* dilettante *m.*

diligence, *n.* diligènza *f.*

diligent, *adj.* diligènte.

dill, *n.* aneto *m.*

dilute, *vb.* diluire.

dilution, *n.* diluzione *f.*

dim, 1. *adj.* oscuro. 2. *vb.* oscurare.

dimension, *n.* dimensione *f.*

diminish, *vb.* diminuire, menomare.

diminution, *n.* diminuzione *f.*

diminutive, *n. and adj.* diminutivo *(m.)*

dimness, *n.* oscurità *f.*

dimple, *n.* fossetta *f.*

din, *n.* rumore *m.*

dine, *vb.* pranzare.

diner, dining-car, *n.* vagone ristorante *m.*

dingy, *adj.* sùdicio.

dinner, *n.* pranzo *m.*

dinosaur, *n.* dinosàuro *m.*

diocese, *n.* diòcesi *f.*

dioxide, *n.* biòssido *m.*

dip, *vb.* immèrgere, tuffare.

diphtheria, *n.* difterite, *f.*

diploma, *n.* diplòma *m.*

diplomacy, *n.* diplomazìa *f.*

diplomat, *n.* diplomàtico *m.*

diplomatic, *adj.* diplomàtico.

dipper, *n.* mèstolo *m.*

dire, *adj.* terribile.

direct, 1. *adj.* dirètto. 2. *vb.* dirigere.

direct current, *n.* corrènte continua *f.*

direction, *n.* direzione *f.,* sènso *m.*

directional, *adj.* direttivo.

directive, *adj.* direttivo.

directly, *adv.* direttamente, immediatamente.

directness, *n.* franchezza *f.*

director, *n.* direttore *m.*

directorate, *n.* direttorato *m.*

directory, *n.* guida *f.;* (telephone d.) elènco telefònico *m.*

dirge, *n.* canto funebre *m.*

dirigible, *n. and adj.* dirigìbile *(m.)*

dirt, *n.* sudiciume *m.*

dirty, *adj.* sùdicio, sporco.

disability, *n.* incapacità *f.*

disable, *vb.* rèndere incapace.

disabled, *adj.* invàlido.

disabuse, *vb.* disingannare.

disadvantage, *n.* svantàggio *m.*

disagree, *vb.* discordare, dissentire.

disagreeable, *adj.* sgradévole, antipàtico.

disagreement, *n.* dissènso *m.*

disappear, *vb.* sparire, scomparire.

disappearance, *n.* scomparsa *f.*

disappoint, *vb.* delùdere.

disappointment, *n.* delusione *f.*

disapproval, *n.* disapprovazione *f.*

disapprove, *vb.* disapprovare.

disarm, *vb.* disarmare.

disarmament, *n.* disarmo *m.*

disarrange, *vb.* scompigliare.

disarray, *n.* scompiglio *m.*

disassemble, *vb.* smontare.

disaster, *n.* disastro *m.*

disastrous, *adj.* disastroso.

disavow, *vb.* disconóscere.

disavowal, *n.* disconoscimento *m.*

disband, *vb.* sbandare.

disbar, *vb.* cancellare dall'albo dell'avvocatura.

disbelieve, *vb.* non credere.

disburse, *vb.* sborsare.

discard, *vb.* scartare.

discern, *vb.* discèrnere, scòrgere.

discerning, *adj.* penetrante.

discernment, 1. *n.* giudizio *m.*

discharge, 1. *n.* scàrico *m.;* (gun) scarica *f.;* (mil., job) licenziamento *m.* 2. *vb.* scaricare; (mil., job) licenziare.

disciple, *n.* discépolo *m.*

disciplinary, *adj.* disciplinare.

discipline, 1. *n.* disciplina *f.* 2. *vb.* disciplinare.

disclaim, *vb.* disconóscere.

disclaimer, *n.* disconoscimento *m.*

disclose, *vb.* rivelare.

disclosure, *n.* rivelazione *f.*

disco, *n.* (musicaccia) disco *f.*

discolor, *vb.* scolorire.

discoloration, *n.* scolorimento *m.*

discomfiture, *n.* sconfitta *f.*

discomfort, *n.* disàgio *m.*

disconcert, *vb.* sconcertare.

disconnect, *vb.* sconnèttere.

disconsolate, *adj.* sconsolato.

discontent, 1. *n.* scontènto *m.* 2. *vb.* scontentare.

discontented, *adj.* scontènto.

discontinue, *vb.* interrómpere, sospèndere.

discord, *n.* discòrdia *f.;* (music) disaccòrdo *m.*

discordant, *adj.* discordante.

discotheque, *n.* discotèca *f.*

discount, 1. *n.* sconto *m.* 2. *vb.* scontare.

discourage, *vb.* scoraggiare.

discouragement, *n.* scoraggiamento *m.*

discourse, 1. *n.* discorso *m.* 2. *vb.* discorrere.

discourteous, *adj.* scortese.

discourtesy, *n.* scortesìa *f.*

discover, *vb.* scoprire.

discoverer, *n.* scopritore *m.*

discovery, n. scopèrta f.

discredit, 1. n. discrèdito m. 2. vb. screditare.

discreditable, adj. disonorévole.

discreet, adj. discreto.

discrepancy, n. discrepanza f.

discrepant, adj. discrepante.

discretion, n. discrezione f.

discriminate, vb. discriminare.

discrimination, n. discriminazione f.

discursive, adj. digressivo.

discuss, vb. discùtere.

discussion, n. discussione f.

disdain, 1. n. disdegno m. 2. vb. disdegnare.

disdainful, adj. disdegnoso.

disease, n. malattìa f.

disembark, vb. sbarcare.

disembarkation, n. sbarco m.

disembodied, adj. incorpòreo.

disenchantment, n. disincanto m.

disengage, vb. disimpegnare.

disentangle, vb. districare.

disfavor, n. sfavore m.

disfigure, vb. disfigurare.

disfranchise, vb. privare della franchigia.

disgorge, vb. vomitare; (intr.) sgorgare.

disgrace, 1. n. disgràzia f., sfavore m., disonore m. 2. vb. disonorare.

disgraceful, adj. disonorante.

disgruntled, adj. scontento.

disguise, 1. n. travestimento m. 2. vb. travestire.

disgust, 1. n. disgusto m. 2. vb. disgustare.

disgusting, adj. disgustante, disgustoso.

dish, n. piatto m.

dishcloth, n. strofinàccio (per piatti) m.

dishearten, vb. scoraggiare.

dishonest, adj. disonèsto.

dishonesty, n. disonestà f.

dishonor, 1. n. disonore m. 2. vb. disonorare.

dishonorable, adj. disonorévole.

dish-towel, n. asciugapiatti m.

disillusion, 1. n. disillusione f. 2. vb. disillùdere.

disinfect, vb. disinfettare.

disinfectant, n. disinfettante m.

disinherit, vb. diseredare.

disintegrate, vb. disintegrare.

disinterested, adj. disinteressato.

disjointed, adj. sconnèsso.

disk, n. disco m.

dislike 1. n. antipatìa f. 2. vb. non piacere (with English subject as indirect object).

dislocate, vb. slogare.

dislodge, vb. sloggiare.

disloyal, adj. sleale.

disloyalty, n. sleltà f.

dismal, adj. melancònico.

dismantle, vb. smantellare.

dismay, 1. n. costernazione f. 2. vb. costernare.

dismember, vb. smembrare.

dismiss, vb. congedare, diméttere.

dismissal, n. congedo m.

dismount, vb. smontare.

disobedience, n. disubbidiènza f.

disobedient, adj. disobbediènte.

disobey, vb. disubbidire.

disorder, 1. n. disòrdine m. 2. vb. disordinare.

disorderly, adj. disordinato.

disorganize, vb. disorganizzare.

disown, vb. disconóscere.

disparage, vb. disprezzare.

disparate, adj. disparato.

disparity, n. disparità f.

dispassionate, adj. spassionato.

dispatch, see despatch.

dispatcher, n. speditore m.

dispel, vb. dissipare.

dispensable, adj. dispensàbile.

dispensary, n. dispensàrio m.

dispensation, n. dispensazione f.

dispense, vb. dispensare; (d. from) esentare (da).

dispersal, n. dispersione f.

disperse, vb. dispèrdere.

displace, vb. spostare.

displaced person, n. rifugiato m.

displacement, n. spostamento m.; (ship) dislocamento m.

display, 1. n. esibizione f.; (showing off) ostentazione f. 2. vb. esibire, ostentare.

displease, vb. dispiacere (a).

displeasure, n. dispiacere m.

disposable, adj. disponìbile.

disposal, n. disposizione f.

dispose, vb. disporre.

disposition, n. disposizione f.

dispossess, vb. spodestare.

disproof, n. confutazione f.

disproportion, n. sproporzione f.

disproportionate, adj. sproporzionato.

disprove, vb. confutare.

disputable, adj. disputàbile.

dispute, 1. n. dìsputa f. 2. vb. disputare.

disqualification, n. squalifica f.

disqualify, vb. squalificare.

disregard, 1. n. indifferènza f. 2. vb. trascurare.

disrepair, n. dilapidazione f.

disreputable, adj. disonorévole.

disrespect, n. mancanza di rispètto f.

disrespectful, adj. irrispetoso.

disrobe, vb. svestirsi.

disrupt, vb. causare una scissione in.

dissatisfaction, n. insoddisfazione f.

dissatisfy, vb. non soddisfare.

dissect, vb. dissecare.

dissection, n. dissezione f.

dissemble, vb. dissimulare.

disseminate, vb. disseminare.

dissension, n. dissènso m.

dissent, 1. n. dissènso m. 2. vb. dissentire.

dissertation, n. dissertazione f.

disservice, n. disservizio m.

dissimilar, adj. dissìmile.

dissipate, vb. dissipare.

dissipated, adj. dissoluto.

dissipation, n. dissipazione f., dissolutezza f.

dissociate, vb. dissociare.

dissolute, adj. dissoluto.

dissoluteness, n. dissolutezza f.

dissolution, n. dissoluzione f.

dissolve, vb. dissòlvere, sciògliere.

dissonance, n. dissonanza f.

dissonant, adj. dissonante.

dissuade, vb. dissuadere.

distance, n. distanza f.

distant, adj. distante, lontano; (be d.) distare.

distaste, n. disgusto m.

distasteful, adj. disgustoso.

distemper, n. indisposizione f.

distend, vb. distèndere.

distill, vb. distillare.

distillation, n. distillazione f.

distiller, n. distillatore m.

distillery, n. distillatòrio m.

distinct, adj. distinto.

distinction, n. distinzione f.

distinctive, adj. distintivo.

distinctly, adv. distintamente.

distinguish, vb. distinguere.

distort, vb. distòrcere.

distract, vb. distrarre.

distraction, n. distrazione f.

distraught, adj. pazzo.

distress, 1. n. afflizione f. 2. vb. affliggere.

distribute, vb. distribuire.

distribution, n. distribuzione f.

distributor, n. distributore m.

district, n. distretto m.

distrust, 1. n. sfidùcia f. 2. vb. non fidarsi di.

distrustful, adj. sospettoso.

disturb, vb. disturbare.

disturbance, n. disturbo m.

disunite, vb. disunire.

disuse, n. disuso m.

ditch, n. fosso m., fossato m.

ditto, n. lo stesso m.

diva, n. diva f.

divan, n. divano m.

dive, 1. n. tuffo m. 2. vb. tuffarsi.

dive-bomber, n. picchiatore m., tuffatore m.

diver, n. tuffatore m.

diverge, vb. divèrgere.

divergence, n. divergènza f.

divergent, adj. divergènte.

diverse, adj. divèrso.

diversion, n. diversione f.

diversity, n. diversità f.

divert, vb. (turn away) stornare; (amuse) divertire.

divest, vb. spogliare.

divide, vb. divìdere.

dividend, n. dividèndo m.

divine, 1. adj. divino. 2. vb. divinare.

divinity, n. divinità f.

divisible, adj. divisìbile.

division, *n.* divisione *f.,* scissione *f.*

divorce, 1. *n.* divòrzio *m.* 2. *vb.* divorziare.

divorcée, *n.* divorziata *f.*

divulge, *vb.* divulgare.

dizziness, *n.* vertigine *f.,* stordimento *m.*

dizzy, *adj.* vertiginoso, stordito.

do, *vb.* fare; **(how do you do?)** come sta?

docile, *adj.* dòcile.

dock, *n.* bacino *m.*

docket, *n.* etichetta *f.;* **(legal)** elenco *m.*

dockyard, *n.* arsenale *m.*

doctor, *n.* dottore *m.,* mèdico *m.*

doctorate, *n.* dottorato *m.*

doctrinaire, *adj.* dottrinàrio.

doctrine, *n.* dottrina *f.*

document, 1. *n.* documento *m.* 2. *vb.* documentare.

documentary, *adj.* documentàrio.

documentation, *n.* documentazione *f.*

dodge, *vb.* elùdere, schivare.

doe, *n.* cèrva *f.*

doeskin, *n.* pelle di cèrva *f.*

dog, *n.* cane *m.*

dogged, *adj.* ostinato, tenace.

doggerel, *n.* versucci *m.pl.*

doghouse, *n.* canile *m.*

dogma, *n.* dògma *m.*

dogmatic, *adj.* dogmàtico.

dogmatism, *n.* dogmatismo *m.*

doily, *n.* tovagliolino *m.*

doldrum, *n.* **(in the d.s)** *adj.* calmo.

dole, 1. *n.* elemòsina *f.* 2. *vb.* **(d. out)** distribuire.

doleful, *adj.* triste.

doll, *n.* bàmbola *f.,* pupàttola *f.*

dollar, *n.* dòllaro *m.*

dolorous, *adj.* doloroso.

dolphin, *n.* delfino *m.*

domain, *n.* dominio *m.*

dome, *n.* cùpola *f.*

domestic, *adj.* domèstico.

domesticate, *vb.* domesticare.

domicile, *n.* domicìlio *m.*

dominance, *n.* predominio *m.*

dominant, *adj.* dominante.

dominate, *vb.* dominare.

domination, *n.* dominazione *f.*

domineer, *vb.* spadroneggiare.

dominion, *n.* dominio *m.*

don, *vb.* indossare.

donate, *vb.* donare.

donation, *n.* donazione *f.*

done, *adj.* fatto; **(food)** còtto.

donkey, *n.* àsino *m.,* somaro *m.*

don't, *vb.* non fare.

doom, 1. *n.* **(condemnation)** condanna *f.;* **(fate)** destino *m.* 2. *vb.* condannare.

doomsday, *n.* giorno del giudìzio universale *m.*

door, *n.* pòrta *f.;* **(auto)** portièra *f.*

doorman, *n.* portinaio *m.*

door-mat, *n.* stuoino *m.*

doorstep, *n.* gradino della pòrta *m.*

doorway, *n.* vano della pòrta *m.*

dope, *n.* **(drug)** narcòtico *m.;* **(fool)** imbecille *m.*

dormant, *adj.* inattivo.

dormer, *n.* abbaino *m.*

dormitory, *n.* dormitòrio *m.*

dosage, *n.* dosatura *f.*

dose, 1. *n.* dòse *f.* 2. *vb.* dosare.

dossier, *n.* incartamento *m.*

dot, *n.* punto *m.*

dotage, *n.* rimbambimento *m.*

dote, *vb.* esser rimbambito; **(d. upon)** adorare.

double, 1. *n.* *and adj.* dóppio *(m.).* 2. *vb.* doppiare.

double-breasted, *adj.* a dóppio pètto.

double-cross, *vb.* ingannare.

double-dealing, *n.* duplicità *f.*

double time, *n.* passo di càrica *m.*

doubly, *adv.* doppiamente.

doubt, 1. *n.* dùbbio *m.* 2. *vb.* dubitare.

doubtful, *adj.* dùbbio, dubbioso.

doubtless, *adv.* senza dùbbio.

dough, *n.* pasta *f.*

dour, *adj.* sevèro.

douse, *vb.* spègnere.

dove, *n.* colombo *m.*

dowager, *n.* vècchia ricca e tirànnica *f.*

dowdy, *adj.* sciatto.

dowel, *n.* tassèllo *m.*

down, 1. *n.* **(on face; bird)** pelùria *f.;* **(feathers)** piumino *m.* 2. *adv.* giù. 3. *prep.* giù per.

downcast, *adj.* abbassato.

downfall, *n.* rovina *f.*

downhearted, *adj.* scoraggiato.

downhill, *adv.* in discesa.

down payment, *n.* antìcipo *m.*

downpour, *n.* rovèscio di piòggia *m.*

downright, *adj.* chiaro, completo.

downstairs, *adv.* giù per le scale.

downtown, *n.* centro della città *m.*

downtrodden, *adj.* opprèsso.

downward, *adv.* in giù.

downy, *adj.* coperto di pelùria.

dowry, *n.* dòte *f.*

doze, 1. *n.* sonnellino *m.,* pisolino *m.* 2. *vb.* sonnecchiare.

dozen, *n.* dozzina *f.*

drab, *adj.* grigio.

draft, 1. *n.* **(plan)** abbozzo *m.;* **(money)** tratta *f.;* **(ship)** pescàggio *m.;* **(air)** corrènte d'aria *f.;* **(military service)** servizio militare *m.* 2. *vb.* **(draw up)** redìgere.

draftee, *n.* rècluta *f.*

draftsman, *n.* disegnatore *m.*

drafty, *adj.* pièno di corrènti d'ària.

drag, *vb.* trascinare.

dragnet, *n.* giacchio *m.*

dragon, *n.* dragone *m.*

drain, 1. *n.* fogna *f.* 2. *vb.* scolare.

drainage, *n.* drenàggio *m.*

dram, *n.* dramma *m.*

drama, *n.* dramma *m.*

dramatic, *adj.* drammàtico.

dramatics, *n.* drammàtica *f.*

dramatist, *n.* drammaturgo *m.*

dramatize, *vb.* drammatizzare.

dramaturgy, *n.* drammaturgia *f.*

drape, 1. *n.* drappéggio *m.* 2. *vb.* drappeggiare.

drapery, *n.* drappéggio *m.*

drastic, *adj.* dràstico.

draught, see draft.

draw, *vb.* **(pull)** tirare; **(picture)** disegnare; **(d. back)** ritirarsi; **(d. up)** stèndere.

drawback, *n.* svantàggio *m.*

drawbridge, *n.* ponte levatòio *m.*

drawer, *n.* cassetto *m.*

drawing, *n.* **(picture)** disegno *m.;* **(lottery)** sortéggio *m.*

drawl, *vb.* parlare lentamente.

dray, *n.* carro *m.*

drayhorse, *n.* cavallo da tiro *m.*

drayman, *n.* carrettière *m.*

dread, 1. *n.* timore *m.* 2. *vb.* temere.

dreadful, *adj.* terribile.

dreadfully, *adv.* terribilmente.

dream, 1. *n.* sogno *m.* 2. *vb.* sognare.

dreamer, *n.* sognatore *m.*

dreamy, *adj.* vago.

dreary, *adj.* fosco.

dredge, 1. *n.* draga *f.* 2. *vb.* dragare.

dregs, *n.* fèccia *f.sg.*

drench, *vb.* inzuppare.

dress, 1. *n.* vestito *m.,* àbito *m.* 2. *vb.* vestire.

dresser, *n.* credènza *f.*

dressing, *n.* **(food)** condimento *m.,* **(medical)** bende *f.pl.*

dressing gown, *n.* vestàglia *f.*

dressmaker, *n.* sarta da dònna *f.*

dress rehearsal, *n.* pròva generale *f.*

drier, *n.* essiccatòio *m.*

drift, 1. *n.* deriva *f.* 2. *vb.* andare alla deriva.

driftwood, *n.* legno flottante *m.*

drill, 1. *n.* **(tool)** tràpano *m.;* **(practice)** esercitazione *f.* 2. *vb.* trapanare; esercitare.

drink, 1. *n.* bevanda *f.,* bibita *f.* 2. *vb.* bere.

drinkable, *adj.* bevìbile.

drip, *vb.* gocciolare.

dripping, *n.* gocciamento *m.*

drive, 1. *n.* **(ride)** passeggiata in carrozza *f.;* **(avenue)** viale *m.* 2. *vb.* costringere; **(auto)** guidare.

drivel, 1. *n.* bava *f.* 2. *vb.* sbavare.

driver, *n.* conducènte *m.,* autista *m.*

driveway, *n.* viale *m.*

drizzle, 1. *n.* pioggerèlla *f.* 2. *vb.* piovigginare.

dromedary, n. dromedàrio m.

drone, 1. n. (bee) fuco m.; (hum) ronzìo m. 2. vb. ronzare.

droop, vb. abbàttersi.

drop, 1. n. góccia f. 2. vb. (fall) cadere; (let fall) lasciar cadere.

dropout, n. studente che lascia definitivamente la scuola m.

dropper, n. contagocce m.

dropsy, n. idropìsia f.

drought, n. siccità f.

drove, n. mandra f.

drown, vb. annegare.

drowse, vb. sonnecchiare, assopirsi.

drowsiness, n. sonnolènza f.

drowsy, adj. sonnolènto.

drudge, vb. lavorare duramente.

drudgery, n. lavoro monòtono m.

drug, n. dròga f.

druggist, n. farmacista m.

drug store, n. farmacìa f.

drum, n. tamburo m.

drum major, n. tamburo maggiore m.

drummer, n. tamburo m.

drumstick, n. (lit.) bacchetta del tamburo m.; (chicken) gamba di pollo f.

drunk, adj. ubbriaco.

drunkard, n. ubbriacone m.

drunken, adj. ubbriaco.

drunkenness, n. ubbriachezza f.

dry, 1. adj. secco, asciutto. 2. vb. seccare, asciugare.

dry cell, n. pila a secco f.

dry-clean, vb. pulire a secco.

dry-cleaner, n. tintore m.

dry-cleaning, n. pulitura a secco f.

dry dock, n. bacino di carenàggio m.

dry goods, n. stoffe f.pl.; tessuti m.pl.

dryness, n. secchezza f.

dual, n. and adj. duale (m.).

dualism, n. dualismo m.

dubious, adj. dùbbio.

duchess, n. duchessa f.

duchy, n. ducato m.

duck, 1. n. ànitra f. 2. vb. tuffare.

duct, n. canale m.

ductile, adj. dùttile.

dud, n. bomba inesplòsa f.; (failure) fiasco m.

due, adj. dèbito, dovuto; (fall d.) scadere.

duel, 1. n. duèllo m. 2. vb. duellare.

duelist, n. duellante m.

dues, n. quòta f.; (tax) diritti m.

duet, n. duetto m.

duffle bag, n. zàino m.

dugout, n. trincèa f.

duke, n. duca m.

dukedom, n. ducato m.

dulcet, adj. armonioso.

dull, 1. adj. monòtono, ottuso, insulso. 2. vb. ottùndere.

dullard, n. stùpido m.

dullness, n. monotonìa f., ottusità f.

duly, adv. debitamente.

dumb, adj. muto; (stupid) sciocco.

dumbfound, vb. sbalordire.

dumbwaiter, n. calapranzi m., calapiatti m.

dummy, n. fantòccio m.

dump, vb. scaricare.

dumpling, n. gnòcco m.

dun, adj. grigio fosco.

dunce, n. stolto m.

dune, n. duna f.

dung, n. stèrco m., letame m.

dungarees, n. tuta f.sg.

dungeon, n. prigione sotterrànea f.

dunk, vb. tuffare, inzuppare.

dupe, n. credulone m.

duplex, n. dóppio.

duplicate, vb. duplicare.

duplication, n. duplicazione f.

duplicity, n. duplicità f.

durable, adj. duràbile.

durability, n. durabilità f.

duration, n. durata f.

duress, n. coercizione f.

during, prep. durante.

dusk, n. crepùscolo m.

dusky, adj. fosco.

dust, n. pólvere m.; (sweepings) spazzatura f.

dustpan, n. paletta per spazzature f.

dusty, adj. polveroso.

Dutch, adj. olandese.

Dutchman, n. olandese m.

dutiful, adj. obbediènte.

dutifully, adv. con ubbidiènza.

duty, n. dovere m.; (tax) imposta f.

duty-free, adj. esente da dogana.

dwarf, n. nano m.

dwell, vb. abitare; (d. upon) diffóndersi su.

dweller, n. abitante m.

dwelling, n. abitazione f., dimora f.

dwindle, vb. diminuire.

dye, 1. n. tintura f. 2. vb. tìngere.

dyer, n. tintore m.

dyestuff, n. matèria colorante f.

dynamic, adj. dinàmico.

dynamics, n. dinàmica f.

dynamite, n. dinamite f.

dynamo, n. dìnamo f.

dynasty, n. dinastìa f.

dysentery, n. dissenterìa f.

dyslexia, n. dislessìa f.

dyspepsia, n. dispepsìa f.

dyspeptic, adj. dispèptico.

E

each, adj. ogni.

each one, pron. ciascuno, cadaùno.

each other, pron. l'un l'altro; or use reflexive.

eager, adj. bramoso, impaziènte.

eagerly, adv. bramosamente, impazientemente.

eagerness, n. brama f., impaziènza f.

eagle, n. àquila f.

eaglet, n. aquilòtto m.

ear, n. orécchio m.; (grain) spiga f.

earache, n. mal d'orecchi (m.)

eardrum, n. tìmpano m.

earl, n. conte m.

early, adv. di buon'ora, prèsto.

earmark, vb. riservare.

earn, vb. guadagnare; (deserve) meritare.

earnest, adj. sèrio; (in e.) sul sèrio.

earnestly, adv. seriamente.

earnestness, n. serietà f.

earnings, n. guadagni m.pl.

earphone, n. cùffia f.

earring, n. orecchino m.

earshot, n. portata di voce f.

earth, n. tèrra f.

earthenware, n. stovìglie f.pl.

earthly, adj. terreno.

earthquake, n. terremòto m.

earthworm, n. lombrico m.

earthy, adj. terreno.

ease, 1. n. àgio m., còmodo m. 2. vb. sollevare.

easel, n. cavalletto m.

easily, adv. facilmente.

easiness, n. facilità f.

east, n. èst m., oriènte m.

Easter, n. Pasqua f.

easterly, adj. ad est, da est.

eastern, adj. orientale.

eastward, adv. vèrso èst.

easy, adj. fàcile.

easygoing, adj. noncurante.

eat, vb. mangiare.

eatable, adj. mangiàbile.

eaves, n. gronda f.sg.

eavesdrop, vb. origliare.

ebb, 1. n. riflusso m.; (ebb-tide) bassa marèa f. 2. vb. rifluire.

ebony, n. èbano m.

ebullient, adj. esuberante.

eccentric, adj. eccèntrico.

eccentricity, n. eccentricità f.

ecclesiastic, n. and adj. ecclesiàstico (m.)

ecclesiastical, adj. ecclesiàstico.

echelon, n. scaglione m.

echo, 1. n. èco m. 2. vb. echeggiare.

eclipse, 1. n. eclissi f. 2. vb. eclissare.

ecology, n. ecologìa f.

ecological, adj. ecològico.

economic, adj. econòmico.

economical, adj. econòmico.

economics, n. economìa polìtica f.

economist, n. economista m.

economize, vb. economizzare.

economy, n. economìa f.

ecru, *adj.* (colore di) seta cruda.

ecumenical, *adj.* ecumènico.

ecstasy, *n.* èstasi *f.*

eczema, *n.* eczèma *m.*

eddy, *n.* vòrtice *m.*

edge, *n.* bordo *m.*, màrgine *m.*; orlo *m.*

edging, *n.* orlatura *f.*

edgy, *adj.* irritàbile.

edible, *adj.* mangiàbile.

edict, *n.* editto *m.*

edifice, *n.* edifício *m.*

edify, *vb.* edificare.

edit, *vb.* (journal) dirigere; (book) curare l'edizione di.

edition, *n.* edizione *f.*

editor, *n.* (journal) direttore *m.*

editorial, 1. *n.* artícolo di fondo *m.* 2. *adj.* editoriale.

educate, *vb.* educare.

education, *n.* educazione *f.*

educational, *adj.* educativo.

educator, *n.* educatore *m.*

eel, *n.* anguilla *f.*

efface, *vb.* cancellare.

effect, 1. *n.* effètto *m.*; (in e.) effettivamente. 2. *vb.* effettuare.

effective, *adj.* effettivo.

effectively, *adv.* effettivamente.

effectiveness, *n.* effettività *f.*

effectual, *adj.* efficace.

effeminate, *adj.* effeminato.

effervescence, *n.* effervescènza *f.*

effete, *adj.* effeminato.

efficacious, *adj.* efficace.

efficacy, *n.* efficàcia *f.*

efficiency, *n.* efficiènza *f.*

efficient, *adj.* efficiènte.

efficiently, *adv.* efficientemente.

effigy, *n.* effigie *f.*

effort, *n.* sforzo *m.*; (make an e.) sforzarsi.

effortless, *adj.* sènza sforzo.

effrontery, *n.* sfrontatezza *f.*

effulgent, *adj.* risplendènte.

effusive, *adj.* espansivo.

egg, *n.* uòvo *m.*

eggplant, *n.* melanzana *f.*

ego, *n.* lo *m.*

egoism, *n.* egoísmo *m.*

egotism, *n.* egotismo *m.*

egotist, *n.* egotista *m.*

Egypt, *n.* l'Egitto *m.*

Egyptian, *adj.* egiziano.

eight, *num.* òtto.

eighteen, *num.* diciòtto.

eighteenth, *adj.* diciottèsimo, decimottavo.

eighth, *adj.* ottavo.

eightieth, *adj.* ottantèsimo.

eighty, *num.* ottanta.

either, 1. *pron.* l'uno o l'altro. 2. *conj.* o; sia; (either . . . or) o . . . o; sia . . . che.

ejaculate, *vb.* (med.) eiaculare; (fig.) esclamare.

eject, *vb.* espèllere.

ejection, *n.* espulsione *f.*

eke out, *vb.* supplire a.

elaborate, 1. *adj.* elaborato. 2. *vb.* elaborare.

elapse, *vb.* trascórrere.

elastic, *n. and adj.* elàstico (*m.*)

elasticity, *n.* elasticità *f.*

elate, *vb.* esaltare.

elated, *adj.* esaltato.

elation, *n.* esaltazione *f.*

elbow, *n.* gómito *m.*

elbowroom, *n.* spàzio libero *m.*

elder, 1. *n.* (older person) maggiore *m.*; (tree) sambuco *m.* 2. *adj.* maggiore.

elderberry, *n.* frutto del sambuco *m.*

elderly, *adj.* vècchio.

eldest, *adj.* (il) maggiore.

elect, *vb.* elèggere.

election, *n.* elezione *f.*

electioneer, *vb.* cercare voti.

elective, *adj.* elettivo.

electorate, *n.* votanti *m.pl.*

electric, electrical, *adj.* elèttrico.

electric eel, *n.* anguilla elèttrica *f.*; gimnòto *m.*

electrician, *n.* elettricista *m.*

electricity, *n.* elettricità *f.*

electrocardiogram, *n.* elettrocardiogramma *m.*

electrocution, *n.* elettrocuzione *f.*

electrode, *n.* elèttrodo *m.*

electrolysis, *n.* elettròlisi *f.*

electron, *n.* elettrone *m.*

electronic, *adj.* elettrònico.

electronics, *n.* elettrònica *f.*

electroplating, *n.* galvanoplàstica *f.*

elegance, *n.* eleganza *f.*

elegant, *adj.* elegante.

elegiac, *adj.* elegíaco.

elegy, *n.* elegía *f.*

element, *n.* elemento *m.*

elemental, elementary, *adj.* elementare.

elephant, *n.* elefante *m.*

elephantine, *adj.* elefantesco.

elevate, *vb.* elevare.

elevation, *n.* elevazione *f.*

elevator, *n.* ascensore *m.*

eleven, *num.* ùndici.

eleventh, *adj.* undicèsimo.

elf, *n.* folletto *m.*

elfin, *adj.* di folletto.

elicit, *vb.* cavar fuòri.

eligibility, *n.* eleggibilità *f.*

eligible, *adj.* eleggibile.

eliminate, *vb.* eliminare.

elimination, *n.* eliminazione *f.*

elixir, *n.* elisir *m.*

elk, *n.* alce *m.*

elm, *n.* olmo *m.*

elocution, *n.* elocuzione *f.*

elongate, *vb.* allungare.

elope, *vb.* fuggire.

eloquence, *n.* eloquènza *f.*

eloquent, *adj.* eloquènte.

eloquently, *adv.* eloquentemente.

else, 1. *adj.* altro. 2. *adv.* altrimenti.

elsewhere, *adv.* altrove.

elucidate, *vb.* elucidare.

elude, *vb.* elùdere.

elusive, *adv.* elusivo.

emancipate, *vb.* emancipare.

emancipation, *n.* emancipazione *f.*

emancipator, *n.* emancipatore *m.*

emasculate, *vb.* castrare.

embalm, *vb.* imbalsamare.

embankment, *n.* àrgine *m.*

embargo, *n.* embargo *m.*

embark, *vb.* imbarcare.

embarrass, *vb.* imbarazzare.

embarrassment, *n.* imbarazzo *m.*

embassy, *n.* ambasciata *f.*

embellish, *vb.* abbellire.

embellishment, *n.* abbellimento *m.*

embers, *n.* brace *f.sg.*

embezzle, *vb.* appropriarsi fraudolentemente.

embitter, *vb.* amareggiare.

emblazon, *vb.* adornare, illustrare.

emblem, *n.* emblèma *m.*

emblematic, *adj.* emblemàtico.

embody, *vb.* incorporare.

emboss, *vb.* stampare in rilièvo.

embrace, 1. *n.* abbràccio *m.*; (sexual) amplèsso *m.* 2. *vb.* abbracciare.

embroider, *vb.* ricamare.

embroidery, *n.* ricamo *m.*

embroil, *vb.* imbrogliare.

embryo, *n.* embrione *m.*

embryology, *n.* embriología *f.*

embryonic, *adj.* embrionale.

emend, *vb.* emendare.

emerald, *n.* smeraldo *m.*

emerge, *vb.* emèrgere.

emergency, *n.* emergènza *f.*

emergent, *adj.* emergènte.

emery, *n.* smeriglio *m.*

emetic, *n. and adj.* emètico (*m.*)

emigrant, *n. and adj.* emigrante (*m.*)

emigrate, *vb.* emigrare.

emigration, *n.* emigrazione *f.*

eminence, *n.* eminènza *f.*

eminent, *adj.* eminènte.

emissary, *n.* emissàrio *m.*

emission controls, *n.pl.* apparècchio per limitare l'emissione di fumi nocivi *m.*

emit, *vb.* emèttere.

emollient, *n. and adj.* emolliènte (*m.*)

emolument, *n.* emolumento *m.*

emotion, *n.* emozione *f.*

emotional, *adj.* emotivo; (easily moved) emozionàbile.

emperor, *n.* imperatore *m.*

emphasis, *n.* ènfasi *f.*

emphasize, *vb.* méttere in rilièvo.

emphatic, *adj.* enfàtico.

empire, *n.* impèro *m.*

empirical, *adj.* empírico.

employ, 1. *n.* impiègo *m.*, servízio *m.* 2. *vb.* impiegare.

employed, *adj.* addetto.

employee, *n.* impiegato *m.*, impiegata *f.*

employer, *n.* datore di lavoro *m.;* (boss) padrone *m.*

employment, *n.* impiègo *m.*

empower, *vb.* autorizzare.

empress, *n.* imperatrice *f.*

emptiness, *n.* vuòto *m.*

empty, 1. *adj.* vuòto. 2. *vb.* vuotare.

emulate, *vb.* emulare.

emulsion, *n.* emulsione *f.*

enable, *vb.* méttere in grado di.

enact, *vb.* decretare.

enactment, *n.* decreto *m.*

enamel, 1. *n.* smalto *m.* 2. *vb.* smaltare.

enamor, *vb.* innamorare.

encamp, *vb.* accamparsi.

encampment, *n.* accampamento *m.*

encephalitis, *n.* encefalite *f.*

encephalon, *n.* encèfalo *m.*

enchant, *vb.* incantare.

enchanting, *adj.* incantévole.

enchantment, *n.* incanto *m.*

encircle, *vb.* accerchiare.

enclose, *vb.* rinchiùdere; (with letter) acclùdere.

enclosure, *n.* recinto *m.*

encompass, *vb.* (surround) circondare; (cause) causare.

encounter, 1. *n.* incontro *m.* 2. *vb.* incontrare.

encourage, *vb.* incoraggiare, confortare.

encouragement, *n.* incoraggiamento *m.*

encroach upon, *vb.* usurpare.

encyclical, *n.* enciclica *f.*

encyclopaedia, *n.* enciclopedia *f.*

end, 1. *n.* fine *f.,* tèrmine *m.;* (aim) scòpo *m.* 2. *adj.* ùltimo. 3. *vb.* finire, terminare.

endanger, *vb.* méttere in pericolo.

endear, *vb.* rèndere caro.

endearment, *n.* carezza *f.*

endeavor, 1. *n.* sforzo *m.* 2. *vb.* sforzarsi.

endemic, *adj.* endèmico.

ending, *n.* fine *f.; (gram.)* desinènza *f.*

endless, *adj.* sènza fine.

endocrine, *adj.* endòcrino.

endorse, *vb.* firmare; (cheques, etc.) girare.

endorsement, *n.* girata *f.*

endow, *vb.* dotare.

endowment, *n.* dotazione *f.*

endurance, *n.* sopportazione *f.*

endure, *vb.* soportare; (last) durare.

enduring, *adj.* durévole.

enema, *n.* clistère *m.;* (colonic irrigation) enteroclisma *m.*

enemy, *n. and adj.* nemico *(m.)*

energetic, *adj.* enèrgico.

energy, *n.* energia *f.*

enervate, *vb.* snervare.

enervation, *n.* snervamento *m.*

enfold, *vb.* avvòlgere.

enforce, *vb.* eseguire.

enforcement, *n.* esecuzione *f.*

enfranchise, *vb.* affrancare.

engage, *vb.* (hire) prèndere a

nolo; (attention) attrarre; (to get married) fidanzare.

engaged, *adj.* (to get married) fidanzato.

engagement, *n.* (to get married) fidanzamento *m.;* (date) appuntamento *m.*

engaging, *adj.* attraènte.

engender, *vb.* generare.

engine, *n.* màcchina *f.;* (locomotive) locomotiva *f.*

engineer, *n.* ingegnère *m.;* (train driver) macchinista *m.*

engineering, *n.* ingegneria *f.*

genio *m.*

England, *n.* Inghilterra *f.*

English, *adj.* inglese.

Englishman, *n.* inglese *m.*

Englishwoman, *n.* inglese *f.*

engrave, *vb.* incìdere.

engraver, *n.* incisore *m.*

engraving, *n.* incisione *f.*

engross, *vb.* (absorb) assorbire; (copy) copiare.

enhance, *vb.* aumentare, accréscere.

enigma, *n.* enimma *m.*

enigmatic, *adj.* enimmàtico.

enjoin, *vb.* (command) ingiùngere; (forbid) vietare.

enjoy, *vb.* godere.

enjoyable, *adj.* godibile, piacévole.

enjoyment, *n.* godimento *m.*

enlace, *vb.* allacciare.

enlargement, *n.* ingrandimento *m.*

enlarger, *n.* ingranditore *m.*

enlighten, *vb.* illuminare.

enlightenment, *n.* chiarimento *m.*

enlist, *vb.* arrolare.

enlisted man, *n.* uòmo di truppa *m.*

enlistment, *n.* arrolamento *m.*

enliven, *vb.* ravvivare.

enmesh, *vb.* invilluppare.

enmity, *n.* inimicizia *f.*

ennoble, *vb.* annobilire.

ennui, *n.* nòia *f.*

enormity, *n.* enormità *f.*

enormous, *adj.* enòrme.

enough, 1. *adj.* sufficiènte. 2. *adv.* abbastanza. 3. *vb.* (be so) bastare.

enrage, *vb.* far arrabbiare.

enrapture, *vb.* estasiare.

enrich, *vb.* arricchire.

enroll, *vb.* iscrivere, registrare; *(mil.)* arruolare.

enrollment, *n.* iscrizione *f.,* registrazione *f.*

ensemble, *n.* insième *m.*

enshrine, *vb.* méttere in un reliquàrio.

ensign, *n.* (flag) bandièra *f.,* insegna *f.;* (rank) alfière *m.*

enslave, *vb.* asservire.

ensnare, *vb.* prèndere in tràppola.

ensue, *vb.* (follow) seguire; (happen) accadere.

entail, *vb.* comportare, richièdere.

entangle, *vb.* imbrogliare.

enter, *vb.* entrare.

enterprise, *n.* impresa *f.*

enterprising, *adj.* avventuroso.

entertain, *vb.* trattenere; (guests) accògliere; (amuse) divertire.

entertainment, *n.* trattenimento *m.;* (amusement) divertimento *m.*

enthrall, *vb.* incantare.

enthusiasm, *n.* entusiasmo *m.*

enthusiast, *n.* entusiasta *m.*

enthusiastic, *adj.* entusiàstico.

entice, *vb.* adescare.

entire, *adj.* intero.

entirely, *adv.* interamente.

entirety, *n.* totalità *f.*

entitle, *vb.* intitolare; (authorize) autorizzare.

entity, *n.* entità *f.*

entomb, *vb.* seppellire.

entrails, *n.* interiora *f.pl.*

entrain, *vb.* prèndere il treno.

entrance, *n.* entrata *f.,* ingresso *m.*

entrant, *n.* concorrènte *m.*

entrap, *vb.* intrappolare.

entreat, *vb.* supplicare.

entreaty, *n.* sùpplica *f.*

entrench, *vb.* trincerare.

entrepreneur, *n.* imprenditore *m.*

entrust, *vb.* affidare.

entry, *n.* entrata *f.,* ingresso *m.*

enumerate, *vb.* enumerare.

enumeration, *n.* enumerazione *f.*

enunciate, *vb.* enunciare.

enunciation, *n.* enunciazione *f.*

envelop, *vb.* avviluppare.

envelope, *n.* busta *f.*

enviable, *adj.* invidiàbile.

envious, *adj.* invidioso.

environment, *n.* ambiente *m.*

environmentalist, *n.* fautore della preservazione dell'ambiente *m.*

environmental protection, *n.* protezione dell'ambiente *f.*

environs, *n.* dintorni *m.pl.*

envisage, *vb.* figurarsi.

envoy, *n.* inviato *m.*

envy, 1. *n.* invidia *f.* 2. *vb.* invidiare.

eon, *n.* eternità *f.*

ephemeral, *adj.* effimero.

epic, 1. *n.* epopèa *f.* 2. *adj.* èpico.

epicure, *n.* epicurèo *m.*

epidemic, 1. *n.* epidemia *f.* 2. *adj.* epidèmico.

epidermis, *n.* epidèrmide *f.*

epigram, *n.* epigramma *m.*

epilepsy, *n.* epilessia *f.*

epilogue, *n.* epilogo *m.*

episode, *n.* episòdio *m.*

epistle, *n.* epistola *f.*

epitaph, *n.* epitàffio *m.*

epithet, *n.* epìteto *m.*

epitome, *n.* epitome *f.*

epitomize, *vb.* epitomare.

epoch, *n.* època *f.*

equable, *adj.* èquo.

equal, 1. *adj.* uguale, pari. 2. *vb.* uguagliare.

equality, n. uguaglianza f.
equalize, vb. uguagliare.
equanimity, n. equanimità f.
equate, vb. uguagliare.
equation, n. equazione f.
equator, n. equatore m.
equatorial, adj. equatoriale.
equestrian, adj. equèstre.
equidistant, adj. equidistante.
equilateral, adj. equilaterale.
equilibrate, vb. equilibrare.
equilibrium, n. equilibrio m.
equinox, n. equinòzio m.
equip, vb. corredare, fornire.
equipment, n. equipàggio m., corrèdo m.
equitable, adj. èquo.
equity, n. equità f.
equivalent, adj. equivalente; (be e.) equivalere.
equivocal, adj. equivoco.
equivocate, vb. giocare sull'equivoco.
era, n. èra f.
eradicate, vb. sradicare.
eradicator, n. sradicatore m.
erase, vb. cancellare, raschiare.
eraser, n. raschino m., cancellino m.
erasure, n. cancellatura f.
erect, 1. adj. erètto. 2. vb. erìgere, costruire.
erection, n. erezione f., costruzione f.
erectness, n. posizione erètta f.
ermine, n. ermellino m.
erode, vb. eródere.
erosion, n. erosione f.
erosive, adj. erosivo.
erotic, adj. eròtico.
err, vb. errare.
errand, n. commissione f.
errant, adj. errante.
erratic, adj. erràtico.
erroneous, adj. erròneo.
error, n. errore m.
erudite, adj. erudito.
erudition, n. erudizione f.
erupt, vb. eruttare.
eruption, n. eruzione f.
escalate, vb. aumentare.
escalator, n. scala mòbile f.
escapade, n. scappata f.
escape, 1. n. fuga f., scampo m. 2. vb. sfuggire, scappare.
escapism, n. desiderio di sfuggire alla realtà m.
eschew, vb. evitare.
escort, 1. n. scòrta f. 2. vb. scortare.
esculent, adj. esculènte.
escutcheon, n. scudo m.
Eskimo pie, n. eschimese m.
esophagus, n. esòfago m.
esoteric, adj. esotèrico.
especial, adj. speciale.
especially, adv. specialmente.
espionage, n. spionàggio m.
espousal, n. sposalizio m.
espouse, vb. sposare.
essay, 1. n. sàggio m. 2. vb. provare.
essayist, n. saggista m.
essence, n. essènza f.
essential, adj. essenziale.

essentially, adv. essenzialmente.
establish, vb. stabilire.
establishment, n. stabilimento m.
estate, n. (inheritance) patrimònio m.; (possessions) bèni m.pl.; (condition) condizione f., stato m.
esteem, 1. n. stima f. 2. vb. stimare.
estimable, adj. stimàbile.
estimate, 1. n. valutazione f., stima f. 2. vb. valutare, stimare.
estimation, n. stima f., valutazione f.
estrange, vb. alienare.
estuary, n. estuàrio m.
etching, n. acquafòrte f.
eternal, adj. etèrno.
eternity, n. eternità f.
ether, n. ètere m.
ethereal, adj. etèreo.
ethical, adj. ètico.
ethics, n. ètica f.
ethnic, adj. ètnico.
etiquette, n. galatèo f.
etymology, n. etimologia f.
eucalyptus, n. eucalitto m.
eugenic, adj. eugènico.
eugenics, n. eugenètica f.
eulogize, vb. elogiare.
eulogy, n. elògio m.
eunuch, n. eunuco m.
euphonious, adj. eufònico.
Europe, n. Europa f.
European, n. and adj. europèo (m.)
euthanasia, n. eutanasia f.
evacuate, vb. evacuare.
evade, vb. evitare, elùdere.
evaluate, vb. valutare.
evaluation, n. valutazione f.
evanescent, adj. evanescènte.
evangelist, n. evangelista m.
evaporate, vb. evaporare.
evaporation, n. evaporazione f.
evasion, n. evasione f.
evasive, adj. evasivo.
eve, n. vigilia f.
even, 1. adj. pari, giusto, uniforme. 2. adv. anche, perfino.
evening, n. sera f.
evenness, n. uniformità f.
event, n. avvenimento m.
eventful, adj. pièno di avvenimenti.
eventual, adj. finale.
ever, adv. sèmpre, mai.
everglade, n. palude f.
evergreen, adj. sempreverde.
everlasting, adj. sempitèrno.
every, adj. ogni.
everybody, pron. ognuno.
everyday, adj. quotidiano.
everyone, pron. ognuno.
everything, pron. tutto.
everywhere, adv. dappertutto.
evict, vb. espèllere.
eviction, n. espulsione f.
evidence, n. evidènza f.
evident, adj. evidènte; (be e.) risultare.
evidently, adv. evidentemente.

evil, 1. n. male m. 2. adj. cattivo.
evince, vb. manifestare.
eviscerate, vb. sviscerare.
evoke, vb. evocare.
evolution, n. evoluzione f.
evolutionist, n. evoluzionista m.
evolve, vb. evòlvere.
ewe, n. pècora f.
exact, 1. adj. esatto. 2. vb. esìgere.
exactly, adv. esattamente.
exaggerate, vb. esagerare.
exaggeration, n. esagerazione f.
exalt, vb. esaltare.
exaltation, n. esaltazione f.
examination, n. esame m.
examine, vb. esaminare.
example, n. esèmpio m.
exasperate, vb. esasperare.
exasperation, n. esasperazione f.
excavate, vb. scavare.
excavation, n. scavo m.
exceed, vb. eccèdere, superare.
exceedingly, adv. estremamente.
excel, vb. eccèllere, superare.
excellence, n. eccellènza f.
Excellency, n. Eccellènza f.
excellent, adj. eccellènte.
except, 1. vb. eccettuare. 2. prep. eccètto, salvo, tranne; (e. for) all'infuòri di.
exception, n. eccezione f.
exceptional, adj. eccezionale.
excerpt, n. brano m.
excess, n. eccèsso m.
excessive, adj. eccessivo.
exchange, 1. n. scàmbio m. 2. vb. scambiare.
exchangeable, adj. scambiàbile.
excise, n. dàzio m.
excitable, adj. eccitàbile.
excite, vb. eccitare.
excitement, n. eccitamento m., eccitazione f.
exclaim, vb. esclamare.
exclamation, n. esclamazione f.
exclamation point or mark, n. punto esclamativo m.
exclude, vb. esclùdere.
exclusion, n. esclusione f.
exclusive, adj. esclusivo.
excogitate, vb. escogitare.
excommunicate, vb. scomunicare.
excommunication, n. scomùnica f.
excoriate, vb. escoriare.
excrement, n. escremento m.
excruciating, adj. tormentoso.
exculpate, vb. scolpare.
excursion, n. escursione f.
excusable, adj. scusàbile.
excuse, 1. n. scusa f. 2. vb. scusare.
execrable, adj. esecràbile.
execute, vb. eseguire; (kill legally) giustiziare.
execution, n. esecuzione f.; (le-

gal killing) esecuzione capitale f.

executioner, n. bòia m., carnéfice m.

executive, 1. n. amministratore m. 2. adj. esecutivo.

executor, n. esecutore m.

exemplary, adj. esemplare.

exemplify, vb. esemplificare.

exempt, 1. adj. esènte. 2. vb. esentare.

exercise, 1. n. esercizio m. 2. vb. esercitare.

exert, vb. esercitare.

exertion, n. sforzo m.

exhale, vb. esalare.

exhaust, vb. esaurire.

exhaustion, n. esaurimento m.

exhaustive, adj. esauriènte.

exhibit, 1. n. mostra f. 2. vb. esibire, mostrare.

exhibition, n. esibizione f., mostra f.

exhibitionism, n. esibizionismo m.

exhilarate, vb. esilarare.

exhort, vb. esortare.

exhortation, n. esortazione f.

exhume, vb. esumare.

exigency, n. esigènza f.

exile, 1. n. esilio m.; (person) fuoruscito m. 2. vb. esiliare.

exist, vb. esistere.

existence, n. esistènza f.

existent, adj. esistènte.

exit, n. uscita f.

exodus, n. èsodo m.

exonerate, vb. esonerare.

exorbitant, adj. esorbitante.

exorcise, vb. esorcizzare; (chase away) scacciare.

exotic, adj. esòtico.

expand, vb. espàndere.

expanse, n. distesa f.

expansion, n. espansione f.

expansive, adj. espansivo.

expatiate, vb. diffóndersi.

expatriate, n. espatriato m.

expect, vb. aspettarsi.

expectancy, n. aspettativa f.

expectation, n. aspettativa f.

expectorate, vb. espettorare.

expediency, n. opportunità f.

expedient, 1. n. espediènte m. 2. adj. espediènte, opportuno.

expedite, vb. sbrigare.

expedition, n. spedizione f.

expel, vb. espèllere.

expend, vb. spèndere, consumare.

expenditure, n. spesa f.

expense, n. spesa f.

expensive, adj. costoso.

expensively, adv. costosamente.

experience, 1. n. esperiènza f. 2. vb. esperimentare.

experienced, adj. espèrto.

experiment, 1. n. esperimento m. 2. vb. sperimentare.

experimental, adj. sperimentale.

expert, n. and adj. espèrto (m.).

expiate, vb. espiare.

expiration, n. espirazione f.

expire, vb. espirare, morire.

explain, vb. spiegare.

explanation, n. spiegazione f.

explanatory, adj. esplicativo.

expletive, 1. n. bestémmia f. 2. adj. espletivo.

explicit, adj. esplicito.

explode, vb. esplòdere, scoppiare.

exploit, vb. sfruttare.

exploitation, n. sfruttamento m.

exploration, n. esplorazione f.

exploratory, adj. esplorativo.

explore, vb. esplorare.

explorer, n. esploratore.

explosion, n. esplosione f., scòppio m.

explosive, n. and adj. esplosivo (m.).

exponent, n. esponènte m.

export, 1. n. esportazione f. 2. vb. esportare.

exportation, n. esportazione f.

expose, vb. esporre.

exposé, n. esposto m., esposizione f.

exposition, n. esposizione f.

expository, adj. espositivo.

expostulate, vb. far rimostranze.

exposure, n. esposizione f., rivelazione f.; (photography) pòsa f.

expound, vb. esporre.

express, 1. n. esprèsso m.; (train) direttissimo m. 2. adj. esprèsso. 3. vb. esprimere.

expressage, n. spese di traspòrto f.pl.

expression, n. espressione f.; (outlet) sfògo m.

expressive, adj. espressivo.

expressly, adv. espressamente.

expressman, n. impiegato della compagnia di traspòrti m.

expropriate, vb. espropriare.

expulsion, n. espulsione f.

expunge, vb. espùngere.

expurgate, vb. espurgare.

exquisite, adj. squisito.

extant, adj. esistènte.

extemporaneous, adj. estemporàneo.

extend, vb. estèndere; (in time) prolungare; prorogare.

extension, n. estensione f.; (in time) prolungamento m.; pròroga f.

extensive, adj. esteso.

extensively, adv. estesamente.

extent, n. estensione f., distesa f.

extenuate, vb. estenuare.

exterior, adj. esteriore.

exterminate, vb. sterminare.

extermination, n. sterminio m.

external, adj. estèrno; (foreign) èstero.

extinct, adj. estinto.

extinction, n. estinzione f.

extinguish, vb. estinguere.

extirpate, vb. estirpare.

extol, vb. estòllere.

extort, vb. estòrcere.

extortion, n. estorsione f.

extortioner, n. ricattatore m.

extra, adj. extra, aggiunto, straordinàrio.

extra-, prefix. estra-, stra-.

extract, 1. n. estratto f. 2. vb. estrarre.

extraction, n. estrazione f.; (race) stirpe f.

extradite, vb. estradare.

extradition, n. estradizione f.

extraneous, adj. estràneo.

extraordinary, adj. straordinàrio.

extravagance, n. stravaganza f., prodigalità f.

extravagant, adj. stravagante, pròdigo.

extravaganza, n. rivista frivola f.

extreme, adj. estrèmo.

extremely, adv. estremamente.

extremity, n. estremità f.

extricate, vb. districare.

extrovert, adj. estrovertito.

exuberant, adj. esuberante.

exudation, n. essudato m.

exult, vb. esultare.

exultant, adj. esultante.

eye, n. òcchio m.

eyeball, n. glòbo dell'òcchio m.

eyebrow, n. sopracciglio m.

eyeglass, n. lènte f.

eyeglasses, n. occhiali m.pl.

eyelash, n. ciglio m.

eyelet, n. occhièllo m.

eyelid, n. pàlpebra f.

eyesight, n. vista f.

eyewitness, n. testimòne oculare m.

F

fable, n. fàvola f.

fabric, n. (cloth) stòffa f.; (architecture) fàbbrica f.

fabricate, vb. fabbricare.

fabrication, n. fabbricazione f.; (lie) bugia f.

fabulous, adj. favoloso.

façade, n. facciata f.

face, 1. n. faccia f., viso m. 2. vb. fronteggiare, affrontare.

facet, n. faccetta f.

facetious, adj. facèto.

face value, n. valore nominale m.

facial, adj. faciale.

facile, adj. fàcile.

facilitate, vb. facilitare.

facility, n. facilità f.

facing, 1. n. rivestitura f. 2. adv. dirimpètto. 3. prep. dirimpètto a.

facsimile, n. facsimile m.

fact, n. fatto m.

faction, n. fazione f.

factor, n. fattore m.

factory, n. fàbbrica f.

factual, adj. obiettivo.

faculty, n. facoltà f.

fad, n. mania f.

fade, vb. appassire; (lose color) impallidire.

faeces, n. fèccie f.pl.

fagged, adj. stanco.

fail, vb. fallire, mancare; (in examination) èsser bocciato.

failing, 1. n. debolezza f. 2. prep. in mancanza di.

faille, n. fàglia f.

failure, n. fiasco m., mancanza f.; (bankruptcy) fallimento m.

faint, 1. n. svenimento m. 2. adj. dèbole. 3. vb. svenire.

faintly, adv. debolmente.

fair, 1. n. fièra f. 2. adj. bèllo; (blond) biondo; (just) giusto, èquo.

fairly, adj. giustamente; (moderately) abbastanza.

fairness, n. giustezza f.

fairy, n. fata f.

fairyland, n. paese delle fate m.

faith, n. fede f.

faithful, adj. fedele.

faithfulness, n. fedeltà f.

faithless, adj. sènza fede.

fake, 1. n. falso m. 2. vb. falsificare.

faker, n. falsificatore m.

falcon, n. falcone m.

falconry, n. falconerìa f.

fall, 1. n. caduta f.; (autumn) autunno m. 2. vb. cadere; (f. asleep) addormentarsi; (f. due) scadere; (f. in love) innamorarsi; (f. upon) attaccare.

fallacious, adj. fallace.

fallacy, n. fallàcia f.

fallible, adj. fallibile.

fallout, n. pioggia radioattiva f.

fallow, adj. a maggese; (f. field) maggese n.m.

false, adj. falso.

falsehood, n. bugìa f.

falseness, n. falsità f.

falsetto, n. falsetto m.

falsification, n. falsificazione f.

falsify, vb. falsificare.

falter, vb. esitare, incespicare.

fame, n. fama f.

famed, adj. famoso.

familiar, adj. familiare; (f. with) pràtico di.

familiarity, n. familiarità f.

familiarize, vb. familiarizzare.

family, n. famiglia f.; (f. tree) àlbero genealògico m.

famine, n. carestìa f.

famished, adj. affamato.

famous, adj. famoso.

fan, 1. n. ventàglio m.; (enthusiast) tifoso m. 2. vb. sventolare.

fanatic, n. and adj. fanàtico (m.).

fanatical, adj. fanàtico.

fanaticism, n. fanatismo m.

fanciful, adj. immaginoso, capriccioso.

fancy, 1. n. immaginazione f. 2. adj. di fantasìa. 3. vb. immaginare.

fanfare, n. fanfara f.

fang, n. zanna f.

fantastic, adj. fantàstico.

fantasy, n. fantasìa f.

far, adj. and adv. lontano; (as far as) fino a; (by far) di gran lunga; (how far?) fino dove?; (in so far as) in quanto che; (so far) finora.

faraway, adj. and adv. lontano.

farce, n. farsa f.

farcical, adj. farsesco.

fare, 1. n. (price) tariffa f.; (passenger) passeggièro m.; (food) cibo m. 2. vb. andare.

farewell, n. and interj. addio (m.).

far-fetched, adj. ricercato.

far-flung, adj. esteso.

farina, n. farina f.

farm, n. fattorìa f.

farmer, n. agricoltore m., colòno m.

farmhouse, n. casa colònica f.

farming, n. agricoltura f.

farmyard, adj. cortile.

far-reaching, adj. esteso.

far-sighted, be, vb. aver vista lunga.

farther, adv. più lontano.

farthest, adv. il più lontano.

fascinate, vb. affascinare.

fascination, n. fàscino m.

fascism, n. fascismo m.

fascist, n. and adj. fascista (m. and f.)

fashion, n. mòda f.; (manner) manièra f.

fashionable, adj. alla mòda.

fast, 1. n. digiuno m. 2. adj. (speedy) ràpido; (firm) fermo; (of clock) avanti. 3. vb. digiunare. 4. adv. (quickly) rapidamente; (firmly) fermamente.

fasten, vb. attaccare, fissare.

fastener, fastening, n. chiusura f., fermatura f.

fastidious, adj. fastidioso.

fat, n. and adj. grasso (m.)

fatal, adj. fatale; (deadly) mortale.

fatality, n. fatalità f.

fatally, adv. fatalmente.

fate, n. fato m.

fateful, adj. fatale.

father, n. padre m.

fatherhood, n. paternità f.

father-in-law, n. suòcero m.

fatherland, n. pàtria f.

fatherless, adj. òrfano di padre.

fatherly, adj. patèrno.

fathom, 1. n. bràccio m. 2. vb. scandagliare.

fatigue, 1. n. fatica f. 2. vb. affaticare.

fatten, vb. ingrassare.

fatty, adj. grasso.

fatuous, adj. fàtuo.

faucet, n. rubinetto m.

fault, n. colpa f.; (defect) difètto m., mènda f.

faultfinding, n. crìtica f.

faultless, adj. irreprensìbile.

faultlessly, adv. irreprensibilmente.

faulty, adj. difettoso.

favor, 1. n. favore m. 2. vb. favorire.

favorable, adj. favorévole, propìzio.

favorite, n. and adj. favorito (m.).

favoritism, n. favoritismo m.

fawn, 1. n. cerbiàttolo m. 2. vb. (f. upon) adulare.

faze, vb. sconcertare.

fear, 1. n. paùra f., timore m. 2. vb. temere, aver paùra di.

fearful, adj. (person) pauroso, timoroso; (thing) spaventoso.

fearless, adj. intrèpido.

fearlessness, n. intrepidezza f.

feasible, adj. fattibile.

feast, n. fèsta f.; (banquet) banchetto m.

feat, n. fatto m.; impresa f.

feather, n.penna f., piuma f.

feather, n. penna f., piuma f.

feathered, adj. pennuto, piumato.

feathery, adj. piumoso.

feature, n. tratto m.

February, n. febbraio m.

fecund, adj. fecondo.

federal, adj. federale.

federation, n. federazione f.

fedora, n. cappèllo flòscio m.

fee, n. (for professional services) onoràrio m.; (membership) quòta f.; (school) tassa f.

feeble, adj. dèbole.

feeble-minded, adj. dèbole di cervèllo.

feebleness, n. debolezza f.

feed, 1. n. nutrimento m. 2. vb. nutrire, alimentare.

feedback, n. informazione ricevuta durante un processo f.

feel, 1. n. tatto m. 2. vb. sentire.

feeling, n. sentimento m.

feign, vb. fìngere.

felicitate, vb. felicitare.

felicitous, adj. felice.

felicity, n. felicità f.

feline, adj. felino.

fell, 1. adj. malvàgio. 2. vb. abbàttere.

fellow, n. indivìduo m.; (associate) sòcio m.

fellowship, n. borsa f.

felon, n. fellone m.

felony, n. fellonìa f.

felt, n. feltro m.

female, 1. n. fèmmina f. 2. adj. femminile.

feminine, adj. femminile.

femininity, n. femminilità f.

fence, 1. n. recinto m. 2. vb. chiùdere con un recinto; (sword, foil) schermire.

fencer, n. schermidore m.

fencing, n. scherma f.

fender, n. (auto) parafango m.

ferment, 1. n. fermento m. 2. vb. fermentare.

fermentation, n. fermentazione f.

fern, n. felce f.

ferocious, adj. feroce.

ferociously, *adv.* ferocemente.

ferocity, *n.* feròcia *f.*

ferry, *n.* traghetto *m.*

fertile, *adj.* fèrtile.

fertility, *n.* fertilità *f.*

fertilization, *n.* fertilizzazione *f.*

fertilize, *vb.* fertilizzare.

fertilizer, *n.* fertilizzante *m.*

fervency, *n.* fervore *m.*

fervent, *adj.* fervènte.

fervently, *adv.* ferventemente.

fervid, *adj.* fèrvido.

fervor, *n.* fervore *m.*

fester, *vb.* suppurare.

festival, *n.* fèsta *f.*

festive, *adj.* festivo.

festivity, *n.* festività *f.*

festoon, *n.* festone *m.*

fetal, *adj.* fetale.

fetch, *vb.* (go and get) andare a cercare; (bring) apportare.

fetching, *adj.* attraènte.

fête, *n.* fèsta *f.*

fetid, *adj.* fètido.

fetish, *n.* feticcio *m.*

fetlock, *n.* nòcca *f.*

fetters, *n.* ceppi *m.pl.*

fetus, *n.* fèto *m.*

feud, *n.* inimicizia *f.;* (historical) feudo *m.*

feudal, *adj.* feudale.

feudalism, *n.* feudalismo *m.*

fever, *n.* fèbbre *f.*

feverish, *adj.* febbrile.

feverishly, *adv.* febbrilmente.

few, *adj. and pron.* pòchi *pl.*

fiancé, *n.* fidanzato *m.*

fiancée, *n.* fidanzata *f.*

fiasco, *n.* fiasco *m.*

fiat, *n.* órdine *m.*

fib, *n.* fandònia *f.*

fiber, *n.* fibra *f.*

fibrous, *adj.* fibroso.

fickle, *adj.* incostante.

fickleness, *n.* incostanza *f.*

fiction, *n.* finzione *f.;* (novel-writing) novellìstica *f.*

fictional, *adj.* finto.

fictitious, *adj.* fittìzio.

fictitiously, *adv.* fittiziamente.

fiddle, 1. *n.* violino *m.* 2. *vb.* suonare il violino.

fiddlesticks, *interj.* fandònie!

fidelity, *n.* fedeltà *f.*

fidget, *vb.* agitarsi.

fief, *n.* feudo *m.*

field, *n.* campo *m.*

fiend, *n.* demònio *m.*

fiendish, *adj.* demonìaco.

fierce, *adj.* feroce.

fiery, *adj.* focoso.

fife, *n.* pìffero *m.*

fifteen, *num.* quìndici.

fifteenth, *adj.* quindicésimo.

fifth, *adj.* quinto.

fifty, *num.* cinquanta.

fig, *n.* fico *m.*

fight, 1. *n.* combattimento *m.;* (struggle) lotta *f.;* (quarrel) lite *f.* 2. *vb.* combàttere.

fighter, *n.* combattènte *m.;* (plane) càccia *m.*

figment, *n.* finzione *f.*

figurative, *adj.* figurato.

figuratively, *adv.* figurata-mente.

figure, 1. *n.* figura *f.;* (of body) linea *f.;* (math.) cifra *f.* 2. *vb.* figurare, calcolare.

figurehead, *n.* uòmo di pàglia *m.*

figure of speech, *n.* figura retòrica *f.*

figurine, *n.* figurina *f.*

filament, *n.* filamento *m.*

filch, *vb.* rubare.

file, 1. *n.* (tool) lima *f.;* (row) fila *f.;* riga *f.;* (papers, etc.) filza *f.;* archìvio *m.;* (cards) schedàrio *m.* 2. *vb.* (tool) limare; (papers) archiviare; (f. off) sfilare.

filial, *adj.* filiale.

filigree, *n.* filigrana *f.*

filings, *n.* limatura *f.sg.*

fill, *vb.* riempire; (tooth) otturare.

fillet, *n.* (band) banda *f.;* (meat) filetto *m.;* (fish) fetta *f.*

filling, *n.* (of tooth) otturazione *f.*

filling station, *n.* stazione di servizio *f.*

film, *n.* pellìcola *f.*

filmy, *adj.* velato.

filter, 1. *n.* filtro *m.* 2. *vb.* filtrare.

filth, *n.* sudiciume *m.*

filthy, *adj.* sùdicio.

fin, *n.* pinna *f.*

final, *adj.* finale.

finale, *n.* finale *m.*

finalist, *n.* finalista *m.*

finality, *n.* finalità *f.*

finally, *adv.* finalmente.

finance, *n.* finanza *f.*

financial, *adj.* finanziàrio.

financier, *n.* finanzière *m.*

find, *vb.* trovare.

finding, *n.* ritrovato *m.*

fine, 1. *n.* fulta *f.* ammènda *f.;* (voluntary) oblazione *f.* 2. *adj.* (beautiful) bèllo; (pure) fino; (excellent) bravo. 3. *vb.* multare.

fine arts, *n.* bèlle arti *f.pl.*

finery, *n.* vestiti eleganti *m.pl.*

finesse, *n.* finezza *f.*

finger, *n.* dito *m.*

fingernail, *n.* ùnghia *f.*

fingerprint, *n.* impronta digitale *f.*

finicky, *adj.* affettato.

finish, 1. *n.* fine *f.* 2. *vb.* finire, terminare.

finite, *adj.* definito.

fir, *n.* abete *m.*

fire, 1. *n.* fuòco *m.;* (burning of house, etc.) incèndio *m.* 2. *vb.* (weapon) sparare; (deprive of job) licenziare.

fire alarm, *n.* allarme d'incèndio *m.*

firearm, *n.* arma da fuòco *f.*

firecracker, *n.* petardo *m.*

firedamp, *n.* grìsou *m.,* mètano *m.*

fire engine, *n.* pompa da incèndio *f.*

fire escape, *n.* uscita di sicurezza *f.*

fire extinguisher, *n.* estintore *m.*

firefly, *n.* lùcciola *f.*

fireman, *n.* pompière *m.;* (locomotive) fuochista *m.*

fireplace, *n.* focolare *m.*

fireproof, *adj.* incombustìbile.

firescreen, *n.* parafuòco *m.*

fireside, *n.* cantùccio del focolare *m.*

firewood, *n.* legna *f.*

fireworks, *n.* fuòchi d'artifìcio *m.pl.*

firm, 1. *n.* ditta *f.* 2. *adj.* fermo.

firmness, *n.* fermezza *f.*

first, *adj.* primo.

first aid, *n.* primo soccorso *m.*

first-class, *adj.* di prima classe.

first-hand, *adj.* di prima mano.

first-rate, *adj.* di prima qualità.

fiscal, *adj.* fiscale.

fish, 1. *n.* pesce *m.* 2. *vb.* pescare.

fisherman, *n.* pescatore *m.*

fishery, *n.* peschièra *f.*

fishhook, *n.* amo *m.*

fishing, *n.* pesca *f.*

fishmonger, *n.* pescivéndolo *m.*

fishwife, *n.* pescivéndola *f.*

fishy, *adj.* di pesce; (strange) strano.

fission, *n.* fissione *f.*

fissure, *n.* fessura *f.*

fist, *n.* pugno *m.*

fistic, *adj.* pugilìstico.

fit, 1. *n.* accèsso *m.* 2. *adj.* adatto, idòneo. 3. *vb.* (befit) convenire a; (clothes) andar bène; (adapt) adattare.

fitful, *adj.* irregolare.

fitness, *n.* idoneità *f.;* (health) salute *f.*

fitting, 1. *n.* adattamento *m.* 2. *adj.* conveniènte.

five, *num.* cinque.

fix, 1. *n.* impìccio *m.* 2. *vb.* acconciare; (repair) riparare; (set) fissare; (f. up) sistemare.

fixation, *n.* fissazione *f.*

fixed, *adj.* fisso.

fixture, *n.* infisso *m.*

flabby, *adj.* flòscio.

flaccid, *adj.* flàccido.

flag, *n.* bandièra *f.;* (stone) lastra di ròccia *f.*

flagellant, *n.* flagellante *m.*

flagellate, *vb.* flagellare.

flagging, *adj.* indebolito.

flagon, *n.* coppa *f.*

flagpole, *n.* asta di bandièra *f.*

flagrant, *adj.* flagrante.

flagrantly, *adv.* flagrante-mente.

flagship, *n.* nave ammiràglia *f.*

flagstone, *n.* lastra di ròccia *f.*

flail, *n.* coreggiato *m.*

flair, *n.* fiuto *m.;* (ability) abilità *f.*

flake, *n.* fiòcco *m.*

flamboyant, *adj.* sgargiante.

flame, 1. *n.* fiamma *f.;* (burst

into f.s) divampare. 2. vb. fiammeggiare.

flame thrower, n. lanciafiamme m.

flaming, adj. fiammante.

flamingo, n. fiammingo m., fenicòttero m.

flank, 1. n. fianco m. 2. vb. fiancheggiare.

flannel, n. flanèlla f.

flap, n. (wing) colpo m.; (envelope) lembo di chiusura m.

flare, vb. fiammeggiare.

flare-up, n. scòppio d'ira m.

flash, 1. n. baleno m. 2. vb. balenare.

flashcube, n. cubo per flash m.

flashiness, n. vistosità f.

flashlight, n. lampadina tascàbile f.

flashy, adj. vistoso.

flask, n. fiasco m.

flat, 1. n. appartamento m.; (music) bemòlle m. 2. adj. piatto, piano.

flatcar, n. carro piatto m.

flatness, n. monotonìa f.

flatten, vb. appiattire.

flatter, vb. adulare, lusingare.

flatterer, n. adulatore m., lusingatore m.

flattering, adj. lusinghièro.

flattery, n. adulazione f., lusinghe f.pl.

flat-top, n. portaèrei m.

flaunt, vb. ostentare.

flavor, 1. n. (taste) sapore m.; (odor) aròma m. 2. vb. insaporire.

flavoring, n. aròma artificiale m.

flavorless, adj. sènza sapore.

flaw, n. difètto m.

flawless, adj. perfètto.

flawlessly, adv. perfettamente.

flax, n. lino m.

flay, vb. scorticare.

flea, n. pulce f.

fleck, n. macchietta f.

fledgling, n. uccellino m.

flee, vb. fuggire.

fleece, n. vèllo m.

fleecy, adj. velloso.

fleet, 1. n. flòtta f. 2. adj. veloce.

fleeting, adj. fugace.

Fleming, n. fiammingo m.

Flemish, adj. fiammingo.

flesh, n. carne f.

fleshy, adj. carnoso.

flex, vb. flèttere.

flexibility, n. flessibilità f.

flexible, adj. flessìbile.

flicker, 1. n. tremolìo m. 2. vb. tremolare.

flier, n. aviatore m.

flight, n. volo m.

flight attendant, n. cameriere m.; cameriera f.

flighty, adj. capriccioso.

flimsy, adj. tènue.

flinch, vb. ritirarsi.

fling, vb. lanciare.

flint, n. (lighter) piètra focaia f.; (stone) selce f.

flip, vb. gettare.

flippant, adj. leggièro.

flippantly, adv. leggieramente.

flirt, 1. n. civetta f. 2. vb. civettare, flirtare.

flirtation, n. flirt m.

float, vb. galleggiare.

flock, 1. n. gregge m. 2. vb. affollarsi.

flog, vb. fustigare.

flood, 1. n. inondazione f. 2. vb. inondare.

floodgate, n. cateratta f.

floodlight, n. riflettore elèttrico m.

floor, n. pavimento m.; (story) piano m.; (take the f.) prèndere la paròla.

flooring, n. pavimentazione f.

floorwalker, n. ispettore di magazzino m.

flop, 1. n. (failure) fiasco m.; (thud) tonfo m. 2. vb. muòversi goffamente; (fail) far fiasco.

floral, adj. floreale.

Florence, n. Firènze f.

Florentine, adj. fiorentino.

florid, adj. rubicondo.

florist, n. fioraio m.

flounce, 1. n. volante m. 2. vb. dimenarsi.

flounder, vb. dibàttersi.

flour, n. farina f.

flourish, vb. fiorire; (wave around) agitare.

flow, vb. scòrrere.

flower, 1. n. fiore m. 2. vb. fiorire.

flowerpot, n. vaso per fiori m.

flowery, adj. fiorito.

fluctuate, vb. fluttuare.

fluctuation, n. fluttuazione f.

flue, n. conduttura f.

fluency, n. scorrevolezza f.

fluent, adj. scorrévole.

fluffy, adj. lanuginoso.

fluid, n. and adj. flùido (m.)

fluidity, adj. fluidità f.

flunk, vb. bocciare.

flunkey, n. lacchè m.

fluorescent, adj. fluorescènte.

fluoroscope, n. fluoroscòpio m.

flurry, n. trambusto m.

flush, 1. adj. a livèllo di. 2. vb. (f. the toilet) tirare lo sciacquone.

flute, n. flàuto m.

flutter, vb. svolazzare.

flux, n. flusso m.

fly, 1. n. mosca f. 2. vb. volare.

foam, 1. n. schiuma f., spuma f. 2. vb. spumare.

focal, adj. focale.

focus, n. fuòco m.

fodder, n. foràggio m.

foe, n. nemico m.

fog, n. foschìa f.

foggy, adj. nebbioso.

foil, 1. n. (fencing) fioretto m.; (metal) fòglia f. 2. vb. frustrare.

foist, vb. far accettare.

fold, 1. n. pièga f. 2. vb. piegare.

solder, n. cartèlla f.

foliage, n. fogliame m.

folio, n. fòlio m.

folk, n. pòpolo m.

folklore, n. folclore m.

folks, n. la gènte f.

follicle, n. follìcolo m.

follow, vb. seguire; (pursue) inseguire.

follower, n. seguace m.

folly, n. follìa f.

foment, vb. fomentare.

fond, adj. amante, tènero.

fondant, n. fondènte m.

fondle, vb. accarezzare.

fondly, adv. teneramente.

fondness, n. tenerezza f., passione f.

food, n. cibo m., alimento m., vitto m.

foodstuffs, n. gèneri alimentari m.pl.

fool, 1. n. citrullo m., sciòcco m., stolto m. 2. vb. ingannare.

foolhardiness, n. temerarietà f.

foolhardy, adj. temeràrio.

foolish, adj. sciòcco, stolto.

foolproof, adj. assolutamente sicuro.

foolscap, n. carta formato protocòllo f.

foot, n. piède m.

footage, n. metràggio m.

football, n. (soccer) càlcio m.

foothill, n. collina bassa f.

foothold, n. appòggio m., sostegno m.

footing, n. appòggio m., base f.

footlights, n. ribalta f.sg.

footman, n. staffière m.

footnote, n. nòta f.

footprint, n. orma f.

footsore, be, vb. aver male ai piedi.

footstep, n. orma f.

footstool, n. sgabèllo m.

fop, n. damerino m.

for, 1. prep. per. 2. conj. perchè, chè.

forage, 1. n. foràggio m. 2. vb. predare.

foray, n. scorrerìa f.

forbear, vb. trattenersi.

forbearance, n. pazìenza f.

forbid, vb. proibire, vietare.

forbidding, adj. repulsivo.

force, 1. n. fòrza f., vigore m. 2. vb. forzare.

forceful, adj. vigoroso.

forcefulness, n. vigorìa f.

forceps, n. fòrcipe m. (sg.)

forcible, adj. forzato; (powerful) potènte.

ford, n. guado m.

fore, adj. anteriore.

fore and aft, adv. a pròra e a poppa.

forearm, n. avambràccio m.

forebears, n. antenati m.pl.

forebode, vb. presentire.

foreboding, n. presentimento m.

forecast, 1. n. previsione f. 2. vb. prevedere, pronosticare.

forecaster, n. pronosticatore m.

forecastle, n. castello di prua m.

foreclosure, n. graduazione f.

forefather, n. antenato m.

forefinger, n. indice m.

forefront, n. primo piano m.

forego, vb. rinunciare a.

foregone, adj. anticipato.

foreground, n. primo piano m.

forehead, n. fronte f.

foreign, adj. straniero, estero.

foreign aid, n. aiuto ai paesi esteri m.

foreigner, n. straniero m.

foreleg, n. gamba anteriore f.

foreman, n. capo operaio m.

foremost, 1. adj. primo. 2. adv. in avanti.

forenoon, n. mattina f.

forensic, adj. forènse.

forerunner, n. precursore m.

foresee, vb. prevedere.

foreseeable, adj. prevedibile.

foreshadow, vb. presagire.

foresight, n. previdénza f.

forest, n. foresta f.

forestall, vb. impedire.

forester, n. silvicultore m.; (guard) guàrdia forestale f.

forestry, n. silvicultura f.

foretaste, 1. n. pregustazione f. 2. vb. pregustare.

foretell, vb. predire.

forever, adv. per sèmpre.

forevermore, adv. eternamente.

forewarn, vb. preavvertire.

foreword, n. prefazione f.

forfeit, vb. demeritare, pèrdere.

forfeiture, n. pèrdita f.

forgather, vb. riunirsi.

forge, 1. n. fucina f. 2. vb. (make) foggiare; (falsify) contraffare.

forger, n. contraffattore m.

forgery, n. contraffazione f.

forget, vb. dimenticare.

forgetful, adj. diméntico.

forget-me-not, n. miosòtide f., non ti scordar di me m.

forgive, vb. perdonare.

forgiveness, n. perdono m.

forgo, vb. rinunziare a.

fork, n. forchetta f.; (in road) bivio m.

forlorn, adj. disperato.

form, 1. n. forma f.; (blank) mòdulo m. 2. vb. formare.

formal, adj. formale.

formaldehyde, n. formaldèide f.

formality, n. formalità f.

formally, adv. formalmente.

format, n. formato m.

formation, n. formazione f.

formative, adj. formativo.

former, 1. adj. precedènte. 2. pron. quello.

formerly, adv. anticamente, già.

formidable, adj. formidàbile.

formless, adj. informe.

formula, n. fòrmula f.

formulate, vb. formulare.

formulation, n. formulazione f.

forsake, vb. abbandonare.

forsythia, n. forsizia f.

fort, n. fortezza f.

forte, n. fòrte m.

forth, adv. (out) fuòri; (onward) via; (and so f.) e così via.

forthcoming, adj. pròssimo.

forthright, adj. onèsto.

forthwith, adv. immediatamente.

fortieth, adj. quarantèsimo.

fortification, n. fortificazione f.

fortify, vb. fortificare.

fortissimo, adv. fortìssimo.

fortitude, n. fortezza f.

fortnight, n. quindici giorni m.pl.

fortress, n. fortezza f., ròcca f.

fortuitous, adj. fortùito.

fortunate, adj. fortunato.

fortune, n. fortuna f.

fortune-teller, n. chiaroveggènte m.

forty, num. quaranta.

forum, n. fòro m.

forward, adv. avanti.

forwardness, n. presuntuosità f.

fossil, n. and adj. fòssile (m.)

fossilize, vb. fossilizzare, tr.

foster, vb. (raise) allevare; (nourish) nutrire.

foul, 1. adj. spòrco; (unfair) disonèsto. 2. vb. sporcare.

found, vb. fondare.

foundation, n. (building) fondamento m.; (fund) fondazione f.

founder, n. fondatore m.

foundling, n. trovatèllo m.; (f. hospital) brefotròfio m.

foundry, n. fonderìa f.

fountain, n. fontana f.

fountainhead, n. punto d'origine m.

fountain pen, n. penna stilogràfica f.

four, num. quattro.

four-in-hand, n. cravatta f.

fourscore, num. ottanta.

foursome, n. gruppo di quattro persone m.

fourteen, num. quattòrdici.

fourth, adj. quarto.

fowl, n. pollo m.

fox, n. volpe f.

foxglove, n. digitale f.

foxhole, n. trincèa f.

foxy, adj. volpino.

foyer, n. idotto m.

fracas, n. fracasso m.

fraction, n. frazione f.

fracture, 1. n. frattura f. 2. vb. fratturare.

fragile, adj. fràgile.

fragment, n. frammento m.

fragmentary, adj. frammentàrio.

fragrance, n. fragranza f.

fragrant, adj. fragrante.

frail, adj. fràgile; (morally) dèbole.

frailty, n. debolezza f.

frame, 1. n. cornice m. 2. vb. incorniciare.

framework, n. ossatura f.

France, n. Frància f.

franchise, n. diritto di voto m.

frank, adj. franco.

frankfurter, n. salsiccia f.

frankincense, n. incènso m.

frankly, adv. francamente.

frankness, n. franchezza f.

frantic, adj. frenètico.

fraternal, adj. fratèrno.

fraternally, adv. fraternamente.

fraternity, n. fraternità f.

fraternize, vb. fraternizzare.

fratricide, n. (act) fratricidio m.; (person) fratricida m.

fraud, n. fròde f.

fraudulent, adj. fraudolento.

fraudulently, adv. fraudolentemente.

fraught, adj. càrico.

fray, n. combattimento m.

freak, 1. n. mostruosità f. 2. adj. mostruoso.

freckle, n. lentiggine f.

freckled, adj. lentigginoso.

free, 1. adj. libero; (without cost) gratùito. 2. vb. liberare.

freedom, n. libertà f.

free lance, n. giornalista o politicante indipendènte m.

freestone, adj. spiccàgnolo.

freeze, vb. gelare.

freezer, n. frigorifero m.; congelatore m.

freezing, n. congelamento m.; (f. point) punto di congelamento m.

freight, n. càrico m.; (f. train) treno mèrci m.; (f. station) scalo mèrci m.

freightage, n. spese di trasporto f.pl.

freighter, n. nave mercantile f.

French, adj. francese.

Frenchman, n. francese m. or f.

frenzied, adj. frenètico.

frenzy, n. frenesia f.

frequency, n. frequènza f.

frequency modulation, n. modulazione di frequènza f.

frequent, 1. adj. frequènte. 2. vb. frequentare.

frequently, adv. frequentemente.

fresco, n. affresco m.

fresh, adj. fresco; (impudent) impudènte.

freshen, vb. rinfrescare.

freshman, n. matricola f.

freshness, n. freschezza f.

fresh-water, adj. d'acqua dolce.

fret, vb. tormentare, tr., irritare, tr.

fretful, adj. irritàbile.

fretfully, adv. irritabilmente.

fretfulness, n. irritabilità f.

friar, n. frate m.

fricassee, n. fricassèa f.

friction, n. frizione f.

Friday, n. venerdì m.

friend, n. amico m., amica f.

friendless, *adj.* sènza amici.

friendliness, *n.* amichevolezza *f.*

friendly, *adj.* amichévole, amíco.

friendship, *n.* amicízia *f.*

frigate, *n.* fregata *f.*

fright, *n.* spavènto *m.*

frighten, *vb.* spaventare.

frightful, *adj.* spaventoso.

frigid, *adj.* frígido.

Frigid Zone, *n.* zona glaciale *f.*

frill, *n.* gala *f.;* affettazione *f.*

frilly, *adj.* increspato.

fringe, *n.* frància *f.*

frisky, *adj.* allegro.

fritter, 1. *n.* frittèlla *f.* 2. *vb.* (f. away) sciupare.

frivolity, *n.* frivolità *f.*

frivolous, *adj.* frívolo.

frivolousness, *n.* frivolezza *f.*

frock, *n.* àbito da donna *f.*

frog, *n.* ranòcchio *m.*, rana *f.*

frolic, *vb.* far capriòle.

from, *prep.* da.

front, *n.* fronte *m.;* parte anteriore *f.;* davanti *m.;* (in f.) davanti; (in f. of) davanti a.

frontage, *n.* facciata *f.*

frontal, *adj.* frontale.

frontier, *n.* frontièra *f.*

frost, *n.* brina *f.*

frostbite, *n.* congelamento *f.*

frosting, *n.* pasta fròlla *f.*

frosty, *adj.* gèlido.

froth, *n.* schiuma *f.*, spuma *f.*

frown, *vb.* aggrottare le ciglia.

frowzy, *adj.* trascurato.

fructify, *vb.* fruttificare.

frugal, *adj.* frugale.

frugality, *n.* frugalità *f.*

fruit, *n.* frutto *m.*

fruitful, *adj.* fruttuoso.

fruition, *n.* fruizione *f.*

fruitless, *adj.* infruttuoso.

frustrate, *vb.* frustrare.

frustration, *n.* frustrazione *f.*

fry, *vb.* friggere.

fryer, *n.* (chicken) pollo gióvane *m.*

frying-pan, *n.* padèlla *f.*

fuchsia, *n.* fùcsia *f.*

fudge, 1. *n.* fondènte *m.* 2. *interj.* sciocchezze!

fuel, *n.* combustibile *m.;* (motor f.) carburante *m.*

fugitive, *n. and adj.* fuggitivo *(m.)*

fugue, *n.* fuga *f.*

fulcrum, *n.* fulcro *m.*

fulfill, *vb.* realizzare.

fulfillment, *n.* realizzazione *f.*

full, *adj.* pieno.

fullback, *n.* estrèmo *m.*

full dress, *n.* àbito da cerimònia *m.*

fullness, *n.* pienezza *f.*

fully, *adv.* pienamente.

fulminate, *vb.* fulminare.

fulmination, *n.* fulminazione *f.*

fumble, *vb.* lasciar cadere.

fume, *n.* esalazione *f.*

fumigate, *vb.* fumigare.

fumigator, *n.* fumigatore *m.*

fun, *n.* divertimento *m.*

function, 1. *n.* funzione *f.* 2. *vb.* funzionare.

functional, *adj.* funzionale.

functionary, *n.* funzionàrio *m.*

fund, *n.* fondo *m.*

fundamental, *adj.* fondamentale.

funeral, 1. *n.* funerale *m.* 2. *adj.* fùnebre.

funereal, *adj.* funèreo.

fungicide, *n.* fungicida *m.*

fungus, *n.* fungo *m.*

funnel, *n.* imbuto *m.;* (smokestack) ciminièra *f.*

funny, *adj.* còmico.

fur, *n.* pellíccia *f.*

furious, *adj.* furioso.

furlough, *n.* licènza *f.*

furnace, *n.* fornace *m.*, caldaia *f.*

furnish, *vb.* fornire; (house) ammobiliare.

furnishings, *n.* mobília *f.*

furniture, *n.* mòbili *m.pl.*

furor, *n.* furore *m.*

furred, *adj.* copèrto di pelliccia.

furrier, *n.* pelliccialo *m.*

furrow, *n.* solco *m.*

furry, *adj.* copèrto di pelliccia; (tongue) patinoso.

further, 1. *adj.* ulteriore. 2. *adv.* oltre, più avanti.

furtherance, *n.* appòggio *m.*

furthermore, *adv.* inoltre.

fury, *n.* fùria *f.*, furore *m.*

fuse, 1. *n.* (electricity) fusíbile *m.;* (explosives) spoletta *f.* 2. *vb.* fòndere.

fuselage, *n.* fusolièra *f.*

fusillade, *n.* fucilería *f.*

fusion, *n.* fusione *f.*

fuss, *n.* chiasso *m.*

fussy, *adj.* difficoltoso.

futile, *adj.* fùtile.

futility, *n.* futilità *f.*

future, 1. *n.* futuro *m.*, avvenire *m.* 2. *adj.* futuro.

futurity, *n.* avvenire *m.*

futurology, *n.* futurologia *f.*

fuzz, *n.* lanùgine *f.*

fuzzy, *adj.* lanuginoso; (confused) confuso.

G

gab, *vb.* chiacchierare.

gabardine, *n.* gabardina *f.*

gadabout, *n.* bighellone *f.*

gadfly, *n.* tafano *m.*

gadget, *n.* congegno *m.*

gag, 1. *n.* bavàglio *m.;* (joke) trovata còmica *f.* 2. *vb.* imbavagliare.

gaiety, *n.* gaiezza *f.*

gaily, *vb.* gaiamente.

gain, 1. *n.* guadagno *m.* 2. *vb.* guadagnare.

gainful, *adj.* lucroso.

gainfully, *adv.* lucrosamente.

gainsay, *vb.* contraddire.

gait, *n.* andatura *f.*

gala, 1. *n.* gala *f.* 2. *adj.* di gala.

galaxy, *n.* galàssia *f.*

gale, *n.* tempèsta *f.*

gall, 1. *n.* (bile) fièle *m.;* (insolence) sfacciatàggine *f.* 2. *vb.* irritare.

gallant, *adj.* galante, coraggioso.

gallantly, *adv.* coraggiosamente.

gallantry, *n.* coràggio *m.*

gall bladder, *n.* vescica del fièle *m.*

galleon, *n.* galeone *m.*

gallery, *n.* gallería *f.;* (top g., theater) loggione *m.*

galley, *n.* (ship) galèa *f.;* (kitchen) cucina *f.;* (typogr.) colonna *f.*

galley proof, *n.* bòzze in colonna *f.pl.*

Gallic, *adj.* gàllico.

gallivant, *vb.* vagare.

gallon, *n.* gallone *m.*

gallop, 1. *n.* galòppo *m.* 2. *vb.* galoppare.

gallows, *n.* forca *f.*

gallstone, *n.* càlcolo biliare *m.*

galore, *adv.* a bizzèffe.

galosh, *n.* galòscia *f.*

galvanize, *vb.* galvanizzare.

gamble, *vb.* giocare d'azzardo.

gambler, *n.* giocatore d'azzardo *m.*

gambling, *n.* giòco d'azzardo *m.*

gambol, 1. *n.* salto *m.* 2. *vb.* saltare.

game, 1. *n.* giòco *m.;* (sports encounter) partita *f.;* (hunting) selvaggina *f.* 2. *adj.* coraggioso.

gamely, *adv.* coraggiosamente.

gameness, *n.* coràggio *m.*

gamin, *n.* monèllo *m.*

gamut, *n.* gamma *f.*

gamy, *adj.* alquanto putrefatto.

gander, *n.* pàpero *m.*

gang, *n.* gruppo *m.*, squadra *f.*

gangling, *adj.* smilzo.

gangplank, *n.* pontile *m.*

gangrene, *n.* cancrena *f.*

gangrenous, *adj.* cancrenoso.

gangster, *n.* gangster *m.*

gangway, *n.* passerèlla *f.*

gap, *n.* apertura *f.*

gape, *vb.* spalancare la bocca.

garage, *n.* autorimessa *f.*

garb, *n.* costume *m.*

garbage, *n.* rifiuti *f.pl.*

garble, *vb.* ingarbugliare.

garden, *n.* giardino *m.*

gardener, *n.* giardinière *m.*

gardenia, *n.* gardènia *f.*

gargle, 1. *n.* gargarismo *m.* 2. *vb.* gargarizzare.

gargoyle, *n.* dóccia con testa grottesca *f.*

garish, *adj.* sgargiante.

garland, *n.* ghirlanda *f.*

garlic, *n.* àglio *m.*

garment, *n.* vestito *m.*

garner, *vb.* cògliere.

garnet, *n.* granato *m.*

garnish, *vb.* guarnire.

garnishee, *vb.* méttere il fermo su.

garnishment, *n.* guarnizione *f.*

garret, *n.* soffitta *f.*

garrison, *n.* guarnigione *f.*

garrote, *n.* garrotta *f.*

garrulous, *adj.* gàrrulo.

garter, *n.* giarrettièra *f.*

gas, *n.* gas *m.;* (gasoline) benzina *f.*

gaseous, *adj.* gassoso.

gash, 1. *n.* squàrcio *m.* 2. *vb.* squarciare.

gasket, *n.* guarnizione *f.*

gasless, *adj.* sènza gas, sènza benzina.

gas mask, *n.* màschera antigas *f.*

gasohol, *n.* benzina ricavata da prodotti alcòlici *f.*

gasoline, *n.* benzina *f.*

gasp, 1. *n.* boccheggiamento *m.* 2. *vb.* boccheggiare.

gassy, *adj.* gassoso.

gastric, *adj.* gàstrico.

gastric juice, *n.* succo gàstrico *m.*

gastritis, *n.* gastrite *f.*

gastronomical, *adj.* gastronòmico.

gastronomy, *n.* gastronomìa *f.*

gate, *n.* (city) pòrta *f.;* (apartment house) portone *m.;* (fence) cancèllo *m.*

gateway, *n.* pòrta *m.,* entrata *f.*

gather, *vb.* raccògliere, radunare; (infer) desùmere.

gathering, *n.* adunata *f.,* assemblèa *f.*

gaudily, *adv.* vistosamente.

gaudiness, *n.* vistosità *f.*

gaudy, *adj.* vistoso.

gauge, 1. *n.* apparécchio misuratore *m.;* (track) scartamento *m.;* (loading g.) sàgoma *f.* 2. *vb.* misurare, stimare.

gaunt, *adj.* magro.

gauntlet, *n.* guanto *m.*

gauze, *n.* garza *f.*

gavel, *n.* martellino *m.*

gavotte, *n.* gavòtta *f.*

gawky, *adj.* goffo.

gay, 1. *adj.* gaio; (homosexual) omosessuale. 2. *n.* finòcchio *m.*

gaze, *vb.* guardare.

gazelle, *n.* gazzèlla *f.*

gazette, *n.* gazzeta *f.*

gazetteer, *n.* dizionàrio geogràfico *m.*

gear, *n.* ingranàggio *m.;* (harness) finimenti *m.pl.;* (g. lever) lèva del cambio *f.*

gearing, *n.* ingranàggio *m.*

gearshift, *n.* càmbio di velocità *m.*

gelatin, *n.* gelatina *f.*

gelatinous, *adj.* gelatinoso.

geld, *vb.* castrare.

gelding, *n.* castrone *m.*

gem, *n.* gèmma *f.*

gender, *n.* gènere *m.*

gene, *n.* gène *m.*

genealogical, *adj.* genealògico.

genealogy, *n.* genealogìa *f.*

general, *n. and adj.* generale (*m.*)

generality, *n.* generalità *f.*

generalization, *n.* generalizzazione *f.*

generalize, *vb.* generalizzare.

generally, *adv.* generalmente.

generalship, *n.* qualità di generale *f.pl.*

generate, *vb.* generare.

generation, *n.* generazione *f.*

generator, *n.* generàtore *m.*

generic, *adj.* genèrico.

generosity, *n.* generosità *f.*

generous, *adj.* generoso.

generously, *adv.* generosamente.

genetic, *adj.* genètico.

genetics, *n.* genètica *f.*

Geneva, *n.* Ginèvra *f.*

Genevan, *adj.* ginevrino.

genial, *adj.* piacévole, cordiale.

geniality, *n.* piacevolezza *f.,* cordialità *f.*

genially, *adv.* piacevolmente, cordialmente.

genital, *adj.* genitale.

genitals, *n.* genitali *m.pl.*

genitive, *n. and adj.* genitivo (*m.*)

genius, *n.* gènio *m.*

Genoa, *n.* Gènova *f.*

Genoese, *adj.* genovese.

genocide, *n.* genicìdio *m.*

genre, *n.* gènere *m.*

genteel, *adj.* eccessivamente raffinato.

gentian, *n.* genziana *f.*

gentile, *n. and adj.* gentile (*m.*); non israelitico.

gentility, *n.* raffinatezza eccessiva *f.*

gentle, *adj.* mite.

gentleman, *n.* signore *m.,* gentiluòmo *m.*

gentlemanly, *adj.* da gentiluòmo.

gentlemen's agreement, *n.* impegno d'onore *m.*

gentleness, *n.* mitezza *f.*

gently, *adv.* mitemente, adagio.

gentry, *n.* piccola nobiltà *f.;* (ironical) gènte *f.*

genuflect, *vb.* genuflèttersi.

genuine, *adj.* genuino.

genuinely, *adv.* genuinamente.

genuineness, *n.* genuinità *f.*

genus, *n.* gènere *m.*

geographer, *n.* geògrafo *m.*

geographical, *adj.* geogràfico.

geography, *n.* geografìa *f.*

geometric, *adj.* geomètrico.

geometry, *n.* geometrìa *f.*

geopolitics, *n.* geopolìtica *f.*

geranium, *n.* gerànio *m.*

germ, *n.* gèrme *m.*

German, *n. and adj.* tedesco (*m.*)

germane, *adj.* rilevante.

Germanic, *adj.* germànico.

German measles, *n.* rosolìa *f.*

Germany, *n.* Germània *f.*

germicide, *n.* germicida *m.*

germinal, *adj.* germinale.

germinate, *vb.* germinare.

gestate, *vb.* portare nell'ùtero.

gestation, *n.* gestazione *f.*

gesticulate, *vb.* gesticolare.

gesticulation, *n.* gesticolazione *f.*

gesture, *n.* gèsto *m.*

get, *vb.* (obtain) ottenere; (receive) ricévere; (take) prèndere; (become) divenire, diventare; (arrive) arrivare; (g. in) entrare; (g. off) scéndere; (g. on, agree) intèndersi; (g. on, go up) montare; (g. out) uscire; (g. up) alzarsi.

getaway, *n.* fuga *f.*

geyser, *n.* geyser *m.*

ghastly, *adj.* orrèndo.

ghost, *n.* spèttro *m.,* larva *f.*

ghost writer, *n.* collaboratore anònimo *m.*

giant, *n. and adj.* gigante (*m.*)

gibberish, *n.* borbottamento *m.*

gibbon, *n.* gibbone *m.*

gibe at, *vb.* beffarsi di.

giblets, *n.* rigàglie *f.pl.*

giddy, *adj.* stordito.

gift, *n.* dono *m.*

gifted, *adj.* dotato.

gigantic, *adj.* gigantesco.

giggle, *vb.* ridere scioccamente.

gigolo, *n.* cicisbèo *m.*

gild, *vb.* dorare, indorare.

gill, *n.* brànchia *f.*

gilt, 1. *n.* doratura *f.* 2. *adj.* dorato.

gilt-edged, *adj.* sicuro.

gimcrack, *n.* cianfrusàglia *f.*

gimlet, *n.* succhiello *m.*

gin, *n.* gin *m.*

ginger, *n.* zènzero *m.*

gingerly, *adj.* càuto.

gingham, *n.* ghingano *m.*

giraffe, *n.* giraffa *f.*

gird, *vb.* cìngere, *tr.*

girder, *n.* trave *f.*

girdle, *n.* cintura *f.*

girl, *n.* ragazza *f.,* fanciulla *f.*

girlish, *adj.* da ragazza.

girth, *n.* circonferènza *f.*

gist, *n.* contenuto essenziale *m.*

give, *vb.* dare; (g. back) rèndere; (g. in) cèdere; (g. out) distribuire; (g. up) rinunziare a.

give-and-take, *n.* scàmbio *m.*

given name, *n.* nome di battèsimo *m.*

giver, *n.* datore *m.,* donatore *m.*

gizzard, *n.* ventriglio *m.*

glacé, *adj.* lùcido.

glacial, *adj.* glaciale.

glacier, *n.* ghiacciaio *m.*

glad, *adj.* contènto, lièto.

gladden, *vb.* allietare.

glade, *n.* radura *f.*

gladiolus, *n.* gladiòlo *m.*

gladly, *adv.* lietamente, con piacere.

gladness, *n.* contentezza *f.*

glamor, *n.* fàscino *m.*

glamorous, *adj.* affascinante.

glance, *n.* sguardo *m.,* occhiata *f.*

gland, *n.* glàndola *f.*

glandular, *adj.* glandolare.

glare, *n.* bagliore *m.*

glaring, *adj.* abbagliante.

glass, *n.* vetro *m.;* (drinking-g.) bicchière *m.*

glass-blowing, *n.* soffiatura del vetro *f.*

glasses, *n.* occhiali *m.*

glassful, *n.* bicchière *m.*

glassware, *n.* cristallerie *f.pl.*

glassy, *adj.* vetroso, vitreo.

glaucoma, *n.* glaucòma *m.*

glaze, 1. *n.* (enamel) smalto *m.;* (varnish) vernice *f.* 2. *vb.* smaltare, verniciare.

glazier, *n.* vetraio *m.*

gleam, *n.* barlume *m.*

glee, *n.* giòia *f.*

glee club, *n.* còro maschile *m.*

gleeful, *adj.* gioioso.

glen, *n.* valletta *f.*

glib, *adj.* fluènte.

glide, *vb.* scivolare.

glider, *n.* aliante *m.*

glimmer, 1. *n.* barlume *m.* 2. *vb.* mandare una luce incèrta.

glimmering, 1. *n.* barlume *m.* 2. *adj.* incèrto.

glimpse, *vb.* intravedere.

glint, *n.* riflèsso *m.*

glisten, *vb.* scintillare.

glitter, 1. *n.* scintillio *m.* 2. *vb.* scintillare, risplèndere.

gloat, *vb.* gioire.

global, *adj.* globale.

globe, *n.* glòbo *m.*

globular, *adj.* globulare.

globule, *n.* glòbulo *m.*

glockenspiel, *n.* campanette *f.pl.*

gloom, *n.* (darkness) oscurità *f.;* (sadness) tristezza *f.*

gloomy, *adj.* oscuro, triste.

glorification, *n.* glorificazione *f.*

glorify, *vb.* glorificare.

glorious, *adj.* glorioso.

glory, 1. *n.* glòria *f.* 2. *vb.* gloriarsi.

gloss, 1. *n.* lucidezza *f.;* (explanation) chiòsa *f.* 2. *vb.* lucidare; chiosare.

glossary, *n.* glossàrio *m.*

glossy, *adj.* lùcido.

glove, *n.* guanto *m.*

glow, 1. *n.* incandescènza *f.* 2. *vb.* èssere incandescènte.

glowing, *adj.* incandescènte.

glowworm, *n.* lùcciola *f.*

glucose, *n.* glucòsio *m.*

glue, 1. *n.* còlla *f.* 2. *vb.* incollare.

glum, *adj.* (frowning) acci-gliato; (sad) triste.

glumness, *n.* tristezza *f.*

glut, *n.* saturazione *f.*

glutinous, *adj.* glutinoso.

glutton, *n.* ghiottone *m.*

gluttonous, *adj.* ghiotto.

glycerine, *n.* glicerina *f.*

gnarl, *n.* nodo *m.*

gnash, *vb.* digrignare.

gnat, *n.* cùlice *m.*

gnaw, *vb.* ródere.

go, *vb.* andare; (become) diventare; (g. away) andàr-sene; (g. back) tornare; (g. by) passare; (g. down) scèn-dere; (g. in) entrare; (g. on) continuare; (g. out) uscire; (g. up) salire; (g. without) fare a meno di.

goad, 1. *n.* pùngolo *m.,* stimolo *m.* 2. *vb.* stimolare.

goal, *n.* mèta *f.;* (soccer) pòrta *f.*

goal-keeper, *n.* portière *m.*

goat, *n.* capra *f.*

goatee, *n.* barbetta *f.*

goatherd, *n.* capraio *m.*

goatskin, *n.* pèlle di capra *f.*

gobble, *vb.* ingollare.

gobbler, *n.* tacchino *m.*

go-between, *n.* intermediàrio *m.*

goblet, *n.* coppa *f.*

goblin, *n.* folletto *m.*

god, *n.* dio *m.,* iddio *m.*

godchild, *n.* figliòccio *m.*

goddess, *n.* dèa *f.*

godfather, *n.* padrino *m.,* com-pare *m.*

godless, *adj.* àteo; (impious) èmpio.

godlike, *adj.* divino.

godly, *adj.* devòto, pio.

godmother, *n.* madrina *f.,* co-mare *f.*

godsend, *n.* dòno del cièlo *m.*

Godspeed, *n.* addìo *m.*

go-getter, *n.* arrivista *m.*

goiter, *n.* gozzo *m.*

gold, *n.* òro *m.*

golden, *adj.* d'òro, àureo.

gold-filled, *adj.* (tooth) ottu-rato d'òro.

goldfinch, *n.* cardellino *m.*

goldfish, *n.* pesce rosso *m.*

goldleaf, *n.* fòglia d'òro *f.*

goldsmith, *n.* oréfice *m.*

gold standard, *n.* parità àurea *f.*

golf, *n.* golf *m.*

gondola, *n.* góndola *f.*

gondolier, *n.* gondolière *m.*

gone, *adj.* (vanished) sparito; (departed) partito.

gong, *n.* gong *m.*

gonorrhea, *n.* gonorrèa *f.*

good, 1. *n.* bène *m.;* (g.s) mèrci *f.pl.* 2. *adj.* buòno.

good-by, *n.* and *interj.* addìo (*m.*)

Good Friday, *n.* venerdì santo *m.*

good-hearted, *adj.* di buòn cuòre.

good-humored, *adj.* di buòn umore.

good-looking, *adj.* bellino.

good-natured, *adj.* di buòn temperamento.

goodness, *n.* bontà *f.*

good will, *n.* buona volontà *f.*

goose, *n.* òca *f.,* pàpera *f.*

gooseberry, *n.* ribes *m.*

gooseneck, *n.* collo di cigna *m.*

goose step, *n.* passo d'òca *m.*

gore, *n.* sangue *m.*

gorge, *n.* gola *f.*

gorgeous, *adj.* splèndido.

gorilla, *n.* gorilla *m.*

gory, *adj.* insanguinato.

gosling, *n.* paperetto *m.*

gospel, *n.* vangèlo *m.*

gossamer, *n.* garza sottile *f.*

gossip, 1. *n.* (talk) diceria *f.,* pettegolezzo *m.;* (person) pettègolo *m.,* pettègola *f.* 2. *vb.* pettegolare.

gossipy, *adj.* pettègolo.

Gothic, *adj.* gótico.

gouge, *n.* sgòrbia *f.*

gourd, *n.* zucca *f.*

gourmand, *n.* ghiottone *m.*

gourmet, *n.* buongustaio *m.*

govern, *vb.* governare.

governess, *n.* governante *f.*

government, *vb.* govèrno *m.*

governmental, *adj.* governa-tivo.

governor, *n.* governatore *m.*

governorship, *n.* governatorato *m.*

gown, *n.* gonnèlla *f.*

grab, *vb.* arraffare, carpire.

grace, *n.* gràzia *f.*

graceful, *adj.* grazioso.

gracefully, *adv.* graziosamente.

graceless, *adj.* sgraziato.

gracious, *adj.* grazioso.

grackle, *n.* gràcchio *m.*

grade, 1. *n.* grado *m.;* (quality) qualità *f.;* (mark) voto *m.* 2. *vb.* classificare.

grade crossing, *n.* passàggio a livèllo *m.*

gradual, *adj.* graduale.

gradually, *adv.* gradualmente.

graduate, *vb.* graduare; (uni-versity) laurearsi.

graft, 1. *n.* innèsto *m.;* (fraud) baratteria *f.* 2. *vb.* innestare.

graham flour, *n.* farina integra-le *f.*

grail, *n.* gradale *m.*

grain, *n.* grano *m.;* (single) chicco *m.*

grain alcohol, *n.* àlcole etilico *m.*

gram, *n.* grammo *m.*

grammar, *n.* grammàtica *f.*

grammarian, *n.* grammàtico *m.*

grammar school, *n.* scuòla ele-mentare *f.*

grammatical, *adj.* grammati-cale.

gramophone, *n.* grammòfono *m.*

granary, *n.* granaio *m.*

grand, *adj.* grande, grandioso.

grandchild, *n.* nipote *m.* or *f.*

granddaughter, *n.* nipote *f.*

grandeur, *n.* grandezza *f.*

grandfather, *n.* nònno *m.*

grandiloquent, *adj.* magnilo-quente.

grandiose, *adj.* grandioso.

grandly, *adj.* grandiosamente.

grandmother, *n.* nònna *f.*

grandparents, *n.* nònni *m.pl.*

grandson, *n.* nipote *m.*

grandstand, n. tribuna f.

grange, n. fattoria f.

granger, n. fattore m.

granite, n. granito m.

granny, n. vècchia f.

grant, 1. n. concessione f.; (gift) dono m. 2. vb. concèdere.

granular, adj. granulare.

granulate, vb. granulare.

granulation, n. granulazione f.

granule, n. granèllo m.

grape, n. uva f.; (g. juice) spremuta d'uva f.

grapefruit, n. pompèlmo m.

grapeshot, n. mitràglia f.

grapevine, n. vite f.

graph, n. gràfico m.

graphic, adj. gràfico.

graphite, n. grafite m.

graphology, n. grafologia f.

grapple, 1. n. uncino m., lotta f. 2. vb. venire alle prese.

grasp, 1. n. presa f. 2. vb. afferrare.

grasping, adj. avaro.

grass, n. èrba f.; (marijuana) marijuana f.

grasshopper, n. cavalletta f.

grassy, adj. erboso.

grate, 1. n. graticola f. 2. vb. (cheese, etc.) grattugiare; (irritate) irritare.

grateful, adj. grato.

grater, n. grattùgia f.

gratify, vb. gratificare.

grating, n. inferriata f.

gratis, 1. adj. gratùito. 2. adv. gratuitamente.

gratitude, n. gratitùdine f.

gratuitous, adj. gratùito.

gratuity, n. mància f.

grave, 1. n. tomba f. 2. adj. grave.

gravel, n. ghiaia f.

gravely, adj. gravemente.

gravestone, n. piètra tombale f.

graveyard, n. camposanto m.

gravitate, vb. gravitare.

gravitation, n. gravitazione f.

gravity, n. gravità f.

gravure, n. incisione f.

gravy, n. sugo di carne m.

gray, adj. grigio.

grayish, adj. grigiastro.

gray matter, n. cervèllo m.

graze, vb. pàscere.

grazing, n. pàscolo m.

grease, 1. n. grasso m. 2. vb. ùngere, lubrificare.

greasy, adj. grasso; untuoso.

great, adj. grande.

greatness, n. grandezza f.

Greece, n. Grècia f.

greed, n. cupidìgia f.

greediness, n. ghiottoneria f.

greedy, adj. ghiottone.

Greek, adj. grèco.

green, adj. verde.

greenery, n. verzura f.

greenhouse, n. sèrra f.

greet, vb. salutare.

greeting, n. saluto m.

gregarious, adj. gregàrio.

grenade, n. granata f.

grenadine, n. granatina f.

greyhound, n. levrière m.

grid, n. graticola f.; (electric power) rete f.

griddle, n. graticola f.

gridiron, n. graticola f.

grief, n. dolore m.

grievance, n. lagnanza f.

grieve, vb. addolorare, tr.

grievous, adj. doloroso, grave.

grill, n. graticola f.

grillroom, n. rosticceria f.

grim, adj. fosco.

grimace, n. smòrfia f.

grime, n. sudiciume m.

grimy, adj. sùdicio.

grin, vb. sorrìdere da un orècchio all'altro.

grind, vb. macinare.

grindstone, n. màcina f.

grip, 1. n. presa f.; (suitcase) valigia f. 2. vb. afferrare.

gripe, 1. n. lagnanza f. 2. vb. lagnarsi.

grippe, n. influènza f.

grisly, adj. orrìbile.

grist, n. grano da macinare m.

gristle, n. cartilàgine f.

grit, n. sàbbia f.

grizzled, adj. grigio.

groan, 1. n. gèmito m. 2. vb. gèmere.

grocer, n. negoziante di gèneri alimentari m.

grocery, n. negòzio di gèneri alimentari m.

grog, n. gròg m.

groggy, adj. intontito.

groin, n. inguine m.

groom, n. palafrenière m.; (footman) staffière m.; (bridegroom) sposo m.

groove, n. solco m.

grope, vb. andare a tastoni.

grosgrain, n. grossagrana f.

gross, adj. grossolano; (blunder) madornale; (weight) lordo.

grossly, adv. grossolanamente; (wholly) totalmente.

grossness, n. grossolanità f.

grotesque, adj. grottesco.

grotto, n. grotta f.

grouch, 1. n. (person) brontolone m. 2. vb. brontolare.

ground, 1. n. tèrra f.; (reason) motivo m.; (basis) base f.; (electrical) presa di tèrra f. 2. vb. basare.

ground hog, n. marmotta f.

groundless, adj. sènza base.

ground swell, n. mare di fondo m.

groundwork, n. fondamento m.

group, 1. n. gruppo m. 2. vb. raggruppare, tr.

groupie, n. membro di un gruppo di ragazze m.

grouse, n. tetraone m.

grove, n. boschetto m.

grovel, vb. umiliarsi.

grow, vb. crèscere; (raise) coltivare.

growl, 1. n. brontolamento m. 2. vb. brontolare.

grown, adj. maturo.

grown-up, n. and adj. adulto (m.)

growth, n. crèscita f., sviluppo m.

grub, 1. n. larva f.; (food) cibo m. 2. vb. scavare.

grubby, adj. sporco.

grudge, n. àstio m.

gruel, n. pappa f.

gruesome, adj. orrèndo.

gruff, adj. bùrbero.

grumble, vb. brontolare.

grumpy, adj. scontento.

grunt, 1. n. grugnito m. 2. vb. grugnire.

guarantee, 1. n. garanzia f. 2. vb. garantire.

guarantor, n. mallevadore m.

guaranty, n. garanzia f.

guard, 1. n. guàrdia f. 2. vb. custodire, guardarsi.

guarded, adj. guardingo.

guardhouse, n. guardina f.

guardian, n. guardiano m.; (legal) tutore m.

guardianship, n. tutèla f.

guardsman, n. guàrdia f.

gubernatorial, adj. governatoriale.

guerilla, n. (war) guerriglia f.; (fighter) guerriglière m.

guess, vb. indovinare.

guesswork, n. congettura f.

guest, n. òspite m.; (hotel, etc.) cliènte m.

guffaw, 1. n. sghignazzata f. 2. vb. sghignazzare.

guidance, n. guida f.

guide, 1. n. guida f. 2. vb. guidare.

guidebook, n. guida f.

guidepost, n. palo indicatore m.

guild, n. arte f., corporazione f.

guile, n. astùzia f.

guillotine, n. ghigliottina f.

guilt, n. colpa f.

guiltily, adv. colpevolmente.

guiltless, adj. sènza colpa.

guilty, adj. colpévole.

guinea fowl, n. faraona f.

guinea pig, n. porcellino d'India m.

guise, n. apparènza f.; (shape) fòggia f.

guitar, n. chitarra f.

gulch, n. burrone m.

gulf, n. golfo m.

gull, n. gabbiano m.

gullet, n. gola f.

gullible, adj. crèdulo.

gully, n. burrone m.

gulp, vb. inghiottire; (g. down) ingollare.

gum, n. gomma f.; (chewing-g.) gomma da masticare f.

gummy, adj. gommoso.

gun, n. fucile m.; (cannon) cannone m.

gunboat, n. cannonièra f.

gunman, n. bandito armato m.

gunner, n. artiglière m.

gunpowder, n. pólvere da sparo m.

gunshot, n. portata di un fucile f.

gunwale, n. parapètto m.

gurgle, 1. n. gorgòlio m. 2. vb. gorgogliare.

guru, n. guru m.

gush, vb. sgorgare, zampillare.

gusher, n. sorgènte di petròlio f.

gusset, n. gherone m.

gust, n. ràffica f.; (rain) scròscio m.

gustatory, adj. gustativo.

gusto, n. gusto m.

gusty, adj. tempestoso.

guts, n. intestino m., minùgia f.; (courage) fégato m.

gutter, n. (street) cunetta f.; (house) grondaia f.

guttural, adj. gutturale.

guy, n. tìzio m.

guzzle, vb. ingozzare.

gym, n. palèstra f.

gymnasium, n. palèstra f.; (school) ginnàsio m.

gymnast, n. ginnasta m.

gymnastic, adj. ginnàstico.

gymnastics, n. ginnàstica f.

gynaecology, n. ginecologìa f.

gypsum, n. gesso m.

gypsy, n. zìngaro m., zìngara f.

gyrate, vb. turbinare.

gyroscope, n. giroscòpio m.

H

haberdasher, n. merciàio m.

haberdashery, n. mercerìa f.

habiliments, n. vestimenta f.pl.

habit, n. abitùdine f.; (dress) àbito m.

habitable, adj. abitàbile.

habitat, n. ambiènte f.

habitation, n. abitazione f.

habitual, adj. abituale.

habituate, vb. abituare.

habitué, n. frequentatore m.

hack, 1. n. cavallo da dipòrto m. 2. vb. tagliare.

hackneyed, adj. banale.

hacksaw, n. sega per metalli f.

haft, n. mànico m.

hag, n. strega f.

haggard, adj. sparuto.

haggle, vb. mercanteggiare.

hag-ridden, adj. tormentato da streghe.

Hague, The, n. l'Aia f.

hail, 1. n. gràndine f. 2. vb. grandinare; (call to) salutare.

Hail Mary, n. avemmarìa f.

hailstone, n. chicco di gràndine m.

hailstorm, n. grandinata f.

hair, n. capelli m.pl., crìne, f.; (single, on head) capello m.; (body, animals) pelo m.

haircut, n. tàglio di capelli m.

hairdo, n. pettinatura f., acconciatura f.

hairdresser, n. parrucchière m.

hairline, n. lìnea sottilissima f.

hairpin, n. forcina f.

hair-raising, adj. orrèndo.

hair's-breadth, n. grossezza di un capello f.

hairspray, n. schiuma per capelli f.

hairy, adj. peloso.

halcyon, adj. felice.

hale, adj. robusto.

half, 1. n. metà f. 2. adj. mèzzo. 3. adv. a metà.

half-and-half, adv. metà e metà.

halfback, n. secondo m.

half-baked, adj. immaturo, imperfètto.

half-breed, n. mesticcio m.

half-brother, n. fratellastro m.

half-dollar, n. mèzzo dòllaro m.

half-hearted, adj. sènza entusiasmo.

half-mast, adv. a mezz'asta.

halfway, adv. a mèzza via.

half-wit, n. imbecille m.

halibut, n. pianuzza f.

hall, n. sala f., àula f.; (hallway) vestìbolo m., corridoio m.

hallmark, n. màrchio m.

hallow, vb. santificare.

Halloween, n. la véglia di Ognissanti f.

hallucination, n. allucinazione f.

hallway, n. vestìbolo m., corridoio m.

halo, n. aurèola f.

halt, 1. n. fermata f. 2. vb. fermare, tr. 3. interj. alt!

halter, n. cavezza f., capestro m.

halve, vb. dimezzare.

halyard, n. drizza f.

ham, n. prosciutto m.

Hamburg, n. Amburgo m.

hamlet, n. vico m.

hammer, 1. n. martèllo m. 2. vb. martellare.

hammock, n. amaca f.

hamper, 1. n. cesta f. 2. vb. impedire.

hamstring, vb. ostacolare.

hand, n. mano f.

handbag, n. (lady's) borsetta f.; (suitcase) valigetta f.

handbook, n. manuale m.

handcuffs, n. manette f.pl.

handful, n. manata f.

handicap, n. svantàggio m.

handicraft, n. lavoro manuale m.

handiwork, n. òpera f.

handkerchief, n. fazzoletto m.

handle, 1. n. mànico m., maniglia f., manovèlla f. 2. vb. maneggiare.

handle bar, n. manùbrio m.

hand-made, adj. fatto a mano.

handmaid, n. ancella f.

handorgan, n. organetto a manovèlla m.

handout, n. (alms) limòsina f.

hand-pick, vb. scégliere con cura.

hand-rail, n. mancorrente m.

handsome, adj. bèllo.

hand-to-hand, adj. còrpo a còrpo.

handwriting, n. calligrafìa f.

handy, adj. (person) dèstro; (thing) còmodo; (at hand) a portata di mano.

handy-man, n. factotum m.

hang, vb. pèndere; (execute) impiccare.

hangar, n. aviorimesssa f.

hangdog, adj. con una fàccia patibolare.

hanger, n. gàncio m.; (coat-h.) attaccapanni m.

hanger-on, n. seguace m.

hang glider, n. aliante ad cui l'utente pende m.

hanging, n. (execution) impiccagione f.; (tapestry) tappezzerìa f.

hangman, n. impiccatore m.

hangnail, n. pipita f.

hangout, n. ritròvo m.

hang-over, n. stanghetta f.

hangup, n. difficoltà psicològica f.

hank, n. matassa f.

hanker, vb. bramare.

haphazard, adv. a casàccio.

happen, vb. (take place) accadere, succèdere; (chance to be) trovarsi.

happening, n. avvenimento m.

happily, adv. felicemente.

happiness, n. felicità f.

happy, adj. felice.

happy-go-lucky, adj. spensierato.

harakiri, n. karakiri m.

harangue, 1. n. arringa f. 2. vb. arringare.

harass, vb. annoiare.

harbinger, n. precursore m.

harbor, n. (refuge) rifùgio m.; (port) pòrto m.

hard, 1. adj. duro; (difficult) difficile. 2. adv. fortemente, duramente.

hard-bitten, adj. tenace.

hard-boiled, adj. sòdo.

hard coal, n. antracite f.

harden, vb. indurire.

hard-headed, adj. pràtico.

hard-hearted, adj. di cuòre duro.

hardiness, n. robustezza f.

hardly, adv. (with difficulty) stentatamente; (scarely) appena; (h. ever) quasi mai.

hardness, n. durezza f.

hardship, n. avversità f.

hardware, n. ferramenta f.pl.

hardwood, n. legno duro m.

hardy, adj. robusto.

hare, n. lèpre f.

hare-brained, adj. scervellato.

hare-lip, n. labbro leporino m.

harem, n. àrem m.

hark, vb. ascoltare.

Harlequin, n. Arlecchino m.

harlot, n. meretrice f.

harm, 1. n. danno m. 2. vb. danneggiare, nuòcere.

harmful, adj. dannoso, nocivo.

harmless, adj. innòcuo, innocènte.

harmonic, adj. armònico.

harmonica, n. armònica f.

harmonious, adj. armonioso.

harmonize, vb. armonizzare.

harmony, n. armonia f.

harness, 1. n. bardatura f. 2. vb. bardare.

harp, n. arpa f.

harpoon, 1. n. fiòcina f. 2. vb. fiocinare.

harpsichord, n. clavicémbalo m.

harridan, n. vecchiàccia f.

harrow, 1. n. èrpice m. 2. vb. erpicare.

harry, vb. spogliare.

harsh, adj. aspro.

harshness, n. asprezza f.

harvest, 1. n. raccòlta f. 2. vb. raccògliere.

hash, n. guazzabùglio m.

hashish, n. hascisc m.

hasn't, vb. non à.

hassle, vb. seccare n., seccatura f.

hassock, n. cuscino m.

haste, 1. n. fretta m. 2. vb. affrettarsi.

hasten, vb. affrettare tr.

hastily, adv. affrettatamente, frettolosamente.

hasty, adj. affrettato, frettoloso.

hat, n. cappèllo m.

hatch, 1. n. (boat) boccapòrto m. 2. vb. (hen) covare; (egg) schiudersi; aprirsi.

hatchery, n. vivaio m.

hatchet, n. accetta f.

hate, 1. n. òdio m. 2. vb. odiare.

hateful, adj. odioso.

hatred, n. òdio m.

haughtiness, n. supèrbia f.

haughty, adj. supèrbo.

haul, vb. trascinare, trasportare.

haunch, n. anca f.

haunt, vb. frequentare.

have, vb. avere; (h. to, necessity) dovere.

haven, n. pòrto m.; (refuge) rifùgio m.

haven't, vb. non ho, etc.

havoc, n. devastazione f.

hawk, n. falco m.

hawker, n. venditore ambulante m.

hawser, n. alzaia f., gòmena f.

hawthorn, n. biancospino m.

hay, n. fièno m.

hay fever, n. asma del fièno m.

hayfield, n. campo da fièno m.

hayloft, n. fienile m.

haystack, n. cùmulo di fièno m.

hazard, 1. n. rischio m. 2. vb. rischiare.

hazardous, adj. rischioso.

haze, n. nébbia f.

hazel, n. (plant) nocciòlo m.; (nut) nocciòla m.

hazy, adj. nebbioso, vago.

he, pron. egli, lùi.

head, n. tèsta f., capo m.

headache, n. mal di tèsta m.

headband, n. bènda f., diadèma m.

headfirst, adv. colla tèsta in avanti.

headgear, n. acconciatura del capo f.

head-hunting, n. càccia alle tèste f.

heading, n. tìtolo m.

headlight, n. fanale anteriore m.

headline, n. tìtolo m.

headlong, adv. a capofitto.

head-man, n. capo m.

headmaster, n. direttore m.

head-on, adj. frontale.

headquarters, n. quartière generale m.

headstone, n. piètra tombale f.

headstrong, adj. ostinato, testardo.

headwaters, n. sorgènti f.pl.

headway, n. progrèsso m.; (trains, etc.) intervallo m.

head-work, n. lavoro intellettuale m.

heady, adj. impetuoso, inebbriante.

heal, vb. guarire, risanare.

health, n. salute f.; (skoal) brindisi m.

healthful, adj. salubre.

healthy, adj. sano.

heap, 1. n. mùcchio m. 2. vb. ammucchiare.

hear, vb. sentire, udire.

hearing, n. (sense) udito m.; (audience) udiènza f.

hearken to, vb. ascoltare.

hearsay, n. (by h.) per sentito dire.

hearse, n. carro fùnebre m.

heart, n. cuòre m.

heartache, n. angòscia f.

heart-break, n. crepacuòre m.

heartbroken, adj. straziato.

heartburn, n. bruciore di stòmaco m.

heartfelt, adj. sincèro.

hearth, n. focolare m.

heartless, adj. sènza cuòre.

heart-rending, adj. straziante.

heart-sick, adj. scoraggiato.

heart-stricken, adj. colpito al cuòre.

heart-to-heart, adj. ìntimo.

hearty, adj. cordiale.

heat, 1. n. calore m., caldo m. 2. vb. riscaldare.

heated, adj. (dwelling-place) riscaldato; (discussion) infiammato.

heater, n. calorifero m.

heath, n. brughièra f.

heathen, n. and adj. pagano (m.)

heather, n. èrica f.

heat-stroke, n. colpo di calore m.

heat wave, n. ondata di caldo f.

heave, vb. sollevare; (utter) eméttere.

heaven, n. cièlo m.

heavenly, adj. celèste.

heavy, adj. pesante.

heavyweight, n. and adj. peso màssimo (m.)

Hebrew, n. and adj. ebrèo (m.); ebràico (m.)

heckle, vb. fare domande imbarazzanti.

hectare, n. èttaro m.

hectic, adj. ètico; (wild) da impazzire.

hectogram, n. ètto m., ettogramma m.

hedge, n. sièpe f.

hedgehog, n. riccio m.

hedge-hop, vb. volare rasentando la tèrra.

hedgerow, n. sièpe di cespùgli o di àlberi.

hedonism, n. edonismo m.

heed, vb. badare a, prestare attenzione a.

heedless, adj. spensierato.

heel, n. calcagno m., tallone m.; (shoes) tacco m.

hefty, adj. pesante, vigoroso.

hegemony, n. egemonia f.

heifer, n. giovènca f.

height, n. altezza f.; (high place) altura f.

heighten, vb. (raise) innalzare; (increase) accréscere.

heinous, adj. atroce.

heir, n. erède m.

heir apparent, n. erède legittimo m.

heirloom, n. oggètto antico di famiglia m.

heir presumptive, n. presunto erède m.

helicopter, n. elicòttero m.

heliocentric, adj. eliocèntrico.

heliograph, n. eliògrafo m.

heliotrope, n. eliotròpio m.

helium, n. èlio m.

hell, n. infèrno m.

Hellenic, adj. ellènico.

Hellenism, n. ellenismo m.

hellish, adj. infernale.

hello, interj. buòn giorno, buòna sera,; (telephone) pronto.

helm, n. timone m.

helmet, n. èlmo m.

helmsman, n. timonière m.

help, 1. n. aiuto m. 2. vb. aiutare; (at table) servire.

helper, n. aiutante m.

helpful, adj. (person) serviziévole; (thing) ùtile.

helpfulness, n. utilità f.

helping, n. porzione f.

helpless, adj. impotènte.

helter-skelter, adv. a casàccio.

hem, 1. n. orlo m. 2. vb. orlare.

hematite, n. ematite f.

hemisphere, n. emisfèro m.

hemlock, n. cicuta f.

hemoglobin, n. emoglobina f.

hemophilia, n. emofilia f.

hemorrhage, n. emorragia f.

hemorrhoid, n. emorròide f.

hemp, n. cànapa f.

hemstitch, n. orlo a giorno m.

hen, n. gallina f.

hence, adv. (time, place) di qui; (therefore) quindi.

henceforth, adv. d'ora in pòi.

henchman, n. bravo m.

henna, n. enné m.

henpecked, adj. dominato dalla móglie.

hepatic, adj. epàtico.

hepatics, n. epàtica f.

her, 1. adj. suo, di lèi. 2. pron. (direct) la; (indirect) le; (alone, stressed, or with prep.) lèi.

herald, n. araldo m.

heraldic, adj. aràldico.

heraldry, n. aràldica f.

herb, n. èrba f.

herbaceous, adj. erbàceo.

herbarium, n. erbàrio m.

herculean, adj. ercùleo.

herd, n. gregge m., mandra f.

here, adv. qui; (h. is) ècco.

hereabout, adv. qui vicino.

hereafter, adv. d'ora in pòi.

hereby, adv. con questo.

hereditary, adj. ereditàrio.

heredity, n. eredità f.

herein, adv. qui dentro.

heresy, n. eresìa f.

heretic, n. erètico m.

heretical, adj. erètico.

hereto, adv. a questo.

heretofore, adv. finora.

herewith, adv. con questo.

heritage, n. eredità f.

hermetic, adj. ermètico.

hermit, n. eremita m.

hermitage, n. eremitàggio m., romitàggio m.

hernia, n. èrnia f.

hero, n. eròe m.

heroic, adj. eròico.

heroically, adv. eroicamente.

heroin, n. eroina f.

heroine, n. eroina f.

heroism, n. eroismo m.

heron, n. airone m.

herpes, n. èrpete m.

herring, n. aringa f.

herringbone, n. lisca d'arenga f.

hers, pron. suo, di lèi.

herself, pron. sè stessa.

hertz, n. hertz m.

hesitancy, n. esitazione f.

hesitant, adj. esitante.

hesitate, vb. esitare.

hesitation, n. esitazione f.

heterodox, adj. eterodòsso.

heterodoxy, n. eterodossìa f.

heterogeneous, adj. eterogèneo.

heterosexual, adj. eterosessuale.

hew, vb. tagliare.

hexagon, n. esàgono m.

heyday, n. apogèo m.

hi! interj. ciao.

hiatus, n. iato m.

hibernate, vb. svernare.

hibernation, n. ibernazione f.

hibiscus, n. ibisco m.

hiccup, n. singulto m.

hickory, n. noce americano m.

hide, 1. n. pèlle f. 2. vb. nascóndere tr.

hideous, adj. spaventoso.

hide-out, n. nascondiglio m.

hierarchical, adj. geràrchico.

hierarchy, n. gerarchìa f.

hieroglyphic, adj. geroglìfico.

high, adj. alto, elevato; (in price) caro.

highbrow, n. and adj. intellettuale (m. or f.)

high fidelity, n. alta fedeltà f.

high-handed, adj. arbitràrio.

high-hat, vb. trattare dall'alto in basso.

highland, n. regione montuosa f.

highlight, vb. mèttere in riliévo.

highly, adv. altamente, estremamente.

high-minded, adj. magnànimo.

Highness, n. Altezza f.

high school, n. licèo m., ginnàsio m.

high seas, n. alto mare m. (sg.).

high-strung, adj. eccitàbile.

high tide, n. alta marèa f.

highway, n. strada maestra f.; (h. robber) grassatore m.

hijacker, n. dirottatore m.

hike, 1. n. gita a pièdi f. 2. vb. fare una gita a pièdi.

hilarious, adj. ilare.

hilarity, n. ilarità f.

hill, n. collina f.

hilt, n. èlsa f.

him, pron. (direct) lo; (indirect) gli; (alone, stressed, or with prep.) lùi.

himself, pron. sè stesso; (refl.) si.

hind, 1. n. cèrva f., dàina f. 2. adj. posteriore.

hinder, vb. impedire, ostacolare.

hindmost, adj. ùltimo.

hindrance, n. impedimento m., ostàcolo m., intràlcio m.

hinge, n. càrdine m., gànghero m.

hint, 1. n. cenno m. 2. vb. accennare.

hinterland, n. retrotèrra f.

hip, n. anca f., fianco m.

hippodrome, n. ippòdromo m.

hippopotamus, n. ippopòtamo m.

hire, 1. n. nòlo m. 2. vb. noleggiare.

hireling, n. mercenàrio m.

his, adj. and pron. suo, di lùi.

Hispanic, adj. ispànico.

hiss, 1. n. sìbilo m. 2. vb. sibilare.

historian, n. stòrico m.

historic, historical, adj. stòrico.

history, n. stòria f.

histrionic, adj. istriònico.

histrionics, n. istriònica f.

hit, 1. n. colpo m.; (success) successo m. 2. vb. colpire; percuòtere; picchiare.

hitch, 1. n. (obstacle) ostàcolo m. 2. vb. attaccare.

hither, adv. qua.

hitherto, adv. finora.

hive, n. alveare m.

hives, n. eruzione cutànea f.

hoard, 1. n. ammasso m. 2. vb. ammassare.

hoarse, adj. fiòco, ràuco.

hoax, 1. n. inganno m. 2. vb. ingannare.

hobble, vb. zoppicare.

hobby, n. passione f.

hobby-horse, n. cavallo a dòndolo m.

hobgoblin, n. folletto m.

hobnail, n. chiòdo gròsso m.

hobnob with, vb. frequentare.

hobo, n. vagabondo m.

hock, vb. impegnare.

hockey, n. hockey m.

hocus-pocus, n. inganno m.

hod, n. sècchia f.

hodge-podge, n. miscùglio m.

hoe, 1. n. zappa f. 2. vb. zappare.

hog, n. pòrco m., maiale m.

hog-tie, vb. legare sicuramente.

hogshead, n. botte f.

hoist, vb. innalzare.

hold, 1. n. presa f.; (boat) stiva f. 2. vb. tenere; (contain) contenere; (h. up, support) règgere.

holder, n. recipiènte m.; (cigarette-h.) portasigarette m.

holdup, n. grassazione f.

hole, n. buco m.

holiday, n. giorno festivo m.; vacanza f., fèsta f.

holiness, n. santità f.

Holland, n. Olanda f.

hollow, n. and adj. cavo (m.).

holly, n. agrifòglio m.

hollyhock, n. malvaròsa f.

holocaust, n. olocàusto m.

hologram, n. ologramma m.

holography, n. olografia f.

holster, n. fondina f.

holy, adj. santo.

holy day, n. fèsta ecclesiàstica f.

Holy See, n. Santa Sede f.

Holy Spirit, n. Spìrito Santo m.

Holy Week, n. settimana santa f.

homage, n. omàggio m.

home, 1. n. casa f. 2. adj. casalingo. 3. adv. a casa.

homeland, n. pàtria f.

homeless, adj. sènza tètto.

homelike, adj. casalingo.

homely, adj. brutto.

home-made, adj. fatto in casa.

home rule, n. autonomìa f.

homesick, be, vb. soffrire di nostalgìa.

homesickness, n. nostalgìa f.

home-spun, adj. filato in casa.

homestead, n. fattorìa f.

homeward, adv. vèrso casa.

homework, n. lavoro di casa m.

homicide, n. (act) omicìdio m.; (person) omicida m.

homily, n. omelìa f.

homing pigeon, *n.* piccione viaggiatore *m.*

hominy, *n.* semolino di granturco *f.*

homogeneous, *adj.* omogèneo.

homogenize, *vb.* omogenizzare.

homonym, *n.* omònimo *f.*

homonymous, *adj.* omònimo.

homosexual, *adj.* omosessuale.

hone, *n.* còte *f.*

honest, *adj.* onèsto.

honestly, *adv.* onestamente.

honesty, *n.* onestà *f.*

honey, *n.* mièle *m.*

honey-bee, *n.* ape da mièle *f.*

honeycomb, *n.* favo *m.*

honeymoon, *n.* luna di mièle *m.*

honeysuckle, *n.* caprifòglio *m.*

honor, 1. *n.* onore *m.* 2. *vb.* onorare.

honorable, *adj.* onorévole.

honorary, *adj.* onoràrio.

hood, *n.* cappùccio *m.;* (auto) còfano *m.*

hoodlum, *n.* teppista *m.*

hoodwink, *vb.* ingannare.

hoof, *n.* zòccolo *m.*

hook, 1. *n.* uncino *m.;* (fish.) amo *m.* 2. *vb.* uncinare; (catch) prèndere all'amo.

hookworm, *n.* anchilòstoma *m.*

hoop, *n.* cérchio *m.*

hoot, *vb.* (auto horn) sonare.

hop, 1. *n.* (plant) lùppolo *m.;* (jump) salto *m.* 2. *vb.* saltare.

hope, 1. *n.* speranza *f.* 2. *vb.* sperare.

hopeful, *adj.* pieno di speranza.

hopeless, *adj.* disperato.

hopelessness, *n.* disperazione *f.*

horde, *n.* òrda *f.*

horehound, *n.* marrùbio *m.*

horizon, *n.* orizzonte *m.*

horizontal, *adj.* orizzontale.

hormone, *n.* ormone *m.*

horn, *n.* còrno *m.;* (auto) clàcson *m.*

hornet, *n.* calabrone *m.*

horny, *adj.* calloso.

horoscope, *n.* oròscopo *f.*

horrendous, *adj.* orrèndo.

horrible, *adj.* orrìbile.

horrid, *adj.* òrrido.

horrify, *vb.* far inorridire; (be horrified) inorridire.

horror, *n.* orrore *m.*

horse, *n.* cavallo *m.;* (cavalry) cavalleria *f.*

horseback, on, *adv.* a cavallo.

horsefly, *n.* mosca cavallina *f.*

horsehair, *n.* crine di cavallo *f.*

horseman, *n.* cavalière *m.*

horsemanship, *n.* equitazione *f.*

horseplay, *n.* giòco rozzo *m.*

horse-power, *n.* cavallovapore *m.*

horse-radish, *n.* ràfano *m.*

horseshoe, *n.* fèrro di cavallo *m.*

horsewhip, *n.* frustino *m.*

hortatory, *adj.* esortativo.

horticulture, *n.* orticultura *f.*

hose, *n.* (tube) tubo flessibile *m.;* (stockings) calze *f.pl.*

hosiery, *n.* calzetteria *f.*

hospitable, *adj.* ospitale.

hospital, *n.* ospedale *m.*

hospitality, *n.* ospitalità *f.*

hospitalization, *n.* ospedalizzazione *f.*

hospitalize, *vb.* ospedalizzare.

host, *n.* (giver of hospitality) òspite *m.;* (innkeeper) òste *m.;* (crowd) moltitùdine *f.;* (Eucharist) òstia *f.*

hostage, *n.* ostàggio *m.*

hostel, *n.* albèrgo *m.*

hostelry, *n.* albèrgo *m.*

hostess, *n.* òspite *f.*

hostile, *adj.* ostile.

hostility, *n.* ostilità *f.*

hot, *adj.* caldo; (on water faucets) C.

hotbed, *n.* terreno concimato *m.;* (fig.) focolare *m.*

hot dog, *n.* salsiccia *f.*

hotel, *n.* albèrgo *m.*

hot-headed, *adj.* eccitàbile.

hothouse, *n.* sèrra *f.*

hound, *n.* cane *m.*

hour, *n.* ora *f.*

hourglass, *n.* orològio a pólvere *m.*

hourly, *adv.* ogni ora.

house, *n.* casa *f.;* (legislative) càmera *f.*

housefly, *n.* mosca *f.*

household, *n.* famiglia *f.*

housekeeper, *n.* massaia *f.*

housekeeping, *n.* economia domèstica *f.*

housemaid, *n.* domèstica *f.*

housewife, *n.* massaia *f.*

housework, *n.* lavoro domèstico *m.*

hovel, *n.* tugùrio *m.*

hover, *vb.* volteggiare.

hovercraft, *n.* aliscafo *f.*

how, *adv.* come; (h. far) fino dove; (h. long) fino a quando; (h. many, h. much) quanto.

however, *adv.* comunque, però, tuttavìa.

howitzer, *n.* òbice *m.*

howl, 1. *n.* urlo *m.* 2. *vb.* urlare.

howsoever, *adv.* comunque.

hub, *n.* mòzzo *m.;* (fig.) cèntro *m.*

hubbub, *n.* tumulto *m.*

huckleberry, *n.* vaccinio *m.*

huddle, 1. *n.* consultazione *f.* 2. *vb.* rannicchiarsi; (go into a h.) tenere una consultazione.

hue, *n.* colore *m.*

huff, *n.* petulanza *f.*

hug, 1. *n.* abbràccio *m.* 2. *vb.* abbracciare.

huge, *adj.* immane.

hulk, *n.* carcassa *f.*

hull, *n.* (boat) scafo *m.;* (fruit) bùccia *f.*

hullabaloo, *n.* chiasso *m.*

hum, 1. *n.* ronzìo *n* 2. *vb.* (insect) ronzare; (sing) canticchiare.

human, *adj.* umano.

humane, *adj.* umanitàrio.

humanism, *n.* umanésimo *m.*

humanist, *n.* umanista *m.*

humanitarian, *adj.* umanitàrio.

humanity, *n.* umanità *f.*

humanly, *adv.* umanamente.

humble, 1. *adj.* ùmile. 2. *vb.* umiliare.

humbug, *n.* impostura *f.*

humdrum, *adj.* monòtono.

humid, *adj.* ùmido.

humidify, *vb.* inumidire.

humidity, *n.* umidità *f.*

humidor, *n.* scàtola per inumidire i sigari *f.*

humiliate, *vb.* umiliare.

humiliation, *n.* umiliazione *f.*

humility, *n.* umiltà *f.*

humor, *n.* umore *m.;* (wit) umorismo *m.*

humorist, *n.* umorista *m.*

humorous, *adj.* umorìstico.

hump, *n.* gobba *f.*

humpback, *n.* gobbo *m.,* gobba *f.*

humus, *n.* humus *m.*

hunch, 1. *n.* gobba *f.;* (suspicion) sospètto *m.* 2. *vb.* curvare, *tr.*

hunchback, *n.* gobbo *m.,* gobba *f.*

hundred, *num.* cènto; (group of a hundred) centinaio *n.m.*

hundredth, *adj.* centèsimo.

Hungarian, *adj.* ungherese.

Hungary, *n.* Ungherìa *f.*

hunger, *n.* fame *f.*

hungry, be, *vb.* aver fame.

hunk, *n.* pèzzo *m.*

hunt, 1. *n.* càccia *f.* 2. *vb.* cacciare; (h. for) cercare.

hunter, *n.* cacciatore *m.*

hunting, *n.* càccia *f.*

huntress, *n.* cacciatrice *f.*

hurdle, 1. *n.* (hedge) sièpe *f.;* (obstacle) ostàcolo *m.* 2. *vb.* saltare.

hurl, *vb.* lanciare, scagliare.

hurrah for, *interj.* viva, evviva (often written W).

hurricane, *n.* uragano *m.*

hurry, 1. *n.* fretta *f.* 2. *vb.* affrettare *tr.*

hurt, 1. *n.* danno *m.;* (wound) ferita *f.* 2. *vb.* far male a.

hurtful, *adj.* dannoso.

hurtle, *vb.* precipitarsi.

husband, *n.* marito *m.*

husbandry, *n.* amministrazione *f.*

hush, 1. *vb.* far tacere. 2. *interj.* zitto!

husk, *n.* bùccia *f.*

husky, *adj.* (strong) fòrte; (hoarse) ràuco.

hustle, 1. *n.* fretta *f.* 2. *vb.* (shove) spingere; (hurry) affrettare, *tr.*

hut, *n.* casùpola *f.*

hutch, *n.* coniglièra *f.*

hyacinth, *n.* giacinto *m.*

hybrid, *adj.* ìbrido.

hydrangea, *n.* ortènsia *f.*

hydrant, *n.* idrante *m.*

hydraulic, *adj.* idràulico.

hydrochloric, *adj.* idroclòrico.
hydroelectric, *adj.* idroelèttrico.
hydrogen, *n.* idrògeno *m.*
hydrophobia, *n.* idrofobìa *f.*
hydroplane, *n.* idrovolante *m.*
hydrotherapy, *n.* idroterapèutica *f.*
hyena, *n.* ièna *f.*
hygiene, *n.* igiène *f.*
hygienic, *adj.* igiènico.
hymn, *n.* inno *m.*
hymnal, *n.* innàrio *m.*
hyperacidity, *n.* iperacidità *f.*
hyperbole, *n.* ipèrbole *f.*
hypercritical, *adj.* ipercrìtico.
hypersensitive, *adj.* ipersensitivo.
hypertension, *n.* ipertensione *f.*
hyphen, *n.* tratto d'unione *m.*
hyphenate, *vb.* scrivere con tratto d'unione.
hypnosis, *n.* ipnòsi *f.*
hypnotic, *adj.* ipnòtico.
hypnotism, *n.* ipnotismo *m.*
hypnotize, *vb.* ipnotizzare.
hypochondria, *n.* ipocondrìa *f.*
hypochondriac, *n. and adj.* ipocondrìaco (*m.*)
hypocrisy, *n.* ipocrisìa *f.*
hypocrite, *n.* ipòcrita *m.*
hypocritical, *adj.* ipòcrita.
hypodermic, *adj.* ipodèrmico.
hypotenuse, *n.* ipotenusa *f.*
hypothesis, *n.* ipòtesi *f.*
hypothetical, *adj.* ipotètico.
hysterectomy, *n.* isterectomìa *f.*
hysteria, hysterics, *n.* isterismo *m.*
hysterical, *adj.* istèrico.

I

I, *pron.* io.
iambic, *adj.* giàmbico.
ice, *n.* ghiàccio *m.*
ice-berg, *n.* borgognone *m.*
ice-box, *n.* ghiacciaia *f.*
ice-cream, *n.* gelato *m.*
ice-skate, *n.* pàttino *m.*
ichthyology, *n.* ittiologìa *f.*
icing, *n.* pasta fròlla *f.*
icon, *n.* icòne *f.*
icy, *adj.* diàccio.
idea, *n.* idèa *f.*
ideal, *adj.* ideale.
idealism, *n.* idealismo *m.*
idealist, *n.* idealista *m.*
idealistic, *adj.* idealìstico.
idealize, *vb.* idealizzare.
ideally, *adv.* idealmente.
identical, *adj.* idèntico.
identifiable, *adj.* identificàbile.
identification, *n.* identificazione *f.*
identify, *vb.* identificare.
identity, *n.* identità *f.*
ideology, *n.* ideologìa *f.*
idiocy, *n.* idiozìa *f.*
idiom, *n.* idiòma *m.*
idiot, *n.* idiòta *m.*
idiotic, *adj.* idiòta.
idle, *adj.* ozioso.

idleness, *n.* òzio *m.*
idol, *n.* ìdolo *m.*
idolator, *n.* idolatra *m. or f.*
idolatry, *n.* idolatrìa *f.*
idolize, *vb.* idolatrare.
idyl, *n.* idìllio *m.*
idyllic, *adj.* idìllico.
if, *conj.* se; (as if) quasi.
ignite, *vb.* accèndere.
ignition, *n.* accensione *f.*
ignition key, *n.* chiavetta d'accensione *f.*
ignoble, *adj.* ignòbile.
ignominious, *adj.* ignominioso.
ignoramus, *n.* ignorantone *m.*
ignorance, *n.* ignoranza *f.*
ignorant, *adj.* ignorante, ignaro.
ignore, *vb.* trascurare.
ill, *adj.* malato.
illegal, *adj.* illegale.
illegible, *adj.* illeggìbile.
illegibly, *adv.* illeggibilmente.
illegitimacy, *n.* illegittimità *f.*
illegitimate, *adj.* illegìttimo.
illicit, *adj.* illécito.
illiteracy, *n.* analfabetismo *m.*
illiterate, *n. and adj.* analfabèta (*m. or f.*)
illness, *n.* malattìa *f.*, malore *m.*
illogical, *adj.* illògico.
ill-omened, *adj.* infàusto.
illuminate, *vb.* illuminare.
illumination, *n.* illuminazione *f.*
illusion, *n.* illusione *f.*
illusive, illusory, *adj.* illusòrio.
illustrate, *vb.* illustrare.
illustration, *n.* illustrazione *f.*
illustrative, *adj.* illustrativo.
illustrious, *adj.* illustre.
ill will, *n.* cattiva volontà *f.*
image, *n.* immàgine *f.*
imagery, *n.* figure retòriche *f.pl.*
imaginable, *adj.* immaginàbile.
imaginary, *adj.* immaginàrio.
imagination, *n.* fantasìa *f.*, immaginazione *f.*
imaginative, *adj.* immaginativo.
imagine, *vb.* immaginare, *tr.*, figurarsi.
imam, *n.* imam *m.*
imbecile, *n. and adj.* imbecille (*m. or f.*)
imitate, *vb.* imitare.
imitation, *n.* imitazione *f.*
imitative, *adj.* imitativo.
immaculate, *adj.* immacolato.
immanent, *adj.* immanènte.
immaterial, *adj.* immateriale.
immature, *adj.* immaturo.
immediate, *adj.* immediato.
immediately, *adv.* immediatamente, sùbito.
immense, *adj.* immènso.
immerse, *vb.* immèrgere.
immigrant, *n. and adj.* immigrante.
immigrate, *vb.* immigrare.
imminent, *adj.* imminènte.
immobile, *adj.* immòbile.
immobilize, *vb.* immobilizzare.

immoderate, *adj.* immoderato.
immodest, *adj.* immodèsto, impùdico.
immodesty, *n.* immodèstia *f.*, impudicìzia *f.*
immoral, *adj.* immorale.
immorality, *n.* immoralità *f.*
immorally, *adv.* immoralmente.
immortal, *adj.* immortale.
immortality, *n.* immortalità *f.*
immortalize, *vb.* immortalare.
immovable, *adj.* immòbile.
immune, *adj.* immune, esento.
immunity, *n.* immunità *f.*
immunize, *vb.* immunizzare.
immutable, *adj.* immutàbile.
impact, *n.* urto *m.*
impair, *vb.* menomare.
impale, *vb.* impalare.
impart, *vb.* impartire.
impartial, *adj.* imparziale.
impatience, *n.* impaziènza *f.*
impatient, *adj.* impaziènte.
impatiently, *adv.* impazientemente.
impeach, *vb.* imputare.
impede, *vb.* impedire.
impediment, *n.* impedimento *m.*
impel, *vb.* impèllere.
impenetrable, *adj.* impenetràbile.
impenitent, *adj.* impenitènte.
imperative, *n. and adj.* imperativo (*m.*)
imperceptible, *adj.* impercettìbile.
imperfect, *adj.* imperfètto.
imperfection, *n.* imperfezione *f.*, mènda *f.*
imperial, *adj.* imperiale.
imperialism, *n.* imperialismo *m.*
imperil, *vb.* méttere in perìcolo.
imperious, *adj.* imperioso.
impersonal, *adj.* impersonale.
impersonate, *vb.* impersonare, contraffare.
impersonation, *n.* contraffazione *f.*
impersonator, *n.* impersonatore *m.*
impertinence, *n.* impertinènza *f.*
impertinent, *adj.* impertinènte.
impervious, *adj.* impèrvio.
impetuous, *adj.* impetuoso.
impetus, *n.* ìmpeto *m.*
implacable, *adj.* implacàbile.
implant, *vb.* implantare.
implement, *n.* strumento *m.*
implicate, *vb.* implicare.
implication, *n.* implicazione *f.*
implicit, *adj.* implìcito.
implied, *adj.* implìcito.
implore, *vb.* implorare.
imply, *vb.* implicare; (suggest) suggerire; (insinuate) insinuare.
impolite, *adj.* scortese.
imponderable, *adj.* imponderàbile.
import, 1. *n.* importazione *f.*;

(meaning) significato *m*. 2. *vb*. importare.
importance, *n*. importanza *f*.
important, *adj*. importante; (be l.) importare.
importation, *n*. importazione *f*.
importune, 1. *adj*. importuno. 2. *vb*. importunare.
impose, *vb*. imporre.
imposition, *n*. imposizione *f*.
impossibility, *n*. impossibilità *f*.
impossible, *adj*. impossibile.
impotence, *n*. impotènza *f*.
impotent, *adj*. impotènte.
impoverish, *vb*. impoverire.
impregnable, *adj*. inespugnàbile.
impregnate, *vb*. impregnare, ingravidare.
impresario, *n*. impresàrio *m*.
impress, *vb*. (imprint) imprimere; (affect) impressionare.
impression, *n*. impressione *f*.
impressive, *adj*. impressionante.
imprison, *vb*. imprigionare.
imprisonment, *n*. prigionia *f*.
improbable, *adj*. improbàbile.
impromptu, 1. *n*. improvviso *m*. 2. *adj*. improvvisato; estemporàneo.
improper, *adj*. impròprio, sconveniènte.
improve, *vb*. migliorare.
improvement, *n*. miglioramento *m*.
improvise, *vb*. improvvisare.
impudent, *adj*. impudènte.
impugn, *vb*. impugnare.
impulse, *n*. impulso *m*.
impulsive, *adj*. impulsivo.
impunity, *n*. impunità *f*.
impure, *adj*. impuro.
impurity, *n*. impurità *f*.
impute, *vb*. imputare.
in, *prep*. in; (within, of time) entro.
inadvertent, *adj*. inavveduto.
inalienable, *adj*. inalienàbile.
inane, *adj*. inano.
inaugural, *adj*. inaugurale; (speech) discorso inaugurale *n.m.*
inaugurate, *vb*. inaugurare.
inauguration, *n*. inaugurazione *f*.
incandescence, *n*. incandescènza *f*.
incandescent, *adj*. incandescènte.
incantation, *n*. incantamento *m*.
incapacitate, *vb*. rèndere incapace.
incapacity, *n*. incapacità *f*.
incarcerate, *vb*. incarcerare.
incarnate, *adj*. incarnato.
incarnation, *n*. incarnazione *f*.
incendiary, *n. and adj*. incendiàrio (*m.*).
incense, *n*. incènso *m*.
incentive, *n*. incentivo *m*.
inception, *n*. inizio *m*.
incessant, *adj*. incessante.

incest, *n*. incèsto *m*.
inch, *n*. pòllice *m*.
incidence, *n*. incidènza *f*.
incident, *n*. incidènte *m*.
incidental, *adj*. incidentale.
incidentally, *adv*. incidentalmente.
incipient, *adj*. incipiènte.
incise, *vb*. incìdere.
incision, *n*. incisione *f*.
incisive, *adj*. incisivo.
incisor, *n*. dènte incisivo *m*.
incite, *vb*. incitare.
inclination, *n*. inclinazione *f*.
incline, 1. *n*. pendìo *m*. 2. *vb*. inclinare; (fig.) propèndere.
inclined, *adj*. (disposed) propènso.
inclose, *vb*. rinchiùdere; (in letter) acclùdere.
include, *vb*. inclùdere.
including, *prep*. compreso (*adj*.), agrees with following noun).
inclusive, *adj*. inclusivo.
incognito, *adj*. incògnito.
income, *n*. rèddito *m*.
incomparable, *adj*. incomparàbile.
inconsiderate, *adj*. strafottènte; villano.
inconvenience, 1. *n*. scomodità *f*. 2. *vb*. incomodare.
inconvenient, *adj*. incòmodo.
incorporate, *vb*. incorporare *tr*.
incorrigible, *adj*. incorreggìbile.
increase, 1. *n*. aumento *m*. 2. *vb*. accréscere, aumentare.
incredible, *adj*. incredìbile.
incredulity, *n*. incredulità *f*.
incredulous, *adj*. incrèdulo.
increment, *n*. incremento *m*.
incriminate, *vb*. incriminare.
incrimination, *n*. incriminazione *f*.
incrust, *vb*. incrostare.
incubator, *n*. incubatrice *f*.
inculcate, *vb*. inculcare.
incumbency, *n*. durata in càrica *f*.
incumbent, 1. *n*. titolare *m*. 2. *adj*. incombènte.
incur, *vb*. incórrere in.
incurable, *adj*. incuràbile.
indebted, *adj*. indebitato.
indeed, *adv*. davvero.
indefatigable, *adj*. infaticàbile.
indefinite, *adj*. indefinito.
indefinitely, *adv*. indefinitamente.
indelible, *adj*. indelèbile.
indemnify, *vb*. indennizzare.
indemnity, *n*. indennità *f*.
indent, *vb*. dentellare; (paragraph) collocare in dentro; (coastline) frastagliare.
indentation, *n*. dentallatura *f*.
independence, *n*. indipendènza *f*.
independent, *adj*. indipendènte.
in-depth, *adj*. profondo; esauriente.
index, *n*. ìndice *m*.

India, *n*. Ìndia *f*.
Indian, 1. *n*. indiano; (American Indian) pellirossa *m*. 2. *adj*. indiano; dei pellirossa.
indicate, *vb*. indicare.
indication, *n*. indicazione *f*.
indicative, *n. and adj*. indicativo (*m.*).
indicator, *n*. indicatore *m*.
indict, *vb*. accusare.
indictment, *n*. accusa *f*.
indifference, *n*. indifferènza *f*.
indifferent, *adj*. indifferènte.
indigenous, *adj*. indigeno.
indigent, *adj*. indigènte.
indigestion, *n*. indigestione *f*.
indignant, *adj*. indignato.
indignation, *n*. indignazione *f*.
indignity, *n*. indegnità *f*., sgarberia *f*.
indirect, *adj*. indiretto.
indiscreet, *adj*. indiscreto.
indiscretion, *n*. indiscrezione *f*.
indispensable, *adj*. indispensàbile.
indisposed, *adj*. indisposto.
indisposition, *n*. indisposizione *f*.
individual, 1. *n*. individuo *m*. 2. *adj*. individuale.
individuality, *n*. individualità *f*.
individually, *adj*. individualmente.
indivisible, *adj*. indivisibile.
indoctrinate, *vb*. addottrinare.
indolent, *adj*. indolènte.
Indonesia, *n*. Indonèsia *f*.
indoor, *adj*. da eseguirsi in casa.
indoors, *adv*. in casa.
indorse, *vb*. firmare; (check, etc.) girare.
induce, *vb*. indurre.
induct, *vb*. (into army) arruolare.
induction, *n*. induzione *f*.
inductive, *adj*. induttivo.
indulge, *vb*. indùlgere.
indulgence, *n*. indulgènza *f*.
indulgent, *adj*. indulgènte.
industrial, *adj*. industriale.
industrialist, *n*. industriale *m*.
industrious, *adj*. industrioso, operoso.
industry, *n*. indùstria *f*.
inebriate, 1. *n*. ubbriacone *m*. 2. *vb*. inebbriare.
ineligible, *adj*. ineleggìbile, inàbile.
inept, *adj*. inètto.
inert, *adj*. inèrte.
inertia, *n*. inèrzia *f*.
inevitable, *adj*. inevitàbile.
inexplicable, *adj*. inesplicàbile.
infallible, *adj*. infallìbile.
infamous, *adj*. infame.
infamy, *n*. infàmia *f*.
infancy, *n*. infànzia *f*.
infant, *n*. infante *m*.
infantile, *adj*. infantile.
infantry, *n*. fanteria *f*.
infantryman, *n*. fante *m*.
infatuate, *vb*. infatuare.
infect, *vb*. infettare.
infected, *adj*. infètto.

infection, n. infezione f.
infectious, adj. infettivo.
infer, vb. inferire, desùmere.
inference, n. inferènza f.
inferior, adj. inferiore.
inferiority, n. inferiorità f.; (i. complex) complesso d'inferiorità.
infernal, adj. infernale.
inferno, n. infèrno m.
infest, vb. infestare.
infidel, n. and adj. infedele; miscredènte.
infidelity, n. infedeltà f.
infiltrate, vb. infiltrare, tr.
infinite, n. and adj. infinito (m.).
infinitesimal, adj. infinitesimale.
infinitive, n. infinito m.
infinity, n. infinità f.
infirm, adj. infermo; (weak) dèbole; (unsure) irresoluto.
infirmary, n. infermería f.
infirmity, n. infermità f.
inflame, vb. infiammare.
inflammable, adj. infiammàbile.
inflammation, n. infiammazione f.
inflammatory, adj. infiammatòrio.
inflate, vb. gonfiare.
inflation, n. gonfiamento m.; (financial) inflazione f.
inflection, n. inflessione f.; (gram.) flessione f.
inflict, vb. infliggere.
infliction, n. inflizione f.
influence, n. influènza f., influsso m.
influential, adj. influènte.
influenza, n. influènza f.
inform, vb. informare.
informal, adj. senza cerimònie.
information, n. informazioni f.pl.
infringe, vb. infràngere.
infuriate, vb. far infuriare; (become i.d) infuriare.
ingenious, adj. ingegnoso.
ingenuity, n. ingegnosità f.
ingredient, n. ingrediènte m.
inhabit, vb. abitare.
inhabitant, n. abitante m.
inhale, vb. inalare.
inherent, adj. inerènte.
inherit, vb. ereditare.
inheritance, n. eredità f., retàggio m.
inhibit, vb. inibire.
inhibition, n. inibizione f.
inhuman, adj. inumano.
inimical, adj. nemico.
inimitable, adj. inimitàbile.
iniquity, n. iniquità f.
initial, n. and adj. iniziale (f.)
initiate, vb. iniziare.
initiation, n. iniziazione f.
initiative, n. iniziativa f.
inject, vb. iniettare.
injection, n. iniezione f.
injunction, n. ingiunzione f.
injure, vb. (harm) danneggiare, nuòcere; (wound) ferire.

injurious, adj. dannoso, nocivo.
injury, n. danno m., ferita f.
injustice, n. ingiustizia f.
ink, n. inchiòstro m.
inland, 1. adj. intèrno; **2.** adv. vèrso l'intèrno.
inlet, n. pòrto m., canale m.
inmate, n. paziènte m.
inn, n. locanda f.
inner, adj. interiore, intèrno.
innermost, adj. più íntimo.
innocence, n. innocènza f.
innocent, adj. innocènte.
innocuous, adj. innòcuo.
innovation, n. innovazione f.
innuendo, n. insinuazione f.
innumerable, adj. innumerévole.
inoculate, vb. inoculare.
inoculation, n. inoculazione f.
input, n. entrata f.; informazioni fornite f.pl.
inquest, n. inchièsta f.
inquire, vb. informarsi.
inquiry, n. ricerca d'informazioni f., investigazione f., inchièsta f.
inquisition, n. inquisizione f.
inquisitive, adj. eccessivament curioso.
inroad, n. incursione f.
insane, adj. insano, pazzo.
insanity, n. insània f., pazzía f.
inscribe, vb. iscrivere.
inscription, n. iscrizione f.
insect, n. insètto m.
insecticide, n. pòlvere insetticida m.
insensible, adj. insensibile.
insensitive, adj. insensíbile.
insensitivity, n. insensibilità f.
inseparable, adj. inseparàbile.
insert, 1. n. cosa inserita f. **2.** vb. inserire.
insertion, n. inserzione f.
inside, 1. n. intèrno m. **2.** adj. intèrno, interiore. **3.** adv., prep. dentro.
insidious, adj. insidioso.
insight, n. penetrazione f.
insignia, n. insegne f.pl.
insignificance, n. insignificanza f.
insignificant, adj. insignificante.
insinuate, vb. insinuare.
insinuation, n. insinuazione f.
insipid, adj. insipido; (dull) insulso.
insist, vb. insistere.
insistence, n. insistènza f.
insistent, adj. insistènte.
insolence, n. insolènza f.
insolent, adj. insolènte.
insolently, adv. insolentemente.
insomnia, n. insònnia f.
inspect, vb. ispezionare.
inspection, n. ispezione f.
inspector, n. ispettore m.
inspiration, n. ispirazione f.
inspire, vb. ispirare.
install, vb. installare; (a person) insediare.

installation, n. installazione f.; (of a person) insediamento m.; (industrial) impianto m.
installment, n. (payment) rata f.; (story, etc.) puntata f.
instance, n. istanza f.; (example) esèmpio m.; (request) richièsta f.; (for i.) per esèmpio.
instant, 1. n. istante m., àttimo m. **2.** adj. immediato; (date) corrènte.
instantaneous, adj. istantàneo.
instantly, adv. immediatamente.
instead, adv. invece; (i. of) invece di.
instigate, vb. istigare.
instill, vb. istillare.
instinct, n. istinto m.
instinctive, adj. istintivo.
institute, n. istituto m.
institution, n. istituzione f.
instruct, vb. istruire.
instruction, n. istruzione f.
instructive, adj. istruttivo.
instructor, n. istruttore m.
instructress, n. istruttrice f.
instrument, n. strumento m.
instrumental, adj. strumentale.
insufferable, adj. insoffribile.
insufficient, adj. insufficiènte.
insular, adj. insulare.
insulate, vb. isolare.
insulation, n. isolamento m.
insulator, n. isolatore m.
insulin, n. insulina f.
insult, 1. n. insulto m., ingiùria f. **2.** vb. insultare, ingiurare.
insulting, adj. insultante, ingiurioso.
insuperable, adj. insuperàbile.
insurance, n. assicurazione f.
insure, vb. assicurare, tr.
insurgent, n. and adj. ribèlle (m.)
insurrection, n. insurrezione f.
intact, adj. intatto.
intangible, adj. intangibile.
integral, adj. integrale.
integrate, vb. integrare.
integrity, n. integrità f.
intellect, n. intellètto m.
intellectual, adj. intellettuale.
intelligence, n. intelligènza f.
intelligent, adj. intelligènte.
intelligentsia, n. intellighènzia f.
intelligible, adj. intelligibile.
intend, vb. aver intenzione di.
intense, adj. intènso.
intensify, vb. intensificare.
intensive, adj. intensivo.
intent, 1. n. intènto m., intendimento m. **2.** adj. intènto; (i. on) intènto a.
intention, n. intenzione f., propòsito m.
intentional, adj. intenzionale.
intentionally, adv. intenzionalmente, apposta.
inter, vb. seppellire.
intercede, vb. intercèdere.
intercept, vb. intercettare.
intercourse, n. rapporto m.

interdict, 1. *n.* interdetto *m.* 2. *vb.* interdire.

interest, 1. *n.* interèsse *m.* 2. *vb.* interessare; (be i.ed in) interessarsi di.

interesting, *adj.* interessante.

interface, *n.* interfàcie *f.*

interfere, *vb.* (i. in) immischiarsi in, intervenire in; (i. with) ostacolare.

interference, *n.* ingerènza *f.;* (physics) interferènza *f.*

interim, 1. *n.* frattèmpo *m.* 2. *adj.* provvisòrio.

interior, *n. and adj.* interiore *(m.)*

interject, *vb.* inframettere.

interjection, *n.* interiezione *f.*

interlude, *n.* interlùdio *m.*

intermarry, *vb.* fare matrimoni misti.

intermediary, *n. and adj.* intermediàrio *(m.)*

intermediate, *adj.* intermèdio.

interment, *n.* sepoltura *f.*

intermission, *n.* intermissione *f.,* intervallo *m.*

intermittent, *adj.* intermittènte.

intern, *vb.* internare.

internal, *adj.* intèrno.

international, *adj.* internazionale.

internationalism, *n.* internazionalismo *m.*

interne, *n.* mèdico intèrno *m.*

interpose, *vb.* interporre.

interpret, *vb.* interpretare.

interpretation, *n.* interpretazione *f.*

interpreter, *n.* intèrprete *m.*

interrogate, *vb.* interrogare.

interrogation, *n.* interrogazione *f.*

interrogative, *adj.* interrogativo.

interrupt, *vb.* interrómpere.

interruption, *n.* interruzione *f.*

intersect, *vb.* intersecare, *tr.;* (cross) incrociarsi.

intersection, *n.* intersezione *f.;* (crossing) incròcio *m.*

intersperse, *vb.* cospàrgere.

interval, *n.* intervallo *m.*

intervene, *vb.* intervenire.

intervention, *n.* intervènto *m.*

interview, 1. *n.* intervista *f.* 2. *vb.* intervistare.

intestine, *n. and adj.* intestino *(m.)*

intimacy, *n.* intimità *f.*

intimate, *adj.* intimo.

intimidate, *vb.* intimidire.

intimidation, *n.* intimidazione *f.*

into, *prep.* in.

intolerant, *adj.* intollerante.

intonation, *n.* intonazione *f.*

intone, *vb.* intonare.

intoxicate, *vb.* (poison) intossicare; (get drunk) inebriare.

intoxication, *n.* intossicazione *f.,* ubbriachezza *f.*

intravenous, *adj.* endovenoso.

intrepid, *adj.* intrèpido.

---

intrepidity, *n.* intrepidità *f.*

intricacy, *n.* complicazione *f.*

intricate, *adj.* intricato, complicato.

intrigue, 1. *n.* intrigo *m.;* (love affair) tresca *f.* 2. *vb.* intrigare.

intrinsic, *adj.* intrinseco.

introduce, *vb.* introdurre; (persons) presentare.

introduction, *n.* introduzione *f.,* presentazione *f.*

introductory, *adj.* introduttivo.

introspection, *n.* introspezione *f.*

introvert, *adj.* introvertito.

intrude, *vb.* intrùdere, *tr.*

intruder, *n.* intruso *m.*

intuition, *n.* intuizione *f.*

intuitive, *adj.* intuitivo.

inundate, *vb.* inondare.

invade, *vb.* invàdere.

invader, *n.* invasore *m.*

invalid, *n. and adj.* invàlido *(m.)*

invariable, *adj.* invariàbile.

invasion, *n.* invasione *f.*

invective, *n.* invettiva *f.*

inveigle, *vb.* sedurre, adescare.

invent, *vb.* inventare.

invention, *n.* invenzione *f.*

inventive, *adj.* inventivo.

inventor, *n.* inventore *m.*

inventory, *n.* inventàrio *m.*

inverse, *adj.* invèrso.

invertebrate, *n. and adj.* invertebrato *(m.)*

invest, *vb.* investire.

investigate, *vb.* investigare.

investigation, *n.* investigazione *f.*

investment, *n.* investimento *m.*

inveterate, *adj.* inveterato.

invidious, *adj.* odioso.

invigorate, *vb.* invigorire.

invincible, *adj.* invincibile.

invisible, *adj.* invisibile.

invitation, *n.* invito *m.*

invite, *vb.* invitare.

invocation, *n.* invocazione *f.*

invoice, 1. *n.* fattura *f.* 2. *vb.* fatturare.

invoke, *vb.* invocare.

involuntary, *adj.* involontàrio.

involve, *vb.* coinvòlgere, implicare.

involved, *adj.* complicato.

invulnerable, *adj.* invulneràbile.

inward, 1. *adj.* intimo. 2. *adv.* vèrso l'interno.

inwardly, *adv.* intimamente.

iodine, *n.* iòdio *m.*

Iran, *n.* Iran *m.*

Iraq, *n.* Iràk *m.*

irate, *adj.* irato.

ire, *n.* ira *f.*

Ireland, *n.* Irlanda *f.*

iridium, *n.* iridio *m.*

iris, *n.* iride *f.;* (flower) iris *f.*

Irish, *adj.* irlandese.

irk, *vb.* infastidire.

iron, 1. *n.* fèrro *m.;* (flat-i.) fèrro da stiro. 2. *adj.* di fèrro, fèrreo. 3. *vb.* stirare.

---

ironical, *adj.* irònico.

ironworks, *n.* ferrièra *f.sg.*

irony, *n.* ironìa *f.*

irrational, *adj.* irrazionale.

irrefutable, *adj.* irrefutàbile.

irregular, *adj.* irregolare.

irregularity, *n.* irregolarità *f.*

irrelevant, *adj.* non pertinènte.

irreprehensible, *adj.* irreprensìbile.

irreprehensibly, *adv.* irreprensìbilmente.

irresistible, *adj.* irresistìbile.

irresponsible, *adj.* irresponsàbile.

irreverent, *adj.* irriverènte.

irrevocable, *adj.* irrevocàbile.

irrigate, *vb.* irrigare.

irrigation, *n.* irrigazione *f.*

irritability, *n.* irritabilità *f.*

irritable, *adj.* irritàbile.

irritant, *adj.* irritante.

irritate, *vb.* irritare.

irritation, *n.* irritazione *f.*

island, *n.* ìsola *f.*

isolate, *vb.* isolare.

isolation, *n.* isolamento *m.;* (politics) isolazione *f.*

isolationist, *n.* isolazionista *m.*

isosceles, *adj.* isòscele.

Israel, *n.* Israèle *m.*

Israeli, *adj.* israeliano.

Israelite, 1. *n.* israelita *m.* 2. *adj.* israelìtico.

issuance, *n.* emissione *f.*

issue, 1. *n.* (offspring) pròle *f.;* (bonds, etc.) emissione *f.;* (river) foce *f.;* (magazine) nùmero *m.* 2. *vb.* (come out) uscire; (publish) pubblicare.

isthmus, *n.* istmo *m.*

it, *pron.* ciò; (subject) esso; (direct object) lo, la.

Italian, *adj.* italiano.

italic, *adj.* itàlico.

italics, *n.* corsivo *m.sg.*

Italy, *n.* Itàlia *f.*

itch, 1. *n.* prudore *m.,* prurito *m.* 2. *vb.* prùdere, prurire.

item, *n.* articolo *m.*

itemize, *vb.* elencare.

itinerant, *adj.* girovago.

itinerary, *n.* itineràrio *m.*

its, *adj.* suo.

itself, *pron.* esso stesso.

ivory, *n.* avòrio *m.*

ivy, *n.* édera *f.*

J

jab, *vb.* pugnalare.

jack, *n.* binda *f.,* cricco *m.,* martinèllo *m.*

jack-of-all-trades, *n.* factotum *m.*

jackal, *n.* sciacallo *m.*

jackass, *n.* àsino *m.*

jacket, *n.* giacca *f.,* giacchetta *f.*

jack-knife, *n.* coltèllo a serra-mànico *m.*

jade, *n.* giada *f.*

jaded, *adj.* sfinito.

jagged, *adj.* seghettato.

jaguar, *n.* giaguaro *m.*

jail, *n.* càrcere *m.,* prigione *f.*

jailer, *n.* carcerière *m.*

jam, *n.* marmellata *f.;* (trouble) impiccio *m.*

jamb, *n.* stipite *m.*

jangle, *n.* rumore aspro *m.*

janitor, *n.* bidèllo *m.*

January, *n.* gennaio *m.*

Japan, *n.* il Giappone *m.*

Japanese, *adj.* giapponese.

jar, 1. *n.* giara *f.;* (glass) bottiglia *f.* 2. *vb.* scuòtere; (displease) offèndere.

jargon, *n.* gèrgo *m.*

jasmine, *n.* gelsomino *m.*

jaundice, *n.* itterìzia *f.*

jaunt, *n.* escursione *f.*

javelin, *n.* giavellòtto *m.*

jaw, *n.* mascèlla *f.*

jay, *n.* ghiandaia *f.*

jaywalk, *vb.* attraversare la strada all'infuòri dei passaggi pedonali.

jazz, *n.* jazz *m.* (pronounced giazz).

jealous, *adj.* geloso.

jealousy, *n.* gelosìa *f.*

jeans, *n.* jeans *m.pl.*

jeer (at), *vb.* beffarsi (di).

jelly, *n.* gelatìna *f.*

jelly-fish, *n.* medusa *f.*

jeopardize, *vb.* méttere in perìcolo.

jeopardy, *n.* perìcolo *m.*

jerk, 1. *n.* strattone *m.,* sbalzellone *m.* 2. *vb.* tirare con strattoni.

jerkin, *n.* giustacuòre *m.*

jerky, *adj.* a sbalzelloni.

jersey, *n.* màglia *f.*

Jerusalem, *n.* Gerusalèmme *f.*

jest, 1. *n.* scherzo *m.* 2. *vb.* scherzare.

jester, *n.* buffone *m.*

Jesuit, *n.* gesuita *m.*

Jesus Christ, *n.* Gesù Cristo *m.*

jet, 1. *n.* (black substance) giavazzo *m.;* (emission) gètto *m.;* (plane) reattore *m.,* aviogètto *m.* 2. *adj.* a reazione. 3. *vb.* sgorgare.

jet lag, *n.* sfasamento prodotto dal passaggio attraverso parecchi fusi orari *m.*

jetsam, *n.* mèrci gettate in mare.

jettison, *vb.* gettare in mare.

jetty, *n.* mòlo *m.*

Jew, *n.* ebrèo *m.,* giudèo *m.*

jewel, *n.* gioièllo *m.*

jeweler, *n.* gioiellière *m.*

jewelry, *n.* gioiellerìa *f.*

Jewish, *adj.* ebrèo, ebràico.

jib, 1. *n.* fiòcco *m.* 2. *vb.* (horse) recalcitrare; (refuse) rifiutarsi.

jibe, 1. *n.* bèffa *f.* 2. *vb.* (j. at) beffarsi di.

jiffy, *n.* istante *m.*

jig, *n.* giga *f.*

jilt, *vb.* abbandonare.

jingle, *vb.* tintinnare.

jinx, *n.* malaugùrio *m.*

jittery, *adj.* nervoso.

job, *n.* impiègo *m.,* occupazione *f.*

jobber, *n.* commerciante all'ingròsso *m.*

jockey, *n.* fantino *m.*

jocular, *adj.* umorìstico.

jocund, *adj.* giocondo.

jog, *vb.* scuòtere.

joggle, *n.* caletta *f.*

join, 1. *n.* congiunzione *f.* 2. *vb.* congiùngere; (associate with) associarsi con; (j. up) arruolarsi.

joiner, *n.* (carpenter) falegname *m.*

joint, 1. *n.* giuntura *f.,* articolazione *f.* 2. *adj.* congiunto, collettivo.

jointly, *adv.* collettivament, congiuntamente.

joist, *n.* travicèllo *m.*

joke, 1. *n.* schèrzo *m.;* (trick) burla *f.* 2. *vb.* scherzare.

joker, *n.* burlone *m.*

jolly, *adj.* allegro.

jolt, 1. *n.* scòssa *f.,* sobbalzo *m.* 2. *vb.* sobbalzare.

jonquil, *n.* giunchiglia *f.*

jostle, *vb.* spingere.

jounce, 1. *n.* sobbalzo *m.* 2. *vb.* sobbalzare.

journal, *n.* giornale *m.*

journalism, *n.* giornalismo *m.*

journalist, *n.* giornalista *m.*

journey, 1. *n.* viàggio *m.* 2. *vb.* viaggiare.

journeyman, *n.* operaio espèrto *m.*

jovial, *adj.* gioviale.

jowl, *n.* guància *f.*

joy, *n.* giòia *f.*

joyful, *adj.* gioioso.

joyous, *adj.* gioioso.

jubilant, *adj.* giubilante.

jubilee, *n.* giubilèo *m.*

Judaism, *n.* giudaismo *m.*

judge, 1. *n.* giùdice *m.* 2. *vb.* giudicare.

judgment, *n.* giudìzio *m.*

judicial, *adj.* giudiziàrio; (impartial) imparziale.

judiciary, 1. *n.* magistratura *f.* 2. *adj.* giudiziàrio.

judicious, *adj.* giudizioso.

jug, *n.* bròcca *f.*

juggle, *vb.* far giòchi di prestigio.

jugular, *adj.* giugulare.

juice, *n.* succo *m.*

juicy, *adj.* succoso.

July, *n.* lùglio *m.*

jumble, *n.* confusione *f.*

jump, 1. *n.* salto *m.* 2. *vb.* saltare.

junction, *n.* bìvio *m.,* diramazione *f.,* biforcazione *f.*

juncture, *n.* giuntura *f.*

June, *n.* giugno *m.*

jungle, *n.* giungla *f.*

junior, *adj.* minore; (in names) iuniore.

juniper, *n.* ginepro *m.*

junk, *n.* ròba da chiòdi *f.*

junket, *n.* (food) giuncata *f.;* (trip) escursione *f.*

jurisdiction, *n.* giurisdizione *f.*

jurisprudence, *n.* giurisprudènza *f.*

jurist, *n.* giurista *m.*

juror, *n.* giurato *m.*

jury, *n.* giurìa *f.*

just, 1. *adj.* giusto 2. *adv.* pròprio; (j. now) or'ora.

justice, *n.* giustìzia *f.*

justifiable, *adj.* giustificàbile.

justification, *n.* giustificazione *f.*

justify, *vb.* giustificare.

jut, *vb.* proiettarsi, spòrgere.

jute, *n.* iuta *f.*

juvenile, *adj.* giovanile.

K

kale, *n.* càvolo *m.*

kaleidoscope, *n.* caleidoscòpio *m.*

kangaroo, *n.* canguro *m.*

karakul, *n.* lince persiana *f.*

karat, *n.* carato *m.*

karate, *n.* karate *m.*

keel, *n.* chìglia *f.*

keen, *adj.* acuto.

keep, *vb.* conservare, serbare, mantenere, tenere; (stay) tenersi.

keeper, *n.* custòde *m.*

keepsake, *n.* ricòrdo *m.*

keg, *n.* barìletto *m.*

kennel, *n.* canìle *m.*

kerchief, *n.* fazzoletto *m.*

kernel, *n.* gherìglio *m.;* (fig.) nòcciolo *m.*

kerosene, *n.* petròlio raffinato *m.*

ketchup, *n.* salsa di pomodoro *f.*

kettle, *n.* péntola *f.*

kettledrum, *n.* tìmpano *m.*

key, *n.* chiave *f.;* (piano) tasto *m.;* (musical structure) tonalità *f.*

keyboard, *n.* tastièra *f.*

keyhole, *n.* buco della serratura *f.*

khaki, *n.* cachi *m.*

kick, 1. *n.* càlcio *m.* 2. *vb.* tirar calci (a).

kid, 1. *n.* (goat) capretto *m.;* (child) ragazzo *m.,* ragazza *f.* 2. *vb.* prèndere in giro.

kidnap, *vb.* rapire.

kidnapper, *n.* rapitore *m.*

kidnapping, *n.* rapimento *m.*

kidney, *n.* rène *f.;* (as food) rognone *m.*

kidney bean, *n.* fagiuòlo reniforme *m.*

kill, *vb.* uccìdere.

killer, *n.* uccisore *m.*

kiln, *n.* fornace *f.*

kilocycle, *n.* chilocìclo *m.*

kilogram, *n.* chilogramma *m.;* chilo *m.; (abbr.)* kg.

kilohertz, *n.* kilohertz *m.*

kilometer, *n.* chilòmetro *m.; (abbr.)* km.

kilowatt, *n.* chilowatt *m.; (abbr.)* kw.

kilt, n. gonnellino m.
kimono, n. chimono m.
kin, n. parentela f.
kind, 1. n. gènere m., razza f. 2. adj. gentile.
kindergarten, n. giardino d'infànzia m.
kindle, vb. accèndere.
kindling, n. legna minuta f.
kindly, adj. benèvolo.
kindness, n. gentilezza f.
kindred, 1. n. parentela f. 2. adj. imparentato; (alike) affine.
kinetic, adj. cinètico.
king, n. re m.
kingdom, n. regno m.
kink, n. nodo m.
kiosk, n. chiòsco m.
kiss, 1. n. bàcio m. 2. vb. baciare.
kitchen, n. cucina f.
kite, n. aquilone m.; (bird) nìbbio m.
kitten, n. gattino m.
kleptomania, n. cleptomanìa f.
kleptomaniac, n. cleptòmane m.
knack, n. facoltà m.
knapsack, n. zàino m.
knead, vb. impastare.
knee, n. ginòcchio m.
knee-cap, n. rotèlla del ginòcchio f.
kneel, vb. inginocchiarsi.
knell, n. rintocco m.
knickers, n. pantaloni m.pl.
knife, n. coltèllo m.
knight, n. cavalière m.; (chess) cavallo m.
knit, vb. lavorare a maglia; (k. one's brows) aggrottare le ciglia.
knock, vb. 1. n. bussata f. 2. vb. bussare; (strike) colpire; (k. down) abbàttere.
knot, n. nodo m.
knotty, adj. nodoso.
know, vb. (from outside in) conòscere; (from inside out) sapere; (k. how to) sapere.
knowledge, n. conoscènza f.; (without the k. of) all'insaputa di.
knuckle, n. nòcca f.
kodak, n. kodak f.
Korea, n. Corèa f.

L

label, n. etichetta f.
labor, 1. n. lavoro m.; (workers) manodòpera f. 2. vb. lavorare.
laboratory, n. laboratòrio m.
laborer, n. lavoratore m.
laborious, adj. laborioso.
labor union, n. sindacato operaio m.
laburnum, n. avorniéllo m.
labyrinth, n. labirinto m.
lace, n. merletto m., pizzo m.
lacerate, vb. lacerare.
laceration, n. lacerazione f.

lack, 1. n. mancanza f. 2. vb. mancare.
lackadaisical, adj. lànguido.
lackey, n. lacchè m.
laconic, adj. lacònico.
lacquer, 1. n. lacca f. 2. vb. laccare.
lactic, adj. làttico.
lactose, n. lattòsio m.
lacy, adj. leggèro come merletti.
lad, n. ragazzo m.
ladder, n. scala a piuòli f.; (stocking) cordiglièra f.
ladies, n. signore f.pl.
ladle, n. mèstola f., ramaiuòlo f.
lady, n. signora f.
ladybug, n. coccinèlla f.
lag, 1. n. ritardo m. 2. vb. indugiare.
lag behind, vb. restare indiètro.
lagoon, n. laguna f.
laid-back, adj. calmo.
lair, n. covo m., tana f.
laity, n. laicato m.
lake, 1. n. lago m. 2. adj. lacuale.
lamb, n. agnèllo m.; (meat) abbàcchio m.
lame, adj. zòppo.
lament, 1. n. lamento m. 2. vb. lamentare.
lamentable, adj. lamentévole.
lamentation, n. lamentazione f.
laminate, vb. laminare.
lamp, n. làmpada f.
lampoon, n. pasquinata f.
lance, 1. n. lància f. 2. vb. tagliare colla lancetta f.
land, 1. n. tèrra f.; (country) paese m. 2. vb. (from boat) sbarcare; (plane) atterrare.
landholder, n. proprietàrio di tèrra f.
landing, n. sbarco m.; (plane) atterràggio m.
landlady, n. padrona f.
landlord, n. padrone m.
landmark, n. monumento m.
landscape, n. paesaggio m.
landslide, n. frana f.
landward, adv. vèrso tèrra.
lane, n. viòttolo m.
language, n. lingua f.; (manner of talking) linguaggio m.
languid, adj. lànguido.
languish, vb. languire.
languor, n. languore m.
lanky, adj. alto e smilzo.
lanolin, n. lanolina f.
lantern, n. lantèrna f.
lap, 1. n. grembo m. 2. vb. lambire.
lapel, n. risvòlta f.
lapin, n. coniglio m.
lapse, 1. n. (mistake) errore m.; (time) percorso m. 2. vb. decadere.
larceny, n. furto m.
lard, n. strutto m.
large, adj. grande.
largely, adv. in gran parte.
largo, n., adj., adv. largo (m.)
lariat, n. làccio m.

lark, n. allòdola f.; (fun) divertimento m.
larkspur, n. consòlida reale f.
larva, n. larva f.
laryngitis, n. laringite f.
larynx, n. laringe f.
lascivious, adj. lascivo.
laser, n. làser m.
lash, 1. n. frusta f., sfèrza f. 2. vb. frustare, sferzare.
lass, n. ragazza f.
lassitude, n. lassitùdine f.
lasso, n. làccio m.
last, 1. n. forma f. 2. adj. ùltimo. 3. vb. durare.
lasting, adj. durévole.
latch, n. saliscendi m.
late, 1. adj. tardo, tardivo. 2. adv. tardi; (delayed) in ritardo.
lately, adv. recentemente.
latent, adj. latènte.
lateral, adj. laterale.
lath, n. listèllo m.
lathe, n. tórnio m.
lather, n. schiuma f.
Latin, n. and adj. latino (m.)
latitude, n. latitùdine f.
Latium, n. Làzio m.; (of L.) laziale.
latrine, n. latrina f.
latter, 1. adj. recènte. 2. pron. (opposed to former) questo.
lattice, n. grata f.
laud, vb. lodare.
laudable, adj. lodévole.
laudanum, n. làudano m.
laudatory, adj. laudativo.
laugh, 1. n. riso m. 2. vb. rìdere; (l. at) derìdere.
laughable, adj. ridìcolo.
laughter, n. riso m.; (burst of l.) risata f.
launch, 1. n. lància f. 2. vb. (throw) lanciare; (boat) varare.
launching, n. varo m.
launder, vb. lavare.
laundress, n. lavandaia f.
laundry, n. (clothes) bucato m.; (establishment) lavanderia f.
laundryman, n. lavandaio m.
laureate, adj. laureato.
laurel, n. allòro m., làuro m.
lava, n. lava f.
lavallière, n. pendènte m.
lavatory, n. latrina f.
lavender, n. lavanda f.
lavish, 1. adj. pròdigo. 2. vb. prodigare.
law, n. legge f., diritto m.
lawful, adj. legale, legìttimo.
lawless, adj. sènza legge.
lawn, n. prato m.
lawsuit, n. càusa f.
lawyer, n. avvocato m.
lax, adj. rilassato.
laxative, n. and adj. lassativo (m.), purgante (m.).
laxity, n. rilassamento m.
lay, 1. adj. làico. 2. vb. méttere, porre, deporre.
layer, n. strato m.
layman, n. làico m.

lazy, adj. pigro.

lead, 1. n. direzione f.; (metal) piombo m. 2. vb. menare; condurre.

leaden, adj. di piombo, plùmbeo.

leader, n. capo m.; (Fascist) duce m.

leadership, n. guida f.

lead pencil, n. matita f.

leaf, n. fòglia f.

leaflet, n. fogliolina f.

leafy, adj. fogliuto.

league, n. lega f.

League of Nations, n. Società delle Nazioni f.

leak, 1. n. falla f. 2. vb. (lose water) pèrdere; (let water in) far acqua.

leakage, n. infiltrazione f.; (loss) pèrdita f.

leaky, adj. che pèrde, che à falle.

lean, 1. adj. magro. 2. vb. appoggiare, tr.

leap, 1. n. salto m. 2. vb. saltare.

leap year, n. anno bisestile m.

learn, vb. imparare.

learned, adj. dòtto.

learning, n. dottrina f.

lease, 1. n. affitto m.; (contract) contratto d'affitto m. 2. vb. affittare.

leash, n. guinzàglio m.

least, 1. adj. mìnimo. 2. adv. minimamente.

leather, n. cuòio m.; (artificial l.) similcuòio m.

leathery, adj. tiglioso.

leave, 1. n. (departure) commiato m., congedo m.; (permission) permesso m.; (furlough) licènza f. 2. vb. lasciare; (depart) partire; (go away) andàrsene; (l. out) omèttere.

leaven, n. lièvito m.

lecherous, adj. lascivo.

lecture, n. conferènza f.

lecturer, n. conferenzière m.

ledge, n. ripiano m.

ledger, n. libro mastro m.

lee, n. sottovènto m.

leech, n. sanguisuga f.

leek, n. pòrro m.

leer, vb. guardare lascivamente.

leeward, adv. sottovènto.

left, 1. n. sinistra. 2. adj. sinistro; (departed) partito. 3. adv. a sinistra.

leftist, adj. di sinistra.

left-over, n. avanzo m.

leg, n. gamba f.

legacy, n. làscito m.

legal, adj. legale.

legalize, vb. legalizzare.

legation, n. legazione f.

legend, n. leggènda f.

legendary, adj. leggendàrio.

Leghorn, n. Livorno m.

legible, adj. leggìbile.

legion, n. legione f.

legislate, vb. fare leggi.

legislation, n. legislazione f.

legislator, n. legislatore m.

legislature, n. parlamento m.

legitimate, adj. legìttimo.

legume, n. legume m.

leisure, n. àgio m., riposo m., còmodo m.

leisurely, adj. còmodo.

lemon, n. limone m.

lemonade, n. limonata f.

lend, vb. prestare.

length, n. lunghezza f.

lengthen, vb. allungare, tr.

lengthwise, adv. per il lungo.

lengthy, adj. molto lungo.

lenient, adj. clemènte.

lens, n. lènte f.

Lent, n. quarésima f.

Lenten, adj. di quarésima.

lentil, n. lenticchia f.

lento, adv. lènto.

leopard, n. leopardo m.

leper, n. lebbroso m.

leprosy, n. lebbra f.

lesbian, adj. lèsbico n., lèsbica f.; tribade f.

lesion, n. lesione f.

less, 1. adj. minore. 2. adv. and prep. meno.

lessen, vb. diminuire.

lesser, adj. minore.

lesson, n. lezione f.

lest, conj. affinchè . . . non.

let, vb. (allow) lasciare, permèttere; (lease) affittare; (l. alone) lasciar stare; (l. up) diminuire.

letdown, n. allentamento m.

lethal, adj. letale.

lethargic, adj. letàrgico.

lethargy, n. letargia f.

letter, n. lèttera f.

letterhead, n. carta intestata f.

lettuce, n. lattuga f.

leukemia, n. leucèmia f.

levee, n. diga f.

level, 1. n. livèllo m. 2. adj. orizzontale, equilibrato. 3. vb. livellare.

lever, n. lèva f.

levity, n. leggerezza f.

levy, 1. n. lèva f.; (tax) imposta f. 2. vb. arruolare; (tax) imporre.

lewd, adj. impùdico.

lexicon, n. lèssico m.

liability, n. responsabilità f.

liable, adj. responsàbile, soggètto.

liaison, n. (mil.) collegamento m.; (love affair) relazione f.

liar, n. bugiardo m.

libation, n. libagione f.

libel, 1. n. libèllo m. 2. vb. diffamare.

libelous, adj. diffamatòrio.

liberal, n. and adj. liberale (m.)

liberalism, n. liberalismo m.

liberality, n. liberalità f.

liberate, vb. liberare.

libertine, n. and adj. libertino (m.)

liberty, n. libertà f.

libidinous, adj. libidinoso.

libido, n. libido f.

librarian, n. bibliotecàrio m.

library, n. bibliotèca f.

libretto, n. libretto m.

license, n. licènza f., permesso m.; (driver's) patènte f.

licentious, adj. licenzioso.

lick, vb. leccare.

licorice, n. liquirizia f.

lid, n. copèrchio m.; (eye) pàlpebra f.

lie, 1. n. bugìa f.; menzogna f. 2. vb. (tell untruths) mentire; (recline) giacere.

lien, n. sequèstro m.

lieutenant, n. tenènte f.; (second l.) sottotenènte m.

life, 1. n. vita f. 2. adj. (for l.) vitalìzio.

life-boat, n. barca di salvatàggio f.

life-buoy, n. salvagente m.

life-guard, n. bagnino m.

life insurance, n. assicurazione sulla vita f.

lifeless, adj. sènza vita.

life-preserver, n. (belt) cintura di salvatàggio f.; salvagènte m.

life style, n. modo di vivere m.

life-time, n. durata della vita f.

lift, 1. n. ascensore m. 2. vb. sollevare.

ligament, n. legamento m.

ligature, n. legatura f.

light, 1. n. luce f. 2. adj. luminoso; (not heavy) leggièro. 3. vb. accèndere; (l. up) illuminare, tr.

lighten, vb. (make less heavy) alleggerire; (flash) lampeggiare.

lighter, n. (cigar, cigarette) accendisigaro m.

light-house, n. faro m.

lightly, adv. leggiermente.

lightness, n. leggerezza f.

lightning, n. lampo m., fùlmine m.; (l.-rod) parafùlmine m.

lightship, n. nave faro f.

lignite, n. lignite f.

Ligurian, adj. ligure.

like, 1. adj. simile. 2. vb. (use piacere with English subject as indirect object). 3. prep. come.

likeable, adj. amàbile, simpàtico.

likelihood, n. probabilità f.

likely, adj. probàbile.

liken, vb. assomigliare.

likeness, n. somiglianza f.

likewise, adv. similmente.

lilac, n. lillà m.

lilt, n. canto m.

lily, n. gìglio m.

lily of the valley, n. mughetto m.

limb, n. (of body) arto m.; mèmbro m.; (of tree) ramo m.

limber, vb. rèndere flessìbile.

limbo, n. limbo m.

lime, n. calce f.; (bird-l.) vischio f.; (fruit) limone f.; (tree) tiglio m.

limelight, n. bagliore m.

limestone, n. pietra calcare f.

lime-water, n. acqua di calce f.

limit, 1. n. limite m. 2. vb. limitare.

limitation, n. limitazione f.

limited, n. (train) ràpido m.

limitless, adj. illimitato.

limousine, n. limousine f.

limp, 1. n. zoppicamento m. 2. adj. fiacco, flessibile. 3. vb. zoppicare.

limpid, adj. limpido.

linden, n. tiglio m.

line, 1. n. linea f.; (row) fila f.; (writing) riga f.; rigo m. 2. vb. (l. up) allineare, tr.

lineage, n. lignàggio m., stirpe f.

lineal, adj. diretto.

linear, adj. lineare.

linen, 1. n. (cloth) tela di lino f.; (household l.) biancheria f. 2. adj. di lino.

liner, n. (boat) transatlàntico m.

linger, vb. indugiare.

lingerie, n. lingeria f.

linguist, n. linguista m.

linguistic, adj. linguístico.

linguistics, n. linguística f.

liniment, n. linimento m.

lining, n. fòdera f.

link, 1. n. (bond) legame m., vincolo m., (in chain) anèllo m. 2. vb. collegare, tr.

linoleum, n. linòleum m.

linseed, n. seme di lino m.

lint, n. filàccia inglese f.

lion, n. leone m.

lip, n. labbro m.

lip-stick, n. rossetto m.

liquefy, vb. liquefare, tr.

liqueur, n. liquore m.

liquid, n. and adj. liquido (m.)

liquidate, vb. liquidare.

liquidation, n. liquidazione f.

liquor, n. liquore m.

lira, n. lira f.

lisle, n. filo di cotone mercerizzato m.

lisp, 1. n. pronùncia blesa f. 2. vb. essere bleso.

lisping, adj. bleso.

list, 1. n. lista f., elenco m., ruòlo m.; (slant) inclinazione f. 2. vb. elencare; (slant) inclinarsi.

listen (to), vb. ascoltare.

listless, adj. svogliato.

litany, n. litania f.

liter, n. litro m.

literacy, n. letteratezza f.

literal, adj. letterale.

literary, adj. letteràrio.

literate, adj. letterato.

literature, n. letteratura f.

lithe, adj. flessuoso.

lithograph, 1. n. litografia f. 2. vb. litografare.

lithography, n. litografia f.

litigant, n. litigante m.

litigation, n. càusa f.

litmus, n. tornasole m.

litter, 1. n. (mess) disòrdine m.; (stretcher) barella f.; (animal's bed) lettièra f.; (kittens, puppies) figliata f. 2. vb. méttere in confusione; (have kittens) figliare.

little, 1. n. poco 2. adj. piccolo m. 3. adv. poco.

liturgical, adj. litùrgico.

liturgy, n. liturgia f.

live, 1. adj. vivo 2. vb. vivere.

livelihood, n. vita f.

lively, adj. vivace, brioso.

liven, vb. ravvivare, tr.

liver, n. fégato m.

livery, n. livrèa f.

livestock, n. bestiame m.

livid, adj. lìvido.

living, 1. n. vita f. 2. adj. vivènte.

lizard, n. lucèrtola f.

lo, interj. ècco.

load, 1. n. càrico m. 2. vb. caricare.

loaf, 1. n. pagnòtta f., pane m. 2. vb. oziare.

loafer, n. bighellone m.; (slipper) pantòfola f.

loam, n. terriccio m.

loan, 1. n. prèstito m. 2. vb. prestare.

loath, adj. riluttante.

loathe, vb. abominare.

loathing, n. ripugnanza f.

loathsome, adj. schifoso.

lobby, n. corridoio m.

lobe, n. lòbo m.

lobster, n. aragosta f.

local, 1. n. (train) òmnibus m.; accelerato m. 2. adj. locale.

locale, n. località f.

locality, n. località f.

localize, vb. localizzare.

locate, vb. collocare; (find) trovare; (be l.d) trovarsi.

location, n. situazione f.

lock, 1. n. serratura f.; (canal) chiusa f. 2. vb. chiùdere a chiave.

locker, n. armadietto m.; (baggage) depòsito bagagli automàtico m.

locket, n. medaglione m.

lockjaw, n. tètano m.

locksmith, n. fabbro di serratura m.

locomotion, n. locomozione f.

locomotive, n. locomotiva f., locomotore m.

locust, n. locusta f.

locution, n. locuzione f.

lode, n. filone m.

lodge, 1. n. casetta f. 2. vb. alloggiare.

lodger, n. òspite m.

lodging, n. allòggio m.

loft, n. solaio m.; (warehouse) magazzino m.

lofty, adj. alto.

log, n. ciòcco m., ceppo m.; (tree-trunk) tronco d'àlbero m.

loge, n. lòggia f.

logic, n. lògica f.

logical, adj. lògico.

loin, n. lombo m.; (food) lombata f.

loiter, vb. andare a zonzo.

Lombard, adj. lombardo.

Lombardy, n. Lombardìa f.

London, n. Londra f.; (of L.) londinese.

lone, lonely, lonesome, adj. solitàrio.

loneliness, n. solitùdine f.

long, 1. adj. lungo 2. vb. (l. for) bramare. 3. adv. lungamente.

longevity, n. longevità f.

longing, n. brama f.

longitude, n. longitùdine f.

longitudinal, adj. longitudinale.

long-lived, adj. longèvo.

look, 1. n. sguardo m.; (appearance) aspètto m. 2. vb. guardare; (l. out, take care) badare, vigilare.

looking glass, n. spècchio m.

loom, n. telaio m.

loop, n. càppio m., làccio m.

loophole, n. feritòia f.; (way out) scappatòia f.

loose, 1. adj. sciòlto. 2. vb. sciògliere.

loosen, vb. allentare, tr., sciògliere, tr.

loot, n. bottino m.

lop off, vb. mozzare.

lopsided, adj. mal equilibrato.

loquacious, adj. loquace.

lord, n. signore m.

lordship, n. signorìa f.

lorry, n. autocarro m.

lose, vb. pèrdere; (mislay) smarrire.

loss, n. pèrdita f.

lot, n. (fate) sòrte f.; (drawing) sortéggio m.; (group) lotto m.; (land) terreno m.; (a l. of, l.s of) molto adj.

lotion, n. lozione f.

lottery, n. lotterìa f.

lotus, n. lòto m.

loud, 1. adj. alto, fòrte. 2. adv. fòrte.

loud-speaker, n. altoparlante m.

lounge, 1. n. divano m., salone m. 2. vb. andare a zonzo.

louse, n. pidòcchio m.

lout, n. zoticone m.

louver, n. ventilatore m.

lovable, adj. amàbile.

love, 1. n. amore m. 2. vb. amare.

lovely, adj. bèllo, leggiadro.

lover, n. amante m. or f.

low, 1. adj. basso. 2. vb. mugghiare.

lowbrow, adj. poco intelligènte.

lower, 1. adj. inferiore. 2. vb. abbassare, tr.

lowly, adj. ùmile.

loyal, adj. leale.

loyalist, n. lealista m.

loyalty, n. lealtà f.

lozenge, n. losanga f.; (pastille) pasticca f.
lubricant, n. and adj. lubrificante (m.)
lubricate, vb. lubrificare.
lucid, adj. chiaro.
luck, n. fortuna f., sòrte f.; (bad l.) sfortuna f.
lucky, adj. fortunato.
lucrative, adj. lucrativo.
ludicrous, adj. ridicolo.
lug, vb. trascinare.
luggage, n. bagagli m.pl.
lukewarm, adj. tièpido.
lull, vb. cullare.
lullaby, n. ninna-nanna f.
lumbago, n. lombàggine f.
lumber, n. legname m.
luminous, adj. luminoso.
lump, 1. n. massa f., protuberanza f. 2. vb. ammassare.
lumpy, adj. pieno di protuberanze.
lunacy, n. pazzia f.
lunar, adj. lunare.
lunatic, n. and adj. lunàtico (m.)
lunch, n. colazione f.
luncheon, n. colazione f.
lung, n. polmone m.
lunge, vb. lanciarsi.
lurch, vb. traballare.
lure, vb. adescare.
lurid, adj. sensazionale.
lurk, vb. nascòndersi.
luscious, adj. saporoso.
lush, adj. lussureggiante.
lust, n. concupiscènza f.
luster, n. lustro m.
lustful, adj. concupiscènte.
lustrous, adj. rillucènte.
lusty, adj. vigoroso.
lute, n. liuto m.
Lutheran, adj. luterano.
luxuriant, adj. lussureggiante, rigoglioso.
luxurious, adj. lussuoso.
luxury, n. lusso m.
lying, adj. menzognèro, bugiardo, mendace.
lymph, n. linfa f.
lynch, vb. linciare.
lyre, n. lira f.
lyric, adj. lirico.
lyricism, n. liricismo m.

M

macabre, adj. màcabro.
macaroni, n. pasta asciutta f., maccheroni m.pl.
machine, n. màcchina f.
machine gun, n. mitragliatrice f.
machinery, n. meccanismo m.
machinist, n. macchinista m.
machismo, n. gallismo m.
macho, adj. fallòcrate.
mackerel, n. sgombro m.
mackinaw, n. impermeàbile m.
mad, adj. pazzo; (angry) furioso.
madam, n. signora f.

madcap, n. and adj. scervellato (m.)
madden, vb. far impazzire.
madrigal, n. madrigale m.
mafia, n. mafia f.
magazine, n. periòdico m., rivista f.
magic, 1. n. magia f. 2. adj. màgico.
magician, n. mago m.
magistrate, n. magistrato m.
magistrature, n. magistratura f.
magnanimous, adj. magnànimo.
magnate, n. magnate m.
magnesium, n. magnèsio m.
magnet, n. magnète m.
magnetic, adj. magnètico.
magnificence, n. magnificènza f.
magnificent, adj. magnifico.
magnify, vb. ingrandire.
magnitude, n. grandezza f.
mahogany, n. mògano m.
maid, n. domèstica f.; (old m.) zitèlla f.
maiden, n. fanciulla f.
mail, 1. n. pòsta f. 2. vb. impostare.
mail-box, n. buca per lettere f.
mailman, n. postino m.
maim, vb. storpiare.
main, adj. principale.
mainframe, n. parte centrale di una calcolatrice f.
mainland, n. tèrra ferma f.
mainspring, n. molla principale f.
maintain, vb. mantenere; (in argument) sostenere.
maintenance, n. mantenimento m.
maize, n. granturco m.
majestic, adj. maestoso.
majesty, n. maestà f.
major, n. and adj. maggiore (m.)
majority, n. maggioranza f.
make, vb. fare.
make-believe, 1. n. finta f. 2. adj. finto. 3. vb. fingere.
maker, n. fattore m.
makeshift, n. espediènte m.
make-up, n. belletto m.
malady, n. malattìa f.
malaria, n. malària f.
male, n. and adj. màschio (m.)
malevolent, adj. malèvolo.
malice, n. malevolènza f.
malicious, adj. maligno.
malign, 1. adj. maligno. 2. vb. diffamare.
malignant, adj. maligno.
malleable, adj. malleàbile.
malnutrition, n. cattiva nutrizione f.
malt, n. malto m.
maltreat, vb. maltrattare.
mammal, n. mammifero m.
man, n. uòmo m.
manage, vb. amministrare, dirigere.
management, n. amministrazione f., direzione f.

manager, n. amministratore m., direttore m.
mandate, n. mandato m.
mandatory, adj. obbligatòrio.
mandolin, n. mandolino m.
mane, n. crinièra f.
maneuver, 1. n. manòvra f. 2. vb. manovrare.
manganese, n. manganese m.
manger, n. mangiatoia f.
mangle, vb. tritare.
manhood, n. virilità f.
mania, n. manìa f.
maniac, n. and adj. maniaco (m.)
manicure, n. manicure f.
manifest, 1. adj. manifèsto. 2. vb. manifestare.
manifesto, n. manifèsto m.
manifold, adj. moltéplice.
manipulate, vb. manipolare.
mankind, n. umanità f.
manly, adj. virile.
manner, n. manièra f., mòdo m.
mannerism, n. manierismo m.
mansion, n. palazzo m.
manslaughter, n. omocidio m.
mantelpiece, n. cornice f.
mantle, n. mantèllo m.
Mantua, n. Màntova f.
Mantuan, n. and adj. mantovano (m.)
manual, n. and adj. manuale (m.)
manufacture, n. fabbricazione f.
manufacturer, n. fabbricante m.
manufacturing, adj. industriale.
manure, n. concime m.
manuscript, n. and adj. manoscritto (m.)
many, adj. molti m.pl.; molte f.pl.
map, n. carta f.
maple, n. àcero m.
mar, vb. danneggiare, guastare.
marble, n. marmo m.
march, 1. n. màrcia f. 2. vb. marciare.
March, n. marzo m.
mare, n. cavalla f.
margarine, n. margarina f.
margin, n. màrgine m.
marginal, adj. marginale.
marijuana, n. marijuana f.
marinate, vb. marinare.
marine, adj. marino, marìttimo.
mariner, n. marinaio m.
marionette, n. marionetta f.
marital, adj. maritale.
maritime, adj. marìttimo.
mark, 1. n. segno m. 2. vb. marcare, segnare.
market, n. mercato m.
market place, n. piazza del mercato m.
marmalade, n. marmellata f.
maroon, n. (color) marrone m.
marquee, n. pensilina f.
marquis, n. marchese m.
marriage, n. matrimònio m.

marrow, *n.* midollo *m.*

marry, *vb.* sposare, *tr.;* (woman) maritare, *tr.*

Marseilles, *n.* Marsiglia *f.*

marsh, *n.* palude *f.*

marshal, *n.* maresciallo *m.*

marital, *adj.* marziale.

martinet, *n.* tiranno *m.*

martyr, *n.* màrtire *m.*

martyrdom, *n.* martìrio *m.*

marvel, **1.** *n.* meraviglia *f.* **2.** *vb.* meravigliarsi.

marvelous, *adj.* meraviglioso.

mascara, *n.* kohl *m.*

mascot, *n.* portafortuna *m.*

masculine, *adj.* maschile.

mash, *vb.* schiacciare.

mask, **1.** *n.* màschera *f.* **2.** *vb.* mascherare.

mason, *n.* muratore *m.*

masquerade, **1.** *n.* mascherata *f.* **2.** *vb.* mascherarsi.

mass, *n.* massa *f.;* (church) messa *f.*

massacre, **1.** *n.* massacro *m.* **2.** *vb.* massacrare.

massage, **1.** *n.* massaggio *m.* **2.** *vb.* massaggiare.

masseur, *n.* massaggiatore *m.*

massive, *adj.* massiccio.

mass meeting, *n.* assemblèa *f.*

mast, *n.* àlbero *m.*

master, *n.* (boss) padrone *m.;* (great artist) maestro *m.;* (workman) mastro *m.*

master-key, *n.* comunèlla *f.*

masterpiece, *n.* capolavoro *m.*

mastery, *n.* padronanza *f.*

masticate, *vb.* masticare.

mat, *n.* stuòia *f.*

match, **1.** *n.* (light) fiammifero *m.;* (contest) incontro *m.;* (equal) uguale *m.;* (marriage) matrimònio *m.* **2.** *vb.* uguagliare.

mate, **1.** *n.* (spouse) consòrte *m. or f.;* (pal) compagno *m.;* (second in command) secondo *m.;* (assistant) assistènte *m.* **2.** *vb.* accoppiare, *tr.*

material, *n. and adj.* materiale *(m.).*

materialism, *n.* materialismo *m.*

materialize, *vb.* materializzare.

maternal, *adj.* matèrno.

maternity, *n.* maternità *f.*

mathematical, *adj.* matemàtico.

mathematics, *n.* matemàtica *f.*

matinée, *n.* mattinata *f.*

matriarchy, *n.* matriarcato *m.*

matrimony, *n.* matrimònio *m.*

matron, *n.* matrona *f.*

matter, **1.** *n.* matèria *f.;* (pus) pus *m.* **2.** *vb.* importare.

mattress, *n.* materasso *m.*

mature, **1.** *adj.* maturo **2.** *vb.* maturare; (fall due) scadere.

maturity, *n.* maturità *f.;* (financial) scadènza *f.*

maudlin, *adj.* piagnucoloso.

maul, *vb.* percuòtere.

mausoleum, *n.* mausolèo *m.*

maxim, *n.* màssima *f.*

maximum, *n. and adj.* màssimo *(m.).*

may, *vb.* potere.

May, *n.* màggio *m.*

maybe, *adv.* forse.

mayhem, *n.* danni *m.pl.*

mayonnaise, *n.* maionese *m.*

mayor, *n.* sìndaco *m.*

maze, *n.* labirinto *m.*

me, *pron.* me, mi.

meadow, *n.* prato *m.*

meager, *adj.* magro, scarso.

meal, *n.* pasto *m.;* (flour) farina *f.*

mean, **1.** *n.* mèdia *f.* **2.** *adj.* (in the middle) mèdio; (base) meschino, spregévole. **3.** *vb.* significare, voler dire.

meaning, *n.* significato *m.*

means, *n.* mèzzo *m.sg.*

meantime, meanwhile, *n.* frattèmpo *m.*

measles, *n.* morbillo *m.*

measure, **1.** *n.* misura *f.* **2.** *vb.* misurare.

measurement, *n.* misuramento *m.*

measuring, *adj.* misuratore.

meat, *n.* carne *f.*

mechanic, *n.* meccànico *m.*

mechanical, *adj.* meccànico.

mechanism, *n.* meccanismo *m.*

mechanize, *vb.* meccanizzare.

medal, *n.* medàglia *f.*

meddle, *vb.* immischiarsi.

medieval, *adj.* medioevale.

median, *adj.* mediano.

mediate, *vb.* fare da intermediàrio.

mediator, *n.* intermediàrio *m.*

medical, *adj.* mèdico.

medicate, *vb.* medicare.

medicine, *n.* medicina *f.*

mediocre, *adj.* mediòcre.

mediocrity, *n.* mediocrità *f.*

meditate, *vb.* meditare.

meditation, *n.* meditazione *f.*

Mediterranean, *n. and adj.* mediterràneo *(m.).*

medium, **1.** *n.* mèzzo *m.* **2.** *adj.* mèdio.

medley, *n.* miscùglio *m.*

meek, *adj.* mite.

meekness, *n.* mitezza *f.*

meet, *vb.* incontrare *tr.*

meeting, *n.* riunione *f.,* assemblèa *f.;* (**n.-place**) ritròvo *m.*

megahertz, *n.* megahertz *m.*

megaphone, *n.* megàfono *m.*

melancholy, **1.** *n.* malinconìa *f.* **2.** *adj.* malincònico, melancònico.

mellow, *adj.* maturato.

melodious, *adj.* melodioso.

melodrama, *n.* melodramma *m.*

melody, *n.* melodìa *f.*

melon, *n.* mellone *m.*

melt, *vb.* fóndere *tr.,* sciògliere *tr.*

meltdown, *n.* fusione *f.*

member, *n.* sòcio *m.,* membro *m.*

membership, *n.* (persons) affiliati *m.pl.*

membrane, *n.* membrana *f.*

memento, *n.* ricòrdo *m.*

memoir, *n.* memòria *f.*

memorable, *adj.* memoràbile.

memorandum, *n.* memorandum *m.*

memorial, **1.** *n.* monumento *m.,* memoriale *m.* **2.** *adj.* commemorativo.

memorize, *vb.* imparare a memòria.

memory, *n.* memòria *f.*

menace, **1.** *n.* minàccia *f.* **2.** *vb.* minacciare.

menagerie, *n.* serràglio *m.*

mend, *vb.* accomodare.

mendacious, *adj.* mendace.

mendicant, **1.** *n.* mèndico *m.* **2.** *adj.* mendicante.

menial, *adj.* servile.

menopause, *n.* menopàusa *f.*

menstruation, *n.* mestruazione *f.;* règole *f.pl.*

menswear, *n.* abbigliamento maschile *m.*

mental, *adj.* mentale.

mentality, *n.* mentalità *f.*

menthol, *n.* mentòlo *m.*

mention, **1.** *n.* menzione *f.* **2.** *vb.* menzionare.

menu, *n.* lista *f.*

mercantile, *adj.* mercantile.

mercenary, *adj.* mercenàrio.

merchandise, *n.* mercanzia *f.*

merchant, *n.* mercante *m.*

merchant marine, *n.* marina mercantile *f.*

merciful, *adj.* pietoso.

merciless, *adj.* spietato.

mercury, *n.* mercùrio *m.*

mercy, *n.* pietà *f.,* misericòrdia *f.*

mere, *adj.* mèro, sémplice.

merely, *adv.* meramente, semplicemente.

merge, *vb.* assorbire.

merger, *n.* fusione *f.*

meringue, *n.* meringa *f.*

merit, **1.** *n.* mèrito *m.* **2.** *vb.* meritare.

meritorious, *adj.* meritòrio.

mermaid, *n.* sirena *f.*

merriment, *n.* allegrezza *f.*

merry, *adj.* allegro.

merry-go-round, *n.* carosèllo *m.*

mesh, **1.** *n.* (fabric) màglia *f.* **2.** *vb.* (gears) ingranare.

mesmerize, *vb.* ipnotizzare.

mess, *n.* pasticcio *m.,* confusione *f.;* (soldiers' meals) ràncio *m.*

message, *n.* messàggio *m.,* ambasciata *f.*

messenger, *n.* messaggèro *m.*

messy, *adj.* confuso, disordinato.

metabolism, *n.* metabolismo *m.*

metal, *n.* metallo *m.*

metallic, *adj.* metàllico.

metamorphosis, *n.* metamòrfosi *f.*

metaphysics, *n.* metafìsica *f.*

meteor, *n.* metèora *f.*

meteorology, n. meteorologìa f.

meter, n. (recording device) contatore m.; (unit of measure) mètro m.

method, n. mètodo m.

meticulous, adj. meticoloso.

metric, adj. mètrico.

metropolis, n. metròpoli f.

metropolitan, adj. metropolitano.

mettle, n. coràggio f.

Mexican, adj. messicano.

Mexico, n. il Mèssico m.

mezzanine, n. mezzanino m.

microbe, n. micròbio m.

microfiche, n. microscheda f.

microfilm, n. mìcrofilm m.

microform, n. microforma f.

microphone, n. micròfono m.

microscope, n. microscòpio m.

microscopic, adj. microscòpico.

mid-, adj. mèdio.

middle, 1. n. mèzzo m. 2. adj. mèdio, intermèdio, mèzzo.

middle-aged, adj. di mèzza età.

Middle Ages, n. medioèvo m.

middle class, n. borghesìa f., ceto mèdio m., classe mèdia f.

Middle East, n. Medio Oriente m.

midget, n. nano m.

midnight, n. mezzanòtte f.

midriff, n. diaframma m.

midwife, n. levatrice f.

mien, n. aspètto m., cera f.

might, 1. n. potènza f. 2. vb. use conditional of potere.

mighty, adj. potènte.

migraine, n. emicrània f.

migrate, vb. migrare.

migration, n. migrazione f.

migratory, adj. migratòrio.

Milan, n. Milano f.

Milanese, adj. milanese.

mild, adj. mite.

mildew, n. muffa bianca f.

mildness, n. mitezza f.

mile, n. miglio m.

mileage, n. chilometràggio m.

milestone, n. piètra miliare f.

militant, adj. militante.

militarism, n. militarismo m.

military, adj. militare.

militia, n. milìzia f.

milk, 1. n. latte m. 2. vb. mùngere.

milk-bar, n. latterìa f.

milkman, n. lattaio m.

milky, adj. làtteo.

mill, 1. n. mulino m.; (factory) fàbbrica f. 2. vb. macinare.

miller, n. mugnaio m.

millimeter, n. millìmetro m.

milliner, n. modista m. or f.

millinery, n. modisterìa f.

million, n. milione m.

millionaire, n. milionàrio m.

mimic, 1. n. imitatore m. 2. adj. imitato. 3. vb. imitare.

mince, vb. triturare.

mind, 1. n. mente f., ànimo m. 2. vb. badare a; (obey) ubbi-

dire a; (never m.) non impòrta.

mindful, adj. mèmore.

mine, 1. n. minièra f.; (explosive) mina f. 2. adj. mìo. 3. vb. minare.

mine field, n. campo minato m.

miner, n. minatore m.

mineral, n. and adj. minerale (m.).

mine-sweeper, n. nave spazzamine f.

mingle, vb. mescolare, tr.

miniature, n. miniatura f.

miniaturize, vb. miniaturizzare.

minimize, vb. ridurre al mìnimo.

minimum, n. and adj. mìnimo (m.).

minimum wage, n. salàrio mìnimo m.

mining, 1. n. coltivazione delle minière f. 2. adj. mineràrio.

minister, 1. n. ministro m. 2. vb. ministrare.

ministry, n. ministèro m.

mink, n. visone m.

minnow, n. pesciolino m.

minor, 1. n. (person under 21) minorènne. 2. adj. minore, minorènne.

minority, n. minoranza f.; (age) minorità f.

minstrel, n. menestrèllo m.

mint, 1. n. (plant) menta f.; (coin factory) zecca f. 2. vb. coniare.

minus, prep. meno.

minute, 1. n. minuto m.; (of meeting) verbale m. 2. adj. minuto.

miracle, n. miràcolo m.

miraculous, adj. miracoloso.

mirage, n. miràggio m.

mire, n. fango m.

mirror, n. spècchio m.

mirth, n. allegrìa f.

misadventure, n. disgràzia f.

misappropriate, vb. appropriare indebitamente.

misbehave, vb. comportarsi male.

miscellaneous, adj. miscellàneo.

mischief, n. cattivèria f., malìzia f.

mischievous, adj. cattivo, malizioso.

misconstrue, vb. fraintèndere.

miscreant, n. and adj. miscredènte.

misdemeanor, n. contravvenzione f.

miser, n. avaro m.

miserable, adj. mìsero.

miserly, adj. avaro.

misery, n. misèria f.

misfit, n. persona inadatta f.

misfortune, n. sfortuna f.

misgiving, n. apprensione f., dùbbio m.

mishap, n. disgràzia f.

mislay, vb. smarrire.

mislead, vb. ingannare.

misplace, vb. smarrire.

misplaced, adj. fuòri di propòsito.

mispronounce, vb. pronunziar male.

miss, 1. n. (unsuccessful shot) colpo mancato m. 2. vb. mancare, pèrdere; (feel the lack of) sentire la mancanza di.

Miss, n. signorina f.

missile, n. missile m.

mission, n. missione f.

missionary, n. and adj. missionàrio (m.).

misspell, vb. scrivere scorrettamente.

mist, n. nèbbia f.

mistake, 1. n. sbàglio m. 2. vb. sbagliare.

mistaken, adj. errato, erròneo, sbagliato.

mister, n. signore m.

mistletoe, n. vìschio m.

mistreat, vb. maltrattare, bistrattare.

mistress, n. padrona f.; (lover) amante f.

mistrust, 1. n. sfidùcia f. 2. vb. diffidare di.

misty, adj. nebbioso.

misunderstand, vb. fraintèndere.

misuse, vb. abusare di.

mite, n. (coin) òbolo m.; (small piece) pezzettino m.; (tot) piccino m.

mitigate, vb. mitigare.

mitten, n. guanto m.

mix, vb. mescolare, tr.

mixture, n. mescolanza f., mistura f.

mix-up, n. confusione f.

moan, 1. n. gèmito m. 2. vb. gèmere.

moat, n. fòssa f.

mob, n. fòlla f., plebàglia f.

mobile, adj. mòbile.

mobilization, n. mobilitazione f.

mobilize, vb. mobilitare.

mock, 1. adj. finto. 2. vb. deridere, beffarsi di, schernire.

mockery, n. derisione f., scherno m.

mod, adj. moderno.

mode, n. (way) mòdo m.; (fashion) mòda f.

model, 1. n. modèllo m. 2. vb. modellare.

moderate, 1. adj. moderato. 2. vb. moderare.

moderation, n. moderazione f.

modern, adj. modèrno.

modernize, vb. rimodernare, tr.

modest, adj. modèsto.

modesty, n. modèstia f.

modify, vb. modificare.

modish, adj. alla mòda.

modulate, vb. modulare.

moist, adj. ùmido.

moisten, vb. inumidire.

moisture, n. umidità f.

molar, adj. molare.

molasses, n. melassa f.

mold, 1. n. forma f., stampo

m.; (must) muffa *f.* **2.** *vb.* formare, modellare.

moldy, *adj.* muffito.

mole, *n.* (animal) talpa *f.;* (pier) mòlo *m.*

molecule, *n.* molècola *f.*

molest, *vb.* molestare.

mollify, *vb.* ammollire.

molten, *adj.* fuso.

moment, *n.* momènto *m.*

momentary, *adj.* momentàneo.

momentous, *adj.* importante.

monarch, *n.* monarca *m.*

monarchy, *n.* monarchìa *f.*

monastery, *n.* monastèro *m.*

Monday, *n.* lunedì *m.*

monetary, *adj.* monetàrio.

money, *n.* denaro *m.*

money-order, *n.* vàglia *m.*

mongrel, *n. and adj.* bastardo *(m.).*

monitor, *n.* monitore *m.*

monk, *n.* mònaco *m.*

monkey, *n.* scimmia *f.*

monocle, *n.* monòcolo *m.*

monologue, *n.* monòlogo *m.*

monoplane, *n.* monoplano *m.*

monopolize, *vb.* monopolizzare.

monopoly, *n.* monopòlio *m.*

monosyllable, *n.* monosìllabo *m.*

monotone, *n.* tono uniforme *m.*

monotonous, *adj.* monòtono.

monotony, *adj.* monotonìa *f.*

monoxide, *n.* monòssido *m.*

monsoon, *n.* monsone *m.*

monster, **1.** *n.* mostro *m.* **2.** *adj.* (huge) immènso.

monstrosity, *n.* mostruosità *f.*

monstrous, *adj.* mostruoso.

month, *n.* mese *m.*

monthly, *adj.* mensile.

monument, *n.* monumento *m.*

monumental, *adj.* monumentale.

mood, *n.* stato d'ànimo *m.*

moody, *adj.* triste.

moon, *n.* luna *f.*

moonlight, *n.* chiaro di luna *m.*

moor, **1.** *n.* brughièra *f.* **2.** *vb.* ormeggiare.

mooring, *n.* ormèggio *m.*

moot, *adj.* discusso.

mop, *n.* scopa di stracci *f.*

moped, *n.* ciclomotore *m.*

moral, *n. and adj.* morale *(f.).*

morale, *n.* morale *m.*

moralist, *n.* moralista *m.*

morality, *n.* moralità *f.*

morally, *adv.* moralmente.

morbid, *adj.* morboso.

more, *adv.* più; (m. and m.) sempre più.

moreover, *adv.* per di più.

mores, *n.* costumi *m.pl.*

morgue, *n.* càmera mortuària *f.*

morning, *n.* mattina *f.*, mattino *m.*

moron, *n.* imbecille *m.*

morose, *adj.* poco sociévole.

morphine, *n.* morfina *f.*

Morse code, *n.* còdice Morse *m.*

morsel, *n.* (food) boccone *m.;* (piece) frammènto *m.*

mortal, *n. and adj.* mortale *(m.).*

mortality, *n.* mortalità *f.*

mortar, *n.* calcina *f.*

mortgage, **1.** *n.* ipotèca *f.* **2.** *vb.* ipotecare.

mortician, *n.* imprenditore di pompe funebri *m.*

mortify, *vb.* mortificare.

mortuary, *adj.* mortuàrio.

mosaic, *n.* mosàico *m.*

mosquito, *n.* zanzara *f.;* (m. net) zanzarièra *f.*

moss, *n.* mùschio *m.*

most, **1.** *adj.* la maggior parte di. **2.** *adj.* maggiormente.

mostly, *adv.* per lo più.

moth, *n.* tarma *f.*

mother, *n.* madre *f.*, mamma *f.*

mother-in-law, *n.* suòcera *f.*

motif, *n.* motivo *m.*

motion, *n.* mòto *m.;* (parliamentary) mozione *f.*

motionless, *adj.* immòbile.

motion-picture, *n.* pellìcola *f.*

motivate, *vb.* motivare.

motive, **1.** *n.* motivo *m.* **2.** *adj.* motore; (m. power) fòrza motrice.

motley, *n.* eterogèneo, multicolore.

motor, *n.* motore *m.*

motorboat, *n.* motoscafo *m.*

motorcycle, *n.* motocicletta *f.*

motorist, *n.* automobilista *m.*

motorize, *vb.* motorizzare.

motorized farming, *n.* motocultura *f.*

motto, *n.* motto *m.*

mound, *n.* tùmulo *m.*

mount, *vb.* montare, salire.

mountain, *n.* montagna *f.*, monte *m.*

mountaineer, *n.* montanaro *m.*

mountainous, *adj.* montagnoso, montuoso.

mountebank, *n.* ciarlatano *m.*

mourn, *vb.* piàngere.

mournful, *adj.* doloroso.

mourning, *n.* lutto *m.*

mouse, *n.* sórcio *m.*, tòpo *m.*

mouth, *n.* bocca *f.*

mouthpiece, *n.* (instrument) imboccatura *f.;* (spokesman) portavoce *m.*

movable, *adj.* mòbile.

move, **1.** *n.* (household goods) traslòco *m.* **2.** *vb.* muòvere, *tr.*

movement, *n.* movimento *m.*

movie, *n.* cinema *m.*, film *m.*

moving, **1.** *n.* (household goods) traslòco *m.* **2.** *adj.* commovènte.

mow, *vb.* falciare.

Mr., *n.* Sig. *m.* (abbr. for Signore).

Mrs., *n.* Sra. *f.* (abbr. for Signora).

much, *adj. and adv.* molto.

mucilage, *n.* gomma liquida *f.*

muck, *n.* letame *m.*, melma *f.*

mucous, *adj.* mucoso.

mucus, *n.* muco *m.*

mud, *n.* fango *m.*, lòto *m.*

muddy, *adj.* fangoso.

muff, **1.** *n.* manicotto *m.* **2.** *vb.* sbagliare.

muffle, *vb.* (wrap up) imbacuccare, *tr.;* (silence) attutire.

muffler, *n.* (scarf) sciarpa *f.;* (auto) silenziatore dello scàrico *m.*

mug, *n.* coppa *f.*

mulatto, *n.* mulatto *m.*

mule, *n.* mulo *m.*

mullah, *n.* mulla(h) *m.*

multicolored, *adj.* multicolore.

multinational, *adj.* multinazionale.

multiple, *adj.* mùltiplo.

multiplication, *n.* moltiplicazione *f.*

multiplicity, *n.* molteplicità *f.*

multiply, *vb.* moltiplicare, *tr.*

multitude, *n.* moltitùdine *f.*

mummy, *n.* mùmmia *f.*

mumps, *n.* orecchioni *m.pl.*

munch, *vb.* sgranocchiare.

Munich, *n.* Mònaco di Bavièra *m.*

municipal, *adj.* municipale.

munificent, *adj.* munificènte.

munition, *n.* munizione *f.*

mural, *adj.* murale.

murder, *n.* assassinio *m.*

murderer, *n.* assassino *m.*

murmur, **1.** *n.* mormorio *m.* **2.** *vb.* mormorare.

muscle, *n.* mùscolo *m.*

muscular, *adj.* muscolare.

muse, **1.** *n.* musa *f.* **2.** *vb.* meditare.

museum, *n.* musèo *m.*

mushroom, *n.* fungo *m.*

music, *n.* mùsica *f.*

musical, *adj.* musicale.

musical comedy, *n.* operetta *f.*, rivista *f.*

musician, *n.* musicista *m.*

muslin, *n.* mussolina *f.*

must, *n.* use present of dovere.

mustache, *n.* baffi *m.pl.*

mustard, *n.* sènape *f.*, mostarda *f.*

muster, **1.** *n.* rivista *f.* **2.** *vb.* radunare.

musty, *adj.* ammuffito.

mutation, *n.* mutazione *f.*

mute, *adj.* muto.

mutilate, *vb.* mutilare.

mutiny, **1.** *n.* ammutinamento *m.* **2.** *vb.* ammutinarsi.

mutter, *vb.* borbottare.

mutton, *n.* carne di montone *f.*

mutual, *adj.* mùtuo.

muzzle, *n.* (gun) bocca *f.;* (animal's mouth) muso *m.;* (mouth covering) museruòla *f.*

my, *adj.* mìo.

myopia, *n.* miopìa *f.*

myriad, **1.** *n.* mirìade *f.* **2.** *adj.* innumerévole.

myrtle, *n.* mirto *m.*

myself, *pron.* me stesso; (I m.) ìo stesso.

mysterious, *adj.* misterioso.

mystery, *n.* mistèro *m.*

mystic, *adj.* mìstico.

mystify, *vb.* mistificare.

myth, *n.* mito *m.*

mythical, *adj.* mìtico.

mythology, *n.* mitologìa *f.*

N

nag, 1. *n.* ronzino *m.* 2. *vb.* tormentare.

nail, 1. *n.* chiòdo *m.* 2. *vb.* inchiodare.

naïve, *adj.* ingènuo.

naked, *adj.* nudo.

name, 1. *n.* nome *m.;* (family n.) cognome *m.* 2. *vb.* chiamare; (nominate) nominare.

namely, *adv.* cioè.

namesake, *n.* omònimo *m.*

nap, 1. *n.* pisolino *m.,* sonnellino *m.* 2. *vb.* sonnecchiare.

naphtha, *n.* nafta *f.*

napkin, *n.* tovagliòlo *m.*

Naples, *n.* Nàpoli *f.*

narcissus, *n.* narciso *m.*

narcotic, *n. and adj.* narcòtico (*m.*)

narrate, *vb.* narrare.

narrative, 1. *n.* racconto *m.* 2. *adj.* narrativo.

narration, *n.* narrazione *f.*

narrow, *adj.* stretto.

nasal, *adj.* nasale.

nasty, *adj.* disgustoso, antipàtico.

natal, *adj.* natale.

nation, *n.* nazione *f.*

national, *adj.* nazionale.

nationalism, *n.* nazionalismo *m.*

nationality, *n.* nazionalità *f.*

nationalization, *n.* nazionalizzazione *f.*

nationalize, *vb.* nazionalizzare.

native, 1. *n.* indìgeno *m.* 2. *adj.* nativo, indìgeno.

nativity, *n.* natività *f.*

natural, *adj.* naturale.

naturalist, *n.* naturalista *m.*

naturalize, *vb.* naturalizzare.

naturalness, *n.* naturalezza *f.*

nature, *n.* natura *f.*

naughty, *adj.* birichino.

nausea, *n.* nàusea *f.*

nauseating, *adj.* nauseante.

nautical, *adj.* nàutico.

naval, *adj.* navale.

nave, *n.* navata *f.*

navel, *n.* ombellico *m.*

navigable, *adj.* navigàbile.

navigate, *vb.* navigare.

navigation, *n.* navigazione *f.*

navigator, *n.* navigatore *m.*

navy, *n.* marina *f.*

navy yard, *n.* arsenale *m.*

Neapolitan, *adj.* napoletano.

near, 1. *adj., adv.* vicino. 2. *prep.* vicino a.

nearby, *adv.* vicino.

nearly, *adv.* quasi.

near-sighted, *adj.* miope.

neat, *adj.* lindo.

neatness, *n.* lindezza *f.*

nebula, *n.* nebulosa *f.*

nebulous, *adj.* nebuloso.

necessary, *adj.* necessàrio; (be n.) bisognare, volerci.

necessity, *n.* necessità *f.*

neck, *n.* collo *m.*

necklace, *n.* collana *f.*

necktie, *n.* cravatta *f.*

nectar, *n.* nèttare *m.*

need, 1. *n.* bisogno *m.* 2. *vb.* aver bisogno di.

needful, *adj.* necessàrio.

needle, *n.* ago *m.;* (phonograph) puntina *f.*

needless, *adj.* inùtile.

needy, *adj.* bisognoso.

nefarious, *adj.* nefàrio.

negative, 1. *n.* negativa *f.* 2. *adj.* negativo.

neglect, *vb.* trascurare.

negligée, *n.* vestàglia *f.*

negligent, *adj.* trascurato.

negligible, *adj.* trascuràbile.

negotiate, *vb.* negoziare.

negotiation, *n.* negoziazione *f.*

Negro, *n.* negro *m.*

neighbor, *n.* vicino *m.,* pròssimo *m.*

neighborhood, *n.* vicinanza *f.*

neither, *conj.* nè.

neon, *n.* nèon *m.*

neophyte, *n.* neòfita *m.*

nephew, *n.* nipote *m.*

nepotism, *n.* nepotismo *m.*

nerve, *n.* nèrvo *m.;* (effrontery) sfrontatezza *f.*

nervous, *adj.* nervoso.

nest, *n.* nido *m.*

nestle, *vb.* annidarsi.

net, *n.* rete *f.*

netting, *n.* rete *f.*

network, *n.* rete *f.*

neuralgia, *n.* nevralgìa *f.*

neurology, *n.* neurologìa *f.*

neurotic, *adj.* nevròtico.

neutral, *n. and adj.* nèutro (*m.*).

neutrality, *n.* neutralità *f.*

neutron, *n.* neutrone *m.*

neutron bomb, *n.* bomba al neutrone *f.*

never, *adv.* mai.

nevertheless, *adv.* nondimeno.

new, *adj.* nuòvo.

news, *n.* notìzie *f.pl.*

news-boy, *n.* giornalaio *m.*

newscast, *n.* radiocorrière *m.*

newspaper, *n.* giornale *m.*

newsreel, *n.* attualità *f.pl.*

next, *adj.* pròssimo, seguènte.

nibble, *vb.* rosicchiare.

nice, *adj.* gentile, buòno.

nick, *n.* tacca *f.*

nickel, *n.* nichel *m.*

nickname, *n.* nomìgnolo *m.*

nicotine, *n.* nicotina *f.*

niece, *n.* nipote *f.*

niggardly, *adj.* taccagno.

night, *n.* nòtte *f.*

night club, *n.* ritròvo notturno *m.*

nightgown, *n.* camìcia da nòtte *f.*

nightingale, *n.* usignuòlo *m.*

nightly, *adv.* ogni nòtte.

nightmare, *n.* incubo *m.*

night-stick, *n.* clava *f.*

nimble, *adj.* àgile.

nine, *num.* nòve.

nineteen, *num.* diciannòve.

nineteenth, *adj.* dècimo nòno, diciannovèsimo.

ninetieth, *adj.* novantèsimo.

ninety, *num.* novanta.

ninth, *adj.* nòno.

nip, *n.* pizzicotto *m.*

nipple, *n.* capézzolo *m.*

nitrate, *n.* nitrato *m.*

nitrogen, *n.* nitrògeno *m.*

no, 1. *adj.* nessuno. 2. *interj.* nò.

nobility, *n.* nobiltà *f.*

noble, *n. and adj.* nòbile (*m.*).

nobleman, *n.* nobiluòmo *m.*

nobly, *adv.* nobilmente.

nobody, *pron.* nessuno.

nocturnal, *adj.* notturno.

nocturne, *n.* notturno *m.*

nod, 1. *n.* cenno del capo *m.* 2. fare un cenno col capo.

node, *n.* nòdo *m.*

no-frills, *adj.* sèmplice.

noise, *n.* rumore *m.*

noiseless, *adj.* silenzioso.

noisome, *adj.* puzzolènte.

noisy, *adj.* rumoroso.

nomad, *n.* nòmade *m.*

nominal, *adj.* nominale.

nominate, *vb.* nominare, designare.

nomination, *n.* nòmina *f.*

nominee, *n.* designato *m.,* candidato *m.*

nonaligned, *adj.* non allineato.

nonchalant, *adj.* incurante.

noncombatant, *n. and adj.* non combattènte (*m.*).

non-commissioned officer, *n.* sottufficiale *m.*

noncommittal, *adj.* che non si compromette.

nondescript, *adj.* sènza caratteristiche speciali.

none, *adj. and pron.* nessuno.

nonentity, *n.* nullità *f.*

nonpartisan, *adj.* nèutro.

nonresident, *adj.* non residènte.

nonsense, *n.* assurdità *f.,* fandònie *f.pl.*

nonstop, *adj.* sènza fermate.

noodles, *n.* tagliatèlle *f.pl.*

nook, *n.* cantùccio *m.*

noon, *n.* mezzogiorno *m.*

noose, *n.* nodo scorsoio *m.*

nor, *conj.* nè.

norm, *n.* nòrma *f.*

normal, *adj.* normale.

normally, *adv.* normalmente.

north, 1. *n.* nord *m.* 2. *adj.* settentrionale.

northeast, *n.* nord-èst *m.*

northern, *adj.* settentrionale.

North Pole, *n.* polo nord *m.*

northwest, *n.* nord-òvest *m.*

Norway, *n.* Norvègia *f.*

Norwegian, *adj.* norvegese.

nose, *n.* naso *m.*

nosebleed, *n.* emorragìa nasale *f.*

nose dive, *n.* picchiata *f.*

nostalgia, *n.* nostalgìa *f.*

nostril, n. narice f.

nostrum, n. rimèdio empìrico m.

not, adv. non.

notable, adj. notévole.

notary, n. notaio m.

notation, n. notazione f.

notch, 1. n. tacca f. 2. vb. intaccare.

note, 1. n. nòta f.; (short letter) biglietto m. 2. vb. notare.

notebook, n. agènda f., taccuino m.

notepaper, n. carta da léttera f.

noted, adj. nòto.

noteworthy, adj. rimarchévole.

nothing, pron. niènte, nulla.

notice, 1. n. avviso m., attenzione f. 2. vb. osservare.

noticeable, adj. notévole.

notification, n. notificazione f., avviso m.

notify, vb. notificare.

notion, n. nozione f.

notoriety, n. notorietà f.

notorious, adj. famigerato, notòrio.

notwithstanding, prep. nonostante.

noun, n. sostantivo m.

nourish, vb. nutrire.

nourishment, n. nutrimento m.

novel, 1. n. romanzo m. 2. adj. originale.

novelist, n. romanzière m.

novelty, n. novità f.

November, n. novèmbre m.

novena, n. novèna f.

novice, n. novìzio m.

Novocaine, n. novocaìna f.

now, adv. ora, adèsso.

nowhere, adv. in nessun luògo.

nozzle, n. imboccatura f.

nuance, n. sfumatura f.

nuclear, adj. nucleare.

nuclear warhead, n. testata càrica nucleare f.

nuclear waste, n. rifiuti nucleari m.pl.

nucleus, n. nùcleo m.

nude, adj. nudo.

nugget, n. pepita f.

nuisance, n. fastìdio m., seccatura f.

nuke, n. arma nucleare f.

nullify, vb. annullare.

number, 1. n. nùmero m. 2. vb. numerare.

numerical, adj. numèrico.

numerous, adj. numeroso.

nun, n. mònaca f., suòra f.

nuncio, n. nùnzio m.

nuptial, adj. nuziale.

nurse, 1. n. (hospital) infermièra f.; (wet-nurse) nutrice f., bàlia f.; (baby-tender) bambinaia f. 2. vb. curare.

nursery, n. stanza dei bambini f.; (plants) vivaio m.

nurture, vb. allevare, curare.

nut, n. nocciòla f.

nut-cracker, n. schiaccionoci m.

nutrition, n. nutrizione f.

nutritious, adj. nutriènte.

nutshell, n. gùscio di noce m.

nylon, n. nàilon m.

nymph, n. ninfa f.

O

oak, n. quèrcia f.

oar, n. remo m.

oasis, n. oasi f.

oath, n. (solemn) giuramento m.; (swear-word) bestèmmia f.

oatmeal, n. fiocchi d'avena m.pl.

oats, n. avena f.sg.

obdurate, adj. ostinato.

obedience, n. obbediènza f.

obedient, adj. obbediènte.

obeisance, n. riverènza f.

obelisk, n. obelisco m.

obese, adj. obèso.

obey, vb. ubbidire.

obituary, n. necrològio m.

object, 1. n. oggetto m. 2. vb. opporsi, obiettare.

objection, n. obiezione f.

objectionable, adj. offensivo.

objective, n. and adj. obiettivo (m.)

obligation, n. òbbligo m., obbligazione f.

obligatory, adj. obbligatòrio.

oblige, vb. obbligare.

obliging, adj. serviziévole.

oblique, adj. obliquo.

obliterate, vb. cancellare.

oblivion, n. oblìo m.

oblong, adj. oblungo.

obnoxious, adj. odioso.

obscene, adj. oscèno.

obscure, adj. oscuro.

obsequious, adj. ossequioso.

observance, n. osservanza f.

observation, n. osservazione f.

observatory, n. osservatòrio m.

observe, vb. osservare.

observer, n. osservatore m.

obsession, n. ossessione f.

obsolete, adj. caduto in disuso.

obstacle, n. ostàcolo m.

obstetrical, adj. ostètrico.

obstetrician, n. ostètrico m.

obstinate, adj. ostinato.

obstreperous, adj. clamoroso, chiassoso.

obstruct, vb. ostruire, ostacolare.

obstruction, n. ostruzione f.

obtain, vb. ottenere.

obtrude, vb. intrùdersi.

obtuse, adj. ottuso.

obviate, vb. evitare.

obvious, adj. òvvio.

occasion, 1. n. occasione f. 2. vb. cagionare.

occasional, adj. occasionale.

occasionally, adv. di quando in quando.

Occident, n. occidènte m.

occidental, adj. occidentale.

occult, adj. occulto.

occupant, n. occupante m., inquilino m.

occupation, n. occupazione f., professione f.

occupy, vb. occupare.

occur, vb. accadere, succèdere.

occurrence, n. avvenimento m.

ocean, n. ocèano m.

o'clock, n. ora f.

octagon, n. ottàgono m.

octave, n. ottava f.

October, n. ottobre m.

octopus, n. ottòpode m.

ocular, adj. oculare.

oculist, n. oculista m.

odd, adj. (numbers) dispari; (queer) strano.

oddity, n. stranezza f.

odds, n. probabilità f.

odious, adj. odioso.

odor, n. odore m.

of, prep. di; (from) da.

off, adv. vìa.

offend, vb. offèndere.

offender, n. offensore m.; (accused) imputato m.

offense, n. offesa f.

offensive, 1. n. offensiva f. 2. adj. offensivo.

offer, 1. n. offèrta f. 2. vb. offrire.

offering, n. offèrta f.

offhand, adv. estemporaneamente.

office, n. ufficio m.; (dentist's, doctor's) gabinetto m.; (o. supplies) oggetti di cancelleria m.pl.

officer, n. ufficiale m.

official, n. and adj. ufficiale (m.).

officiate, vb. officiare.

officious, adj. inframmettènte.

offshore, adv. vicino alla tèrra.

offspring, n. pròle f.

often, adv. spesso.

oil, 1. n. òlio m. 2. vb. ùngere, lubrificare.

oil-cloth, n. tela cerata f.

oily, adj. oleoso.

ointment, n. unguènto m.

okay, interj. va bene.

old, adj. vècchio.

old-fashioned, adj. passato di mòda.

olfactory, adj. olfattòrio.

oligarchy, n. oligarchìa f.

olive, n. (tree) olivo m.; (fruit) oliva f.

ombudsman, n. mediatore m.

omelet, n. frittata f.

omen, n. presàgio m.

ominous, adj. infausto.

omission, n. omissione f.

omit, vb. omèttere.

omnibus, n. àutobus m.

omnipotent, adj. omnipotènte.

on, adv. and prep. su, sopra.

once, adv. una vòlta; (formerly) un tèmpo.

one, num. uno.

oneself, pron. sè stesso (sg.); sè stessi (pl.).

one-sided, adj. unilaterale.

one-way, adj. (fare) di corsa sèmplice; (street) a sènso ùnico.

onion, n. cipolla f.

onion-skin, n. carta velina f.

only, 1. adj. ùnico. 2. adv. solamente, soltanto; (but) ma.

onslaught, n. attacco m.

onus, n. ònere m.

onward, adv. avanti.

ooze, 1. n. melma f. 2. vb. trasudare.

opacity, n. opacità f.

opal, n. opale m.

opaque, adj. opaco.

open, 1. adj. apèrto. 2. vb. aprire.

opening, n. (breach) apertura f.; (start) inizio m.; inaugurazione f.

opera, n. òpera f.

opera-glasses, n. binòcolo da teatro m.(sg.)

operate, vb. operare.

operatic, adj. lìrico.

operation, n. operazione f.

operative, adj. operativo.

operator, n. operatore m.

operetta, n. operetta f.

ophthalmic, adj. oftàlmico.

opinion, n. opinione f., parere m.

opponent, n. antagonista m.

opportunism, n. opportunismo m.

opportunity, n. occasione f.

oppose, vb. opporre, tr.

opposite, 1. n. and adj. oppòsto (m.). 2. adv. dirimpètto. 3. prep. dirimpètto a.

opposition, n. opposizione f.

oppress, vb. opprìmere.

oppression, n. oppressione f.

oppressive, adj. oppressivo.

oppressor, n. oppressore m.

optic, adj. òttico.

optician, n. òttico m.

optics, n. òttica f.

optimism, n. ottimismo m.

optimistic, adj. ottimìstico.

option, n. opzione f.

optional, adj. facoltativo.

optometry, n. optometria f.

opulence, n. opulènza f.

opulent, adj. opulènto.

or, conj. o (before o, od); sia, ossia.

oracle, n. oràcolo m.

oral, adj. orale.

orange, n. (tree) aràncio m.; (fruit) arància f.

orangeade, n. aranciata f.

oration, n. orazione f.

orator, n. oratore m.

oratory, n. oratòria f.

orbit, n. òrbita f.

orchard, n. òrto m., frutteto m.

orchestra, n. orchèstra f.

orchid, n. orchidèa f.

ordain, vb. ordinare.

ordeal, n. ordàlia f.; (fig.) pròva f.

order, 1. n. òrdine m. 2. vb. ordinare.

orderly, adj. ordinato.

ordinance, n. ordinanza f.

ordinary, adj. ordinàrio.

ordination, n. ordinazione f.

ore, n. minerale m.

organ, n. òrgano m.

organdy, n. organza f.

organic, adj. orgànico.

organism, n. organismo m.

organist, n. organista m.

organization, n. organizzazione f.

organize, vb. organizzare.

orgy, n. òrgia f.

orient, vb. orientare.

Orient, n. Oriènte m.

Oriental, adj. orientale.

orientation, n. orientazione f.

origin, n. origine f.

original, adj. originale; (former) primitivo.

originality, n. originalità f.

ornament, 1. n. ornamento m. 2. vb. ornare.

ornamental, adj. ornamentale.

ornate, adj. ornato.

ornithology, n. ornitologia f.

orphan, n. and adj. òrfano (m.).

orphanage, n. orfanotròfio m.

orthodox, adj. ortodòsso.

orthography, n. ortografia f.

orthopedic, adj. ortopèdico.

oscillate, vb. oscillare.

osmosis, n. osmòsi f.

ostensible, adj. ostensìbile.

ostentation, n. ostentazione f.

ostentatious, adj. ostentato.

ostracize, vb. ostracizzare.

ostrich, n. struzzo m.

other, adj. altro.

otherwise, adv. altrimenti.

ouch, interj. ahi!

ought, vb. use conditional of dovere.

ounce, n. óncia f.

our, adj. nòstro.

ours, pron. nòstro.

ourselves, pron. noi stessi m., noi stesse f.

oust, vb. espèllere.

ouster, n. espulsione f.

out, adv. fuòri.

outbreak, n. scòppio m.

outburst, n. scòppio m.

outcast, n. pària m.

outcome, n. evènto m.

outdoors, adv. all'apèrto.

outer, adj. esteriore.

outfit, 1. n. corredo m. 2. vb. corredare, fornire.

outgrowth, n. risultato m.

outing, n. escursione f., gita f.

outlandish, adj. curioso, strano.

outlaw, n. bandito m.

outlet, n. sbocco m., sfògo m.; (electrical) presa elèttrica f.

outline, n. schizzo m.

outlive, vb. sopravvìvere a.

out of, prep. fuòri di; (motion) fuòri da.

out-of-date, adj. arretrato.

outpost, n. avamposto m.

output, n. produzione f.; rendimento m.

outrage, n. oltràggio m.

outrageous adj. oltraggioso.

outrank, vb. precèdere.

outright, adv. completamente.

outrun, vb. oltrepassare.

outside, 1. n. and adj. estèrno (m.). 2. adv. fuòri. 3. prep. fuòri di; (except) all'infuòri di.

outskirts, n. sobborghi m.pl., periferia f.

outward, 1. adj. esteriore. 2. adv. vèrso l'estèrno.

outwardly, adv. esteriormente.

oval, n. and adj. ovale m.

ovary, n. ovàia f.

ovation, n. ovazione f.

oven, n. forno m.

over, adv. and prep. sopra; (o. again) di nuòvo; (o. and o.) ripetutamente.

overbearing, adj. prepotènte.

overcoat, n. soprabìto m.

overcome, vb. sopraffare, superare.

overdue, adj. scaduto.

overflow, vb. strarìpare, traboccare.

overhaul, vb. rimèttere a nuòvo.

overhead, 1. n. spese ordinàrie f.pl. 2. adj. and adv. in alto.

overkill, n. esagerazione rettòrica f.

overlook, vb. omèttere, trascurare.

overnight, 1. adj. notturno. 2. adv. durante la nòtte.

overpass, n. cavalcavìa m.

overpower, vb. vìncere.

overrule, vb. decìdere contro; (law) cassare.

overrun, vb. invàdere.

oversee, vb. sorvegliare.

oversight, n. negligènza f.

overstuffed, adj. imbottito.

overt, adj. apèrto.

overtake, vb. raggiùngere.

overthrow, 1. n. sconvolgimento m. 2. vb. sconvòlgere, sovvertire.

overtime, adj. straordinàrio.

overture, n. sinfonia f.

overturn, vb. capovòlgere.

overview, n. quadro generale m.

overweight, n. peso eccessivo m.

overwhelm, vb. sopraffare.

overwork, 1. n. lavoro eccessivo m. 2. vb. lavorare troppo.

owe, vb. dovere.

owing, adj. dovuto; (o. to) dovuto a.

owl, n. civetta f., gufo m.; (o. service) servizio notturno m.

own, 1. adj. pròprio. 2. vb. possedere.

owner, n. possessore m.

ox, n. bue m.

oxygen, n. ossìgeno m.

oyster, n. òstrica f.

P

pa, n. babbo m.

pace, n. passo m.

pacific, adj. pacifico.

pacifier, n. pacificatore m.

pacifism, n. pacifismo m.

pacifist, n. pacifista m.

pacify, vb. pacificare.

pack, 1. n. pacco m.; (gang) banda m.; (cards) mazzo m.; (dogs) muta f. 2. vb. imballare; (suitcases) fare le valigie.

package, n. pacco m.

packing, n. imballàggio m.

pact, n. patto m.

pad, 1. n. cuscinetto m. 2. vb. imbottire.

padding, n. imbottitura f.

paddle, 1. n. remo m. 2. vb. remare; (splash) guazzare; (spank) sculacciare.

paddock, n. campo m.

padlock, n. lucchetto m.

Padua, n. Pàdova f.

Paduan, adj. padovano.

pagan, n. and adj. pagano (m.).

page, 1. n. pàgina f.; (servant) pàggio m. 2. vb. chiamare.

pageant, n. cortèo m.

pagoda, n. pagòda f.

pail, n. sécchia f.

pain, n. dolore m., pena f.

painful, adj. doloroso.

painstaking, adj. coscienzoso.

paint, 1. n. colore m.; (makeup) belletto m. 2. vb. dipingere.

painter, n. pittore m.

painting, n. pittura f., dipinto m.

pair, n. paio m.

pajamas, n. pigiama m.pl.

palace, n. palazzo m.

palatable, adj. gustoso.

palate, n. pàlato m.

palatial, adj. magnifico.

pale, 1. adj. pàllido. 2. vb. impallidire.

paleness, n. pallidezza f.

palette, n. tavolòzza f.

pall, vb. perder sapore m.

pallbearer, n. persona che règge i cordoni f.

pallid, adj. pàllido.

palm, n. palma f.

palpitate, vb. palpitare.

paltry, adj. meschino.

pamper, vb. trattare con indulgènza.

pamphlet, n. opùscolo m.

pan, 1. n. padèlla f. 2. vb. criticare aspramente; (p. out) riuscire.

panacea, n. panacèa f.

pan-cake, n. frittèlla f.

pane, n. (p. of glass) vetro m.

panel, n. pannèllo m.

pang, n. spàsimo m.

panic, n. pànico m.

panorama, n. panorama m.

pant, vb. anelare, ansare.

panther, n. pantèra f.

panties, n. mutandine (da dònna) f.pl.

pantomime, n. pantomima f.

pantry, n. dispènsa f.

pants, n. pantaloni m.pl.

panty hose, n. collant m.

(Italy); ghette f.pl. (Switzerland)

papa, n. papà m.

papal, adj. papale.

paper, n. carta f.; (newsp.) giornale m.; (wall-p.) carta da parati f.

paperback, n. libro in brossura m.

paper-hanger, n. tappezzière in carta m.

par, n. pari f.

parable, n. paràbola f.

parachute, n. paracadute m.

parade, n. parata f.

paradise, n. paradiso m.

paradox, n. paradòsso m.

paraffin, n. paraffina f.

paragraph, n. paràgrafo m.

parakeet, n. pappagallo m.

parallel, n. and adj. parallèlo (m.).

paralysis, n. paràlisi f.

paralyze, vb. paralizzare.

paramedic, n. paramèdico m.; assistente mèdico m.

parameter, n. paràmetro m.

paramount, adj. suprèmo.

paraphrase, 1. n. paràfrasi f. 2. vb. parafrasare.

parasite, n. parassita m.

parcel, n. pacco m.

parch, vb. inaridire.

parchment, n. pergamena f.

pardon, 1. n. perdono m. 2. vb. perdonare.

pare, vb. (nails) tagliare; (fruit) sbucciare.

parent, n. genitore m.

parentage, n. paternità f.

parenthesis, n. parèntesi f.

parish, n. pària m.

Paris, n. Parigi f.

parish, n. parròcchia f.; (priest) pàrroco m.

Parisian, adj. parigino.

parity, n. parità f.

park, 1. n. parco m. 2. vb. parcare.

parking, n. postéggio m., parcamento m.; (p. area) autoparchéggio m.; (p. lights) luci di città f.pl.

parkway, n. viale m.; (superhighway) autostrada f.

parley, 1. n. parlamento m. 2. vb. parlamentare.

parliament, n. parlamento m.

parliamentary, adj. parlamentare.

parlor, n. salòtto m.

Parmesan, adj. parmigiano.

parochial, adj. parrocchiale.

parody, 1. n. parodìa f. 2. vb. parodiare.

parole, n. paròla d'onore f.

paroxysm, n. parossismo m.

parrot, n. pappagallo m.

parsimony, n. parsimònia f.

parsley, n. prezzèmolo m.

parson, n. pàrroco m.

part, 1. n. parte f. 2. vb. separare, tr.

partake, vb. partecipare.

partial, adj. parziale.

partiality, n. parzialità f.

participant, n. partecipante m.

participate, vb. partecipare.

participation, n. partecipazione f.

participle, n. participio m.

particle, n. particèlla f.

particular, adj. particolare; (fussy) esigènte.

parting, n. separazione f.

partisan, n. and adj. partigiano (m.).

partition, n. partizione f.; (wall) muro divisòrio m.

partly, adv. in parte.

partner, n. compagno m., sòcio m.

part of speech, n. parte del discorso f.

partridge, n. pernice f.

party, n. (political) partito m.; (social) ricevimento m. (legal) parte in càusa f.; (person) individuo m.; (group) gruppo m.

pass, 1. n. passo m. 2. vb. passare; (auto) sorpassare; (exam.) superare; (go beyond) oltrepassare.

passable, adj. (road) praticàbile; (work) passàbile.

passage, n. passàggio m.

passé, adj. fuòri di mòda f. (faded) appassito.

passenger, n. passeggèro m.

passer-by, n. passante m.

passing, n. (auto) sorpasso m.

passion, n. passione f.

passionate, adj. appassionato.

passive, n. and adj. passivo (m.).

passport, n. passapòrto m.

past, n. and adj. passato (m.).

paste, 1. n. pasta f., còlla f. 2. vb. incollare.

pasteurize, vb. pasteurizzare.

pastille, n. pastiglia f., pasticca f.

pastime, n. passatèmpo m.

pastor, n. pastore m.

pastry, n. pasticceria f.

pastry shop, n. pasticceria f.

pasture, n. pàscolo m.

pasty, n. pasticcio m. 2. adj. (color) pàllido.

pat, 1. n. colpetto m.; (butter, etc.) panetto m. 2. vb. bàttere leggieramente.

patch, 1. n. pèzza f. 2. vb. rappezzare, rattoppare.

patchwork, n. raffazzonamento m.

patent, 1. n. brevetto m. 2. vb. brevettare.

patent leather, n. pèlle verniciata f.

paternal, adj. patèrno.

paternity, n. paternità f.

path, n. sentièro m., pista f.

pathetic, adj. patètico.

pathology, n. patologia f.

pathos, n. pàtos m.

patience, n. paziènza f.

patient, adj. paziènte.

patio, n. cortile m.

patriarch, n. patriarca m.
patrimony, n. patrimònio m.
patriot, n. patriòta m.
patriotic, adj. patriòttico.
patriotism, n. patriòttismo m.
patrol, n. pattùglia f.
patrolman, n. poliziòtto m.
patron, n. patròno m.
patronage, n. patronato m.
patronize, vb. comprare da.
pattern, n. modèllo m.
pauper, n. pòvero m.
pause, n. pàusa f.
pave, vb. pavimentare.
pavement, n. selciato m.
pavilion, n. padiglione m.
paw, n. zampa f.
pawn, 1. n. pegno m.; (chess) pedina f. **2.** impegnare.
pay, 1. n. paga f. **2.** vb. pagare; (p. in) versare.
payment, n. pagamento m., versamento m.
pea, n. pisèllo m.
peace, n. pace f.
peaceable, adj. pacifico.
peaceful, adj. tranquillo.
peach, n. (tree) pèsco m.; (fruit) pèsca f.
peacock, n. pavone m.
peak, n. cima f., picco m.
peal, 1. n. scampanìo m. **2.** vb. scampanare.
peanut, n. aràchide f.
pear, n. (tree) pero m.; (fruit) pera f.
pearl, n. pèrla f.
peasant, n. contadino m.
pebble, n. ciòttolo m.
peck, vb. beccare.
peculiar, adj. (special) peculiare; (queer) strano.
peculiarity, n. peculiarità f.
pecuniary, adj. pecuniàrio.
pedagogue, n. pedagògo m.
pedagogy, n. pedagogìa f.
pedal, 1. n. pedale m. **2.** vb. pedalare.
pedant, n. pedante m.
peddle, vb. vèndere al minuto.
peddler, n. venditore ambulante m.
pedestal, n. piedestallo m.
pedestrian, 1. n. pedone m. **2.** adj. pedèstre; (pertaining to pedestrians) pedonale.
pediatrician, n. pediàtra m.
pedigree, n. genealogìa f.
peek, vb. sbirciare.
peel, vb. sbucciare, pelare.
peep, 1. n. occiata f. **2.** vb. (look) dare un' occhiata; (appear) spuntare.
peer, 1. n. pari m. **2.** vb. guardare curiosamente.
peevish, adj. stizzoso.
peg, n. piuòlo m.
pelt, 1. n. (skin) pèlle f. **2.** vb. assalire.
pelvis, n. pèlvi f.
pen, 1. n. penna f.; (fountain p.) penna stilogràfica. **2.** vb. scrivere.
penalty, n. pena f.
penance, n. penitènza f.

penchant, n. inclinazione f.
pencil, n. làpis m., matita f.
pendant, n. pendènte m.
pending, 1. adj. pendènte. **2.** prep. in attesa di.
penetrate, vb. penetrare.
penetration, n. penetrazione f.
penicillin, n. penicillina f.
peninsula, n. penisola f.
penitence, n. penitènza f.
penitent, n. and adj. penitènte (m.).
pen-knife, n. temperino m.
penniless, adj. al verde.
penny, n. sòldo m.
pension, n. pensione f.
pensive, adj. pensoso.
pent-up, adj. rinchiuso.
penury, n. penùria f.
people, n. (folks) gènte f.; (nation) pòpolo m.
pepper, n. pepe m.
per, prep. per.
perambulator, n. carrozzèlla f.
perceive, vb. scòrgere.
per cent, adv. per cènto.
percentage, n. percentuale m.
perceptible, adj. percettìbile.
perception, n. percezione f.
perch, 1. n. (fish) pesce pèrsico m.; (pole) pèrtica f.; (for birds) posatòio m. **2.** vb. posarsi; (roost) appollaiarsi.
perdition, n. perdizione f.
peremptory, adj. perentòrio.
perennial, adj. perènne.
perfect, 1. adj. perfètto. **2.** vb. perfezionare.
perfection, n. perfezione f.
perforation, n. perforazione f.
perform, vb. eseguire; (a play) rappresentare; (sing) cantare; (instrumental music) suonare.
performance, n. esecuzione f., rappresentazione f.
perfume, 1. n. profumo m. **2.** vb. profumare.
perfunctory, adj. casuale.
perhaps, adv. forse; (p. even) magari.
peril, n. pericolo m.
perilous, adj. pericoloso.
perimeter, n. perìmetro m.
period, n. periodo m.
periodic, adj. periòdico.
periodical, n. and adj. periòdico (m.).
periphery, n. periferìa f.
perish, vb. perire.
perishable, adj. deperìbile.
perjure oneself, vb. spergiurare.
perjury, n. spergiuro m.
permanent, adj. permanènte.
permeate, vb. permeare.
permissible, adj. permissìbile.
permission, n. permesso m.
permit, 1. n. permesso m. **2.** vb. permèttere.
pernicious, adj. pernicioso.
perpendicular, n. and adj. perpendicolare (m.).
perpetrate, vb. perpetrare.
perpetual, adj. perpètuo.

perplex, 1. adj. perplèsso. **2.** vb. rèndere perplèsso.
perplexity, n. perplessità f.
persecute, vb. perseguitare.
persecution, n. persecuzione f.
perseverance, n. perseveranza f.
persevere, vb. perseverare.
persist, vb. persìstere.
persistent, adj. persistènte.
person, n. persona f.
personage, n. personàggio m.
personal, adj. personale.
personality, n. personalità f.
personally, adv. personalmente.
personnel, n. personale m.
perspective, n. prospettiva f.
perspiration, n. sudore m.
perspire, vb. sudare.
persuade, vb. persuadere.
persuasive, adj. persuasivo.
pertain, vb. appartenere.
pertinent, adj. pertinènte.
perturb, vb. perturbare.
peruse, vb. scòrrere.
pervade, vb. pervàdere.
perverse, adj. pervèrso.
perversion, n. perversione f.
pervert, vb. pervertire.
pessimism, n. pessimismo m.
pessimist, n. pessimista m.
pestilence, n. pestilènza f.
pet, 1. n. and adj. favorito (m.); (animal) animale domèstico m. **2.** vb. vezzeggiare.
petal, n. pètalo m.
petition, n. petizione f.
petrify, vb. pietrificare.
petrol, n. benzina f.
petroleum, n. petròlio m.
petticoat, n. sottana f.
petty, adj. meschino, piccolo.
petulance, n. petulanza f.
petulant, adj. petulante.
pew, n. banco in chièsa m.
phantom, n. fantasma m.
pharmacist, n. farmacista m.
pharmacy, n. farmacìa f.
phase, n. fase f.
pheasant, n. fagiano m.
phenomenal, adj. fenomenale.
phenomenon, n. fenòmeno m.
philanthropy, n. filantropìa f.
philately, n. filatèlica f.
philosopher, n. filòsofo m.
philosophical, adj. filosòfico.
philosophy, n. filosofìa f.
phlegm, n. flèmma m.
phlegmatic, adj. flemmàtico.
phobia, n. fobìa f.
phonetic, adj. fonètico.
phonograph, n. grammòfono m.
phosphorus, n. fòsforo m.
photocopier, n. fotocopiatore m.
photocopy, n. fotocopia f.
photoelectric, adj. fotoelèttrico.
photogenic, adj. fotogènico.
photograph, 1. n. fotografìa f. **2.** vb. fotografare.
photographer, n. fotògrafo m.
photography, n. fotografìa f.

photostat, n. riproduzione anastàtica f.

phrase, n. frase f.

physical, adj. fisico.

physician, n. mèdico m.

physicist, n. fisico m.

physics, n. fisica f.

physiology, n. fisiologia f.

physiotherapy, n. fisioterapia f.

physique, n. fisico m.

pianist, n. pianista m.

piano, n. pianofòrte m.

picayune, adj. meschino.

piccolo, n. ottavino m.

pick, 1. n. piccone m. 2. vb. (gather) raccògliere; (select) scègliere.

picket, n. picchetto m.

pickle, n. salamòia f.; (trouble) impiccio m.

pickpocket, n. borsaiòlo m.

picnic, n. gita f.

picture, n. quadro m.

picturesque, adj. pittoresco.

pie, n. tòrta f.

piece, n. pèzzo m.

Piedmont, n. Piemonte m.

Piedmontese, adj. piemontese.

pier, n. (dock) banchina f., mòlo m.; (pillar) pilone m.

pierce, vb. forare, traforare.

piety, n. pietà f.

pig, n. pòrco m.; maiale m.

pigeon, n. piccione m.

pigeonhole, n. casèlla f.

pigment, n. pigmento m.

pile, 1. n. (heap) ammasso m., mucchio m.; (post) palafitta f. 2. vb. ammucchiare.

pilfer, vb. rubacchiare.

pilgrim, n. pellegrino m.

pilgrimage, n. pellegrinàggio m.

pill, n. pillola f.

pillage, 1. n. sacchéggio m. 2. vb. saccheggiare.

pillar, n. pilastro m., pilone m.

pillow, n. guanciale m.

pillowcase, n. fèdera f.

pilot, n. pilòta m.

pimple, n. forùncolo m.

pin, n. spillo m.

pinch, 1. n. pizzicòtto m. 2. vb. pizzicare.

pine, 1. n. pino m. 2. vb. languire.

pineapple, n. ananàs m.

ping-pong, n. tennis da tàvola m.

pink, adj. ròsa.

pinnacle, n. pinnàcolo m.

pint, n. pinta f.

pioneer, n. pionière f.

pious, adj. pio.

pipe, n. tubo m.; (tobacco) pipa f.

piper, n. piffero m.

piquant, adj. piccante.

pirate, n. pirata m.

pistol, n. pistola f.

piston, n. pistone m., stantuffo m.

pit, n. buca f.

pitch, 1. n. (tar) pece f.; (throw) lància m.; (music)

tone m. 2. vb. (hurl) lanciare.

pitchblende, n. pechblenda f., uraninite f.

pitcher, n. bròcca f.; (thrower) lanciatore m.

pitchfork, n. forca f.

pitfall, n. tràppola f.

pitiful, adj. pietoso.

pitiless, adj. spietato.

pity, n. pietà f.; (shame) peccato m.; (what a p.) che peccato!

pivot, n. pèrnio m.

pizza, n. pizza f.

placard, n. cartèllo m.

placate, vb. placare.

place, 1. n. posto m., luògo m.; (take p.) aver luògo; accadere. 2. vb. méttere; porre.

placid, adj. plàcido.

plagiarism, n. plàgio m.

plague, n. pèste f.

plain, 1. n. pianura f. 2. adj. (clear) chiaro; (simple) sèmplice, modèsto.

plaintiff, n. attore m.

plan, 1. n. piano m., progètto m., (map) pianta f. 2. vb. progettare.

plane, 1. n. piano m.; (airplane) aeroplano m.; (carpenter's) pialla f. 2. vb. piallare.

planet, n. pianeta m.

planetarium, n. planetàrio m.

planetary, adj. planetàrio.

plank, n. asse f., tàvola f.

plant, 1. n. pianta f.; (factory) installation) impianto m. 2. vb. piantare.

plantation, n. piantagione f.

planter, n. piantatore m.; (plantation owner) proprietàrio di piantagione m.

plasma, n. plasma m.

plaster, 1. n. intònaco m.; (medical) empiastro m. 2. vb. intonacare.

plastic, n. plàstica f. 2. adj. plàstico.

plate, n. piatto m.; (photographic) lastra f.; (auto) targa f.

plateau, n. altopiano m.

platform, n. piattaforma f.

platinum, n. plàtino m.

platitude, n. banalità f.

platoon, n. drappèllo m., plotone m.

platter, n. piatto grande m.

plaudit, n. applàuso m.

plausible, adj. plausibile.

play, 1. n. (game) giòco m.; (joke) schèrzo m.; (theater) dramma m. 2. vb. giocare; (on stage) recitare; (instrument) suonare.

player, n. (game) giocatore m.; (instrument) suonatore m.

playful, adj. scherzoso.

playground, n. campo per ricreazione m.

playmate, n. compagno di giòchi m.

playwright, n. drammaturgo m.

plea, n. preghièra f.; (excuse) scusa f.

plead, vb. esortare, implorare; (give as excuse) addurre come scusa.

pleasant, adj. piacévole.

please, 1. vb. piacere a. 2. adv., interj. per favore.

pleasing, adj. piacévole, grato.

pleasure, n. piacere m.

pleat, n. pièga f.

plebiscite, n. plebiscito m.

pledge, 1. n. pegno m. 2. vb. impegnare.

plentiful, adj. abbondante.

plenty, 1. n. abbondanza f. 2. adj. (p. of) molto.

pleurisy, n. pleurite f.

pliable, pliant, adj. pieghévole.

pliers, n. pinze f.pl., pinzette f.pl.

plight, n. situazione f.

plot, 1. n. (conspiracy) complòtto m.; (story) intréccio m.; (land) appezzamento m.; (plan) pianta f.

plow, 1. n. aratro m. 2. vb. arare.

pluck, 1. n. fégato m. 2. vb. cògliere.

plug, 1. n. tappo m.; (electric) spina f. 2. vb. tappare.

plum, n. (tree) susino m.; (fruit) susina f., prugna f.

plumage, n. piumàggio m.

plumber, n. trombàio m., stagnino m.; idràulico m.

plume, n. penna f.

plump, adj. grassòccio.

plunder, 1. n. bottino m., prèda f. 2. vb. saccheggiare, predare.

plunge, 1. n. tuffo m. 2. vb. tuffare, tr.

plural, n. and adj. plurale (m.).

plus, prep. più.

plutocrat, n. plutòcrate m.

pneumatic, adj. pneumàtico.

pneumonia, n. polmonite f.

poach, vb. (hunt illegally) andare a càccia di fròdo; (eggs) cuòcere in camicia; (poached eggs) uòva affogate.

poacher, n. cacciatore di fròdo m.

pocket, 1. n. tasca f. 2. vb. intascare.

pocket-book, n. portafògli m.

pocket-size, adj. tascàbile.

pod, n. baccèllo m.

podiatry, n. cura dei pièdi f.

poem, n. poesia f., poèma m.

poet, n. poèta m., poetéssa f.

poetic, adj. poètico.

poetry, n. poesia f.

poignant, adj. doloroso.

point, 1. n. punto m. 2. vb. puntare; (p. to) indicare; (p. out) additare.

pointed, adj. acuto.

pointless, adj. privo di senso.

poise, n. equilibrio m.

poison, 1. n. veleno m. 2. vb. avvelenare.

poisonous, adj. velenoso.

poke, *vb.* spingere; (fire) attizzare.

Poland, *n.* Polònia *f.*

polar, *adj.* polare.

pole, *n.* (post) palo *m.;* (rod) pertica *f.;* (wagon) timone *m.;* (electrical, geographical) pòlo *m.*

police, *n.* polizìa *f.*

policeman, *n.* vìgile *m.,* poliziòtto *m.*

policy, *n.* politica *f.;* (insurance) polizza *f.*

polish, 1. *n.* (material) lùcido *m.;* (gloss) lucidatura *f.* 2. *vb.* lucidare.

Polish, *adj.* polacco.

polite, *adj.* cortese.

politeness, *n.* cortesìa *f.*

politic, political, *adj.* politico.

politician, *n.* politico *m.*

politics, *n.* politica *f.*

poll, 1. *n.* (head) tèsta *f.;* (voting) votazione *f.;* (p.-tax) testàtico *m.* 2. *vb.* (get, in voting) ottenere.

pollen, *n.* pòlline *f.*

pollute, *vb.* contaminare.

polonaise, *n.* polacca *f.*

polygamy, *n.* poligamìa *f.*

polygon, *n.* poligono *m.*

pomp, *n.* pompa *f.,* fasto *m.*

pompous, *adj.* pomposo, fastoso.

poncho, *n.* impermeàbile *m.*

pond, *n.* stagno *m.*

ponder, *vb.* ponderare.

ponderous, *adj.* ponderoso.

pontiff, *n.* pontéfice *m.*

pontoon, *n.* pontone *m.*

pony, *n.* cavallino *m.*

pool, *n.* stagno *m.;* (money) fondo comune *m.*

poor, *adj.* pòvero.

pop, 1. *n.* scòppio *m.;* (father) babbo *m.* 2. *vb.* scoppiettare.

pope, *n.* papa *m.*

popular, *adj.* popolare.

popularity, *n.* popolarità *f.*

population, *n.* popolazione *f.*

porcelain, *n.* porcellana *f.*

porch, *n.* veranda *f.;* (church) pòrtico *m.*

pore, *n.* pòro *m.*

pork, *n.* maiale *m.*

pornography, *n.* pornografìa *f.*

porous, *adj.* poroso.

port, *n.* pòrto *m.*

portable, *adj.* portàtile.

portal, *n.* portale *m.*

portend, *vb.* presagire.

portent, *n.* presàgio *m.*

porter, *n.* facchino *m.,* portabagagli *m.;* (hotel) portière *m.*

portfolio, *n.* cartèlla *f.,* portafòglio *m.*

porthole, *n.* oblò *m.*

portico, *n.* pòrtico *m.*

portion, *n.* porzione *f.*

portly, *adj.* corpulènto.

portrait, *n.* ritratto *m.*

portray, *vb.* ritrattare.

Portugal, *n.* il Portogallo *m.*

Portuguese, *adj.* portoghese.

pose, 1. *n.* pòsa *f.* 2. *vb.* posare; (p. as) atteggiarsi a.

position, *n.* posizione *f.*

positive, *adj.* positivo.

possess, *vb.* possedere.

possession, *n.* possèsso *m.*

possessive, *adj.* possessivo.

possessor, *n.* possessore *m.*

possibility, *n.* possibilità *f.*

possible, *adj.* possibile.

possibly, *adv.* possibilmente, forse.

post, 1. *n.* (pole) palo *m.;* (place) posto *m.;* (mail) pòsta *f.* 2. *vb.* (put up) affiggere; (mail) impostare.

postage, *n.* affrancatura *f.;* (p.-stamp) francobollo *m.*

postal, *adj.* postale.

post-card, *n.* cartolina postale *f.*

poster, *n.* cartèllo *m.*

poste restante, *adv.* fermo pòsta.

posterior, 1. *n.* culo *m.* 2. *adj.* posteriore.

posterity, *n.* posterità *f.,* pòsteri *m.pl.*

post-graduate, *adj.* di perfezionamento.

postman, *n.* postino *m.*

post-mark, *n.* timbro postale, *m.*

post office, *n.* ufficio postale *m.*

postpone, *vb.* posporre, rimandare.

postscript, *n.* poscritto *m.*

posture, *n.* posizione *f.*

pot, *n.* pèntola *f.;* (marijuana) marijuana *f.*

potassium, *n.* potàssio *m.*

potato, *n.* patata *f.*

potent, *adj.* potènte.

potential, *n.* and *adj.* potenziale *(m.)*

pot-hole, *n.* buca *f.*

potion, *n.* pozione *f.*

pottery, *n.* stoviglie *f.pl.*

pouch, *n.* borsa *f.*

poultry, *n.* pollame *m.*

pound, 1. *n.* libbra *f.;* (p. sterling) sterlina *f.* 2. *vb.* pestare.

pour, *vb.* versare; (p. off) travasare.

poverty, *n.* povertà *f.,* misèria *f.*

powder, 1. *n.* pòlvere *m.;* (facep.) cìpria *f.;* (p.-puff) fiòcco da cìpria *f.* 2. *vb.* polverizzare; (one's face) incipriare, *tr.*

power, *n.* potere *m.,* potènza *f.*

powerful, *adj.* potènte.

powerless, *adj.* impotènte.

practicable, *adj.* praticàbile.

practical, *adj.* praticàmente.

practice, 1. *n.* pràtica *f.* 2. *vb.* praticare, esercitare, *tr.*

practiced, *adj.* espèrto.

practitioner, *n.* professionista *m.*

pragmatic, *adj.* prammàtico.

prairie, *n.* prateria *f.*

praise, 1. *n.* lòde *f.* 2. *vb.* lodare.

prank, *n.* birichinata *f.,* burla *f.*

pray, *vb.* pregare.

prayer, *n.* preghièra *f.*

preach, *vb.* predicare.

preacher, *n.* predicatore *m.*

preamble, *n.* preàmbolo *m.*

precarious, *adj.* precàrio.

precaution, *n.* precauzione *f.*

precede, *vb.* precèdere.

precedence, *n.* precedènza *f.*

precedent, *n.* precedènte *m.*

precept, *n.* precètto *m.*

precinct, *n.* precinto *f.*

precious, *adj.* prezioso.

precipice, *n.* precipìzio *m.*

precipitate, *vb.* precipitare.

precise, *adj.* preciso.

precision, *n.* precisione *f.*

preclude, *vb.* preclùdere.

precocious, *adj.* precòce.

precursor, *n.* precursore *m.*

predatory, *adj.* predatòrio, di prèda.

predecessor, *n.* predecessore *m.*

predestination, *n.* predestinazione *f.*

predicament, *n.* impiccio *m.*

predicate, *n.* predicato *m.*

predict, *vb.* predire.

predilection, *n.* predilezione *f.*

predispose, *vb.* predisporre.

predominant, *adj.* predominante.

prefabricated, *adj.* prefabbricato.

preface, *n.* prefazione *f.*

prefect, *n.* prefètto *m.*

prefer, *vb.* preferire.

preferable, *adj.* preferìbile.

preference, *n.* preferènza *f.*

prefix, *n.* prefisso *m.*

pregnancy, *n.* gravidanza *f.*

pregnant, *adj.* gràvida *f.,* incinta *f.;* (animals only) prègna *f.*

prehistoric, *adj.* preistòrico.

prejudice, 1. *n.* pregiudìzio *m.* 2. *vb.* pregiudicare.

prejudiced, *adj.* pregiudicato.

preliminary, *adj.* preliminare.

prelude, *n.* prelùdio *m.*

premature, *adj.* prematuro.

premeditate, *vb.* premeditare.

premier, *n.* primo ministro *m.*

premiere, *n.* prima *f.*

premise, *n.* premessa *f.*

premium, *n.* prèmio *m.*

premonition, *n.* premonizione *f.*

prenatal, *adj.* prenatale.

preparation, *n.* preparazione *f.*

preparatory, *adj.* preparatòrio.

prepare, *vb.* preparare.

preponderant, *adj.* preponderante.

preposition, *n.* preposizione *f.*

preposterous, *adj.* assurdo.

prerequisite, *n.* primo requisito *m.*

prerogative, *n.* prerogativa *f.*

prescribe, *vb.* prescrivere.

prescription, *n.* prescrizione *f.*

presence, *n.* presènza *f.*

present, 1. *n.* dono *m.*, regalo *m.*, omàggio *m.* 2. *adj.* presènte; (the p.) assistere. 3. *vb.* presentare; regalare.

presentable, *adj.* presentàbile.

presentation, *n.* presentazione *f.*

presently, *adv.* fra pòco, immediatamente.

preservation, *n.* conservazione *f.*

preservative, *adj.* conservativo.

preserve, *vb.* preservare, conservare, serbare.

preside, *vb.* presièdere.

presidency, *n.* presidènza *f.*

president, *n.* presidènte *m.*

press, 1. *n.* prèssa *f.;* (newspapers) stampa *f.* 2. *vb.* prèmere; stringere; (urge) insistere.

pressing, *adj.* urgènte.

pressure, *n.* pressione *f.*

pressure cooker, *n.* pèntola a pressione *f.*

prestige, *n.* prestigio *m.*

presume, *vb.* presùmere.

presumption, *n.* presunzione *f.*

presumptuous, *adj.* presuntuoso.

presumptuousness, *n.* presuntuosità *f.*

presuppose, *vb.* presupporre.

pretend, *vb.* fingere, far finta; (claim) pretèndere.

pretense, *n.* finta *f.*

pretension, *n.* pretesa *f.*

pretentious, *adj.* pretenzioso.

pretext, *n.* pretèsto *m.*

pretty, *adj.* grazioso, bellino.

prevail, *vb.* prevalere.

prevalent, *adj.* prevalènte.

prevent, *vb.* impedire.

prevention, *n.* prevenzione *f.*

preventive, *adj.* preventivo.

preview, *n.* anteprima *f.*

previous, *adj.* precedènte.

prey, *n.* prèda *f.*

price, *n.* prèzzo *m.*

priceless, *adj.* inestimàbile.

prick, *vb.* pùngere.

pride, *n.* orgòglio *m.*

priest, *n.* prète *m.*

prim, *adj.* affettato.

primary, *adj.* primàrio.

prime, *adj.* primo, principale.

prime minister, *n.* primo ministro *m.*

primitive, *adj.* primitivo.

prince, *n.* principe *m.*

princess, *n.* principessa *f.*

principal, 1. *n.* capo *m.*, direttore *m.* 2. *adj.* principale.

principally, *adv.* principalmente.

principle, *n.* principio *m.*

print, 1. *n.* stampa *f.;* (impression) impronta *f.* 2. *vb.* stampare.

printing, *n.* stampa *f.;* (pressrun) tiratura *f.*

printing-press, *n.* màcchina per stampare *f.*

printout, *n.* foglio stampato prodotto da un calcolatore elettrònico *m.*

priority, *n.* priorità *f.*

prism, *n.* prisma *m.*

prison, *n.* prigione *f.*

prisoner, *n.* prigionièro *m.*

privacy, *n.* intimità *f.*, solitùdine *f.*

private, 1. *n.* soldato sèmplice *m.* 2. *adj.* privato.

privation, *n.* privazione *f.*

privet, *n.* ligustro *m.*

privilege, *n.* privilègio *m.*

privy, *n.* latrina *f.*

prize, 1. *n.* prèmio *m.* 2. *vb.* apprezzare.

probability, *n.* probabilità *f.*

probable, *adj.* probàbile.

probate, 1. *n.* omologazione *f.* 2. *vb.* omologare.

probation, *n.* pròva *f.*

probe, *vb.* sondare.

probity, *n.* probità *f.*

problem, *n.* problèma *m.*

procedure, *n.* procedimento *m.;* (legal) procedura *f.*

proceed, *vb.* procèdere.

process, *n.* procèsso *m.*

procession, *n.* processione *f.*

proclaim, *vb.* proclamare.

proclamation, *n.* proclamazione *f.*

procrastinate, *vb.* procrastinare.

procure, *vb.* procurare.

prodigal, *adj.* pròdigo.

prodigy, *n.* prodìgio *m.*

produce, *vb.* produrre.

product, *n.* prodotto *m.*

production, *n.* produzione *f.*

productive, *adj.* produttivo.

profane, 1. *adj.* profano. 2. *vb.* profanare.

profanity, *n.* bestèmmie *f.pl.*

profess, *vb.* professare.

profession, *n.* professione *f.*

professional, 1. *n.* professional *m.* 2. *adj.* professionale.

professor, *n.* professore *m.*

proficient, *adj.* espèrto.

profile, *n.* profilo *m.*

profit, 1. *n.* guadagno *m.*, profitto *m.*, vantàggio *m.* 2. *vb.* approfittare.

profitable, *adj.* vantaggioso.

profiteer, *n.* pescecane *m.*

profound, *adj.* profondo.

profoundly, *adv.* profondamente.

profundity, *n.* profondità *f.*

profuse, *adj.* profuso.

prognosis, *n.* prògnosi *f.*

program, *n.* programma *m.*

progress, 1. *n.* progrèsso *m.* 2. *vb.* progredire.

progressive, *adj.* progressivo.

prohibit, *vb.* proibire.

prohibition, *n.* proibizione *f.*, divièto *m.*

prohibitive, *adj.* proibitivo.

project, 1. *n.* progètto *m.* 2. *vb.* (plan) progettare; (stick out) spòrgere.

projectile, *n.* proièttile *m.*

projection, *n.* proiezione *f.*

projector, *n.* proiettore *m.*

proliferation, *n.* proliferazione *f.*

prolific, *adj.* prolifico.

prologue, *n.* pròlogo *m.*

prolong, *vb.* prolungare.

prolongation, *n.* prolungamento *m.*

prominent, *adj.* prominènte.

promiscuous, *adj.* promiscuo.

promise, 1. *n.* promessa *f.* 2. *vb.* promèttere.

promote, *vb.* promuòvere.

promotion, *n.* promozione *f.*

prompt, *adj.* pronto.

prompter, *n.* suggeritore *m.*

promulgate, *vb.* promulgare.

pronoun, *n.* pronome *m.*

pronounce, *vb.* pronunciare.

pronunciation, *n.* pronùncia *f.*

proof, *n.* pròva *f.;* (printing) bòzze *f.pl.*

proof-read, *vb.* corrèggere le bòzze di.

prop, 1. *n.* puntèllo *m.* 2. *vb.* puntellare.

propaganda, *n.* propaganda *f.*

propagate, *vb.* propagare.

propel, *vb.* spingere innanzi.

propeller, *n.* elica *f.*

propensity, *n.* propensione *f.*

proper, *adj.* pròprio.

property, *n.* proprietà *f.*

prophecy, *n.* profezìa *f.*

prophesy, *vb.* profetizzare.

prophet, *n.* profèta *m.*

prophetic, *adj.* profètico.

propitious, *adj.* propizio.

proponent, *n.* proponènte *m.*

proportion, *n.* proporzione *f.*

proportionate, *adj.* proporzionato.

proposal, *n.* propòsta *f.*

propose, *vb.* proporre, *tr.*

proposition, *n.* propòsta *f.*

proprietor, *n.* proprietàrio *m.*

propriety, *n.* conveniènza *f.*

prosaic, *adj.* prosàico.

proscribe, *vb.* proscrivere.

prose, *n.* pròsa *f.*

prosecute, *vb.* intentare giudizio contro.

prospect, *n.* prospètto *m.*

prospective, *adj.* prospettivo.

prosper, *vb.* prosperare.

prosperity, *n.* prosperità *f.*

prosperous, *adj.* pròspero.

prostitute, *n.* prostituta *f.*

prostrate, 1. *adj.* prostrato. 2. *vb.* prostrare.

protect, *vb.* protèggere.

protection, *n.* protezione *f.*

protective, *adj.* protettivo.

protector, *n.* protettore *m.*

protégé, *n.* protètto *m.*

protein, *n.* proteìna *f.*

protest, 1. *n.* protèsta *f.* 2. *vb.* protestare.

Protestant, *n. and adj.* protestante (*m.*).

Protestantism, *n.* protestantésimo *m.*

protocol, *n.* protocòllo *m.*

proton, *n.* protone *m.*

protract, *vb.* protrarre.
protrude, *vb.* spingere fuòri, *tr.*
protuberance, *n.* protuberanza *f.*
proud, *adj.* orgoglioso.
prove, *vb.* comprovare.
proverb, *n.* provèrbio *m.*
proverbial, *adj.* proverbiale.
provide, *vb.* provvedere.
provided, *conj.* purchè.
providence, *n.* provvidènza *f.*
province, *n.* provincia *f.*
provincial, *adj.* provinciale.
provision, *n.* provvista *f.*
provocation, *n.* provocazione *f.*
provoke, *vb.* provocare.
prowess, *n.* prodezza *f.*
prowl, *vb.* vagare intorno.
proximity, *n.* prossimità *f.*
proxy, *n.* (person) procuratore *m.;* (document) procura *f.*
prudence, *n.* prudènza *f.*
prudent, *adj.* prudènte.
prune, *n.* prugna secca *f.*
pry, *vb.* ficcare il naso.
psalm, *n.* salmo *m.*
pseudonym, *n.* pseudònimo *m.*
psychedelic, *adj.* psichedèlico.
psychiatrist, *n.* psichiatra *m.*
psychiatry, *n.* psichiatria *f.*
psychoanalysis, *n.* psicoanàlisi *f.*
psychological, *adj.* psicològico.
psychology, *n.* psicologia *f.*
psychosis, *n.* psicòsi *f.*
ptomaine, *n.* ptomaina *f.*
public, *n.* and *adj.* pùbblico (*m.*).
publication, *n.* pubblicazione *f.*
publicity, *n.* pubblicità *f.*
publish, *vb.* pubblicare.
publisher, *n.* editore *m.*
pudding, *n.* budino *m.*
puddle, *n.* pozzànghera *f.*
puff, 1. *n.* sbuffo *m.;* (powder-p.) fiòcco da cìpria *m.* 2. *vb.* sbuffare.
pugnacious, *adj.* pugnace.
pull, 1. *n.* tirata *f.* 2. *vb.* tirare.
pulley, *n.* puléggia *f.*
pulmonary, *adj.* polmonare.
pulp, *n.* polpa *f.*
pulpit, *n.* pùlpito *m.*
pulsar, *n.* pùlsar *m.*
pulsate, *vb.* pulsare.
pulse, *n.* polso *m.*
pump, 1. *n.* pompa *f.* 2. *vb.* pompare.
pumpkin, *n.* zucca *f.*
pun, *n.* freddura *f.*
punch, 1. *n* (drink) pònce *m.;* (blow) pugno *m.* 2. *vb.* (make hole) perforare; (hit) colpire; dar pugni a.
punctual, *adj.* puntuale.
punctuate, *vb.* punteggiare.
punctuation, *n.* punteggiatura *f.*
puncture, 1. *n.* puntura *f.;* (tire) foratura *f.* 2. *vb.* forare.
pungent, *adj.* pungènte.
punish, *vb.* punire.
punishment, *n.* punizione *f.*
punitive, *adj.* punitivo.
puny, *adj.* débole.

pupil, *n.* alunno *m.,* scolaro *m.*
puppet, *n.* burattino *m.*
puppy, *n.* cùcciolo *m.*
purchase, 1. *n.* compra *f.;* (grasp) presa *f.* 2. *vb.* comprare.
pure, *adj.* puro.
purée, *n.* passato *m.*
purgative, *n.* and *adj.* purgante (*m.*).
purge, 1. *n.* purga *f.* 2. *vb.* purgare.
purify, *vb.* purificare.
puritanical, *adj.* da puritano.
purity, *n.* purezza *f.,* purità *f.*
purple, *n.* pórpora *f.*
purport, 1. *n.* significato *m.* 2. *vb.* use future of verb which in English is dependent on "purport".
purpose, *n.* fine *m.,* scòpo *m.,* propòsito *m.;* (on p.) appòsta.
purposely, *adv.* appòsta.
purse, *n.* borsa *f.*
pursue, *vb.* inseguire, perseguire.
pursuit, *n.* inseguimento *m.*
push, 1. *n.* spinta *f.* 2. *vb.* spingere.
put, *vb.* méttere, porre, ficcare; (p. back) riméttere; (p. down, suppress) sopprimere; (p. in) inserire; (p. off) rimandare; (p. on) indossare; (p. out, extinguish) spégnere; (p. up with) soffrire.
putrid, *adj.* pùtrido.
puzzle, *n.* indovinello *m.;* (cross-word p.) crucivèrba *m.*
pyjamas, *n.* pigiama *m.pl.*
pyramid, *n.* piràmide *f.*

Q

quadrangle, *n.* quadràngolo *m.*
quadraphonic, *adj.* quadrafònico.
quadruped, *n.* quadrùpede *m.*
quail, 1. *n.* quàglia *f.* 2. *vb.* scoraggiarsi.
quaint, *adj.* strano.
quake, 1. *n.* trèmito *m.* 2. *vb.* tremare.
qualification, *n.* qualificazione *f.,* qualifica *f.,* requisito *m.*
qualified, *adj.* idòneo.
qualify, *vb.* qualificare; (be fit) essere idòneo.
quality, *n.* qualità *f.*
qualm, *n.* nàusea *f.;* (fig.) scrùpolo *m*
quandary, *n.* perplessità *f.*
quantity, *n.* quantità *f.,* somma *f.*
quarantine, *n.* quarentena *f.*
quarrel, 1. *n.* lite *f.* 2. *vb.* litigare.
quarry, *n.* cava *f.*
quarter, *n.* (one fourth) quarto *m.;* (region; mercy) quartière *f.;* (three months) trimèstre *m.*
quarterly, *adj.* trimestrale.
quartet, *n.* quartetto *m.*

quartz, *n.* quarzo *m.*
quasar, *n.* quàsar *m.*
quaver, *vb.* tremolare.
queen, *n.* regina *f.*
queer, *adj.* strano.
quell, *vb.* sopprimere.
quench, *vb.* estinguere; (q. one's thirst) dissetare.
query, 1. *n.* domanda *f.* 2. *vb.* domandare.
quest, *n.* ricerca *f.*
question, 1. *n.* domanda *f.,* questione *f.* 2. *vb.* interrogare; (doubt) dubitare di.
questionable, *adj.* dùbbio.
question mark, *n.* punto interrogativo *m.*
questionnaire, *n.* questionàrio *m.*
quick, 1. *adj.* ràpido, pronto, svelto. 2. *adv.* prèsto.
quicken, *vb.* affrettare, *tr.*
quicksand, *n.* banco mòbile di sàbbia *m.*
quiet, 1. *n.* quiète *f.* 2. *adj.* quièto; (be, keep q.) tacere.
quilt, *n.* trapunta *f.,* coltrone *m.,* imbottita *f.*
quinine, *n.* chinino *m.*
quintet, *n.* quintètto *m.*
quip, *n.* motto *m.*
quit, *vb.* (leave) lasciare; (stop) cessare, sméttere; (resign) méttersi.
quite, *adv.* completamente, pròprio.
quiver, 1. *n.* farètra *f.* 2. *vb.* tremare; (shiver) rabbrividire.
quixotic, *adj.* donchisciottesco.
quiz, 1. *n.* esame *m.* 2. *vb.* esaminare.
quorum, *n.* quorum *m.*
quota, *n.* quòta *f.*
quotation, *n.* citazione *f.*
quote, *vb.* citare.

R

rabbi, *n.* rabbino *m.*
rabbit, *n.* coniglio *m.*
rabble, *n.* plebàglia *f.,* volgo *m.*
rabid, *adj.* rabbioso.
rabies, *n.* ràbbia *f.*
race, 1. *n.* (contest) corsa *f.;* (breed) razza *f.* 2. *vb.* córrere.
race-track, *n.* ippòdromo *m.*
rack, 1. *n.* (torture) ruòta *f.;* (for feed) rastrellièra *f.;* (luggage) reticella *f.;* (railroad) cremaglièra *f.* 2. *vb.* torturare.
racket, *n.* (tennis) racchetta *f.;* (uproar) frastuòno *m.,* baccano *m.*
radar, *n.* (instrument) radiotelèmetro *m.;* (science) radiotelemetria *f.*
radiance, *n.* fulgore *m.*
radiant, *adj.* raggiante.
radiate, *vb.* irradiare, *tr.*
radiation, *n.* irradiazione *f.*
radiator, *n.* radiatore *m.*
radical, *n.* and *adj.* radicale (*m.*).

radio, 1. *n.* ràdio *f.* 2. *adj.* (pertaining to r.) radiofònico.

radioactive, *adj.* radioattivo.

radish, *n.* ramolàccio *m.*, ravanèllo *m.*

radium, *n.* ràdio *m.*

radius, *n.* ràggio *m.*

raffle, *n.* lotterìa *f.*

raft, *n.* zàttera *f.*

rafter, *n.* travicèllo *m.*

rag, *n.* cèncio *m.*, stràccio *m.*

ragamuffin, *n.* straccione *m.*

rage, 1. *n.* ràbbia *f.* 2. *vb.* infuriare.

ragged, *adj.* cencioso.

raid, *n.* incursione *f.*

rail, *n.* rotaia *f.;* (bar) sbarra *f.*

railcar, *n.* automotrice *f.;* (electric r.) elettromotrice *f.*

railing, *n.* ringhièra *f.*

railroad, 1. *n.* ferrovìa *f.* 2. *adj.* (pertaining to r.s) ferroviàrio.

rain, 1. *n.* piòggia *f.* 2. *vb.* piòvere; (r. cats and dogs) diluviare.

rainbow, *n.* arcobaleno *m.*

raincoat, *n.* impermeàbile *m.*

rainfall, *n.* precipitazione atmosfèrica *f.*

rainy, *adj.* piovoso.

raise, *vb.* (bring up) allevare; (erect) erìgere; (grow) coltivare; (increase) aumentare; (hoist) innalzare; (lift) levare; (collect) raccògliere; (intensify) alzare.

raisin, *n.* uva secca *f.;* (sultana r.) uva sultanina *f.*

rake, 1. *n.* rastrèllo *m.* 2. *vb.* rastrellare.

rally, 1. *n.* (recovery) ricùpero di fòrze *m.;* (meeting) raduno *m.* 2. *vb.* riunire, *tr.*

ram, 1. *n.* (animal) montone *m.;* (post) battipalo *m.* 2. *vb.* bàttere; cacciare.

ramble, *vb.* divagare.

ramp, *n.* piano inclinato *m.*

rampart, *n.* bastione *m.*

ranch, *n.* fattorìa *f.*

rancid, *adj.* ràncido.

rancor, *n.* rancore *m.*

random, *n.* (at r.) a casàccio.

range, 1. *n.* (distance) portata *f.;* (mountains) catena *f.;* (scope) estensione *f.;* (sphere) sfèra *f.;* (stove) cucina econòmica *f.* 2. *vb.* (arrange) disporre; (vary) variare.

rank, *n.* rango *m.;* (line) fila *f.;* (position) grado *m.*

ransack, *vb.* frugare dappertutto.

ransom, 1. *n.* riscatto *m.* 2. *vb.* riscattare.

rap, 1. *n.* colpo *m.*, picchio *m.* 2. *vb.* colpire, picchiare.

rape, *vb.* violare.

rapid, *adj.* ràpido.

rapport, *n.* rappòrto *m.*

rapture, *n.* èstasi *f.*

rare, *adj.* raro; (underdone) pòco còtto.

rarely, *adv.* raramente.

rascal, *n.* briccone *m.*

rash, 1. *n.* eruzione *f.* 2. *adj.* inconsiderato.

raspberry, *n.* lampone *m.;* (Bronx cheer) pernàcchia *f.*

rat, *n.* ratto *m.*

rate, 1. *n.* (price) prèzzo *m.;* (speed) velocità *f.* 2. *vb.* classificare, *tr.*

rather, *adv.* piuttosto.

ratify, *vb.* ratificare.

ratio, *n.* rappòrto *m.*

ration, 1. *n.* razione *f.;* (r.-card) tèssera annonària *f.* 2. *vb.* razionare.

rational, *adj.* razionale.

rattle, *n.* ràntolo *m.*, rumore secco *m.*

raucous, *adj.* ràuco.

ravage, 1. *n.* devastazione *f.* 2. *vb.* devastare.

rave, *vb.* delirare.

ravel, *n.* groviglio *m.*

raven, 1. *n.* corvo *m.* 2. *adj.* corvino.

ravenous, *adj.* affamato.

raw, *adj.* grezzo, crudo.

ray, *n.* ràggio *m.*

rayon, *n.* ràion *m.*

razor, *n.* rasòio *m.*

reach, 1. *n.* portata *f.* 2. *vb.* (get to) arrivare a; raggiùngere; (extend) allungare.

react, *vb.* reagire.

reaction, *n.* reazione *f.*

reactionary, *adj.* reazionàrio.

reactor, *n.* reattore *m.*

read, *vb.* lèggere.

reader, *n.* (person) lettore *m.;* (book) libro di lettura *m.*

readily, *adj.* prontamente.

reading, *n.* lettura *f.*

ready, *adj.* pronto; (r.-made) già fatto.

real, *adj.* reale, vero.

realist, *n.* realista *m.*

reality, *n.* realtà *f.*

realization, *n.* realizzazione *f.*

realize, *vb.* (make real) realizzare; (be, become aware of) rendersi conto di.

really, *adv.* realmente, veramente, davvero.

realm, *n.* reame *m.*, regno *m.*

reap, *vb.* mietere, raccògliere.

rear, 1. *n.* (back) parte posteriore *f.;* (r.-guard) retroguàrdia *f.* 2. *vb.* (bring up) allevare; (raise) alzare; (erect) èrgere, *tr.;* (lift) sollevare; (of horse) impennarsi.

rear-view mirror, *n.* spècchio retrovisore *m.*

reason, 1. *n.* ragione *f.* 2. *vb.* ragionare.

reasonable, *adj.* ragionévole.

reassure, *vb.* rassicurare.

rebate, *n.* sconto *m.*

rebel, 1. *n.* and *adj.* ribèlle *(m.)*. 2. *vb.* ribellarsi.

rebellion, *n.* ribellione *f.*

rebellious, *adj.* ribèlle.

rebirth, *n.* rinàscita *f.*

reborn, be, *vb.* rinàscere.

rebound, 1. *n.* rimbalzo *m.* 2. *vb.* rimbalzare.

rebuff, *n.* ripulsa *f.*

rebuild, *vb.* ricostruire.

rebuke, 1. *n.* rimpròvero *m.* 2. *vb.* rimproverare.

rebuttal, *n.* confutazione *f.*

recalcitrant, *adj.* ricalcitrante.

recall, *vb.* richiamare.

recapitulate, *vb.* ricapitolare.

recede, *vb.* recèdere.

receipt, *n.* ricevuta *f.;* (document) quietanza *f.*

receive, *vb.* ricévere.

receiver, *n.* ricevitore *m.*

recent, *adj.* recènte.

recently, *adv.* recentemente.

receptacle, *n.* ricettàcolo *m.*, recipiènte *m.*

reception, *n.* accogliènza *f.;* (party) ricevimento *m.*

receptive, *adj.* ricettivo.

recess, *n.* (in wall) rientranza *f.;* (vacation) vacanze *f.*

recipe, *n.* ricètta *f.*

recipient, *n.* ricevènte *f.*

reciprocate, *vb.* ricambiare.

recitation, *n.* recitazione *f.*

recite, *vb.* recitare.

reckless, *adj.* avventato.

reckon, *vb.* (count) contare; (deem) stimare; (think) pensare.

reclaim, *vb.* redimere; (land) bonificare.

reclamation, *n.* bonifica *f.*

recline, *vb.* reclinare.

recognition, *n.* riconoscimento *m.*

recognize, *vb.* riconóscere.

recoil, *vb.* indietreggiare.

recollect, *vb.* ricordare, rammentarsi.

recommend, *vb.* raccomandare.

recommendation, *n.* raccomandazione *f.*

recompense, 1. *n.* ricompènsa *f.* 2. *vb.* ricompensare.

reconcile, *vb.* riconciliare.

recondition, *vb.* riparare.

reconsider, *vb.* riprèndere in esame.

reconstruct, *vb.* ricostruire.

record, 1. *n.* memòria *f.*, ricordo *m.*, registro *m.;* (top achievement) primato *m.;* (phonograph) disco *m.;* (r. library) discoteca *f.;* (r. player) giradischi *m.* 2. *vb.* registrare; (phonograph) incidere.

recording, *n.* incisione *f.*

recount, *vb.* (tell) raccontare; (count again) contare di nuòvo.

recourse, *n.* ricorso *m.;* (have r.) ricórrere.

recover, *vb.* ricuperare.

recovery, *n.* ricùpero *m.;* (medical) guarigione *f.*

recruit, 1. *n.* rècluta *f.* 2. *vb.* reclutare.

rectangle, *n.* rettàngolo *m.*

rectifier, *n.* rettificatrice *f.*

rectify, *vb.* rettificare.

recuperate, *vb.* ricuperare.

recur, *vb.* ricórrere, ritornare.

recycle, *vb.* riciclare.

red, *adj.* rosso.

redeem, *vb.* redimere.

redeemer, *n.* redentore *m.*

redemption, *n.* redenzione *f.*

redress, *n.* riparazione *f.*

reduce, *vb.* ridurre.

reduction, *n.* riduzione *f.*

reed, *n.* canna *f.;* (for instrument) ància *f.*

reef, *n.* scòglio *m.*

reel, 1. *n.* (bobbin) naspo *m.;* (spool) rocchetto *m.;* (dance) trescone *m.* 2. *vb.* traballare; (r. off) dipanare.

refer, *vb.* riferire, *tr.*

referee, *n.* àrbitro *m.*

reference, *n.* allusione *f.*, riferimento *m.;* (cross-r.) rimando *m.;* (r. room) sala di consultazione *f.*

refill, *vb.* riempire di nuòvo.

refine, *vb.* raffinare.

refinement, *n.* raffinatezza *f.*

reflect, *vb.* riflèttere.

reflection, *n.* riflessione *f.*, riflèsso *m.*

reflex, *n.* riflèsso *m.*

reform, 1. *n.* riforma *f.* 2. *vb.* riformare.

reformation, *n.* riforma *f.*

refractory, *adj.* ribèlle.

refrain, *vb.* trattenere, *tr.*

refresh, *vb.* rinfrescare, ristorare.

refreshment, *n.* ristòro *m.*

refrigerator, *n.* frigorífero *m.*

refuge, *n.* rifùgio *m.;* (take r.) rifugiarsi.

refugee, *n.* rifugiato *m.*

refund, *vb.* restituire.

refusal, *n.* rifiuto *m.*

refuse, 1. *n.* (waste matter) rifiuti *m.pl.* 2. *vb.* rifiutare.

refutation, *n.* confutazione *f.*

refute, *vb.* confutare.

regain, *vb.* ritornare a.

regal, *adj.* regale.

regard, 1. *n.* riguardo *m.*, rispètto *m.* 2. *vb.* (look at) guardare; (concern) riguardare; (consider) considerare.

regarding, *prep.* riguardo a.

regardless, *adv.* ciò nonostante; (r. of) malgrado.

regent, *n.* reggènte *m.*

regime, *n.* regime *m.*

regiment, *n.* reggimento *m.*

region, *n.* regione *f.*

register, 1. *n.* registro *m.* 2. *vb.* registrare.

registration, *n.* registrazione *f.*

regret, 1. *n.* rimpianto *m.*, rincrescimento *m.* 2. *vb.* rimpiàngere, rincréscere (with English subject in dative).

regular, *adj.* regolare.

regularity, *n.* regolarità *f.*

regulate, *vb.* regolare.

regulation, *n.* regolamento *m.*

regulator, *n.* regolatore *m.*

rehabilitate, *vb.* riabilitare.

rehearsal, *n.* pròva *f.*

rehearse, *vb.* provare.

reign, 1. *n.* regno *m.* 2. *vb.* regnare.

reimburse, *vb.* rimborsare.

rein, *n.* rèdina *f.*

reincarnation, *n.* nuòva incarnazione *f.*

reindeer, *n.* rènna *f.*

reinforce, *vb.* rinforzare.

reinforcement, *n.* rinfòrzo *m.*

reinstate, *vb.* rimèttere.

reiterate, *vb.* reiterare.

reject, *vb.* rigettare, respingere.

rejoice, *vb.* rallegrare, *tr.*

rejoin, *vb.* (answer) replicare; (join again) ricongiùngersi.

rejoinder, *n.* rèplica *f.*

rejuvenate, *vb.* ringiovanire.

relapse, 1. *n.* ricaduta *f.* 2. *vb.* ricadere.

relate, *vb.* (tell) narrare; (be connected with) riferirsi a; riguardare; (connect) mèttere in relazione. r. to, entrare in rapporto con.

related, *adj.* affine, connèsso.

relation, *n.* (story) narrazione *f.;* (connection) rappòrto *m.;* relazione *f.;* (person) parènte *m.*

relationship, *n.* rappòrto *m.;* (kinship) parentela *f.*

relative, 1. *n.* parènte *m.* 2. *adj.* relativo.

relativity, *n.* relatività *f.*

relax, *vb.* allentare, *tr.*

relay, *vb.* ritrasmèttere.

release, 1. *n.* liberazione *f.* 2. *vb.* liberare, sprigionare.

relent, *vb.* aver pietà.

relevant, *adj.* pertinente.

reliable, *adj.* fededegno.

reliant, *adj.* fidènte.

relic, *n.* avanzo *m.;* (religious) reliquia *f.*

relief, *n.* sollièvo *m.;* (social work) assistènza *f.;* (diversion) diversivo *m.;* (replacement) càmbio *m.;* (help) soccorso *m.*

relieve, *vb.* sollevare; (help) soccórrere; (free) liberare; (alleviate) alleviare.

religion, *n.* religione *f.*

religious, *adj.* religioso.

relinquish, *vb.* abbandonare.

relish, 1. *n.* gusto *m.;* (sauce) condimento *m.* 2. *vb.* gustare.

reluctance, *n.* riluttanza *f.*

reluctant, *adj.* riluttante.

rely, *vb.* confidare.

remain, *vb.* restare, rimanere.

remainder, *n.* rèsto *m.*

remark, 1. *n.* osservazione *f.* 2. *vb.* osservare.

remarkable, *adj.* notévole, rimarchévole.

remedy, 1. *n.* rimèdio *m.* 2. *vb.* rimediare a.

remember, *vb.* ricordarsi di.

remembrance, *n.* ricòrdo *m.*

remind, *vb.* rammentare.

reminiscence, *n.* reminiscènza *f.*

remiss, *adj.* negligènte.

remit, *vb.* (send) spedire; (forgive) rimèttere.

remittance, *n.* spedizione *f.*

remnant, *n.* rèsto *m.*, rimanènte *m.*

remorse, *n.* rimòrso *m.*

remote, *adj.* remòto.

removable, *adj.* amovìbile.

removal, *n.* rimozione *f.*

remove, *vb.* tògliere, rimuòvere.

renaissance, *n.* rinascimento *m.*

rend, *vb.* strappare.

render, *vb.* rèndere.

rendezvous, *n.* appuntamento *m.*

rendition, *n.* esecuzione *f.*

renege, *vb.* rifiutare.

renew, *vb.* rinnovare.

renewal, *n.* rinnovamento *m.*

renounce, *vb.* rinunciare a.

renovate, *vb.* rimodernare.

renown, *n.* rinomanza *f.*

renowned, *adj.* rinomato.

rent, 1. *n.* affitto *m.*, pigione *f.* 2. *vb.* affittare, noleggiare.

rental, *n.* nolèggio *m.*

repair, 1. *n.* riparazione *f.* 2. *vb.* riparare.

reparation, *n.* riparazione *f.*

repatriate, *vb.* rimpatriare.

repay, *vb.* ripagare, rimborsare.

repeat, 1. *n.* (music) ripresa *f.* 2. *vb.* ripètere, replicare.

repel, *vb.* respingere.

repent, *vb.* pentirsi di.

repentance, *n.* pentimento *m.*

repercussion, *n.* ripercussione *f.*

repertoire, *n.* repertòrio *m.*

repetition, *n.* ripetizione *f.;* (theater) rèplica *f.*

replace, *vb.* sostituire, rimpiazzare.

replenish, *vb.* riempire di nuòvo.

reply, 1. *n.* risposta *f.;* (rebuttal) rèplica *f.* 2. *vb.* rispóndere; replicare.

report, 1. *n.* (bang) detonazione *f.;* (news) notizia *f.;* (rumor) voce *f.;* (memoir) rappòrto *m.* 2. *vb.* dare notizia di; (complain of) denunciare.

reporter, *n.* cronista *m.*, giornalista *m.*

repose, 1. *n.* ripòso *m.* 2. *vb.* riposare.

reprehend, *vb.* riprèndere.

reprehensible, *adj.* riprensìbile.

represent, *vb.* rappresentare.

representation, *n.* rappresentazione *f.*

representative, 1. *n.* deputato *m.* 2. *adj.* rappresentativo.

repress, *vb.* reprimere.

repression, *n.* repressione *f.*

reprimand, 1. *n.* rimpròvero *m.* 2. *vb.* rimproverare.

reprisal, *n.* rappresàglia *f.*

reproach, 1. *n.* rimpròvero *m.* 2. *vb.* rimproverare.

reproduce, vb. riprodurre, tr.

reproduction, n. riproduzione f.

reproof, n. rimpròvero m.

reprove, vb. rimproverare.

reptile, n. rèttile m.

republic, n. repùbblica f.

republican, adj. repubblicano.

repudiate, vb. ripudiare.

repudiation, n. ripùdio m.

repulse, 1. n. ripulsa f. 2. vb. respingere.

repulsive, adj. repellènte.

reputation, n. riputazione f.

repute, vb. riputare.

request, 1. n. richièsta f., domanda f. 2. vb. richièdere, domandare.

require, vb. richièdere, esigere.

requirement, n. esigènza f., requisito m.

requisite, 1. n. requisito m. 2. adj. necessàrio.

requisition, 1. n. requisizione f. 2. vb. requisire.

rescind, vb. rescindere.

rescue, 1. n. liberazione f. 2. vb. liberare.

research, n. ricerche f.pl.

resemble, vb. rassomigliare a.

resent, vb. offèndersi di.

reservation, n. risèrva f.; (tickets) prenotazione f.

reserve, 1. n. risèrva f. 2. vb. riservare; (tickets) prenotare.

reservoir, n. serbatòio m.

reside, vb. risièdere, abitare.

residence, n. residènza f., abitazione f.

resident, 1. n. abitante m. 2. adj. residènte.

residue, n. resìduo m.

resign, vb. dimèttersi; (r. oneself, give up hope) rassegnarsi.

resignation, n. dimissione f.; (loss of hope) rassegnazione f.

resist, vb. resìstere.

resistance, n. resistènza f.

resolute, adj. risoluto.

resolution, n. risoluzione f.

resolve, 1. n. decisione f. 2. vb. risòlvere, sciògliere; (decide) decidersi.

resonance, n. risonanza f.

resonant, adj. risonante.

resort, 1. n. (recourse) ricorso m.; (vacation place) stazione f.; luògo di soggiorno m. 2. vb. ricòrrere.

resound, vb. risonare.

resource, n. risorsa f.

respect, 1. n. rispètto m. 2. vb. rispettare.

respectable, adj. rispettàbile.

respectful, adj. rispettoso.

respective, adj. rispettivo.

respiration, n. respirazione f.

respite, n. trègua f.

respond, vb. rispóndere.

response, n. risposta f.

responsibility, n. responsabilità f.

responsible, adj. responsàbile.

responsive, adj. responsivo.

rest, 1. n. (remainder) rimanènte m.; (repose) ripòso m. 2. vb. riposare.

restaurant, n. ristorante m., ristoratore m., trattorìa f.; (r.-keeper) trattore m.

restful, adj. riposante.

restitution, n. restituzione f.

restless, adj. irrequièto.

restoration, n. restaurazione f.

restore, vb. restaurare.

restrain, vb. trattenere.

restraint, n. contròllo m.

restrict, vb. restringere.

restriction, n. restrizione f.

result, 1. n. risultato m. 2. vb. risultare.

resume, vb. riassùmere, riprèndere.

résumé, n. riassunto m.

resurgent, adj. risorgènte.

resurrect, vb. esumare.

resurrection, n. risurrezione f.

retail, 1. adv. al minuto, al dettàglio. 2. vb. vèndere al minuto, vèndere al dettàglio.

retain, vb. ritenere, conservare.

retake, vb. riprèndere.

retaliate, vb. ricambiare.

retaliation, n. rappresàglia f.

retard, vb. ritardare.

retention, n. ritenzione f.; (remembering ability) memòria f.

reticence, n. reticènza f.

reticent, adj. reticènte.

retina, n. rètina f.

retinue, n. sèguito m.

retire, vb. ritirare, tr.

retort, vb. replicare, ribàttere.

retract, vb. (pull back) ritrarre; (withdraw) ritrattare.

retreat, 1. n. ritirata f. 2. vb. ritirarsi.

retribution, n. retribuzione f.

retrieve, vb. ricuperare.

retroactive, adj. retroattivo.

retrospect, n. sguardo retrospettivo m.

retrospective, adj. retrospettivo.

return, 1. n. ritorno m.; (r. ticket) biglietto d'andata e ritorno m. 2. vb. tornare; ritornare.

reunion, n. riunione f.

reunite, vb. riunire.

reveal, vb. rivelare.

revel, 1. n. (noisy good time) baldòria f.; (drunken rout) gozzovìglia f. 2. vb. far baldòria; gozzovigliare.

revelation, n. rivelazione f.

revelry, n. baldòria f.

revenge, 1. n. vendetta f. 2. vb. vendicare.

revenue, n. entrata f.

reverberate, vb. riverberare.

revere, vb. riverire.

reverence, n. riverènza f.

reverend, adj. reverèndo.

reverent, adj. riverènte.

reverie, n. fantasticherìa f.

reverse, 1. n. rovèscio m., contràrio m.; (auto) màrcia indiètro f. 2. vb. rovesciare; (direction) invertire.

revert, vb. ritornare.

review, 1. n. rivista f., riesame m.; (book r.) recensione f. 2. vb. passare in rivista; riesaminare; (book) recensire.

revise, vb. rivedere.

revision, n. revisione f.

revival, n. ravvivamento m.; (theater) ripresa f.

revive, vb. ravvivare.

revocation, n. rèvoca f.

revoke, vb. revocare.

revolt, 1. n. rivòlta f. 2. vb. rivoltare. tr.

revolution, n. rivoluzione f.; (turn) giro m.

revolutionary, adj. rivoluzionàrio.

revolve, vb. girare.

revolver, n. rivoltèlla f.

reward, 1. n. ricompènsa f. 2. vb. ricompensare.

rhetoric, n. rettòrica f.

rhetorical, adj. rettòrico.

rheumatic, adj. reumàtico.

rheumatism, n. reumatismo m.

rhinoceros, n. rinoceronte m.

rhubarb, n. rabàrbaro m.

rhyme, 1. n. rima f. 2. vb. rimare.

rhythm, n. ritmo m.

rhythmical, adj. ritmico.

rib, n. còstola f.

ribbon, n. nastro m.

rice, n. riso m.

rich, adj. ricco.

riches, n. ricchezza f.

rid, vb. sbarazzare.

riddle, n. enimma m.

ride, 1. n. corsa f. 2. vb. (on horse) cavalcare; (other transport) andare.

rider, n. cavalière m.

ridge, n. (between furrows) pòrca f.; (mountain) cresta f.

ridicule, 1. n. ridicolo m. 2. vb. deridere.

ridiculous, adj. ridìcolo.

rifle, n. fucile m.

rig, 1. n. equipàggio m.; (ship) atrezzatura f. 2. vb. equipaggiare; attrezzare.

right, 1. n. (side) dèstra f.; (justice) giusto m. 2. adj. (side) dèstro; (straight) diretto; (correct) corrètto; (be r.) aver ragione. 3. vb. (set upright) drizzare; (correct) corrèggere.

righteous, adj. giusto.

righteousness, n. giustizia f.

right of way, n. precedènza f.

rigid, adj. rigido.

rigidity, n. rigidezza f.

rigor, n. rigore m.

rigorous, adj. rigoroso.

rim, n. bordo m., orlo m.

ring, 1. n. (circle) cèrchio m.; (for finger) anèllo m.; (boxing) quadrato m.; (on bell) suòno m., scampanellata f. 2. vb. sonare; (r. out) risonare;

(form a r. around) accerchiare.

rinse, *vb.* risciacquare.

riot, 1. *n.* tumulto *m.* 2. *vb.* tumultuare.

rip, *vb.* strappare.

ripe, *adj.* maturo.

ripen, *vb.* maturare.

ripoff, 1. *n.* furto *m.* 2. *vb.* rubare.

ripple, *n.* increspatura *f.*

rise, 1. *n.* (increase) aumènto *m.;* (origin) origine *f.* 2. *vb.* alzarsi, levarsi, sorgere.

risk, 1. *n.* rischio *m.* 2. *vb.* arrischiare, rischiare.

rite, *n.* rito *m.*

ritual, *n. and adj.* rituale *(m.).*

rival, 1. *n. and adj.* rivale. 2. *vb.* rivaleggiare con.

rivalry, *n.* rivalità *f.*

river, *n.* fiume *m.*

rivet, 1. *n.* chiòdo ribadito *m.* 2. *vb.* ribadire.

road, 1. *n.* cammino *m.*, strada *f.*, via *f.* 2. *adj.* (pertaining to roads) stradale.

roam, *vb.* vagare.

roar, 1. *n.* ruggito *m.* 2. *vb.* ruggire.

roast, 1. *n.* arròsto *m.* 2. *vb.* arrostire.

roasting, (of coffee) *n.* torrefazione *f.*

rob, *vb.* derubare; (r. completely) svaligiare.

robber, *n.* ladrone *m.*

robbery, *n.* furto *m.*

robe, *n.* vèste *f.*

robin, *n.* pettirosso *m.*

robot, *n.* autòma *m.*

robust, *adj.* robusto.

rock, 1. *n.* ròccia *f.;* (music) (musicaccia) rock *f.;* (fortress) ròcca *f.;* (pertaining to r.) roccioso. 2. *vb.* dondolare.

rocker, *n.* (rocking-chair) sèdia a dòndolo *f.*

rocket, *n.* razzo *m.*

rocky, *adj.* roccioso.

rod, *n.* verga *f.*

rodent, *n.* roditore *m.*

roe, *n.* cèrva *f.*

rogue, *n.* briccone *m.*

roguish, *adj.* bricconesco.

role, *n.* ruòlo *m.*

roll, 1. *n.* ròtolo *m.;* (bread) panino *m.;* (list) ruòlo *m.;* (of ship) rullio *m.* 2. *vb.* rotolare; (ship) rullare.

roller, *n.* rotèlla *m.*, rullo *m.*

roller-bearing, *n.* cuscinetto a rotolamento *m.*

Roman, *adj.* romano.

romance, *n.* romanzo *m.*

romantic, *adj.* romàntico.

Rome, *n.* Roma *f.*

romp, *vb.* giocare vigorosamente.

roof, *n.* tètto *m.*

room, *n.* (in house) càmera *f.*, stanza *f.;* (space) posto *m.*, spàzio *f.*

roommate, *n.* compagno di stanza *m.*, compagna di stanza *f.*

rooster, *n.* gallo *m.*

root, *n.* radice *f.*

rope, *n.* còrda *f.*, fune *f.*

rosary, *n.* rosàrio *m.*

rose, *n.* ròsa *f.*

rosin, *n.* rèsina *f.*

rosy, *adj.* ròseo.

rot, 1. *n.* putrefazione *f.* 2. *vb.* marcire, imputridire, *tr.*

rotary, *adj.* rotatòrio.

rotate, *vb.* rotare.

rotation, *n.* rotazione *f.*

rotten, *adj.* pùtrido.

rouge, *n.* rossetto *m.*

rough, *adj.* rùvido, rozzo.

round, 1. *n.* giro *m.* 2. *adj.* rotondo, tondo. 3. *adv.* intorno. 4. *prep.* intorno a.

rouse, *vb.* svegliare, risvegliare.

rout, *n.* rotta *f.*

route, *n.* percorso *m.*

routine, *n.* abitùdini fisse *f.pl.*

rove, *vb.* errare.

row, 1. *n.* (fight) lite *f.;* (uproar) baccano *m.;* (series) fila *f.;* (boat ride) remata *f.* 2. *vb.* (raise a row) litigare; (use oars) remare.

rowboat, *n.* battèllo a remi *m.*

rowdy, *adj.* litigioso.

royal, *adj.* reale, règio.

royalty, *n.* regalità *f.*

rub, 1. *n.* fregata *f.* 2. *vb.* fregare, strofinare.

rubber, *n.* gomma *f.;* (overshoe) scarpa di gomma *f.*

rubbish, *n.* scarti *m.pl.;* (nonsense) fandònie *f.pl.*

ruby, *n.* rubino *m.*

rudder, *n.* timone *m.*

ruddy, *adj.* rubicondo.

rude, *adj.* rude.

rudiment, *n.* rudimento *m.*

rue, *vb.* pentirsi di.

ruffian, *n.* malfattore *m.*

ruffle, 1. *n.* increspatura *f.* 2. *vb.* increspare.

rug, *n.* (for floor) tappeto *m.;* (blanket) copèrta *f.*

rugged, *adj.* scabroso.

ruin, 1. *n.* rovina *f.;* (remain) rùdere *m.* 2. *vb.* rovinare.

ruinous, *adj.* ravinoso.

rule, 1. *n.* règola *f.* 2. *vb.* regolare; (reign) regnare.

ruler, *n.* (lawgiver) sovrano *m.;* (measuring-stick) règolo *m.*

rum, *n.* rum *m.*

rumble, 1. *n.* brontolìo *m.* 2. *vb.* brontolare.

rumor, *n.* diceria *f.*, voce *f.*

run, 1. *n.* (in stocking) cordiglièra *f.* 2. *vb.* còrrere; (work) funzionare; (flow) scórrere; (r. across) incontrare; (r. away) fuggire; (r. into) investire.

run-down, *adj.* indebolito.

rung, *n.* piuòlo *m.*

runner, *n.* corridore *m.*

runway, *n.* pista *f.*

rupture, *n.* rottura *f.*

rural, *adj.* rurale.

rush, 1. *n.* afflusso *m.;* (hurry) fretta *f.;* (reed) giunco *m.* 2. *vb.* affluire; precipitarsi.

Russia, *n.* Rùssia *f.*

Russian, *adj.* russo.

rust, 1. *n.* rùggine *f.* 2. *vb.* arrugginire, *tr.*

rustic, *n. and adj.* rùstico *(m.).*

rustle, 1. *n.* fruscìo *m.* 2. *vb.* frusciare.

rust-proof, *adj.* inossidàbile.

rusty, *adj.* arrugginito, rugginoso.

rut, *n.* solco *m.*

ruthless, *adj.* spietato.

rye, *n.* ségale *f.*

S

Sabbath, *n.* giorno di ripòso *m.*

saber, *n.* sciàbola *f.*

sable, *n.* zibellino *m.*

sabotage, 1. *n.* sabotàggio *m.* 2. *vb.* sabotare.

saboteur, *n.* sabotatore *m.*

saccharine, 1. *n.* saccarina *f.* 2. *adj.* saccarino.

sachet, *n.* sacchetto di profumo *m.*

sack, 1. *n.* sacco *m.;* (pillage) sacchèggio *m.* 2. *vb.* (discharge) licenziare; (plunder) saccheggiare.

sacrament, *n.* sacramento *m.*

sacred, *adj.* sacro.

sacrifice, 1. *n.* sacrificio *m.* 2. *vb.* sacrificare.

sacrilege, *n.* sacrilègio *m.*

sacrilegious, *adj.* sacrilego.

sacristan, *n.* sagrestano *m.*

sacristy, *n.* sagrestìa *f.*

sad, *adj.* triste.

sadden, *vb.* rattristare.

saddle, 1. *n.* sèlla *f.* 2. *vb.* sellare.

sadism, *n.* sadismo *m.*

safe, 1. *n.* cassaforte *f.* 2. *adj.* sicuro, salvo; (s. and sound) sano e salvo.

safeguard, 1. *n.* salvaguàrdia *f.* 2. *vb.* salvaguardare.

safety, *n.* sicurezza *f.*

safety island, *n.* isolòtto salvagente *m.*

safety-pin, *n.* spillo di sicurezza *f.*

sage, *n. and adj.* sàggio *(m.).*

sail, 1. *n.* vela *f.* 2. *vb.* navigare; (depart) salpare.

sailboat, *n.* battèllo a vela *m.*

sailor, *n.* marinaio *m.*

saint, *n.* santo *m.*

sake, *n.* motivo *m.*

salad, *n.* insalata *f.*

salary, *n.* stipèndio *m.*

sale, *n.* véndita *f.*, spàccio *m.*

salesman, *n.* commesso di negòzio *m.;* (traveling s.) commesso viaggiatore *m.*

sales tax, *n.* tassa di scambio *f.*

saliva, *n.* saliva *f.*

salmon, *n.* salmone *m.*

salon, *n.* salone *m.*

salt, 1. n. sale m. 2. adj. salso. 3. vb. salare.

salty, adj. salso, salato.

salutation, n. saluto m., salutazione f.

salute, 1. n. saluto m. 2. vb. salutare.

salvage, 1. n. salvatàggio m. 2. vb. salvare.

salvation, n. salvezza f.

salve, n. unguento m.

same, adj. stesso.

sample, 1. n. campione m.; (s. fair) fièra campionària f.

sanatorium, n. sanatòrio m.

sanctify, vb. santificare.

sanction, 1. n. sanzione f. 2. vb. sanzionare.

sanctity, n. santità f.

sanctuary, n. santuàrio m.

sand, n. rena f., sàbbia f.

sandal, n. sàndalo m.

sandwich, n. sandwich m., tramezzino m.

sandy, adj. renoso, sabbioso.

sane, adj. sano.

sanguinary, adj. sanguinàrio.

sanitary, adj. igiènico, sanitàrio.

sanitation, n. igiène f.

sanity, n. sanità f.

Santa Claus, n. Befana f. (old woman who brings presents on Twelfth Night).

sap, 1. n. linfa f.; (fool) citrullo m. 2. vb. (weaken) indebolire.

sapphire, n. zaffiro m.

sarcasm, n. sarcasmo m.

sarcastic, adj. sarcàstico.

sardine, n. sardèlla f.

Sardinia, n. Sardegna f.

Sardinian, adj. sardo.

sash, n. cintura f.

satellite, n. satèllite m.

satin, n. raso m.

satire, n. sàtira f.

satirize, vb. satireggiare.

satisfaction, n. soddisfazione f.

satisfactory, adj. soddisfacènte f.

satisfy, vb. soddisfare.

saturate, vb. saturare.

saturation, n. saturazione f.

Saturday, n. sàbato m.

sauce, n. salsa f.

saucer, n. piattino m.

saucy, adj. impertinènte.

sausage, n. salsiccia f.

savage, n. and adj. selvàggio (m.).

save, 1. vb. (preserve) salvare; (economize) risparmiare. 2. prep. salvo.

savings, n. rispàrmio m.; (s.-bank) cassa di rispàrmio f.

savior, n. salvatore m.

savor, 1. n. sapore m. 2. vb. sapere.

savory, adj. saporito.

saw, 1. n. sega f.; (proverb) provèrbio m. 2 vb. segare.

say, vb. dire; (s. again) ridire.

saying, n. provèrbio m.

scab, n. crosta f.; (nonstriker) crumire m.

scaffold, n. patibolo m.

scaffolding, n. impalcatura f.

scald, 1. n. scottatura f. 2. vb. scottare.

scale, 1. n. scala f.; (balance) bilància f.; (fish, etc.) squama f.; (music) gamma f. 2. vb. scrostare; (climb) arrampicarsi su.

scalp, n. pèlle del crànio f.

scan, vb. scrutare; (poetry) scandire.

scandal, n. scàndalo m.; (gossip) maldicènza f.

scandalous, adj. scandaloso.

scant, adj. scarso.

scar, 1. n. cicatrice f. 2. vb. cicatrizzare, tr.

scarce, adj. scarso; (be s.) scarseggiare.

scarcely, adv. appena.

scarcity, n. scarsità f.

scare, 1. n. spavento m. 2. vb. spaventare.

scarecrow, n. spauràcchio m.

scarf, n. sciarpa f.

scarlet, n. and adj. scarletto (m.).

scarlet fever, n. scarlattina f.

scathing, adj. mordace.

scatter, vb. spàrgere.

scavenger, n. spazzino m.

scenario, n. scenàrio m.

scene, n. scèna f.

scenery, n. paesàggio m.

scent, n. odore m., fiuto m., profumo m.; (track) pista f.

schedule, n. oràrio m.

scheme, n. progètto m.

scholar, n. dòtto m., erudito m.

scholarship, n. borsa di stùdio f.; (knowledge) erudizione f.

school, n. scuòla f.

sciatica, n. sciàtica f.

science, n. sciènza f.

science fiction, n. fantascienza f.

scientific, adj. scientifico.

scientist, n. scienziato m.

scissors, n. fòrbici f.pl.

scoff, vb. schernire, farsi beffe.

scold, vb. sgridare.

scolding, n. ramanzina f.

scoop, 1. n. cucchiàia f., ramaiuòlo m. 2. vb. travasare.

scope, n. (extent) portata f.; (outlet) sfògo m.

scorch, vb. bruciare.

score, 1. n. (points) punti m.pl.; (twenty) ventina f.; (music) partitura f. 2. vb. segnare.

scorn, 1. n. disprèzzo m., disdegno m. 2. vb. disprezzare, disdegnare.

scornful, adj. sprezzante, disdegnoso.

Scotch, adj. scozzese.

Scotland, n. Scòzia f.

scour, vb. lavare strofinando.

scourge, 1. n. sfèrza f. 2. vb. sferzare.

scout, n. esploratore m.

scowl, vb. aggrottare le ciglia.

scramble, 1. n. parapiglia m. 2. vb. (climb) arrampicarsi.

scrambled eggs, n. uòva strapazzate f.pl.

scrap, 1. n. pezzetto m.; (fight) tafferùglio m. 2. vb. scartare; (fight) azzuffarsi.

scrape, 1. n. (trouble) impiccio m. 2. vb. raschiare.

scratch, 1. n. graffiatura f. 2. vb. graffiare.

scream, 1. n. strillo m. 2. vb. strillare.

screen, 1. n. (furniture) paravènto m.; (sieve) crivèllo m.; (movie) schèrmo m. 2. vb. (protect) protèggere; (sift) crivellare.

screw, 1. n. vite f. 2. vb. avvitare.

screw-driver, n. cacciavite m.

scribble, vb. scribacchiare.

scribe, n. scriba m.

scripture, n. scrittura f.

scroll, n. ròtolo m.

scrub, vb. strofinare.

scruple, n. scrùpolo m.

scrupulous, adj. scrupoloso.

scrutinize, vb. scrutare.

sculptor, n. scultore m.

sculpture, n. scultura f.

scythe, n. falce f.

sea, n. mare m.

seabed, n. letto del mare m.

seal, 1. n. sigillo m.; suggèllo m. (animal) fòca f. 2. vb. sigillare; suggellare.

sealing-wax, n. ceralacca f.

seam, n. cucitura f.

seaport, n. pòrto di mare m.

search, 1. n. ricerca f. 2. vb. ricercare.

seasick, adj. (be s.) soffrire di mal di mare.

seasickness, n. mal di mare m.

season, 1. n. stagione f.; (s. ticket) biglietto d'abbonamento m. 2. vb. condire.

seasoning, n. condimento m.

seat, 1. n. (chair) sèdia f.; (place) posto m.; (headquarters) sede f. 2. vb. far sedere.

second, n. and adj. secondo (m.).

secondary, adj. secondàrio.

secret, n. and adj. segreto (m.).

secretary, n. segretàrio m., segretària f.

sect, n. sètta f.

section, n. sezione f.

sectional, adj. sezionale.

secular, adj. secolare.

secure, adj. sicuro.

security, n. sicurezza f.

sedative, n. and adj. sedativo (m.).

seduce, vb. sedurre.

seductive, adj. seducènte.

see, vb. vedere.

seed, n. seme m.

seek, vb. cercare.

seem, vb. parere, sembrare.

seep, vb. trasudare.

seesaw, n. altalena f.

segment, n. segmento m.

segregate, vb. segregare.

seize, vb. afferrare.

seldom, adv. di rado, raramente.

select, 1. adj. scelto. 2. vb. scégliere.

selection, n. scelta f., selezione f.

selective, adj. selettivo.

self, pron. stesso; **self-**, di sè stesso.

selfish, adj. egoìstico.

selfishness, n. egoismo m.

sell, vb. véndere.

semantic, adj. semàntico.

semantics, n. semàntica f.

semester, n. semèstre m.

semicircle, n. semicérchio m.

semicolon, n. punto e virgola, m.sg.

seminary, n. seminàrio m.

senate, n. senato m.

senator, n. senatore m.

send, vb. mandare, spedire, inviare.

senile, adj. senile.

senior, adj. maggiore; (father) padre.

senior citizen, n. persona anziana f.

sensation, n. sensazione f.

sensational, adj. sensazionale.

sense, 1. n. sènso m.; (intelligence) senno m. 2. vb. intuire.

sensible, adj. assennato.

sensitive, adj. sensitivo, sensibile.

sensual, adj. sensuale.

sentence, 1. n. frase f., proposizione f.; (court) condanna f. 2. vb. condannare.

sentiment, n. sentimento m.

sentimental, adj. sentimentale.

separate, 1. adj. separato. 2. vb. separare.

separation, n. separazione f.

September, n. settèmbre m.

sequence, n. sèrie f.

serenade, n. serenata f.

serene, adj. sereno.

sergeant, n. sergènte m.

serial, adj. in sèrie, periòdico.

series, n. sèrie f.

serious, adj. sèrio.

sermon, n. sermone m.

serpent, n. serpènte m.

serum, n. sièro m.

servant, n. domèstico m., sèrvo m.; (s.s, collectively) servitù f.

serve, vb. servire.

service, n. servizio m.

servile, adj. servile.

servitude, n. servitù f.

session, n. sessione f.

set, 1. n. sèrie f.; (clique) cricca f. 2. adj. fisso. 3. vb. (put) méttere; (regulate) regolare; (fix) fissare; (mount) montare.

settle, vb. (establish) stabilire, tr.; (fix) fissare; (decide) decidere; (arrange) sistemare; (pay) saldare; (s. down to) méttersi a.

settlement, n. (colony) colònia

f.; (hamlet) borgo m.; (accounts) regolamento m.; (affairs) sistemazione f.

settler, n. colòno m.

seven, num. sètte.

shell, 1. n. (egg) gùscio m.; (pod) baccèllo m.; (conch) conchiglia f.; (explosive) bomba f. 2. vb. bombardare.

seventeen, num. diciassètte.

seventeenth, adj. diciassettèsimo.

seventh, adj. sèttimo.

seventieth, adj. settantèsimo.

seventy, num. settanta.

sever, vb. staccare, tr.

several, adj. parecchi.

severe, adj. sevèro.

severity, n. severità f.

sew, vb. cucire.

sewer, n. fogna f.

sex, n. sèsso m.

sexism, n. sessismo m.

sexist, n. and adj. sessista.

sexton, n. sagrestano m.

sexual, adj. sessuale.

shabby, adj. (worn-out) lògoro; (mean) gretto, meschino.

shack, n. capanna f.

shade, 1. n. ombra f.; (color) tinta f.; (against light) paralume m. 2. vb. ombreggiare; (darken) oscurare.

shadow, n. ombra f.

shady, adj. ombroso.

shaft, n. (mine) pozzo m.; (transmission) àlbero m.; (wagon) stanga f.; (ray) ràggio m.; (arrow) strale m.

shaggy, adj. ispido.

shake, 1. n. scòssa f.; (hand-s.) stretta di mano f. 2. vb. scuòtere, tr.; (quiver) tremare; (s. hands with) stringere la mano a.

shall, vb. dovere; or use future tense of verb.

shallow, adj. pòco profondo.

shame, 1. n. vergogna f.; (pity) peccato m.; (what a s.) che peccato! 2. vb. gettar vergogna su.

shameful, adj. vergognoso.

shampoo, n. sciampò f.

shape, 1. n. forma f., fòggia f. 2. vb. formare, foggiare.

share, 1. n. parte f., porzione f.; (stock) azione f. 2. vb. condividere.

shark, n. pescecane m.

sharp, 1. n. (music) dièsis m. 2. adj. acuto.

sharpen, vb. aguzzare.

sharply, adv. acutamente; (harshly) aspramente.

sharpness, n. acutezza f.

shatter, vb. frantumare.

shave, vb. ràdere, tr., fare la barba a, tr.

shawl, n. scialle m.

she, pron. ella f., essa f., lèi f.

sheaf, n. fàscio m., covone m.

shear, vb. tosare.

shears, n. cesòie f.pl.

sheath, n. fòdero m., guaìna f.

shed, 1. n. tettòia f. 2. vb. versare; (lose) lasciar cadere.

sheep, n. pècora f.

sheet, n. (bed) lenzuòlo m.; (paper) fòglio m.; (metal) lastra f.

shelf, n. scaffale m.

shellac, n. gomma lacca f.

shelter, 1. n. ricòvero m. 2. vb. ricoverare, tr.

shepherd, n. pastore m.

sherbet, n. sorbetto m.

sherry, n. vino di Xeres m.

shield, 1. n. scudo m. 2. vb. protèggere.

shift, 1. n. (change) cambiamento m.; (turn) turno m. 2. vb. cambiare.

shin, n. stinco m.

shine, vb. brillare, splèndere; (shoes) lucidare.

shingles, n. èrpete f.

shiny, adj. lùcido.

ship, 1. n. nave f. 2. vb. spedire.

shipment, n. spedizione f.

shipper, n. speditore m.

shipping agent, n. spedizionière m.

shipwreck, n. naufràgio m.

shirk, vb. sottrarsi a.

shirt, n. camicia f.

shiver, 1. n. brìvido m. 2. vb. rabbrividire.

shock, 1. n. scòssa f., urto m. 2. vb. urtare.

shoe, 1. n. scarpa f. 2. vb. calzare; (horse) terrare.

shoelace, n. làccio per scarpe m.

shoemaker, n. calzolaio m.

shoot, 1. n. (sprout) germóglio m. 2. vb. (gun) sparare; (a person) fucilare; (s. down) abbàttere.

shop, 1. n. bottega f., negòzio m., spàccio m. 2. vb. far compre.

shopping, n. compre f.pl., spese f.pl.

shore, n. spiàggia f., sponda f.

short, adj. brève, corto; (s. circuit) corto circùito m.; (run s.) scarseggiare.

shortage, n. mancanza f.

shorten, vb. abbreviare, tr.

shorthand, n. stenografia f.

shortly, adv. fra pòco.

shorts, n. calzoncini corti m.pl.

shot, n. colpo m., sparo m.; (bullets) pallini m.pl.; (distance) portata f.

should, vb. use conditional of dovere.

shoulder, n. spalla f.

shout, 1. n. grido m. 2. vb. gridare.

shove, 1. n. spinta f. 2. vb. spingere.

shovel, n. pala f.

show, 1. n. mostra f., esposizione f.; (theater) spettàcolo m. 2. vb. mostrare.

shower, n. (rain) acquazzone m.; (bath) dòccia f.

shrapnel, n. shràpnel m.

shrewd, adj. acuto, furbo.

shriek, 1. n. strillo m. 2. vb. strillare.

shrill, adj. stridulo.

shrimp, n. gamberetto m.; (small person) nano m.

shrine, n. santuàrio m.

shrink, vb. contrarsi; (s. from) rifuggire da.

shroud, n. sudàrio m.

shrub, n. arbusto m.

shudder, 1. n. brivido m. 2. vb. rabbrividire.

shun, vb. schivare.

shut, vb. chiùdere.

shutter, n. scuretto m.; (camera) otturatore m.

shy, adj. tìmido.

Sicilian, adj. siciliano.

Sicily, n. Sicìlia f.

sick, adj. ammalato, malato.

sickness, n. malattìa f.

side, n. lato m., fianco m.

side-car, n. carrozzino m.

side-dish, n. contorno m.

sidewalk, n. marciapiède m.

siege, n. assèdio m.

sieve, n. crivèllo m., stàccio m., vàglio m.

sift, vb. stacciare, crivellare.

sigh, 1. n. sospiro m. 2. vb. sospirare.

sight, n. vista f.

sightseeing, n. turismo m.

sign, 1. n. segno m. 2. vb. firmare, sottoscrivere.

signal, 1. n. segnale m.; (directional s.) fréccia f. 2. vb. segnalare.

signature, n. firma f.

significance, n. significato m.

significant, adj. significativo.

signify, vb. significare.

silence, 1. n. silènzio m. 2. vb. far tacere.

silencer, n. silenziatore m.

silent, adj. silenzioso, zitto.

silk, n. seta f.

silken, silky, adj. setàceo.

sill, n. davanzale m.

silly, adj. sciòcco.

silo, n. silo m.

silver, 1. n. argènto m. 2. adj. argènteo.

silverware, n. posaterìa d'argento m.

silvery, adj. argentino.

similar, adj. simile.

similarity, n. somiglianza f.

similarly, adv. similmente.

simple, adj. sémplice.

simplicity, n. semplicità f.

simplify, vb. semplificare.

simply, adj. semplicemente.

simulate, vb. simulare.

simultaneous, adj. simultàneo.

sin, 1. n. peccato m 2. vb. peccare.

since, 1. prep. sino da. 2. conj. da quando; (because) giacchè, poichè.

sincere, adj. sincèro.

sincerely, adv. sinceramente.

sincerity, n. sincerità f.

sinew, n. nèrbo m.

sinful, adj. peccaminoso.

sing, vb. cantare.

singe, vb. strinare.

singer, n. cantatore m., cantatrice f.

single, adj. solo, ùnico; (unmarried) cèlibe.

single file, n. fila indiana f.

singular, adj. singolare.

sinister, adj. sinistro.

sink, 1. n. acquàio m., lavandino m. 2. vb. affondare; (ground) sprofondarsi.

sinner, n. peccatore m.

sinuous, adj. sinuoso.

sinus, n. seno frontale m.

sinusitis, n. sinusite f.

sip, 1. n. sorso m. 2. vb. sorseggiare.

siphon, n. sifone m.

sir, n. signore m.

siren, n. sirèna f.

sirloin, n. lombo m.

sister, n. sorèlla f.

sister-in-law, n. cognata f.

sit, vb. sedere.

site, n. sito m.

sitting, n. seduta f.

situate, vb. situare.

situation, n. situazione f.

six, num. sèi.

sixteen, num. sédici.

sixteenth, adj. sedicésimo, decimosèsto.

sixth, adj. sèsto.

sixtieth, adj. sessantésimo.

sixty, num. sessanta.

size, n. grandezza f.; (apparel) misura f.

sizing, n. incollatura f.

skate, n. 1. pàttino m. 2. vb. pattinare.

skateboard, n. asse a rotelle m.

skein, n. matassa f.

skeleton, n. schèletro m.

skeptic, n. scèttico m.

skeptical, adj. scèttico.

sketch, 1. n. abbozzo m., schizzo m. 2. vb. abbozzare, schizzare.

ski, 1. n. sci m. 2. vb. sciare.

skid, 1. n. slittamento m. 2. vb. slittare.

ski-lift, n. seggiovia f.

skill, n. abilità f., destrezza f.

skilful, adj. àbile, dèstro.

skim, vb. (remove cream) scremare; (go over lightly) sfiorare, rasentare.

skin, 1. n. pèlle f. 2. vb. pelare; (fruit) sbucciare.

skip, vb. saltare.

skirmish, 1. n. scaramùccia f. 2. vb. scaramucciare.

skirt, 1. n. gònna f., sottana f. 2. vb. rasentare.

skull, n. crànio m.

skunk, n. moffetta f.; (person) puzzone m.

sky, n. cièlo m.

skylight, n. lucernàrio m.

skyscraper, n. grattacièlo m.

slab, n. lastra f.

slack, adj. lento.

slacken, vb. rallentare.

slacks, n. calzoni m.pl.

slam, vb. sbàttere.

slander, 1. n. calùnnia f. 2. vb. calunniare.

slang, n. gèrgo m.

slant, 1. n. pendìo m. 2. adj. obliquo. 3. vb. inclinarsi.

slap, 1. n. schiaffo m. 2. vb. schiaffeggiare.

slash, 1. n. squàrcio m. 2. vb. squarciare.

slat, n. stecca f.

slate, n. ardèsia f., lavagna f.

slaughter, 1. n. massacro m., carneficina f., macèllo m. 2. vb. massacrare, macellare.

slave, n. schiavo m.

slavery, n. schiavitù f.

Slavic, adj. slavo.

slay, vb. trucidare.

sled, n. slitta f.

sleek, adj. lìscio.

sleep, 1. n. sonno m. 2. vb. dormire.

sleeper, sleeping car, n. vagone lètti m., carrozza lètti m.

sleepy, adj. sonnolento.

sleet, n. nevischio m.

sleeve, n. mànica f.

sleigh, n. slitta f.

slender, adj. svelto.

slice, 1. n. fetta f. 2. vb. affettare.

slide, vb. scivolare, sdrucciolare.

slide rule, n. régolo calcolatore m.

slight, 1. n. disprèzzo m. 2. adj. esìguo, insufficiènte; (thin) èsile.

slim, adj. sottile.

slime, n. melma f.

sling, 1. n. fionda f. 2. vb. lanciare, scagliare.

slink, vb. andare furtivamente.

slip, 1. n. scivolone m.; (mistake) errore m.; (paper) striscia f.; (underwear) sottovèste f. 2. vb. scivolare, sdrucciolare; (make a mistake) sbagliare.

slipper, n. pantòfola f.

slippery, adj. sdrucciolévole.

slit, n. fessura f.

slogan, n paròla d'òrdine f.; (advertising) motto m.

slope, n. pendènza f., pendìo m.

sloppy, adj. trasandato.

slot, n. fessura f.

slot machine, n. distributore automàtico m.

slouch, vb. stare scomposto.

slovenly, adj. trascurato.

slow, adj. lento; (behind time) indiètro, in ritardo.

slowly, adv. lentamente.

slowness, n. lentezza f.

sluggish, adj. lento.

slum, n. bassofondo m.

slumber, n. sonno m.

slur, 1. n. calùnnia f.; (music) legatura f. 2. vb. calunniare.

slush, n. fanghìglia f.

sly, *adj.* furbo.

smack, 1. *n.* (blow) pacca *f.;* (boat) battèllo *m.* 2. *vb.* (hit) schiaffeggiare; (taste) sapere.

small, *adj.* piccolo.

smallpox, *n.* vaiòlo *m.*

smart, *adj.* elegante, intelligènte.

smash, *vb.* fracassare, frantumare.

smear, *vb.* spalmare.

smell, 1. *n.* odore *m.;* (stench) puzzo *m.;* (sense) fiuto *m.* 2. *vb.* fiutare; (stink) puzzare.

smelt, 1. *n.* (fish) eperlano *m.* 2. *vb.* (melt) fóndere.

smile, 1. *n.* sorriso *m.* 2. *vb.* sorridere.

smite, *vb.* colpire.

smock, *n.* (workman's) camiciòtto *m.;* (hospital) càmice *m.*

smoke, 1. *n.* fumo *m.* 2. *vb.* fumare.

smokestack, *n.* fumaiòlo *m.*

smolder, *vb.* covare.

smooth, 1. *adj.* levigato, liscio. 2. *vb.* levigare, lisciare.

smother, *vb.* asfissiare, soffocare.

smug, *adj.* contento di sè stesso.

smuggler, *n.* contrabbandière *m.*

smuggling, *n.* contrabbando *m.*

snack, *n.* spuntino *m.*

snag, *n.* ostàcolo *m.*

snail, *n.* lumaca *f.*

snake, *n.* sèrpe *m.*

snap, *vb.* schioccare; (break) rómpere.

snapshot, *n.* istantànea *f.*

snare, *n.* tràppola *f.*

snarl, 1. *n.* (growl) ringhio *m.;* (tangle) groviglio *m.* 2. *vb.* ringhiare, aggrovigliare, *tr.*

snatch, *vb.* afferrare, ghermire.

sneak, *vb.* andare furtivamente.

sneaker, *n.* scarpa di tela *f.*

sneer, 1. *n.* sogghigno *m.* 2. *vb.* sogghignare.

sneeze, 1. *n.* starnuto *m.* 2. *vb.* starnutire.

snicker, *n.* risatina *f.*

snob, *n.* snob *m.*

snore, *vb.* russare.

snow, 1. *n.* neve *f.* 2. *vb.* nevicare.

snowdrift, *n.* ammasso di neve *m.*

snub, *vb.* non salutare.

snug, *adj.* còmodo.

so, *adv.* così; (so far, in time) finora; (so far, in space) fin qui; (so as to) così da.

soak, *vb.* bagnare, inzuppare.

soap, *n.* sapone *m.*

soar, *vb.* volare in alto.

sob, 1. *n.* singhiozzo *m.* 2. *vb.* singhiozzare.

sober, *adj.* moderato, non ubriaco; (serious) sòbrio.

sociable, *adj.* sociévole.

social, *adj.* sociale; (s. work) assistènza sociale *n.f.*

socialism, *n.* socialismo *m.*

socialist, *n. and adj.* socialista.

society, *n.* società *f.*

sociology, *n.* sociologia *f.*

sock, 1. *n.* calzino *m.;* (blow) pugno *m.* 2. *vb.* (hit) colpire.

socket, *n.* òrbita *f.;* (electric) presa *f.*

sod, *n.* piòta *f.,* zòlla *f.;* (with grass) zòlla erbosa *f.*

soda, *n.* sòda *f.*

sodium, *n.* sòdio *m.*

sofa, *n.* sofà *m.*

soft, *adj.* molle, mòrbido.

soft drink, *n.* bibita non alcoòlica *f.*

soften, *vb.* ammollire.

soil, 1. *n.* suolo *m.,* terreno *m.* 2. *vb.* sporcare.

soiled, *adj.* spòrco.

sojourn, 1. *n.* soggiorno *m.* 2. *vb.* soggiornare.

solace, 1. *n.* consolazione *f.* 2. *vb.* consolare.

solar, *adj.* solare.

solder, 1. *n.* saldatura *f.* 2. *vb.* saldare.

soldier, *n.* soldato *m.*

sole, 1. *n.* (of foot, shoe) suòla *f.;* (fish) sògliola *f.* 2. *adj.* ùnico.

solemn, *adj.* solènne.

solemnity, *n.* solennità *f.*

solicit, *vb.* sollecitare.

solicitous, *adj.* sollécito.

solid, *n. and adj.* sòlido (*m.*).

solidify, *vb.* solidificare, *tr.*

solidity, *n.* solidità *f.*

solitary, *adj.* solitàrio.

solitude, *n.* solitùdine *f.*

solo, *n.* assolo *m.*

soloist, *n.* solista *m. or f.*

so long, *interj.* ciao.

soluble, *adj.* solùbile.

solution, *n.* soluzione *f.*

solve, *vb.* risòlvere.

solvent, *n. and adj.* solvènte (*m.*).

somber, *adj.* fosco, sòbrio.

some, 1. *pron.* ne. 2. *adj.* qualche, alcuni; (a little) un po'.

somebody, *pron.* qualcuno.

somehow, *adv.* in qualche mòdo.

someone, *pron.* qualcuno.

somersault, *n.* capriòla *f.,* salto mortale *m.*

something, *pron.* qualcosa, qualche cosa.

sometime, *adj.* (former) già.

sometimes, *adv.* qualche vòlta.

somewhat, *adv.* un po'.

somewhere, *adv.* in qualche luògo.

son, *n.* figlio *m.*

song, *n.* canto *m.,* canzone *f.*

son-in-law, *n.* gènero *m.*

soon, *adv.* prèsto, fra pòco.

soot, *n.* fuliggine *f.*

soothe, *vb.* calmare.

soothingly, *adv.* dolcemente.

sophisticated, *adj.* sofisticato.

soprano, *n.* soprano *m.*

sorcery, *n.* stregoneria *f.*

sordid, *adj.* sòrdido.

sore, 1. *n.* piaga *f.* 2. *adj.* dolènte; (angry) adirato.

sorrow, 1. *n.* dolore *m.* 2. *vb.* addolorarsi.

sorrowful, *adj.* addolorato.

sorry, *adj.* dispiacènte.

sort, 1. *n.* sòrta *f.* 2. *vb.* assortire.

soul, *n.* ànima *f.*

sound, 1. *n.* suòno *m.* 2. *adj.* sano, giusto. 3. *vb.* suonare; (take soundings) sondare.

soup, *n.* minèstra *f.,* zuppa *f.*

sour, *adj.* àcido; (unripe) acèrbo.

source, *n.* fonte *f.,* sorgènte *f.*

south, *n.* sud *m.,* mezzogiorno *m.*

southeast, `n. sud-èst *m.*

southern, *adj.* meridionale.

South Pole, *n.* pòlo sud *m.*

southwest, *n.* sud-òvest *m.*

souvenir, *n.* ricòrdo *m.*

sovereign, *n. and adj.* sovrano (*m.*).

soviet, 1. *n.* sovièt *m.* 2. *adj.* soviètico.

sow, 1. *n.* scrofa *f.,* tròia *f.* 2. *vb.* seminare.

space, *n.* spàzio *m.*

space shuttle, *n.* spola spaziale *f.*

spacious, *adj.* spazioso.

spade, *n.* vanga *f.*

spaghetti, *n.* spaghetti *m.pl.*

Spain, *n.* Spagna *f.*

span, 1. *n.* (measure) spanna *f.;* (bridge) ponte *m.* 2. *vb.* stèndersi su.

Spaniard, *n.* spagnuòlo *m.*

Spanish, *adj.* spagnuòlo.

spank, *vb.* sculacciare.

spanking, *n.* sculacciata *f.*

spar, 1. *n.* àlbero *m.* 2. *vb.* (box) fare il pugilato.

spare, 1. *n.* pèzzo di ricàmbio *m.* 2. *adj.* (extra) di ricàmbio; (thin) magro; (available) disponibile. 3. *vb.* aver disponibile; (save) risparmiare.

spark, *n.* scintilla *f.*

sparkle, *vb.* scintillare.

spark-plug, *n.* candela d'accensione *f.*

sparrow, *n.* pàssero *m.*

sparse, *adj.* rado.

spasm, *n.* spàsimo *m.*

spasmodic, *adj.* spasmòdico.

spatter, 1. *n.* spuzzo *m.* 2. *vb.* spruzzare.

speak, *vb.* parlare; (s. ill) sparlare.

speaker, *n.* oratore *m.;* (presiding officer) presidènte *m.*

spear, 1. *n.* lància *f.* 2. *vb.* trafiggere.

special, *adj.* speciale.

specialist, *n.* specialista *m.*

specially, *adv.* specialmente.

specialty, *n.* specialità *f.*

species, *n.* spècie *f.*

specific, *adj.* specifico.

specify, *vb.* specificare.

specimen, *n.* sàggio *m.*

spectacle, *n.* spettàcolo *m.; (pl.* eyeglasses) occhiali *m.pl.*

spectacular, *adj.* spettacolare.

spectator, *n.* spettatore *m.*

spectrum, *n.* spèttro *m.*

speculate, *vb.* speculare.

speculation, *n.* speculazione *f.*

speech, *n.* discorso *m.*

speechless, *adj.* interdetto.

speed, 1. *n.* velocità *f.* 2. *vb.* affrettare, *tr.;* (s. up) accelerare, *tr.*

speedometer, *n.* tachìmetro *m.*

speedy, *adj.* veloce.

spell, 1. *n.* incantésimo *m.* 2. *vb.* scrivere.

spelling, *n.* ortografìa *f.*

spend, *vb.* (money) spèndere; (time) passare.

spendthrift, *n.* sciupone *m.*

sphere, *n.* sfèra *f.*

spice, *n.* spèzie, *f.pl.*

spider, *n.* ragno *m.; (s.-web)* ragnatelo *m.*

spike, *n.* chiòdo *m.*

spill, *vb.* rovesciare.

spillway, *n.* scàrico *m.*

spin, 1. *n.* (excursion) giretto *m.* 2. *vb.* filare; (whirl) girare.

spinach, *n.* spinaci *m.pl.*

spine, *n.* spina dorsale *f.*

spinet, *n.* spinetta *f.*

spinster, *n.* zitèlla *f.*

spiral, *n.* and *adj.* spirale *(m.)*

spire, *n.* gùglia *f.*

spirit, *n.* spirito *m.*

spiritual, *adj.* spirituale.

spiritualism, *n.* spiritismo *m.*

spit, *vb.* sputare.

spite, 1. *n.* dispètto *m.;* (in s. of) malgrado. 2. *vb.* contrariare.

splash, 1. *n.* tonfo *m.,* spruzzo *m.* 2. *vb.* spruzzare.

splendid, *adj.* splèndido.

splendor, *n.* splendore *m.*

splice, *vb.* congiùngere.

splint, *n.* stecca *f.*

splinter, 1. *n.* schéggia *f.* 2. *vb.* scheggiare, *tr.*

split, 1. *n.* (crack) fessura *f.;* (division) scissione *f.* 2. *vb.* (wood) spaccare; (crack) fèndere, *tr.;* (divide) dividere, *tr.,* scindere, *tr.*

splurge, *vb.* spèndere molto denaro.

spoil, *vb.* guastare.

spoke, *n.* ràggio *m.*

spokesman, *n.* portavoce *m.*

sponge, *n.* spugna *f.*

sponsor, *n.* mallevadore *m.;* (backer) sostenitore *m.*

spontaneity, *n.* spontaneità *f.*

spontaneous, *adj.* spontàneo.

spool, *n.* bobina *f.;* (film) rocchetto *m.*

spoon, *n.* (large) cucchiaio *m.;* (small) cucchiaino *m.*

spoonful, *n.* cucchiaiata *f.*

sporadic, *adj.* sporàdico.

spore, *n.* spòra *f.*

sport, 1. *n.* sport *m.,* dipòrto *m.* 2. *adj.* sportivo.

sportsman, *n.* sportivo *m.*

spot, *n.* (place) posto *m.;* (blot) màcchia *f.*

spouse, *n.* sposo *m.,* sposa *f.*

spout, 1. *n.* becco *m.* 2. *vb.* spruzzare.

sprain, 1. *n.* stòrta *f.* 2. *vb.* stòrcere.

sprawl, *vb.* sdraiarsi.

spray, *vb.* sprizzare, nebulizzare.

spread, 1. *n.* distesa *f.;* (food) banchetto *m.* 2. *adj.* disteso, spiegato. 3. *vb.* stèndere, *tr.;* spiegare, *tr.;* (diffuse) diffóndere, *tr.*

spree, *n.* baldòria *f.*

sprig, *n.* ramoscèllo *m.*

sprightly, *adj.* brioso.

spring, 1. *n.* (season) primavera *f.;* (source) fonte *f.,* sorgènte *f.;* (leap) salto *m.;* (metal) mòlla *f.* 2. *vb.* sórgere, saltare; (leap up) scattare.

springboard, *n.* trampolino *m.*

sprinkle, *vb.* cospàrgere.

sprint, 1. *n.* corsa veloce. 2. *vb.* córrere velocemente.

sprinter, *n.* velocista *m.*

sprout, 1. *n.* germóglio *m.* 2. *vb.* germogliare.

spry, *adj.* arzillo.

spur, 1. *n.* sprone *m.,* sperone *m.* 2. *vb.* spronare.

spurious, *adj.* spùrio.

spurn, *vb.* disdegnare.

spurt, 1. *n.* scatto *m.* 2. *vb.* scattare; (pour out) spruzzare.

spy, 1. *n.* spione *m.* 2. *vb.* spiare; (perceive) scòrgere.

squabble, *n.* battibecco *m.*

squad, *n.* squadra *f.*

squadron, *n.* squadrone *f.*

squalid, *adj.* squàllido.

squall, *vb.* sbraitare.

squalor, *n.* squallore *m.*

squander, *vb.* scialacquare.

square, 1. *n.* quadrato *m.;* (open place) piazza *f.* 2. *adj.* quadrato. 3. *vb.* quadrare.

squash, 1. *n.* (drink) spremuta *f.;* (vegetable) zucca *f.* 2. *vb.* spiaccicare.

squat, 1. *adj.* tarchiato. 2. *vb.* accosciarsi.

squeak, 1. *n.* cigolìo *m.* 2. *vb.* cigolare.

squeamish, *adj.* schizzinoso.

squeeze, 1. *n.* stretta *f.* 2. *vb.* stringere; (juice) sprèmere.

squirrel, *n.* scoiàttolo *m.*

squirt, *vb.* schizzare, zampillare.

stab, 1. *n.* pugnalata *f.* 2. *vb.* pugnalare.

stability, *n.* stabilità *f.*

stabilize, *vb.* stabilizzare.

stable, 1. *n.* stalla *f.* 2. *adj.* stàbile.

stack, 1. *n.* mùcchio *m.* 2. *vb.* ammucchiare.

stadium, *n.* stàdio *m.*

staff, *n.* (stick) bastone *m.;* (personnel) personale *m.;* (music) rigo *m.*

stag, *n.* cèrvo *m.*

stage, *n.* (theater) palcoscènico *m.;* (phase) fase *f.,* stàdio *m.*

stagflation, *n.* inflazione in un'economìa stagnante *f.*

stagger, *vb.* barcollare.

stagnant, *adj.* stagnante.

stagnate, *vb.* stagnare.

stain, 1. *n.* màcchia *f.;* (color) colore *m.* 2. *vb.* colorare; macchiare.

staircase, stairs, *n.* scala *f.*

stake, 1. *n.* (post) palo *m.;* (sum, bet) posta *f.* 2. *vb.* rischiare; (bet) puntare.

stale, *adj.* raffermo.

stalemate, *n.* punto mòrto *m.*

stalk, *n.* gambo *m.*

stall, 1. *n.* stallo *m.;* (vendor's) banco *m.* 2. *vb.* (stop) arrestarsi.

stallion, *n.* stallone *m.*

stalwart, *adj.* robusto.

stamen, *n.* stame *m.*

stamina, *n.* vigore *m.*

stammer, *vb.* balbettare.

stamp, 1. *n.* (adhesive) bollo *m.;* (embossed, impressed) timbro *m.;* (postage-s.) francobollo *m.* 2. *vb.* bollare, timbrare.

stampede, *n.* fuga precipitosa *f.*

stamp pad, *n.* cuscinetto *m.*

stand, 1. *n.* (position) posizione *f.;* (vendor's) padiglione *m.;* (grandstand) tribuna *f.* 2. *vb.* stare; (put) méttere; (suffer) soffrire, tollerare; (s. up) stare in pièdi.

standard, 1. *n.* nòrma *f.* 2. *adj.* normale.

standardize, *vb.* standardizzare.

standing, 1. *n.* riputazione *f.* 2. *adj.* permanènte; (s. up) in pièdi.

standpoint, *n.* punto di vista *m.*

staple, *n.* (fiber) fibra *f.;* (comm.) prodotto principale *m.*

star, *n.* stella *f.*

starboard, *n.* tribordo *m.*

starch, 1. *n.* àmido *m.* 2. *vb.* inamidare.

stare, *vb.* guardare fisso.

stark, *adv.* completamente.

start, 1. *n.* inizio *m.;* (departure) partènza *f.;* (jump) sussulto *m.* 2. *vb.* cominciare, iniziare; (depart) partire; (jump) sussultare, trasalire.

startle, *vb.* allarmare, far trasalire.

starvation, *n.* fame *f.*

starve, *vb.* morire di fame.

state, 1. *n.* stato *m.* 2. *vb.* affermare.

statement, *n.* affermazione *f.;* (bank) rendiconto *m.;* (legal) deposizione *f.*

stateroom, *n.* cabina *f.*

statesman, n. uòmo di stato m.

static, adj. stàtico.

station, n. stazione f., fattoria f.

stationary, adj. stazionàrio.

stationer, n. cartolàio m.

stationery, n. oggetti di cancelleria m.pl.; (s. store) cartoleria f.

station wagon, n. giardinetta f.

statistics, n. (science) statistica f.; (data) statistiche f.pl.

statue, n. stàtua f.

stature, n. statura f.

status, n. condizione f.

statute, n. statuto m.

staunch, adj. fedele.

stay, 1. n. (sojourn) permanènza f.; (delay) sospensione f. 2. vb. restare; (hold back) fermare.

steadfast, adj. saldo.

steady, adj. fermo, saldo.

steak, n. bistecca f.

steal, vb. rubare; (go furtively) andare in soppiatto.

stealth, n. (by s.) furtivamente.

stealthily, adv. di soppiatto.

stealthy, adj. furtivo.

steam, n. vapore m.

steamboat, n. piròscafo m.

steamship, n. piròscafo m.

steel, 1. n. acciàio m. 2. vb. indurire.

steel wool, n. lana di acciàio f., pàglia di acciàio f.

steep, adj. èrto, rìpido, scosceso.

steeple, n. campanile m.

steeplechase, n. corsa ad ostàcoli f.

steer, vb. dirìgere.

stellar, adj. stellare.

stem, n. stelo m.

stencil, n. stampino m.

stenographer, n. stenògrafa f.

stenography, n. stenografìa f.

step, 1. n. (pace) passo m.; (footprint) orma f.; (stair) gradino m. 2. vb. camminare.

stepfather, n. patrigno m.

stepladder, n. scalèo m.

stepmother, n. matrigna f.

stereotype, n. stereotipia f.

stereophonic, adj. stereofònico.

sterile, adj. stèrile.

sterility, n. sterilità f.

sterilize, vb. sterilizzare.

sterling, adj. puro; (pound s.) sterlina f.

stern, 1. n. poppa f. 2. adj. sevèro.

stethoscope, n. stetoscòpio m.

stevedore, n. stivatore m.

stew, 1. n. stufato m. 2. vb. stufare.

steward, n. camerière m.

stewardess, n. (boat) camerièra f.; (plane) stewardess f.

stick, 1. n. bastone m. 2. vb. (adhere) aderire; (attach) appiccicare, attaccare; (shove) cacciare, ficcare.

sticker, n. etichetta f.

sticky, adj. attaccatìccio, viscoso.

stiff, adj. rìgido.

stiffen, vb. irrigidire, tr.

stiffness, n. rigidezza f.

stifle, vb. soffocare.

stigma, n. stigma m.

stigmata, n. stìmmate f.pl.

still, 1. n. alambicco m. 2. adj. calmo. 3. vb. calmare. 4. adv. ancora.

still-born, adj. nato mòrto.

still life, n. natura mòrta f.

stillness, n. quiète f., calma f.

stilted, adj. ampolloso.

stimulant, n. and adj. stimolante (m.)

stimulate, vb. stimolare.

stimulus, n. stìmolo m.

sting, 1. n. (body-part) pungiglione m.; (wound) puntura f. 2. vb. pùngere.

stingy, adj. avaro, tìrchio.

stipulate, vb. stipulare.

stir, 1. n. agitazione f., commozione f. 2. vb. agitare, tr., muòvere, tr.

stitch, 1. n. punto m. 2. vb. cucire.

stock, 1. n. (supply) provvista f.; (lineage) stirpe f.; (animals) bestiame m.; (of gun) càlcio m.; (financial) azioni f. 2. vb. tenere in magazzino.

stockbroker, n. agènte di càmbio m.

stock exchange, n. borsa f.

stockholder, n. azionista m.

Stockholm, n. Stoccolma f.

stocking, n. calza f.

stockyard, n. mattatòio m.

stodgy, adj. ottuso.

stoic, n. stòico m.

stoical, adj. stòico.

stole, n. stòla f.

stolid, adj. stòlido.

stomach, n. stòmaco m. 2. vb. tollerare.

stone, 1. n. piètra f., sasso m. 2. vb. lapidare.

stool, n. sgabèllo m.

stoop, vb. curvarsi; (demean oneself) abbassarsi.

stooped, adj. curvo.

stop, 1. n. fermata f. 2. vb. fermare, tr.; (close) otturare, tappare; (cease) smèttere; (cease moving) sostare.

stopgap, n. temporàneo m.

stop-over, n. fermata intermèdia f.

stopper, n. tappo m.

stopping, n. sosta f.

storage, n. magazzinàggio m.

store, 1. n. negòzio m.; (supply) provvista f. 2. vb. immagazzinare, conservare; (fill) riempire.

storehouse, n. magazzino m.

storm, n. tempèsta f.

stormy, adj. tempestoso.

story, n. racconto m., stòria f.

stout, adj. grasso; (strong) fòrte.

stove, n. fornèllo m., stufa f.

straight, 1. adj. diritto, rètto. 2. adv. direttamente, diritto.

straight-away, n. rettilìneo m.

straighten, vb. raddrizzare.

straightforward, adj. franco.

strain, 1. n. tensione f. 2. vb. sforzare, tr.; (filter) colare.

strainer, n. colino m.

strait, n. stretto m.

strand, 1. n. riva f. 2. vb. arenarsi.

strange, adj. strano; (foreign) stranièro.

stranger, n. stranièro m.

strangle, vb. strangolare.

strap, n. cinghia f.

stratagem, n. stratagèmma m.

strategic, adj. stratègico.

strategy, n. strategìa f.

stratosphere, n. stratosfèra f.

stratum, n. strato m.

straw, n. pàglia f.; (for drinking) cannùccia di pàglia f.

strawberry, n. fràgola f.

stray, 1. adj. smarrito. 2. vb. allontanarsi.

streak, n. strìa f.

stream, 1. n. corrènte f., fiòtto m.

streamlined, adj. aerodinàmico.

street, n. vìa f., strada f.

streetcar, n. tram m.

strength, n. fòrza f.

strengthen, vb. rafforzare.

strenuous, adj. strènuo.

streptococcus, n. streptocòcco m.

stress, 1. n. sfòrzo m., tensione f.; (accent) accènto m. 2. vb. accentare.

stretch, 1. n. tratto m. 2. vb. tèndere.

stretcher, n. barèlla f.

strew, vb. cospàrgere.

stricken, adj. colpito.

strict, adj. sevèro.

stride, 1. n. passo lungo m. 2. vb. camminare a passi lunghi.

strident, adj. strìdulo.

strife, n. conflitto m.

strike, 1. n. (workers') sciòpero m. 2. vb. scioperare; (hit) colpire.

strike-breaker, n. crumiro m.

string, 1. n. filo m., còrda f. 2. vb. infilare.

string bean, n. fagiòlo m.

stringent, adj. rigoroso.

strip, 1. n. strìscia f. 2. vb. spogliare, tr.

stripe, n. lista f., striscia f.

strive, vb. sforzarsi.

stroke, 1. n. colpo m. 2. vb. accarezzare.

stroll, 1. n. passeggiata f. 2. vb. passeggiare.

stroller, n. passeggiatore m.

strong, adj. fòrte.

stronghold, n. roccafòrte f.

structure, n. struttura f.

struggle, 1. n. lotta f. 2. vb. lottare.

strut, vb. pavoneggiarsi.

stub, n. mozzicone m.; (checkbook) madre f.

stubborn, *adj.* testardo.

stucco, *n.* stucco *m.*

student, *n.* studènte *m.*, studentessa *f.*

studio, *n.* stùdio *m.*

studious, *adj.* studioso.

study, 1. *n.* stùdio *m.* 2. *vb.* studiare.

stuff, 1. *n.* (cloth) stoffa *f.*; (junk) ròba *f.* 2. *vb.* rimpinzare, imbottire; (food) infarcire.

stuffed, *adj.* ripièno.

stuffing, *n.* ripièno *m.*

stumble, *vb.* inciampare.

stump, *n.* (tree) ceppo *m.*; (arm, leg) moncone *m.*

stun, *vb.* stordire.

stunt, *n.* impresa fuòri del consuèto *f.*

stupendous, *adj.* stupèndo.

stupid, *adj.* stùpido.

stupidity, *n.* stupidità *f.*

stupor, *n.* stupore *m.*

sturdy, *adj.* gagliàrdo.

stutter, *vb.* tartagliare.

Stuttgart, *n.* Stoccarda *f.*

sty, *n.* porcile *m.*; (eye) orzaiòlo *m.*

style, *n.* stile *m.*

stylish, *adj.* di mòda.

suave, *adj.* blando.

subconscious, *adj.* subcosciènte.

subdue, *vb.* soggiogare.

subject, 1. *n.* soggètto *m.*; (of king) suddito *m.* 2. *adj.* soggètto. 3. *vb.* sottoporre, assoggettare.

subjugate, *vb.* soggiogare.

subjunctive, *n.* and *adj.* congiuntivo *(m.)*

sublimate, 1. *n.* and *adj.* sublimato *(m.)* 2. *vb.* sublimare.

sublime, *adj.* sublime.

submarine, 1. *n.* sommergìbile *m.* 2. *adj.* sottomarino.

submerge, *vb.* sommèrgere.

submersion, *n.* sommersione *f.*

submission, *n.* sottomissione *f.*

submit, *vb.* sottomèttere, *tr.*

subnormal, *adj.* subnormale.

subordinate, *n.* and *adj.* subordinato *(m.)*

subscribe, *vb.* (write name) sottoscrivere; (take regularly) abbonarsi; (agree with) aderire.

subscription, *n.* abbonamento *m.*

subsequent, *adj.* successivo.

subservient, *adj.* servile.

subside, *vb.* diminuire; (building) sprofondarsi; (earth) cédere; (water) abbassarsi.

subsidy, *n.* sussidio *m.*

substance, *n.* sostanza *f.*

substantial, *adj.* sostanziale.

substitute, 1. *n.* sostituto *m.* 2. *vb.* sostituire.

substitution, *n.* sostituzione *f.*

subterfuge, *n.* sotterfùgio *m.*

subtle, *adj.* sottile.

subtract, *vb.* sottrarre.

suburb, *n.* sobborgo *m.*

subvention, *n.* sovvenzione *f.*

subversive, *adj.* sovversivo.

subvert, *vb.* sovvertire.

subway, *n.* metropolitana *f.*

succeed, *vb.* (come after) succèdere a; (be successful) riuscire.

success, *n.* succèsso *m.*, riuscita *f.*

successful, *adj.* riuscito.

succession, *n.* successione *f.*, sèrie *f.*

successive, *adj.* successivo.

successor, *n.* successore *m.*

succor, 1. *n.* soccorso *m.* 2. *vb.* soccórrere.

succumb, *vb.* soccómbere.

such, *adj.* tale.

suck, *vb.* succhiare.

suction, *n.* aspirazione *f.*

sudden, *adj.* improvviso.

suds, *n.* schiuma *f.*

sue, *vb.* citare in giudìzio.

suffer, *vb.* soffrire.

suffice, *vb.* bastare.

sufficient, *adj.* sufficiènte.

suffocate, *vb.* soffocare.

sugar, *n.* zùcchero *m.*

suggest, *vb.* suggerire.

suggestion, *n.* suggerimento *m.*

suicide, *n.* suicìdio *m.*; (commit s.) suicidarsi.

suit, 1. *n.* (clothes) àbito *m.*; (cards) colore *m.*; (request) domanda *f.*; (law) càusa *f.* 2. *vb.* convenire a, andàr bène a.

suitable, *adj.* conveniènte.

suitcase, *n.* valigia *f.*

suite, *n.* sèrie *f.*; (followers) sèguito *m.*; (music) suite *f.*

suitor, *n.* corteggiatorre *m.*

sullen, *adj.* cupo.

sultana raisin, *n.* uva sultanina *f.*

sum, 1. *n.* somma *f.* 2. *vb.* sommare; (s. up) riassùmere.

summarize, *vb.* riassùmere.

summary, *n.* and *adj.* sommàrio *(m.)*

summer, 1. *n.* estate *f.* 2. *adj.* estivo.

summit, *n.* sommità *f.*, cima *f.*, vetta *f.*

summon, *vb.* chiamare, citare.

summons, *n.* chiamata *f.*; (court) citazione *f.*

sumptuous, *adj.* sontuoso.

sun, *n.* sole *m.*

sunburn, *n.* abbronzatura *f.*

sunburned, *adj.* abbronzato.

Sunday, *n.* domènica *f.*

sunken, *adj.* infossato.

sunny, *adj.* solatìo.

sunshine, *n.* sole *m.*

superb, *adj.* supèrbo.

superficial, *adj.* superficiale.

superfluous, *adj.* supèrfluo.

super-highway, *n.* autostrada *f.*

superhuman, *adj.* sovrumano.

superintendent, *n.* sovrintendènte *m.*

superior, *adj.* superiore.

superiority, *n.* superiorità *f.*

superlative, *n.* and *adj.* superlativo *(m.)*

superman, *n.* superuòmo *m.*

supernatural, *adj.* soprannaturale.

supersede, *vb.* soppiantare.

superstar, *n.* superstar *m.*

superstition, *n.* superstizione *f.*

superstitious, *adj.* superstizioso.

supervise, *vb.* sorvegliare.

supper, *n.* cena *f.*

supplant, *vb.* soppiantare.

supplement, *n.* supplemento *m.*

supply, 1. *n.* fornitura *f.*, provvista *f.* 2. *vb.* fornire, provvedere.

support, 1. *n.* sostegno *m.* 2. *vb.* appoggiare, sostenere.

suppose, *vb.* supporre.

suppress, *vb.* supprimere.

suppression, *n.* soppressione *f.*

supreme, *adj.* suprèmo.

sure, *adj.* sicuro.

surely, *adv.* sicuramente.

surety, *n.* sicurezza *f.*

surf, *n.* frangènti *m.pl.*

surface, *n.* superficie *f.*

surge, *vb.* ondare.

surgeon, *n.* chirurgo *m.*

surgery, *n.* chirurgìa *f.*

surmise, 1. *n.* congettura *f.* 2. *vb.* congetturare.

surmount, *vb.* sormontare.

surname, *n.* cognome *m.*

surpass, *vb.* sorpassare.

surplus, *n.* avanzo *m.*

surprise, 1. *n.* sorpresa *f.* 2. *vb.* sorprèndere.

surrender, *vb.* (hand over) cédere; (yield) arrèndersi.

surround, *vb.* circondare.

surroundings, *n.* dintorni *m.pl.*

surveillance, *n.* sorveglianza *f.*

survey, 1. *n.* esame *m.*; (geographical) rilevamento *m.* 2. *vb.* esaminare.

surveyor, *n.* agrimensore *m.*

survival, *n.* sopravvivènza *f.*

survive, *vb.* sopravvivere.

susceptible, *adj.* suscettibile.

suspect, 1. *adj.* sospètto. 2. *vb.* sospettare.

suspend, *vb.* sospèndere.

suspense, *n.* incertezza *f.*

suspension, *n.* sospensione *f.*

suspension bridge, *n.* ponte sospeso *m.*

suspicion, *n.* sospètto *m.*

suspicious, *adj.* sospettoso; (questionable) sospètto.

sustain, *vb.* sostenere.

swallow, 1. *n.* (bird) róndine *f.*; (food) beccone *m.*; (drink) sorso *m.* 2. *vb.* inghiottire.

swamp, 1. *n.* palude *f.* 2. *vb.* inondare.

swan, *n.* cigno *m.*

swap, 1. *n.* baratto *m.* 2. *vb.* barattare.

swarm, 1. *n.* sciame *m.* 2. *vb.* sciamare; (be crowded) formicolare.

sway, *vb.* oscillare; (influence) dominare.

swear, *vb.* giurare; (curse) be-

stemmiare; (s.-word) bestémmia f.
sweat, 1. n. sudore m. **2.** vb. sudare.
sweater, n. golf m.
Swede, n. svedese m.
Sweden, n. Svèzia f.
Swedish, adj. svedese.
sweep, vb. spazzare.
sweet, adj. dolce.
sweetheart, n. innamorato m.,
innamorata f.
sweetness, n. dolcezza f.
swell, 1. adj. magnifico. **2.** vb.
gonfiare, tr.
swelter, vb. sudare.
swift, adj. veloce.
swim, vb. nuotare.
swindle, vb. truffare.
swindler, n. truffatore m.
swine, n. pòrco m.
swing, 1. n. (children's) altalena f. **2.** vb. dondolare, penzolare.
swirl, vb. turbinare.
Swiss, adj. svizzero.
switch, 1. n. (rod) verga f.;
(railway) scàmbio m.; (electric) interruttore m. **2.** vb.
(whip) sferzare; (s. on) accèndere; (s. off) spègnere.
switchboard, n. centralino m.
Switzerland, vb. Svizzera f.
sword, n. spada f.
sword-fish, n. pesce spada m.
syllable, n. sillaba f.
symbol, n. simbolo m.
symbolic, adj. simbòlico.
sympathetic, adj. sensibile.
sympathize, vb. simpatizzare.
sympathy, n. simpatìa f.
symphonic, adj. sinfònico.
symphony, n. sinfonìa f.; (s. orchestra) orchèstra sinfònica f.
symptom, n. sìntomo m.
symptomatic, adj. sintomàtico.
synchronous, adj. sìncrono.
synchronize, vb. sincronizzare.
syndicate, n. consòrzio m.
syndrome, n. sindrome f.
synonym, n. sinònimo m.
synonymous, adj. sinònimo.
synthesis, n. sìntesi f.
synthetic, adj. sintètico.
syphilis, n. sìfilide f.
syphilitic, adj. sifilìtico.
syringe, n. siringa f.
syrup, n. sciròppo m.
system, n. sistèma m.
systematic, adj. sistemàtico.

T

tabernacle, n. tabernàcolo m.
table, n. tàvola f.
tablecloth, n. tovàglia f.
tablespoon, n. cucchiaio m.
tablespoonful, n. cucchiaiata f.
tablet, n. tavoletta f.; (pastille)
pastìcca f.
tack, 1. n. bulletta f. **2.** vb.
attaccare; (turn) virare.
tact, n. tatto m.
tag, n. etichetta f.

tail, n. coda f.
tailor, n. sarto m.
take, vb. prèndere; (carry) portare; (lead) condurre.
tale, n. racconto m.
talent, n. talènto m.
talk, 1. n. discorso m. **2** vb.
parlare.
talkative, adj. loquace.
tall, adj. alto.
tallow, n. sego m.
tame, 1. adj. addomesticato,
mansuèto. **2.** vb. addomesticare, domare.
tamper, vb. immischiarsi.
tan, 1. n. (sun) abbronzatura f.
2. adj. castagno. **3.** vb. abbronzare; (leather) conciare.
tangible, adj. tangìbile.
tangle, 1. n. garbùglio m. **2.** vb.
ingarbugliare.
tank, n. serbatòio m.; (armored vehicle) carro armato
m.
tap, 1. n. (blow) colpetto m.;
(faucet) rubinetto m. **2.** vb.
percuòtere.
tape, n. nastro m.
tape recorder, n. magnetòfono
m., registratore magnètico m.
tapestry, n. tappezzerìa f.
tar, 1. n. catrame m. **2.** vb. incatramare.
target, n. bersàglio m.
tariff, n. tariffa f.
tarnish, 1. n. appannatura f. **2.**
vb. appannare, tr.
tart, 1. n. tòrta f.; (harlot) puttana f. **2.** adj. acre.
task, n. còmpito m., incàrico
m.
taste, 1. n. gusto m. **2.** vb. gustare.
tasty, adj. gustoso, saporito,
saporoso.
taunt, vb. schernire.
taut, adj. teso.
tavern, n. osterìa f., tavèrna f.
tax, n. imposta f., tassa f.
taxi, n. tassì m.
taxpayer, n. contribuènte m.
tea, n. thè (tè) m.
teach, vb. insegnare.
teacher, n. insegnante m. or f.,
maestro m., maestra f.
team, n. squadra f.
tea-pot, n. teièra f.
tear, 1. n. làgrima f. **2.** vb.
strappare.
tease, vb. tormentare.
teaspoon, n. cucchiaino da thè
m.
technical, adj. tècnico.
technique, n. tècnica f.
tedious, adj. tedioso.
tedium, n. tèdio m.
telegram, n. telegramma m.
telegraph, 1. n. telègrafo m. **2.**
vb. telegrafare.
telephone, 1. n. telèfono m.;
(t.-call) telefonata f. **2.** vb. telefonare.
telescope, n. telescòpio m.
teletype, n. telescrivènte f.

televise, vb. trasméttere per televisione.
television, n. televisione f.; (t.
screen) teleschermo m.; (t.
set) televisore m.
tell, vb. raccontare.
teller, n. cassière m.
temper, 1. n. (anger) còllera f.
2. vb. temperare.
temperament, n. temperamento m.
temperamental, adj. capriccioso.
temperance, n. temperanza f.
temperate, adj. temperato.
temperature, n. temperatura f.
tempest, n. tempèsta f.
tempestuous, adj. tempestoso.
temple, n. tèmpio m.; (forehead) tèmpia f.
temporary, adj. provvisòrio.
tempt, vb. tentare.
temptation, n. tentazione f.
ten, num. dièci.
tenant, n. inquilino m.
tend, vb. tèndere; (care for) curare.
tendency, n. tendènza f.
tender, 1. n. carro di scòrta m.
2. adj. tènero. **3.** vb. offrire.
tenderly, adv. teneramente.
tenderness, n. tenerezza f.
tendon, n. tèndine m.
tennis, n. tènnis m.
tenor, n. tenore m.
tense, adj. teso.
tension, n. tensione f.
tent, n. tènda f.
tentative, 1. n. tentativo m. **2.**
adj. sperimentale, tentativo.
tenth, adj. dècimo.
term, n. perìodo m.; (school)
trimèstre m.
terminal, adj. terminale.
terminate, vb. terminare.
terminus, n. capolìnea m., tèrmine m.
terrace, n. terrazza f.
terrible, adj. terrìbile.
terribly, adv. terribilmente.
terrify, vb. atterrire.
territory, n. territòrio m.
terror, n. terrore m.
test, 1. n. pròva f. **2.** vb. provare, collaudare.
testament, n. testamento m.
testify, vb. testimoniare.
testimony, n. testimonianza f.
text, n. tèsto m.
textile, 1. n. tessuto m. **2.** adj.
tèssile.
texture, n. tessitura f.
than, prep. (before nouns, pronouns) di; (elsewhere) che.
thank, vb. ringraziare.
thankful, adj. grato.
that, 1. adj. quel, quello,
quella. **2.** pron. quello, quella.
3. conj. che.
the, def. art. il, lo, la, l'; i, gli,
gl', le.
theater, n. teatro m.
thee, pron. te, ti.
theft, n. furto m.
their, adj. loro.

theirs, *pron.* loro.

them, *pron.* li, le; loro.

theme, *n.* tèma *m.*

themselves, *pron.* si, sè; essi, stessi.

then, *adv.* (at that time) allora; (therefore) dunque; (afterward) pòi.

thence, *adv.* di là.

theologian, *n.* teòlogo *m.*

theology, *n.* teologìa *f.*

theoretical, *adj.* teòrico.

theory, *n.* teorìa *f.*

therapy, *n.* terapìa *f.*

there, *adv.* lì, là; ci, vi.

therefore, *adv.* perciò.

thermometer, *n.* termòmetro *m.*

these, *adj. and pron.* questi *m.pl.*, queste *f.pl.*

they, *pron.* loro; essi *m.pl.*; esse *f.pl.*

thick, *adj.* spesso, folto, dènso, fitto.

thicken, *vb.* infoltire, condensare.

thickness, *n.* spessore *m.*

thief, *n.* ladro *m.*

thigh, *n.* còscia *f.*

thimble, *n.* ditale *m.*

thin, *adj.* sottile; (meager) magro.

thing, *n.* còsa *f.*

thingumajig, *n.* còso *m.*

think, *vb.* pensare.

thinker, *n.* pensatore *m.*

third, *adj.* tèrzo.

Third World, *n.* Tèrzo Mondo *m.*

thirst, *n.* sete *f.*

thirsty, *adj.* (be t.) aver sete.

thirteen, *num.* trédici.

thirteenth, *adj.* tredicèsimo, decimotèrzo.

thirtieth, *adj.* trentèsimo.

thirty, *num.* trenta.

this, *adj. and pron.* questo *m.sg.*, questa *f.sg.*; (t. man) questi *pron.m.sg.*

thorough, *adj.* complèto.

those, 1. *adj.* quei, quegli *m.pl.*; quelle *f.pl.* 2. *pron.* quelli *m.pl.*; quelle *f.pl.*

thou, *pron.* tu.

though, 1. *adj.* però. 2. *conj.* sebbène.

thought, *n.* pensièro *m.*

thoughtful, *adj.* pensoso; (careful) attènto.

thousand, *num.* mille.

thread, 1. *n.* filo *m.* 2. *vb.* infilare.

threat, *n.* minàccia *f.*

threaten, *vb.* minacciare.

three, *num.* tre.

thrift, *n.* economìa *f.*

thrill, *n.* frèmito *m.*

thrive, *vb.* prosperare.

throat, *n.* gola *f.*

throne, *n.* tròno *m.*

through, 1. *adj.* (direct) dirètto. 2. *prep.* per, attravèrso; (go t., pass t.) attraversare.

throughout, *adv.* dappertutto, completamente.

throw, *vb.* gettare, lanciare, buttare.

thrust, 1. *n.* spinta *f.* 2. *vb.* spingere.

thumb, *n.* pòllice *m.*

thunder, 1. *n.* tuòno *m.* 2. *vb.* tuonare.

Thursday, *n.* giovedì *m.*

thus, *adv.* così.

thwart, *vb.* frustrare.

thy, *adj.* tuo.

ticket, *n.* biglietto *m.*

tickle, *vb.* solleticare.

ticklish, *adj.* delicato.

tide, *n.* marèa *f.*

tidy, 1. *n.* (bond) legame *m.*; (neck-tie) cravatta *f.* 2. *vb.* legare; (make equal score) èssere pari con.

tier, *n.* fila *f.*

tiger, *n.* tigre *f.*

tight, *adj.* stretto, teso; (drunk) ubriaco.

tighten, *vb.* stringere.

tile, *n.* tègola *f.*

till, 1. *n.* cassetto *m.* 2. *vb.* coltivare. 3. *prep.* fino a; sino a. 4. *conj.* finchè.

tilt, 1. *n.* inclinazione *f.* 2. *vb.* inclinare.

timber, *n.* legname *m.*

time, 1. *n.* tèmpo *m.*; (o'clock) ora *f.*; (occasion) vòlta *f.*

timetable, *n.* oràrio *m.*

timid, *adj.* tìmido.

timidity, *n.* timidezza *f.*

timidly, *adv.* timidamente.

tin, *n.* stagno *m.*; (metal can) latta *f.*

tint, *n.* tinta *f.*

tiny, *adj.* minùscolo.

tip, 1. *n.* (end) punta *f.*; (reward) mància *f.* 2. *vb.* (tilt) inclinare; (give money to) dare una mància a.

tire, 1. *n.* pneumàtico *m.* 2. *vb.* stancare.

tired, *adj.* stanco.

tissue, *n.* tessuto *m.*; (facial) fazzoletti detergenti *m.pl.*

title, *n.* tìtolo *m.*

to, *prep.* a, ad (before a and, optionally, before other vowels).

toast, 1. *n.* pane abbrustolito *m.*; (health) brindisi *m.* 2. *vb.* abbrustolire; (drink health) brindare.

tobacco, *n.* tabacco *m.*

today, *n. and adv.* òggi *(m.)*

toe, *n.* dito del piède *m.*; (big t.) pòllice *m.*

together, *adv.* insième.

toil, 1. *n.* fatica *f.* 2. *vb.* faticare.

toilet, *n.* latrina *f.*, gabinetto *m.*

token, *n.* segno *m.*; (metal) gettone *m.*

tolerance, *n.* tolleranza *f.*

tolerant, *adj.* tollerante.

tolerate, *vb.* tollerare.

tomato, *n.* pomodoro *m.*

tomb, *n.* tomba *f.*

tomorrow, *n. and adv.* domani *(m.)*

ton, *n.* tonnellata *f.*

tone, *n.* tòno *m.*

tongue, *n.* lingua *f.*

tonic, *n. and adj.* tònico *(m.)*; (music) tònica *(f.)*

tonight, *adv.* stasera.

tonsil, *n.* tonsilla *f.*

too, *adv.* (also) anche; (excessively) troppo.

tool, *n.* utensile *m.*

too many, too much, *adj.* troppo.

tooth, *n.* dènte *m.*

toothache, *n.* mal di denti *m.*

toothbrush, *n.* spazzolino per i denti *m.*

top, 1. *n.* sommità *f.* 2. *vb.* superare.

topcoat, *n.* sopràbito *m.*

topic, *n.* argomento *m.*

topical, *adj.* d'attualità.

topsy-turvy, *adv.* sottosopra.

torch, *n.* fiàccola *f.*

torment, 1. *n.* tormento *m.* 2. *vb.* tormentare.

torrent, *n.* torrènte *m.*

torture, 1. *n.* tortura *f.* 2. *vb.* torturare.

toss, *vb.* buttare, agitare, *tr.*

total, *n. and adj.* totale *(m.)*

totalitarian, *adj.* totalitàrio.

totter, *vb.* barcollare.

touch, 1. *n.* tocco *m.* 2. *vb.* toccare.

tough, *adj.* (meat) tiglioso; (hard) difficile.

tour, 1. *n.* viàggio *m.* 2. *vb.* viaggiare.

touring, tourism, *n.* turismo *m.*

tourist, 1. *n.* turista *m. or f.* 2. *adj.* turìstico.

tournament, *n.* concorso *m.*

tow, *vb.* rimorchiare.

toward, *prep.* vèrso.

towel, *n.* asciugatòio *m.*; (hand-t.) asciugamani *m.*

tower, *n.* torre *f.*

town, *n.* città *f.*; (small t.) cittadina *f.*

toy, 1. *n.* giocàttolo *m.*, trastullo *m.* 2. *vb.* trastullarsi.

trace, 1. *n.* tràccia *f.* 2. *vb.* rintracciare.

track, *n.* binàrio *m.*; (for running) pista *f.*

tract, *n.* tratto *m.*

tractor, *n.* trattrice *f.*

trade, 1. *n.* commèrcio *m.* 2. *vb.* commerciare.

trader, *n.* commerciante *m.*

tradition, *n.* tradizione *f.*

traditional, *adj.* tradizionale.

traffic, *n.* tràffico *m.*

traffic light, *n.* semàforo *m.*

tragedy, *n.* tragèdia *f.*

tragic, *adj.* tràgico.

trail, *n.* sentièro *m.*

trailer, *n.* rimòrchio *m.*; (house-t.) carovana *f.*; (t. truck) autotreno *m.*

train, 1. *n.* treno *m.* 2. *vb.* allenare.

traitor, n. traditore m.

tram, n. tram m.

tramway, 1. n. tranvìa f. **2.** adj. tranviàrio.

tramp, n. vagabondo m.

tranquil, adj. tranquillo.

tranquillity, n. tranquillità f.

transaction, n. operazione f.

transfer, 1. n. trasferimento m. **2.** vb. trasferire.

transfix, vb. trafiggere.

transform, vb. trasformare.

transfusion, n. trasfusione f.

transition, n. transizione f.

translate, vb. tradurre.

translation, n. traduzione f.

transmit, vb. trasméttere.

transparent, adj. trasparènte.

transport, 1. n. trasporto m. **2.** vb. trasportare.

transportation, n. trasporto m.

transsexual, n. persona che ha cambiato sesso f.

transvestite, adj. transvestito.

trap, n. tràppola f.

trash, n. cianfrusàglia f.

travel, 1. n. viàggio m.; (t. agency) agenzia viaggi f. **2.** vb. viaggiare.

traveler, n. viaggiatore m.

traveler's check, n. assegno (per) viaggiatori m.

tray, n. vassòio m.

treacherous, adj. proditòrio; (deceptive) ingannévole.

tread, 1. n. passo m. **2.** vb. calpestare.

treason, n. tradimento m.

treasure, n. tesòro m.

treasurer, n. tesorière m.

treasury, n. tesòro m.

treat, vb. trattare.

treatise, n. trattato m.

treatment, n. trattamento m.

treaty, n. trattato m.

tree, n. àlbero m.

tremble, vb. tremare.

tremendous, adj. tremèndo.

trench, n. trincèa f.

trend, n. tendènza f.

trespass, n. violazione di confine f.

triage, n. scelta f.

trial, n. pròva f.; (law) procèsso m.

triangle, n. triàngolo m.

tribulation, n. tribolazione f.

tributary, n. and adj. tributàrio (m.); (river) affluènte (m.)

tribute, n. tributo m.

trick, 1. n. tiro m.; trucco m. **2.** vb. ingannare.

tricky, adj. ingannévole.

trifle, n. bazzècola f.

trigger, n. grilletto m.

trim, 1. adj. ordinato. **2.** vb. (clip) cimare; (make neat) ordinare.

trinket, n. ninnolo m.

trip, 1. n. viàggio m. **2.** vb. incespicare.

triple, 1. adj. trìplice. **2.** vb. triplicare, tr.

trite, adj. trito.

triumph, 1. n. trionfo m. **2.** vb. trionfare.

triumphal, adj. trionfale.

triumphant, adj. trionfante.

trivial, adj. meschino.

trolley-bus, n. fìlobus m.; (t.-b. line) filovìa f.

trolley-car, n. tram m.

troop, n. truppa f.

trophy, n. trofèo m.

tropic, n. tròpico m.

tropical, adj. tròpico.

trot, 1. n. tròtto m. **2.** vb. trottare.

trouble, 1. n. guaio m.; (jam) impiccio m.; (bother) disturbo m.; fastidio m. **2.** vb. disturbare, infastidire.

troublesome, adj. fastidioso.

trough, n. trògolo m.

trousers, n. calzoni m.pl.

trousseau, n. corredo nuziale m.

trout, n. tròta f.

truce, n. trégua f.

truck, n. camione m., autocarro m.

true, adj. vero; (loyal) fedele.

truly, adv. veramente; (yours t.) Vostro devmo.

trumpet, n. tromba f.

trumpeter, n. trombettière m.

trunk, n. (tree) tronco m.; (luggage) baùle m.

trust, n. fidùcia f.; (comm.) consòrzio m.

trustworthy, adj. fededegno.

truth, n. verità f.

truthful, adj. verìdico.

try, vb. provare, tentare.

tryst, n. appuntamento m.

T-shirt, n. maglietta f.

tub, n. vasca f.

tube, n. tubo m.; (radio) vàlvola f.

tuberculosis, n. tuberculòsi f.

tuck, 1. n. pièga f. **2.** vb. rimboccare.

Tuesday, n. martedì m.

tuft, n. ciuffo m.

tug, vb. tirare.

tug-boat, n. rimorchiatore m.

tuition, n. (fee) tassa scolàstica f.

tulip, n. tulipano m.

tumble, 1. n. capitómbolo m. **2.** vb. capitombolare.

tumor, n. tumore m.

tumult, n. tumulto m.

tuna, n. tonno m.

tune, 1. n. melodìa f. **2.** vb. accordare; (t. in) sintonizzare.

tuneful, adj. melodioso.

tunnel, 1. n. galleria f., traforo m. **2.** vb. traforare.

turban, n. turbante m.

turbine, n. turbina f.

turbo-jet, n. turboreattore m.

turbo-prop, n. turbo-èlica f.

turf, n. pìota f.

Turin, n. Torino m.

Turinese, adj. torinese.

Turk, n. Turco m.

turkey, n. tacchino m.

Turkey, n. Turchìa f.

Turkish, adj. turco.

turmoil, n. confusione f.

turn, 1. n. giro m.; (vehicle) svòlta f.; (time around) turno m. **2.** vb. girare.

turnip, n. rapa f.

turn signal, n. fréccia f.

turret, n. torretta f.

turtle, n. tartaruga f.

Tuscan, adj. toscano.

Tuscany, n. Toscana f.

tutor, n. insegnante privato m.

twelfth, adj. dodicésimo.

twelve, num. dódici.

twentieth, adj. ventèsimo.

twenty, num. venti.

twice, adv. due vòlte.

twig, n. ramoscèllo m.

twilight, n. crepùscolo m.

twin, n. gemèllo m.

twine, n. spago m.

twinkle, vb. luccicare.

twist, vb. tòrcere, tr.

two, num. due.

type, 1. n. tipo m. **2.** vb. dattilografare.

typewriter, n. màcchina da scrivere f.

typhoid fever, n. febbre tifoidèa f.

typhus, n. tifo m.

typical, adj. tìpico.

typist, n. dattilògrafa f.

tyranny, n. tirannìa f.

tyrant, n. tiranno m.

U

udder, n. mammèlla f.

ugliness, n. bruttezza f.

ugly, adj. brutto.

ulcer, n. ùlcera f.

ulterior, adj. ulteriore.

ultimate, adj. ùltimo.

umbrella, n. ombrèllo m.

Umbrian, adj. umbro.

umpire, n. àrbitro m.

un-, 1. with adjectives, non, in-. **2.** with verbs, s-, dis-.

unable, adj. incapace.

unanimous, adj. unànime.

unbecoming, adj. sconveniènte.

unbounded, adj. sconfinato.

uncertain, adj. incèrto.

uncertainty, n. incertezza f.

uncle, n. zìo m.

unconscious, adj. incònscio.

uncork, vb. sturare.

uncouth, adj. gòffo.

uncover, vb. scoprire, tr.

under, 1. adj. inferiore. **2.** adv. and prep. sotto.

underestimate, vb. sottovalutare.

undergo, vb. subire.

underground, adj. sotterràneo.

underline, vb. sottolineare.

underneath, adv. and prep. sotto.

underpass, n. sottopassàggio m.

undershirt, n. camiciòla f.

undersigned, adj. sottoscritto.

understand, vb. capire.

understanding, n. comprensione f.

undertake, vb. intraprèndere.

undertaker, n. imprenditore di pompe fùnebri m.

underwear, n. sottovèsti f.pl.

underworld, n. malavita f.

undo, vb. disfare.

undress, vb. svestire, tr.

undulate, vb. ondeggiare.

unearth, vb. dissotterrare.

uneasy, adj. inquièto.

unemployed, adj. disoccupato.

unequal, adj. ineguale.

uneven, adj. disuguale.

unexpected, adj. inaspettato.

unexpectedly, adv. inaspettatamente.

unfair, adj. ingiusto.

unfamiliar, adj. pòco nòto.

unfavorable, adj. sfavorévole.

unfit, adj. inàbile, disadatto.

unfold, vb. spiegare, tr.

unforgettable, adj. indimenticàbile.

unfortunate, adj. disgraziato, sfortunato.

unfurl, vb. spiegare.

unhappy, adj. infelice.

uniform, i. n. divisa f., uniförme m. 2. adj. uniförme.

unify, vb. unificare.

unilateral, adj. unilaterale.

union, n. unione f.

unique, adj. ùnico.

unisex, adj. unisessuale.

unit, n. unità f.

unite, vb. unire.

United Nations, n. Nazioni Unite f.pl.

United States, n. Stati Uniti m.pl.

unity, n. unità f.

universal, adj. universale.

universe, n. univèrso m.

university, n. università f.

unjust, adj. ingiusto.

unknown, adj. ignòto, sconosciuto.

unleaded, adj. senza piombo.

unless, conj. a meno che . . . non.

unlike, adj. dissimile.

unlikely, adj. improbàbile.

unload, vb. scaricare.

unlock, vb. disserrare, aprire.

unlucky, adj. disgraziato, infelice.

unmarried, adj. cèlibe.

unmask, vb. smascherare.

unpack, vb. disimballare.

unpleasant, adj. spiacévole.

unqualified, adj. (unfit) incompetènte; (unreserved) incondizionato.

unravel, vb. districare, tr.

unrecognizable, adj. irriconoscibile.

unrighteous, adj. iniquo.

unseemly, adj. sconveniènte.

unsettle, vb. sconvòlgere.

unsteady, adj. instàbile.

unsuccessful, adj. infruttuoso.

untie, vb. sciògliere.

until, 1. prep. fino a, sino a. 2. conj. finchè . . . non.

untruth, n. menzogna f.

untruthful, adj. menzognèro.

unusable, adj. inservìbile.

unusual, adj. insòlito.

unwarranted, adj. ingiustificato.

unwell, adj. indisposto.

unwind, vb. dipanare.

unworthiness, n. indegnità f.

unworthy, adj. indegno.

up, 1. adv. su. 2. prep. su per.

upbraid, vb. rimproverare.

uphill, 1. adj. (hard) àrduo. 2. adv. all'insù.

uphold, vb. sostenere.

upholder, n. sostenitore m.

upholster, vb. tappezzare.

upholsterer, n. tappezzière m.

upon, prep. sopra, su.

upper, adj. superiore.

upright, adj. and adv. diritto.

uprising, n. sollevazione f.

uproar, n. baccano m.

uproot, vb. sradicare.

upset, 1. n. sconvolgimento m. 2. vb. sconvòlgere.

upside down, adv. sottosopra.

upstairs, adv. su dalle scale.

uptight, adj. teso.

upward, adv. in alto.

urban, adj. urbano.

urchin, n. monèllo m.

urge, vb. spingere, sollecitare.

urgency, n. urgènza f.

urgent, adj. urgènte.

urinal, n. orinatòio m.; (public) vespasiano m.

urinate, vb. orinare.

urine, n. orina f.

urn, n. urna f.

us, pron. noi, ci.

usage, n. usanza f.

use, 1. n. uso m. 2. vb. usare, adoperare, servirsi di.

useful, adj. ùtile.

useless, adj. inùtile.

user, n. utènte m.

usher, n. màschera f.

usual, adj. sòlito, usuale; (as u.) come di sòlito.

usurp, vb. usurpare.

usury, n. usura f.

utensil, n. utensile m.

uterus, n. ùtero m.

utility, n. utilità f.; (light truck) camioncino m.

utilize, vb. utilizzare.

utmost, adj. estrèmo.

utter, 1. adj. complèto. 2. vb. proferire, emèttere.

utterance, n. espressione f.

utterly, adv. completamente.

uvula, n. ùgola f.

V

vacancy, n. posto vacante m.; (hotel) stanza lìbera f.

vacant, adj. vacante, lìbero, vuòto.

vacate, vb. abbondonare, lasciar lìbero.

vacation, n. vacanze f.pl.; (rest) ripòso m.

vaccinate, vb. vaccinare.

vaccination, n. vaccinazione f.

vaccine, n. vaccino m.

vacillate, vb. vacillare.

vacuous, adj. vàcuo.

vacuum, n. vuòto m.

vagrant, n. and adj. vagabondo (m.).

vague, adj. vago.

vain, adj. vano; (in v.) in vano.

valet, n. camerière m.

valiant, adj. valoroso.

valid, adj. vàlido.

valise, n. valìgia f.

valley, n. valle f.

valor, n. valore m.

valuable, adj. prezioso; (expensive) costoso.

value, 1. n. valore m. 2. vb. stimare, valutare.

value-added tax, n. imposta sul valore aggiunto f.

valve, n. vàlvola f.

vampire, n. vampiro m.

van, n. (vehicle) carro m.; furgone m.; (front) avanguàrdia f.; (moving v.) furgone per traslòchi m.

vandal, n. vàndalo m.

vanguard, n. avanguàrdia f.

vanilla, n. vaniglia f.

vanish, vb. svanire.

vanity, n. vanità f.

vanquish, vb. vìncere.

vapor, n. vapore m.

variance, n. disaccòrdo m.

variation, n. variazione f.

varied, adj. svariato.

variety, n. varietà f.

various, adj. vàrio.

varnish, n. vernice f.

vary, vb. variare.

vase, n. vaso m.

vasectomy, n. vasectomìa f.

vassal, n. vassallo m.

vast, adj. vasto.

vat, n. tino m.

vaudeville, n. spettacolo di varietà m.

vault, 1. n. (of roof) vòlta f.; (jump) salto. 2. vb. saltare.

veal, n. vitèllo m.

vegetable, 1. n. legume m.; (v.s) verdura f. 2. adj. vegetale.

vehemence, n. veemènza f.

vehement, adj. veemènte.

vehicle, n. veìcolo m.

veil, n. velo m.

vein, n. vena f.; (geology) filone m.

velocity, n. velocità f.

velvet, 1. n. velluto m. 2. adj. di velluto.

veneer, 1. n. piallàccio m. 2. vb. impiallacciare.

venereal, adj. venèreo.

Venetian, adj. veneziano.

vengeance, n. vendetta f.

Venice, n. Venèzia f.

venom, n. veleno m.

venomous, *adj.* velenoso.

vent, 1. *n.* foro *m.;* (expression) sfogo *m.* 2. *vb.* sfogare.

ventilate, *vb.* ventilare.

ventilation, *n.* ventilazione *f.*

venture, 1. *n.* ventura *f.;* (risk) rischio *m.* 2. *vb.* rischiare; (dare) osare.

venturesome, *adj.* avventuroso.

verb, *n.* vèrbo *m.*

verbal, *adj.* verbale.

verbose, *adj.* verboso.

verdict, *n.* verdetto *m.*

verge, 1. *n.* orlo *m.* 2. *vb.* (v. on) confinare con.

verify, *vb.* verificare.

vermilion, *adj.* vermiglio.

vernacular, *n. and adj.* vernàcolo (*m.*), volgare (*m.*).

versatile, *adj.* versàtile.

verse, *n.* vèrso *m.*

versify, *vb.* versificare.

version, *n.* versione *f.*

versus, *prep.* contro.

vertebrate, *n. and adj.* vertebrato (*m.*)

vertical, *adj.* verticale.

vertigo, *n.* vertigine *f.*

verve, *n.* brio *m.*

very, 1. *adj.* vero; (selfsame) stesso. 2. *adv.* molto; or add suffix -ìssimo.

vespers, *n.* vèspri *m.pl.*

vessel, *n.* (container) recipiènte *m.;* (boat) nave *f.*

vest, *n.* gilè *m.,* panciòtto *m.*

vestige, *n.* vestìgio *m.*

vestry, *n.* sagrestìa *f.*

Vesuvius, *n.* Vesùvio *m.*

veteran, *n.* veterano *m.*

veterinary, *n. and adj.* veterinàrio (*m.*)

veto, 1. *n.* vèto *m.* 2. *vb.* vietare.

vex, *vb.* irritare.

via, *prep.* vìa.

viaduct, *n.* viadotto *m.*

vibrate, *vb.* vibrare.

vibration, *n.* vibrazione *f.*

vicar, *n.* vicàrio *m.*

vice, *n.* vìzio *m.*

vicinity, *n.* vicinanza *f.*

vicious, *adj.* vizioso.

victim, *n.* vìttima *f.*

victorious, *adj.* vittorioso.

victory, *n.* vittòria *f.*

victuals, *n.* vettovàglie *f.pl.,* vitto *m.*

videodisc, *n.* videodisco *m.*

videotape, *n.* nastro televisivo *m.*

view, *n.* vista *f.,* veduta *f.*

vigil, *n.* vèglia *f.,* vigilia *f.*

vigilant, *adj.* vigilante.

vigor, *n.* vigore *m.*

vigorous, *adj.* vigoroso.

vile, *adj.* vile.

village, *n.* villàggio *m.*

villain, *n.* furfante *m.;* (in play) antagonista *m.*

vim, *n.* brio *m.*

vindicate, *vb.* rivendicare.

vine, *n.* vite *f.*

vinegar, *n.* aceto *m.*

vineyard, *n.* vigna *f.*

vintage, *n.* vendémmia *f.*

viol, viola, *n.* vìola *f.*

violate, *vb.* violare.

violation, *n.* violazione *f.,* contravvenzione *f.*

violator, *n.* violatore *m.,* contravventore *m.*

violence, *n.* violènza *f.*

violent, *adj.* violènto.

violet, *n.* vìola *f.*

violin, *n.* violino *m.*

virgin, *n.* vèrgine *f.*

virile, *adj.* virile.

virility, *n.* virilità *f.*

virtual, *adj.* virtuale.

virtue, *n.* virtù *f.*

virtuous, *adj.* virtuoso.

virus, *n.* virus *m.*

visa, 1. *n.* visto *m.* 2. *vb.* vistare.

viscous, *adj.* viscoso.

vise, *n.* mòrsa *f.*

visible, *adj.* visìbile.

vision, *n.* visione *f.;* (of v.) visivo.

visit, 1. *n.* visita *f.* 2. *vb.* visitare.

visitor, *n.* òspite *m. or f.*

visual, *adj.* visuale.

vital, *adj.* vitale.

vitality, *n.* vitalità *f.*

vitamin, *n.* vitamina *f.*

vitiate, *vb.* viziare.

vivacious, *adj.* vivace.

vivid, *adj.* vìvido.

vocabulary, *n.* vocabolàrio *m.*

vocal, *adj.* vocale.

vociferate, *vb.* vociare.

vogue, *n.* voga *f.*

voice, *n.* voce *f.*

void, *adj.* nullo; (devoid) privo.

volcano, *n.* vulcano *m.*

voltage, *n.* voltàggio *m.*

volume, *n.* volume *m.*

voluntary, *adj.* volontàrio.

volunteer, *n.* volontàrio *m.*

vomit, 1. *n.* vòmito *m.* 2. *vb.* vomitare.

vote, 1. *n.* voto *m.* 2. *vb.* votare.

voter, *n.* votante *m.*

voting, *n.* votazione *f.*

vouch for, *vb.* attestare.

vow, *n.* voto *m.*

vowel, *n.* vocale *f.*

voyage, 1. *n.* viàggio *f.* 2. *vb.* viaggiare.

vulgar, *adj.* volgare.

vulgarity, *n.* volgarità *f.*

vulnerable, *adj.* vulneràbile.

W

wad, *n.* batùffolo *m.;* (roll) ròtolo *m.*

wadding, *n.* ovatta *f.*

wade, *vb.* attraversare a guado.

wag, 1. *n.* bellumore *m.* 2. *vb.* dimenare, scuòtere.

wage, *vb.* (war) fare.

wager, 1. *n.* scommessa *f.* 2. *vb.* scomméttere.

wages, *n.* salàrio *m.*

wagon, *n.* carro *m.*

wail, *vb.* lamentarsi.

waist, *n.* cintura *f.,* vita *f.*

waistcoat, *n.* gilè *m.,* panciòtto *m.*

wait, *vb.* aspettare.

waiter, *n.* camerière *m.*

waitress, *n.* camerièra *f.*

waive, *vb.* rinunciare a.

waiver, *n.* rinùncia *f.*

wake, 1. *n.* (vigil) vèglia *f.;* (of boat) scia *f.* 2. *vb.* svegliare; (be awake) vegliare.

walk, 1. *n.* passeggiata *f.* 2. *vb.* camminare, passeggiare.

wall, *n.* muro *m.*

wallcovering, *n.* tapezzerìa *f.*

wallet, *n.* portafògli *m.*

wallpaper, *n.* carta da parati *f.*

walnut, *n.* noce *f.*

walrus, *n.* trichèco *m.*

waltz, *n.* vàlzer *m.*

wander, *vb.* vagare.

want, 1. *n.* bisogno *m.;* (poverty) misèria *f.* 2. *vb.* desiderare.

war, *n.* guèrra *f.*

ward, *n.* pupillo *m.;* (city) rione *m.*

ware, *n.* mèrce *f.*

warlike, *adj.* guerresco.

warm, *adj.* caldo, caloroso.

warmth, *n.* calore *m.*

warn, *vb.* ammonire, avvertire.

warning, *n.* avviso *m.,* ammonimento *m.*

warp, *vb.* curvare *tr.,* viziare.

warrant, *n.* mandato *m.*

warrior, *n.* guerrièro *m.*

warship, *n.* nave da guerra *f.*

wash, 1. *n.* (laundry) bianchería *f.* 2. *vb.* lavare.

wash-basin, *n.* lavabo *m.*

washing machine, *n.* lavabiancherìa *m.*

washroom, *n.* lavatòio *m.*

wasp, *n.* vèspa *f.*

waste, 1. *n.* sprèco *m.* 2. *vb.* sprecare.

watch, 1. *n.* (timepiece) orológio *m.;* (guard) guàrdia *f.* 2. *vb.* guardare.

watchful, *adj.* vigilante.

watchmaker, *n.* orologiaio *m.*

watchman, *n.* guardiano *m.*

water, 1. *n.* acqua *f.* 2. *vb.* innaffiare.

waterbed, *n.* letto ad acqua *m.*

water-color, *n.* acquarèllo *m.*

waterfall, *n.* cascata *f.*

waterproof, *adj.* impermeàbile.

wave, 1. *n.* onda *f.* 2. *vb.* sventolare.

wax, 1. *n.* cera *f.* 2. *vb.* incerare.

way, *n.* via *f.;* (manner) manièra *f.*

we, *pron.* noi.

weak, *adj.* dèbole.

weaken, *vb.* indebolire.

weakly, *adv.* debolmente.

weakness, *n.* debolezza *f.*

wealth, *n.* ricchezza *f.*

wealthy, *adj.* ricco.

weapon, *n.* arma *f.*

wear, 1. n. consumo m. 2. vb. portare; (w. out) consumare; logorare.

weary, adj. stanco.

weasel, n. dònnola f.

weather, n. tèmpo m.

weave, vb. tèssere.

weaver, n. tessitore m.

weaving, n. tessitura f.

web, n. tela f.

wedding, n. nòzze f.pl.

wedge, 1. n. bietta f., cùneo m. 2. vb. incuneare.

Wednesday, n. mercoledì m.

weed, n. erbàccia f.

week, n. settimana f.

weekday, n. giorno feriale m.

week end, n. fine di settimana f.

weekly, n. and adj. settimanale (m.)

weep, vb. piàngere.

weigh, vb. pesare.

weight, n. peso m.

weird, adj. strano.

welcome, adj. benvenuto.

welfare, n. benèssere m.

well, 1. n. pozzo m. 2. vb. sgorgare. 3. adv., interj. bène.

well-known, adj. nòto.

west, n. òvest m.

western, adj. occidentale.

westward, adv. vèrso òvest.

wet, 1. adj. ùmido. 2. vb. inumidire.

whale, n. balena f.

what, pron. che?, che còsa?

whatever, 1. adj. qualunque. 2. pron. qualunque còsa.

wheat, n. frumento m.

wheel, n. ruòta f.

when, adv. quando.

whence, adv. donde.

whenever, adv. ogniqualvòlta.

where, adv. dove.

wherever, adv. dovunque.

whether, conj. se.

which, 1. interrog. pron., adj. quale. 2. rel. pron. che, il quale; (after prep.) cùi; (to w.) cùi.

whichever, adj. and pron. qualunque.

while, conj. mentre.

whim, n. capriccio m.

whip, 1. n. frusta f. 2. vb. frustare.

whirl, vb. girare.

whirlpool, n. vòrtice m.

whirlwind, n. tùrbine m.

whisk broom, n. scopetta f.

whisker, n. basetta f.

whiskey, n. vìschi m.

whisper, 1. n. bisbiglio m. 2. vb. bisbigliare.

whistle, 1. n. fischio m. 2. vb. fischiare.

white, adj. bianco.

who, whom, pron. 1. interrog. chi. 2. rel. che, il quale; (after prep.) cùi.

whoever, whomever, pron. chiunque.

whole, adj. intèro, tutto.

wholesale, adj., adv. all'ingròsso.

wholesome, adj. sano.

wholly, adv. completamente.

whom, see who.

whore, n. puttana f.

whose, pron. 1. interrog. di chi?. 2. rel. cùi.

why, adv. perchè.

wicked, adj. malvàgio.

wickedness, n. malvagità f.

wide, adj. largo.

widen, vb. allargare, tr.

widespread, adj. diffuso.

widow, n. védova f.

widower, n. védovo m.

width, n. larghezza f.

wield, vb. règgere.

wife, n. móglie f.

wig, n. parrucca f.

wild, adj. selvàggio; (plants) selvàtico; (mad) furioso.

wilderness, n. desèrto m.

wildlife, n. selvaticume m.

wilful, adj. capàrbio.

will, 1. n. volontà f.; (testament) testamento m. 2. vb. (leave) lasciare; (future) use future tense.

willing, adj. pronto.

willow, n. sàlice m.

wilt, vb. appassire.

win, vb. vincere.

wind, 1. n. vènto m. 2. vb. avvòlgere; (watch) caricare.

window, n. finèstra f.

windshield, n. parabrezza m.; paravènto m.; (w.-wiper) tergicristallo m.

windy, adj. ventoso.

wine, n. vino m.

wing, n. ala f.

wink, vb. ammiccare.

winner, n. vincitore m.

winter, 1. n. invèrno m. 2. adj. (of w.) invernale.

wintry, adj. invernale.

wipe, vb. asciugare.

wire, 1. n. filo m.; (telegram) telegramma m. 2. vb. telegrafare.

wireless, 1. n. (radio) ràdio f. 2. adj. sènza fili.

wire recorder, n. regiastratore a filo m.

wisdom, n. saggezza f.

wise, adj. saggio.

wish, 1. n. desidèrio m. 2. vb. desiderare.

wit, n. intelligènza f.; (humor) spirito m. (wag) bellumore m.

witch, n. strega f.

with, prep. con.

withdraw, vb. ritirare, tr.

wither, vb. avvizzire.

withhold, vb. trattenere.

within, 1. adv. dentro. 2. prep. entro.

without, prep. sènza.

witness, n. testimone m.

witty, adj. spiritoso.

wizard, n. stregone m.

woe, n. calamità f., guaio m.

wolf, n. lupo m., lupa f.

woman, n. dònna f.

womb, n. ùtero m.

wonder, 1. n. meraviglia f. 2. vb. meravigliarsi, domandarsi.

wonderful, adj. meraviglioso.

woo, vb. corteggiare.

wood, n. legno m.; (forest) bòsco m., forèsta f.

wooded, adj. boscoso.

wooden, adj. di legno.

wool, n. lana f.

woolen, adj. di lana.

word, n. paròla f.

wordy, adj. verboso.

work, 1. n. lavoro m., òpera f. 2. vb. lavorare; (function) funzionare.

worker, n. lavoratore m.

workman, n. operaio m.

world, n. mondo m.

worldly, adj. mondano.

world-wide, adj. mondiale.

worm, n. vèrme m.

worn-out, adj. lògoro.

worry, 1. n. preoccupazione f. 2. vb. preoccupare, tr.

worse, 1. adj. peggiore. 2. adv. pèggio.

worship, 1. n. adorazione f., culto m. 2. vb. adorare.

worst, 1. adj. il peggiore. 2. adv. il pèggio.

worth, 1. n. valore m. 2. adj. (be w.) valere.

worthless, adj. sènza valore.

worthy, adj. degno.

would, vb. use conditional tense.

wound, 1. n. ferita f. 2. vb. ferire.

wrap, 1. n. mantèllo m. 2. vb. avvòlgere.

wrapping, n. involucro m.

wrath, n. ira f.

wreath, n. ghirlanda f.

wreck, 1. n. (ship) naufràgio m.; (ruin) rovina f. 2. vb. naufragare, rovinare.

wrench, 1. n. (tool) chiave inglese f. 2. vb. strappare.

wrestle, vb. lottare.

wretched, adj. mìsero.

wring, vb. tòrcere.

wrinkle, 1. n. ruga f. 2. vb. corrugare.

wrist, n. polso m.

wrist-watch, n. orològio da polso m.

write, vb. scrivere.

writer, n. scrittore m.

writhe, vb. contòrcersi.

writing, n. scrittura f., scritto m.

wrong, 1. n. tòrto m. 2. adj. errato; (be w.) aver tòrto.

X, Y, Z

x-rays, n. raggi x (pron. ics) m.pl.

xylophone, n. silòfono m.

yacht, n. pànfilo m.

yard, n. cortile m.; (railroad)

scalo di smistamento *m.;* (measure) jarda *f.*

yarn, *n.* filato *m.;* (tale) stòria *f.*

yawn, 1. *n.* sbadìglio *m.* **2.** *vb.* sbadigliare.

year, *n.* anno *m.*

yearly, 1. *adj.* annuale. **2.** *adv.* ogni anno.

yearn, *vb.* bramare.

yell, 1. *n.* urlo *m.* **2.** *vb.* urlare.

yellow, *adj.* giallo.

yes, *interj.* sì.

yesterday, *n. and adv.* ièri *(m.)*

yet, 1. *adv.* ancora. **2.** *conj.* tuttavia.

yield, 1. *n.* produzione *f.* **2.** *vb.* cèdere; (produce) produrre.

yoke, *n.* giogo *m.*

yolk, *n.* torlo *m.*

you, *pron.* tu, te, ti; voi, vi, Lei; La, Lo, Loro.

young, *adj.* gióvane.

your, *adj.* tuo; vòstro; Suo; Loro.

yours, *pron.* tuo; vòstro; Suo; Loro.

yourself, *pron.* tu stesso; te stesso, voi stessi, Lei stesso; Loro stessi.

youth, *n.* giovinezza *f.*

youthful, *adj.* giovanile.

Yugoslav, *adj.* jugoslavo.

Yugoslavia, *n.* Jugoslàvia *f.*

zap, *vb.* colpire repentinamente e inaspettatamente.

zeal, *n.* zèlo *m.*

zealous, *aj.* zelante.

zebra, *n.* zèbra *f.*

zephyr, *n.* zèffiro *m.*

zero, *n.* zèro *m.*

zest, *n.* entusiasmo *m.*

zinc, *n.* zinco *m.*

zip code, *n.* còdice di avviamento postale *m.*

zipper, *n.* chiusura lampo *f.*

zone, *n.* zòna *f.*

zoo, *n.* giardino zoològico *m.*

zoological, *adj.* zoològico.

zoology, *n.* zoologìa *f.*

Zurich, *n.* Zurigo *m.*